ONE-WAY WITHIN-SUBJECTS ANALYSIS OF VARIANCE (CHAPTER 13)

Within-Subjects Design

$F_{obt} = \dfrac{MS_{BG}}{MS_E}$ (Test statistic for the one-way within-subjects ANOVA)

Effect Size (Within-Subjects Design)

$\eta_P^2 = \dfrac{SS_{BG}}{SS_T - SS_{BP}}$ (Partial eta-squared for proportion of variance)

$\omega_P^2 = \dfrac{SS_{BG} - df_{BG}(MS_E)}{(SS_T - SS_{BP}) + MS_E}$ (Partial omega-squared for proportion of variance)

TWO FACTOR ANALYSIS OF VARIANCE (CHAPTER 14)

$F_A = \dfrac{MS_A}{MS_E}$ (Test statistic for the main effect on factor A)

$F_B = \dfrac{MS_B}{MS_E}$ (Test statistic for the main effect on factor B)

$F_{A \times B} = \dfrac{MS_{A \times B}}{MS_E}$ (Test statistic for the A × B interaction)

CORRELATION AND REGRESSION (CHAPTERS 15 & 16)

Correlation Coefficient

$r = \dfrac{SS_{XY}}{\sqrt{SS_X SS_Y}}$ (Pearson correlation coefficient)

Analysis of Regression with One Predictor Variable

$F_{obt} = \dfrac{MS_{regression}}{MS_{residual}}$ (Test statistic for analysis of regression)

CHI-SQUARE TESTS (CHAPTER 17)

One-Way and Two-Way Chi-Square Tests

$\chi_{obt}^2 = \sum \dfrac{(f_o - f_e)^2}{f_e}$ (Test statistic for the chi-square goodness-of-fit and the chi-square test for independence)

Effect Size (Test For Independence)

$V = \sqrt{\dfrac{\chi^2}{n \times df_{smaller}}}$ (Cramer's V effect size estimate)

TESTS FOR ORDINAL DATA (CHAPTER 18)

The Sign Test

$z = \dfrac{x - np}{\sqrt{np(1-p)}}$ (Test statistic for the normal approximation for the sign test)

Wilcoxon Signed-Ranks T Test

$z = \dfrac{T - \mu_T}{\sigma_T}$ (Test statistic for the normal approximation of the Wilcoxon T)

Mann-Whitney U Test

$z = \dfrac{U - \mu_U}{\sigma_U}$ (Test statistic for the normal approximation of the Mann-Whitney U)

The Kruskal-Wallis H Test

$H = \dfrac{12}{N(N+1)} \left(\sum \dfrac{R^2}{n} \right) - 3(N+1)$ (Test statistic for the Kruskal-Wallis H test)

The Friedman Test

$\chi_R^2 = \dfrac{12}{nk(k+1)} \sum R^2 - 3n(k+1)$ (Test statistic for the Friedman test)

Bring statistics into focus with Privitera's *Statistics for the Behavioral Sciences*

DO YOUR STUDENTS FOCUS ON THE IMPORTANCE AND RELEVANCE OF STATISTICS?

"Statistics is not something static or antiquated that we used to do in times past; **statistics is an ever-evolving discipline with relevance to our daily lives.** This book is designed not only to engage students in using statistics to summarize data and make decisions about behavior but also to emphasize the ongoing spirit of discovery that emerges when using today's technologies to understand the application of statistics to modern-day research problems."

—Gregory Privitera, Author,
Statistics for the Behavioral Sciences

HOW DOES THIS TEXT ACHIEVE THIS FOCUS?

Unlike statistics texts first written 20 to 30 years ago, Gregory Privitera writes with today's student in mind. The author presents the most current examples and up-to-date research, integrating IBM SPSS Statistics* throughout the text. More important, he engages students with real and interesting research examples that demonstrate the importance of statistics to understanding modern-day research problems.

- **Current research problems:** These problems show students how research is used in the field today.
- **Numerous exercises:** The book includes 32 to 38 problems per chapter, divided into types of problem for flexibility.
- **Today's technology:** Step-by-step SPSS screenshots support students as they work the problems.
- **Abundant, current, and relevant pedagogy:** The book features Research in Focus, SPSS in Focus, and APA in Focus sections.

*IBM SPSS® Statistics was formerly called PASW® Statistics.

HOW DO YOUR COLLEAGUES BELIEVE
THIS TEXT ACHIEVES THIS FOCUS?

"Overall I think this is one of the best statistics books that I have seen and hope that I can use it in the future."

—Charlie L. Law,
Penn State University, Schuylkill

"I am extremely impressed with the stated Learning Objectives at the beginning of each chapter, followed by succinct answers to these same Learning Objectives in place of simply summarizing the chapter . . . this text has more effective organization, has more effective problems and problem solutions, and is more reader-friendly [than my current text]."

—John M. Spores,
Purdue University North Central

FOCUS ON RESEARCH

Research in Focus sections provide context by reviewing the most current research that illustrates the most important statistical concepts.

"The Research in Focus is a very valuable feature of this textbook. It prepares students to read research articles by providing examples on how a particular statistical method is reported in the journals. These not only seem very helpful in preparing students to work with reports of empirical studies but also create a meaningful and interesting context in which course material can be discussed."

—Maria Czyzewska,
Texas State San Marcos

FOCUS ON SPSS

SPSS in Focus sections provide step-by-step, classroom-tested instruction using practical research examples for how the concepts taught in each chapter can be applied using SPSS. Students are supported with screenshot figures and explanations for how to read SPSS output.

"The inclusion of SPSS activities increases the likelihood that I would adopt this book."

—Lisa Kilanowski-Press,
Niagara University

FOCUS ON APA FORMAT

APA in Focus sections explain how to summarize statistical results. These APA sections support student learning by putting statistics into context with research and explaining how to read and report statistical results in research journals using current APA style.

"The inclusion of the APA in Focus section is a fantastic addition and I think an incredible strength of this book."

—Stephanie L. Simon-Dack,
Ball State University

FOCUS ON PRACTICE AND RESULTS

Making Sense sections break down the most difficult concepts in statistics for students.

MAKING SENSE: Populations and Samples

A population is identified as any group of interest, whether that group is all students worldwide or all students in a professor's class. Think of any group you are interested in. Maybe you want to understand why college students join fraternities and sororities. So students who join fraternities and sororities is the group you're interested in. Hence, this group is now a population of interest, to you anyways. You identified a population of interest just as researchers identify populations they are interested in.

Remember that researchers collect samples only because they do not have access to all individuals in a population. Imagine having to identify every person who has fallen in love, experienced anxiety, been attracted to someone else, suffered with depression, or taken a college exam. It's ridiculous to consider that we can identify all individuals in such populations. So researchers use data *... from the population*

Learning Objectives and Checks are thoroughly integrated throughout the text and revisited in the chapter summary.

True or false: The types of data researchers measure fall into two categories: (1) continuous or discrete and (2) quantitative or qualitative.

State whether each of the following are continuous or discrete.

a. Delay (in seconds) it takes drivers to make a left-hand turn when a light turns green
b. The number of questions that participants ask during a research study
c. Type of drug use (none, infrequent, moderate, or frequent)
d. Season of birth (spring, summer, fall, or winter)

State whether the variables listed in Question 2 are quantitative or qualitative.

True or false: Qualitative variables can be continuous or discrete.

A researcher is interested in the effects of stuttering on social behavior with children. He records the number of peers a child speaks to during a typical school day. In this example, would the data be qualitative or quantitative?

✓ **LEARNING CHECK 4**

> "I found the consistent theme of integration of chapter content, examples, learning checks, and Making Sense aspects with the end-of-chapter problems and learning chapter summaries to be very beneficial in promoting a sense of unity of explanation that may not be found in other textbooks."
>
> —Duane Shuttlesworth,
> *Delta State University*

End-of-chapter problems are divided into factual problems, concept and application problems, and problems in research, providing flexibility to students and instructors.

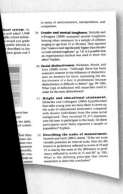

> "I like the three types of [end-of-chapter] problems. This is a nice feature, as students who only know how to perform hand calculations can master the factual and concept/application problems."
>
> —Osvaldo F. Morera,
> *University of Texas, El Paso*

...oblems in Research The book offers excellent quantity, variety, and accuracy of exercises, examples, and ...oblems.

> "The author provides a great number of very good problems at the end of each chapter. These problems are accurate and effective. [Privitera] chose a good variety of questions for students to practice."
>
> —Bryan Myers,
> *UNC Wilmington*

> "I think that this book has several strengths. It has a LOT of problems for the students to solve at the end of the chapters that are both factual and mathematical, and I think the inclusion of so many factual/conceptual questions as separate from 'solution' questions is a huge benefit to this text."
>
> —Stephanie L. Simon-Dack,
> *Ball State University*

FOCUS ON SUPPORT

As you have come to expect, SAGE provides the most comprehensive free and open-access online resources at **www.sagepub.com/priviterastats** designed to support and enhance both instructors' and students' experiences.

Instructors benefit from access to the password-protected **Instructor Teaching Site**, wh PowerPoint slides, course syllabi, lecture notes, a test bank, solutions for the problems in the guide, and solutions for all end-of-chapter problems in the text.

Students maximize their understanding of statistics through the free, open-access **Studer** which presents valuable resources such as e-flashcards, "Learning From SAGE Journal Articles full-text journal articles and discussion questions, web quizzes, and more.

To further improve students' learning experience, the **Student Study Guide** contains objectives, chapter outlines, key formulas, tips and cautions, self-tests and quizzes, and exercis students' understanding of APA style and SPSS.

FOCUS ON SUPPORT

As you have come to expect, SAGE provides the most comprehensive free and open-access online resources at **www.sagepub.com/priviterastats** designed to support and enhance both instructors' and students' experiences.

Instructors benefit from access to the password-protected **Instructor Teaching Site**, which contains PowerPoint slides, course syllabi, lecture notes, a test bank, solutions for the problems in the student study guide, and solutions for all end-of-chapter problems in the text.

Students maximize their understanding of statistics through the free, open-access **Student Study Site**, which presents valuable resources such as e-flashcards, "Learning From SAGE Journal Articles" activities with full-text journal articles and discussion questions, web quizzes, and more.

To further improve students' learning experience, the **Student Study Guide** contains chapter learning objectives, chapter outlines, key formulas, tips and cautions, self-tests and quizzes, and exercises designed to test students' understanding of APA style and SPSS.

FOCUS ON PRACTICE AND RESULTS

Making Sense sections break down the most difficult concepts in statistics for students.

MAKING SENSE: Populations and Samples

A population is identified as any group of interest, whether that group is all students worldwide or all students in a professor's class. Think of any group you are interested in. Maybe you want to understand why college students join fraternities and sororities. So students who join fraternities and sororities is the group you're interested in. Hence, this group is now a population of interest, to you anyways. You identified a population of interest just as researchers identify populations they are interested in.

Remember that researchers collect samples only because they do not have access to all individuals in a population. Imagine having to identify every person who has fallen in love, experienced anxiety, been attracted to someone else, suffered with depression, or taken a college exam. It's ridiculous to consider that we can identify all individuals in such populations. So researchers use data ... (from the population)

Learning Objectives and Checks are thoroughly integrated throughout the text and revisited in the chapter summary.

1. True or false: The types of data researchers measure fall into two categories: (1) continuous or discrete and (2) quantitative or qualitative.
2. State whether each of the following are continuous or discrete.
   a. Delay (in seconds) it takes drivers to make a left-hand turn when a light turns green
   b. The number of questions that participants ask during a research study
   c. Type of drug use (none, infrequent, moderate, or frequent)
   d. Season of birth (spring, summer, fall, or winter)
3. State whether the variables listed in Question 2 are quantitative or qualitative.
4. True or false: Qualitative variables can be continuous or discrete.
5. A researcher is interested in the effects of stuttering on social behavior with children. He records the number of peers a child speaks to during a typical school day. In this example, would the data be qualitative or quantitative?

✓ **LEARNING CHECK 4**

"I found the consistent theme of integration of chapter content, examples, learning checks, and Making Sense aspects with the end-of-chapter problems and learning chapter summaries to be very beneficial in promoting a sense of unity of explanation that may not be found in other textbooks."

—Duane Shuttlesworth,
Delta State University

End-of-chapter problems are divided into factual problems, concept and application problems, and problems in research, providing flexibility to students and instructors.

END-OF-CHAPTER PROBLEMS

Factual Problems

1. What is the difference between descriptive and inferential statistics?
2. Distinguish between data and a raw score.
3. By definition, how is a sample related to a population?
4. State three commonly used research methods in behavioral science.
5. In an experiment, researchers measure two types of variables: independent and dependent variables.
   a. Which variable is manipulated to create the groups?
   b. Which variable is measured in each group?
6. State the four scales of measurement. Which scale of measurement is the most informative?
7. Can a nominal variable be numeric? Explain.
8. What is the main distinction between variables on an interval and ratio scale of measurement?
9. A quantitative variable varies by _____; a qualitative variable varies by _____.
10. What are the two types of data that are collected and measured quantitatively?

Concepts and Application Problems

11. State whether each of the following words best describes descriptive statistics or inferential statistics.

a. Describe
b. Infer
c. Summarize
12. State whether each of the following is true or false.
   a. Graphs, tables, and summary statistics all illustrate the application of inferential statistics.
   b. Inferential statistics are procedures used to make inferences about a population, given only a limited amount of data.
   c. Descriptive statistics can be used to describe populations and samples of data.
13. A researcher measured behavior among all individuals in some small population. Are inferential statistics necessary to draw conclusions concerning this population? Explain.
14. Appropriately use the terms *sample* and *population* to describe the following statement: A statistics class has 25 students enrolled, but only 23 students attended class.
15. On occasion, samples can be larger than the population from which it was selected. Explain why this can't be true.
16. A researcher demonstrates that eating breakfast in the morning causes increased alertness throughout the day. What research design must the researcher have used in this example? Explain.
17. A researcher measures the height and income of participants and finds that taller men tend to earn greater incomes than shorter men. What type of research method did the researcher use in this example? Explain.

"I like the three types of [end-of-chapter] problems. This is a nice feature, as students who only know how to perform hand calculations can master the factual and concept/application problems."

—Osvaldo F. Morera,
University of Texas, El Paso

Problems in Research The book offers excellent quantity, variety, and accuracy of exercises, examples, and problems.

Problems in Research

27. **Grading the public school system.** In December 2009, a CBS News poll asked 1,048 Americans to grade the U.S. public school system. In the poll, they asked, "How would you grade the U.S. on the quality of the public schools in this country?" The results are described in the table below, with A being the best grade and F being the worst grade:

Grade	%
A	6
B	33
C	32
D	18
F	12

Source: Reported at http://www.pollingreport.com/ed.htm

a. What was the sample size for this poll?
b. Based on the percentages given in the table, how well was the U.S. public school system graded in general?

28. **Racial attitudes in college.** Shook and Fazio (2008) randomly assigned White freshman college students to live with a White (same-race group) or Black (different-race group) roommate in a college dormitory. After a few months, researchers measured racial attitudes and compared differences between groups. Is this study an example of an experiment? Explain your answer

in terms of randomization, manipulation, and comparison.

29. **Gender and mental toughness.** Nicholls and colleagues (2009) measured mental toughness (among other measures) in a sample of athletes ranging in age from 15 to 58 years. They reported that "males scored significantly higher than females on total mental toughness" (p. 76). Is it possible that an experimental method was used to show this effect? Explain.

30. **Facial distinctiveness.** Wickham, Morris, and Fritz (2000) wrote, "Although there has been extensive interest in the influence of distinctiveness on memory for faces, measuring the distinctiveness of a face is problematic because distinctiveness is difficult to define" (pp. 99–100). What type of definition will researchers need to make for the term distinctiveness?

31. **Height and educational attainment.** Szklarska and colleagues (2004) hypothesized that taller young men are more likely to move up the scale of educational attainment compared with shorter individuals from the same social background. They recruited 91,373 nineteen-year-old men to participate in the study. Do these participants most likely represent a sample or population? Explain.

32. **Describing the scales of measurement.** Harwell and Gatti (2001) stated, "If the test score variable possesses an interval scale, then the difference in proficiency reflected in scores of 10 and 15 is exactly the same as the difference in proficiency reflected in scores of 15 and 20" (p. 105). What is the defining principle that allows researchers to draw this conclusion?

"The author provides a great number of very good problems at the end of each chapter. These problems are accurate and effective. [Privitera] chose a good variety of questions for students to practice."

—Bryan Myers,
UNC Wilmington

"I think that this book has several strengths. It has a LOT of problems for the students to solve at the end of the chapters that are both factual and mathematical, and I think the inclusion of so many factual/conceptual questions as separate from 'solution' questions is a huge benefit to this text."

—Stephanie L. Simon-Dack,
Ball State University

Statistics

for the BEHAVIORAL SCIENCES

Gregory J. Privitera

St. Bonaventure University

Los Angeles | London | New Delhi
Singapore | Washington DC

Los Angeles | London | New Delhi
Singapore | Washington DC

FOR INFORMATION:

SAGE Publications, Inc.
2455 Teller Road
Thousand Oaks, California 91320
E-mail: order@sagepub.com

SAGE Publications Ltd.
1 Oliver's Yard
55 City Road
London EC1Y 1SP
United Kingdom

SAGE Publications India Pvt. Ltd.
B 1/I 1 Mohan Cooperative Industrial Area
Mathura Road, New Delhi 110 044
India

SAGE Publications Asia-Pacific Pte. Ltd.
33 Pekin Street #02-01
Far East Square
Singapore 048763

Acquisitions Editor: Christine Cardone
Associate Editor: Eve Oettinger
Editorial Assistant: Sarita Sarak
Developmental Editor: Marjorie Anderson
Typesetter: C&M Digitals (P) Ltd.
Proofreader: Wendy Jo Dymond
Indexer: Diggs Publication Services
Cover Designer: Bryan Fishman
Permissions Editor: Karen Ehrmann
Marketing Manager: Liz Thornton

Printed in the United States of America

Library of Congress Cataloging-in-Publication Data

Privitera, Gregory J.
Statistics for the behavioral sciences/Gregory J. Privitera.

p. cm.
Includes bibliographical references and index.

ISBN 978-1-4129-6931-4 (cloth)

1. Social sciences—Statistical methods. 2. Psychology—Statistical methods. I. Title.

HA29.P755 2012
519.5—dc23   2011024471

This book is printed on acid-free paper.

11 12 13 14 15 10 9 8 7 6 5 4 3 2 1

BRIEF CONTENTS

DETAILED CONTENTS

► **PART III** : **PROBABILITY AND THE FOUNDATIONS OF INFERENTIAL STATISTICS**   **224**

8.   Introduction to Hypothesis Testing   **225**

► **PART IV**   **MAKING INFERENCES ABOUT
THE VARIABILITY OF TWO OR MORE MEANS**   **346**

12.   Analysis of Variance: One-Way Between-Subjects Design 347

ABOUT THE AUTHOR

 **Gregory J. Privitera** is an Assistant Professor of Psychology at Saint Bonaventure University and a veteran of the U.S. Marines. Dr. Privitera received his PhD in Psychology at the State University of New York at Buffalo. He went on to complete a postdoctoral research position at Arizona State University before coming to Saint Bonventure University in 2009. He is an author of a book on the psychology of eating and of multiple peer-reviewed articles on the role of learning and cognition on eating behavior and health. His research work examines a variety of important questions related to factors involved in the acquisition/development of diet, the long-term and short-term consequences of dietary food selection, and the role of cognition on hunger and fullness. He oversees a variety of undergraduate research projects at St. Bonaventure University and teaches courses in statistics and research methods each year. Dr. Privitera is also working on a new text, *Methods for the Behavioral Sciences.*

ACKNOWLEDGMENTS

In no particular order, I want to thank many individuals. To my family, I want to thank my wife Alisha for her loving support; my mother Donna for her resilient example of faith; my father James for his strength and positive spirit; my twin brother Andrew, a First Sergeant in the U.S. Army, who ironically leads not by statistics, but by trust; my sister Rachel who gracefully survived childhood with four brothers; my brother Stephen whose work ethic has largely inspired my own; and my brother Joseph who was in the gym with me everyday as I prepared for Marine Corps boot camp many years ago—he was only five!

To my son Aiden Andrew and daughter Grace Ann—every moment I am with you is the greatest moment of my life. I often teach that confidence in the absence of humility is arrogance. It is in those moments that I share with my children that I find my humility each day.

To all the men and women I served with in the U.S. Marine Corps—being a U.S. Marine was an experience that inevitably shaped my character and instilled in me the belief that there is no greater honor than to serve something greater than yourself.

To all those at SAGE Publications, know that your contributions are immeasurably larger than many people will recognize. I am so grateful to be able to share in and work with all of you. It is your vital contributions that have made this book possible and so special to me. Thank you.

To my many colleagues throughout the years, thank you for your collaborative spirit and commitment to academic excellence; and in particular, to the faculty and administration at Saint Bonaventure University for giving me the opportunity to grow, teach, and serve in such a wonderful community.

I especially want to thank the thousands of statistics students across the country. It is your pursuit of education that has inspired this contribution. My hope is that you take away as much from reading this book as I have in writing it.

I also don't want to forget all those who are not mentioned by name but have been supportive and endearing throughout. To my family, friends, acquaintances, and colleagues—thank you for contributing to my perspective in way that is indubitably recognized and appreciated.

Last, but certainly not least, I'd also like to thank the many reviewers who gave me feedback during the development process.

Rebecca Campbell, *Michigan State University*

Osvaldo F. Morera, *University Of Texas-El Paso*

Linda Bastone, *Suny College at Purchase*

Kelly Brennan-Jones, *Suny Brockport*

PREFACE TO THE INSTRUCTOR

PHILOSOPHICAL APPROACH

On the basis of years of experience and student feedback, I was inspired to write a book that professors could truly teach from—one that related statistics to science using current, practical research examples and one that was approachable (and dare I say interesting!) to students. I write this book in that spirit to give the reader one clear message: Statistics is not something static or antiquated that we used to do in times past; statistics is an ever-evolving discipline with relevance to our daily lives. This book is designed not only to engage students in using statistics to summarize data and make decisions about behavior but also to emphasize the ongoing spirit of discovery that emerges when using today's technologies to understand the application of statistics to modern-day research problems. How does the text achieve this goal? It exposes students to statistical applications in current research, tests their knowledge using current research examples, gives them step-by-step instruction for using SPSS with examples, and makes them aware of how statistics is important for their generation—all through the use of the following key themes, features, and pedagogy.

THEMES, FEATURES, AND PEDAGOGY

EMPHASIS ON STUDENT LEARNING

- **Conversational writing style.** I write in a conversational tone that speaks to the reader as if he or she is the researcher. It empowers students to view statistics as something they are capable of understanding and using. It is a positive psychology approach to writing that involves students in the process and decisions made using statistics. The goal is to motivate and excite students about the topic by making the book easy to read and follow without "dumbing down" the information they need to be successful.
- **Learning objectives.** Clear learning objectives are provided at the start of each chapter to get students focused and thinking about the material they will be learning. At the close of each chapter, the chapter summaries reiterate these learning objectives and then summarize the key chapter content related to each objective.
- **Learning Checks** are inserted throughout each chapter (for students to review what they learn, as they learn it), and many figures and tables

are provided to illustrate statistical concepts and summarize statistical procedures.

- **Making Sense** sections support critical and difficult material. In many years of teaching statistics, I have found certain areas of statistics where students struggle with the most. To address this, I include Making Sense sections in each chapter to break down difficult concepts, review important material, and basically "make sense" of the most difficult material taught in this book. These sections are aimed at easing student stress and making statistics more approachable. Again, this book was written with student learning in mind.
- **Review problems.** At least 32 review problems are included at the end of each chapter. The review questions include *factual problems, concepts and application problems,* and *problems in research.* Unlike most statistics textbooks, these questions are categorized for you, so that you can easily identify and specifically test the type of knowledge you want to assess in the classroom. This format tests student knowledge and application of chapter material while also giving students more exposure to how current research applies to the statistics they learn.
- **Additional features.** Additional features in each chapter are aimed at helping students pull out key concepts and recall important material. For example, key terms are bolded, boxed, and defined as they are introduced to make it easier for students to find these terms when reviewing the material and grab their attention as they read the chapters. At the end of the book, each key term is summarized in a glossary. Also, marginal notes are placed throughout each chapter for students to review important material in each chapter. They provide simple explanations and summaries based on those given in detail in the text.

FOCUS ON CURRENT RESEARCH

- **Research in Focus.** To introduce the context for using statistics, Chapters 1 to 6 include Research in Focus sections that review pertinent research that makes sense of or illustrates important statistical concepts discussed in the chapter. By giving students current research examples, I help them "see" statistics as they are applied today, not as they were done 20 years ago.
- **APA in Focus.** As statistical designs are introduced in Chapters 7 to 18, I present APA in Focus sections that explain how to summarize statistical results for each inferential statistic taught. Together, these sections support student learning by putting statistics into context with research and also explaining how to read and report statistical results in research journals that follow American Psychological Association (APA) style.
- **Current research examples.** Many of the statistics computed in this book are based on or use data from published research. This allows students to see the types of questions that behavioral researchers ask while learning about the statistics researchers use to answer research questions. Students don't need a background in research methods to read through the research examples, which is important since most students have not taken research methods prior to taking a statistics course.
- **Problems in Research.** The end-of-chapter review questions include a section of Problems in Research that come straight from the literature. These

classroom-tested problems use the data or conclusions drawn from published research to test knowledge of statistics and are taken from a diverse set of research journals and behavioral disciplines. The problems require students to think critically about published research in a way that reinforces statistical concepts taught in each chapter.

- **Balanced coverage of recent changes in the field of statistics.** I take into account recent developments in the area of statistics. For example, while eta-squared is still the most popular estimate for effect size, there is a great deal of research showing that it overestimates the size of an effect. That being said, a modification to eta-squared, called omega-squared, is considered a better estimate for effect size and is being used more and more in published articles. I teach both, giving students a full appreciation for where statistics currently stands and where it is likely going in the future. Other examples include a full chapter on confidence intervals and detailed reviews of factors that influence power (a key requirement for obtaining grant money and conducting effective research).

INTEGRATION OF SPSS

- **Guide to how to use SPSS with this book.** For professors who teach statistics and SPSS, it can be difficult to teach from a textbook and a separate SPSS manual. The manual often does not include research examples or language that is consistent with that in the textbook and overall can make it difficult for students to follow. This book changes all that by nesting SPSS coverage into the textbook. It begins with the guide at the front of the book, "How to Use SPSS With This Book," which provides students with an easy-to-follow, classroom-tested overview of how SPSS is set up, how to read the data view and variable view screens, and how to use the SPSS in Focus sections in the book.
- **SPSS in Focus.** Many statistics textbooks for behavioral science omit SPSS, include it in an appendix separate from the main chapters in the book, include it at the end of chapters with no useful examples or context, or include it in ancillary materials that often are not included with course content. In *Statistics for the Behavioral Sciences*, SPSS is included in each chapter as statistical concepts are taught. This instruction is given in the SPSS in Focus sections. These sections provide step-by-step, classroom-tested instruction using practical research examples for how the concepts taught in each chapter can be applied using SPSS. Students are supported with screenshot figures and explanations for how to read SPSS outputs.

In addition, there is one more overarching feature that I refer to as *teachability*. While this book is comprehensive and a great reference for any undergraduate student, it is often too difficult to cover every topic in this book. For this reason, the chapters are organized into sections, each of which can largely stand alone. This gives professors the ability to more easily manage course content by assigning students particular sections in each chapter when they don't want to teach all topics covered in the entire chapter. So this book wasn't only written with the student in mind; it was also written with the professor in mind. Here are some brief highlights of what you'll find in each chapter:

CHAPTER OVERVIEWS

CHAPTER 1. INTRODUCTION TO STATISTICS

Students are introduced to scientific thinking and basic research design relevant to the statistical methods discussed in this book. In addition, the types of data that researchers measure and observe are introduced in this chapter. The chapter is to-the-point and provides an introduction to statistics in the context of research.

CHAPTER 2. SUMMARIZING DATA: TABLES, GRAPHS, AND DISTRIBUTIONS

This chapter provides a comprehensive introduction to frequency distributions and graphing using research examples that give students some context for when these tables and graphs are used. In addition, students are exposed to summaries for two-variable data. Throughout the chapter, an emphasis is placed on showing students how to decide between the various tables and graphs used to summarize data.

CHAPTER 3. SUMMARIZING DATA: CENTRAL TENDENCY

This chapter places particular emphasis on what measures of central tendency are, how they are computed, and when they are used. A special emphasis is placed on interpretation and use of the mean, the median, and the mode. Students learn to appropriately use these measures to describe data for many different distributions.

CHAPTER 4. SUMMARIZING DATA: VARIABILITY

Variability is often difficult to conceptually understand. So I begin immediately with an illustration for how this chapter will show students what variability is actually measuring. I clarify immediately that variability can never be negative, and I give a simple explanation for why. These are difficult obstacles for students, so I begin with this to support student learning from the very beginning of the chapter.

CHAPTER 5. PROBABILITY

This is a true probability chapter with many current research examples. This chapter does not ask about the probability of rolling dice; it looks at how probability problems—from simple probability, to Bayes' Theorem, to expected values—are applied to answer questions about behavior. After reading this chapter, students won't feel like they have to gamble in order to apply probability.

CHAPTER 6. PROBABILITY AND NORMAL DISTRIBUTIONS

At an introductory level, the normal distribution is center stage. It is at least mentioned in almost every chapter of this book. It is the basis for statistical theory and the precursor to most other distributions students will learn about. For this reason, I dedicate an entire chapter to its introduction. This chapter uses a variety of research examples to help students work through locating probabilities above the mean, below the mean, between two scores, and even z-scores.

CHAPTER 7. PROBABILITY AND SAMPLING DISTRIBUTION

This is a comprehensive chapter for sampling distributions of both the mean and variance. This chapter introduces the sampling distribution and standard error in a way that helps students to see how the sample mean and sample variance can inform us about the characteristics we want to learn about in some otherwise unknown population. In addition, the chapter is organized in a way that allows professors to easily manage reading assignments for students that are consistent with what they want to discuss in class.

CHAPTER 8. INTRODUCTION TO HYPOTHESIS TESTING

In my experience, shifting from descriptive statistics to inferential statistics is particularly difficult for students. For this reason, this chapter provides a comprehensive introduction to hypothesis testing, significance, effect size, power, and more. In addition, students are introduced to power in the context that emphasizes how essential this concept is for today's research. Two sections are devoted to this topic, and this chapter uses data from published research to introduce hypothesis testing.

CHAPTER 9. TESTING MEANS: INDEPENDENT SAMPLE *T*-TESTS

This chapter introduces students to *t*-tests for one and two independent samples using current research examples. This allows students to apply these tests in context with the situations in which they are used. In addition, students are introduced to two measures for proportion of variance—one that is most often used (eta-squared) and one that is less biased and becoming more popular (omega-squared). This gives students a real sense of where statistics is and where it is likely going.

CHAPTER 10. TESTING MEANS: RELATED SAMPLES *T*-TEST

Many textbooks teach the related samples *t*-test and spend almost the entire chapter discussing the repeated-measures design. This is misleading since the matched-pairs design is also analyzed using this *t*-test. It unnecessarily leads students to believe that this test is limited to a repeated-measures design, and it is not. For this reason, I teach the related samples *t*-test for both designs, explaining that the assumptions, advantages, and disadvantages vary depending on the design used. Students are clearly introduced to the context for using this test and the research situations that require its use.

CHAPTER 11. ESTIMATION AND CONFIDENCE INTERVALS

Confidence intervals and estimation have become increasing emphasized among behavioral scientists and statisticians. Although they have a lot in common with significance testing, there are many who believe that someday confidence intervals will replace significance testing. Maybe, maybe not; but regardless, this emphasis justifies dedicating a full chapter to reviewing this topic. Particular emphasis is placed on describing the similarities and differences between significance testing and confidence intervals.

CHAPTER 12. ANALYSIS OF VARIANCE: ONE-WAY BETWEEN-SUBJECTS DESIGN

The one-way between-subjects analysis of variance (ANOVA) and its assumptions, hypotheses, and calculations are all reviewed. A particular emphasis is placed on reviewing post hoc designs and what should be done following a significant result. Two post hoc tests are reviewed in order of how powerful they are at detecting an effect. This gives students a decision-focused introduction by showing them how to choose statistics that increase the power of detecting an effect.

CHAPTER 13. ANALYSIS OF VARIANCE: ONE-WAY WITHIN-SUBJECTS DESIGN

The one-way within-subjects ANOVA and its assumptions, hypotheses, and calculations are all reviewed. Students are also introduced to post hoc tests that are most appropriate in situations where samples are related. This is important since many statistics textbooks fail to even recognize that other commonly published post hoc tests are not well adapted for related samples. In addition, a full discussion of consistency and power is included to help students see how this design can increase the power of detecting an effect.

CHAPTER 14. ANALYSIS OF VARIANCE: TWO-WAY BETWEEN-SUBJECTS FACTORIAL DESIGN

This chapter provides students with an introduction to the two-way between-subjects factorial design. Students are given illustrations showing exactly how to interpret main effects and interactions, as well as given guidance as to which effects are more important and how to describe these effects. This is a decision-focused chapter, helping students understand the various effects in a two-way ANOVA design and how they can be analyzed and interpreted to answer a variety of research questions.

CHAPTER 15. CORRELATION

This chapter is unique in that it is organized in a way that introduces the Pearson correlation coefficient, effect size, significance, assumptions, and additional considerations up front in the beginning of the chapter. This makes it easy for professors who only want to discuss that design (or any other design) to assign students readings that are specific to those discussed in lectures. This minimizes confusion among students and gives professors more control to manage course content. The SPSS in Focus sections really drive home the point that a Pearson correlation can be used to compute any of the additional tests taught in this chapter.

CHAPTER 16. LINEAR REGRESSION

This chapter provides a comprehensive review for defining how a straight line is used to predict behavioral outcomes. Many figures and tables are included to illustrate and conceptualize regression and how it describes behavior. Also, an analysis of regression is introduced, and parallels between this test and ANOVA are drawn. This is aimed at helping students see how this analysis relates to other tests taught in previous chapters.

CHAPTER 17. NONPARAMETRIC TESTS: CHI-SQUARE TESTS

One of the most difficult parts of teaching chi-square tests can be in explaining their interpretation. Much of the interpretation of the results of a chi-square is intuitive or speculative. These issues and the purposes for using these tests are included. In addition, this chapter is linked with the previous chapter by showing students how measures of effect size for the chi-square test are linked with phi correlations. This gives students an appreciation for how these measures are related.

CHAPTER 18. NONPARAMETRIC TESTS: TESTS FOR ORDINAL DATA

This final chapter is aimed at introducing alternative tests for ordinal data. A key emphasis is to relate each test to those already introduced in previous chapters. The tests taught in this chapter are alternatives for tests taught in Chapters 9, 10, 12, and 13. The tests are introduced in separate sections that make it easier for professors to assign sections of readings for only those tests they want to teach. Again, this minimizes confusion among students and gives the professor more control to manage course content.

APPENDIXES

Appendix A gives students a basic math review specific to the skills they need for the course. The appendix is specifically written to be unintimidating. From the beginning, students are reassured that the level of math is basic and that they don't need a strong background in mathematics to be successful in statistics. Learning checks are included throughout this appendix, and more than 100 end-of-chapter review problems are included to give students all the practice they need to feel comfortable. In addition, Appendix B gives the tables needed to find critical values for the test statistics taught in this book. Appendix C gives the answers for even-numbered problems for the end-of-chapter questions. This allows students to practice additional questions and be able to check their answers in Appendix C.

SUPPLEMENTS

Ancillaries for this book include the following:

- **Student Study Guide:** Contains chapter learning objectives, chapter outlines, key formulas, tips and cautions, self-tests and quizzes, and exercises designed to test students' understanding of APA style and SPSS.
- **Instructor Teaching Site:** Contains PowerPoint slides, course syllabi, lecture notes, a test bank, solutions for the problems in the student study guide, and solutions for all end-of-chapter problems in the text.
- **Student Study Site:** Contains e-flashcards, "Learning From SAGE Journal Articles" activities with full-text journal articles and discussion questions, web quizzes, and more.

Thank you for choosing *Statistics for the Behavioral Sciences* and best wishes for a successful semester!

Gregory J. Privitera
St. Bonaventure, NY

TO THE STUDENT—HOW TO USE SPSS WITH THIS BOOK

The Statistical Package for the Social Sciences (SPSS) is an innovative statistical computer program used to compute most statistics taught in this book. This preface provides you with an overview to familiarize you with how to open, view, and understand this software. The screenshots in this book show IBM SPSS Version 19.0 for the PC. Still, even if you use a MAC or different version, the figures and instructions should provide a rather effective guide for helping you use this statistical software (with some minor differences, of course). SPSS is introduced throughout this book, so it will be worthwhile to read this preface before moving into future discussions of SPSS. Included in this preface is a general introduction to familiarize you with this software.

Understanding this software is especially important for those interested in research careers because it is the most widely used statistical program in the social and behavioral sciences. That is not to minimize the importance of understanding how to compute a mean or plot a bar graph by hand—but knowing how to enter, analyze, and interpret statistics using SPSS is equally important for no other reason than you will need it. This is an essential complement to your reading and work. By knowing how and why you compute certain statistics, you will better understand and interpret the output from SPSS software.

OVERVIEW OF SPSS: WHAT ARE YOU LOOKING AT?

When you open SPSS, you will see a window that looks similar to an Excel spreadsheet. (In many ways, you will enter and view the data similar to that in Microsoft Excel.) At the bottom of the window, you will see two tabs as shown in Figure P.1. The **data view** tab is open by default. The **variable view** tab to the right of it is used to view and define the variables being studied.

DATA VIEW

The data view screen includes a **menu bar** (located at the top of the screen), which displays commands that perform most functions that SPSS provides. These commands include **file, edit, view, data, transform, analyze, graphs, utilities,**

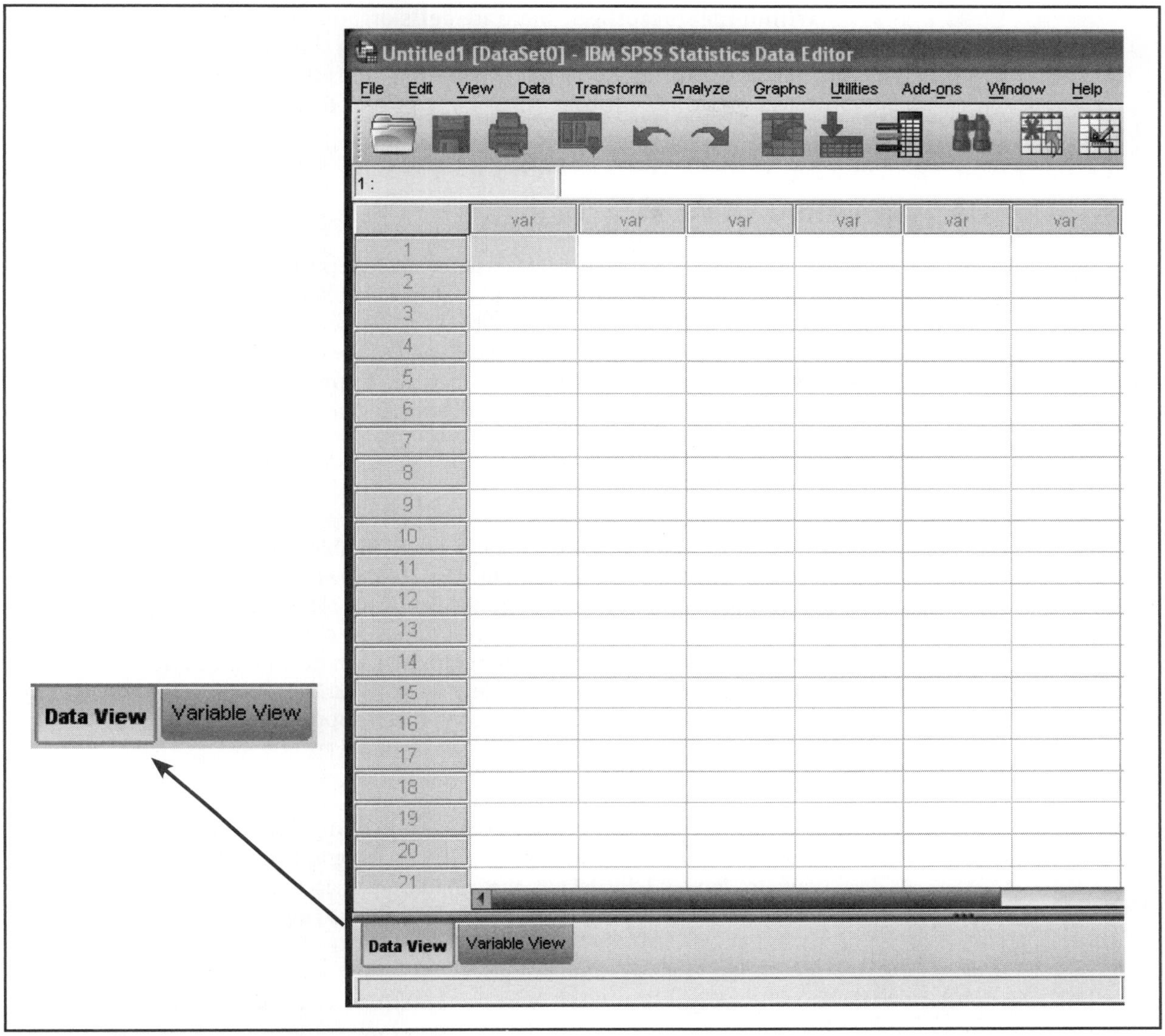

FIGURE P.1

The data view default view in SPSS. The highlighted tab (pulled out with an arrow in this figure) indicates which view you are looking at. In this figure, the data view tab is highlighted.

windows, and **help.** Each command is introduced as needed in each chapter in the SPSS in Focus sections.

Below the menu bar is where you will find the **toolbar,** which includes a row of icons that perform various functions. We use some of these icons, whereas others are beyond the scope of this book. The purpose and function of each icon are introduced as needed in each chapter (again, in the SPSS in Focus sections).

Within the spreadsheet, there are **cells** organized in columns and rows. The rows are labeled numerically from 1, whereas each column is labeled *var*. Each column will be used to identify your variables, so *var* is short for *variable*. To label your variables with something other than *var*, you need to access the variable view tab—this is a unique feature to SPSS.

VARIABLE VIEW

When you click the variable view tab, a new screen appears. Some features remain the same. For example, the menu bar and toolbar remain at the top of your screen. What changes is the spreadsheet. Notice that the rows are still labeled numerically beginning with 1. What changed are the labels across the columns. There are 11 columns in this view, as shown in Figure P.2: **Name, Type, Width, Decimals, Label, Values, Missing, Columns, Align, Measure,** and **Role**. We will look at each column.

Name

In this column, you enter the names of your variables (but no spaces are allowed). Each row identifies a single variable. Also, once you name your variable, the columns label in the data view will change. For example, while in variable view, enter the word *stats* in the first cell of this column. Now click on the data view tab at the bottom left. Notice that the label for column 1 has now changed from *var* to *stats*. Also, notice that once you enter a name for your variable, the row is suddenly filled in with words and numbers. Don't worry; this is supposed to happen.

Type

This cell identifies the type of variable you are defining. When you click in the box, a small gray box with three dots appears. Click on the gray box and a dialog box appears, as shown in Figure P.3. By default, the variable type selected is numeric. This is because your variable will almost always be numeric, so we usually just leave this cell alone.

Name	Type	Width	Decimals	Label	Values	Missing	Columns	Align	Measure	Role

FIGURE P.2

The variable view page with 11 columns. Each column allows you to label and characterize variables.

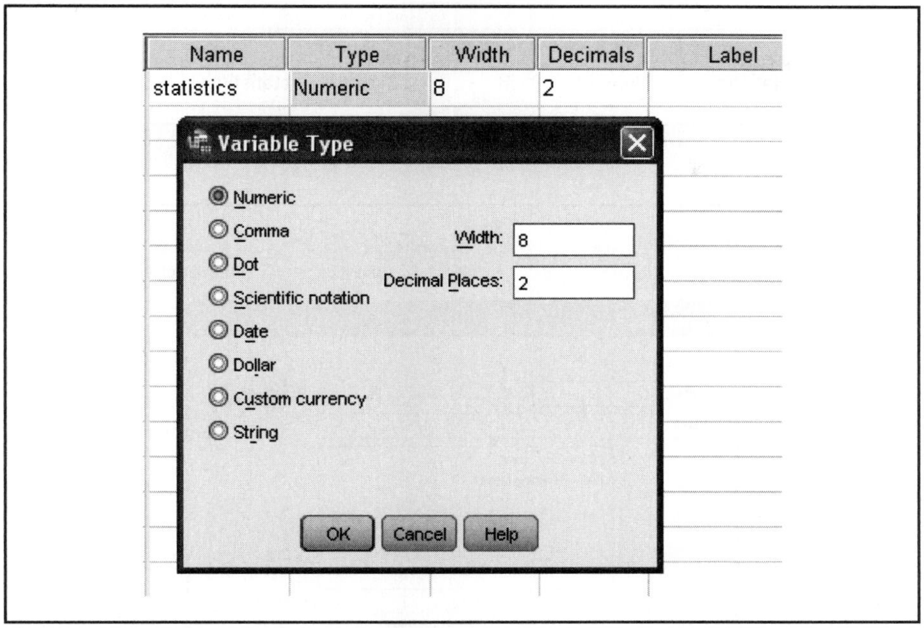

Name	Type	Width	Decimals	Label
statistics	Numeric	8	2	

Variable Type

- ● Numeric
- ○ Comma   Width: 8
- ○ Dot
- ○ Scientific notation   Decimal Places: 2
- ○ Date
- ○ Dollar
- ○ Custom currency
- ○ String

OK   Cancel   Help

FIGURE P.3

The dialog box shown here appears by clicking the small gray box with three dots in the Type column. This allows you to define the type of variable being measured.

Width

The width column is used to identify the largest number or longest string of your variable. For example, GPA would have a width of 4: two digits to the left of the decimal, one space for the decimal, and one digit to the right. The default width is 8. So if none of your variables are longer than 8 digits, you can just leave this alone. Otherwise, when you click in the box, you would select the up and down arrows that appear to the right of the cell to change the width.

Decimals

This cell allows you to identify the number of places beyond the decimal point your variables are. Like the width cell, when you click in the decimal box, you can select the up and down arrows that appear to the right of the cell to change the decimals. If you enter whole numbers, for example, you would simply set this to 0.

Label

The label column allows you to label any variable whose meaning is not clear. For example, we can label the variable name *stats* as *statistics* in the label column, as shown in Figure P.4. This clarifies the meaning of the *stats* variable name.

Values

This column allows you to identify the levels of your variable. This is especially useful for coded data. Since SPSS recognizes numeric values, nominal data are often coded numerically in SPSS. For example, *gender* could be coded as *1 = male, 2 = female*; *seasons* would be coded as *1 = spring, 2 = summer, 3 = fall,* and *4 = winter.*

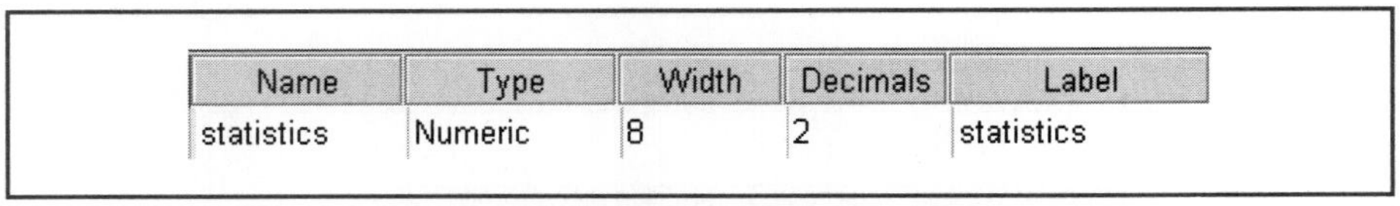

FIGURE P.4

Labeling variables. In this example, we labeled the variable name *stats* as *statistics* in the label column.

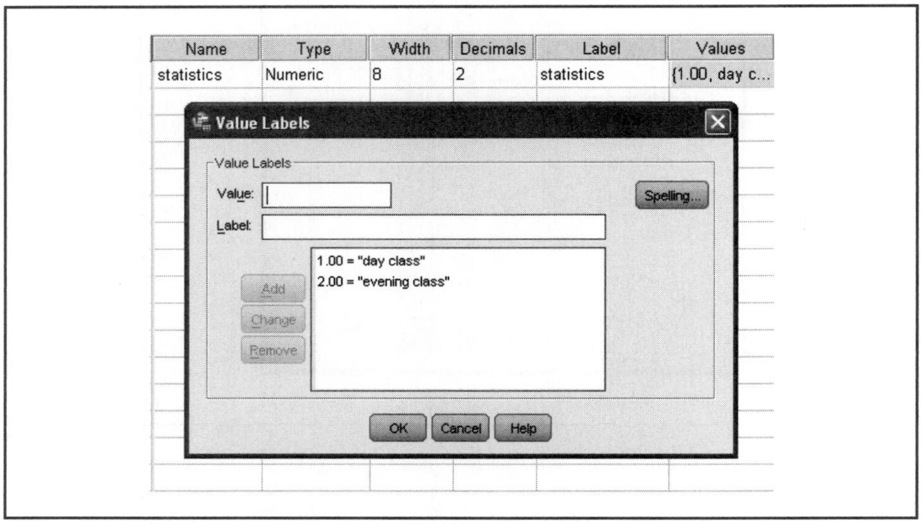

Name	Type	Width	Decimals	Label
statistics	Numeric	8	2	statistics

FIGURE P.5

The dialog box shown here appears by clicking the small gray box with three dots in the **Values column.** This function allows you to code data that are not inherently numeric.

Name	Type	Width	Decimals	Label	Values
statistics	Numeric	8	2	statistics	{1.00, day c...

Value Labels

Value Labels

Value: | |

Label: | |

Spelling...

1.00 = "day class"
2.00 = "evening class"

Add
Change
Remove

OK   Cancel   Help

Click on the small gray box with three dots to display a dialog box where we can label the variable, as shown in Figure P.5. Let's label *day class* as *1* and *evening class* as *2* for our *stats* variable. To do this, enter *1* in the value box and *day class* in the label box; then click the **add** option. Follow these same instructions for the *evening class* label. When both labels have been entered, click **OK** to finish.

Missing

It is at times the case that some data researchers collect are missing. In these cases, you can enter a value that, when entered, means the data are missing. A common value used to represent missing data is *99*. To enter this value, click on the small gray box with three dots that appears to the right of the cell when you click in it. In the dialog box, it is most common to click on the second open circle and enter a *99* in the first cell. When this has been entered, click **OK** to finish. Now, whenever you enter *99* for that variable in the data view spreadsheet, SPSS will recognize it as missing data.

Columns

The columns column lets you identify how much room to allow for your data and labels. For example, the *stats* label is five letters long. If you go to the data view spreadsheet, you will see *stats* as the column label. If you wrote *statisticscourse* in the name column, then this would be too long—notice that this name continues on to a second line in the data view column label, since the columns default value is only 8. You can click the up and down arrows to increase or decrease how much room to allow for your column name label.

Align

The align column allows you to choose where to align the data you enter. You can change this by selecting the drop-down menu that appears after clicking in the cell. The alignment options are right, left, and center. By default, numeric values are aligned to the right, and string values are aligned to the left.

Measure

This column allows you to select the scale of measurement for the variable (scales of measurement are introduced in Chapter 1). By default, all variables are considered scale (i.e., an interval or ratio scale of measurement). If your variable is an ordinal or nominal variable, you can make this change by selecting the drop-down menu that appears after clicking in the cell.

Role

The role column is a new column that SPSS has added in recent versions. The drop down menu in the cell allows you to choose the following commands: input, target, both (input and target), none, partition, or split. Each of these options in the drop-down menu generally allows you to organize the entry and appearance of data in the data view tab. While each option is valuable, these are generally needed for data sets that we will not work with in this book.

PREVIEW OF SPSS IN FOCUS

This book is unique in that you will learn how to use SPSS to perform statistics as they are taught in this book. Most statistics textbooks for behavioral science omit such information, include it in an appendix separate from the main chapters in the book, include it at the end of chapters with no useful examples or context, or include them in ancillary materials that often are not included with course content. Instead, this book provides instructions for using SPSS in each chapter as statistical concepts are taught using practical research examples and screen shots to support student learning. You will find this instruction in the SPSS in Focus sections. These sections provide step-by-step instruction for how the concepts taught in each chapter can be applied to research problems using SPSS.

The reason for this inclusion is simple: Most researchers use some kind of statistical software to analyze statistics, and in behavioral science, the most common statistical software used by researchers is SPSS. This textbook brings statistics in research to the 21st century, giving you both the theoretical and computational instruction needed to understand how, when, and why you perform certain statistics under different conditions and the technical instruction you need to succeed in the modern era of data collection, data entry, data analysis, and statistical interpretation using SPSS statistical software. This preface has familiarized you with this software. Each subsequent SPSS in Focus section will show you how to use SPSS to perform most any application and statistic taught in this book.

PART I

Introduction and Descriptive Statistics

Introduction to Statistics

LEARNING OBJECTIVES

After reading this chapter, you should be able to:

1 Distinguish between descriptive and inferential statistics.

2 Explain how samples and populations, as well as a sample statistic and population parameter, differ.

3 Describe three research methods commonly used in behavioral science.

4 State the four scales of measurement and provide an example for each.

5 Distinguish between qualitative and quantitative data.

6 Determine whether a value is discrete or continuous.

7 Enter data into SPSS by placing each group in separate columns and each group in a single column (coding is required).

1.1   DESCRIPTIVE AND INFERENTIAL STATISTICS

Why should you study statistics? The topic can be intimidating, and rarely does anyone tell you, "Oh, that's an easy course . . . take statistics!" **Statistics** is a branch of mathematics used to summarize, analyze, and interpret what we observe—to make sense or meaning of our observations. A family counselor may use statistics to describe patient behavior and the effectiveness of a treatment program. A social psychologist may use statistics to summarize peer pressure among teenagers and interpret the causes. A college professor may give students a survey to summarize and interpret how much they like (or dislike) the course. In each case, the counselor, psychologist, and professor make use of statistics to do his or her job.

The reason it is important to study statistics can be described by the words of Mark Twain: *There are lies, damned lies and statistics.* He meant that statistics can be deceiving—and so can interpreting them. Statistics are all around you—from your college grade point average (GPA) to a *Newsweek* poll predicting which political candidate is likely to win an election. In each case, statistics are used to inform you. The challenge as you move into your careers is to be able to identify statistics and to interpret what they mean. Statistics are part of your everyday life, and they are subject to interpretation. The interpreter, of course, is YOU.

DEFINITION

Statistics is a branch of mathematics used to summarize, analyze, and interpret a group of numbers or observations.

We begin by introducing two general types of statistics:

- Descriptive statistics: statistics that summarize observations
- Inferential statistics: statistics used to interpret the meaning of descriptive statistics

This book describes how to apply and interpret both types of statistics in science and in practice to make you a more informed interpreter of the statistical information you encounter inside and outside of the classroom. Figure 1.1 is a schematic diagram of the chapter organization of this book, showing which chapters focus on descriptive statistics and which focus on inferential statistics.

DESCRIPTIVE STATISTICS

Researchers can measure many behavioral variables, such as love, anxiety, memory, and thought. Often, hundreds or thousands of measurements are made, and procedures were developed to organize, summarize, and make sense of these measures. These procedures, referred to as **descriptive statistics,** are specifically used to describe or summarize numeric observations, referred to as **data.** To illustrate, suppose we want to study anxiety among college students. We could describe anxiety, then, as a state or feeling of worry and nervousness. This certainly describes anxiety, but not numerically (or in a way that allows us to measure anxiety). Instead, we could state that anxiety is the number of times students fidget during a class presentation. Now anxiety is defined as a number. We may observe 50, 100, or 1,000 students give a class presentation and record the number of times each

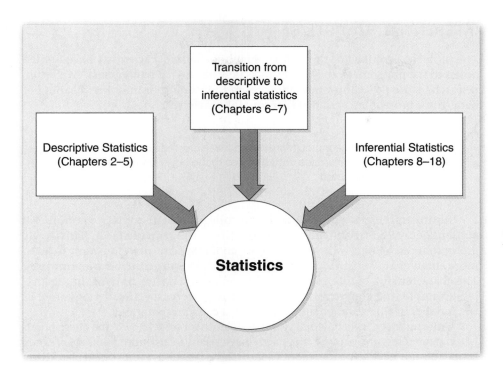

FIGURE 1.1

A general overview of this book. This book begins with an introduction to descriptive statistics (Chapters 2–5) and then uses descriptive statistics to transition (Chapters 6–7) to a discussion of inferential statistics (Chapters 8–18).

student fidgeted. Presenting a spreadsheet with the number for each individual student is not very clear. For this reason, researchers use descriptive statistics to summarize sets of individual measurements so they can be clearly presented and interpreted.

> **Descriptive statistics** are procedures used to summarize, organize, and make sense of a set of scores or observations.
> Descriptive statistics are typically presented graphically, in tabular form (in tables), or as summary statistics (single values).
>
> **Data** (plural) are measurements or observations that are typically numeric. A **datum** (singular) is a single measurement or observation, usually referred to as a **score** or **raw score**.

DEFINITION

Data are generally presented in summary. Typically, this means that data are presented graphically, in tabular form (in tables), or as summary statistics (e.g., an average). For example, the number of times each individual fidgeted is not all that meaningful, whereas the average (mean), middle (median), or most common (mode) number of times among all individuals is more meaningful. Tables and graphs serve a similar purpose to summarize large and small sets of data.

Most often, researchers collect data from a portion of individuals in a group of interest. For example, the 50, 100, or 1,000 students in the anxiety example would not constitute all students in college. Hence, these researchers collected anxiety data from some students, not all. So researchers require statistical procedures that allow them to infer what the effects of anxiety are among all students of interest using only the portion of data they measured.

NOTE: Descriptive statistics summarize data to make sense or meaning of a list of numeric values.

INFERENTIAL STATISTICS

The problem described in the last paragraph is that most scientists have limited access to the phenomena they study, especially behavioral phenomena. As a result, researchers use procedures that allow them to interpret or infer the meaning of data. These procedures are called **inferential statistics.**

DEFINITION

Inferential statistics are procedures used that allow researchers to infer or generalize observations made with samples to the larger population from which they were selected.

To illustrate, let's continue with the college student anxiety example. All students enrolled in college would constitute the **population.** This is the group that researchers want to learn more about. Specifically, they want to learn more about characteristics in this population, called **population parameters.** The characteristics of interest are typically some descriptive statistic. In the anxiety example, the characteristic of interest is anxiety, specifically measured as the number of times students fidget during a class presentation.

Unfortunately, in behavioral research, scientists rarely know what these population parameters are because they rarely have access to an entire population. They simply do not have the time, money, or other resources to even consider studying all students enrolled in college.

DEFINITION

A **population** is defined as the set of all individuals, items, or data of interest. This is the group about which scientists will generalize.

A characteristic (usually numeric) that describes a population is referred to as a **population parameter**.

NOTE: Inferential statistics are used to help the researcher infer how well statistics in a sample reflect parameters in a population.

The alternative is to select a portion or **sample** of individuals in the population. Selecting a sample is more practical, and most scientific research you read comes from samples and not populations. Going back to our example, this means that selecting a portion of students from the larger population of all students enrolled in college would constitute a sample. A characteristic that describes a sample is called a **sample statistic**—this is similar to a parameter, except it describes characteristics in a sample and not a population. Inferential statistics use the characteristics in a sample to infer what the unknown parameters are in a given population. In this way, as shown in Figure 1.2, a sample is selected from a population to learn more about the characteristics in the population of interest.

DEFINITION

A **sample** is defined as a set of selected individuals, items, or data taken from a population of interest.

A characteristic (usually numeric) that describes a sample is referred to as a **sample statistic**.

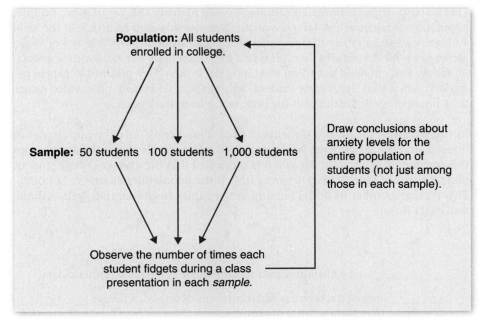

Population: All students enrolled in college.

Sample: 50 students   100 students   1,000 students

Draw conclusions about anxiety levels for the entire population of students (not just among those in each sample).

Observe the number of times each student fidgets during a class presentation in each *sample*.

FIGURE 1.2

Samples and populations. In this example, levels of anxiety are measured in a *sample* of 50, 100, or 1,000 college students. Researchers will observe anxiety in each sample. Then they will use inferential statistics to generalize their observations in each sample to the larger *population*, from which each sample was selected.

MAKING SENSE: Populations and Samples

A population is identified as any group of interest, whether that group is all students worldwide or all students in a professor's class. Think of any group you are interested in. Maybe you want to understand why college students join fraternities and sororities. So students who join fraternities and sororities is the group you're interested in. Hence, this group is now a population of interest, to you anyways. You identified a population of interest just as researchers identify populations they are interested in.

Remember that researchers collect samples only because they do not have access to all individuals in a population. Imagine having to identify every person who has fallen in love, experienced anxiety, been attracted to someone else, suffered with depression, or taken a college exam. It's ridiculous to consider that we can identify all individuals in such populations. So researchers use data gathered from samples (a portion of individuals from the population) to make inferences concerning a population.

To make sense of this, suppose you want to get an idea of how people in general feel about a new pair of shoes you just bought. To find out, you put your new shoes on and ask 20 people at random throughout the day whether or not they like the shoes. Now, do you really care about the opinion of only those 20 people you asked? Not really—you actually care more about the opinion of people in general. In other words, you only asked the 20 people (your sample) to get an idea of the opinions of people in general (the population of interest). Sampling from populations follows a similar logic.

EXAMPLE 1.1

On the basis of the following example, we will identify the population, sample, population parameter, and sample statistic: Suppose you read an article in the local college newspaper citing that the average college student plays 2 hours of video games per week. To test whether this is true for your school, you randomly approach 20 fellow students and ask them how long (in hours) they play video games per week. You find that the average student, among those you asked, plays video games for 1 hour per week. Distinguish the population from the sample.

In this example, all college students at your school constitute the population of interest, and the 20 students you approached is the sample that was selected from this population of interest. Because it is purported that the average college student plays 2 hours of video games per week, this is the population parameter (2 hours). The average number of hours playing video games in the sample is the sample statistic (1 hour).

LEARNING CHECK 1

1. _____ are techniques used to summarize or describe numeric data.

2. _____ describe(s) how a population is characterized, whereas _____ describe(s) the characteristics of samples.
   a. Statistics; parameters
   b. Parameters; statistics
   c. Descriptive; inferential
   d. Inferential; descriptive

3. A psychologist wants to study a small population of 40 students in a local private school. If the researcher was interested in selecting the entire population of students for this study, then how many students must the psychologist include?
   a. None, since it is not possible to study an entire population in this case.
   b. At least half, because this would constitute the majority of the population.
   c. All 40 students, because all students constitute the population.

4. True or false: Inferential statistics are used to help the researcher *infer* whether observations made with samples are reflective of the population.

Answers: 1. Descriptive statistics; 2. b; 3. c; 4. True.

1.2 STATISTICS IN RESEARCH

This book will describe many ways of measuring and interpreting data. Yet, simply collecting data does not make you a scientist. To engage in science, you must follow specific procedures for collecting data. Think of this as playing a game. Without the rules and procedures for playing, the game itself would be lost. The same is true in science; without the rules and procedures for collecting data, the ability to draw scientific conclusions would be lost. Ultimately, statistics are used in the context of **science,** and so it is necessary to introduce you to the basic procedures of scientific inquiry.

To illustrate the basic premise of engaging in science, suppose you come across the following problem first noted by the famous psychologist Edward Thorndike in 1898:

> Dogs get lost hundreds of times and no one ever notices it or sends an account of it to a scientific magazine, but let one find his way from Brooklyn to Yonkers and the fact immediately becomes a circulating anecdote. Thousands of cats on thousands of occasions sit helplessly yowling, and no one takes thought of it or writes to his friend, the professor; but let one cat claw at the knob of a door supposedly as a signal to be let out, and straightway this cat becomes the representative of the cat-mind in all books. . . . In short, the anecdotes give really . . . *supernormal* psychology of animals. (pp. 4–5)

Science is the study of phenomena, such as behavior, through strict observation, evaluation, interpretation, and theoretical explanation.

DEFINITION

Here the problem was to determine the animal mind. Edward Thorndike posed the question of whether animals were truly smart, based on the many observations he made. This is where the scientific process typically begins—with a question. To answer questions in a scientific manner, researchers need more than just statistics; they need a set of strict procedures for making the observations and measurements. In this section, we introduce three research methods commonly used in behavioral research: experimental, quasi-experimental, and correlational methods. Each research method involves examining the relationship between variables. Each method is introduced here because we will apply these methods throughout the book.

EXPERIMENTAL METHOD

Any study that demonstrates cause is called an **experiment.** To demonstrate cause, though, an experiment must follow strict procedures to ensure that the possibility of all other possible causes have been minimized or eliminated. So researchers must control the conditions under which observations are made to isolate cause-and-effect relationships between variables. Figure 1.3 shows the steps in a typical experiment based on a sample taken from a population. We will work through this example to describe the basic structure of an experiment.

To conduct an **experiment,** a researcher must specifically control the conditions under which observations are made to isolate cause-and-effect relationships between variables.

   Three requirements must be satisfied for a study to be regarded as an experiment: randomization, manipulation, and comparison.

DEFINITION

The experiment illustrated in Figure 1.3 was designed to determine the effect of distraction on student test scores. A sample of students was selected from a population of all undergraduates. In one group, the professor sat quietly while students took the exam (low-distraction group); in the other, the professor rattled papers, tapped her foot, and made other sounds during the exam (high-distraction group). Exam scores in both groups were measured and compared.

For this study to be called an experiment, researchers must satisfy three requirements. These requirements are regarded as the necessary steps to ensure enough

FIGURE 1.3

The basic structure of an experiment that meets each requirement for demonstrating cause and effect: randomization, manipulation, and comparison. In this example, a random sample of students was selected from a population of all undergraduates to study the effects of distraction on exam performance. To qualify as an experiment, (1) students were randomly assigned to experience a low- or high-distraction condition while taking an exam (randomization), (2) the researcher created each level of distraction (manipulation), and (3) a comparison group was included where distraction was minimal or absent (comparison).

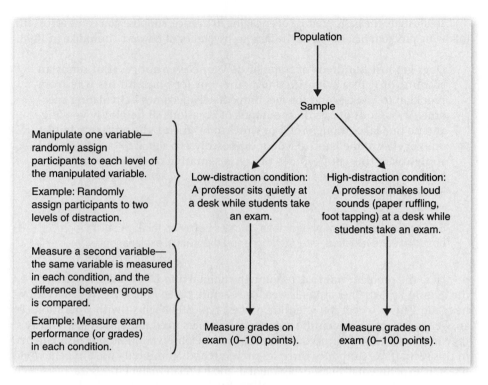

control to allow researchers to draw cause-and-effect conclusions. These requirements are the following:

1. Randomization (of assigning participants to conditions)
2. Manipulation (of variables that operate in an experiment)
3. Comparison (or a control group)

To meet the requirement of randomization, researchers must use **random assignment** (Requirement 1) to assign participants to groups. To do this, a researcher must be able to manipulate the levels of an **independent variable (IV)** (Requirement 2) to create the groups. Referring back to the test distraction example shown in Figure 1.3, the independent variable was distraction. The researcher first manipulated the levels of this variable (low, high), meaning that she created the conditions. She then assigned each student at random to experience one of the levels of distraction.

DEFINITION

Random assignment is a random procedure used to ensure that participants in a study have an equal chance of being assigned to a particular group or condition.

An **independent variable (IV)** is the variable that is manipulated in an experiment. This variable remains unchanged (or "independent") between conditions being observed in an experiment. It is the "presumed cause."

The specific conditions of an IV are referred to as the **levels of the IV**.

Random assignment and manipulation ensure that characteristics of participants in each group (such as their age, intelligence level, or study habits) vary entirely by chance. Because participant characteristics between groups now occur at random, we can assume that these characteristics are about the same between groups. This makes it more likely that any differences observed between groups were caused by the manipulation (low vs. high levels of distraction) and not participant characteristics.

Notice also that there are two groups in the experiment shown in Figure 1.3. So tests scores for students experiencing high levels of distraction were compared to those experiencing low levels of distraction. By comparing test scores between groups, we can determine whether high levels of distraction caused lower scores (compared to scores in the low-distraction group). This satisfies the requirement of comparison (Requirement 3), which requires that at least two groups be observed in an experiment. This allows scores in one group to be compared to those in at least one other group.

In this example, test scores were measured in each group. The measured variable in an experiment is referred to as the **dependent variable (DV).** Dependent variables can often be measured in many ways, and therefore require an **operational definition.** This is where a dependent variable is defined in terms of how it will be measured. For example, here we operationally defined *exam performance* as a score between 0 and 100 on a test. To summarize the experiment in Figure 1.3, levels of distraction (IV) were presumed to cause an effect or difference in exam grades (DV) between groups. This is an experiment because the researchers satisfied the requirements of randomization, manipulation, and comparison, thereby allowing them to draw cause-and-effect conclusions.

NOTE: An experiment is one where researchers satisfy three requirements to ensure enough control to allow researchers to draw cause-and-effect conclusions. These are randomization, manipulation, and comparison.

> The **dependent variable (DV)** is the variable that is believed to change in the presence of the independent variable. It is the "presumed effect."
>
> An **operational definition** is a description of some observable event in terms of the specific process or manner by which it was observed or measured.

DEFINITION

QUASI-EXPERIMENTAL METHOD

A study that lacks randomization, manipulation, or comparison is called a quasi-experiment. This most often occurs in one of two ways:

1. The study includes a quasi-independent variable.
2. The study lacks a comparison group.

In a typical quasi-experiment, the variables being studied can't be manipulated, which makes random assignment impossible. This occurs when variables are preexisting or inherent to the participants themselves. These types of variables are called quasi-independent variables. Figure 1.4 shows an example of a quasi-experiment that measured differences in multitasking ability by gender. Because the levels of gender (male, female) can't be randomly assigned (it is a **quasi-independent variable**), this study is regarded as a quasi-experiment.

> A **quasi-independent variable** is a variable whose levels are not randomly assigned to participants (nonrandom). This variable differentiates the groups or conditions being compared in a quasi-experiment.

DEFINITION

NOTE: A quasi-experiment is a study that (1) includes a quasi-independent variable or (2) lacks a comparison group.

A study is also regarded as a quasi-experiment when only one group is observed. With only one group, there is no comparison group, which means that differences between two levels of an independent variable can't be compared. In

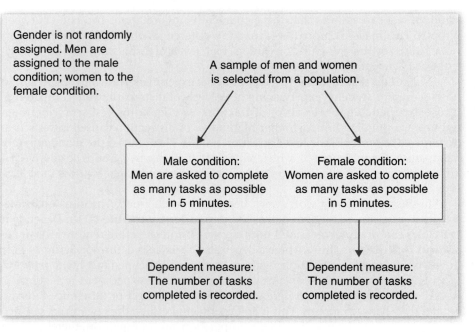

FIGURE 1.4

The basic structure of a quasi-experiment. In this example, researchers measured differences in multitasking behavior by gender. The grouping variable (gender) is preexisting. That is, participants were already male or female prior to the study. For this reason, researchers can't manipulate the variable or randomly assign participants to each level of gender, so this study is regarded as a quasi-experiment.

this way, failing to satisfy any of the three requirements for an experiment (randomization, manipulation, or comparison) makes the study a quasi-experiment.

CORRELATIONAL METHOD

Another method for examining the relationship between variables is to measure pairs of scores for each individual. This method can determine whether a relationship exists between variables, but it lacks the appropriate control needed to demonstrate cause and effect. To illustrate, suppose you test for a relationship between time spent using a computer and exercising per week. The data for such a study appear in tabular form and plotted as a graph in Figure 1.5. Using the correlational method, we can examine the extent to which two variables change in a related fashion. In the example shown in Figure 1.5, as computer use increases, time spent exercising decreases. This pattern suggests that computer use and time spent exercising are related.

NOTE: The correlational method involves measuring the relationship between pairs of scores.

Notice that no variable is manipulated to create different conditions or groups to which participants can be randomly assigned. Instead, two variables are measured for each participant, and the extent to which those variables are related is measured. This book describes many statistical procedures used to analyze data using the correlational method (Chapters 15–17) and the experimental and quasi-experimental methods (Chapters 9–14, 17–18).

EXAMPLE 1.2

A researcher conducts the following study: Participants are presented with a list of words written on a white background on a PowerPoint slide. In one group, the words are written in red (Group Color); in a second group, the words are written in black (Group Black). Participants are allowed to study the words for 1 minute. After that time, the slide is removed and participants are allowed 1 minute to write down as many words as they can recall. The number of words correctly recalled will be recorded for each group. Explain how this study can be an experiment.

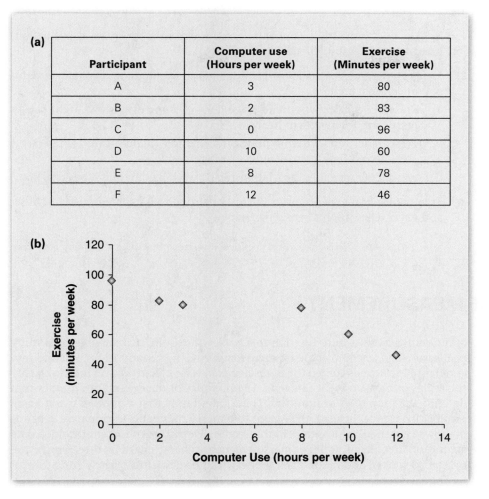

(a)

Participant	Computer use (Hours per week)	Exercise (Minutes per week)
A	3	80
B	2	83
C	0	96
D	10	60
E	8	78
F	12	46

(b)

FIGURE 1.5

An example of the correlational method. In this example, researchers measured the amount of time students spent using the computer and exercising each week. (a) The table shows two sets of scores for each participant. (b) The graph shows the pattern of the relationship between these scores. From the data, we can see that the two variables (computer use and exercise) change in a related fashion. That is, as computer use increases, time spent exercising decreases.

To create an experiment, we must satisfy the three requirements for demonstrating cause and effect: randomization, manipulation, and comparison. To satisfy each requirement, the researcher can

1. Randomly assign participants to experience one of the conditions. This ensures that some participants read colored words and others read black words entirely by chance.

2. Create the two conditions. The researcher could write 20 words on a PowerPoint slide. On one slide, the words are written in red; on the second slide, the same words are written in black.

3. Include a comparison group. In this case, the number of colored words correctly recalled will be compared to the number of black words correctly recalled, so this study has a comparison group.

Remember that each requirement is necessary to demonstrate that the levels of an independent variable are causing changes in the value of a dependent variable. If any one of these requirements is not satisfied, then the study is not an experiment.

✔ **LEARNING CHECK 2**

1. _____ is the study of phenomena through strict observation, evaluation, interpretation, and theoretical explanation.

2. State whether each of the following describes an experiment, quasi-experiment, or correlational method.
   a. A researcher tests whether dosage level of some drug (low, high) causes significant differences in health.
   b. A researcher tests whether political affiliation (Republican, Democrat) is associated with different attitudes toward morality.
   c. A researcher measures the relationship between income and life satisfaction.

3. True or false: An experiment is the only method that can demonstrate cause-and-effect relationships between variables.

Answers: 1. Science; 2. a. Experiment; b. Quasi-experiment; c. Correlational method; 3. True.

1.3   SCALES OF MEASUREMENT

Many statistical tests introduced in this book will require that variables in a study be measured on a certain **scale of measurement.** In the early 1940s, Harvard psychologist S. S. Stevens coined the terms *nominal, ordinal, interval,* and *ratio* to classify the scales of measurement (Stevens, 1946). Scales of measurement are rules that describe the properties of numbers. These rules imply that a number is not just a number in science. Instead, the extent to which a number is informative depends on how it was used or measured. In this section, we discuss the extent to which data are informative. In all, scales of measurement are characterized by three properties: order, differences, and ratios. Each property can be described by answering the following questions:

1. *Order:* Does a larger number indicate a greater value than a smaller number?
2. *Differences:* Does subtracting two numbers represent some meaningful value?
3. *Ratio:* Does dividing (or taking the ratio of) two numbers represent some meaningful value?

DEFINITION

Scales of measurement are rules for how the properties of numbers can change with different uses.

Table 1.1 summarizes the answers to the questions for each scale of measurement. You can think of each scale as a gradient of the informativeness of data. In this section, we begin with the least informative scale (nominal) and finish with the most informative scale (ratio).

NOMINAL SCALES

Numbers on a **nominal scale** identify something or someone; they provide no additional information. Common examples of nominal numbers include ZIP codes,

TABLE 1.1 Scales of measurement. Different scales of measurement and the information they provide concerning the order, difference, and ratio of numbers.

		Scale of Measurement			
		Nominal	**Ordinal**	**Interval**	**Ratio**
Property	**Order**	No	Yes	Yes	Yes
	Difference	No	No	Yes	Yes
	Ratio	No	No	No	Yes

license plate numbers, credit card numbers, country codes, telephone numbers, and Social Security numbers. These numbers simply identify locations, vehicles, or individuals and nothing more. One credit card number, for example, is not greater than another; it is simply different.

DEFINITION

Nominal scales are measurements where a number is assigned to represent something or someone.

In science, nominal variables are typically categorical variables that have been coded—converted to numeric values. Examples of nominal variables include a person's race, gender, nationality, sexual orientation, hair and eye color, season of birth, marital status, or other demographic or personal information. A researcher may code men as 1 and women as 2. They may code the seasons of birth as 1, 2, 3, and 4 for spring, summer, fall, and winter, respectively. These numbers are used to identify gender or the seasons and nothing more. We often code words with numeric values when entering them into statistical programs such as SPSS. **Coding** is largely done because it is often easier to compute data using statistical programs, such as SPSS, when data are entered as numbers, not words.

NOTE: Nominal values represent something or someone. They often reflect coded data in behavioral science.

Coding refers to the procedure of converting a nominal value to a numeric value.

DEFINITION

ORDINAL SCALES

An **ordinal scale** of measurement is one that conveys order alone. This scale indicates that some value is greater or less than another value. Examples of ordinal scales include finishing order in a competition, education level, and rankings. These scales only indicate that one value is greater than or less than another, so differences between ranks do not have meaning. Consider, for example, the *U.S. News & World Report* rankings for the top psychology graduate school programs in the United States. Table 1.2 shows the rank, college, and actual score for the top 25 programs, including ties, in 2009. Based on ranks alone, can we say that the difference between the psychology graduate programs ranked 1 and 11 is the same as the difference between those ranked 13 and 23? In both cases, 10 ranks separate

NOTE: Ordinal values convey order alone.

TABLE 1.2   Ordinal scale. A list of the top 25 ranked psychology graduate school programs in 2009, including ties (left column), and the actual points used to determine their rank (right column). The *U.S. News & World Report* published these rankings.

Rank	College Name	Actual Score
1	Stanford University	4.7
1	University of California, Berkeley	4.7
3	Harvard University	4.6
3	University of California, Los Angeles	4.6
3	University of Michigan, Ann Arbor	4.6
3	Yale University	4.6
7	University of Illinois, Urbana-Champaign	4.5
8	Princeton University	4.4
8	University of Minnesota, Twin Cities	4.4
8	University of Wisconsin, Madison	4.4
11	Massachusetts Institute of Technology	4.3
11	University of Pennsylvania	4.3
13	University of North Carolina, Chapel Hill	4.2
13	University of Texas, Austin	4.2
13	University of Washington	4.2
13	Washington University in St. Louis	4.2
17	Carnegie Mellon University	4.1
17	Columbia University	4.1
17	Cornell University	4.1
17	Northwestern University	4.1
17	Ohio State University	4.1
17	University of California, San Diego	4.1
23	Duke University	4.0
23	Indiana University, Bloomington	4.0
23	John Hopkins University	4.0

the schools. Yet, if you look at the actual scores for determining rank, you find that the difference between ranks 1 and 11 is 0.4 points, whereas the difference between ranks 13 and 23 is 0.2 points. So the difference in points is not the same. Ranks alone don't convey this difference. They simply indicate that one rank is greater or less than another rank.

DEFINITION

Ordinal scales are measurements where values convey order or rank alone.

INTERVAL SCALES

An **interval scale** measurement, on the other hand, can be understood readily by two defining principles: equidistant scales and no true zero. A common example for this in behavioral science is the rating scale. Rating scales are taught here as an interval scale because most researchers report these as interval data in published research. This type of scale is a numeric response scale used to indicate a participant's level of agreement or opinion with some statement. An example of a rating scale is given in Figure 1.6. Here we will look at each defining principle.

> **Interval scales** are measurements where the values have no true zero and the distance between each value is equidistant.

DEFINITION

An **equidistant scale** is a scale distributed in units that are equidistant from one another. Many behavioral scientists assume that scores on a rating scale are distributed in equal intervals. For example, if you are asked to rate your satisfaction with a spouse or job on a 7-point scale from 1 (*completely unsatisfied*) to 7 (*completely satisfied*), like in the scale shown in Figure 1.6, then you are using an interval scale. Because the distance between each point (1 to 7) is assumed to be the same or equal, it is appropriate to compute differences between scores on this scale. So a statement such as "The difference in job satisfaction among men and women was 2 points," is appropriate with interval scale measurements.

> **Equidistant scales** are those values whose intervals are distributed in equal units.

DEFINITION

However, an interval scale does not have a **true zero.** A common example of a scale without a true zero is temperature. A temperature equal to zero for most measures of temperature does not mean that there is no temperature; it is just an arbitrary zero point. Values on a rating scale also have no true zero. In the example shown in Figure 1.6, a 1 was used to indicate no satisfaction, not 0. Each value (including 0) is arbitrary. That is, we could use any number to represent none of something. Measurements of latitude and longitude also fit this criterion. The implication is that without a true zero, there is no value to indicate the absence of the phenomenon you are observing (so a zero proportion is not meaningful). For this reason, stating a ratio such as "Satisfaction ratings were three times greater among men compared to women" is not appropriate with interval scale measurements.

NOTE: Interval values have equidistant scales but no true zero.

> A **true zero** describes values where the value 0 truly indicates nothing. Values on an interval scale do *not* have a true zero.

DEFINITION

Satisfaction Ratings

1	2	3	4	5	6	7
Completely Unsatisfied						Completely Satisfied

FIGURE 1.6

An example of a 7-point rating scale for satisfaction used for scientific investigation.

NOTE: Ratio values have equidistant scales and a true zero. This scale of measurement does not limit the conclusions researchers can state.

RATIO SCALES

Ratio scales are similar to interval scales in that scores are distributed in equal units. Yet, unlike interval scales, a distribution of scores on a ratio scale has a true zero. This is an ideal scale in behavioral research because any mathematical operation can be performed on the values that are measured. Common examples of ratio scales include counts and measures of length, height, weight, and time. For scores on a ratio scale, order is informative. For example, a person who is 30 years old is older than another who is 20. Differences are also informative. For example, the difference between 70 and 60 seconds is the same as the difference between 30 and 20 seconds (the difference is 10 seconds). Ratios are also informative on this scale because a true zero is defined—it truly means nothing. Hence, it is meaningful to state that 60 pounds is twice as heavy as 30 pounds.

DEFINITION

Ratio scales are measurements where a set of values has a true zero and are equidistant.

In science, researchers often go out of their way to measure variables on a ratio scale. For example, if they want to measure eating, they may choose to measure the amount of time between meals or the amount of food consumed (in ounces). If they measure memory, they may choose to measure the amount of time it takes to memorize some list or the number of errors made. If they measure depression, they may choose to measure the dosage (in milligrams) that produces the most beneficial treatment or the number of symptoms reported. In each case, the behaviors were measured using values on a ratio scale, thereby allowing researchers to draw conclusions in terms of order, differences, and ratios—there are no restrictions with ratio scale variables.

LEARNING CHECK 3

1. The _____ are rules for how the properties of numbers can change with different uses.

2. In 2010, *Fortune 500* magazine ranked Apple as the most admired company in the world. This ranking is on a(n) _____ scale of measurement.

3. What are two characteristics of rating scales that allow some researchers to use these values on an interval scale of measurement?
   a. Values on an interval scale have a true zero, but are not equidistant.
   b. Values on an interval scale have differences and a true zero.
   c. Values on an interval scale are equidistant and have a true zero.
   d. Values on an interval scale are equidistant and do not have a true zero.

4. Which of the following is not an example of a ratio scale variable?
   a. Age (in days)
   b. Speed (in seconds)
   c. Height (in inches)
   d. Movie ratings (1 to 4 stars)

TYPES OF DATA 1.4

The scales of measurement reflect the informativeness of data. With nominal scales, researchers can conclude little; with ratio scales, researchers can conclude just about anything in terms of order, differences, and ratios. Researchers also distinguish between the types of data they measure. The types of data researchers measure fall into two categories: (1) continuous or discrete and (2) quantitative or qualitative. Each category is discussed in this section. Many examples we use for these types of data are given in Table 1.3.

CONTINUOUS AND DISCRETE VARIABLES

NOTE: Continuous variables are measured along a continuum, whereas discrete variables are measured in whole units or categories.

Variables can be categorized as continuous or discrete. A **continuous variable** is measured along a continuum. So continuous variables are measured at any place beyond the decimal point. Consider, for example, that Olympic sprinters are timed to the nearest hundredths place (in seconds), but if the Olympic judges wanted to clock them to the nearest millionths place, they could.

> A **continuous variable** is measured along a continuum at any place beyond the decimal point. Continuous variables can be measured in whole units or fractional units.

DEFINITION

A **discrete variable,** on the other hand, is measured in whole units or categories. So discrete variables are not measured along a continuum. For example, the number of brothers and sisters you have and your family's socioeconomic class (working class, middle class, upper class) are examples of discrete variables. Refer to Table 1.3 for more examples of continuous and discrete variables.

> A **discrete variable** is measured in whole units or categories that are not distributed along a continuum.

DEFINITION

QUANTITATIVE AND QUALITATIVE VARIABLES

Variables can be categorized as quantitative or qualitative. A **quantitative variable** varies by amount. The variables are measured in numeric units, and so both continuous and discrete variables can be quantitative. For example, we can measure food intake in calories (a continuous variable), or we can count the number of pieces of food consumed (a discrete variable). In both cases, the variables are measured by amount (in numeric units).

> A **quantitative variable** varies by amount. This variable is measured numerically and is often collected by measuring or counting.

DEFINITION

A **qualitative variable,** on the other hand, varies by class. The variables are often labels for the behaviors we observe—so only discrete variables can fall into this category. For example, socioeconomic class (working class, middle class, upper class) is discrete and qualitative; so are many disorders such as depression (unipolar, bipolar) or drug use (none, experimental, abusive). Refer to Table 1.3 for more examples of quantitative and qualitative variables.

> A **qualitative variable** varies by class. This variable is often represented as a label and describes nonnumeric aspects of phenomena.

DEFINITION

TABLE 1.3   A list of 20 variables showing how they fit into the three categories that describe them.

Variables	Continuous vs. Discrete	Qualitative vs. Quantitative	Scale of Measurement
Gender (male, female)	Discrete	Qualitative	Nominal
Seasons (spring, summer, fall, winter)	Discrete	Qualitative	Nominal
Number of dreams recalled	Discrete	Quantitative	Ratio
Number of errors	Discrete	Quantitative	Ratio
Duration of drug abuse (in years)	Continuous	Quantitative	Ratio
Ranking of favorite foods	Discrete	Quantitative	Ordinal
Ratings of satisfaction (1 to 7)	Discrete	Quantitative	Interval
Body type (slim, average, heavy)	Discrete	Qualitative	Nominal
Score (from 0 to 100%) on an exam	Continuous	Quantitative	Ratio
Number of students in your class	Discrete	Quantitative	Ratio
Temperature (degrees Fahrenheit)	Continuous	Quantitative	Interval
Time (in seconds) to memorize a list	Continuous	Quantitative	Ratio
The size of a reward (in grams)	Continuous	Quantitative	Ratio
Position standing in line	Discrete	Quantitative	Ordinal
Political Affiliation (Republican, Democrat)	Discrete	Qualitative	Nominal
Type of distraction (auditory, visual)	Discrete	Qualitative	Nominal
A letter grade (A, B, C, D, F)	Discrete	Qualitative	Ordinal
Weight (in pounds) of an infant	Continuous	Quantitative	Ratio
A college student's SAT score	Discrete	Quantitative	Interval
Number of lever presses per minute	Discrete	Quantitative	Ratio

EXAMPLE 1.3

For each of the following examples, we (1) name the variable being measured, (2) state whether the variable is continuous or discrete, and (3) state whether the variable is quantitative or qualitative.

a.   A researcher records the month of birth among patients with schizophrenia. The month of birth (the variable) is discrete and qualitative.

b.   A professor records the number of students absent during a final exam. The number of absent students (the variable) is discrete and quantitative.

c.   A researcher asks children to choose which type of cereal they prefer (one with a toy inside or one without). He records the choice of cereal for each child. The choice of cereal (the variable) is discrete and qualitative.

d.   A therapist measures the time (in hours) that clients continue a recommended program of counseling. The time in hours (the variable) is continuous and quantitative.

1. True or false: The types of data researchers measure fall into two categories: (1) continuous or discrete and (2) quantitative or qualitative.

2. State whether each of the following are continuous or discrete.

    a. Delay (in seconds) it takes drivers to make a left-hand turn when a light turns green

    b. The number of questions that participants ask during a research study

    c. Type of drug use (none, infrequent, moderate, or frequent)

    d. Season of birth (spring, summer, fall, or winter)

3. State whether the variables listed in Question 2 are quantitative or qualitative.

4. True or false: Qualitative variables can be continuous or discrete.

5. A researcher is interested in the effects of stuttering on social behavior with children. He records the number of peers a child speaks to during a typical school day. In this example, would the data be qualitative or quantitative?

Answers: 1. True; 2. a. Continuous. b. Discrete. c. Discrete. d. Discrete; 3. a. Quantitative. b. Quantitative. c. Qualitative. d. Qualitative; 4. False; 5. Quantitative.

RESEARCH IN FOCUS: TYPES OF DATA AND SCALES OF MEASUREMENT 1.5

While qualitative variables are often measured in behavioral research, this book will focus largely on quantitative variables. The reason is twofold: (1) Quantitative measures are more common in behavioral research, and (2) most statistical tests taught in this book are adapted for quantitative measures. Indeed, many researchers who measure qualitative variables will also measure those that are quantitative in the same study.

For example, Jones and colleagues (2010) explored the costs and benefits of social networking among college students. The researchers used a qualitative method to interview each student in their sample. In the interview, students could respond openly to questions asked during the interview. These researchers then summarized responses into categories related to learning, studying, and social life. For example, the following student response was categorized as an example of independent learning experience for employability: "I think it [social software] can be beneficial . . . in the real working environment" (p. 780).

The limitation for this analysis is that categories are on a nominal scale (the least informative scale). So many researchers who record qualitative data also use some quantitative measures. For example, researchers in this study also asked students to rate their usage of a variety of social software technologies, such as PowerPoint and personal websites, on a scale from 1 (*never*) to 4 (*always*). A fifth choice (*not applicable*) was also included on this rating scale. These ratings are on an interval scale, which allowed the researchers to also discuss *differences* related to how much students use social software technologies.

Inevitably, the conclusions we can draw with qualitative data are rather limited because these data are typically on a nominal scale. On the other hand, most statistics introduced in this book require that variables are measured on the more informative scales. For this reason, this book mainly describes statistical procedures for quantitative variables measured on an ordinal, interval, or ratio scale.

1.6   SPSS IN FOCUS: ENTERING AND DEFINING VARIABLES

Throughout this book, we present instructions for using the statistical software program SPSS by showing you how this software can make all the work you do by hand as simple as point and click. Before you read this SPSS section, please take the time to read the section titled "How To Use SPSS With This Book" at the beginning of this book. This section provides an overview of the different views and features in SPSS. This software is an innovative statistical computer program that can compute almost any statistic taught in this book.

In this chapter, we discussed how variables are defined, coded, and measured. Let's see how SPSS makes this simple. Keep in mind that the variable view is used to define the variables you measure, and the data view is used to enter the scores you measured. When entering data, make sure that all values or scores are entered in each cell of the data view spreadsheet. The biggest challenge is making sure you enter the data correctly. Entering even a single value incorrectly can alter the data analyses that SPSS computes. For this reason, always double-check the data to make sure the correct values have been entered.

Let's use a simple example. Suppose you record the average GPA of students in one of three statistics classes. You record the following GPA scores for each class, given in Table 1.4.

TABLE 1.4   GPA scores in three statistics classes.

Class 1	Class 2	Class 3
3.3	3.9	2.7
2.9	4.0	2.3
3.5	2.4	2.2
3.6	3.1	3.0
3.1	3.0	2.8

There are two ways you can enter these data: by column or by row. To **enter data by column:**

1. Open the **variable view** tab (see Figure 1.7). In the **name column,** enter your variable names as *class1, class2,* and *class3* (note that spaces are not allowed) in each row. Three rows should be active.

2. Because the data are to the tenths place, go to the **decimal column** and reduce that value to 1 in each row.

Name	Type	Width	Decimals
class1	Numeric	8	1
class2	Numeric	8	1
class3	Numeric	8	1

FIGURE 1.7

SPSS variable view.

1. Open the **data view** tab. Notice that the first three columns are now labeled with the group names (see Figure 1.8). Enter the data, given in Table 1.4, for each class in the appropriate column. The data for each group are now listed down each column.

class1	class2	class3
3.3	3.9	2.7
2.9	4.0	2.3
3.5	2.4	2.2
3.6	3.1	3.0
3.1	3.0	2.8

FIGURE 1.8

Data entry in data view for SPSS.

There is another way to enter these data in SPSS: You can **enter data by row.** This requires *coding* the data.

1. Open the **variable view** tab (see Figure 1.9). Enter *classes* in the first row in the **name column.** Enter *GPA* in the second row in the name column.

2. Go to the **decimal column** and reduce that value to 0 for the first row. You will see why we did this in the next step. Reduce the decimal column to 1 in the second row because we will enter GPA scores for this variable.

Name	Type	Width	Decimals	Label	Values
classes	Numeric	8	0		{1, class 1}...
GPA	Numeric	8	1		None

FIGURE 1.9

SPSS variable view.

1. Go to the **values column** and click on the small gray box with three dots. In the **dialog box,** enter *1* in the **value cell** and *class 1* in the **label cell,** and then select **add.** Repeat these steps by entering *2* for *class 2* and *3* for *class 3*; then select **OK.** When you go back to the data view tab, SPSS will now recognize *1* as *class 1, 2* as *class 2,* and so on in the column you labeled *classes.*

2. Open the **data view** tab. In the first column, enter *1* five times, *2* five times, and *3* five times (see Figure 1.10). This tells SPSS that there are five students in each class. In the second column, enter the GPA scores for each class by row. The data for each class are now listed across the rows next to the corresponding codes (1, 2, and 3) for each class.

classes	GPA
1	3.3
1	2.9
1	3.5
1	3.6
1	3.1
2	3.9
2	4.0
2	2.4
2	3.1
2	3.0
3	2.7
3	2.3
3	2.2
3	3.0
3	2.8

FIGURE 1.10

Data entry in data view for SPSS.

The data for all the variables are labeled, coded, and entered. So long as you do this correctly, SPSS will make summarizing, computing, and analyzing any statistic taught in this book fast and simple.

CHAPTER SUMMARY ORGANIZED BY LEARNING OBJECTIVE

LO 1–2: Distinguish between descriptive and inferential statistics; explain how samples and populations, as well as a sample statistic and population parameter, differ.

- Statistics is a branch of mathematics used to summarize, analyze, and interpret a group of numbers or observations. **Descriptive statistics** are procedures used to make sense of observations by summarizing them numerically. **Inferential statistics** are procedures that allow researchers to infer whether observations made with samples can be generalized to the population.
- A **population** is a set of all individuals, items, or data of interest. A characteristic that describes a population is referred to as a **population parameter**. A **sample** is a set of selected individuals, items, or data taken from a population of interest. A characteristic that describes a sample is referred to as a **sample statistic.**

LO 3: Describe three research methods commonly used in behavioral science.

- The experimental design uses randomization, manipulation, and comparison to control variables to demonstrate cause-and-effect relationships. The quasi-experimental design is structured similar to an experiment but lacks randomization or a comparison group.
- The correlational method is used to measure pairs of scores for each individual and examine the relationship between the variables.

LO 4: State the four scales of measurement and provide an example for each.

- The **scales of measurement** refer to how the properties of numbers can change

with different uses. They are characterized by three properties: order, differences, and ratios. There are four scales of measurement: **nominal, ordinal, interval,** and **ratio.** Nominal values are typically coded (e.g., seasons, months, gender), ordinal values indicate order alone (e.g., rankings, grade level), interval values have equidistant scales and no true zero (e.g., rating scale values, temperature), and ratio values are also equidistant but have a true zero (e.g., weight, height, calories).

LO 5–6: Distinguish between qualitative and quantitative data; determine whether a value is discrete or continuous.

- A **continuous variable** is measured along a continuum, whereas a **discrete variable** is measured in whole units or categories. Hence, continuous but not discrete variables are measured at any place beyond the decimal point. A **quantitative variable** varies by amount, whereas a **qualitative variable** varies by class.

SPSS LO 7: Enter data into SPSS by placing each group in separate columns and by placing each group in a single column (coding is required).

- SPSS can be used to enter and define variables. All variables are defined in the **variable view** tab. The values recorded for each variable are listed in the **data view** tab. Data can be entered by column or by row in the data view tab. Listing data by row requires coding the variable. Variables are coded in the variable view tab in the **values column** (for more details, see Section 1.6).

KEY TERMS

coding	interval scale	ratio scale
continuous variable	levels of the independent variable	raw score
data	nominal scale	sample
datum	operational definition	sample statistic
dependent variable (DV)	ordinal scale	scales of measurement
descriptive statistics	population	science
discrete datavariable	population parameter	score
equidistant scale	qualitative variable	statistics
experiment	quantitative variable	true zero
independent variable (IV)	quasi-independent variable	
inferential statistics	random assignment	

END-OF-CHAPTER PROBLEMS

Factual Problems

1. What is the difference between descriptive and inferential statistics?

2. Distinguish between data and a raw score.

3. By definition, how is a sample related to a population?

4. State three commonly used research methods in behavioral science.

5. In an experiment, researchers measure two types of variables: independent and dependent variables.
   a. Which variable is manipulated to create the groups?
   b. Which variable is measured in each group?

6. State the four scales of measurement. Which scale of measurement is the most informative?

7. Can a nominal variable be numeric? Explain.

8. What is the main distinction between variables on an interval and those on a ratio scale of measurement?

9. A quantitative variable varies by _____; a qualitative variable varies by _____.

10. What are the two types of data that are collected and measured quantitatively?

Concepts and Application Problems

11. State whether each of the following words best describes descriptive statistics or inferential statistics.
   a. Describe
   b. Infer
   c. Summarize

12. State whether each of the following is true or false.
   a. Graphs, tables, and summary statistics all illustrate the application of inferential statistics.
   b. Inferential statistics are procedures used to make inferences about a population, given only a limited amount of data.
   c. Descriptive statistics can be used to describe populations and samples of data.

13. A researcher measured behavior among all individuals in some small population. Are inferential statistics necessary to draw conclusions concerning this population? Explain.

14. Appropriately use the terms *sample* and *population* to describe the following statement: A statistics class has 25 students enrolled, but only 23 students attended class.

15. On occasion, samples can be larger than the population from which it was selected. Explain why this can't be true.

16. A researcher demonstrates that eating breakfast in the morning causes increased alertness throughout the day. What research design must the researcher have used in this example? Explain.

17. A researcher measures the height and income of participants and finds that taller men tend to earn greater incomes than do shorter men. What type of research method did the researcher use in this example? Explain.

18. State whether each of the following variables are examples of an independent variable or quasi-independent variable. Only answer *quasi-independent* for variables that can't be randomized.
    a. Marital status
    b. Political affiliation
    c. Time of delay prior to recall
    d. Environment of research setting
    e. Years of education
    f. Type of feedback (negative, positive)

19. To determine whether a new sleeping pill was effective, adult insomniacs received a pill (either real or fake), and their sleeping times were subsequently measured (in minutes) during an overnight observation period.
    a. Identify the independent variable in this study.
    b. Identify the dependent variable in this study.

20. A researcher tests whether cocaine use increases impulsive behavior in a sample of cocaine-dependent and cocaine-inexperienced mice.
    a. Identify the independent variable in this study.
    b. Identify the dependent variable in this study.

21. Researchers are interested in studying whether personality is related to the month in which someone was born.
    a. What scale of measurement is the month of birth?
    b. Is it appropriate to code the data? Explain.

22. Rank the scales of measurement in order from least informative to most informative.

23. What is the main disadvantage of measuring qualitative data? In your answer, explain why quantitative research is most often applied in the behavioral sciences.

24. State whether each of the following describes a study measuring qualitative or quantitative data.
    a. A researcher distributed open-ended questions to participants asking how they feel when they are in love.
    b. A researcher records the blood pressure of participants during a task meant to induce stress.
    c. A psychologist interested in drug addiction injects rats with an attention-inducing drug and then measures the rate of lever pressing.
    d. A witness to a crime gives a description of the suspect to the police.

25. State whether each of the following are continuous or discrete data.
    a. Time in seconds to memorize a list of words
    b. Number of students in a statistics class
    c. The weight in pounds of newborn infants
    d. The SAT score among college students

26. Fill in the table below to identify the characteristics of each variable.

Variable	Type of Data (qualitative vs. quantitative)	Type of Number (continuous vs. discrete)	Scale of Measurement
Gender			
Seasons			
Time of day			
Rating scale score			
Movie ratings (one to four stars)			
Number of students in your class			
Temperature (degrees Fahrenheit)			
Time (in minutes) to prepare dinner			
Position standing in line			

Problems in Research

27. **Grading the public school system.** In December 2009, a CBS News poll asked 1,048 Americans to grade the U.S. public school system. In the poll, they asked, "How would you grade the U.S. on the quality of the public schools in this country?" The results are described in the table below, with A being the best grade and F being the worst grade:

Grade	%
A	5
B	23
C	32
D	26
F	12

Source: Reported at http://www.pollingreport.com/ed.htm

   a. What was the sample size for this poll?
   b. Based on the percentages given in the table, how well was the U.S. public school system graded in general?

28. **Racial attitudes in college.** Shook and Fazio (2008) randomly assigned White freshman college students to live with a White (same-race group) or Black (different-race group) roommate in a college dormitory. After a few months, researchers measured racial attitudes and compared differences between groups. Is this study an example of an experiment? Explain your answer in terms of randomization, manipulation, and comparison.

29. **Gender and mental toughness.** Nicholls and colleagues (2009) measured mental toughness (among other measures) in a sample of athletes ranging in age from 15 to 58 years. They reported that "males scored significantly higher than females on total mental toughness" (p. 74). Is it possible that an experimental method was used to show this effect? Explain.

30. **Facial distinctiveness**. Wickham, Morris, and Fritz (2000) wrote that "Although there has been extensive interest in the influence of distinctiveness on memory for faces, measuring the distinctiveness of a face is problematic because *distinctiveness* is difficult to define" (pp. 99–100). What type of definition will researchers need to make for the term *distinctiveness?*

31. **Height and educational attainment.** Szklarska, Koziel, Bielicki, and Malina (2007) hypothesized that taller young men are more likely to move up the scale of educational attainment compared with shorter individuals from the same social background. They recruited 91,373 nineteen-year-old men to participate in the study. Do these participants most likely represent a sample or population? Explain.

32. **Describing the scales of measurement.** Harwell and Gatti (2001) stated, "If the test score variable possesses an interval scale, then the difference in proficiency reflected in scores of 10 and 15 is exactly the same as the difference in proficiency reflected in scores of 15 and 20" (p. 105). What is the defining principle that allows researchers to draw this conclusion?

Answers for even numbers are in Appendix C.

Summarizing Data

Tables, Graphs, and Distributions

LEARNING OBJECTIVES

After reading this chapter, you should be able to:

1. Construct a simple frequency distribution for grouped and ungrouped data.

2. Determine whether data should be grouped or ungrouped.

3. Identify when it is appropriate to distribute the cumulative frequency, relative frequency, relative percent, cumulative relative frequency, and cumulative percent.

4. Construct and interpret graphs for distributions of continuous data.

5. Construct and interpret graphs for distributions of discrete data, including two-variable data.

6. Construct frequency distributions for quantitative and categorical data using SPSS.

7. Construct histograms, bar charts, and pie charts using SPSS.

CHAPTER 2

2.1   WHY SUMMARIZE DATA?

Suppose you scored 90% on your first statistics exam. How could you determine how well you did in comparison to the rest of the class? First you'd need to consider the scores of the other students. If there were 20 students in the class, the listing of scores may look like Figure 2.1a. This listing is not particularly helpful because you cannot see at a glance how a score of 90% compares to the other grades. A more meaningful arrangement is to place the data in a summary table that shows the **frequency** of exam scores, which in this case is the number of scores for each grade range. When you arrange the scores in this way, as shown in Figure 2.1b, you can see that an exam score of 90% is extremely good. Only three other students fared as well or better, and most of the class had lower scores.

DEFINITION

A **frequency** describes the number of times or how often a category, score, or range of scores occurs.

This simple example illustrates the need to summarize data (recall in Chapter 1 that summarization is part of descriptive statistics), in that it can make the presentation and interpretation of a distribution of data clearer. Today, computers can construct just about any table or graph we need. But to understand what computers do, it helps to work through smaller data sets by hand. We do that in this chapter, starting with a discussion of frequency distribution tables and concluding with graphs of distributions for one- and two-variable data. In all, this chapter will help you appropriately construct and accurately interpret many of the tables and graphs used to summarize data in behavioral research.

Exam Scores	
90%	80%
59%	72%
64%	84%
77%	87%
88%	60%
78%	66%
94%	78%
96%	73%
65%	81%
79%	55%

(a)

Exam Scores (%)	Frequency
90–99	3
80–89	5
70–79	6
60–69	4
50–59	2

(b)

FIGURE 2.1

This figure shows (a) a list of 20 exam scores and (b) a summary table of the frequency of scores from that list.

FREQUENCY DISTRIBUTIONS FOR GROUPED DATA   2.2

Frequency distributions summarize how often (or frequently) scores occur in a data set. Frequency distributions are most often published when researchers measure counts of behavior. Indeed, to find the frequency of values, we must quite literally count the number times that scores occur. Consider the following list of scores in Table 2.1, which represent the average times (in minutes, rounded to the nearest tenths place) that 50 healthy American children watched television per day in the previous year.

TABLE 2.1   The average time (in minutes) that 50 healthy American children watched television per day in the previous year.

30	70	7	47	13
60	0	91	33	44
40	9	67	55	65
12	140	77	49	77
110	98	21	22	44
33	44	18	10	33
30	20	110	109	54
17	40	102	33	17
55	16	90	12	175
44	33	33	7	82

A **frequency distribution** is a summary display for a distribution of data organized or summarized in terms of how often a category, score, or range of scores occurs.

DEFINITION

Table 2.1 is not really informative as presented. It's only a listing of 50 numbers. To make sense of this list, researchers will consider what makes these data interesting—that is, by determining how the results of this study can be more meaningful to someone wanting to learn something about children's TV habits.

SIMPLE FREQUENCY DISTRIBUTIONS

One way to make these data more meaningful is to summarize how often scores occur in this list using a **simple frequency distribution.** In a simple frequency distribution, we can summarize how often each individual score occurs (ungrouped data—defined in Section 2.4) or how often scores occur in defined groups or intervals (**grouped data**). Often we collect hundreds or even thousands of scores.

With such large data sets, it is generally clearer to summarize the frequency of scores in groups or **intervals.** When summarizing data this way, the data are called grouped data.

<table>
<tr><td>DEFINITION</td><td>A **simple frequency distribution** is a summary display for (1) the frequency of each individual score or category (ungrouped data) in a distribution or (2) the frequency of scores falling within defined groups or intervals (grouped data) in a distribution.

Grouped data are a set of scores distributed into intervals, where the frequency of each score can fall into any given interval.

An **interval** is a discrete range of values within which the frequency of a subset of scores is contained.</td></tr>
</table>

NOTE: Simple frequency distributions summarize how often scores occur. With larger data sets, the frequency of scores contained in discrete intervals is summarized (grouped data).

Table 2.1 lists 50 scores, which is a rather large data set. For this reason, we will summarize this list of scores in groups or intervals. To construct a simple frequency distribution for grouped data, follow three steps:

Step 1: Find the real range.

Step 2: Find the interval width.

Step 3: Construct the frequency distribution.

We will follow these three steps to construct a frequency distribution for the data given in Table 2.1.

Step 1: Find the real range. The **real range** is one more than the difference between the largest and smallest number in a list of data. In Table 2.1, the smallest value is 0 and the largest value is 175; therefore, $175 - 0 = 175$. The *real range* is $175 + 1 = 176$.

<table>
<tr><td>DEFINITION</td><td>The **real range** is one more than the difference between the largest and smallest value in a data set.</td></tr>
</table>

Step 2: Find the interval width. The **interval width** is the range of values contained in each interval of a grouped frequency distribution. To find this, we divide the real range by the number of intervals chosen. The recommended number of intervals is between 5 and 20. Anything less provides too little summary; anything more is often too confusing. Regardless, *you* choose the number of intervals. The computation for the interval width can be stated as

$$\text{Interval width} = \frac{\text{real range}}{\text{number of intervals}}.$$

If we decide to split the data in Table 2.1 into 10 intervals, then the computation is $\frac{176}{10}$; hence, the interval width is 17.6. Rounding is necessary when the value for the interval width is not the same degree of accuracy as the original list. For example, the data listed in Table 2.1 are rounded to the ones place (or the nearest whole number). This means that the interval width should also be a whole number. If it is not, then the interval width should be *rounded up* to the nearest whole number. For this example, we round 17.6 up to an interval width of 18 (the nearest whole number).

DEFINITION

The **interval width** or **class width** is the range of values contained in each interval of a grouped frequency distribution.

Step 3: Construct the frequency distribution. To construct the frequency distribution, we distribute the same number of intervals that we chose in Step 2. In this case, we chose 10 intervals. Table 2.2 shows that each interval has a width of 18. Notice that the first interval contains 18 times in seconds (0, 1, 2, 3, 4, 5, 6, 7, 8, 9, 10, 11, 12, 13, 14, 15, 16, 17) so it does have a width of 18. In a frequency distribution, the **interval boundaries** mark the cutoffs for a given interval. The **lower boundary** is the smallest value in each interval, and the **upper boundary** is the largest value in each interval.

TABLE 2.2   A simple frequency distribution for the average time in minutes that 50 healthy American children watched television per day in the previous year. In this table, $f(x)$ denotes the column heading for the frequencies (f) of scores (x) in each interval.

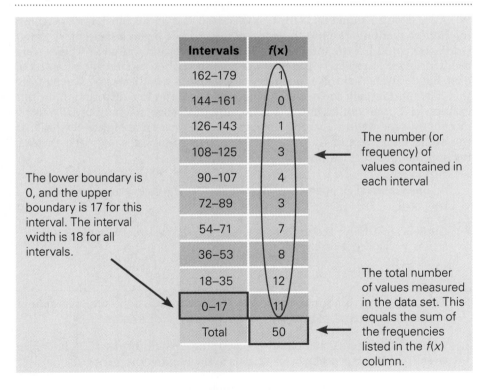

Intervals	f(x)
162–179	1
144–161	0
126–143	1
108–125	3
90–107	4
72–89	3
54–71	7
36–53	8
18–35	12
0–17	11
Total	50

The number (or frequency) of values contained in each interval

The lower boundary is 0, and the upper boundary is 17 for this interval. The interval width is 18 for all intervals.

The total number of values measured in the data set. This equals the sum of the frequencies listed in the $f(x)$ column.

Table 2.2 shows that each lower boundary begins one degree of accuracy greater than the previous upper boundary. This means that we add one whole number because this is the degree of accuracy of the data. (If the data were to the tenths place, then add .1; if to the hundredths place, then add .01; and so on.) We again make the interval width 18 for the second interval and repeat this process until all 10 intervals are constructed. In all, there are four rules for creating a simple frequency distribution:

NOTE: For grouped data, the frequencies of scores are distributed into equal-sized intervals that do not overlap. Hence, each score falls into one and only one interval.

1. Each interval is defined (it has a lower and upper boundary). Intervals such as "or more" or "less than" should not be expressed.

2. Each interval is equidistant (the interval width is the same for each interval).

3. No interval overlaps (the same score cannot occur in more than one interval).

4. All values are rounded to the same degree of accuracy measured in the original data (or to the ones place for the data listed in Table 2.1).

DEFINITION

Interval boundaries are the upper and lower limits for each interval in a grouped frequency distribution.

The **lower boundary** is the smallest value in each interval of a frequency distribution; the **upper boundary** is the largest value in each interval of a frequency distribution.

The total counts in a frequency distribution should sum to the total number of counts made. Because we recorded data for 50 children, the frequency distribution must sum to 50; otherwise, we made a counting error. In all, the simple frequency distribution in Table 2.2 paints a picture of the data, so to speak—it conveys a more descriptive and meaningful way to look at the data.

Also, Table 2.2 shows that only two values fall at or above 126. It may be tempting here to combine the top three intervals into one **open interval.** In other words, we could list the interval as "126–above" because only two values were counted. Often you will see open intervals published when **outliers** exist in a set of data, but be aware that this is not very informative. An outlier is an extreme score that falls substantially above or below most other scores in a distribution. In this example, 175 is an outlier in the data because this value falls substantially above most of the other values recorded. An open interval would make it less obvious that this outlier exists because the upper boundary of the interval is not given; instead, the upper boundary is left open.

NOTE: Open intervals violate the first rule for simple frequency distributions and make it difficult to identify when outliers exist in a data set.

DEFINITION

An **open interval**, or **open class**, is an interval with no defined upper or lower boundary.

Outliers are extreme scores that fall substantially above or below most of the scores in a particular data set.

✓ LEARNING CHECK 1

1. A _____ is a summary display for a distribution of data organized or summarized in terms of how often (or frequently) scores occur.

2. True or false: A researcher observes that a single parent works 42.25 hours per week. The degree of accuracy of 42.25 is to the hundredths place (.01).

3. Each of the following is a rule for the simple frequency distribution except:
   a. Each interval is equidistant.
   b. The same score cannot occur in more than one interval.
   c. Each interval is defined (it has a lower and an upper boundary).
   d. The interval width is equal to the number of intervals in a frequency distribution.

4. What is the recommended number of intervals that should be included in a simple frequency distribution?

5. Why is it generally inappropriate to include an open interval in a simple frequency distribution?

The following example applies the steps for distributing the frequency of scores in a data set.

An industrial organizational psychologist is interested in studying issues of worker safety on the job. To study this, she records the number of complaints about safety filed by employees of 45 local small businesses over the previous 3 years. The results are listed in Table 2.3. In this example, let's construct a frequency distribution of these data.

EXAMPLE 2.1

TABLE 2.3   The number of safety complaints that employees at 45 local small businesses filed over the previous 3 years.

45	98	83	50	86
66	66	88	95	73
88	55	76	115	66
92	110	79	105	101
101	85	90	92	81
55	95	91	92	
78	66	73	58	
86	92	51	63	
91	77	88	86	
94	80	102	107	

Step 1: Find the real range. The smallest value in Table 2.3 is 45 and the largest value is 115; therefore, 115 − 45 = 70. The real range is 70 + 1 = 71.

Step 2: Find the interval width. Let's split the data into eight intervals (again, *you* choose the number of intervals). The interval width is the real range divided by the number of intervals: $\frac{71}{8} = 8.88$. The original data are listed as whole numbers, so we round up to the nearest whole number. The nearest whole number is the degree of accuracy of the data. The interval width is 9.

Step 3: Construct the frequency distribution. The frequency distribution table is shown in Table 2.4. The first interval will start with the smallest value (45) and contain nine values. To construct the next interval, add one degree of accuracy, or one whole number in this example, and repeat the steps to construct the remaining intervals.

TABLE 2.4 A simple frequency distribution with eight intervals and an interval width of 9. The data are the number of complaints about safety that employees of 45 local small businesses filed over the previous 3 years.

Intervals	$f(x)$
108–116	2
99–107	5
90–98	11
81–89	9
72–80	7
63–71	5
54–62	3
45–53	3

One important rule of thumb is to always summarize data in terms of how you want to describe them. For example, if you want to describe the frequency of safety complaints in discrete intervals, then a simple frequency distribution is a great way to summarize the data. But often, researchers want to describe frequencies "at or above" a certain value, or the percentage of people scoring "at least" a certain score. In these cases, it can be more effective to summarize frequency data cumulatively or as percents. Many of these additional summaries for frequency data are described here.

CUMULATIVE FREQUENCY

When researchers want to describe frequencies above or below a certain value, they often report a **cumulative frequency.** A cumulative frequency distributes the sum of frequencies across a series of intervals. You can add from the top or from the bottom; it really depends on how you want to discuss the data. To illustrate, we will use to the data summarized in Table 2.4 (Example 2.1), which shows the frequencies of the number of complaints about safety for 45 small local businesses.

Suppose the researcher wants to describe these businesses as safe, at risk, or dangerous. She uses the following criteria to categorize these businesses: safe (fewer than 72 complaints filed), at risk (between 72 and 89 complaints filed), or dangerous (at least 90 complaints filed). Let's see how a cumulative frequency distribution can be a clearer way to describe these safety categories.

DEFINITION

> A **cumulative frequency** is a summary display that distributes the sum of frequencies across a series of intervals.

Adding From the Bottom Up

We can sum the frequencies beginning with the bottom frequency and adding up the table. Table 2.5 shows this summary in the shaded column. In the table, we began with the frequency in the bottom interval (3) and added the frequency above it to get 6 (3 + 3), added again to get the next frequency 11 (3 + 3 + 5), and repeated these steps until all frequencies were summed. The top frequency is equal to the total number of measures recorded (the total was 45 businesses in this example). This type of summary is more meaningful if we want to discuss data in terms of "less than" or "at or below" a certain value or "at most." For example, "safe" businesses are those that report *fewer than* 72 complaints. Based on the bottom-up cumulative frequency column, we find that 11 businesses are categorized as safe.

TABLE 2.5   A cumulative frequency from the bottom up (shaded, middle column) and the top down (unshaded, far-right column). Arrows are included to show the direction that each cumulative frequency column should be read.

Intervals	Frequency, $f(x)$	Cumulative Frequency (Bottom Up)	Cumulative Frequency (Top Down)
108–116	2	45	2
99–107	5	43	7
90–98	11	38	18
81–89	9	27	27
72–80	7	18	34
63–71	5	11	39
54–62	3	6	42
45–53	3	3	45
	$N = 45$		

Adding From the Top Down

When adding from the top down, begin with the top and add down, as shown in the rightmost column of Table 2.5. We use the same steps described for a bottom-up summary, except we start at the top of the table and add down. This type of summary is more meaningful if we want to discuss data in terms of "greater than" or "at or above" a certain value or "at least." For example, "dangerous" businesses are those that report *at least* 90 complaints filed in the previous 3 years. On the basis of the top-down cumulative frequency column, we find that 18 businesses are categorized as being dangerous. By default, the remaining businesses (not falling into the safe or dangerous categories) would be categorized as "at risk."

NOTE: The cumulative frequency distribution describes the sum of scores across each range and always sums to the total number of scores in a distribution.

LEARNING CHECK 2

1. A _____ is a summary display that distributes the sum of frequencies across a series of intervals.

2. Cumulative frequencies can be added from the top _____ and the bottom _____.

3. When cumulating frequencies from the bottom up, you typically want to discuss the data in terms of:
   a. "At most"
   b. "Less than"
   c. "At or below"
   d. All of the above

4. True or false: Whether you cumulate a frequency distribution from the bottom up or the top down depends on how you want to discuss the data.

5. When cumulating frequencies from the top down, you typically want to discuss the data in terms of:
   a. "Less than"
   b. "At or above"
   c. "At most"
   d. All of the above

Answers: 1. Cumulative frequency; 2. Down, Up; 3. (d); 4. True; 5. (b).

RELATIVE FREQUENCY

When researchers summarize larger data sets (with thousands or even millions of counts), they often distribute the **relative frequency** of scores rather than counts. A relative frequency is a **proportion** from 0 to 1.0 that describes the portion of data in each interval. It is often easier to list the relative frequency of scores because a list with very large frequencies in each interval can be more confusing to read.

For simplicity, we will continue to use the data listed in Table 2.5 to illustrate this type of summary. To calculate the relative frequency, divide the frequency value for each interval by the total number of frequencies recorded. The relative frequencies for each interval listed in Table 2.5 (from the top down) are $\frac{2}{45} = 0.04$, $\frac{5}{45} = 0.11$, $\frac{11}{45} = 0.24$, $\frac{9}{45} = 0.20$, $\frac{7}{45} = 0.16$, $\frac{5}{45} = 0.11$, $\frac{3}{45} = 0.07$, and $\frac{3}{45} = 0.07$. Table 2.6 lists the relative frequency of scores in each interval.

DEFINITION

The **relative frequency** is a summary display that distributes the proportion of scores in each interval. It is computed as the frequency in each interval divided by the total number of frequencies recorded.

A **proportion** is a part or portion of all measured data. The sum of all proportions for a distribution of scores is 1.00.

TABLE 2.6   The relative frequency of scores in each interval (shaded column).

Intervals	Frequency, $f(x)$	Relative Frequency
108–116	2	0.04
99–107	5	0.11
90–98	11	0.24
81–89	9	0.20
72–80	7	0.16
63–71	5	0.11
54–62	3	0.07
45–53	3	0.07
	$N = 45$	1.00

The sum of relative frequencies across all intervals is 1.00, or, in this example, $\frac{45}{45} = 1.00$. Again, a table of relative frequencies can give a clearer summary of frequencies for summarizing larger data sets.

LEARNING CHECK 3

1. When would a researcher construct a relative frequency table?

2. True or false: Relative frequencies are calculated by dividing the frequency value for each interval by the total number of frequencies recorded.

3. The sum of relative frequencies across all intervals is _____.

Answers: 1. To summarize large data sets; 2. True; 3. 1.00

RELATIVE PERCENT

A common way to summarize relative frequencies is to convert them to relative percents—most readers find it easier to understand percents than decimals, perhaps because percents are the basis for awarding grades from grade school through college. To compute the **relative percent,** multiply each relative frequency times 100, which moves the decimal point two places to the right. The shaded column in Table 2.7 lists the relative percent of scores in each interval.

TABLE 2.7   The relative percent of scores in each interval (shaded column).

Intervals	Frequency, $f(x)$	Relative Frequency	Relative Percent
108–116	2	0.04	4%
99–107	5	0.11	11%
90–98	11	0.24	24%
81–89	9	0.20	20%
72–80	7	0.16	16%
63–71	5	0.11	11%
54–62	3	0.07	7%
45–53	3	0.07	7%
	$N = 45$	1.00	100%

DEFINITION

The **relative percent** is a summary display that distributes the percentage of scores occurring in each interval relative to all scores distributed.

NOTE: Relative percents and relative frequencies summarize the percentage or proportion of scores falling into each range.

Percents range from 0% to 100% and can never be negative. A relative percent informs the reader the same as a relative frequency; it's just that many people find it easier to read percents than decimals. The choice of which to use is up to the person compiling the data; there is no right or wrong approach because both provide the same information.

✔ LEARNING CHECK 4

1.   A relative percent:
   a.   Is a relative frequency times 100
   b.   Is the percent of scores recorded in each interval
   c.   Totals 100%
   d.   All of the above

2.   Relative frequencies are commonly reported in academic journals as percents. Why?

3.   True or false: Relative frequencies are summed from the top down or the bottom up.

Answers: 1. (d); 2. Readers find percents easier to read than decimals; 3. False, relative frequencies are listed in each interval and not summed across intervals.

CUMULATIVE RELATIVE FREQUENCY AND CUMULATIVE PERCENT

It is also useful to summarize relative frequencies and percents cumulatively for the same reasons described for cumulative frequencies. To distribute the **cumulative relative frequency,** add each relative frequency beginning at the top or bottom of the table. Table 2.8 lists the top-down and the bottom-up cumulative relative frequencies for the business safety data. For the top-down summary, we begin in the table with the relative frequency for the top interval (.04). Add the relative frequency below it to obtain .15 (.04 + .11); repeat this process to obtain .39 (.04 + .11 + .24), and continue repeating these steps for all intervals. The bottom cumulative relative frequency is equal to 1.00 (give or take rounding errors). Follow these same steps starting at the bottom interval to distribute the cumulative relative frequency from the bottom up.

DEFINITION

The **cumulative relative frequency** is a summary display that distributes the sum of relative frequencies across a series of intervals.

TABLE 2.8   A cumulative relative frequency of scores from the top down and the bottom up (shaded). Arrows are included to show the direction that each cumulative relative frequency column should be read.

Intervals	Frequency, $f(x)$	Relative Frequency	Cumulative Relative Frequency (Top Down)	Cumulative Relative Frequency (Bottom Up)
108–116	2	0.04	0.04	1.00
99–107	5	0.11	0.15	0.96
90–98	11	0.24	0.39	0.85
81–89	9	0.20	0.59	0.61
72–80	7	0.16	0.75	0.41
63–71	5	0.11	0.86	0.25
54–62	3	0.07	0.93	0.14
45–53	3	0.07	1.00	0.07
	$N = 45$	1.00		

To distribute **cumulative percents,** we typically sum from the bottom up, same as described for a cumulative relative frequency, but not the top down. In a cumulative percent distribution, intervals are summed from the smallest to the largest score in a distribution (bottom up). The total cumulative percent is equal to 100% (give or take rounding errors). Table 2.9 lists the cumulative percents for the business safety data. This presentation is called a **percentile rank** and is most often used to summarize standardized exam scores. If a student scored in the 75th percentile on his or her SATs, it means that the student's score was better than 75% of those taking the exam. In Table 2.9, we find that a business at the 85th percentile rank, for example, received more safety complaints than 85% of businesses in the sample.

DEFINITION

Cumulative percents are a summary display that distributes the sum of relative percents across a series of intervals. This summary is presented from the bottom up and is called a percentile rank.

Percentile ranks are a cumulative percent summary. The ranks indicate the percentage of scores at or below a given value and must be summed from the smallest value.

TABLE 2.9   A cumulative percentage of scores, also called percentile ranks, from the bottom up (shaded). An arrow is included to show the direction that the cumulative percent column should be read.

Intervals	Frequency, $f(x)$	Relative Percent	Cumulative Percent (Bottom Up)
108–116	2	4%	100% ↑
99–107	5	11%	96%
90–98	11	24%	85%
81–89	9	20%	61%
72–80	7	16%	41%
63–71	5	11%	25%
54–62	3	7%	14%
45–53	3	7%	7%
	$N = 45$	100%	

NOTE: Cumulative relative frequencies and cumulative percents are a sum of the proportion or percent of scores across intervals. These sum to 1.00 or 100%, respectively.

LEARNING CHECK 5

1. True or false: Cumulative relative frequencies are added from the top down or the bottom up.

2. Cumulative relative frequencies sum to _____ (give or take rounding error).

3. A student learns that his score on an exam is at the 82nd percentile rank. What does this mean in comparison to all other students?

Answers: 1. True; 2. 1.00; 3. This result means that the student scored higher than 82% of all other students on the exam.

2.3   SPSS IN FOCUS: FREQUENCY DISTRIBUTIONS FOR QUANTITATIVE DATA

Although SPSS is not a very popular program for constructing frequency tables, the program can be used for this purpose. In this section, we will construct a frequency distribution table for the continuous data first summarized in Table 2.4.

1. Click on the **variable view** tab and enter *complaints* in the **name column.** We will enter whole numbers, so go to the **decimals column** and reduce that value to 0.

2. Click on the **data view** tab and enter the 45 values from Table 2.3 in the column labeled *complaints*. You can enter the data in any order you wish, but make sure all the data are entered correctly.

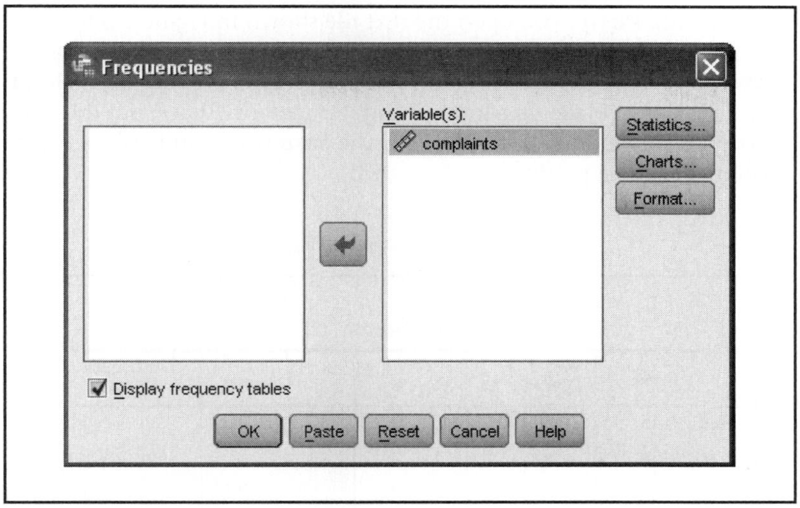

FIGURE 2.2

SPSS dialog box.

3. Go to the **menu bar** and click **Analyze,** then **Descriptive Statistics** and **Frequencies,** to bring up the dialog box shown in Figure 2.2.

4. In the **dialog box,** select the *complaints* variable. When you click the arrow in the center, it will move *complaints* into the **Variable(s):** box to the right. Make sure the option to display frequency tables is selected and click **Paste.**

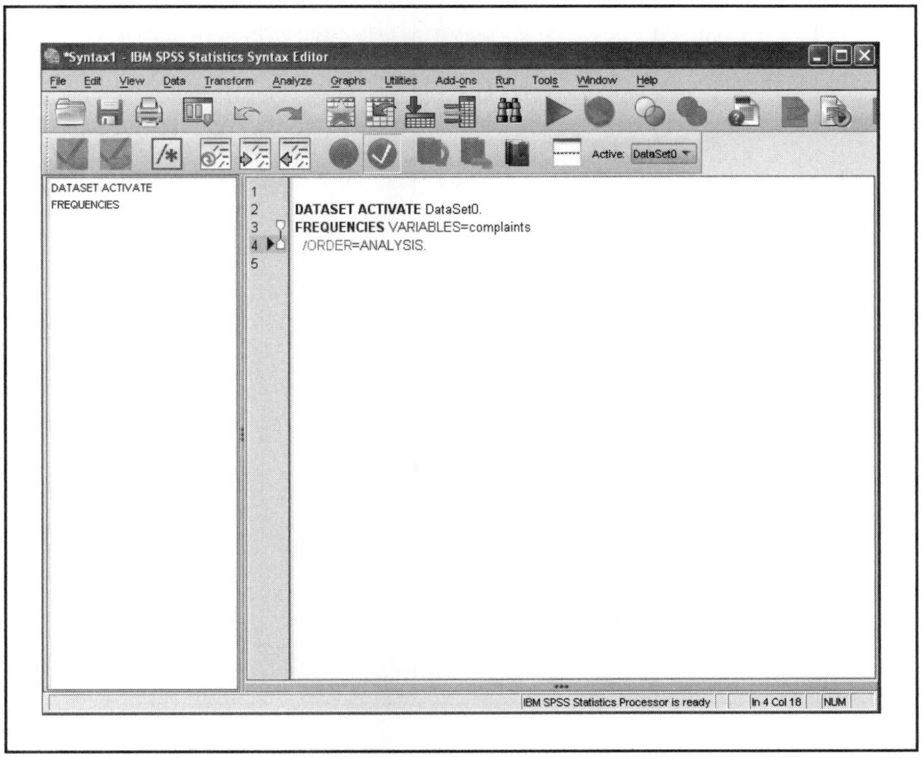

FIGURE 2.3

SPSS text file.

5. By clicking **Paste,** you open the text file shown in Figure 2.3 with the code SPSS will use to run your commands. The text file is what you want to save instead of the output file we are about to create. The reason is simple: The text file doesn't take up a lot of computer memory space, but the output file does. To create the output file, click the **Run** command on the toolbar (the colored triangle pointing to the right).

complaints

		Frequency	Percent	Valid Percent	Cumulative Percent
Valid	45	1	2.2	2.2	2.2
	50	1	2.2	2.2	4.4
	51	1	2.2	2.2	6.7
	55	2	4.4	4.4	11.1
	58	1	2.2	2.2	13.3
	63	1	2.2	2.2	15.6
	66	4	8.9	8.9	24.4
	73	2	4.4	4.4	28.9
	76	1	2.2	2.2	31.1
	77	1	2.2	2.2	33.3
	78	1	2.2	2.2	35.6
	79	1	2.2	2.2	37.8
	80	1	2.2	2.2	40.0
	81	1	2.2	2.2	42.2
	83	1	2.2	2.2	44.4
	85	1	2.2	2.2	46.7
	86	3	6.7	6.7	53.3
	88	3	6.7	6.7	60.0
	90	1	2.2	2.2	62.2
	91	2	4.4	4.4	66.7
	92	4	8.9	8.9	75.6
	94	1	2.2	2.2	77.8
	95	2	4.4	4.4	82.2
	98	1	2.2	2.2	84.4
	101	2	4.4	4.4	88.9
	102	1	2.2	2.2	91.1
	105	1	2.2	2.2	93.3
	107	1	2.2	2.2	95.6
	110	1	2.2	2.2	97.8
	115	1	2.2	2.2	100.0
	Total	45	100.0	100.0	

FIGURE 2.4

SPSS output display.

Figure 2.4 shows the SPSS output file display. SPSS did not distribute these data into intervals as we did. Instead, every value in the original data set is listed (in numerical order from least to most) with frequencies, relative percents (middle two columns), and cumulative percents given for each value. Note that SPSS automatically groups data into intervals only with very large data sets.

FREQUENCY DISTRIBUTIONS FOR UNGROUPED DATA   2.4

Although we've focused on grouped data (i.e., data grouped into intervals), it's not always necessary to group data when you summarize study results. When the dependent variable is qualitative or categorical, or the number of different scores is small, then the frequency of each individual score or category can be summarized. For data of this type, called **ungrouped data,** each measured score is listed in a frequency table; intervals are not constructed. Let's look at an example.

> **Ungrouped data** are a set of scores or categories distributed individually, where the frequency for each individual score or category is counted.

DEFINITION

Many health professionals suggest that children younger than age 3 should take at least two naps a day. To see if mothers actually follow this advice, you ask a sample of 40 mothers with children younger than age 3 how many naps their children take per day on average. Table 2.10 lists the hypothetical results. For these data, mothers gave one of five responses: 0, 1, 2, 3, or 4 naps per day. Grouping data with only five different responses makes little sense, especially because the recommended minimum number of intervals is five. Instead, the data should remain ungrouped. The frequency of ungrouped data is simply listed in a frequency table. We skip all the steps for creating the intervals and go straight to counting the frequency of each value. Each score, as listed in Table 2.11, represents its own count. Notice the important distinction: Grouped data have intervals, and ungrouped data do not.

TABLE 2.10   A list of the number of naps that children, younger than age 3, take per day.

0	2	1	0
0	2	1	0
2	3	2	2
3	3	2	3
1	4	3	2
2	1	2	0
3	2	2	1
0	3	3	2
2	2	1	0
2	1	0	1

TABLE 2.11   A simple frequency distribution for ungrouped data. The data are the number of naps that children, younger than age 3, take per day.

Classes	f(x)
0	8
1	8
2	15
3	8
4	1
	N = 40

NOTE: Data are typically ungrouped for data sets with only a few different scores and for qualitative or categorical variables. For ungrouped data, the frequency of each individual score or category is counted.

Ungrouped data can be summarized using relative frequency, cumulative relative frequency, relative percent, and cumulative relative percent, just as grouped data are. It again depends on how you want to describe the data. Summarizing ungrouped data is especially practical for data sets with only a few different scores and for qualitative or categorical variables. Data obtained for opinion and marketing polls, health categories (lean, healthy, overweight, and obese), or college year (freshman, sophomore, junior, and senior) are often summarized as ungrouped data. A research example for summarizing demographic data is given in Section 2.5.

2.5   RESEARCH IN FOCUS: SUMMARIZING DEMOGRAPHIC INFORMATION

Edenborough, Jackson, Mannix, and Wilkes (2008) conducted a qualitative study to better understand child-to-mother violence. They asked a sample of 185 mothers of children between ages 10 and 24 years to complete questionnaires about their experiences with their children. To describe general characteristics of the mothers they sampled, they included a table, shown in Table 2.12, summarizing their age range (grouped, quantitative data) and type of household (ungrouped, categorical data). Table 2.12 includes the frequencies and relative percents for each variable.

TABLE 2.12   Demographic information of participant ages (grouped) and type of households (ungrouped). These data are adapted from Edenborough et al. (2008).

Variable		Frequency	Relative Percent
Age group	20–29 years	6	3.2
	30–39 years	30	16.2
	40–49 years	94	50.8
	50–59 years	42	22.7
	Not reported	13	7.1
Household	Two parent	101	55.0
	Single parent	54	29.0
	Foster or step family	10	5.4
	Extended family	5	2.6
	Not reported	15	8.0

Most academic journals require that researchers report relevant demographic information of human participants. In this study, researchers reported both grouped and ungrouped demographic data. This study showed that mothers predominantly struggle in silence with violence initiated by their children. The researchers suggested that mothers need a safe and nonjudgmental environment to disclose their experiences and to seek appropriate services and support.

SPSS IN FOCUS: FREQUENCY DISTRIBUTIONS FOR CATEGORICAL DATA   2.6

SPSS can be used to summarize categorical data that are ungrouped. Let's use SPSS to create a frequency distribution for the following hypothetical example: A group of health practitioners want to classify children in public schools as being lean, healthy, overweight, or obese. To do this, they calculated the body mass index (BMI) score of 100 children. Based on the BMI scores, they classified 15 children as lean, 30 as healthy, 35 as overweight, and 20 as obese.

1. Click on the **variable view** tab and enter *categories* in the **name column.** In the second row, enter *frequencies* in the **name column.** We will enter whole numbers, so go to the **decimals column** and reduce that value to 0 for both rows.

2. We must code the data for the categorical variable. Click on the **Values** column and click on the small gray box with three dots. In the **dialog box,** enter *1* in the value cell and *lean* in the label cell, and then click **add.** Repeat these steps by entering *2* for *healthy*, *3* for *overweight*, and *4* for *obese*, and then select **OK.** Now each level for the categorical variable is coded.

3. Click on the **data view** tab and enter *1, 2, 3,* and *4* in the *categories* column. In the *frequencies* column, enter *15, 30, 35,* and *20* next to the corresponding numeric code.

4. Go to **Data,** then **Weight cases . . .** to open up a dialog box. Select **Weight cases by** and move *frequencies* into the **Frequency Variable:** box. Now each frequency is matched to each level of the variable.

5. Go to the **menu bar** and click **Analyze,** then **Descriptive Statistics,** and **Frequencies** to bring up a dialog box.

6. In the **dialog box,** select the *categories* variable and click the arrow in the center to move *categories* into the box labeled **Variable(s):** to the right. Make sure the option to display frequency tables is selected.

7. Select **Paste,** then **Run** (the triangle pointing to the right in the toolbar).

Notice that SPSS does not list the values as 1, 2, 3, and 4 in the output table shown in Figure 2.5, although you entered these values in the "categories" column in the data view. Instead, SPSS lists the data as you labeled them in Step 2 in the variable view. This format makes it much easier to read the output file. Also, every category in the original data set is listed with frequencies, relative percents, and cumulative percents given.

Statistics

categories

N	Valid	100
	Missing	0

categories

		Frequency	Percent	Valid Percent	Cumulative Percent
Valid	lean	15	15.0	15.0	15.0
	healthy	30	30.0	30.0	45.0
	overweight	35	35.0	35.0	80.0
	obese	20	20.0	20.0	100.0
	Total	100	100.0	100.0	

FIGURE 2.5

SPSS output display.

2.7 PICTORIAL FREQUENCY DISTRIBUTIONS

Pictures often help people make sense of frequency data. Economic or health-related data across regions are often presented as pictures. To illustrate, Figure 2.6 shows a map of the United States with the distribution of overweight and obese Americans given as a percentage for each state. This map groups the relative percent for each state into one of four groups: Each interval is coded by color at the bottom. Although not recommended, the intervals are not equal in this example. The reason is probably that the original percents were published with this distribution, and readers could see the actual relative percent for each state in the list in addition to viewing the map. To find out where your state stands on this or other health-related

FIGURE 2.6

A map showing the percentage of adults who are overweight and obese by state in the United States as of 2009.

Source: "Percent of Adults Who are Overweight or Obese, 2009", statehealthfacts.org, The Henry J. Kaiser Family Foundation, 2009. This information was reprinted with permission from the Henry J. Kaiser Family Foundation. The Kaiser Family Foundation is a non-profit private operating foundation, based in Menlo Park, California, dedicated to producing and communicating the best possible analysis and information on health issues.

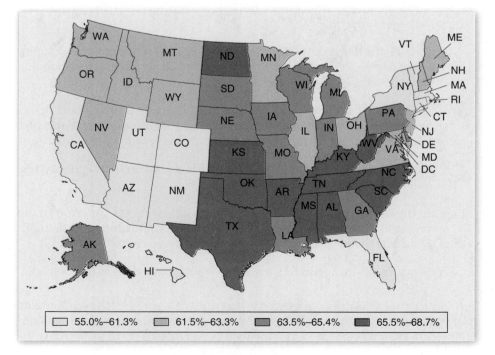

topics, visit http://statehealthfacts.org and click on the *50 state comparisons* tab. If you visit that website, pay attention to the graphs and tables to see how they measure up to the standards described in this chapter.

A **pictogram** is also an effective way to summarize frequency data. A pictogram uses symbols or illustrations to represent a concept, object, place, or event. Pictograms are often seen in magazines, newspapers, government documents or reports, and even research journal articles. For instance, Figure 2.7, which was published in the academic journal *Genetics,* illustrates the percent distribution frequencies for each nucleotide (adenine [A], thymine [T], cytosine [C], and guanine [G]) in a section of human DNA. Hence, researchers can use pictures instead of tables to distribute everything from health facts to nucleotides in human DNA.

A **pictogram** is a summary display that uses symbols or illustrations to represent a concept, object, place, or event.

DEFINITION

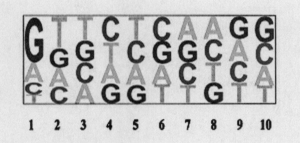

1   2   3   4   5   6   7   8   9   10

FIGURE 2.7

A pictogram of a specific section of human DNA. The size of a letter on the pictogram is proportional to the frequency of the relevant nucleotide.

Source: Adapted from Eskesen, Eskesen, and Ruvinsky (2004).

LEARNING CHECK 6

1. What are the data called when the frequency of each individual score or category is listed?

2. A _____ is a summary display that uses symbols or illustrations to represent a concept, an object, a place, or an event.

3. When is it appropriate to summarize frequencies for ungrouped data?

4. True or false: A pictogram is an effective way to summarize frequency data.

NOTE: Pictures and pictograms can be used to effectively summarize frequency data.

Answers: 1. Ungrouped data; 2. Pictogram; 3. When data sets have only a few different scores and for qualitative or categorical variables; 4. True.

GRAPHING DISTRIBUTIONS: CONTINUOUS DATA   2.8

Researchers can also display frequency data graphically instead of in a table. Although using a table or graph to summarize frequency data is equally effective for the most part, graphs have the main advantage of being more visual and less intimidating than tables in many cases. In this section, we look at several ways to graph distributions of continuous data: histograms, frequency polygons, ogives, and stem-and-leaf displays.

HISTOGRAMS

Grouped data are often summarized graphically using **histograms.** Histograms are graphs that distribute the intervals along the horizontal scale (*x*-axis) and list the frequency of scores in each interval on the vertical scale (*y*-axis). To illustrate, let's construct a histogram for the data given in Figure 2.8, which shows the frequency table and the respective histogram for the time (in months) it took a sample of 200 college graduates to find employment. To construct a histogram, we follow three rules:

FIGURE 2.8

A frequency table (left) and histogram (right) summarizing the frequency distribution for the time (in months) that it took a sample of 200 college graduates to find employment.

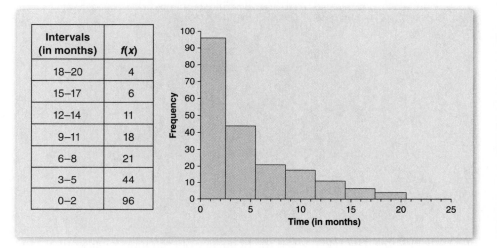

Intervals (in months)	f(x)
18–20	4
15–17	6
12–14	11
9–11	18
6–8	21
3–5	44
0–2	96

DEFINITION

A **histogram** is a graphical display used to summarize the frequency of continuous data that are distributed in numeric intervals (grouped).

Rule 1: A vertical rectangle represents each interval, and the height of the rectangle equals the frequency recorded for each interval. This rule implies that the *y*-axis should be labeled as a number or count. The *y*-axis reflects the frequency of scores for each interval.

Rule 2: The base of each rectangle begins and ends at the upper and lower boundaries of each interval. This rule means that histograms can't be constructed for open intervals because open intervals don't have an upper or a lower boundary. Also, each rectangle should have the same interval width.

Rule 3: Each rectangle touches adjacent rectangles at the boundaries of each interval. Histograms are used to summarize continuous data, such as the time (in months) it takes to find employment. The adjacent rectangles touch because it is assumed that the data are continuous. In other words, it is assumed that the data were measured along a continuum.

FREQUENCY POLYGONS

Another graph that can be used to summarize grouped data is the **frequency polygon.** A frequency polygon is a dot-and-line graph where the dot is the midpoint of each interval, and the line connects each dot. The midpoint of an interval is distributed along the *x*-axis and is calculated by adding the upper and lower boundary of an interval and then dividing by 2. Figure 2.9 illustrates a frequency polygon for the same data used to construct the histogram in Figure 2.8. A histogram and a frequency polygon are equally effective at summarizing these data—the choice between the two depends on how you prefer to summarize the data.

NOTE: Histograms summarize the frequency of continuous data that are quantitative.

A **frequency polygon** is a dot-and-line graph used to summarize the frequency of continuous data at the midpoint of each interval.

DEFINITION

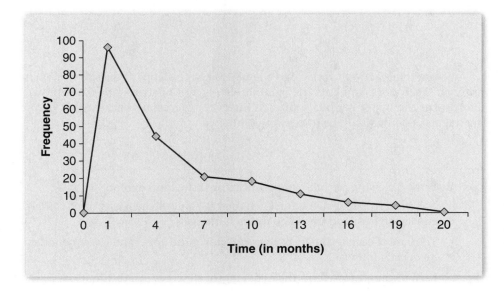

FIGURE 2.9

A frequency polygon summarizing the frequency distribution for the time (in months) that it took a sample of 200 college graduates to find employment.

OGIVES

A dot-and-line graph can also be used to summarize cumulative percents. This type of graph, called an **ogive** (pronounced *oh-jive*), is used to summarize the cumulative percents of continuous data at the upper boundary of each interval. Figure 2.10 shows an ogive for the cumulative percent distribution, from the bottom up, for the same data used to construct the histogram in Figure 2.8. The *y*-axis of an ogive always ranges from 0% to 100% of the data.

NOTE: Frequency polygons are dot-and-line graphs used to summarize the same types of data as histograms.

An **ogive** is a dot-and-line graph used to summarize the cumulative percent of continuous data at the upper boundary of each interval.

DEFINITION

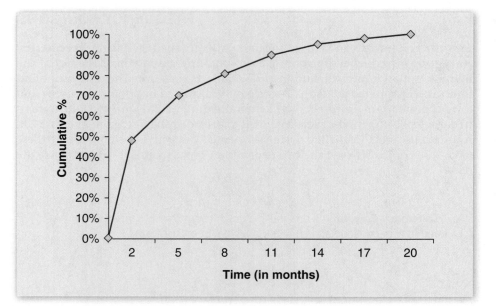

FIGURE 2.10

An ogive summarizing the cumulative percent distribution for the time (in months) that it took a sample of 200 college graduates to find employment.

NOTE: An ogive is a dot-and-line graph used to summarize the cumulative percent of continuous scores.

Notice that each dot in an ogive is plotted at the upper boundary of each interval. Each dot represents the cumulative percent of scores at each interval. Plotting at the upper boundary of each interval is necessary because this point represents or contains all the scores in that interval.

 **LEARNING CHECK 7**

1. All of the following are rules for constructing histograms except:

   a. A vertical rectangle represents each interval, and the height of the rectangle equals the frequency recorded for each interval.

   b. The base of each rectangle begins and ends at the upper and lower boundaries of each interval.

   c. Each rectangle represents the frequency of all scores in a distribution.

   d. Each rectangle touches adjacent rectangles at the boundaries of each interval.

2. True or false: Histograms are used to summarize ungrouped data, which is why each vertical rectangle touches the other.

3. A(n) _____ is a dot-and-line graph plotted at the midpoint of each interval, whereas a(n) _____ is a dot-and-line graph plotted at the upper boundary of each interval.

4. An ogive graphically summarizes what type of frequency distribution?

Answers: 1. (c); 2. False, histograms are used to summarize grouped data; 3. frequency polygon, ogive; 4. A cumulative percent distribution.

STEM-AND-LEAF DISPLAYS

A **stem-and-leaf display** is another graphic method of displaying data. This type of display is particularly useful with smaller data sets because each individual score is listed in the display. Constructing a stem-and-leaf display requires grouping values into stems, then listing them across each row.

> A **stem-and-leaf display**, also called a **stem-and-leaf plot**, is a graphical display where each individual score from an original set of data is listed. The data are organized such that the common digits shared by all scores are listed to the left (in the stem), with the remaining digits for each score listed to the right (in the leaf).

To illustrate this type of display, consider the data listed in Table 2.13 for the number of times per day that 20 patients with obsessive-compulsive disorder washed their hands.

TABLE 2.13   A list of the number of times per day that 20 patients with obsessive-compulsive disorder washed their hands.

12	14	10	47
33	23	16	52
24	32	26	44
42	46	29	19
11	50	30	15

To construct the stem-and-leaf display for these data, we must first recognize the beginning digits of these numbers. For example, 12 begins with the number 1, and 50 begins with a 5. Therefore, let's reorganize the data so that every number with the same first digit is placed in the same row, as shown in panel a of Table 2.14. Here we can see that seven numbers begin with the digit 1 (10, 11, 12, 14, 15, 16, and 19), four begin with 2 (23, 24, 26, and 29), three begin with 3 (30, 32, and 33), four begin with 4 (42, 44, 46, and 47), and two begin with 5 (50 and 52). To simplify this further, let's place the first digit in its own column (separated by a vertical line) so that it's never repeated in a single row, as shown in panel a of Table 2.14. This arrangement of data is called a stem-and-leaf display.

TABLE 2.14   A stem-and-leaf-display where every number with the same first digit is placed in the same row (a) and the first digit in each row is placed in its own column (b). Using new data, (c) displays two digits in the stem, and (d) displays two digits in the leaf.

(a)

10	11	12	14	15	16	19
23	24	26	29			
30	32	33				
42	44	46	47			
50	52					

(Continued)

TABLE 2.14   (Continued)

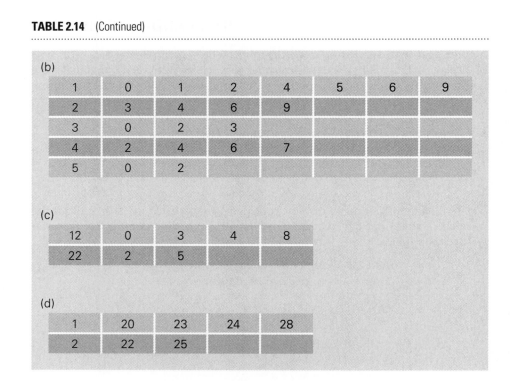

(b)

1	0	1	2	4	5	6	9
2	3	4	6	9			
3	0	2	3				
4	2	4	6	7			
5	0	2					

(c)

12	0	3	4	8
22	2	5		

(d)

1	20	23	24	28
2	22	25		

NOTE: Stem-and-leaf displays organize a set of data by the common digits shared by values.

In a stem-and-leaf display, numbers to the right of the vertical line are the **leaf,** and numbers to the left of the vertical line are the **stem.** The names *stem* and *leaf* derive from their appearance, which in many cases looks like half a leaf, with a stem to the left. There are many ways to display data in a stem-and-leaf display. For example, stems can be more than one digit, as shown in panel (a) of Table 2.14, which displays 120, 123, 124, 128, 222, and 225 with two-digit stems. Also, the leaves can have more than one digit, as shown in panel (a) of Table 2.14, which displays the same numbers, but this time with leaves that have two digits.

A **stem** is located to the left of the vertical line in a stem-and-leaf display. A stem lists the first digit or digits for each number in each row.

A **leaf** is located to the right of the vertical line in a stem-and-leaf display. A leaf lists the last digit or digits for each number in each row.

In all, a stem-and-leaf display is similar to a histogram in that both display the shape of a distribution. Unlike histograms, though, the stem-and-leaf display lists the actual scores in the distribution, instead of frequencies, allowing a person to read the raw data immediately from the display and usually in ascending order. In this way, the stem-and-leaf display retains the value of each data point. The only information we lose is the order that the data were originally obtained. This makes stem-and-leaf displays a very useful tool for displaying data.

1. In a stem-and-leaf display, define the stem. Define the leaf.

2. What is a key distinction between a stem-and-leaf display and a histogram?

3. Identify the original scores listed in the following stem-and-leaf display.

1	3	3	7
5	4	5	

Answers: 1. A stem lists the first digit or digits in each row to the left of the vertical line, and the leaf lists the last digit for each number in each row to the right of the vertical line; 2. A stem-and-leaf display lists actual scores in a distribution; a histogram lists frequencies; 3. 13, 13, 17, 54, and 55.

GRAPHING DISTRIBUTIONS:
DISCRETE AND CATEGORICAL DATA 2.9

Researchers often measure discrete variables—variables measured in whole units. For example, the number of traffic accidents or the number of college graduates are discrete variables because these variables are measured by counting one traffic accident or college graduate at a time. Researchers often measure categorical variables, which vary by class. Examples include race, gender, or marital status. Discrete and categorical data are graphed differently from continuous data because the data are measured in whole units or classes and not along a continuum. Three types of graphs for discrete and categorical data described here are bar charts, pie charts, and scatter grams.

BAR CHARTS

Bar charts are much like histograms, except that the bars are separated from one another, whereas the vertical rectangles or bars on histograms touch each other. The separation between bars reflects the separation or "break" between the whole numbers or categories being summarized. For this reason, bar charts are appropriate for summarizing distributions of discrete and categorical data.

> A **bar chart**, or **bar graph**, is a graphical display used to summarize the frequency of discrete and categorical data that are distributed in whole units or classes.

DEFINITION

To construct a bar chart, list the whole units or categories along the *x*-axis, and distribute the frequencies along the *y*-axis. To illustrate, Figure 2.11 gives the frequency distribution and the respective bar chart for the number of naps that mothers give their children daily. (The original data for Figure 2.11 are given in Table 2.10.) The bar chart has two characteristics: (1) Each class or category is represented by a rectangle, and (2) each rectangle is separated along the *x*-axis. Again, the bar chart is nothing more than a histogram with the bars separated, which makes it more appropriate for summarizing discrete and categorical data.

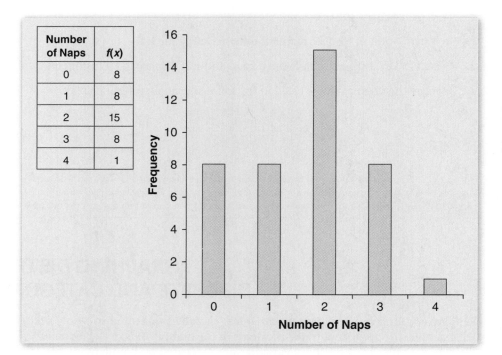

Number of Naps	f(x)
0	8
1	8
2	15
3	8
4	1

FIGURE 2.11

A frequency table (left) and a bar chart (right) summarizing the average number of naps per day that mothers give their children, who are younger than age 3.

NOTE: Bar charts are used to summarize discrete and categorical data. Bar charts are similar to histograms, except that the bars are separated to indicate discrete units or classes.

DEFINITION

NOTE: Pie charts look like a pie, with each slice typically representing the relative percent of scores in some category.

PIE CHARTS

The **pie chart** is another graphical summary used almost exclusively for discrete and categorical data. Educators often teach children subtraction and other mathematical operations by "slicing up pieces of pie." Similarly, you can think of pie charts as slices or pieces of data. To construct a pie chart, we typically distribute data as relative percents. Consider Table 2.15, which displays the educational attainment in the United States of a sample of Americans in 2005.

A **pie chart** is a graphical display in the shape of a circle that is used to summarize the relative percent of discrete and categorical data into sectors.

TABLE 2.15   The relative percent of educational attainment in the United States in 2005.

Level of Education	f(x)	Relative Percent
High school graduate (or less)	127,732.00	67.3%
Associate's degree	15,269.00	8.1%
Bachelor's degree	31,083.00	16.4%
Master's degree	10,936.00	5.8%
Professional/doctoral degree	4,601.00	2.4%
Total	189,621.00	100.0%

Source: Table created based on data from the U.S. Census Bureau, Educational Attainment.

Converting this distribution to a pie chart is simply a matter of finding the correct angles for each slice of pie. There are 360 degrees in a complete circle; therefore, we multiply each percentage times 3.6 (because 100% × 3.6 = 360°) to find the central angles of each **sector** (or category). The central angles for the data in Table 2.15 (from the top down and rounded to the nearest tenths place) are 67.3% × 3.6 = 242.3, 8.1% × 3.6 = 29.2, 16.4% × 3.6 = 59.0, 5.8% × 3.6 = 20.9, and 2.4% × 3.6 = 8.6. The total of all central angles will equal 360 degrees. Now dust off your protractor or use a computer program (such as Excel or SPSS) to construct the pie chart by slicing the pie into each angle you just calculated. The result is shown in Figure 2.12.

A **sector** is the particular portion of a pie chart that represents the relative percent of a particular class or category.

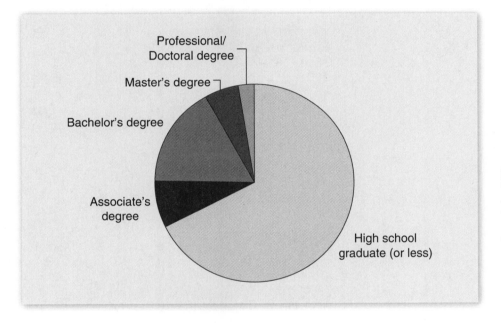

DEFINITION

FIGURE 2.12

A pie chart for the distribution of educational attainment in the United States among citizens (male and female of all races/ethnicities) in 2005.

Source: Table created based on data from the U.S. Census Bureau, Educational Attainment.

SCATTER GRAMS

A great deal of psychological research asks questions about how two factors are related. These studies look for discrete relationships between two variables. For example, psychologists may ask whether race and education, self-esteem and attitudes toward love, gender and parenting styles, culture and diet, or behavior and genetics are related. This research is often graphically summarized using scatter grams.

A **scatter gram**, also called a **scatter diagram** or **scatter plot**, is a graphical display of discrete data points (x, y) used to summarize the relationship between two variables.

DEFINITION

Scatter grams can be used to illustrate the relationship between two variables, denoted (x, y). The x variable (typically the independent variable) is plotted along the x-axis of a graph, and the y variable is plotted along the y-axis. Pairs of values for x and y are called **data points** or **bivariate plots.** The data points are plotted along the x- and y-axis of a graph to see whether a pattern emerges. As Example 2.2

shows, these graphs are useful tools for discerning any relationship or visual pattern between one variable, *x*, and another, *y*.

Data points, also called **bivariate plots**, are the *x*- and *y*-coordinates for each plot in a scatter gram.

EXAMPLE 2.2

Table 2.16 lists the high school averages, *x*, and the freshman college grade point averages (GPA), *y*, of 10 college students using the 4.00 GPA scale. We will construct a scatter gram for these data points and determine whether a visual pattern in the data is apparent.

TABLE 2.16   A list of high school, *y*, and college freshman, *x*, GPA scores.

x	y
2.88	3.02
3.22	3.78
2.20	1.60
3.00	3.05
1.25	1.60
2.44	2.99
2.77	2.66
3.13	3.03
1.98	2.00
3.66	3.70

Each pair of scores constitutes a single data point on the scatter gram. In this example, it would appear that high school averages are predictive of college averages, so we will plot the high school averages (the independent variable) along the *x*-axis. The data points (*x*, *y*) for each pair of scores are (2.88, 3.02), (3.22, 3.78), (2.20, 1.60), (3.00, 3.05), (1.25, 1.60), (2.44, 2.99), (2.77, 2.66), (3.13, 3.03), (1.98, 2.00), and (3.66, 3.70). For the first data point, you move 2.88 points to the right of the *x*-axis, then 3.02 points up the *y*-axis. Follow the same procedure for each additional (*x*, *y*) point: Move along the *x*-axis first, then up the *y*-axis.

NOTE: Scatter grams display pairs of data as individual (x, y) data points. The visual pattern of many plotted data points can be used to infer whether two variables are related.

Once you have plotted each data point, you can look for a visual pattern in the data to see if the two variables are related (or change in a related fashion). Figure 2.13 shows a typical linear (straightline) pattern, where higher scores on the *x*-axis tend to be associated with higher scores on the *y*-axis and vice versa. So the visual pattern is that as scores increase along the *x*-axis, scores also increase along the *y*-axis. Hence, the general pattern in this scatter gram is that higher high school GPAs are associated with better freshman college GPAs.

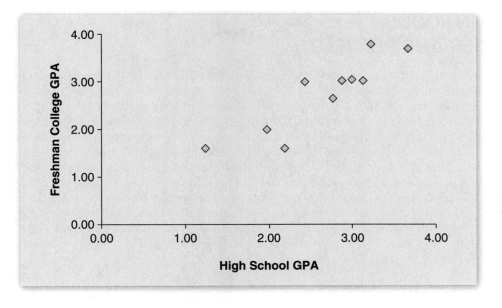

LEARNING CHECK 9

1. _____ are graphical displays similar to histograms, except that the vertical bars or rectangles do not touch.

2. In the following bar chart summarizing the frequency of exercise among a sample of college students, which category of exercise has the largest frequency?

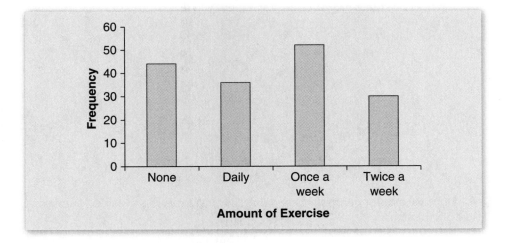

3. True or false: The 360 degrees in a pie chart correspond to 100% of a data distribution.

4. True or false: Scatter grams can be used to determine whether two variables are related or change in a related fashion.

Answers: 1. Bar charts; 2. Most college students exercised once a week; 3. True; 4. True.

2.10 RESEARCH IN FOCUS: FREQUENCIES AND PERCENTS

Although graphs are often used to help the reader understand frequency data, bar charts and histograms are not always equally effective at summarizing percent data. For example, Hollands and Spence (1992, 1998) asked adult participants to identify relative percents displayed in bar charts and pie charts (similar to those presented in this chapter). Their studies showed that participants required more time and made larger errors looking at bar charts than when they looked at pie charts. They went on to show that participants also required more time as the number of bars in the graph increased, whereas increasing the number of slices in a pie chart did not have this effect. They explained that most bar graphs, especially for frequency data, are not distributed in percentage units; hence, the reader cannot clearly estimate a proportion by simply viewing the scale. This research suggests that when you want to convey data as percents, pie charts (and even ogives) would be a better choice for displaying the data.

2.11 SPSS IN FOCUS: HISTOGRAMS, BAR CHARTS, AND PIE CHARTS

To review, histograms are used for continuous or quantitative data, and bar charts and pie charts are used for discrete, categorical, or qualitative data. As an exercise to compare histograms, bar charts, and pie charts, let's construct these graphs for the same data, even though we would never do this in practice. Suppose we measure the following data shown in Table 2.17.

TABLE 2.17   A sample of 20 values.

1	4	5	7
2	3	6	8
3	6	7	9
2	6	5	4
4	5	8	5

Since we are not defining these values, let's just call the variable "numbers." Here are the steps:

1. Click on the **variable view** tab and enter *numbers* in the **name column.** We will enter whole numbers, so go to the **decimals column** and reduce the value to 0.

2. Click on the **data view** tab and enter the 20 values in the column you labeled numbers. You can enter the data in any order you wish, but make sure all the data are entered correctly.

3. Go to the **menu bar** and click **Analyze,** then **Descriptive Statistics** and **Frequencies,** to bring up a dialog box.

4. In the **dialog box,** select the *numbers* variable and click the arrow in the center to move *numbers* into the box labeled **Variable(s):** to the right. Because we only want the graphs and charts in this example, make sure the option to display frequency tables is not selected.

5. Click the **Charts** option in the dialog box, which is shown in Figure 2.14. In the dialog box you have the option to select **bar charts, pie charts,** or **histograms.** Select each option to see how each is displayed, however you can only select one option at a time. After you make your selection, click **Continue.**

6. Select **Paste,** and then **Run** to construct each graph.

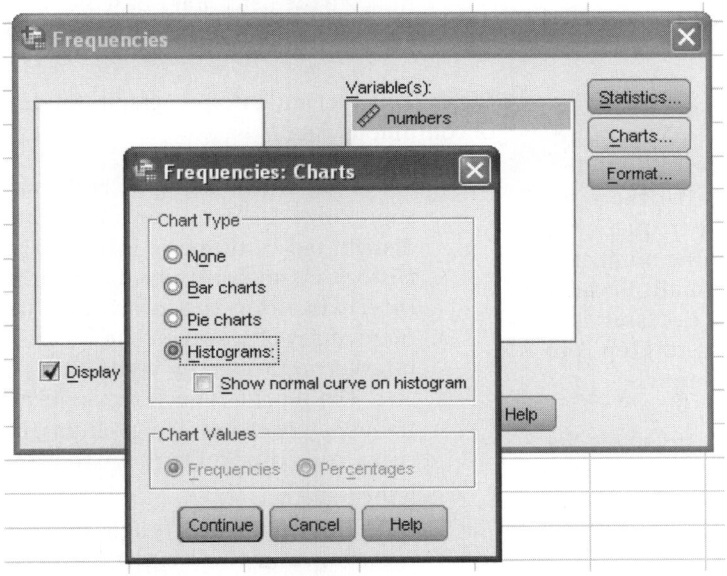

FIGURE 2.14

A screenshot of the dialog boxes for Step 5.

In this example, you can also display the frequency table with the graph by keeping the "Display frequency tables" option selected. In this way, SPSS gives you many options for summarizing data using tables and graphs.

CHAPTER SUMMARY ORGANIZED BY LEARNING OBJECTIVE

LO 1–2: Construct a simple frequency distribution for grouped and ungrouped data; determine whether data should be grouped or ungrouped.

- A **frequency distribution** is a summary display for a distribution of data organized or summarized in terms of how often or frequently scores occur.
- A **simple frequency distribution** for **grouped data** displays the frequency of data in intervals. Each interval is equidistant, no interval overlaps, and the degree of accuracy for each interval is the same as in the original data. This distribution can be constructed using three steps:

Step 1: Find the real range.

Step 2: Find the interval width.

Step 3: Construct the frequency distribution.

- A **simple frequency distribution** for **ungrouped data** displays the frequency of categories or whole units when the number of different values collected is small. Because constructing intervals is not necessary for ungrouped data, skip straight to Step 3 to construct this frequency distribution.

LO 3: Identify when it is appropriate to distribute the cumulative frequency, relative frequency, relative percent, cumulative relative frequency, and cumulative percent.

- A **cumulative frequency** is a summary display that distributes the sum of frequencies across a series of intervals. You can sum from the top or the bottom depending on how you want to discuss the data. You add from the bottom up when discussing the data in terms of "less than" or "at or below" a certain value or "at most." You add from the top down when discussing the data in terms of "greater than" or "at or above" a certain value or "at least."
- A **relative frequency** is a summary display that distributes the proportion of scores in each interval. To compute a relative frequency, divide the frequency in each interval by the total number of scores counted. The relative frequency is reported when summarizing large

data sets. To convert relative frequencies to **relative percents,** multiply each relative frequency times 100. Both summary displays convey the same information.

- **Cumulative relative frequencies** are summary displays for the sum of relative frequencies from the top down or the bottom up. These can be converted to cumulative relative percents by multiplying the cumulative relative frequency in each interval times 100. Cumulative relative percents can be distributed as **percentile ranks,** which indicate the percentage of scores at or below a given score.

LO 4: Construct and interpret graphs for distributions of continuous data.

- A **histogram** is a graphical display used to summarize the frequency of continuous data distributed in numeric intervals (grouped). Histograms are constructed by distributing the intervals along the x-axis and listing the frequencies of scores on the y-axis, with each interval connected by vertical bars or rectangles. The height of each rectangle reflects the frequency of scores in a given interval. Three rules for constructing histograms are as follows:

Rule 1: A vertical rectangle represents each interval, and the height of the rectangle equals the frequency recorded for each interval.

Rule 2: The base of each rectangle begins and ends at the upper and lower boundaries of each interval.

Rule 3: Each rectangle touches adjacent rectangles at the boundaries of each interval.

- A **frequency polygon** is a dot-and-line graph where the dot is the midpoint of each interval, and the line connects each dot. The midpoint of an interval is distributed along the x-axis and is calculated by adding the upper and lower boundary of an interval and then dividing by 2.
- An **ogive** is a dot-and-line graph used to summarize the cumulative percent of

continuous data at the upper boundary of each interval.

- A **stem-and-leaf display** is a graphical display where each individual score from an original set of data is listed. The data are organized such that the common digits shared by all scores are listed to the left (in the stem), with the remaining digits for each score listed to the right (in the leaf).

LO 5: Construct and interpret graphs for distributions of discrete data, including two-variable data.

- **Bar charts** are used to summarize discrete and categorical data. Bar charts are similar to histograms, except that the bars or rectangles are separated to indicate discrete units or classes. To construct a bar chart, list the whole units or categories along the *x*-axis, and distribute the frequencies along the *y*-axis.
- The **pie chart** is a graphical display in the shape of a circle that is used to summarize the relative percent of discrete and categorical data into sectors. Converting proportions to a pie chart requires finding the correct angles for each slice of the pie. To find the central angles of each sector (or category), multiply each relative percent times 3.6 (100% × 3.6 = 360°).
- **Scatter grams,** also called **scatter diagrams** and **scatter plots,** can be used to show the direction of the relationship between two variables, denoted (*x*, *y*). The *x* variable (typically the independent variable) is plotted along the *x*-axis of a graph, and the *y* variable is plotted along the *y*-axis. Pairs of values (*x*, *y*) are called **data points.**

SPSS LO 6–7: Construct frequency distributions for quantitative and categorical data using SPSS; construct histograms, bar charts, and pie charts using SPSS.

- SPSS can be used to create frequency distributions for quantitative and categorical data. Quantitative data are typically entered by column, whereas categorical data (which typically requires coding) are entered by row. Frequency distributions for quantitative and categorical data are created using the **Analyze, Descriptive Statistics,** and **Frequencies** options in the menu bar. Whenever the levels of a variable are coded, a **weight cases** option must also be selected from the menu bar (for more details, see Sections 2.3 and 2.6).
- SPSS can be used to create histograms, bar charts, and pie charts. Each graph is created using the **Analyze, Descriptive Statistics,** and **Frequencies** options in the menu bar. This option will bring up a dialog box that will allow you to identify your variable and select the **Charts** option that gives you the option to select bar charts, pie charts, or histograms. Select each option to see how each summary is displayed (for more details, see Section 2.11).

KEY TERMS

bar chart	interval	real range
bar graph	interval boundaries	relative frequency
bivariate plots	interval width	relative percent
class width	leaf	scatter diagram
cumulative frequency	lower boundary	scatter gram
cumulative percents	ogive	scatter plot
cumulative relative frequency	open class	sector
data points	open interval	simple frequency distribution
frequency	outliers	stem
frequency distribution	percentile rank	stem-and-leaf display
frequency polygon	pictogram	stem-and-leaf plot
grouped data	pie chart	ungrouped data
histogram	proportion	upper boundary

END-OF-CHAPTER PROBLEMS

Factual Problems

1. What are the three steps used to construct a simple frequency distribution?

2. What is the key distinction between grouped and ungrouped data?

3. Is it necessary to compute the observed range to construct a frequency distribution for (a) ungrouped data and (b) grouped data?

4. The upper boundary of one interval and the lower boundary of the next interval do not overlap in a simple frequency distribution. Why?

5. Researchers often prefer to report cumulative percents from the bottom up to explain how certain scores rank at or below other scores in a distribution. What is this type of summary called?

6. Frequency data are not always distributed in intervals. What types of data are not distributed in intervals?

7. What are the three rules for constructing a histogram?

8. Frequency polygons are plotted at the _____ of each interval, whereas ogives are plotted at the _____ of each interval.

9. Why would a researcher summarize data with a bar chart instead of a histogram?

10. When plotting a scatter gram, the independent variable is typically distributed along which axis?

Concepts and Application Problems

11. Below is the number of hand-washing episodes 20 patients with obsessive-compulsive disorder reported having the previous day.

    21, 8, 11, 9, 12, 10, 10, 5, 9, 18,

    17, 3, 6, 14, 18, 16, 19, 3, 22, 7

    (a) Create a simple frequency distribution for these grouped data with four intervals.

    (b) Which interval had the largest frequency?

12. A researcher observed a rat respond for a food reward by pressing one of three levers in a cage.

Pressing the lever to the right (R) produced no food reward, pressing the lever to the left (L) produced a single food pellet, and pressing the lever at the center (C) produced two food pellets. Because the center level produced the largest reward, the researcher hypothesized that the rat would press this lever most often. Each trial ended when the rat pressed a lever. The researcher recorded lever pressing for 30 trials:

    L, L, R, L, R, C, R, L, C, L,
    L, C, C, C, R, C, R, C, L, C,
    C, L, C, C, C, L, C, C, C, C

    (a) Create an ungrouped frequency distribution for these data.

    (b) Do these data support the hypothesis? Explain.

13. The following table shows a frequency distribution for grouped data. Notice that the frequency of scores, $f(x)$, does not add up to 15. If a total of 15 scores were actually counted, give a possible explanation for why the frequencies do not add up to 15.

Intervals	Frequency
0–5	4
5–10	6
10–15	3
15–20	5

14. A researcher reports the following frequency distribution for the time (in minutes) that college students spent on social networking websites during class time. Identify three errors in this simple frequency distribution.

Class Time	Frequency
0–9	14
9–20	18
21–40	26
40+	12

15. The upper boundaries for a distribution of waiting times (in seconds) in a grocery store aisle are 45, 56, 67, and 78. List the value for each lower boundary in this distribution.

16. The lower boundaries for the number of tattoos among prison inmates are 1, 4, 7, 10, 13, and 16. List the value for each upper boundary in this distribution.

17. In a study on romantic relationships, 240 romantically involved men were asked to choose their preference for an ideal night out with their partner. The frequency of men choosing (1) dinner and a movie, (2) a sporting event, (3) gambling/gaming, or (4) going out for drinks was recorded. Should these frequency data be grouped? Explain.

18. The frequency of alcohol-related arrests during a single season at a sporting arena ranged from 0 to 17 arrests per game. What is the interval width if you choose to create a frequency distribution with six intervals?

19. A researcher records the number of dreams that 50 college freshman students recalled during the night prior to a final exam.

Number of Dreams	Cumulative Frequency
4	50
3	44
2	30
1	12
0	5

(a) Convert this table to a percentile rank distribution.

(b) What is the number of dreams at the 60th percentile?

20. The following table shows the relative percent distribution for the time in seconds that it took 200 children with attention-deficit disorder (ADD) to show symptoms of the disorder after a manipulation.

Time (in seconds)	Relative Percent
1–6	5%
7–12	5%
13–18	20%
19–24	20%
25–30	30%
31–36	20%

Assume that researchers determined that children who showed symptoms of ADD in 18 seconds or less qualified to participate in a new cognitive-behavioral therapy trial thought to help reduce ADD symptoms. How many children qualify for this new treatment? *Hint:* First convert the data to a cumulative frequency distribution.

21. Organize the following data into a stem-and-leaf display where (a) the *leaf* has one digit and (b) the *stem* has one digit.
225, 114, 153, 117, 223, 152, 159, 227, 110, 119
155, 159, 226, 153, 223, 114, 158, 221, 115, 220

22. The following set of scores was summarized in a stem-and-leaf display.
(a) List the raw scores that are summarized in this display.
(b) How many scores are summarized?

1	3	7	
3	2	2	2
4	0	1	9
6	6	8	

23. What type of graph for frequency data should you construct when distributing each of the following? Note that there may be more than one right answer.
(a) The number of students falling into an A, B, C, D, or F grade range
(b) The number of men and women suffering from depression

(c) The number of autistic children showing improvement following one of three behavioral therapies

(d) The time it takes a sample of college students to complete some memory task

24. Would it be most appropriate to use a bar chart or a histogram to summarize the frequency distribution of:

(a) The delay to start a game in minutes

(b) The number of students in each of three classrooms

(c) The age (in years) that a sample of women first conceived

(d) The direction of a person's eye movement (right, left, or center) when he or she is telling a lie

25. The following is an incomplete simple frequency distribution table for the number of mistakes made during a series of military combat readiness training exercises. Find the missing values for A, B, and C.

Number of Mistakes	Frequency
6–A	1
B–5	3
0–2	C
	N = 16

26. The following is an incomplete simple frequency distribution table for student grades on a college professor's statistics exam.

Grades (%)	Frequency
87–95	4
A–B	11
69–77	5
60–C	7
51–59	D
	N = 40

(a) Find the missing values for A, B, C, and D.

(b) If students scoring less than 69% on this exam receive a failing grade, was this a difficult test? Explain.

27. The following bar graph summarizes the number of nights per week a sample of college students spent studying.

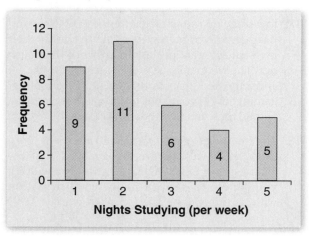

(a) How many students were observed in this study?

(b) How many students studied 3 nights per week?

(c) How many students studied *at least* 3 nights per week?

28. In a study on marital satisfaction, a researcher asks a sample of men to estimate how many times per week they say "I love you" to their spouse. The relative frequency distribution is given below for these data. Construct an ogive for these data. *Hint:* Convert these relative frequencies to cumulative percents before constructing an ogive.

Intervals	Relative Frequency
1–2	.20
3–4	.13
5–6	.17
7–8	.22
9–10	.18
11–12	.10

29. A researcher records the season of birth in a sample of patients with schizophrenia. The seasons recorded were winter, spring, spring, fall, summer, winter, fall, winter, winter, spring, winter, spring, winter, winter, summer, spring, winter, winter, fall, spring.

   (a) Construct a bar chart to summarize these data.

   (b) Construct a pie chart to summarize these data.

30. Convert the following histogram to a frequency polygon. *Hint:* You must plot the midpoints of each interval to distribute a frequency polygon.

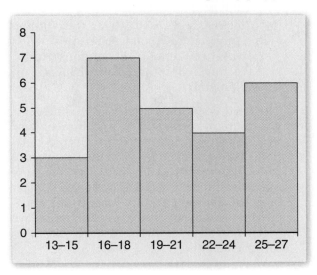

31. A health psychologist measures the amount of sleep (in hours) per night and the amount of time spent exercising (in minutes) per week in a sample of parents. The data points are given below.

   (a) Plot the data points.

   (b) Is there an identifiable pattern in these data? Explain.

Sleep	Exercise
6	30
5	35
8	50
4	15
3	20
7	65
6	50

32. A researcher reports that increased partying in college (nights per week) is associated with a lower grade point average (on the 4.0 grading scale). Does the scatter gram confirm this claim? Explain.

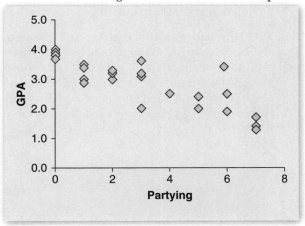

Problems in Research

33. **The "new" employee.** Keith Rollag (2007) noticed that coworkers evaluate and treat "new" employees differently from other staff members. He was interested in how long a new employee is considered "new" in an organization. He surveyed four organizations ranging in size from 34 to 89 employees. He found that the "new" employee status was mostly reserved for the 30% of employees in the organization with the lowest tenure.

   (a) In this study, what was the real range of employees hired by each organization surveyed?

   (b) What was the cumulative percent of "new" employees with the lowest tenure?

34. **Women in psychology then and now.** The following table lists the distribution of degrees in psychology conferred by degree-granting institutions, by sex and year. These and similar data are reported by the National Center for Education Statistics (NCES) at http://nces.ed.gov/programs/digest/.

Bachelor's Degrees	Males	Females
1970–1971	21,227	14,602
1980–1981	14,332	26,736
1990–1991	16,067	42,588
2000–2001	16,585	57,060
2005–2006	19,865	68,269

(a) Based on the data in this table, how has the number of degrees conferred in psychology changed by sex since 1970–1971?

(b) Is this a frequency distribution for grouped or ungrouped data? Explain.

35. **Talking and gender.** Pastizzo and Carbone (2007) reviewed 152 transcripts of lectures, meetings, advisement sessions, public addresses, and other public records to see how many different words (Type Count) and how many words overall (Token Count) were spoken. The following table shows the frequency distribution of their findings by gender.

Participant Characteristics	Count	
	Type	Token
Gender		
Women	24,541	878,261
Men	23,617	751,188
Unknown	479	927
Total		1,630,376

(a) Do men or women speak more words overall (Token Count)?

(b) Do men or women speak more different words (Type Count)?

36. **Talking and age.** Pastizzo and Carbone (2007) also looked at Type Count and Token Count by age (from the previous question). The following table shows the frequency distribution of their findings by age.

Participant Characteristics	Count	
	Type	Token
Age (years)		
17–23	15,002	400,584
24–30	10,740	253,385
31–50	21,085	590,815
51+	15,659	345,945
Unknown	4,171	39,647
Total		1,630,376

(a) Which age group speaks the most?

(b) Identify two problems with this table that could influence how you interpret the data.

37. **Power, influence, faith, and politics.** In February 2009, the Harris Poll asked a sample of Americans whether they thought churches and religious groups have too much or too little power and influence on Washington (reported at www.pollingreport.com). The opinions of Americans were 34% too much, 57% too little, 4% just right, and 5% unsure.

(a) What type of distribution is this?

(b) Knowing that 1,010 adults were polled nationwide, how many Americans polled felt that churches and religious groups have too little power and influence on Washington?

38. **The Gini coefficient.** The Gini coefficient is a measure of the extent to which income or wealth is equally distributed in a given population. The coefficient values range between 0 and 1. The lower the Gini coefficient, the more equally distributed wealth is in a given population. The following figure represents the distribution of wealth based on this measure (reported at http://en.wikipedia.org/wiki/Gini_coefficient).

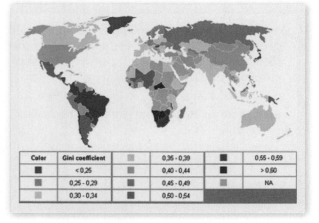

(a) What type of frequency distribution table is this?

(b) Is this an effective presentation of the data? Justify your answer.

NOTE: Answers for even numbers are in Appendix C.

Summarizing Data

Central Tendency

LEARNING OBJECTIVES

After reading this chapter, you should be able to:

1. Distinguish between a population mean and sample mean.

2. Calculate and interpret the mean, the median, and the mode.

3. Calculate and interpret the weighted mean for two or more samples with unequal sample sizes.

4. Identify the characteristics of the mean.

5. Identify an appropriate measure of central tendency for different distributions and scales of measurement.

6. Compute the mean, the median, and the mode using SPSS.

3.1   INTRODUCTION TO CENTRAL TENDENCY

Suppose before registering for a statistics class, a friend told you that students in Professor Smith's class earned higher grades on average than those in Professor Jones's class. On the basis of this information, you may decide to register for Professor Smith's class. You didn't need to know all the individual grades for each student in both classes to make your decision. Instead, your decision was based on knowledge of a single score, or class average.

The class average in this example is a measure of **central tendency.** Measures of central tendency are single values that have a "tendency" to be near the "center" of a distribution. Although we lose some meaning any time we reduce a set of data to a single score, statistical measures of central tendency ensure that the single score meaningfully represents a set of data. In this chapter, we will use three measures of central tendency to describe samples and populations of data: the mean, the median, and the mode.

DEFINITION

Measures of **central tendency** are statistical measures for locating a single score that is most representative or descriptive of all scores in a distribution.

NOTE: Measures of central tendency are values at or near the center of a distribution. Three common measures of central tendency are the mean, the median, and the mode.

Measures of central tendency are stated differently for populations and samples. Calculations of central tendency are largely the same for populations and samples of data, except for the notation used to represent the size of a population and the size of a sample. A population, as you may recall from Chapter 1, is a set of all scores from a given group; a sample is a subset of scores from this group or population. The size of a population is represented with a capital N; the size of a sample or subset of scores from a population is represented with a lowercase n. This notation, summarized here, distinguishes the size of a population from the size of a sample:

$$N = \text{Population size}$$

$$n = \text{Sample size}$$

DEFINITION

Population size is the number of individuals that constitute an entire group or population. The population size is represented by a capital N.

Sample size is the number of individuals that constitute a subset of those selected from a larger population. The sample size is represented by a lowercase n.

NOTE: The size of a population is represented with a capital N; the size of a sample is represented with a lowercase n.

In the sections that follow, we describe how measures of central tendency convey different information regarding scores in both populations and samples. We begin with the mean.

LEARNING CHECK 1

1. All measures of central tendency have a tendency to be at or near the _____ of a distribution

2. The size of a population is symbolized as ___, whereas the size of a sample is symbolized as ___.

Answers: 1. Center; 2. *N, n.*

MEASURES OF CENTRAL TENDENCY 3.2

Although we use different symbols to represent the number of scores (x) in a sample (n) versus a population (N), the computation of central tendency is the same for samples and populations. Three measures of central tendency are introduced in this section: the mean, the median, and the mode.

THE MEAN

The most commonly reported measure of central tendency is the mean. The **mean,** also called an **arithmetic mean** or **average,** is the sum of (Σ) a set of scores (x) divided by the number of scores summed, either in a sample (n) or population (N). The formulas for the population mean and the sample mean are

The **population mean** is the sum of N scores divided by N:

$$\mu = \frac{\sum x}{N} \text{(Population mean)}.$$

The **sample mean** is the sum of n scores divided by n:

$$M = \frac{\sum x}{n} \text{(Sample mean)}.$$

The symbol Σ (sigma) means "sum of," and the numbers or expression to the right of sigma are the items summed. In this formula, x represents each score (x) in a data set. The population mean is identified by the Greek letter mu, μ (pronounced "mew"); the sample mean is identified by an italicized M. You may sometimes see the sample mean identified with $\bar{X}$ (read "*x*-bar"). Although both notations are acceptable, M is the more common notation in published research and is used in this book.

DEFINITION

The **mean**, also called an **arithmetic mean** or **average**, is the sum of a set of scores in a distribution, divided by the total number of scores summed.

The mean for a set of scores in an entire population is referred to as a **population mean**; the mean for a sample (or subset of scores from a population) is referred to as a **sample mean**.

The mean is often referred to as the "balance point" in a distribution. The balance point is not always at the exact center of a distribution, as this analogy will demonstrate. Pick up a pen with a cap and remove the cap. Then place the pen sideways on your index finger until it is balanced and parallel with the floor. Once you have steadied the pen, your finger represents the "balance point" of the distribution of the weight of that pen. In the same way, the mean is the balance point of a distribution of data. Now, put the cap back on the pen and balance it again on your index finger. To balance the pen, you had to move your finger toward the side with the cap, right? Now your finger isn't at the center of the pen but closer to the cap. In the same way, the mean is not necessarily the middle value; it is the value that balances an entire distribution of numbers.

Remember that the computation of the mean does not change for samples and populations, just the notation used in the formula. To calculate the mean of a sample or a population, we do the same thing: We sum a set of scores and divide by the number of scores summed. Example 3.1 illustrates the computation of a population mean, and Example 3.2 illustrates the computation of a sample mean. Notice that the method of solution is the same in both examples.

EXAMPLE 3.1

A clinical psychologist records the number of symptoms expressed for attention-deficit disorder by a group of five children ($N = 5$) in a teacher's classroom. Suppose this group is the only group of interest to the researcher. So this group constitutes the population of children that the researcher is interested in. The psychologist records the following number of symptoms in this population: 3, 6, 4, 7, and 5. To compute the population mean:

First, sum the recorded values:

$$\sum x = 3 + 6 + 4 + 7 + 5 = 25.$$

Then divide the total by the number of scores summed ($N = 5$):

$$\frac{\sum x}{N} = \frac{25}{5} = 5.0.$$

Children in this population expressed a mean of five symptoms ($\mu = 5.0$) for attention-deficit disorder.

EXAMPLE 3.2

Suppose we create an experimental situation where a sample of participants must walk past a presumably scary portion of campus after dark. To measure fear, we record how quickly (in seconds) participants walk through the scary portion of campus after dark. The following times were recorded: 8, 9, 5, 5, 5, 1, 6, and 8. To compute the sample mean:

First, sum the recorded values:

$$\sum x = 8 + 9 + 5 + 5 + 5 + 1 + 6 + 8 = 47.$$

Then divide this total by the number of values summed ($n = 8$):

$$\frac{\sum x}{n} = \frac{47}{8} = 5.9.$$

Participants in this sample had a mean time of 5.9 seconds ($M = 5.9$) to walk past the presumably scary portion of campus after dark.

1. The notation used in the formulas for sample mean and population mean differs. What notation differs in these formulas?

2. The calculation of a population mean and sample mean is the same. State in words how to compute the mean.

3. A scientist records the following sample of scores ($n = 6$): 3, 6, 4, 1, 10, and 12. What is the sample mean of these scores?

Answers: 1. The term N is used in the denominator for the population mean, and the term n is used in the denominator for the sample mean; 2. The mean is the sum of a set of scores, divided by the total number of scores summed; 3. $M = 6.0$.

THE WEIGHTED MEAN

Another popular measure of central tendency is the **weighted mean.** This statistic measures the mean of a group of disproportionate scores or samples of scores. A common application of this in behavioral science is when scores are collected from two or more samples with unequal sample sizes. The term *disproportionate* refers to the fact that some samples have more scores than others (the samples are of disproportionate sizes). In this section, we will use the weighted mean in such a circumstance.

DEFINITION

> A **weighted mean** (denoted M_W) is the combined mean of two or more groups of scores, where the number of scores in each group is disproportionate or unequal.

The formula for the weighted mean for samples of unequal size can be expressed as follows:

$$M_W = \frac{\sum (M \times n)}{\sum n} = \frac{\text{weighted sum}}{\text{combined } n} .$$

M represents the mean of each sample, and n represents the size of each sample. In this formula, the sample size (n) is the weight for each mean. Using this formula, we will compute the combined mean for two or more samples of scores, where the number of scores in each sample is disproportionate or unequal. We will use the data in Table 3.1, which shows the mean fitness score for three samples consisting of participants who are lean, overweight, or obese.

TABLE 3.1   The mean fitness score and sample size for lean, overweight, and obese participants.

Sample	M	n
Lean	46	12
Overweight	58	14
Obese	73	30

NOTE: A weighted mean can be used to compute the mean for multiple groups of scores where the size of each group is unequal.

Notice that the sample size for each group is not the same; more scores were used to compute the mean for some samples than others. If we computed the arithmetic mean, we would get the following result:

$$\text{Arithmetic mean: } \frac{46+58+73}{3} = 59.0.$$

The combined mean is 59.0. But this calculation is incorrect. It does not account for the number of scores that contributed to the calculation of each mean. As a general rule, larger sample sizes carry more weight in determining the overall weighted mean. Because more scores contributed to the mean in the sample of obese participants, for example, the sample mean in this group contributed more to the combined mean of all samples and is therefore given more weight.

To compute the weighted mean, we find the product, $M \times n$, for each sample. This gives us a weight for the mean of each sample. By adding these products, we arrive at the weighted sum:

$$\text{Weighted sum} = (46 \times 12) + (58 \times 14) + (73 \times 30) = 3,554.$$

Then, we divide the weighted sum by the combined sample size (n), which is computed by adding the sample sizes in the denominator:

$$M_W = \frac{3,554}{12+14+30} = 63.5.$$

The weighted mean for these samples is 63.5.

The weighted mean is larger than the arithmetic mean (63.5 vs. 59.0) because the larger sample (the sample of obese participants) scored higher on the fitness measure. Hence, the value of the weighted mean shifted toward the mean from the larger sample (or the sample with more weight). This makes the weighted mean an accurate statistic for computing the mean for samples of unequal sizes.

MAKING SENSE: Making the Grade

Instructors often weight grades for college courses. Suppose your statistics course includes an exam, a quiz, and a final class project. The instructor considers the exam to be the most important measure of learning and so gives it the greatest weight. Table 3.2 shows this weighted distribution.

TABLE 3.2 Grading distribution for students in a hypothetical statistics course.

Type of Measure	Points	Weight
Exam	100	60%
Quiz	100	20%
Final project	100	20%

In this example, we have three class assignments with unequal weights. The score for each assignment is represented as x in the formula, and the weight is represented as w (instead of n for sample size). Notice that the sum of the weights is 100% or 1.00, which means that the denominator will always sum to 1.00. The weighted mean is calculated by computing the weighted sum:

$$\text{Weighted mean} = \sum(x \times w).$$

The exam, quiz, and final project are each worth the same number of points (100), but they are weighted differently. Suppose you score 70 points on the exam, 98 points on the quiz, and 100 points on the final project. If you compute an arithmetic mean to determine your grade, you would be wrong:

$$\frac{70 + 98 + 100}{300} = 0.89 \text{ or } 89\%.$$

Instead, you apply the formula for weighted means to calculate your final average because each grade was weighted. Without doing the calculation, you might guess (correctly) that it's going to be lower than 89%. After you multiply each grade times its weight, then sum each product, you can verify your hunch:

$$\sum(x \times w) = (70 \times .60) + (98 \times .20) + (100 \times .20) = 0.816 \text{ or } 81.6\%.$$

Your grade dropped from a B+ to a B– because your lowest score was on the most important (or most heavily weighted) measure of learning—the exam. You should be aware of this for any class you take. If an instructor puts particular weight on a certain graded assignment, then you should too. A weighted mean can significantly change a grade.

THE MEDIAN

Suppose you measure the following set of scores: 2, 3, 4, 5, 6, 6, and 100. The mean of these scores is 18 (add up the seven scores and divide by 7). Yet, the score of 100 is an outlier in this data set, which causes the mean value to increase so much that the mean fails to reflect most of the data. The mean can be misleading when a data set has an outlier because the mean will shift toward the value of that outlier. For this reason, there is a need for alternative measures of central tendency. One measure is the **median,** which is the middle value in a distribution. The median value represents the midpoint of a distribution of scores where half the scores in a distribution fall above and half below its value. To find the median position, list a set of scores in numeric order and compute this formula:

$$\text{Median position} = \frac{n+1}{2}.$$

The **median** is the middle value in a distribution of data listed in numeric order.

DEFINITION

NOTE: *The median is the midpoint in a distribution. If you list a set of scores in numeric order, the median is the middle score.*

Locating the median is different for odd- and even-numbered sample sizes (n). Example 3.3 illustrates how to find the median for an odd-numbered sample size, and in Example 3.4 we will calculate the median for an even-numbered sample size.

EXAMPLE 3.3

When the number of scores in a distribution is odd, order the set of scores from least to most (or vice versa) and find the middle number. Let's find the median for each of these lists.

(a) 3, 6, 5, 3, 8, 6, 7 ($n = 7$)

(b) 99, 66, 44, 13, 8 ($n = 5$)

(c) 51, 55, 105, 155, 205, 255, 305, 355, 359 ($n = 9$)

(a) First, place each score in numeric order: 3, 3, 5, $\boxed{6}$, 6, 7, and 8. Then locate the position of the middle score: $\dfrac{7+1}{2} = 4$. Count four scores in (from the left or right; it doesn't matter); the median is 6.

(b) These values are already in order from most to least ($n = 5$), so locate the position of the middle score: $\dfrac{5+1}{2} = 3$. Count three places in; the median is 44.

(c) These values are already in order from least to most ($n = 9$), so locate the position of the middle score: $\dfrac{9+1}{2} = 5$. Count five places in; the median is 205.

EXAMPLE 3.4

When the number of scores in a distribution is even, list the scores in numeric order and then average the middle two scores. Let's find the median for each of these lists.

(a) 3, 6, 5, 3, 8, 6 ($n = 6$)

(b) 99, $\boxed{66, 44}$, 13 ($n = 4$)

(c) 55, 105, $\boxed{155, 205}$, 255, 305 ($n = 6$)

(a) First, place each score in numeric order: 3, 3, $\boxed{5, 6}$, 6, and 8. The position of the median score is $\dfrac{6+1}{2} = 3.5$. Any time you obtain a value to the tenths place (i.e., 0.5), you must average the two positions surrounding this answer. In this case, you average the third and fourth positioned values: $\dfrac{5+6}{2} = 5.5$. The median is 5.5.

(b) These values are already in order from most to least. The position of the median is $\dfrac{4+1}{2} = 2.5$. In this case, you average the second and third positioned values: $\dfrac{66+44}{2} = 55$. The median is 55.

(c) These values are already in order from least to most. The position of the median is $\dfrac{6+1}{2} = 3.5$. In this case, you average the third and fourth positioned values: $\dfrac{205+155}{2} = 180$. The median is 180.

Notice that to find the median, we find the middle score. The value of an outlier has little influence over the median. At the beginning of this section, we measured the following set of scores: 2, 3, 4, 5, 6, 6, and 100. The mean of these scores is $M = 18$. If you find the middle score, the median is 5. The value of the outlier did not distort the value of the median. In this example, the median is more reflective of the data for this distribution.

NOTE: Outliers in a data distribution influence the value of the mean but not the median.

Graphically, the median can be estimated by a cumulative percent distribution. Because the median is located in the middle of a distribution, it is approximately at the 50th percentile of a cumulative percent distribution. To illustrate, suppose we measure the 20 scores listed in Table 3.3. The median of this distribution is 16. Figure 3.1 shows an ogive of the cumulative percent distribution for these data. Notice in the figure that the 50th percentile closely approximates the median of this distribution.

NOTE: The 50th percentile of a cumulative percent distribution estimates the value of the median.

TABLE 3.3   A hypothetical list of 20 scores.

2	7	18	29
3	8	21	34
4	11	21	34
4	12	26	37
5	14	29	44

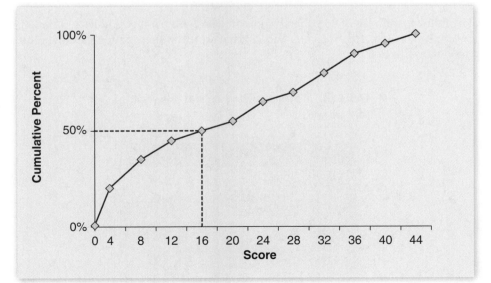

FIGURE 3.1

An ogive for the cumulative percent distribution of scores with a median of 16. The 50th percentile approximates the median of this distribution.

1. The _____ is the combined mean of two or more groups of scores, where the number of scores in each group is disproportionate or unequal.

2. A researcher collects two samples of data. He finds the first sample ($n = 8$) has a mean of 5; the second sample ($n = 2$) has a mean of 10. What is the weighted mean of these samples?

3. What type of distribution is used to approximate the median?

4. The _____ is the preferred measure of central tendency when a data set has outliers.

Answers: 1. weighted mean; 2. $M_w = \dfrac{(5 \cdot 8) + (10 \cdot 2)}{8 + 2} = 6.0$; 3. Cumulative percent distribution; 4. median.

NOTE: The mode reflects the score or scores that occur most often in a distribution. The mode is often reported in research journals with the mean or median.

THE MODE

In addition to the mean and median, a third common measure of central tendency is the **mode.** The mode is the score that occurs most often in a data set. One advantage of the mode is that it is simply a count; no calculations or formulas are necessary to compute a mode. To find the mode, list a set of scores in numeric order and count the score that occurs most often.

DEFINITION

The **mode** is the value in a data set that occurs most often or most frequently.

The mode is generally reported in research journals with other measures of central tendency, such as the mean and median. It is rarely used as the sole way of describing data. Let's work through Examples 3.5 and 3.6 to find the mode.

EXAMPLE 3.5

The following is a list of 20 golfers' scores on a difficult par-4 golf hole: 2, 3, 3, 3, 3, 3, 4, 4, 4, 4, 4, 4, 4, 4, 5, 5, 5, 5, 6, and 7. What score did these golfers card the most (mode) on this hole?

TABLE 3.4 The frequency of scores on a hypothetical par-4 golf hole.

Score	f(x)
Eagle (2)	1
Birdie (3)	5
Par (4)	8
Bogey (5)	4
Double-bogey (6)	1
Triple-bogey (7)	1

Table 3.4 lists these scores in a frequency distribution table. From this table, it is clear that most golfers scored a par 4 on this difficult hole. Therefore, the mode, or most common score on this hole, was par.

A researcher recorded the number of symptoms for major depressive disorder (MDD) expressed in a small sample of 20 "at-risk" participants: 0, 4, 3, 6, 5, 2, 3, 3, 5, 4, 6, 3, 5, 6, 4, 0, 0, 3, 0, and 1. How many symptoms of MDD did participants in this sample most commonly express?

First list these scores in numeric order: 0, 0, 0, 0, 1, 2, 3, 3, 3, 3, 3, 4, 4, 4, 5, 5, 5, 6, 6, and 6. In doing so, we find that 3, which occurred five times, is the mode in this data set. Participants in this "at-risk" sample most often reported three symptoms of MDD.

---

1. The _____ is the value in a data set that occurs most often or most frequently.

2. Identify the mode: A study reports that women are more likely to ask for directions than men.

3. Identify the mode: A researcher observes that most participants in her study were extroverted, not introverted.

LEARNING CHECK 4

Answers: 1. mode; 2. Women; 3. Extroverted participants.

CHARACTERISTICS OF THE MEAN   3.3

Although each measure of central tendency is important for different reasons, the mean is the most reported statistic in behavioral science. Indeed, each subsequent chapter in this book will at least make mention of it. For this reason, it is important to introduce five key characteristics of the mean. Note in this discussion that the five characteristics emphasize that the mean reflects every score in a distribution.

CHANGING AN EXISTING SCORE

Changing an existing score will change the mean. In essence, every score in a distribution affects the mean. Therefore, changing any existing score in a distribution will change the value of the mean. Let's work with a sample of 10 quiz scores: 1, 6, 4, 2, 5, 9, 7, 4, 8, and 4. In this sample $n = 10$ and $\sum x = 50$. The mean is 5.0:

$$M = \frac{\sum x}{n} = \frac{50}{10} = 5.0.$$

If we change one of the scores, the mean will change. For example, let's say that the instructor made a mistake grading one quiz and realized that the first score of 1 should be a 6. Although the number of scores is unchanged at $n = 10$, the sum of scores $\left(\sum x\right)$ increases from 50 to 55. The mean increased from 5.0 to 5.5:

$$M = \frac{\sum x}{n} = \frac{55}{10} = 5.5.$$

If you change the value of the numerator without changing the sample size n, then the value of the mean will change. In this example, the mean increased. As a rule, when you increase the value of an existing score, the mean will increase; when you decrease the value of an existing score, the mean will decrease.

ADDING A NEW SCORE OR REMOVING AN EXISTING SCORE

Adding a new score or completely removing an existing score will change the mean, unless that value equals the mean. Let's work with the same sample of $n = 10$ quiz scores: 1, 6, 4, 2, 5, 9, 7, 4, 8, and 4, where $M = 5.0$. Suppose another student takes the quiz and scores a 2. The new list, with the added score, is $n = 11$ with the following values: 1, 6, 4, 2, 5, 9, 7, 4, 8, 4, and 2. Because this new score ($x = 2$) is less than the mean ($M = 5$), the mean will *decrease* or shift toward that smaller score. The mean decreased from 5.0 to 4.7:

$$M = \frac{\sum x}{n} = \frac{52}{11} = 4.7.$$

Now suppose the additional student scored an 8 instead. The new list, with the added score, is $n = 11$ with the following values: 1, 6, 4, 2, 5, 9, 7, 4, 8, 4, and 8. Because this new score ($x = 8$) is greater than the mean ($M = 5$), the mean will *increase* or shift toward that larger score. The mean increased from 5.0 to 5.3:

$$M = \frac{\sum x}{n} = \frac{58}{11} = 5.3.$$

Deleting a score from the original list of 10 quiz scores will also change the mean in a predictable way. Deleting a score below the mean will *increase* the value of the mean. Suppose one student drops out of the class, so we delete his score of 1 from the data set. The new list, after removing the deleted score, is $n = 9$ with the following values: 6, 4, 2, 5, 9, 7, 4, 8, and 4. The mean increased from 5.0 to 5.4:

$$M = \frac{\sum x}{n} = \frac{49}{9} = 5.4.$$

Deleting a score above the mean will *decrease* the value of the mean. Suppose the student who scored a 9 on the quiz drops out of the class. The new list, after removing the deleted score, is $n = 9$ with the following values: 1, 6, 4, 2, 5, 7, 4, 8, and 4. The mean decreased from 5.0 to 4.6:

$$M = \frac{\sum x}{n} = \frac{41}{9} = 4.6.$$

The only time that a change in a distribution of scores *does not change* the value of the mean is when the value that is added or removed is exactly equal to the mean. For example, here is the original list of quiz scores: 1, 6, 4, 2, 5, 9, 7, 4, 8, and 4, where $M = 5.0$.

Adding a 5 to this data set makes $n = 11$, and the $\sum x = 55$. The mean remains 5.0.

$$M = \frac{\sum x}{n} = \frac{55}{11} = 5.0.$$

Subtracting a 5 from this same data set makes $n = 9$, and the $\sum x = 45$. The mean again remains unchanged.

$$M = \frac{\sum x}{n} = \frac{45}{9} = 5.0.$$

In sum, the *mean* reflects the distance that each individual score deviates from the balance point of a distribution. The farther scores are from the mean, the more they pull the mean toward them to balance the distribution. Values exactly equal to the mean are zero distance from the mean, so the value of the mean doesn't need to change to keep the distribution balanced. This rule has many parts:

NOTE: The mean is a balance point of a distribution of scores. Its value shifts in a direction that balances a set of scores.

Part 1. Add a score above the mean and the mean will *increase*.

Part 2. Add a score below the mean and the mean will *decrease*.

Part 3. Delete a score below the mean and the mean will *increase*.

Part 4. Delete a score above the mean and the mean will *decrease*.

Part 5. Add or delete a score equal to the mean and the mean *does not change*.

ADDING, SUBTRACTING, MULTIPLYING, OR DIVIDING EACH SCORE BY A CONSTANT

Adding, subtracting, multiplying, or dividing each score in a distribution by a constant will cause the mean to change by that constant. To illustrate this, we will work through one example where we subtract a constant from each score and a second example where we multiply each score times a constant. Let's begin with an example where we subtract a constant from each score. Suppose you have five favorite meals consisting of 450, 500, 525, 550, and 600 calories (cal), respectively. For these data, $M = 525$ cal, as shown in the middle column in Table 3.5.

Suppose that each of these meals includes a 100-calorie portion of French fries. In a stunning series of research reports, though, you learn that fried foods aren't good for your heart, so you subtract the French fries portion from each meal. In the rightmost column in Table 3.5, the 100-calorie portion of French fries is subtracted from the total calories in each meal. The reduction in calories is a constant: $C = 100$. Notice that when each value (measured in calories) is changed by the same constant (100 cal), the mean is also changed by that constant. The mean is exactly 100 calories less without the French fries ($M = 425$). This rule applies when *every* score in the distribution is changed by the *same* constant.

TABLE 3.5 The calories in each meal with and without the 100-calorie portion of French fries.

Meal	Meal With French Fries	Meal Without French Fries
1	450	350
2	500	400
3	525	425
4	550	450
5	600	500
$n = 5$	$M = 525$	$M = 425$

To further illustrate this rule, let's use an example where we multiply a constant times each score. Suppose you are a health practitioner conducting a study to determine whether people who eat more fat in their diets also tend to consume more calories. You find that five astonishingly health-conscious adults eat only 2, 3, 4, 5, and 6 grams of fat in their diets per week, respectively. For this study, the mean amount consumed is $M = 4$ grams of fat per week.

NOTE: Changing each score in a distribution by the same constant will likewise change the mean by that constant.

Suppose you want to know how many calories of fat each adult consumed per week (instead of grams of fat). Fat contains 9 calories per gram, so we can multiply the weight (in grams) times 9 to find the number of calories consumed. Table 3.6 shows that multiplying each value in the original distribution times 9 also changes the mean by a multiple of 9. The mean is $M = 36$ calories (4 mean grams of fat × 9 cal per gram = 36 mean calories). Again, this rule applies when *every* score in the distribution is changed by the *same* constant.

TABLE 3.6   The grams of fat and calories of fat consumed per week.

Participants	Grams of Fat	Calories
A	2	18
B	3	27
C	4	36
D	5	45
E	6	54
$n = 5$	$M = 4$	$M = 36$

SUMMING THE DIFFERENCES OF SCORES FROM THEIR MEAN

The sum of the differences of scores from their mean is zero. We can think of the mean as the balance point of a distribution of scores. What logically follows from this is to think of the mean as a zero point for a distribution as well. It's the only constant that you can subtract from every score in a distribution, where the sum of the differences is zero. Think of this as balancing weights on a scale. Only when the difference between the weights on each side of the scale is the same (difference = 0) will the weights on each side of a scale be balanced. Similarly, the balance point of a distribution of scores is the point where the difference of scores above the mean is the same as the difference of scores below the mean (difference = 0). The notation for describing the sum of (Σ) the differences of scores (x) from their mean (M) is $\sum x - M$.

NOTE: The difference of each score from the mean always sums to zero, similar to placing weights on both sides of a scale. The mean would be located at the point that balances both ends—the difference in weight on each side would be zero.

To illustrate, let's use the following scores ($n = 5$): 1, 2, 5, 7, and 10. The mean of this distribution is $M = 5.0$. Now subtract 5 (the mean) from each score. Notice that the sum of the differences above the mean (the positive differences) is the same as the sum of the differences below the mean (the negative differences) in Table 3.7. The differences basically cancel out; the sum of the differences of scores from their mean is 0 $\left(\sum x - M = 0\right)$, as shown in Table 3.7. No other constant produces this result.

Only when the mean is subtracted from each score in a distribution is the sum of the differences equal to zero. We will examine this characteristic again in Chapter 4.

TABLE 3.7 A set of five scores (left column) with a mean of 5. When this mean is subtracted from each score, then summed, the solution is always zero (right column).

x	x – M
1	(1 – 5) = –4
2	(2 – 5) = –3
5	(5 – 5) = 0
7	(7 – 5) = 2
10	(10 – 5) = 5
$\sum x = 25$	$\sum x - M = 0$

SUMMING THE SQUARED DIFFERENCES OF SCORES FROM THEIR MEAN

The sum of the squared differences of scores from their mean is minimal. Suppose that we want to measure how far scores deviate from the mean. We could subtract each score from the mean and sum the deviations, but that will always produce a result equal to 0, as shown in Table 3.7. If we did this, then we would erroneously conclude that scores do not deviate from their mean. The solution to obtain a value greater than 0 is to square each deviation before summing. This produces the smallest possible positive number greater than 0, where larger outcomes indicate that scores deviate further from their mean. The notation for describing the sum of ($\sum$) the squared differences of scores (x) from their mean (M) is $\sum (x - M)^2$.

To illustrate, suppose we measure the same five scores ($n = 5$) from the previous example: 1, 2, 5, 7, and 10, where $M = 5.0$. If we substitute the values of x and M we will obtain the following solution:

$$\sum (x - M)^2 = (1 - 5)^2 + (2 - 5)^2 + (5 - 5)^2 + (7 - 5)^2 + (10 - 5)^2$$
$$= (-4)^2 + (-3)^2 + (0)^2 + (2)^2 + (5)^2 = 16 + 9 + 0 + 4 + 25 = 54.$$

Table 3.8 shows the details of this calculation. The solution is 54, which is the smallest (or minimal) value for the sum of the differences of scores from their mean. Subtracting scores from any constant other than the mean will produce a greater value. If you substitute any positive or negative value other than the mean ($M = 5$), you will always obtain a solution greater than 54. We will examine this characteristic again in Chapter 4.

NOTE: Summing the squared difference of each score from its mean produces a minimal solution. If you replace the mean with any other value, the solution will be larger.

TABLE 3.8   The sum of the differences of scores from their mean. In this example, 54 is the smallest possible solution. Subtracting any other value than the mean will produce a larger solution.

x	$(x - M)^2$
1	$(1 - 5)^2 = 16$
2	$(2 - 5)^2 = 9$
5	$(5 - 5)^2 = 0$
7	$(7 - 5)^2 = 4$
10	$(10 - 5)^2 = 25$
$\Sigma x = 25$	$\Sigma(x - M)^2 = 54$

LEARNING CHECK 5

1. Which of the following will *decrease* the value of the mean?
   a. Delete a score below the mean
   b. Add a score below the mean
   c. Add a score exactly equal to the mean
   d. None of the above

2. From the choices in Question 1, which will *increase* the value of the mean?

3. From the choices in Question 1, which will have *no effect* on the mean?

4. State the characteristic of the mean that indicates that the mean is the "zero point" for a distribution of scores.

5. Suppose that you sum the squared differences of scores from their mean. What is always true about the result you obtain?

Answers: 1. (b); 2. (a); 3. (c); 4. The sum of the differences of scores from their mean is zero; 5. The result is the smallest possible solution. Substituting any other constant (other than the mean) will produce a larger result.

3.4   CHOOSING AN APPROPRIATE MEASURE OF CENTRAL TENDENCY

The measures of central tendency we've discussed—the mean, the median, and the mode—are used to summarize different types of data. The choice of which measure to select depends largely on the type of distribution and the scale of measurement of the data. In this section, we consider both factors to decide which measures of central tendency are most appropriate to describe a given set of data.

USING THE MEAN TO DESCRIBE DATA

The mean is typically used to describe data that are normally distributed and measures on an interval or ratio scale.

Describing Normal Distributions

The **normal distribution** is a distribution where half of all scores fall above the mean, the median, and the mode, and half fall below these measures. Hence, the mean, the median, and the mode are all located at the center of a normal distribution, as illustrated in Figure 3.2. (We will discuss other characteristics of normal distributions in Chapter 6.) In cases where the mean is approximately equal to all other measures of central tendency, the mean is used to summarize the data. We could choose to summarize a normal distribution with the median or mode, but the mean is most often used because all scores are included in its calculation (i.e., its value is most reflective of all the data).

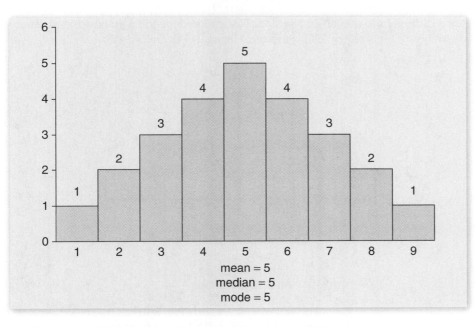

mean = 5
median = 5
mode = 5

FIGURE 3.2

A normal distribution. Notice that the mean, the median, and the mode are the same, and all occur at the center of the distribution: Each measure is equal to 5.

DEFINITION

The **normal distribution** (also called the **symmetrical, Gaussian,** or **bell-shaped distribution**) is a theoretical distribution with data that are symmetrically distributed around the mean, the median, and the mode.

Describing Interval and Ratio Scale Data

The mean is used for data that can be described in terms of the *distance* that scores deviate from the mean. After all, one of the characteristics of the mean (described in Section 3.3) is that the mean balances a set of scores—in other words, the sum of the differences of scores from their mean is 0. For this reason, data that are described by the mean should meaningfully convey differences (or deviations) from the mean. Differences between two scores are meaningfully conveyed for data on an interval or ratio scale only. Hence, the mean is an appropriate measure of central tendency used to describe interval and ratio scale data.

NOTE: The mean is typically used to describe interval and ratio scale data that are normally distributed.

USING THE MEDIAN TO DESCRIBE DATA

The median is typically used to describe skewed distributions of data and measures on an ordinal scale.

Describing Skewed Distributions

Some data can have outliers that skew (or distort) a data set. A **skewed distribution** occurs whenever a data set includes a score or group of scores that fall substantially above (**positively skewed**) or substantially below (**negatively skewed**) most other scores in a distribution. Figure 3.3 illustrates how a skewed distribution shifts the value of the mean. In a normal distribution, the mean and mode are equal (they are both at the center of the distribution). Notice in Figure 3.3 that the value of the mean in a skewed distribution is pulled toward the skewed data points. In a positively skewed distribution, the mean is greater than the mode; in a negatively skewed distribution, the mean is less than the mode. The location of the median is actually unpredictable, and can fall on any side of the mode, depending on how the scores are distributed (Ottenbacher, 1993; Sinacore, Chang, & Falconer, 1992).

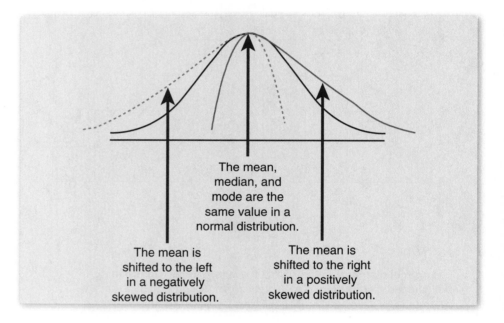

FIGURE 3.3

The position of the mean and mode for positively skewed and negatively skewed distributions, relative to the normal distribution. Notice that in each distribution shown here, the mode does not change, but the mean is pulled in the direction of the tail of a skewed distribution.

The mean, median, and mode are the same value in a normal distribution.

The mean is shifted to the left in a negatively skewed distribution.

The mean is shifted to the right in a positively skewed distribution.

Outliers distort the value of the mean, making it a less meaningful measure for describing all data in a distribution. The value of the median, on the other hand, is not influenced by the value of outliers. For this reason, the median is more representative of all data in a skewed distribution and is therefore the most appropriate measure of central tendency to describe these types of distributions.

DEFINITION

A **skewed distribution** is a distribution of scores that includes outliers or scores that fall substantially above or below most other scores in a data set.

A **positively skewed distribution** is a distribution of scores where a few outliers are substantially larger (toward the right tail in a graph) than most other scores.

A **negatively skewed distribution** is a distribution of scores where a few outliers are substantially smaller (toward the left tail in a graph) than most other scores.

Describing Ordinal Scale Data

The median is used to describe ranked or ordinal data that convey *direction* only. For example, the fifth person to finish a task took longer than the first person to finish a task; an individual with a bachelor's degree is more educated than an individual with an associate's degree. In both examples, the ordinal data convey direction (greater than or less than) only. Because the *distance* (or deviation) of ordinal scale scores from their mean is not meaningful, the median is an appropriate measure used to describe ordinal scale data.

NOTE: The median is typically used to describe skewed distributions and ordinal scale data.

USING THE MODE TO DESCRIBE DATA

The mode is typically used to describe modal distributions of data and measures on a nominal scale.

Describing Modal Distributions

The mode can be used to describe most data that are measured. Sometimes it can complement other measures of central tendency. At the start of this chapter, we considered what you'd need to know to choose between two professors teaching the same course. In addition to knowing the average grade that students earned in each class (the mean), you might also want to know the grade that most students earn in each class (the mode). Both measures would be informative. Any distribution where one or more scores occur most frequently or most often is called a **modal distribution.** Modal distributions can come in a variety of shapes and sizes.

A **modal distribution** is a distribution of scores where one or more scores occur most often or most frequently.

DEFINITION

Unimodal distributions have a single mode. The normal distribution and skewed distribution both have one mode—both distributions are examples of a unimodal shape. The mode can be used with the mean to describe normal distributions. Likewise, the mode can be used with the median to describe skewed distributions.

A **unimodal distribution** is a distribution of scores where one score occurs most often or most frequently. A unimodal distribution has one mode.

DEFINITION

A **bimodal distribution** is a distribution of scores where two scores occur most often or most frequently. A bimodal distribution has two modes.

Bimodal distributions, such as the one in Figure 3.4, have two modes. The mean and median are typically located between the two modes in a bimodal distribution, which often occurs when the data for two groups with unique characteristics are combined. For example, if you measured the height of adult American men and women, you would find a roughly bimodal distribution, with most men reporting a height around 71 inches and most women reporting a height around 66 inches. The modes would be located at 71 inches and 66 inches, with the mean and median height generally falling somewhere between the two modes.

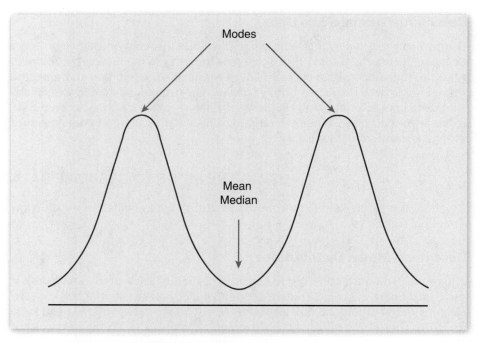

FIGURE 3.4

The location of the mean, the median, and the mode for bimodal distributions. Note that the mean and median can be different values, but they are typically located between the two modes in a bimodal distribution.

Multimodal distributions have more than two modes; **nonmodal distributions,** such as the one in Figure 3.5, have no mode at all. For distributions such as these, the mode would be used to describe multimodal distributions only. Nonmodal distributions are essentially a straight line, with the frequency of each score being the same, so there is no mode. In this rare case, the mean or median, which are both located toward the center of a nonmodal distribution, can be used to describe these data.

DEFINITION

A **multimodal distribution** is a distribution of scores where more than two scores occur most often or most frequently. A multimodal distribution has more than two modes.

A **nonmodal (rectangular) distribution** is a distribution of scores where all scores occur at the same frequency. A nonmodal distribution has no mode.

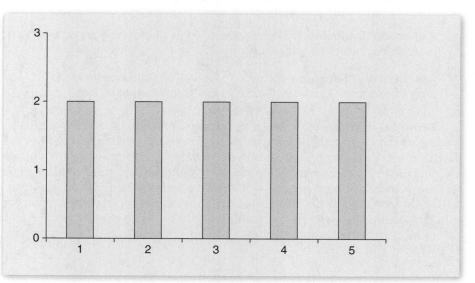

FIGURE 3.5

A nonmodal or rectangular distribution. Notice that nonmodal distributions have no identifiable peak, or mode, in the distribution

Describing Nominal Scale Data

The mode is used to describe nominal data that identify something or someone, nothing more. Because a nominal scale value is not a *quantity,* it does not make sense to use the mean or median to describe these data. The mode is used instead. For example, the mean or median season of birth for patients with schizophrenia is not very meaningful or sensible. But describing these nominal data with the mode is meaningful by saying, for example, that most patients with schizophrenia are born in winter months. Any time you see phrases such as *most often, typical,* or *common,* the mode is being used to describe these data. Table 3.9 summarizes when it is appropriate to use each measure of central tendency.

NOTE: The mode is typically used to describe modal distributions and nominal scale data.

TABLE 3.9 A summary for when it is appropriate to use each measure of central tendency to describe data based on the shape of the distribution and the measurement scale for the data.

Measure of Central Tendency	Shape of Distribution	Measurement Scale
Mean	Normal	Interval, ratio
Median	Skewed	Ordinal
Mode	Modal	Nominal

LEARNING CHECK 6

1. The mean is a preferred descriptive statistic:
    a. For describing normal distributions
    b. For summarizing interval scale measures
    c. For summarizing ratio scale measures
    d. All of the above

2. True or false: When the mean is greater than the mode, the distribution is negatively skewed.

3. True or false: The mean is a preferred measure for describing skewed distributions.

4. Which type of modal distribution would *not* be described using the mode?
    a. Unimodal
    b. Bimodal
    c. Multimodal
    d. Nonmodal

Answers: 1. (d); 2. False, when the mean is greater than the mode, the distribution is positively skewed; 3. False, the median is the preferred measure; 4. (d).

RESEARCH IN FOCUS: DESCRIBING CENTRAL TENDENCY 3.5

Gulledge, Stahmann, and Wilson (2004) used the mean, the median, and the mode to describe several types of nonsexual romantic physical affection among dating and married students at Brigham Young University (BYU). They defined nonsexual romantic physical affection as "any touch intended to arouse feelings of love in the giver or the recipient" (p. 609). They recorded the amount of time, or the number of times, students engaged in seven forms of affection (per week) based on self-reports. Table 3.10 shows a portion of their results.

TABLE 3.10   Data as reported by Gulledge, Stahmann, and Wilson (2004).

Type of Affection	n	Mean	Median	Mode
Backrubs/massages[a]	177	30	20	0, 30
Caressing/stroking[a]	167	88	30	30
Cuddling/holding[a]	171	189	120	120
Holding hands[a]	168	138	60	60
Hugging[b]	174	34	21	20
Kissing on the face[b]	170	30	15	10
Kissing on the lips[b]	169	66	40	50

a. Measured as minutes per week.
b. Measured as times per week.

Table 3.10 shows the sample size (*n*) for each type of affection, in addition to the mean, the median, and the mode. By knowing these measures of central tendency, we can identify how participants generally responded in this study. Looking at the data in Table 3.10, we can see that the distribution of backrubs/massages is bimodal (it has two modes: 0 and 30). Also, the mean is greater than the median and mode for each type of affection, indicating that the distribution for each type of affection is approximately positively skewed. The mean is larger because of outliers—or a few respondents who apparently are very affectionate. The median indicates that most participants are responding below the mean (in most cases, well below the mean).

We were able to identify all this information based solely on three measures. Now suppose the researchers claim that the average student holds hands with a romantic partner for 138 minutes per week. While this is certainly true, you, being an informed reader, would quickly recognize that this conclusion is misleading. The median and mode indicate that most people are actually spending less than half that time per week holding hands with romantic partners because the median and mode for this type of affection was only 60 minutes. Hence, understanding central tendency allows you to clearly describe and accurately interpret behavioral data in ways not otherwise possible.

3.6   SPSS IN FOCUS: MEAN, MEDIAN, AND MODE

SPSS can be used to measure the mean, the median, and the mode for all sorts of data. In this section, we will work through a new example to compute each measure of central tendency. Suppose a researcher gives students a creativity test. Students are given a paper clip, and the time (in seconds) it takes them to list 10 uses for the paper clip is recorded. Faster times are presumed to reflect greater creativity. Using the data shown in Table 3.11, let's use SPSS to compute the mean, the median, and the mode.

1. Click on the **variable view** tab and enter *creativity* in the **name column.** We will enter whole numbers, so go to the **decimals column** and reduce that value to 0.

TABLE 3.11 The time (in seconds) that it took 20 participants to write down 10 uses for a paper clip on a creativity test.

41	80
65	80
123	64
46	59
48	51
87	36
38	80
90	143
132	122
115	100

2. Click on the **data view** tab and enter the 20 values in the column labeled *creativity.*

3. Go to the **menu bar** and click **Analyze,** then **Descriptive Statistics** and **Frequencies,** to bring up a dialog box.

4. In the **dialog box,** select the *creativity* variable and click the arrow in the center to move *creativity* into the box labeled **Variable(s):** to the right. Make sure the option to display frequency tables is not selected, and then select **Statistics** to bring up another dialog box.

5. In the dialog box, select **Mean, Median** and **Mode** to the right; then select **Continue.**

6. Select **Paste,** and then **Run**.

TABLE 3.12 SPSS output table showing the mean, the median, and the mode.

Statistics

creativity

N	Valid	20
	Missing	0
Mean		80.00
Median		80.00
Mode		80

Notice in Table 3.12 that the mean, the median, and the mode are the same—the value of each measure of central tendency is 80. Also, note that when multiple modes exist in the data, which is not the case for this data set, SPSS does not list the value for every mode. Instead, SPSS gives the value for the smallest mode and places the superscript *a* next to that modal value to indicate that other modes exist in the data.

CHAPTER SUMMARY ORGANIZED BY LEARNING OBJECTIVE

LO 1: Distinguish between a population mean and sample mean.

- The mean for a set of scores in an entire population is called a **population mean;** the mean for a sample (or subset of scores from a population) is called a **sample mean.** Each mean is computed the same but with different notation used to identify the sample size (n) and population size (N).

LO 2: Calculate and interpret the mean, the median, and the mode.

- Measures of **central tendency** are statistical measures for locating a single score that is most representative or descriptive of all scores in a distribution. Three measures of central tendency are the mean, the median, and the mode.
- The **mean** is the sum of a set of scores divided by the total number of scores summed:

  The population mean is the sum of N scores divided by N: $\mu = \dfrac{\sum x}{N}$.

  The sample mean is the sum of n scores divided by n: $M = \dfrac{\sum x}{n}$.

- The **median** is the middle score in a data set that is listed in numerical order, where half of all scores fall above and half fall below its value. Unlike the mean, the value of the median is not shifted in the direction of outliers—the median is always at the center or midpoint of a data set. To find the median position, list scores in numerical order and apply this formula:

$$\text{Median position} = \frac{n+1}{2}.$$

- The **mode** is the value in a data set that occurs most often or most frequently. The mode is often reported with the mean or the median.

LO 3: Calculate and interpret the weighted mean for two or more samples with unequal sample sizes.

- The **weighted mean** is the combined mean of two or more groups of scores, where the number of scores in each group is disproportionate or unequal. The formula for the weighted mean of two or more samples with unequal sample sizes is $M_W = \dfrac{\sum (M \times n)}{\sum n}$.

LO 4: Identify the characteristics of the mean.

- The mean has the following characteristics:
  a. Changing an existing score will change the mean.
  b. Adding a new score or completely removing an existing score will change the mean, unless that value equals the mean.
  c. Adding, subtracting, multiplying, or dividing each score in a distribution by a constant will cause the mean to change by that constant.
  d. The sum of the differences of scores from their mean is zero.
  e. The sum of the squared differences of scores from their mean is minimal.

LO 5: Identify an appropriate measure of central tendency for different distributions and scales of measurement.

- The *mean* is used to describe (1) data that are normally distributed and (2) interval and ratio scale data.
- The *median* is used to describe (1) data in a skewed distribution and (2) ordinal scale data.
- The *mode* is used to describe (1) any type of data with a value that occurs the most, although it is typically used together with the mean or the median, and (2) nominal scale data.

SPSS LO 6: Compute the mean, the median, and the mode using SPSS.

- SPSS can be used to compute the mean, median, and mode. Each measure of central tendency is computed using the **Analyze,** then **Descriptive Statistics,** and **Frequencies** options in the menu bar. These actions will bring up a dialog box that will allow you to identify the variable and select the **Statistics** option to select and compute the mean, the median, and the mode (for more details, see Section 3.6).

KEY TERMS

arithmetic mean
average
bell-shaped distribution
bimodal distribution
central tendency
Gaussian distribution
mean
median

modal distribution
mode
multimodal distribution
negatively skewed
nonmodal (rectangular) distribution
normal distribution
population mean
population size

positively skewed
sample mean
sample size
skewed distribution
symmetrical distribution
unimodal distribution
weighted mean

END-OF-CHAPTER PROBLEMS

Factual Problems

1. State the statistical notation for each of the following terms:
   (a) Population size
   (b) Sample size
   (c) Population mean
   (d) Sample mean

2. What is central tendency?

3. Explain why the median is always the score at the *center* of a distribution.

4. How do the sample mean and population mean differ?

5. List five characteristics of the mean.

6. When is the weighted mean equal to the arithmetic mean for combining the mean for two or more samples?

7. The mean is an appropriate measure for describing what types of data?

8. The median is an appropriate measure for describing what types of data?

9. The mode is an appropriate measure for describing what types of data?

10. What value represents:
    (a) The midpoint of a distribution? Explain.
    (b) The balance point of a distribution? Explain.
    (c) The zero point of a distribution? Explain.

Concepts and Application Problems

11. The following frequency distribution table lists the time (in minutes) that participants were late for an experimental session. Compute the sample mean, median, and mode for these data.

Time (min)	Frequency
0	5
2	2
6	1
8	3
9	2

12. The following table lists the number of text messages sent per day in a sample of college students and a sample of their parents.

College Students		Parents	
43	7	24	21
12	50	0	17
14	15	20	19
13	21	21	5
54	21	3	10

(a) Compute the mean, the median, and the mode for the college students' and parents' data.

(b) Based on the shape of the distribution for each sample, which measure of central tendency is most appropriate for describing each sample? Explain how describing each sample with only the most appropriate measure might be misleading.

13. A researcher records the number of hours (per week) that single mothers spend at work and states that the data are distributed normally. Which measure of central tendency is most appropriate for describing these data?

14. A psychologist records the duration of natural labor (in hours) in a sample of 36 first-pregnancy mothers. Based on the duration data given in the following table, which measure of central tendency is most appropriate for describing these data? *Hint:* Draw the shape of this distribution first.

1	5	6	2
7	3	4	7
10	7	5	6
4	3	2	11
5	9	8	5
6	6	9	7
4	5	6	4
8	8	10	9
8	7	6	3

15. A researcher records the levels of attraction for various fashion models among college students. He finds that mean levels of attraction are much higher than the median and mode for these data.

(a) What is the shape of the distribution for the data described in this study?

(b) Which measure of central tendency is most appropriate for describing these data? Explain.

16. A colleague measures the following heights (in inches) of 10 CEOs selected at random: 72, 75, 75, 66, 64, 79, 79, 75, 70, and 72. Which measure of central tendency is most appropriate for describing these data? *Hint:* Draw the shape of this distribution first.

17. A sports psychologist uses the body mass index (BMI) score to measure health in a sample of 60 athletes and determines that 20 are normal, 26 are overweight, and 14 are obese. Which measure of central tendency is most appropriate for describing these data?

18. A family counselor records the number of sessions required for children to complete counseling following the loss of a family member. The counselor finds that most boys completed counseling in 12 sessions, whereas most girls required 15 sessions to complete counseling. If the data for boys and girls are combined, what type of distribution best describes the combined data?

19. A neuroscientist measures the reaction times (in seconds) during an experimental session in a sample of cocaine-addicted ($n = 8$), morphine-addicted ($n = 12$), and heroin-addicted rats ($n = 6$). Mean reaction times in each sample were 11, 18, and 13 seconds, respectively. What is the weighted mean for all three samples? *Hint:* The overall mean is not 14.0 seconds.

20. A cognitive psychologist is interested in the ability of men and women to multitask—a cognitive skill thought to engage short-term or working memory. The psychologist observed a sample of 5 men ($n = 5$) and 8 women ($n = 8$) and measured the number of tasks they could accurately complete within a short time frame. He found that men completed 2.3 tasks on average ($M = 2.3$), whereas women completed 4.5 tasks on average ($M = 4.5$). What is the weighted mean for both samples? *Hint:* The overall mean is not 3.4 tasks.

21. Based on the scale of measurement for each variable listed below, which measure of central tendency is most appropriate for describing the data?

(a) The time (in years) it takes a sample of students to graduate college

(b) The blood type (e.g., Type A, B, AB, O) of a group of participants

(c) The rankings of college undergraduate academic programs

22. A instructor gives students a surprise quiz and records a mean grade of 12 points. What is the new mean value if the instructor:

    (a) Adds 10 points to each quiz

    (b) Subtracts 2 points from each quiz

    (c) Doubles each quiz score

    (d) Divides each quiz score in half

23. Children participating at a 1-week summer camp made five new friends on average during the first 6 days of camp. If each child made one more friend on the last day of camp, then how many friends on average did the children make during the 1-week summer camp?

24. A sample of 26 patients with major depressive disorder (MDD) showed an average of five symptoms of the disorder prior to diagnosis. What is the sum of the differences of scores from the mean in this example?

    Based on the example below, answer Questions 25 to 28:

    A group of researchers measure the weight of five participants prior to a clinical weight loss intervention. They record the following weights (in pounds): 200, 250, 150, 100, and 300 pounds. The mean is 200 pounds.

25. The researchers realize that the scale was not accurate for the individual weighing 300 pounds, so they reweighed that individual and recorded 250 pounds. Will the mean increase or decrease in this situation?

26. Instead, the researchers reweighed the 300-pound individual and recorded a new weight of 350 pounds. Will the mean increase or decrease in this situation?

27. Using the original example of five weights, the researchers added a sixth participant to the sample.

    (a) If the sixth participant weighed 240 pounds, will the mean increase, decrease, or not change?

    (b) If the sixth participant weighed 200 pounds, will the mean increase, decrease, or not change?

    (c) If the sixth participant weighted 180 pounds, will the mean increase, decrease, or not change?

28. The researchers implemented their weight loss intervention with the original five participants and found that each participant lost exactly 10 pounds in the first 3 weeks. Without recalculating the mean, what is the new mean weight?

Problems in Research

29. **General life satisfaction across culture.** Gilman and colleagues (2008) measured general life satisfaction in 1,338 adolescents from two individualistic nations (Ireland, United States) and two collectivist nations (China, South Korea) using the Multidimensional Students' Life Satisfaction Scale (MSLSS). Mean participant scores on the MSLSS are given in the following table.

Nation	Gender	
	Men	Women
United States	4.39	4.61
Ireland	4.37	4.64
China	4.41	4.56
South Korea	3.92	3.78

Mean MSLSS scores by gender and nation in this study.

    (a) Among which group was general life satisfaction lowest on average?

    (b) Among which group was general life satisfaction highest on average?

30. **Weight loss, walking, and dementia.** Miyoshi and colleagues (2008) showed that increased walking among institutionalized patients with dementia was associated with greater weight loss. In their study, they reported that the *median* distance walked per day for all patients was 1,042.7 meters (m). Because the median was reported, what can we assume about the shape of the distribution of walking among patients in this study?

31. **Alcohol abuse and self-esteem.** Malcolm (2004) stated that "although heavy [alcohol] drinking was associated with low self-esteem for

women [on average]; the opposite was true for men" (p. 41). Based on this citation, was the mean self-esteem score larger for heavy-drinking men or heavy-drinking women?

32. **Helping smokers quit by race.** Patten and colleagues (2008) stated that "among nonsmokers who indicated they were close to a smoker whom they thought should quit, Black [participants] were most often concerned about a family member whereas White [participants] endorsed concern most often for a friend" (p. 496). What are the most common concerns (or mode) for each race?

33. **The convenience of eating.** Painter, Wansink, and Hieggelke (2002) tested whether increasing the visibility and convenience of chocolates increases consumption of that product. They placed 30 Hershey kisses in an uncovered container on top of a desk (convenient and visible), in a desk drawer (convenient but not visible), or on a shelf far enough away that participants would have to get up from the desk to reach the chocolates (visible but not convenient). They hypothesized that the more inconvenient the location of the chocolate, the fewer chocolates that participants would eat. Do these findings support the researcher's hypothesis? Explain.

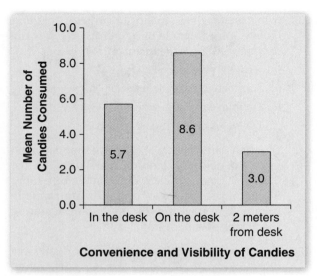

34. **Social support and stroke-induced aphasia.** Hilari and Northcott (2006) used a Social Support Survey (SSS) to gauge how well supported individuals suffering from stoke-induced aphasia (a language disorder) felt more than one year following the stroke. They reported that "in terms of social support, the SSS scores were *negatively skewed* with a mean of 3.69, suggesting that participants felt overall well supported" (p. 17). Based on their findings, what additional measure of central tendency would be appropriate to report with these data? Explain.

NOTE: Answers for even numbers are in Appendix C.

Summarizing Data
Variability

LEARNING OBJECTIVES

After reading this chapter, you should be able to:

1. Compute and interpret a range, interquartile range, and semi-interquartile range.

2. Compute and interpret the variance and standard deviation for a population and sample of data using the definitional formula.

3. Compute and interpret the variance and standard deviation for a population and sample of data using the computational formula.

4. Explain why the sample variance and population variance are computed differently.

5. State the characteristics of the standard deviation and explain the empirical rule.

6. Compute the range, variance, and standard deviation using SPSS.

4.1   MEASURING VARIABILITY

Suppose you learn that the average college graduate earns about $50,000 per year within 6 months of graduating. This may seem like a fair starting income, but what about the income for all other graduates? Each graduate earns a college degree that qualifies him or her for a different type of job that can earn well above or well below the average income. What is the highest income a college graduate can expect to earn? What is the lowest income? What percentage of college graduates earn above or below a certain income level? The idea here is that the mean, like the median and mode, informs you only of scores (or income in this example) at or near the center of a distribution but little to nothing of the remaining scores in a set of data.

Once we know the mean, we need to determine where all the other scores are in relation to the mean. As illustrated in Figure 4.1, we need a measure of **variability,** that is, a way to measure the dispersion or spread of scores around the mean. By definition, the variability of scores can never be negative; variability ranges from 0 to +∞. If four students receive the same scores of 8, 8, 8, and 8 on some assessment, then their scores do not vary because they are all the same value—the variability is 0. However, if the scores were 8, 8, 8, and 9, then they do vary because at least one of the scores differs from the others. Thus, scores can either not vary (variability is 0) or vary (variability is greater than 0). A negative variability is meaningless.

NOTE: Researchers measure variability to determine how dispersed scores are in a set of data. Measures of variability include the range, variance, and standard deviation.

DEFINITION

Variability is a measure of the dispersion or spread of scores in a distribution and ranges from 0 to +∞.

FIGURE 4.1

What we don't know about a distribution even when we know the mean. Notice that although we know the mean score in this distribution, we know nothing of the remaining scores. By computing measures of variability, we can determine how scores vary around the mean and how they vary in general.

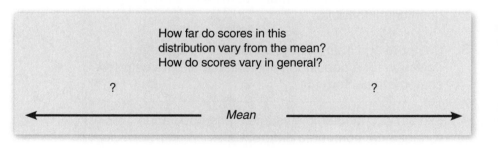

The focus of this chapter is measures of variability: the range, variance, and standard deviation. As with central tendency, we explain how measures of variability are informative, descriptive, and useful for making sense of data.

4.2   THE RANGE

The simplest way to describe how dispersed scores are is to identify the range of scores in a distribution. The **range** is the difference between the largest value (L) and smallest value (S) in a data set. The formula for the range can be stated as follows:

$$\text{Range} = L - S.$$

The **range** is the difference between the largest value (L) and smallest value (S) in a data set.

DEFINITION

NOTE: The range is the difference between the largest and smallest value in a distribution. It is most informative for describing data sets without outliers.

The range is most informative for data sets without outliers. For example, suppose you measure five scores: 1, 2, 3, 4, and 5. The range of these data is 5 – 1 = 4. In this example, the range gives a fair description of the variability of these data. Now suppose your friend also measures five scores: 2, 4, 6, 8, and 100. The range is now 100 – 2 = 98 because the outlier is the largest value in the data set. In this example, a range of 98 is misleading because only one value is greater than 8.

Although the range provides a simple measure of variability, the range accounts for only two values (the largest value and smallest value) in a distribution. Whether the data set has five scores or five million scores, calculations of the range consider only the largest value and smallest value in that distribution. The range in a data set of $n = 3$ may be very informative, but a typical data set for human participant research can be in the hundreds or even thousands. For this reason, many researchers favor other measures of variability to describe data sets.

NOTE: Calculations of the range consider only the largest value and smallest value in a data set.

RESEARCH IN FOCUS: REPORTING THE RANGE   4.3

Because we use only two values to find the range, it is seldom used as a primary measure of variability in behavioral science. The range is included in many research studies to summarize demographic information and to support other reported measures. For instance, researchers often use the range to evaluate human participants who vary in age, weight, income level, order of birth, or any other characteristics of particular interest in the study. These values are often reported in summary tables such as Table 4.1.

Table 4.1 shows a summary table for five characteristics of interest in a study conducted by Agrawal, Madden, Buchholz, Heath, and Lynskey (2008). In this table, the researchers reported the mean and range of each characteristic. Notice that the

TABLE 4.1   The sample characteristics for 3,787 young adult women participating in a twin study testing for links between cannabis use and nicotine dependence/regular smoking (Agrawal, Madden, Buchholz, Heath, & Lynskey, 2008).

Participant Characteristics	Mean (Range)
Age (years)	21.7 (18–29)
Antagonism	0.31 (0.0–0.85)
Impulsivity	0.41 (0.15–0.75)
Aggression	0.26 (0.0–0.96)
Neuroticism	0.43 (0.0–0.98)

range adds greater detail to our understanding of participant characteristics. The range for measures of aggression and neuroticism are about the same, but the means differ. From these values, we can surmise that mean scores for aggression are low, with only a few high scores. Mean scores for neuroticism are closer to the middle of the range, indicating more of a balance among high and low scores in that range. Researchers who list both the mean and the range are giving readers more information for each measure than they would if they reported the mean or the range alone.

LEARNING CHECK 1

1. _____ is a measure of the dispersion or spread of scores in a distribution and ranges from 0 to +∞.

2. What is the formula for computing the range?

3. A researcher collects the following scores: 1, 2, 3, 4, 5, 6, 7, and 8. What is the range of these scores?

4. A researcher reports that participants in her study had a mean age of 21.3 years, with a range equal to 3. Based on this information, is it possible that one of the participants was 25 years old in her study?

Answers: 1. Variability; 2. The range is the largest value (L) minus the smallest value (S) in a data set; 3. Range = 8 − 1 = 7; 4. No, the range is too small.

4.4 QUARTILES AND INTERQUARTILES

Fractiles are measures that divide data sets into two or more equal parts. The median is one example of a fractile because the **median** splits data in half or into two equal parts. Other fractiles include **quartiles, deciles,** and **percentiles,** which split data into four parts, 10 parts, and one hundred parts, respectively. Quartiles, which split data into four equal parts, will be introduced in this section because they are commonly used to split data sets in behavioral research.

NOTE: Fractiles are measures that split data into two or more parts. Examples include the median (2 parts), quartiles (4 parts), deciles (10 parts), and percentiles (100 parts).

The quartiles of a distribution are the range of scores split into four equal parts: In terms of percentiles, the four quartiles are the 25th percentile (Q_1), the 50th percentile (Q_2), the 75th percentile (Q_3), and the 100th percentile (Q_4) of a distribution. Each quartile contains 25% of the data, such that 100% of data are split into four equal parts, with 25% of scores falling in each quartile. The 25th percentile is called the **lower quartile,** the 50th percentile is called the **median quartile,** and the 75th percentile is called the **upper quartile.** The middle score in a distribution is at the 50th percentile, which is why the 50th percentile is called the median quartile.

DEFINITION

Fractiles are measures that divide a set of data into two or more equal parts. Fractiles include the **median**, **quartiles**, **deciles**, and **percentiles**, which split data into 2 parts, 4 parts, 10 parts, and 100 parts, respectively.

The **lower quartile** is the portion of data that falls in the bottom 25 percent of a distribution of scores.

The **median quartile** is the portion of data that falls between the 25th and 50th percentile of a distribution of scores.

The **upper quartile** is the portion of data that falls between the 50th and 75th percentile of a distribution of scores.

By separating data into quartiles, we divide the data set into four parts or four percentiles, thereby organizing the distribution of the data. If your college grade point average (GPA) is above the median quartile, for example, then you know that your GPA is higher than more than 50% of your peers. The quartiles basically define the percentile boundaries in a distribution. To locate each quartile in a data set, follow three steps:

Step 1: Locate the median for all data. This is the median quartile (Q_2).

Step 2: Locate the median for scores below Q_2. This is the lower quartile (Q_1).

Step 3: Locate the median for scores above Q_2. This is the upper quartile (Q_3).

Example 4.1 applies the three steps used to locate each quartile in a data set. Remember from Chapter 3 that to locate the position of the median in each step, we will use the following formula: $\dfrac{n+1}{2}$.

A researcher records the time (in seconds) that 14 patrons waited to be served after ordering their meal. The times recorded were 62, 68, 74, 76, 80, 84, 85, 87, 87, 88, 92, 93, 96, and 98. We will use the three steps to locate the lower, median, and upper quartiles for this data set.

EXAMPLE 4.1

Step 1: Compute $\dfrac{n+1}{2}$, where n is all scores in the data set. Because $n = 14$, the median position is $\dfrac{14+1}{2} = 7.5$. Now list the scores in numerical order. The median is the average of the seventh and eighth positioned scores: $Q_2 = \dfrac{85+87}{2} = 86$.

Step 2: Compute $\dfrac{n+1}{2}$, where n is all scores below Q_2. For scores below Q_2, use only 62, 68, 74, 76, 80, 84, and 85 in the calculation. Because $n = 7$ scores below Q_2, the median position is $\dfrac{7+1}{2} = 4$. Now list the scores below Q_2 in numerical order. The median is the fourth positioned score: $Q_1 = 76$.

Step 3: Compute $\dfrac{n+1}{2}$, where n is all scores above Q_2. For scores above Q_2, use only 87, 87, 88, 92, 93, 96, and 98 in the calculation. Because $n = 7$ scores above Q_2, the median position is $\dfrac{7+1}{2} = 4$. Now list the scores above Q_2 in numerical order. The median is the fourth positioned score: $Q_3 = 92$.

| 62 | 68 | 74 | 76 | 80 | 84 | 85 | 87 | 87 | 88 | 92 | 93 | 96 | 98 |

$Q_1 = 76$ $Q_2 = 86$ $Q_3 = 92$

FIGURE 4.2

The data for Example 4.1 listed in numerical order with the value for each quartile.

The quartiles in Example 4.1 are shown in Figure 4.2. In sum, this example demonstrates that identifying each quartile in a distribution requires locating a median for all data, as well as for only data above and below Q_2.

Using quartiles to describe data also allows us to compute an **interquartile range (IQR).** An IQR is the range of a distribution of scores after the top and the bottom 25% of scores in that distribution are removed. The cutoff for the top 25% of scores is at the 75th percentile, and the cutoff for the bottom 25% of scores is at the 25th percentile. To compute an IQR, we subtract the upper quartile (or 75th percentile) from the lower quartile (or 25th percentile):

$$IQR = Q_3 - Q_1.$$

DEFINITION

Interquartile range (IQR) is the range of a distribution of scores falling within the upper and lower quartiles of a distribution.

NOTE: The interquartile range (IQR) is the variability of scores falling within the upper and lower quartiles of a distribution.

Some statisticians also use the **semi-interquartile range (SIQR),** also called the **quartile deviation:**

$$SIQR = \frac{Q_3 - Q_1}{2}, \text{ also represented as } SIQR = \frac{IQR}{2}.$$

DEFINITION

Semi-interquartile range (SIQR) or **quartile deviation** is a measure of half the distance between the cutoffs for the upper and lower quartiles of a distribution. The SIQR is computed by dividing the IQR in half.

The semi-interquartile range is used as a measure of half the distance between the cutoffs for the upper (Q_3) and lower (Q_1) quartiles of a distribution. You can think of the SIQR as the mean IQR, with smaller SIQR values indicating less spread or variability. Because the IQR excludes the top and the bottom 25% of scores in a distribution, outliers have little influence over this estimate of variability. However, while the SIQR is a good estimate of variability, it is also limited in that its estimate excludes half the scores in a distribution.

LEARNING CHECK 2

1. _____ is/are measures used to divide data into two or more parts.

2. When data are divided into four equal parts, the data are split into four _____.

3. A researcher records the number of times that 10 students cough during a final exam. He records the following data: 0, 0, 0, 3, 3, 5, 5, 7, 8, and 11. True or false: In this example, the range will be smaller than the interquartile range.

Answers: 1. Fractiles; 2. Quartiles; 3. False, the range will be larger than the IQR.

4.5   THE VARIANCE

A preferred estimate of variability is the variance because it includes all scores, not just two extreme scores, to estimate variability. The **variance** measures the average squared distance that scores deviate from their mean. The value of the variance can be 0 (no variability) or greater than 0 (there is variability). A negative variance is meaningless. Unlike calculations of the mean, the formula for variance does change for samples and populations, both in terms of notation and calculation.

NOTE: The variance is a preferred measure of variability because all scores are included in its computation. Variance can be computed for data in populations and samples.

Variance is a measure of variability for the average squared distance that scores deviate from their mean.

DEFINITION

POPULATION VARIANCE

The **population variance** is represented by the Greek symbol σ^2 (stated as "sigma squared"). Calculations of population variance are used to measure the dispersion of scores from their mean. A population variance, which is computed only for an entire population of scores, is defined by the following formula:

$$\sigma^2 = \frac{\Sigma(x-\mu)^2}{N} \text{ or } \frac{SS}{N}.$$

Population variance is a measure of variability for the average squared distance that scores in a population deviate from the mean. It is computed only when all scores in a given population are known.

DEFINITION

A **deviation** is the difference of each score from its mean.

The **sum of squares (SS)** is the sum of the squared deviations of scores from their mean the *SS* is the numerator in the variance formula.

In this formula, the expression $x-\mu$ is a **deviation;** it is the difference of each score from its mean. This value is squared, then summed, in the numerator: $\Sigma(x-\mu)^2$. The numerator for the variance formula is also called the **sum of squares (SS)** or the sum of the squared deviations of scores from their mean. The term N is the population size. To compute the population variance, follow two steps:

NOTE: To compute the population variance, the SS is divided by the population size (N).

Step 1: Calculate the *SS* (the numerator).

Step 2: Divide the *SS* by the population size (*N*).

EXAMPLE 4.2

Suppose you want to determine how much your six closest friends actually know about you. This is the group of interest to you; your six closest friends constitute the population of interest. You quiz each close friend about 10 facts you think they should know about you. The scores on the quiz are: 5, 10, 3, 7, 2, and 3. We will follow the steps to calculate the population variance (σ^2) of these scores.

Step 1: Calculate the *SS*. To compute *SS,*

(1) Identify each score: 5, 10, 3, 7, 2, and 3.

(2) Compute the population mean:

$$\mu = \frac{5+10+3+7+2+3}{6} = 5.$$

(3) Compute the squared deviation of each score from the mean. For each score, subtract the mean, and then square the result. The computation for each score is

$x = 5$: $(5-5)^2 = 0$

$x = 10$: $(10-5)^2 = 25$

$x = 3$: $(3-5)^2 = 4$

$x = 7$: $(7-5)^2 = 4$

$x = 2$: $(2-5)^2 = 9$

$x = 3$: $(3-5)^2 = 4$

(4) Sum the squared deviations. Add the answers from (3) to find the *SS*:

$$SS = 0 + 25 + 4 + 4 + 9 + 4 = 46.$$

Step 2: Divide the *SS* by the population size. The population variance is *SS* divided by *N*:

$$\sigma^2 = \frac{SS}{N} = \frac{46}{6} = 7.67.$$

The population variance for the data in this example is $\sigma^2 = 7.67$.

LEARNING CHECK 3

1. Why is the variance a preferred measure of variability?

2. A researcher selects a population of 8 scores with an $SS = 72$. What is the population variance in this example?

3. Describe the sum of squares (*SS*) in words.

4. A researcher measures the following scores: 12, 14, 16, 18, and 20. Compute the *SS* for these data.

5. True or false: When all scores in a population are the same, the variance will always be equal to 0.

Answers: 1. Because it includes all scores in its computation; 2. $\sigma^2 = 9$; 3. *SS* is the sum of the squared deviations of scores from their mean.; 4. $SS = 40$; 5. True

SAMPLE VARIANCE

The **sample variance** is likewise used to measure how dispersed scores are from their mean when the data consist of less than an entire population of scores. The sample variance (denoted s^2) is defined by the following formula:

$$s^2 = \frac{\Sigma(x - M)^2}{n - 1} \text{ or } \frac{SS}{n - 1}.$$

Sample variance is a measure of variability for the average squared distance that scores in a sample deviate from the mean. It is computed when only a portion or sample of data is measured in a population.

DEFINITION

Figure 4.3 shows that the numerator for sample variance is computed the same as that for the population variance: The numerator is the *SS*. It is calculations in the denominator that differ for populations and samples. To compute the sample variance, we divide the *SS* by the sample size (n) minus 1. The notations for the mean (M) and the sample size (n) have also changed to account for the fact that the data are from a sample and not a population. To compute sample variance, we again follow two steps:

NOTE: To compute the sample variance, we divide the SS *by one less than the sample size (n – 1).*

Step 1: Calculate the *SS* (the numerator).

Step 2: Divide *SS* by ($n - 1$).

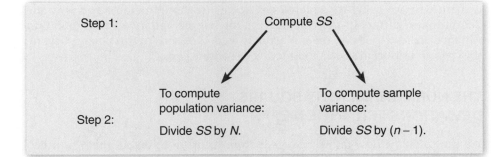

FIGURE 4.3

The steps to compute the sample variance and population variance. Notice that Step 1 is the same for computing the sample and population variance. Only computations in the denominator of the variance formula (Step 2) differ for sample variance and population variance.

We will compute the sample variance using the same data from Example 4.2. This will allow us to directly compare calculations for both measures of variability.

Suppose you have more than just six close friends. So the six close friends you quizzed in Example 4.2 now constitute a sample or portion of all your close friends. The sample of six scores from Example 4.2 was 5, 10, 3, 7, 2, and 3. We will follow the steps to calculate the sample variance (s^2) of these scores.

EXAMPLE 4.3

Step 1: Calculate the *SS*. Follow the same steps shown for Step 1 in Example 4.2. The steps to compute *SS* are the same for population variance and sample variance: $SS = 46$.

Step 2: Divide *SS* by ($n - 1$). The sample variance is $s^2 = \dfrac{SS}{n - 1} = \dfrac{46}{(6 - 1)} = 9.20$.

NOTE: Computations of SS are the same for population variance and sample variance. The change in computation is whether we divide SS by N (population variance) or n – 1 (sample variance).

The sample variance for the data in this example is $s^2 = 9.20$.

For populations and samples of data, the larger the value of the variance, the more dispersed or spread out scores are from their mean. For variance, keep in mind that values of sample variance and population variance can be very large—much larger than scores in the original data set.

LEARNING CHECK 4

1. How does calculating the sample variance differ from calculating the population variance?

2. A researcher measures the following data: 3, 3, 3, 4, 4, and 4. What is the sample variance for these data?

3. True or false: A scientist measures the following data: 23, 23, 23, 23, 23, and 23. The value for the sample variance and population variance will be the same.

Answers: 1. The denominator for sample variance is $(n - 1)$, not N; 2. $s^2 = 0.3$; 3. True because the variance is 0.

4.6. EXPLAINING VARIANCE FOR POPULATIONS AND SAMPLES

In this section, we look at the variance calculation in depth. In particular, we explain why we compute squared deviations in the numerator and why the denominator differs in the calculations for sample variance and population variance. Believe it or not, there is actually a good reason for this change beyond the cynical statistician's goal of just trying to confuse you.

THE NUMERATOR: WHY SQUARE DEVIATIONS FROM THE MEAN?

We can calculate how far each score is from its mean to determine how much variability there is in a data set. For example, suppose a set of data has a mean of 5. As shown in Figure 4.4, a score of 10 will deviate further from the mean than a score of 3 in this data set. The idea here is that scores in a given data set will be at various distances from the mean. Some scores will deviate further than others. Regardless of whether we have a sample or population of scores, in both cases we want to measure variability by determining how far a group of scores deviates from the mean. To compute variance, we square each deviation in the numerator. There are three reasons we square each deviation to compute *SS:*

1. The sum of the differences of scores from their mean is zero.

2. The sum of the squared differences of scores from their mean is minimal.

3. Squaring scores can be corrected by taking the square root.

The most straightforward way to measure variability would be to subtract each score from its mean and to sum each deviation. The problem is that the sum will always be equal to 0 (this was the fourth characteristic of the mean listed in Chapter 3).

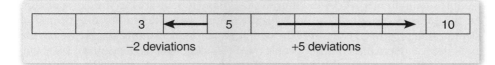

Table 4.2 shows an example of a small population of scores: 3, 5, and 7. Notice that the sum of the differences of scores from their mean is zero in the table. Here we would conclude that these scores do not vary from one another, but they do. To avoid this result, each deviation is squared to produce the smallest positive solution that is not zero.

TABLE 4.2   A list of scores (left column) with a mean of 5. The sum of the differences of each score from their mean is 0 (right column). The sum of the differences of scores from their mean will always equal 0.

x	x – Mean
3	3 – 5 = –2
5	3 – 5 = 0
7	3 – 5 = 2
	Sum of deviations = 0

The reason we square each deviation before summing is largely because of Reasons 2 and 3 listed on the previous page: We want to compute how far scores are from their mean without ending up with a solution equal to 0 every time. Basically, we need to compute a positive value for variance that is not 0. Think of any solution to avoid this 0 result as intentionally making an error. To minimize error, we need to ensure that the result we obtain is the smallest possible positive value—or the value with minimal error. The last characteristic of the mean listed in Chapter 3 showed that squaring each deviation before summing each deviation will produce the smallest possible positive solution. This is one reason for squaring deviations: It provides a solution with minimal error.

Another reason for squaring is that we can correct for this by taking the square root of the solution for variance (we will do this when we calculate *standard deviation* in Section 4.9). This is not a perfect correction, but it is a simple and appropriate way to correct for squaring each deviation. Whether we have a sample or population of scores, these rules are the same: In both cases, squaring each deviation provides a solution with minimal error that can be corrected by taking the square root of the variance.

NOTE: The SS produces the smallest possible positive value for deviations of scores from their mean. The SS is computed the same for sample variance and population variance.

THE DENOMINATOR: SAMPLE VARIANCE AS AN UNBIASED ESTIMATOR

The population variance is computed by dividing the *SS* by the population size (*N*), whereas the sample variance is computed by dividing the *SS* by sample size (n) minus 1. Why did statisticians choose to subtract 1 in the denominator of the sample variance? The following example will illustrate the reason and demonstrate why ($n - 1$) improves the sample variance calculation. Suppose we have a hypothetical population of three people ($N = 3$) who scored an 8 (Person A), 5 (Person B), and 2 (Person C) on a quiz. This hypothetical population has a variance of 6:

$$\sigma^2 = \frac{(8-5)^2 + (5-5)^2 + (2-5)^2}{3} = \frac{9+0+9}{3} = \frac{18}{3} = 6.$$

We know that this population has a variance of 6. On average, any sample we select from this population should also have a variance of 6. To determine this, we will take all samples of size two ($n = 2$) from this population of three. On average, we should find that the sample variance is equal to 6—it should be the same as the variance in the population. If it is not, then the sample variance is biased. Table 4.3 lists the nine possible samples of size two that could be selected from this population.

The last two columns in Table 4.3 show two ways to calculate sample variance. In column C, SS is divided by n (not $n - 1$). Notice that when we do not subtract 1 in the denominator, the sample variance will underestimate the population variance on average. Hence, the sample variance is a **biased estimator** in that it will be less than the population variance on average ($3 < 6$). The following statement describes this rule:

The sample variance is biased: If $s^2 = \dfrac{SS}{n}$, then $s^2 < \sigma^2$ on average.

In column D of Table 4.3, notice that, on average, the sample variance equals the population variance when we subtract 1 from n in the denominator ($6 = 6$). Making this change in the denominator makes the sample variance an **unbiased estimator**—its value will equal the population variance on average. The following statement describes this rule:

The sample variance is unbiased: If $s^2 = \dfrac{SS}{n-1}$, then $s^2 = \sigma^2$ on average.

DEFINITION

A **biased estimator** is any sample statistic, such as a sample mean, obtained from a randomly selected sample that does not equal the value of its respective population parameter, such as a population mean, on average.

An **unbiased estimator** is any sample statistic, such as a sample mean, obtained from a randomly selected sample that equals the value of its respective population parameter, such as a population mean, on average.

NOTE: When we divide SS *by (n – 1), the sample variance is an unbiased estimator of the population variance. This is one reason why researchers place (n – 1) in the denominator of sample variance.*

On the basis of this example, you can see that only when we divide SS by ($n - 1$) to compute the sample variance will we produce a value that equals the population variance on average. This makes the sample variance unbiased in that, on average, the variance of the sample will equal the variance of the population from which the sample was selected. Therefore, to ensure that the sample variance is an unbiased estimator, we divide by ($n - 1$) to calculate sample variance.

TABLE 4.3   The computation of sample variance (last two columns) using n and $(n-1)$ in the denominator. To compute the average sample variance in columns C and D, we add up all possible values for sample variance listed in that column and divide by 9 (or the total number of samples that can be selected). In this example, each sample was selected from a population with a variance of 6. Notice that only when we divide SS by $(n-1)$ do we find that, on average, the sample variance is equal to the population variance—it is an unbiased estimator.

A Participants Sampled ($n = 2$)	B Scores for Each Participant	C s^2 Using (n)	D s^2 Using ($n-1$)
A,A	8,8	0	0
A,B	8,5	2.25	4.50
A,C	8,2	9.00	18.00
B,A	5,8	2.25	4.50
B,B	5,5	0	0
B,C	5,2	2.25	4.50
C,A	2,8	9.00	18.00
C,B	2,5	2.25	4.50
C,C	2,2	0	0
Mean sample variance:		$\dfrac{27}{9} = 3.0$	$\dfrac{54}{9} = 6.0$

THE DENOMINATOR: DEGREES OF FREEDOM

The denominator $(n-1)$ also tells us the **degrees of freedom (df) for sample variance,** which are the number of scores that are free to vary in a sample. Basically, if you know the mean of a data set and the value of all scores in that data set except one, you can perfectly predict the last score (i.e., the last score is not free to vary). Suppose, for example, we have a sample of three participants with a mean score of 4 ($M = 4$). Table 4.4 shows a distribution with these three scores: 3, 4, and x. We know two scores (3 and 4) but not the last score (x). But the last score is not free, so we can find its value.

> The **degrees of freedom (df) for sample variance** are the number of scores in a sample that are free to vary. All scores except one are free to vary in a sample: $n-1$.

DEFINITION

TABLE 4.4 The degree's of freedom for variance: Each score is free to vary in a distribution, except one $(n-1)$.

x	M	$x - M$
3	4	−1
4	4	0
x	4	?
		$\sum(x - M) = 0$

NOTE: Degrees of freedom for sample variance tell us that all scores are free to vary in a sample except one (n − 1). This term is placed in the denominator of sample variance.

Remember that the sum of the deviations of scores from their mean is zero. The deviation of the first score from its mean is −1 $(3 - 4 = -1)$, and the deviation of the second score from its mean is 0 $(4 - 4 = 0)$. Therefore, it must be the case that $-1 + 0 + (x - 4) = 0$. Thus, $x = 5$ because it is the only value for x that can make the solution to this equation equal to 0. Therefore, we can say that one score is not free to vary when the sample mean is known. This example illustrates that the scores used to compute sample variance are free to vary with 1 degree of freedom or $(n - 1)$. Because all scores in a sample (n) are free to vary except one (-1), we calculate the sample variance by dividing SS by only those scores that are free to vary in a sample $(n - 1)$.

✔ **LEARNING CHECK 5**

1. Why do we square each deviation in the numerator of variance?

2. How many scores are free to vary in a sample?

3. True or false: The sample variance is unbiased when dividing SS by $(n - 1)$. This is one reason that sample variance is computed with $(n - 1)$ in the denominator.

4. A researcher records five scores: 3, 4, 5, 6, and x. If the mean in this distribution is 5, then what is the value for x?

Answers: 1. We want to compute how far scores are from their mean without ending up with a solution equal to 0 every time, and taking the square root of variance can correct for squaring each deviation in the numerator; 2. All scores, except one, are free to vary; 3. True; 4. $x = 7$.

4.7 THE COMPUTATIONAL FORMULA FOR VARIANCE

The formula we've used thus far to compute variance is called the **definitional formula for variance.** This formula literally defines the SS in the numerator, which is the sum of the squared differences of scores from their mean. The definitional formula for variance is as follows:

DEFINITION

The **definitional formula for variance** is a way to calculate the population variance and sample variance that requires summing the squared differences of scores from their mean to compute the SS in the numerator.

Definitional formula (population):

$$SS = \sum (x - \mu)^2, \text{ where } \sigma^2 = \frac{SS}{N}.$$

Definitional formula (sample):

$$SS = \sum (x - M)^2, \text{ where } s^2 = \frac{SS}{n-1}.$$

Computationally, there is a disadvantage to using the definitional formula—it is prone to rounding errors, especially when the mean has a decimal remainder. Squaring decimals often requires rounding, and the mean is often a decimal, resulting in rounding errors. As an alternative to this problem, statisticians derived the **computational formula for variance,** also called the **raw scores method for variance.** Notice in the formula that the computational method does not require us to calculate the mean to compute the *SS*. The computational formula for variance is as follows:

> The **computational formula for variance**, or the **raw scores method for variance**, is a way to calculate the population variance and sample variance without needing to sum the squared differences of scores from their mean to compute the *SS* in the numerator.

DEFINITION

Computational formula (population):

$$SS = \sum x^2 - \frac{\left(\sum x\right)^2}{N}, \text{ where } \sigma^2 = \frac{SS}{N}.$$

Computational formula (sample):

$$SS = \sum x^2 - \frac{\left(\sum x\right)^2}{n}, \text{ where } s^2 = \frac{SS}{n-1}.$$

The notation in each formula distinguishes between a population (*N*) and a sample size (*n*). Before proceeding, keep in mind that with identical data sets, the computational formula will always produce the same solution as the definitional formula, give or take rounding error. The computational formula is actually a quicker way to calculate variance with large data sets. Example 4.4 demonstrates the equivalence of the two forms of the variance formula.

NOTE: The computational formula for variance is a quicker way to compute variance by hand.

A social psychologist studying emotion presented 20 participants (*n* = 20) with five pictures showing personal loss or tragedy and recorded the amount of time (in seconds) each participant spent looking at these pictures. Using the hypothetical data for this study given in Table 4.5, we will calculate the *SS* (or the numerator for variance) using both formulas.

EXAMPLE 4.4

Calculate *SS* using the definitional formula. To compute the *SS*, (1) identify each score, (2) compute the population mean, (3) compute the squared deviation of each score from the mean, and (4) sum the squared deviations. These calculations are shown in Table 4.6. For this example, *SS* = 11,199.20.

Although we found the answer, it took a lot of work. We had to calculate the mean, calculate 20 deviations from the mean, square 20 deviations from the mean, and

TABLE 4.5 A list of the amount of time (in seconds) each participant ($n = 20$) spent looking at pictures showing personal loss or tragedy.

46	35	28	44
33	40	14	43
45	39	88	51
110	55	74	92
30	52	54	23

then sum 20 squared deviations from the mean just to find the *SS*. To compute population variance, we divide *SS* by *N;* to compute sample variance, we divide *SS* by ($n - 1$). You can imagine how complex the calculation would be if the study had 100 or 1,000 scores. Let's solve the same problem using the computational formula to see whether it is any easier to compute.

TABLE 4.6 Calculations required for computing the sum of squares (*SS*) using the definitional formula in Example 4.4.

x	M	x – M	(x – M)²
14	49.80	−35.80	1,281.64
23	49.80	−26.80	718.24
28	49.80	−21.80	475.24
30	49.80	−19.80	392.04
33	49.80	−16.80	282.24
35	49.80	−14.80	219.04
39	49.80	−10.80	116.64
40	49.80	−9.80	96.04
43	49.80	−6.80	46.24
44	49.80	−5.80	33.64
45	49.80	−4.80	23.04
46	49.80	−3.80	14.44

x	M	x – M	(x – M)²
51	49.80	1.20	1.44
52	49.80	2.20	4.84
54	49.80	4.20	17.64
55	49.80	5.20	27.04
74	49.80	24.20	585.64
88	49.80	38.20	1,459.24
92	49.80	42.20	1,780.84
110	49.80	60.20	3,624.04
		$\sum(x-M)=0$	$\sum(x-M)^2 = 11,199.20$

Calculate *SS* using the computational formula. To compute *SS*, (1) identify each score and the size of the sample or population, (2) square each score, and (3) substitute the value in the formula. These calculations are shown in Table 4.7. Notice that we didn't calculate the mean. We found all the information we need to compute the computational formula in only three steps. When we substitute the values given in Table 4.7, we get the following solution:

$$SS = \sum x^2 - \frac{\left(\sum x^2\right)}{n} = 60,800 - \frac{(996)^2}{20} = 11,199.20.$$

As with the definitional formula, *SS* = 11,199.20, verifying that both formulas (definitional and computational) produce the same solution.

LEARNING CHECK 6

1. How is the computational formula different from the definitional formula for variance?

2. True or false: With identical data sets, the definitional and computational formula for variance will always produce the same solution, give or take rounding error.

3. A researcher measures the following sample of scores (*n* = 3): 1, 4, and 7. (a) Use the definitional formula to calculate variance. (b) Use the computational formula to calculate variance. (c) Are your answers the same?

Answers: 1. The computational formula does not require that we compute the mean to compute *SS* in the numerator. 2. True; 3. (a) 9. (b) 9. (c) Yes.

TABLE 4.7 Calculations required for computing the sum of squares (SS) using the computational formula in Example 4.4.

x	x^2
14	196
23	529
28	784
30	900
33	1,089
35	1,225
39	1,521
40	1,600
43	1,849
44	1,936
45	2,025
46	2,116
51	2,601
52	2,704
54	2,916
55	3,025
74	5,476
88	7,744
92	8,464
110	12,100
$\sum x = 996$	$\sum x^2 = 60,800$

4.8 THE STANDARD DEVIATION

The **standard deviation,** also called the **root mean square deviation,** is the square root of the variance. Taking the square root of the variance basically "unsquares" the variance, and it is used as a measure for the average distance that scores deviate from their mean. The distance that scores deviate from their mean is measured as the number of standard deviations that scores deviate from their mean. The **population standard deviation** is represented by the Greek letter for lowercase *s*, called sigma: σ. The **sample standard deviation** is represented by a lowercase *s*. In research reports, you may also see the sample standard deviation stated as *SD*. The notation for each type of standard deviation is as follows:

The **standard deviation**, also called the **root mean square deviation**, is a measure of variability for the average distance that scores deviate from their mean. It is calculated by taking the square root of the variance.

The **population standard deviation** is a measure of variability for the average distance that scores in a population deviate from their mean. It is calculated by taking the square root of the population variance.

The **sample standard deviation** is a measure of variability for the average distance that scores in a sample deviate from their mean. It is calculated by taking the square root of the sample variance.

DEFINITION

$$\sigma = \sqrt{\sigma} = \sqrt{\frac{SS}{N}} \text{ (Population standard deviation)}$$

$$s = \sqrt{s^2} = \sqrt{\frac{SS}{n-1}} \text{ (Sample standard deviation)}$$

To find the standard deviation, we first compute the variance and then take the square root of that answer. Remember that our objective is to find the average distance that scores deviate from their mean (the standard deviation) and not the average *squared* distance that scores deviate from their mean (the variance). Taking the square root of the variance will allow us to reach this objective. We will compute the standard deviation in Example 4.5. To compute the standard deviation, we follow two steps:

NOTE: The standard deviation is the square root of the variance. It is used to determine the average distance that scores deviate from their mean.

Step 1: Compute the variance.

Step 2: Take the square root of the variance.

A psychologist assumes that students will really miss their parents when they first leave for college. To test this assumption, she records the time (in minutes) that 10 freshman students ($n = 10$) talked to their parents during their first month of college. Using the data for this study given in Table 4.8, let's compute the variance and standard deviation.

EXAMPLE 4.5

Step 1: Compute the variance. Using the computational formula to calculate variance, we find n, $\sum x$, and $\sum x^2$. We know that $n = 10$, and Table 4.9 shows that $\sum x = 4,300$ and $\sum x^2 = 2,064,750$. When we substitute these values into the

TABLE 4.8 The number of minutes that 10 students ($n = 10$) spent talking to their parents in their first month of college.

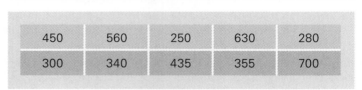

450	560	250	630	280
300	340	435	355	700

formula for sample variance, we find that $SS = 215{,}750$ (the numerator), and the sample variance is $s^2 = 23{,}972.22$.

$$s^2 = \frac{SS}{n-1} = \frac{2{,}064{,}750 - \frac{(4{,}300)^2}{10}}{10-1} = \frac{215{,}750}{9} = 23{,}972.22.$$

Step 2: Take the square root of the variance. We take the square root of the sample variance to find the standard deviation.

$$SD = \sqrt{s^2} = \sqrt{23{,}972.22} = 154.83.$$

TABLE 4.9 Calculations for the sum of squares (SS) using the computational formula for Example 4.5.

x	x^2
250	62,500
280	78,400
300	90,000
340	115,600
355	126,025
435	189,225
450	202,500
560	313,600
630	396,900
700	490,000
$\sum x = 4{,}300$	$\sum x^2 = 2{,}064{,}750$

The standard deviation is 154.83 minutes in this example. If you compute the mean for this sample, you will find that the mean time is 430 minutes. The standard deviation tells us that the distribution of times for all other students (other than those responding at the mean) deviates an average distance of 154.83 minutes from the mean. In the next section, we explain how to interpret this result.

LEARNING CHECK 6

1. How do you compute standard deviation?

2. The standard deviation is a measure used to determine the average distance that each score deviates from _____.

3. The sample variance is 121. What is the standard deviation for this sample?

4. The population variance is 121. What is the standard deviation for this population?

Answers: 1. Take the square root of the variance; 2. The mean; 3. 11; 4. 11.

WHAT DOES THE STANDARD DEVIATION TELL US? 4.9

The standard deviation is an estimate for the average distance that scores deviate from the mean. When scores are concentrated near the mean, the standard deviation is small; when scores are scattered far from the mean, the standard deviation is larger. Yet, the standard deviation is more informative than this, particularly for data that are normally distributed. For normal distributions with any mean and any variance, we can make the following three statements:

1. At least 68% of all scores lie within one standard deviation of the mean.

2. At least 95% of all scores lie within two standard deviations of the mean.

3. At least 99.7% of all scores lie within three standard deviations of the mean.

These statements are often called the **empirical rule.** Empiricism is *to observe*. The name of this rule arises because many of the behaviors that researchers *observe* are approximately normally distributed. The empirical rule, then, is an approximation—the percentages are correct, give or take a few fractions of a standard deviation. Nevertheless, this rule is critical because of how specific it is for describing behavior.

The **empirical rule** states that for any normally distributed set of data, at least 99.7% of data lie within three standard deviations of the mean, at least 95% of data lie within two standard deviations of the mean, and at least 68% of data lie within one standard deviation of the mean.

DEFINITION

NOTE: For normal distributions, most scores fall within one standard deviation (68%) of the mean, and almost all scores fall within three standard deviations (99.7%) of the mean.

To illustrate how useful the empirical rule is, consider how we can apply it to a sample data set and can come to some immediate conclusions about the distribution of scores. Suppose that a researcher selects a sample of 5,000 full-time employees and records the time (in hours per week) that they spend thinking about work when they are not working. These data are normally distributed with a mean equal to 12 ($M = 12$) and a standard deviation equal to 4 ($SD = 4$). Without knowing the time for each employee, we still know a lot about this sample. In fact, because the data are normally distributed, we can distribute at least 99.7% of the data simply by plotting three standard deviations above and below the mean, as shown in Figure 4.5. Notice that we add the SD value to M to plot standard deviations above the mean; to plot standard deviations below the mean, we subtract the SD value from M.

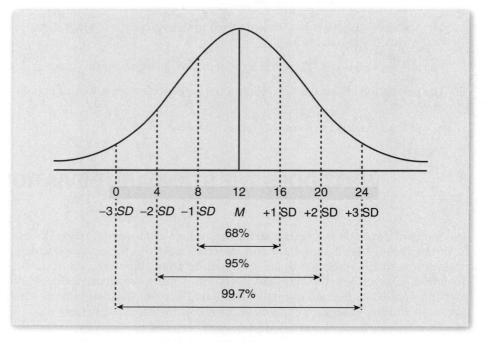

FIGURE 4.5

The empirical rule. The proportion of scores under a normal curve at each standard deviation above and below the mean. The data are distributed as 12 ± 4 ($M \pm SD$).

Although the researcher did not report the time (in hours) recorded for each individual employee in this sample, we know a lot about these data because we know the mean and the standard deviation. For example, we know that at least 68% of employees spent between 8 and 16 hours thinking about work when they were not working, and we know that any time (in hours) beyond three standard deviations from the mean is rare. This makes the standard deviation a very descriptive measure for determining the average distance that each score is from the mean for data that are normally distributed.

> **MAKING SENSE:** Standard Deviation and Nonnormal Distributions
>
> The standard deviation (SD) also tells us about distributions that are not normally distributed. The Russian mathematician Pafnuty Chebyshev devised the theorem that explains the standard deviation for any distribution.
>
> **DEFINITION**
>
> **Chebyshev's theorem** defines the percentage of data from any distribution that will be contained within any number of standard deviations (where $SD > 1$).

Chebyshev explained that the proportion of all data for any distribution (sample or population; normal or not) must lie within k standard deviations above and below the mean, where k is greater than 1. His theorem is defined as

$$1 - \frac{1}{k^2}, \text{where } k \text{ is greater than } 1.$$

Notice that if k were 1 standard deviation (1 SD), the solution would be 0%. So this theorem can describe only the proportion of data falling within *greater* than 1 SD of the mean. Let's see how this theorem compares to the empirical rule. First, this theorem explains that *at least* 75% of the data fall within 2 SD of the mean:

$$1 - \frac{1}{k^2} = 1 - \frac{1}{2^2} = 0.75 \text{ or } 75\%.$$

Recall that 95% of all data fall within 2 SD of the mean for normal distributions. The Chebyshev theorem explains that *at least* 89% of the data fall within 3 SD of the mean:

$$1 - \frac{1}{k^2} = 1 - \frac{1}{3^2} = 0.89 \text{ or } 89\%.$$

Recall that 99.7% of all data fall within 3 SD of the mean for normal distributions. In fact, it would take 10 standard deviations (10 SD) from the mean to account for *at least* 99% of the data for nonnormal distributions according to Chebyshev's theorem:

$$1 - \frac{1}{k^2} = 1 - \frac{1}{10^2} = 0.99 \text{ or } 99\%.$$

While the standard deviation is most precise for normal distributions, because most data fall within 3 SD of the mean, it is also informative for any other distribution. We can still define the percentage of scores that will fall within each standard deviation from the mean for any distribution. The informativeness of the standard deviation for any type of distribution makes it one of the most complete and meaningful measures for determining the variability of scores from their mean.

CHARACTERISTICS OF THE STANDARD DEVIATION 4.10

Although the standard deviation has many characteristics, we focus on four of the most fundamental ones for samples and populations.

1. **The standard deviation is always positive:** $SD \geq 0$. The standard deviation is a measure of variability. Data sets can either vary (be greater than 0) or not vary (be equal to 0) from the mean. A negative variability is meaningless.

2. **The standard deviation is used to describe quantitative data.** The standard deviation is a numeric value—it is the square root of the variance. For this reason, the standard deviation is used to describe quantitative data, which are data measured in numeric units.

3. **Standard deviations are typically reported with the mean.** The standard deviation is the average distance that scores deviate from their mean. It therefore makes sense to report the mean and the standard deviation together. For normally distributed data, knowing just the mean and standard deviation can inform the reader of the distribution for close to all the recorded data (99.7% of data fall within 3 SD of the mean).

Although the mean and standard deviation can be reported in many ways, they are often reported as the mean plus or minus the standard deviation ($M \pm SD$). For example, in a study on cigarette use among men and women (Wan, Friedman, Boutros, & Crawford, 2008), "of those who reported smoking, men (16.02 ± 1.73 years) and women (16.13 ± 1.89 years) reported a similar age for starting to smoke" (p. 428). This style of reporting the mean and standard deviation provides a concise way to summarize a lot of information for the behavior measured.

4. **The value for the standard deviation is affected by the value of each score in a distribution.** To change the standard deviation, you must change the distance of scores from the mean and from each other. To illustrate this, consider two cases: one where changing scores in a distribution has no effect on standard deviation and another where the standard deviation is changed.

NOTE: Adding or subtracting the same constant to each score will not change the distance that scores deviate from the mean. Hence, the standard deviation remains unchanged.

Adding or subtracting the same constant to each score will not change the value of the standard deviation. Suppose, for example, an instructor gives a quiz to eight students ($n = 8$) and obtains the following scores: 3, 5, 6, 6, 7, 7, 9, and 10. If we calculate the sample standard deviation of this distribution of quiz scores, we get $SD = 2.20$.

After grading all the quizzes, the instructor decides that one of the questions was misleading, so he adds one point to every score. The distribution of scores is now shifted by +1; the new scores are 4, 6, 7, 7, 8, 8, 10, and 11. If we now recalculate the sample standard deviation of this new distribution of quiz scores, we again get $SD = 2.20$.

Figure 4.6 illustrates the reason the standard deviation is unchanged. Adding (or subtracting) the same constant to each score will not change the distance that scores deviate from the mean because the mean also changes by that constant. (In Chapter 3, we discussed how the mean changes.) Despite the change in each score, the average distance of each score from its mean remains the same, and so the standard deviation also remains unchanged.

NOTE: Multiplying or dividing each score using the same constant will cause the standard deviation to change by that constant.

Multiplying or dividing each score using the same constant will cause the standard deviation to change by that constant. Suppose we throw a party for a friend with five balloons ($n = 5$); the balloons have radii of 1, 2, 3, 4, and 5 units. If we calculate the sample standard deviation for this distribution, we obtain $s = 1.58$.

FIGURE 4.6

A list of the original distribution of scores (top row) and the new distribution created by increasing each score +1 (bottom row). Adding one point to each score in the original data set did not change the distance each score was from its mean. Hence, the value of the standard deviation does not change.

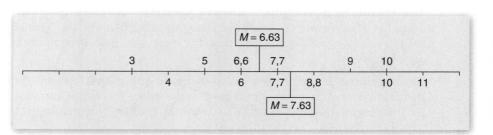

Yet after much deep and profound consideration, we realize that the friend will never be happy with such inadequately blown-up balloons. We decide to blow up the balloons to double their size. The new radii are 2, 4, 6, 8, and 10 units (all we did was multiply each radius times 2). Notice in Figure 4.7 that the distance between each radius has doubled; each score is now separated by two units, not one. If we now recalculate the standard deviation for this new distribution of radii, we get $s = 3.16$ or $(1.58)^2$. Dividing all scores by the same constant will produce a similar result—the value for the standard deviation will be divided by that constant.

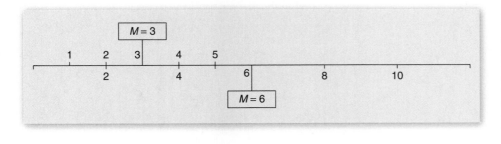

FIGURE 4.7

A list of the original distribution of scores (top row) and the new distribution created by multiplying each score times 2 (bottom row). Multiplying each score times 2 doubled the distance each score was from its mean. Hence, the value for the standard deviation also doubled.

 **LEARNING CHECK 8**

1. The empirical rule is stated for data with what type of distribution?

2. How many standard deviations from the mean will contain at least 99% of data for any type of distribution?

3. Each of the following is a characteristic of standard deviation, except:
   a. The standard deviation is always positive.
   b. The standard deviation is affected by the value of every score in a distribution.
   c. The standard deviation is used to describe qualitative variables.
   d. Standard deviations are almost always reported with the mean.

4. An instructor measures the following quiz scores: 6, 8, 7, and 9 ($SD = 1.29$). If the instructor subtracts two points from each quiz score, how will the value for the standard deviation change?

Answers: 1. Data that are normally distributed; 2. $\pm 10 \, SD$; 3. c; 4. The standard deviation will not change ($SD = 1.29$).

SPSS IN FOCUS: RANGE, VARIANCE, AND STANDARD DEVIATION 4.11

In the SPSS in Focus section of Chapter 3, we computed the mean, the median, and the mode for creativity, measured as the time (in seconds) in took participants to list 10 uses for a paper clip. The data for this example, originally given in Table 3.11, are reproduced here in Table 4.10. In this section, we will use these same data to compute the range, variance, and standard deviation.

1. Click on the **variable view** tab and enter *creativity* in the **name column.** We will enter whole numbers, so reduce the value in the **decimals column** to 0.

TABLE 4.10 The time (in seconds) that it took a group of 20 participants to write down 10 uses for a paper clip on a creativity test. This table originally appeared as Table 3.11 in Chapter 3.

41	80
65	80
123	64
46	59
48	51
87	36
38	80
90	143
132	122
115	100

2. Click on the **data view** tab and enter the 20 values in the *creativity* column.

3. Go to the **menu bar** and click **Analyze,** then **Descriptive Statistics** and **Frequencies,** to display a dialog box.

4. When you select the *creativity* variable and click the arrow in the center of the dialog box, *creativity* will move into the box labeled **Variable(s):** to the right. Make sure the option to display frequency tables is not selected, and then click on **Statistics** to bring up another dialog box.

5. In this dialog box, select **Std. deviation, Variance** and **Range;** then select **Continue.**

6. Select **Paste,** and then **Run.** Table 4.11 shows the SPSS output table.

TABLE 4.11 SPSS output table displaying the range, variance, and standard deviation for the creativity data.

Statistics

creativity

N	Valid	20
	Missing	0
Std. Deviation		33.422
Variance		1117.053
Range		107

CHAPTER SUMMARY ORGANIZED BY LEARNING OBJECTIVE

LO 1: Compute and interpret a range, interquartile range, and semi-interquartile range.

- The **range** is the difference between the largest value (L) and smallest value (S) in a data set. Although the range provides a simple measure for variability, it accounts for only two values (the largest value and smallest value) in a distribution.
- The **interquartile range (IQR)** is the range of a distribution of scores after the top and bottom 25% of scores in that distribution are removed.

$$IQR = Q_3 - Q_1.$$

- Scores in a distribution can be split into four sections or **quartiles** of equal size: The 25th percentile is called the **lower quartile,** the 50th percentile is called the **median quartile,** and the 75th percentile is called the **upper quartile.**
- The **semi-interquartile range (SIQR)** is used as a measure of half the distance between Q_3 and Q_1.

$$\text{SIQR} = \frac{Q_3 - Q_1}{2}, \text{ also represented as SIQR} = \frac{IQR}{2}.$$

LO 2–3: Compute and interpret the variance and standard deviation for a population and sample of data using the definitional formula and the computational formula.

- The **variance** is a measure of variability for the average squared distance that scores deviate from their mean. Its value is always greater than or equal to zero. The numerator in the variance formula is the **sum of squares (SS).** The denominator for population variance is N; the denominator for sample variance is $(n-1)$.
- The **population variance** is a measure of variability for the average squared distance that scores in a population deviate from the mean.

$$\text{Population variance}: \sigma^2 = \frac{\Sigma(x-\mu)^2}{N} \text{ or } \frac{SS}{N}.$$

- The **sample variance** is a measure of variability for the average squared distance that scores in a sample deviate from the mean.

$$\text{Sample variance}: s^2 = \frac{\Sigma(x-M)^2}{n-1} \text{ or } \frac{SS}{n-1}.$$

- The **computational formula for variance** is a way to calculate the population variance and sample variance without needing to compute the mean to compute SS in the numerator.

Computational formula (population):

$$SS = \sum x^2 - \frac{(\sum x)^2}{N}, \text{ where } \sigma^2 = \frac{SS}{N}.$$

Computational formula (sample):

$$SS = \sum x^2 - \frac{(\sum x)^2}{n}, \text{ where } s^2 = \frac{SS}{n-1}.$$

- The **standard deviation** is a measure of variability for the average distance that scores deviate from their mean and is calculated by taking the square root of the variance.

$$\text{Population standard deviation}: \sigma = \sqrt{\sigma^2} = \sqrt{\frac{SS}{N}}.$$

$$\text{Sample standard deviation}: s = \sqrt{s^2} = \sqrt{\frac{SS}{n-1}}.$$

LO 4: Explain why the sample variance and population variance are computed differently.

- The numerator for the sample variance and population variance does not differ. SS is the numerator in both formulas; only the denominator differs for two reasons. First, the sample variance is unbiased when we divide SS by $(n-1)$—on average, the variance of the sample will equal the variance of the population from which the sample was selected. Second, all scores in a sample are free to vary except one when the mean is known. So we divide the SS by 1 less than the sample size, called the **degrees of freedom (df) for sample variance.**

LO 5: State the characteristics of the standard deviation and explain the empirical rule.

- The standard deviation is always positive, and it is used to describe quantitative data, typically reported with the mean, and affected by the value of each score in a distribution.

Adding or subtracting the same constant to each score will not change the standard deviation. Multiplying or dividing each score using the same constant will cause the standard deviation to change by the constant.

- For normal distributions with any mean and any variance, we can make the following three statements using on the **empirical rule:** (1) at least 68% of all scores lie within one standard deviation of the mean, (2) at least 95% of all scores lie within two standard deviations of the mean, and (3) at least 99.7% of all scores lie within three standard deviations of the mean.

SPSS LO 6: Compute the range, variance, and standard deviation using SPSS.

- SPSS can be used to compute the range, variance, and standard deviation. Each measure of variability is computed using the **Analyze, Descriptive Statistics,** and **Frequencies** options in the menu bar. These actions will bring up a dialog box that will allow you to identify the variable and select the **Statistics** option to select and compute the range, variance, and standard deviation (for more details, see Section 4.11).

KEY TERMS

biased estimator
Chebyshev's theorem
computational formula for
   variance
deciles
definitional formula for variance
degrees of freedom (*df*)
   for sample variance
deviation
empirical rule
fractiles

interquartile range (IQR)
lower quartile
median
median quartile
percentiles
population standard deviation
population variance
quartile deviation
quartiles
range
raw scores method for variance

root mean square deviation
sample standard deviation
sample variance
semi-interquartile
   range (SIQR)
standard deviation
sum of squares (SS)
unbiased estimator
upper quartile
variability
variance

END-OF-CHAPTER PROBLEMS

Factual Problems

1. Can variability be negative? Explain.

2. How many scores are included in the computation of the range?

3. What is the interquartile range?

4. Why is variance, as a measure of variability, preferred to the range, the IQR, and the SIQR?

5. Explain why deviations from the mean are squared in the formula for variance.

6. What does it mean to say that the sample variance is unbiased?

7. What are the degrees of freedom for sample variance?

8. What does the standard deviation measure?

9. Based on the empirical rule, what percentage of data fall within 1 *SD*, 2 *SD*, and 3 *SD* of the mean for data that are distributed normally?

10. State four characteristics of the standard deviation.

Concepts and Application Problems

11. A social scientist measures the number of minutes (per day) that a small hypothetical population of college students spends online.

Student	Score	Student	Score
A	98	F	92
B	77	G	94
C	88	H	98
D	65	I	88
E	24	J	82

(a) What is the range of data in this population?

(b) What is the IQR of data in this population?

(c) What is the SIQR of data in this population?

(d) What is the population variance?

(e) What is the population standard deviation?

12. Suppose the researcher selects a sample of eight students from the population in Question 11. The sample consists of persons A, B, C, F, G, H, I, and J.

(a) What is the range of data in this sample?

(b) What is the IQR of data in this sample?

(c) What is the SIQR of data in this sample?

(d) What is the sample variance?

(e) What is the sample standard deviation?

13. If Sample 1 has a variance of 4 and Sample 2 has variance of 32, can we tell which sample had a larger range? If so, which sample had a greater range?

14. An animal researcher records the time (in seconds) it takes a group of maze-bright rats to complete a maze. Locate the lower, median, and upper quartiles for the following times. *Hint:* First arrange the data in numerical order.

Time (seconds)	Frequency
4	5
5	3
6	1
8	6
12	1
	$N = 16$

15. A sociologist records the annual household income (in thousands of dollars) among a sample of families living in a high-crime neighborhood. Locate the lower, median, and upper quartiles for the times listed below. *Hint:* First arrange the data in numerical order.

23	19
34	38
52	42
44	38
35	40

16. A behavioral scientist measures attention in a sample of 31 participants. To measure the variance of attention, she computes $SS = 120$ for this sample. (a) What are the degrees of freedom for variance? (b) Compute the variance and standard deviation.

17. A psychopathologist records the number of criminal offenses among teenage drug users in a nationwide sample of 1,201 participants. To measure the variance of criminal offenses, he computes $SS = 10,800$ for this sample. (a) What are the degrees of freedom for variance? (b) Compute the variance and standard deviation.

18. A student computes a variance of 9. Will the standard deviation differ if 9 is the value for a population versus a sample variance? Explain.

19. A student computes a standard deviation of 12. Will the variance differ if 12 is the value for a population versus a sample standard deviation? Explain.

20. If the value of the SS remains constant, state whether each of the following will increase, decrease, or have no effect on the sample variance.

(a) The sample size increases

(b) The degrees of freedom decrease

(c) The size of the population increases

21. State whether each of the following will increase, decrease, or have no effect on the population variance.

(a) The sum of squares (SS) increases

(b) The sample size decreases

(c) The size of the population increases

22. A researcher selects a sample with a sample variance of 36. If she computed the sample variance by dividing SS by $(n - 1)$, then what other value will also be equal to 36 on average?

23. A researcher measures the time (in seconds) it takes a sample of five participants to complete a memory task. It took four of the participants is 5, 6, 6, and 7 seconds. If $M = 6$, then what must be the fifth time recorded?

24. A sample of 60 scores is distributed with an $SS = 240$. What is the sample variance and sample standard deviation for this distribution?

25. If the example in Question 24 were a population of scores, would the value for the variance and standard deviation change? If so, how?

26. A psychologist measures a sample of scores on a love quiz, where $SD = 4$ points on this quiz. State the new value for SD if the psychologist (a) adds 2 points to each quiz score and (b) doubles each quiz score.

27. An expert reviews a sample of 10 scientific articles ($n = 10$) and records the following number of errors in each article: 0, 4, 2, 8, 2, 3, 1, 0, 5, and 7. Compute SS, variance, and standard deviation for this sample using the definitional and computational formula.

28. A social psychologist records the age (in years) that a sample of eight participants first experienced peer pressure. The recorded ages for the participants were 14, 20, 17, 16, 12, 16, 15, and 16. Compute the SS, the variance, and the standard deviation for this sample using the definitional and computational formula.

29. A professor records the time (in minutes) that it takes 16 students to complete an exam. Compute the SS, the variance, and the standard deviation (a) assuming the 16 students constitute a population and (b) assuming the 16 students constitute a sample.

23	32	44	20
25	14	29	41
43	21	39	33
48	38	50	40

30. A school administrator has students rate the quality of their education on a scale from 1 (*poor*) to 7 (*exceptional*). She claims that 99.7% of students rated the quality of their education between 3.5 and 6.5. If the mean rating is 5.0, then what is the standard deviation assuming the data are normally distributed? *Hint:* Use the empirical rule.

31. To study bonding between mothers and infants, a researcher places each mother and her infant in a playroom and has the mother leave for 10 minutes. The researcher records crying time in the sample of infants during this time that the mother was not present and finds that crying time is normally distributed with $M = 4$ and $SD = 1.2$. Based on the empirical rule, state the range of crying times within which (a) 68% of infants cried, (b) 95% of infants cried, and (c) 99.7% of infants cried.

Problems in Research

32. **Smoking and gender.** Wan and colleagues (2008) studied the links between smoking and schizophrenia by gender. In a description of their participants ($M \pm SD$), they stated that "of those who reported smoking, men ($n = 61$) and women ($n = 93$) reported . . . similar daily cigarette consumption per day (men: 4.25 ± 6.25 cigarettes per day; women: 3.84 ± 5.26 cigarettes per day)" (p. 428).

    (a) State the degrees of freedom for variance for men and for women.

    (b) Assume these data are normally distributed. Is it more likely that men or women smoked at least half a pack (10 cigarettes) per day? Explain.

33. **Sex and submission among women.** Sanchez, Kiefer, and Ybarra (2006) presented data suggesting that women implicitly associate a submissive role with sexual content and behavior. In their study, they reported that "women's responses to sex-primed submissive words ($M = 687.73$ milliseconds, $SD = 164.90$) were significantly faster than their responses to neutral-primed submissive words ($M = 771.58$ milliseconds, $SD = 246.04$)" (p. 515). They interpreted these findings as supporting their hypothesis that women associate submission specifically with sex-based content and behavior.

    (a) These data show that, on average, women responded faster to the sex-primed words. Assuming these data were normally distributed, distribute the data for each group (the neutral-primed and sex-primed groups) 3 SD above and 3 SD below the mean. In which group were individual participant responses (not average participant responses) the fastest?

34. **Total wellness among Citadel cadets.** Gibson and Myers (2006) investigated perceived wellness among freshman military cadets at the Citadel academy. Cadets completed the Five Factor Wellness Inventory to measure their perceived wellness pertaining to creative, coping, social, essential, and physical wellness. Total wellness scores ranged from 14.84 to 71.60, with $M \pm SD$ being 50.00 ± 9.99. Are these data approximately normally distributed? Explain.

35. **Acceptable height preferences.** Salska and colleagues (2008) studied height preferences among dating partners. In their first study, they reviewed Yahoo personals for heterosexual individuals living with 250 miles of Los Angeles, California, and recorded the acceptable range of heights for their dating partners. The following table lists some of the results. Overall, did men or women show greater variability in their responses? Explain.

Preferences	Women		Men	
	M	*SD*	*M*	*SD*
Shortest acceptable height, inches	68.9	2.6	60.6	3.7
Tallest acceptable height, inches	75.3	2.2	69.8	2.7

36. **Ideal height preferences.** In a second study, Salska and colleagues (2008) distributed a survey to a group of men and women to see what each participant's ideal height would be for a partner. Based on the data given in the table, which gender (men or women) reported ideal height preferences (first row) that most closely approximated the mean height of participants (second row)? Explain.

Preferences	Women		Men	
	M	*SD*	*M*	*SD*
Ideal height, inches	71.3	2.5	65.7	2.6
Mean participant height, inches	65.0	2.5	69.1	2.9

NOTE: Answers for even numbers are in Appendix C.

Probability

LEARNING OBJECTIVES

After reading this chapter, you should be able to:

1. Compute a simple probability and explain the relationship between probability and relative frequency.

2. Describe four types of relationships between multiple outcomes.

3. Define and compute Bayes' theorem for conditional outcomes.

4. Construct a probability distribution for a given random variable.

5. Compute the mean and expected value of a probability distribution.

6. Compute the variance and standard deviation of a probability distribution.

7. Compute the mean, variance, and standard deviation of a binomial probability distribution.

8. Construct a probability table and conditional probability table using SPSS.

5.1 INTRODUCTION TO PROBABILITY

Although you don't hear much about variances and standard deviations in everyday life, you do come across probabilities, the topic of this chapter. **Probability** is used to describe the likelihood that an outcome will occur. A weather forecaster may tell you that there is a 30% chance of rain, the favored horse in the Kentucky Derby might have 2 to 1 odds of winning, or an all-star baseball player has a 3 in 10 chance of getting a hit. Probabilities are important in research as well. Researchers may report that the likelihood of detecting a disorder is 72%, that 1 in 4 women marry by their 20th birthday, or that about 24% of Americans age 25 or older have earned a bachelor's degree.

DEFINITION

Probability (symbolized as *p*) is the frequency of times an outcome occurs divided by the total number of possible outcomes.

Probability can be used to predict any **random event**—any event where the outcomes observed in that event can vary. For example, if you flip a coin one time (the event), then it can land heads or tails (the outcomes). We can predict the likelihood of one outcome or the other, but the outcome itself can vary from one observation to the next. Probability is unnecessary in a **fixed event**—any event where the outcome observed in that event does not change. For example, what is the probability that a life (the event) will end (the outcome)? The event is fixed: All living things die eventually. Estimating the probability of this event is not valuable. Yet, suppose we ask what the probability is that a life (the event) will end (the outcome) in a car accident? Now the event is random: Not all car accidents result in death.

NOTE: Probability allows us to make predictions regarding random events.

DEFINITION

A **random event** is any event where the outcomes observed in that event can vary.

A **fixed event** is any event where the outcome observed in that event is always the same.

5.2 CALCULATING PROBABILITY

NOTE: Probability is a measure for the likelihood of observing an outcome in a random event.

In this section, we will demonstrate how probabilities are calculated. By definition, probability is the frequency of times an outcome occurs divided by the total number of possible outcomes.

To calculate probability, we need to know two things. First, we need to know the number of total possible outcomes. For example, if we flip a fair coin one time, then the total outcomes possible are two: heads or tails. The total number of possible outcomes is called the **sample space.** Second, we need to know how often an outcome of interest occurs. If we want to know how often heads occurs in one flip of a fair coin, we can count the number of times heads occurs in the total sample space. In this case, heads can occur one time per flip of a fair coin.

DEFINITION

The **sample space**, also called the **outcome space**, is the total number of possible outcomes that can occur in a given random event.

For any given random event, the probability, *p*, of an outcome, *x*, is represented as $p(x)$. The frequency, *f*, of times an outcome, *x*, occurs is represented as $f(x)$. The formula for probability then is the frequency of times an outcome occurs, $f(x)$, divided by the sample space or the total number of possible outcomes:

$$p(x) = \frac{f(x)}{\text{sample space}}.$$

To compute probability, we follow two steps: (1) find the sample space and (2) find $f(x)$. We will use these steps to compute probability in two experiments.

Suppose in Experiment 1, we flip a fair coin one time and want to know what the probability is that we will flip heads. In Step 1, we find the sample space. The sample space for all possible outcomes is two: heads or tails:

Sample space: 2 (Heads, Tails).

In Step 2, we find $f(x)$. In this example, we want to know the probability of flipping heads. Hence, we want to know how often heads will be the outcome. When we count the number of times heads occurs in our sample space, we find that heads occurs one time. We can now state the probability of flipping heads (the outcome) with one flip of a fair coin (the event) as

$$p(\text{flipping heads}) = \frac{1}{2}.$$

Now let's work through an example related to conducting research. Suppose in Experiment 2, we select a sample of one participant ($n = 1$) from a population of 10 participants ($N = 10$). We want to know the probability of selecting a man from this population, when the population consists of 4 men and 6 women. In Step 1, we find the sample space. The sample space for all possible outcomes is 10: 4 men and 6 women in the population:

Sample space: 10 (4 men, 6 women).

In Step 2, we find $f(x)$. In this example, we want to know the probability of selecting a man from this population. Hence, we want to know how often selecting a man will be the outcome. When we count the number of men our sample space, we find that there are 4 men. We can now state the probability of selecting a man (the outcome) with one selection from this population (the event) as

$$p(\text{selecting a man}) = \frac{4}{10}.$$

Again, probability is the frequency of a given outcome, *x*, divided by all possible outcomes or sample space. Flip a fair coin once, and you have a 1 in 2 probability of flipping heads; select a sample of size one from a population of size 10, where there are 4 men and 6 women in the population, and you have a 4 in 10 probability of selecting a male participant.

NOTE: Probability is the frequency of times an outcome occurs divided by the total number of possible outcomes.

When you solve the probability formula, you can use two rules about probability to verify your answer:

1. **Probability varies between 0 and 1.** There are various ways to express a probability: It can be written as a fraction, decimal, percent, or proportion.

No matter how you express the probability, its value must vary between 0 and 1. The probability of flipping heads in Experiment 1 was written as a fraction, but it would have been just as accurate if you wrote it as a decimal ($p = .50$), a percent ($p = 50\%$), or a proportion ($p = 1:1$, where the proportion is stated as heads:tails). Similarly, the probability of selecting a man in Experiment 2 was stated as a fraction, but it would have been just as accurate if you wrote it as a decimal ($p = .40$), a percent ($p = 40\%$), or a proportion ($p = 4:6$, where the proportion is stated as men:women). The closer to 1, the more probable an event is; the closer to 0, the less probable an event is.

NOTE: Probability varies between 0 and 1 and is never negative. Hence, a specified outcome is either probable ($0 < p \leq 1$) or improbable ($p = 0$).

2. **Probability can never be negative.** Similar to the logic given in Chapter 4 for variance, a negative probability is meaningless. An event is either probable (its probability is greater than 0) or improbable (its probability is equal to 0).

To this point, each step used to compute probability has been elaborated to help you see the sample space and count the frequency of times an outcome occurs. Now let's work through two examples where we determine the value of the sample space and $f(x)$ without writing out the sample space.

EXAMPLE 5.1

A researcher selects a sample from a population of 432 people, 212 of whom are women. What is the probability of selecting a woman as the first participant in this study?

Step 1: Find the sample space. The sample space consists of a population of 432 people; the sample space is 432.

Step 2: Find $f(x)$. The outcome, x, is the number of women who can be selected from this population. There are 212 women; $f(x) = 212$. Thus, the probability of selecting a woman as the first participant is $p = .49$:

$$p(\text{selecting a woman}) = \frac{212}{432} = .49.$$

EXAMPLE 5.2

Miltenberger and colleagues (2003) conducted a study on compulsive buying. As part of their study, they asked participants whether they felt satisfaction or relief when engaging in compulsive shopping. Of the 19 participants who completed their survey, 5 said satisfaction, 3 said relief, and 11 said both. What is the probability that participants in this study felt satisfaction, relief, or both from compulsive buying?

Step 1: Find the sample space. In this study, Miltenberger and colleagues (2003) observed 19 participants; the sample space is 19.

Step 2: Find f(x). We know that 5 participants felt satisfaction, $f(x) = 5$; 3 felt relief, $f(x) = 3$; and 11 felt both, $f(x) = 11$. Therefore, the probabilities for each response can be stated as

$$p(\text{satisfaction}) = \frac{5}{19} = .26.$$

$$p(\text{relief}) = \frac{3}{19} = .16.$$

$$p(\text{both}) = \frac{11}{19} = .58.$$

LEARNING CHECK 1

1. _____ is the proportion or fraction of times an outcome is likely to occur.

2. What is the distinction between a random event and a fixed event?

3. A researcher has participants complete a computer task where they can choose to play one of 200 games. Of the 200 games, only 80 of them are set up so that participants can win the game.

   (a) What is the event in this example?

   (b) What is the outcome, x, in this example?

   (c) What is the probability that a participant will choose a game that he or she can win?

4. State whether each of the following is an appropriate probability.

   (a) $p = .88$ (b) $p = -.26$ (c) $p = 1.45$ (d) $p = 1.00$

Answers: 1. Probability; 2. Outcomes in a random event can vary, whereas outcomes in a fixed event are always the same; 3. (a) Selecting one game, (b) Selecting a game that a participant can win, (c) $p(x) = .40$; 4. (a) Yes, (b) No, (c) No, (d) Yes.

PROBABILITY AND RELATIVE FREQUENCY   5.3

The probability formula looks strikingly similar to the calculation of a relative frequency, which was first introduced in Chapter 2. Indeed, the relative frequency of an event is the probability of its occurrence. Both probability and relative frequency vary between 0 and 1 and can never be negative. To find the relative frequency and therefore the probability of an outcome, we follow two steps: (1) distribute the frequencies and (2) distribute the relative frequencies.

NOTE: For a given event, the relative frequency of an outcome is the probability of its occurrence.

Step 1: Distribute the frequencies. Table 5.1 shows how we could distribute the frequency of a coin flip. Table 5.2 shows how we could distribute the frequency of selecting men from a population consisting of 4 men and 6 women. Notice that the sum of the frequencies equals the sample space. So, by distributing frequencies in Step 1, you can find the sample space, which is the denominator of the probability formula.

TABLE 5.1   The frequency of a coin flip.

Sides of a Coin	$f(x)$
Heads	1
Tails	1
	Sample space = 2

TABLE 5.2   Frequency of selecting men and women.

Gender	$f(x)$
Men	4
Women	6
	Sample space = 10

Step 2: Distribute the relative frequencies. Table 5.3 shows how we could distribute the relative frequency of a coin flip. Table 5.4 shows how we could distribute the relative frequency of selecting a man from a population consisting of 4 men and 6 women. In both examples, the relative frequency is the probability of observing each outcome.

TABLE 5.3   The relative frequency of a coin flip.

Sides of a Coin	f(x)	p(x)
Heads	1	0.50
Tails	1	0.50
	Sample space = 2	$\sum p(x) = 1.00$

TABLE 5.4   The relative frequency of selecting men and women.

Gender	f(x)	p(x)
Men	4	0.40
Women	6	0.60
	Sample space = 10	$\sum p(x) = 1.00$

NOTE: *The relative frequency of an outcome is the probability of observing that outcome.*

Relative frequencies are often given in a figure. Example 5.3 is an example of relative frequencies displayed in a bar chart.

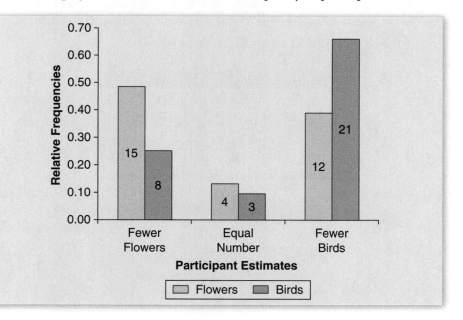

EXAMPLE 5.3

Dai, Wertenbroch, and Brendl (2008) showed participants 57 pictures of flowers and 57 pictures of birds on a computer screen. Participants, not being told how many of each picture was shown, were then asked to estimate how many pictures of flowers and birds were shown. Thirty-one participants were given payment for closely estimating the number of pictures of flowers (Group Flowers), and 32 were given payment for closely estimating the number of pictures of birds (Group Birds). Figure 5.1 displays a bar chart for the relative frequency of participant choices in

FIGURE 5.1

A bar chart showing the relative frequency of participant choices in one of two conditions. The corresponding frequency of participant choices is given in each bar.

Source: Adapted from Dai, Wertenbroch, and Brendl (2008).

each group. Using this figure, what is the probability that participants in each group of this study underestimated the number of pictures of flowers in this study?

The outcome, *x*, is the number of participants in each group who underestimated the number of pictures of flowers. In Group Flowers, we can see from Figure 5.1 that 15 of 31 participants estimated fewer flowers than were actually shown. The total number of participants is the sample space, and the number of participants underestimating the number of pictures of flowers is the frequency of *x*, or $f(x)$. Hence, when participants expected payment for closely estimating the number of pictures of flowers, the probability of underestimating the number of pictures of flowers was

$$p(\text{fewer flowers}) = \frac{15}{31} = .48.$$

In Group Birds, we can see from Figure 5.1 that 8 of 32 participants estimated fewer flowers. The total number of participants is again the sample space, and the number of participants underestimating the number of pictures of flowers is $f(x)$. Hence, when participants expected payment for closely estimating the number of pictures of birds, the probability of underestimating the number of pictures of flowers was

$$p(\text{fewer flowers}) = \frac{8}{32} = .25.$$

LEARNING CHECK 2

1. True or false: The probability of an outcome is the same as the relative frequency of its occurrence.

2. Below is the relative frequency distribution for whether an employee comes to work on time at a local business. What is the probability that an employee comes in late to work?

On Time?	Relative Frequency
Yes	0.82
No	0.18

Answers: 1. True; 2. $p = .18$.

THE RELATIONSHIP BETWEEN MULTIPLE OUTCOMES 5.4

So far, we've considered the probability of each individual outcome for a given event—such as the probability of flipping heads (the outcome) with one flip of a fair coin or selecting a male participant (the outcome) from a population. In the behavioral sciences, it is often necessary to compute the probability of two or more outcomes for a given event. How we compute probabilities for multiple outcomes depends on the relationship between each outcome. In this section, we describe four relationships that can exist between two outcomes. The probabilities for two outcomes can be mutually exclusive, independent, complementary, and conditional.

MUTUALLY EXCLUSIVE OUTCOMES

The probabilities for two outcomes are **mutually exclusive** when two outcomes cannot occur together. For example, in one flip of a fair coin (the event), it is not possible to flip a head (Outcome 1) and a tail (Outcome 2). The two outcomes for this event are mutually exclusive. The probability that they occur together is 0. We can represent the probabilities of two mutually exclusive outcomes (A and B) symbolically as

$$p(A \cap B) = 0, \text{ where } \cap \text{ is the symbol for "and."}$$

When two outcomes are mutually exclusive, they can't occur together, but one or the other can occur. For example, in one flip of a fair coin (the event), it is possible to flip a head (Outcome 1) or a tail (Outcome 2). We can calculate the probability that one or another outcome (A or B) occurs by using the **additive rule.** The additive rule can be represented symbolically as

$$p(A \cup B) = p(A) + p(B), \text{ where } \cup \text{ is the symbol for "or."}$$

DEFINITION

Two outcomes (A and B) are **mutually exclusive** when the two outcomes can't occur together. The probability of two mutually exclusive outcomes occurring together is 0.

NOTE: For two mutually exclusive outcomes, one or the other outcome can occur (A or B) but not both (A and B).

The **additive rule**, also called the **additive law**, states that when two outcomes for a given event are mutually exclusive, the probability that any one of these outcomes occurs is equal to the sum of their individual probabilities.

Example 5.4 illustrates the additive rule for mutually exclusive events.

EXAMPLE 5.4

The probability that someone in the human population has an AB blood type is approximately $p = .08$; the probability that someone in the human population has an O blood type is approximately $p = .25$. Knowing that each individual can have one and only one blood type: (a) What is the probability that a person has an AB and an O blood type? (b) What is the probability that a person has an AB or an O blood type?

(a) Remember that the outcomes (AB and O blood type) are mutually exclusive. An individual can't have both blood types. The probability that a person has an AB and an O blood type is 0:

$$p(AB \cap O) = 0.$$

(b) Because these are mutually exclusive outcomes, we can use the additive rule to find the probability that a person has an AB or an O blood type:

$$p(AB \cup O) = .08 + .25 = .33.$$

Each individual can have one and only one blood type, so blood types are mutually exclusive. In Example 5.4, the probability that an individual has an AB and an O blood type is 0. To compute the probability that a person has an AB or an O blood type, we used the additive rule and found that there is a 33% probability that an individual has an AB or an O blood type.

NOTE: While two mutually exclusive outcomes can't occur together (p = 0), the sum of their probabilities is equal to the probability that one or the other outcome occurs (the additive rule).

LEARNING CHECK 3

1. Two outcomes are mutually exclusive when: [complete the sentence].

2. Two outcomes (A and B) are mutually exclusive, where $p(A) = .45$ and $p(B)$ is .28. (a) What is the probability of A and B? (b) What is the probability of A or B?

3. What rule states that the sum of the individual probabilities for two mutually exclusive outcomes is equal to the probability that one or the other outcome occurs?

Answers: 1. Two outcomes cannot occur together; 2. (a) $p = 0$, (b) $p = .45 + .28 = .73$; 3. The additive rule.

INDEPENDENT OUTCOMES

The probabilities for two outcomes are **independent** when the probability of one outcome does not affect the probability of the second outcome. For example, if we flip a fair coin two times (the event), it is possible to flip a head (Outcome 1) on the first flip and a head (Outcome 2) on the second flip. The probability of the first outcome has no effect on the probability of the second outcome. The two outcomes are independent.

Two outcomes (A and B) are **independent** when the probability of one outcome does not affect the probability of the second outcome.

DEFINITION

When two outcomes (A and B) are independent, the probability that both outcomes occur is equal to the product of their individual probabilities. This is called the **multiplicative rule** and can be stated as

$$p(A \cap B) = p(A) \times p(B).$$

NOTE: When two outcomes are independent, the probability of one outcome does not affect the probability of the second outcome.

The **multiplicative rule**, also called the **multiplicative law**, states that when two outcomes for a given event are independent, the probability that both outcomes occur is equal to the product of their individual probabilities.

DEFINITION

Example 5.5 illustrates the multiplicative rule for independent events.

A researcher is interested in detecting a particular effect or change in some population. She determines that 80% of the sample she selects from this population will show the effect she is looking for. So the probability that one sample will detect the effect is $p = .80$. What is the probability that two samples, chosen at random from the population, will show the effect she is trying to detect?

EXAMPLE 5.5

(a) Here we are asking for the probability that the researcher will detect an effect in one sample *and* a second sample. These outcomes are independent because each time she selects a sample, she selects from the entire population—each selection is associated with the sample probability ($p = .80$) of selecting a sample that will detect the effect. Because these outcomes are independent, we use the multiplicative rule. The probability that two samples will show the effect she is trying to detect:

$$p(\text{Sample 1} \cap \text{Sample 2}) = .80 \times .80 = .64.$$

NOTE: The probability that two independent outcomes occur is equal to the product of their individual probabilities.

There is a 64% probability that both samples will detect the effect she is looking for. So long as you know the individual probability for two independent outcomes, according to the multiplicative rule, their product will be equal to the probability that they both occur.

✔ **LEARNING CHECK 4**

1. Two outcomes are _____ when the probability of one outcome does not affect the probability of the second outcome.

2. Two outcomes (A and B) are independent, where $p(A) = .45$ and $p(B)$ is .28. What is the probability of A and B?

3. What rule states that the product of the individual probabilities for two independent outcomes is equal to the probability that both outcomes occur?

Answers: 1. independent; 2. $p = .45 \times .28 = .126$; 3. The multiplicative rule.

COMPLEMENTARY OUTCOMES

The probabilities for two outcomes are **complementary** when the sum of their probabilities is equal to 1.00. For example, if we flip a fair coin one time (the event), the probability of flipping a head (Outcome 1) or a tail (Outcome 2) is 1.00. The outcomes (head, tail) are exhaustive of all possible outcomes for this event—the two outcomes are complementary.

DEFINITION

Two outcomes (A and B) are **complementary** when the sum of their probabilities is equal to 1.00. When two outcomes are complementary, they are exhaustive of all possible outcomes—so the two outcomes constitute 100% of the sample space.

NOTE: When two outcomes are complementary, the sum of their probabilities is equal to 1.0.

When two outcomes (A and B) are complementary, we can state the probability of one or the other outcome occurring as

$$p(A) + p(B) = 1.00.$$

To illustrate, recall that in Experiment 2 (in Section 5.2), we computed the probability of selecting a man from a population with 4 men and 6 women. This experiment is an example of complementary outcomes, where the sum of their probabilities is equal to 1:

$$p(\text{men}) + p(\text{women}) = \frac{4}{10} + \frac{6}{10} = 1.00.$$

Because the sum of the probabilities for two complementary outcomes is equal to 1, it will also be true that subtracting 1 from the probability of one outcome will equal the probability of the second outcome. For two complementary outcomes, the probability of A is

$$p(A) = 1 - p(B).$$

For two complementary outcomes, the probability of B is

$$p(B) = 1 - p(A).$$

To illustrate, in Experiment 2, we will substitute the probability of selecting a man for $p(A)$, and we will substitute the probability of selecting a woman for $p(B)$. To find the probability of A, we subtract 1 from the probability of B:

$$p(A) = 1 - \frac{6}{10} = \frac{4}{10}.$$

To find the probability of B, we subtract 1 from the probability of A:

$$p(B) = 1 - \frac{4}{10} = \frac{6}{10}.$$

NOTE: When two outcomes are complementary, subtracting 1 from the probability of one outcome will give you the probability for the second outcome.

LEARNING CHECK 5

1. Two outcomes are _____ when the sum of their probabilities is equal to 1.00.

2. State whether each of the following two events are complementary.
    (a) The probability of winning, losing (assuming no ties) a game.
    (b) The probability of studying or playing a video game on the day of an exam.
    (c) The probability of donating money to a charity (yes, no).

Answers: 1. complementary; 2. (a) Complementary, (b) Not complementary, (c) Complementary.

CONDITIONAL OUTCOMES

The probabilities for two outcomes are **conditional** when the probability of one outcome is dependent on the occurrence of the other outcome. An outcome is dependent when the probability of its occurrence is changed by the occurrence of the other outcome. For example, suppose you want to determine the probability of drawing two heart cards from a fair deck of cards. A fair deck has 52 cards, of which 13 cards are hearts, 13 are diamonds, 13 are spades, and 13 are clubs. On your first draw, $p = \frac{13}{52}$ that you will draw a heart card. On your second draw, the fair deck now has 51 cards, only 12 of which are heart cards because you are now holding one heart card. On the second draw, the probability of selecting a heart card changes: The probability is $p = \frac{12}{51}$. These two outcomes are conditional because selecting a heart card on the first draw changed the probability of selecting a heart card on the second draw.

DEFINITION

NOTE: Two outcomes are conditional when the occurrence of one outcome changes the probability that the other outcome will occur.

Two outcomes are **conditional** or **dependent** when the probability of one outcome is dependent on the occurrence of the other outcome. An outcome is dependent when the probability of its occurrence is changed by the occurrence of the other outcome.

In behavioral research, conditional outcomes commonly appear when we want to know the probability that a certain outcome will occur within a subset of a given sample space. For example, a developmental psychologist may study the type of hospitals (public vs. private) where pregnant women give birth, among insured and uninsured mothers. Table 5.5 displays hypothetical data in a crosstabulation, where the type of hospital variable is listed in the rows, and the insurance status variable is listed in the columns.

TABLE 5.5 A crosstabulation for the type of hospital and insurance status of 200 women who gave birth.

		Insurance Status		
		Insured	**Uninsured**	**Totals**
Type of hospital	Public	50	80	130
	Private	40	30	70
	Totals	90	110	200

Suppose the 200 mothers listed in the crosstabulation are a population of interest. If we select one of these mothers at random, then what is the probability of selecting an uninsured mother (*U*) who gave birth in a public hospital (*P*)?

$$p(P \cap U) = \frac{80}{200} = 0.40.$$

The probability we computed was for two independent outcomes because the sample space included all 200 mothers in the sample. These data indicate a 40% probability that we will select an uninsured mother who gave birth in a public hospital. But if we limit the sample space to only those mothers giving birth in public hospitals, this makes the probability question conditional. We are now asking, What is the probability of selecting an uninsured mother, *given* that she gave birth in a public hospital? Now the sample space includes only those mothers giving birth in a public hospital. The probability of selecting an uninsured mother is now dependent on whether she gave birth in a public hospital. The new sample space is 130 mothers.

NOTE: Conditional probabilities are stated as the probability of one event (A), given that another event (B) occurred.

For a conditional probability we are asking about the probability of one outcome, *given* that another outcome occurred. Using the data given in Table 5.5, then, we can state the probability of selecting an uninsured mother, *given* that she gave birth in a public hospital, as

$$p(U / P) = \frac{80}{130} = 0.62.$$

The / symbol in the parentheses is read "given that." Although there is a 40% probability of selecting an uninsured mother who gave birth in a public hospital, there is a 62% probability of selecting an uninsured mother, *given* that she gave birth in a public hospital. The formula for this type of conditional probability can be stated as

$$p(U / P) = \frac{p(P \cap U)}{p(P)}.$$

We can check our work using this new formula. Notice that we already calculated the numerator in this formula: $p(P \cap U) = 0.40$. The denominator would be the number of mothers giving birth in a public hospital (130) over the total number of women (200). The probability is

$$p(P) = \frac{130}{200} = 0.65.$$

We now know the probability to substitute into the numerator ($p = .40$) and the denominator ($p = .65$). The conditional probability for selecting a mother who is uninsured, given that she gave birth in a public hospital, is

$$p(U / P) = \frac{p(P \cap U)}{p(P)} = \frac{.40}{.65} = 0.62 \sqrt{}.$$

This solution matches (indicated by $\sqrt{}$) with the conditional probability we found initially. Researchers often select diverse samples that can be separated into subsets. Any time researchers consider these subsets of data, they are mostly asking questions about the conditional probabilities in their samples—such as in our example, where we considered the conditional probability of selecting an uninsured mother, given that she gave birth in a public hospital.

CONDITIONAL PROBABILITIES AND BAYES' THEOREM 5.5

A modified version of the conditional probability formula that we presented in Section 5.4 has broader applications for statistical inference. The modified formula can be applied to situations where we want to determine the conditional probability of obtaining samples of data, given that a parameter in some population is known. So the modified formula can be used to make inferences concerning parameters in a given population. This alternative formula for conditional probabilities is known as **Bayes' theorem** or **Bayes' law:**

$$p(U / P) = \frac{p(P / U) p(U)}{p(P)}.$$

DEFINITION

Bayes' theorem, or **Bayes' law**, is a mathematical formula that relates the conditional and marginal (unconditional) probabilities of two conditional outcomes that occur at random.

NOTE: Bayes' theorem is often applied to a variety of conditional probability situations, including those related to statistical inference.

Let's use Bayes' theorem to find the probability of selecting a mother who is uninsured, given that she gave birth in a public hospital. In Section 5.4, we determined using the data given in Table 5.5 that the conditional probability is 62%.

To apply Bayes' theorem, we first have to determine the reverse conditional probability: the probability that a mother gave birth in a public hospital, given that she is uninsured. In this case, we limit the sample space to only those mothers who are uninsured, making the new sample space 110 mothers. Notice that the row total for uninsured mothers is 110 mothers:

$$p(P/U) = \frac{80}{110} = 0.73.$$

Second, we compute the probability of a mother being uninsured, which is given in the table. We divide the number of uninsured mothers (110) by the full sample space (200):

$$p(U) = \frac{110}{200} = 0.55.$$

Third, we compute the probability of a mother giving birth in a public hospital, which is also given in the table. We divide the number of mothers giving birth in a public hospital (130) by the full sample space (200):

$$p(P) = \frac{130}{200} = 0.65.$$

Finally, we substitute these values into the Bayes' theorem formula:

$$p(U/P) = \frac{p(P/U)p(U)}{p(P)} = \frac{0.73 \times 0.55}{0.65} = 0.62\sqrt{}.$$

This solution matches (indicated by √) the conditional probability we computed in Section 5.4. Whether we used values given directly in the table, computed the basic conditional probability formula, or computed Bayes' theorem, each alternative produced the same solution—the probability of selecting a mother who is uninsured, given that she gave birth in a public hospital, is 62%.

LEARNING CHECK 6

1. Two outcomes are _____ when the probability of one outcome is dependent on the occurrence of the other outcome.

2. The probability that a participant is married is $p(M) = .60$. The probability that a participant is married and "in love" is $p(M \cap L) = .46$. Assuming that these are random events, what is the probability that a participant is in love, given that the participant is married?

Answers: 1. Conditional; 2. $p(L/M) = \frac{p(M \cap L)}{p(M)} = \frac{.46}{.60} = 0.77.$

SPSS IN FOCUS: PROBABILITY TABLES 5.6

Table 5.5 displayed a crosstabulation for the frequency of births based on the type of hospital (public vs. private) and insurance status (insured vs. uninsured) of mothers. We will use SPSS to covert these data to a conditional probability table.

CONSTRUCT A PROBABILITY TABLE

1. Click on the **variable view** tab and enter *hospital* in the **name column.** In the second row, enter *insurance,* and in the third row, enter *frequencies* in the same column. The data are whole numbers, so reduce the value in each row to 0 in the **decimals column.**

2. Coding hospital: To code *hospital,* click the small gray box with three dots in the **Values** column to display a dialog box. In the dialog box, enter *1* in the value cell and *public* in the label cell, and then click **add.** Then enter *2* in the value cell and *private* in the label cell, and then click **add.**

3. Coding insurance: To code *insurance,* we follow the same general instructions given in Step 2. Click the small gray box with three dots in the **Values** column to display a dialog box. In the dialog box, enter *1* for *insured* and *2* for *uninsured.* Select **OK.**

4. Go to the data view and enter 1, 1, 2, 2 down the first column. Then enter 1, 2, 1, 2 down the second column. In the *frequencies* column, list the frequencies for each coded cell: Enter 50, 80, 40, 30 down the third column.

5. Go to **Data,** then **Weight cases . . .** to open up a dialog box. Select **Weight cases by** and move *frequencies* into the **Frequency Variable:** box. Now each frequency is linked to each cell.

6. Go to the **menu bar** and click **Analyze,** then **Descriptive Statistics,** and **Crosstabs** to display a dialog box.

7. In the **dialog box,** select the *hospital* variable and click the top arrow to move it into the box labeled **Row(s):** to the right. Next, select the *insurance* variable and click the arrow to move it into the box labeled **Column(s):** to the right.

8. Select **Paste,** and then **Run.**

SPSS converts the coded data into the probability table shown in Table 5.6. The SPSS output table gives a probability display identical to that given in Table 5.5.

TABLE 5.6 An SPSS output of the crosstabulation shown in Table 5.5.

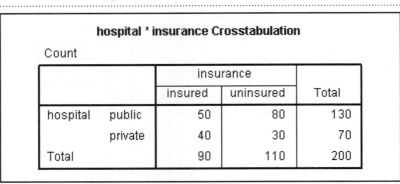

hospital * insurance Crosstabulation				
Count				
		insurance		Total
		insured	uninsured	
hospital	public	50	80	130
	private	40	30	70
Total		90	110	200

CONSTRUCT A CONDITIONAL PROBABILITY TABLE

We can also construct a conditional probability table with these same data. Having SPSS compute conditional probabilities listed directly in a table is easier than having to compute these by hand using the probabilities displayed in Table 5.6.

1. Follow Steps 1 to 7 for constructing a probability table.
2. Click **Cells . . .** to display the new dialog box shown in Figure 5.2. Select the **Row, Column,** and **Total** options under the **Percentages** heading to the left and select **Continue.**
3. Select **Paste,** and click the **Run** command.

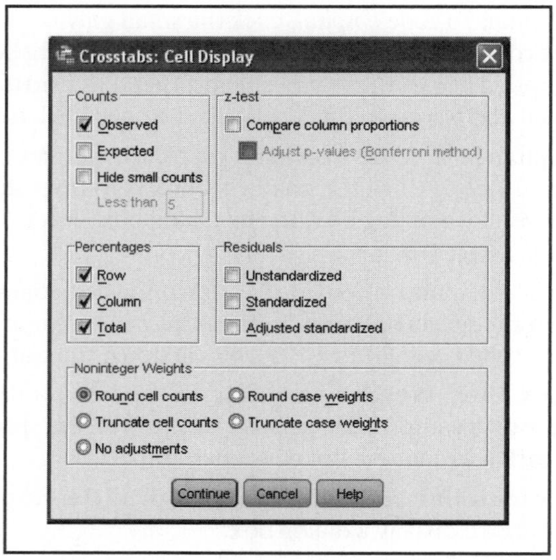

FIGURE 5.2

The dialog box showing the appropriate selection to make in Step 2.

The SPSS output table shown in Table 5.7 lists many probability values for the contingency between type of hospital and type of insurance. We computed by hand that the conditional probability is 62% for selecting a mother who is uninsured, given that she gave birth in a public hospital. This conditional probability is circled in the table and confirms our computation.

TABLE 5.7 An SPSS output of the conditional and independent (total column) probabilities for the original data in Table 5.5.

hospital * insurance Crosstabulation

| | | | insurance | | |
			insured	uninsured	Total
hospital	public	Count	50	80	130
		% within hospital	38.5%	61.5%	100.0%
		% within insurance	55.6%	72.7%	65.0%
		% of Total	25.0%	40.0%	65.0%
	private	Count	40	30	70
		% within hospital	57.1%	42.9%	100.0%
		% within insurance	44.4%	27.3%	35.0%
		% of Total	20.0%	15.0%	35.0%
Total		Count	90	110	200
		% within hospital	45.0%	55.0%	100.0%
		% within insurance	100.0%	100.0%	100.0%
		% of Total	45.0%	55.0%	100.0%

The value of the conditional probability of selecting a mother who is uninsured, given that she gave birth in a public hospital.

PROBABILITY DISTRIBUTIONS 5.7

As the four relationships indicate, researchers are typically interested in a specific outcome. For example, a clinical psychologist may be interested in the number of symptoms expressed by patients with a certain disorder, a social psychologist may be interested in the number of cars sold in a day by salespeople using various persuasion techniques, and an evolutionary psychologist may be interested in the number of years a certain species survives. In each case, the variable of interest to the researcher is a **random variable** in that the variable can lead to any number of possible outcomes in a random experiment. A random experiment is any type of experiment where a random variable is observed. A random variable can describe the outcomes for any behavior that varies from person to person or from situation to situation.

NOTE: *Researchers measure random variables, which describe the possible, as-yet-undetermined outcomes in a random experiment.*

DEFINITION

A **random variable** is a variable obtained or measured in a random experiment. Unlike other mathematical variables, a random variable is not the actual outcome of a random experiment but rather describes the possible, as-yet-undetermined outcomes in a random experiment.

In a random experiment, researchers are often interested in the **probability distribution** of a random variable. That is, they are interested in the probability of obtaining each possible outcome of a random variable. Each probability in a probability distribution ranges between 0 and 1 and can never be negative. The sum of probabilities in a probability distribution for a given random variable, x (where x is the range of possible outcomes for a random variable), must sum to 1:

NOTE: *Probability distributions display the probability of each possible outcome for a given random variable.*

$$\sum p(x) = 1.00.$$

A **probability distribution** is the distribution of probabilities for each outcome of a random variable. The sum of probabilities in a probability distribution is equal to 1.

DEFINITION

Examples 5.6 and 5.7 illustrate how to distribute the probabilities of each outcome of a random variable.

A researcher tests the ability of participants to time the occurrence of a sound. She has participants press a clicker every time they hear a sound. Unbeknownst to participants, the sound occurs every 20 seconds. To test how well participants can time the sound, she gives participants one trial where no sound is presented. In this trial, participants are asked to press the clicker at the time they think the sound should occur. In this study, she finds that 34% of participants pressed the clicker before 20 seconds passed, 26% pressed it at 20 seconds, and 40% pressed it after 20 seconds passed. Construct the probability distribution for the timing accuracy of participants in this study.

EXAMPLE 5.6

To distribute the probabilities of each outcome, we first identify the random variable. The random variable, x, is the timing accuracy of participants: Participants timed the sound too early (prior to 20 seconds), correctly (at 20 seconds), or too late (after 20 seconds). Second, we list the probabilities of each outcome of the random variable, as shown in Table 5.8.

TABLE 5.8 The probability distribution for the accuracy of participants to time a sound that occurs every 20 seconds.

	Timing of Sound		
x	**<20 Seconds**	**20 Seconds**	**>20 Seconds**
$p(x)$	0.34	0.26	0.40

EXAMPLE 5.7

A researcher records the number of participants rating a certain situation as stressful on a 5-point scale from 1 (not stressful at all) to 5 (very stressful). Table 5.9 displays the frequency distribution of the results. Construct the probability distribution for participant ratings on this scale in this study.

TABLE 5.9 The frequency distribution for participant ratings.

Ratings	$f(x)$
1	20
2	28
3	14
4	10
5	8
	$\Sigma x = 80$

To distribute the probabilities for each outcome, we first identify the random variable. The random variable, *x,* is the participant ratings: 1, 2, 3, 4, 5. In this example, though, we are given frequencies, not percents. So to distribute probabilities for each outcome of the random variable, we must first convert each frequency to a relative frequency.

To convert each frequency to a relative frequency, we divide the frequency of each outcome given in Table 5.9 by the total number of participants (or sample space) in the study. The sample space in this study is 80. Table 5.10 shows the frequencies ($f(x)$) for each outcome and the relative frequency ($p(x)$) for each outcome. Table 5.11 reorganizes the relative frequencies to display the probability distribution of participant ratings in this study.

TABLE 5.10 The frequency ($f(x)$) and relative frequency ($p(x)$) distribution of participant ratings.

Ratings	$f(x)$	$p(x)$
1	20	0.250
2	28	0.350
3	14	0.175
4	10	0.125
5	8	0.100
	$\Sigma x = 80$	$\Sigma p(x) = 1.00$

TABLE 5.11 The probability distribution of participant ratings. The distribution sums to 1.00.

x	1	2	3	4	5
p(x)	0.250	0.350	0.175	0.125	0.100

LEARNING CHECK 7

1. A _____ is the distribution of probabilities for each outcome of a random variable.

2. The probabilities for all possible outcomes of a given random variable sum to what value?

3. State whether each of the following probability distributions is correct. If the probability distribution is incorrect, then explain why.

   (a) .35, −.10, .40, .25.

   (b) .15, .26, .54, .05.

   (c) 0.18, 0.32, 0.34, 0.36

Answers: 1. probability distribution; 2. The probabilities sum to 1.0; 3. (a) Incorrect, because one of the probabilities is negative. (b) Correct. (c) Incorrect, because the sum of the probabilities does not equal 1.

THE MEAN OF A PROBABILITY DISTRIBUTION AND EXPECTED VALUE 5.8

In addition to using probability distributions to identify the probabilities for each outcome of a random variable, we can also use them to predict the outcome (or value of the outcome) of a random variable that we can expect to occur, on average. For example, you may read an article reporting that one murder is expected to occur in the United States every 32.6 minutes or that we can expect the average mother to have 3.14 children in her lifetime. Of course, murders do not occur exactly every 32.6 minutes, and it is not even possible for a mother to have 3.14 children. Instead, you should interpret these statistics as averages.

The use of probability to predict the expected mean value of a random variable is called **mathematical expectation**, or **expected value.** To compute the mean value, μ, of a random variable, we (1) multiply each possible outcome, *x*, times the probability of its occurrence, *p*, and (2) sum each product:

$$\mu = \sum(xp).$$

NOTE: The expected value of a given random variable is equal to the mean of the probability distribution of that random variable.

A **mathematical expectation**, or **expected value**, is the mean, or average expected outcome, of a given random variable. The expected outcome of a random variable is the sum of the products for each random outcome times the probability of its occurrence.

DEFINITION

By definition, to determine the expected value of a random variable, we compute the mean of a probability distribution of that random variable. The mean of a probability distribution, then, is the value we predict will occur on average. Examples 5.8, 5.9, and 5.10 illustrate how to compute and interpret the expected value of a random variable.

EXAMPLE 5.8

The probabilities are .24, .16, .40, and .20 that participants in a cognitive learning study will forget 0, 1, 2, or 3 items, respectively, in a memory test. How many items should the researchers expect participants to forget on the test?

In this example, the random variable is forgetting. The possible outcomes of the random variable are 0, 1, 2, or 3 items. To find the expected value, we multiply the value of each outcome of the random variable times its corresponding probability and then sum the products:

$$\mu = (0 \times .24) + (1 \times .16) + (2 \times .40) + (3 \times .20) = 1.56.$$

We expect participants, on average, to forget 1.56 items on this cognitive learning test. A more practical interpretation is that we expect participants to forget between 1 or 2 items on this test.

EXAMPLE 5.9

Richard Tunney (2006) ran a study to determine if the way in which odds were presented, either as probabilities or relative frequencies, affects participants' betting preferences. As part of his study, he ran a series of different probability conditions, where P-bets were associated with a high probability of winning a modest amount and £-bets were associated with a low probability of winning a larger amount (in pounds sterling). Below is one example of each betting condition in his study. Using the values in Table 5.12, confirm that the expected values given in the last column are correct.

TABLE 5.12 Two betting conditions from the Tunney (2006) study. The expected value is given for each betting condition (P and £).

Pair	Probability of Winning	Amount to Win	Amount to Lose	Expected Value
P	.75	6.00	3.00	3.75
£	.35	17.00	3.50	3.68

P-bet. Table 5.12 shows that the probability of winning 6.00 pounds is $p = .75$. The probability of losing 3.00 pounds must then be $p = .25$. In this example, the random variable, *x,* is gambling. The possible outcomes of this random variable are winning 6 pounds (+6.00) or losing 3 pounds (–3.00). To find the expected value for wining or losing money, we multiply the value of each outcome of the random variable times its corresponding probability and then sum the products:

$$\mu = 6.00(.75) - 3.00(.25) = +3.75.$$

In this example, we had a 25% chance of losing 3.00 pounds and a 75% chance of winning 6.00 pounds. If a gambler played these odds for an infinite number of trials, we can expect that he would win 3.75 pounds per bet.

£-bet. Table 5.12 shows that the probability of winning 17.00 pounds is $p = .35$. The probability of losing 3.50 pounds then must be $p = .65$. In this example, the random variable, *x,* is gambling. The possible outcomes of this random variable are winning

17.00 pounds (+17.00) or losing 3.50 pounds (–3.50). To find the expected value of winning or losing money, we multiply the value of each outcome of the random variable times its corresponding probability and then sum the products:

$$\mu = (17.00 \times .35) - (3.50 \times .65) = +3.68.$$

Despite low odds of winning ($p = .35$), we still can expect a gambler who played these odds for an infinite number of trials to win 3.68 pounds per bet.

From Example 5.9, suppose a gambler places 100 P-bets and 100 £-bets. How much money should we expect a gambler to win or lose per P-bet? Per £-bet?

Expected value per P-bet: Table 5.12 shows that the expected value for P-bets is 3.75 pounds per bet. Therefore, if a gambler places 100 bets, then we would expect the gambler to win

$$100 \times 3.75 = +375 \text{ pounds}.$$

Expected value per £-bet: Table 5.12 shows that the expected value for £-bets is 3.68 pounds per bet. Therefore, if a gambler places 100 bets, then we would expect the gambler to win

$$100 \times 3.68 = +368 \text{ pounds}.$$

NOTE: Expected value can be used to assess risk by estimating the amount we can expect to gain or lose based on the known probabilities of outcomes for a given random variable.

EXAMPLE 5.10

MAKING SENSE: Expected Value and the "Long-Term Mean"

We can think of expected value as a long-term mean. To illustrate, suppose we flip two fair coins three times and observe two heads face-up on each flip. The random variable is the number of heads per coin flip. The possible outcomes of the random variable are 0, 1, or 2 heads. In three flips, we observed two heads face-up on each flip. On the basis of these observations, can we say that we should expect to observe two heads on every flip? No, because we only flipped the coins three times. On average, we did observe two heads on each flip, but with a finite number of flips, the mean is a short-term mean—it is the mean for a finite number of observations of a random variable.

Expected value, on the other hand, is an estimate of the mean outcome for a random variable assuming the random variable was observed an infinite number of times. An expected value is not based on making three observations; instead, the expected value is based on the assumption that the two fair coins were flipped an infinite number of times—it is a long-term mean. Table 5.13 shows the probability distribution for flipping heads with two fair coins.

To find the expected value, we multiply the value of each outcome of the random variable times its corresponding probability and then sum the products:

$$\mu = (0 \times .25) + (1 \times .50) + (2 \times .25) = 1.00.$$

(Continued)

NOTE: Expected value is the long-term mean—it is the average outcome for a random variable that is observed an infinite number of times.

(Continued)

TABLE 5.13 The probability distribution for the number of heads showing per flip of two fair coins.

Number of Heads	0	1	2
$p(x)$	0.25	0.50	0.25

On average, we expect to flip one head each time we flip two fair coins. Of course, in three flips, we may not observe this outcome, but if you flipped the two coins an infinite number of times, we would expect to flip one head per flip. So expected value is really a long-term mean—it is the average expected outcome for a random variable, assuming the random variable is observed an infinite number of times.

5.9 RESEARCH IN FOCUS: WHEN ARE RISKS WORTH TAKING?

In his book *Against the Gods: The Remarkable Story of Risk,* Peter Bernstein (1998) explores how the average person approaches expectations of risk and reward. He describes an experiment showing how expectations for certain outcomes are not always consistent with expectations derived mathematically. Here are the procedures for the situations he described:

Situation 1: Suppose you are offered the choice between having a 100% chance of receiving $3,000 or an 80% chance of receiving $4,000 with a 20% chance of receiving nothing. Which do you choose?

Situation 2: Suppose you have a choice between a 100% chance of losing $3,000 or an 80% chance of losing $4,000 with a 20% chance of breaking even. Which do you choose?

Take the time to select which option you would choose in each situation. Then, let's see how our decision compares with the mathematical expectation, or expected value, for each outcome.

Situation 1

The mathematical expectation for a 100% chance of receiving $3,000 is

$$\$3,000 \times 1.00 = \$3,000.$$

The mathematical expectation for an 80% chance of receiving $4,000 and a 20% chance of breaking even is

$$(\$4,000 \times .80) + (0 \times .20) = \$3,200.$$

Because the second riskier choice has a greater mathematical expectation, that would be the best choice. Instead, 80% of those surveyed chose the 100% guarantee of receiving $3,000, not the riskier option with the larger mathematical expectation.

Situation 2

The mathematical expectation for a 100% chance of losing $3,000 is

$$-\$3,000 \times 1.00 = -\$3,000.$$

The mathematical expectation for an 80% chance of losing $4,000 and a 20% chance of breaking even is

$$(-\$4,000 \times .80) + (0 \times .20) = -\$3,200.$$

Now the second, riskier choice has a lower mathematical expectation, so the optimal choice would be to take the $3,000 loss and not take the risk. In this situation, though, 92% of those surveyed chose to take the risk with a 20% chance of breaking even. Thus, in both situations, the majority of those surveyed answered wrong—that is, based on the mathematical expectation. By the way, what did you choose?

THE VARIANCE AND STANDARD DEVIATION OF A PROBABILITY DISTRIBUTION 5.10

Expected value is a mean for a probability distribution, but tells us nothing of the distribution for all other outcomes. To determine the distribution of all other outcomes for a given random variable, we will compute the variance and standard deviation of all other outcomes in a probability distribution in this section. The standard deviation of a probability distribution is the mean distance that all other possible outcomes for a random variable deviate from the mean. To estimate the **variance of a probability distribution,** σ^2, for a random variable, x, we use the following formula:

$$\sigma^2 = \sum \left((x - \mu)^2 \, p \right).$$

To estimate the **standard deviation of a probability distribution,** σ, for a random variable, x, we take the square root of the variance:

$$\sigma = \sqrt{\sigma^2} = \sqrt{\sum \left((x - \mu)^2 \, p \right)}.$$

DEFINITION

The **variance of a probability distribution** is a measure of variability for the average squared distance that outcomes for a given random variable deviate from the expected value or mean of a probability distribution.

The **standard deviation of a probability distribution** is a measure of variability for the average distance that outcomes for a given random variable deviate from the expected value or mean of a probability distribution. It is calculated by taking the square root of the variance of a probability distribution.

Example 5.11 will demonstrate how to use these formulas to calculate the variance and standard deviation of outcomes in a probability distribution.

NOTE: While the expected value of the mean is the average outcome, the standard deviation of a probability distribution is the distance that all other outcomes deviate from the mean.

EXAMPLE 5.11

In Example 5.8, we measured the expected value of forgetting on a memory quiz (the random variable). The possible outcomes for the random variable were 0, 1, 2, or 3 items. We found that the expected value of forgetting was 1.56 items on the memory quiz ($\mu = 1.56$). Calculate the variance and standard deviation of all the possible outcomes for forgetting.

TABLE 5.14 Computations for calculating the variance of a probability distribution.

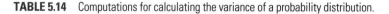

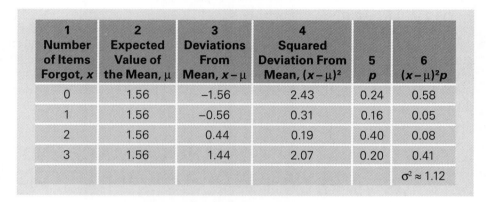

1 Number of Items Forgot, x	2 Expected Value of the Mean, μ	3 Deviations From Mean, $x - \mu$	4 Squared Deviation From Mean, $(x - \mu)^2$	5 p	6 $(x - \mu)^2 p$
0	1.56	−1.56	2.43	0.24	0.58
1	1.56	−0.56	0.31	0.16	0.05
2	1.56	0.44	0.19	0.40	0.08
3	1.56	1.44	2.07	0.20	0.41
					$\sigma^2 \approx 1.12$

Because we know μ, we can arrange the calculation of the variance as shown in Table 5.14. The calculations for columns 1 to 4 are needed to compute the squared deviations of outcomes from the expected value of the mean: $(x - \mu)^2$. The values in column 6 were calculated by multiplying each squared deviation from the mean times its respective probability. The sum of values in column 6 is the variance of the probability distribution for the random variable forgetting:

$$\sigma^2 = \sum \left((x - \mu)^2 p \right) \approx 1.12.$$

The standard deviation of the probability distribution for the random variable forgetting is the square root of the variance:

$$\sigma = \sqrt{\sigma^2} = \sqrt{1.12} \approx 1.06.$$

For this problem, we can conclude that, on average, we expect students to forget 1.56 items on the memory quiz, with all other outcomes for forgetting distributed at 1.06 standard deviations from the mean.

In Example 5.11, there were only four possible outcomes for the random variable: 0, 1, 2, or 3. Yet, in cases where we distribute a large number of possible outcomes for a random variable, it is often sensible to use the computing formula for the variance of a probability distribution. The computing formula allows us to compute the variance and standard deviation of a probability distribution without needing to compute the squared deviation of each outcome from the mean. The computing formula for the variance of a probability distribution is

$$\sigma^2 = \left(\sum \left(x^2 p \right) - \mu^2 \right).$$

The computing formula for the standard deviation of a probability distribution is the square root of the variance:

$$\sigma = \sqrt{\sigma^2} = \sqrt{\left(\sum \left(x^2 p \right) - \mu^2 \right)}.$$

NOTE: The computing formulas for the variance and standard deviation of a probability distribution do not require us to compute the squared deviation of each outcome from the mean.

Example 5.12 uses the computing formulas to find the expected value of the variance and standard deviation of a probability distribution.

EXAMPLE 5.12

Table 5.15 shows the probability distribution for the proportion of words recalled in a list of 20 words, published in a study by Donald Laming (2006). The mean of this probability distribution is 7.89 ($\mu = 7.89$) words recalled. What are the variance and standard deviation of this probability distribution?

TABLE 5.15   The probability distribution for the proportion of words recalled in a list of 20 words.

Words	Probability
1	0.197
2	0.053
3	0.051
4	0.066
5	0.207
6	0.049
7	0.002
8	0.005
9	0.004
10	0.004
11	0.043
12	0.048
13	0.005
14	0.055
15	0.039
16	0.007
17	0.011
18	0.014
19	0.090
20	0.050

Source: Adapted from Laming (2006).

First we calculate the expression in the parentheses of the computing formula, and then we subtract μ^2 from the result to obtain the variance:

Step 1: Calculate $\sum x^2 p$.

$$\sum x^2 p = [1^2(0.197)] + [2^2(0.053)] + [3^2(0.051) + 4^2(0.066)]$$
$$+[5^2(0.207)] + [6^2(0.049)] + [7^2(0.002)] + [8^2(0.005)] + [9^2(0.004)]$$
$$+[10^2(0.004)] + [11^2(0.043)] + [12^2(0.048)] + [13^2(0.005)] + [14^2(0.055) = 104.336.$$
$$+[15^2(0.039)] + [16^2(0.007)] + [17^2(0.011)] + [18^2(0.014)]$$
$$+[19^2(0.090)] + [20^2(0.050)]$$

Step 2: Subtract μ^2 from the answer in Step 1: $\sigma^2 = (\sum(x^2 p) - \mu^2)$:

$$\sigma^2 = 104.336 - (7.89)^2 \approx 42.08.$$

The variance is approximately 42.08. The standard deviation of this probability distribution is

$$\sigma = \sqrt{\sigma^2} = \sqrt{42.084} \approx 6.49.$$

For this example, we expect that students will recall 7.89 words, on average, with all other outcomes of recall distributed at 6.49 standard deviations from the mean.

LEARNING CHECK 8

1. A _____ is the average expected outcome, for a given random variable.

2. There is a 75% chance that a store will earn a profit of $1,000 and a 25% chance it will lose $2,000 by marking all items half off. Using mathematical expectation, do we expect the store to earn a profit by marking all items half off?

3. Calculate the mean and standard deviation of the following probability distribution.

x	0	1	2
$p(x)$	0.35	0.30	0.35

4. When is it sensible to use the computing formula to compute the variance and standard deviation of a probability distribution?

Answers: 1. mathematical expectation or expected value; 2. Yes, the mathematical expectation is an average profit of $250; 3. $\mu = 1.0$, $\sigma = \sqrt{0.7} = 0.84$; 4. When there are a large number of possible outcomes for a random variable.

5.11 EXPECTED VALUE AND THE BINOMIAL DISTRIBUTION

In cases where there are only two behavioral outcomes, we can use shortcuts to calculate the mean and standard deviation of a probability distribution. The distribution of probabilities for each outcome of a random variable with two possible outcomes is called a **binomial probability distribution.** A binomial probability distribution can occur by natural occurrence—for example, the outcomes for flipping one fair coin are heads, tails. A binomial probability distribution can also occur by manipulation—for example, the level of self-esteem among children (self-esteem: low, high) or the number of students graduating college (graduated: yes, no). We could define self-esteem and graduation rates as having more than two outcomes, but we manipulated the data such that only two outcomes were possible.

NOTE: *A random variable with only two possible outcomes will have a binomial probability distribution.*

> A **binomial probability distribution**, or **binomial distribution**, is the distribution of probabilities for each outcome of a bivariate random variable.
>
> A **bivariate random variable** or **dichotomous variable** is any random variable with only two possible outcomes.

DEFINITION

Binomial probability distributions are common in behavioral research. In this section, we introduce how researchers compute the mean, variance, and standard deviation of random variables with only two possible outcomes.

THE MEAN OF A BINOMIAL DISTRIBUTION

When a random variable has only two possible outcomes, we can use a simple formula to estimate the expected value or expected outcome of the random variable. When there are only two outcomes for a random variable, x, we calculate the mean of the binomial probability distribution as

$$\mu = np.$$

The mean of a binomial distribution is the product of the number of times the random variable is observed (n) times the probability of the outcome of interest on an individual observation (p). For example, if we flip one fair coin 10 times ($n = 10$), then the expected value of flipping heads is

NOTE: *The mean of a binomial probability distribution is the expected value of a random variable with two possible outcomes.*

$$\mu = 10 \times \frac{1}{2} = 5 \text{ heads, where } p(\text{heads}) = \frac{1}{2} \text{ per flip.}$$

We expect to flip 5 heads in 10 flips of one fair coin.

THE VARIANCE AND STANDARD DEVIATION OF A BINOMIAL DISTRIBUTION

As with the mean, we can also simplify calculations of variance and standard deviation when there are only two outcomes of a random variable. The formula for the variance of a binomial probability distribution is

$$\sigma^2 = np\,(1 - p)$$

or

$$\sigma^2 = npq.$$

NOTE: The standard deviation of a binomial probability distribution is the average distance that bivariate outcomes deviate from the expected value or mean of a binomial probability distribution.

The formula for the standard deviation of a binomial probability distribution is the square root of the variance:

$$\sigma = \sqrt{\sigma^2} = \sqrt{np(1-p)}$$

or

$$\sigma = \sqrt{\sigma^2} = \sqrt{npq}.$$

In each formula, n is the number of times the random variable is observed, p is the probability of the outcome of interest, and q is the probability of the complementary binomial outcome. Keep in mind that p and q are complementary outcomes, so $q = (1 - p)$. Example 5.13 applies these formulas to calculate the variance and the standard deviation of a binomial probability distribution.

EXAMPLE 5.13

In the study described in Example 5.8, the probabilities that participants in a cognitive learning study will forget 0, 1, 2, or 3 items in a memory test were .24, .16, .40, and .20, respectively. We can convert this information into a binomial distribution by defining forgetting as missing at least one item on the memory quiz. When we do so, we find that the probability of forgetting at least one item on the memory quiz is $p = .76$ $(.16 + .40 + .20 = .76)$, and the probability of not forgetting is $p = .24$. If a researcher observes 88 participants in the study, then we expect 21.12 participants $(\mu = 88 \times .24 = 21.12)$ to recall every item on the memory test. What are the variance and the standard deviation of this binomial probability distribution?

Because we know that $n = 88$ and p(not forgetting) $= .24$, then the variance of this binomial probability distribution is

$$\sigma^2 = 88 \times .24(1 - .24) \approx 16.05.$$

The standard deviation is the square root of the variance:

$$\sigma = \sqrt{\sigma^2} = \sqrt{16.05} \approx 4.01.$$

We expect an average of 21.12 participants to recall every item on the memory test (not forget), with all other outcomes being distributed 4.01 standard deviations from the mean.

 **LEARNING CHECK 9**

1. A _____ is the distribution of probabilities for each outcome of a bivariate random variable.

2. A local report indicates that the probability of a suburbanite committing a violent crime is .09. If the local suburb has 192 residents, how many suburbanites would we expect to commit a violent crime?

3. Based on the same example given in Question 2, what are the variance and standard deviation of violent crime given that $n = 192$, $p = .09$, and $q = .91$?

Answers: 1. binomial probability distribution. 2. $\mu = np = 192(.09) = 17.28$ suburbanites. 3. $\sigma^2 = npq = 192 (.09)(.91) = 15.725$, $\sigma = \sqrt{15.725} = 3.97$.

A FINAL THOUGHT ON THE LIKELIHOOD
OF RANDOM BEHAVIORAL OUTCOMES 5.12

Probabilities are used to predict the occurrence of behavioral outcomes. But behavior is not always as "neat" as the probability calculations would lead us to believe. Consider the causes of emotions such as love, happiness, or frustration. Can we predict when or how often these emotions will be expressed? Sure, but the answer depends on many factors: Buying a significant other flowers, for example, may facilitate love in some but not all people; being promoted at work may cause happiness in some but not all people; and waiting in line may cause frustration in some but not all people. Behavior is not an all-or-nothing phenomenon; it is not as simple as saying it occurs or doesn't occur. To put it another way, behavioral outcomes are not equally likely.

NOTE: Using probability to predict the occurrence of behavioral outcomes can be challenging because it is often the case that the outcomes are not equally likely—one behavioral outcome can be influenced by a multitude of known and unknown factors.

For example, can we say that the probability of life on any other planet is $p = .50$, because life either exists or does not? No; of the eight planets in our solar system, only one has life, but even that knowledge alone makes it unlikely that the probability of planetary life is truly $p = .50$. In fact, many planets have a near 0 probability of supporting life due to factors such as the shape of their orbit, their location from the sun, or the type of star they orbit.

In the same way, behavior is complex, and predicting its occurrence can be even more challenging. There are just so many factors that contribute to the likelihood of observing the behavioral outcomes that researchers study. Consider, for example, many of the factors that contribute to the probability of illegal drug use. Some factors include an individual's gender, genetics, socioeconomic status, family involvement, age, and education level. Including or excluding any of these factors can change the probabilities we use to predict its occurrence. For this reason, calculating probabilities of any type of behavior, as well as interpreting them appropriately, requires some intuition and common sense. As perhaps best stated by the late mathematician and astronomer Pierre Simon Laplace: *Probability theory is nothing but common sense reduced to calculation.*

CHAPTER SUMMARY ORGANIZED BY LEARNING OBJECTIVE

LO 1: Compute a simple probability and explain the relationship between probability and relative frequency.

- **Probability** (symbolized as *p*) is the frequency of times an outcome occurs divided by the total number of possible outcomes. Probability varies between 0 and 1 and is never negative.
- To calculate the probability of an outcome for a random variable, *x*, use the formula for $p(x)$, where $f(x)$ is the frequency of times an outcome occurs, and the **sample space** is the total number of outcomes possible:

$$p(x) = \frac{f(x)}{\text{sample space}}.$$

- The two steps to compute the probability formula are (1) find the sample space and (2) find $f(x)$.
- A probability is the same as a relative frequency. To find a probability using the relative frequency, we follow two steps: (1) distribute the frequencies and (2) distribute the relative frequencies.

LO 2: Describe four types of relationships between multiple outcomes.

- Four types of relationships between multiple outcomes are mutually exclusive, independent, complementary, and conditional or dependent outcomes.
- When two outcomes (A and B) are **mutually exclusive,** the outcomes can't occur together, but one or the other can occur. Hence, the probability of A and B is equal to 0, and the probability of A or B is stated by the **additive rule,** where $\cup$ is the symbol for *or:* $p(A \cup B) = p(A) + p(B)$.
- Two outcomes (A and B) are **independent** when the probability of one outcome does not affect the probability of the second outcome. To compute the probability that two independent outcomes occur together, we follow the **multiplicative rule,** where $\cap$ is the symbol for *and:* $p(A \cap B) = p(A) \times p(B)$.
- Two outcomes (A and B) are **complementary** when the sum of their probabilities is

equal to 1.0, so the probability of A or B is $p(A) + p(B) = 1.00$.
- Two outcomes (A and B) are **conditional** when the probability of one outcome is dependent on the occurrence of the other. We can compute the conditional probability of A, given that B occurred, using the following formula:

$$p(A / B) = \frac{p(B \cap A)}{p(B)}.$$

LO 3: Define and compute Bayes' theorem for conditional outcomes.

- **Bayes' theorem,** or **Bayes' law,** is a mathematical formula that relates the conditional and marginal (unconditional) probabilities of two conditional outcomes that occur at random. Bayes' formula has broader applications for inferential statistics than other formulas for conditional probabilities. We can compute the conditional probability of A, given that B occurred, using the following Bayes' formula:

$$p(A / B) = \frac{p(B / A) p(A)}{p(B)}.$$

LO 4–5: Construct a probability distribution for a given random variable and compute the mean and expected value of a probability distribution.

- The **probability distribution** is the distribution of probabilities for each outcome of a random variable. The sum of probabilities for a probability distribution is equal to 1.
- **Mathematical expectation,** or **expected value,** is the mean, or average expected outcome, for a random variable. The expected outcome of a random variable is the sum of the products for each random outcome times the probability of its occurrence: $\mu = \Sigma(xp)$.

LO 6: Compute the variance and standard deviation of a probability distribution.

- To estimate the **variance of a probability distribution,** σ^2, for the outcomes of a random variable, *x*, compute the following formula:

$$\sigma^2 = \sum \left((x - \mu)^2 p \right), \text{ or } \sigma^2 = \left(\sum \left(x^2 p \right) - \mu^2 \right).$$

- To estimate the **standard deviation of a probability distribution,** σ, for the outcomes of a random variable, x, take the square root of the variance: $\sigma = \sqrt{\sigma^2}$.

LO 7: Compute the mean, variance, and standard deviation of a binomial probability distribution.

- A **binomial probability distribution** is the distribution of probabilities for each outcome of a bivariate random variable. A bivariate or dichotomous random variable is one with only two possible outcomes.
- The mean of a binomial probability distribution is the product of the number of trials (n) times the probability of the outcome of interest on an individual trial (p):

$$\mu = np.$$

- The variance of a binomial probability distribution is

$$\sigma^2 = np(1-p), \text{ or } \sigma^2 = npq.$$

- The standard deviation of a binomial distribution is the square root of the variance: $\sigma = \sqrt{\sigma^2}$.

SPSS LO 8: Construct a probability table and conditional probability table using SPSS.

- SPSS can be used to construct probability tables for one or more variables. To construct a probability table, each variable should be coded in the variable view table. In the data view tab, the combination of each level for each factor should be arranged across the rows. The corresponding frequencies for each combination of levels are then entered in the last column. Probability and conditional probability tables are created using the **Analyze, Descriptive Statistics,** and **Crosstabs** options in the menu bar. A **weight cases** option must also be selected from the menu bar (for more details, see Section 5.6).

KEY TERMS

additive law
additive rule
Bayes' law
Bayes' theorem
binomial distribution
binomial probability distribution
bivariate random variable
complementary outcomes
conditional outcomes
dependent outcomes

dichotomous variable
expected value
fixed events
independent outcomes
mathematical expectation
multiplicative law
multiplicative rule
mutually exclusive outcomes
outcome space
probability

probability distribution
random events
random variables
sample space
standard deviation of a
   probability distribution
variance of a probability
   distribution

END-OF-CHAPTER PROBLEMS

Factual Problems

1. Describe in words how to compute $p(x)$.

2. Distinguish between random events and fixed events.

3. State two characteristics of a probability.

4. Explain how probability and relative frequency are related.

5. State the rule or law associated with the following types of relationships:

   a. Two outcomes are mutually exclusive.

   b. Two outcomes are independent.

6. State the conditions that make two outcomes complementary.

7. Given two outcomes, A and B, state their relationship as a conditional probability using a "given" statement.

8. What is a probability distribution? What makes a binomial probability distribution unique?

9. State the formula for calculating the following:

   (a) The mean of a probability distribution

   (b) The variance of a probability distribution

   (c) The standard deviation of a probability distribution

10. State the formula for calculating the following:

    (a) The mean of a binomial probability distribution

    (b) The variance of a binomial probability distribution

    (c) The standard deviation of a binomial probability distribution

Concepts and Application Problems

11. A hypothetical population consists of eight individuals ages 13, 14, 17, 20, 21, 22, 24, and 30 years.

    (a) What is the probability that a person in this population is a teenager?

    (b) What is the probability of selecting a participant who is at least 20 years old?

    (c) What is the probability of selecting a participant older than 30?

12. On the basis of statistics from the previous 3 years, a maternity ward states that 97% of patients say they are satisfied with their birthing experience. If 100,000 patients gave birth in that maternity ward over the previous 3 years, then how many patients do we expect will not satisfied with their visit?

13. Researchers often enter a lot of data into statistical software programs. The probability of making zero to two errors per 1,000 keystrokes is 0.51, and the probability of making three to five errors per 1,000 keystrokes is 0.24. Find the probabilities (per 1,000 keystrokes) associated with each of the following.

    (a) At most two errors

    (b) At least three errors

    (c) At most five errors

    (d) More than five errors

14. The probabilities that a student will attain a 3.6 GPA, at least a 3.0 GPA, at least a 2.5 GPA, and at least a 2.0 GPA are 0.08, 0.47, 0.69, and 0.81, respectively. Find the probabilities associated with each of the following.

    (a) A GPA worse than 3.0 but greater than 2.5

    (b) A GPA worse than 2.0

    (c) At least a GPA of 2.5

    (d) A GPA worse than 3.0

15. In a study on reinforcement, a researcher allows a rat to choose between four arms of a plus maze. A plus maze is a maze shaped like a plus sign, with each extension from the center being called an "arm" in the maze. Upon being placed in the center of the maze, the probability on any given trial that a subject is reinforced in the left arm is 0.30, the right is 0.30, the front arm is 0.20, and the back arm is 0.20.

    (a) What is the probability the rat will be reinforced when entering the left or right arm?

    (b) To make the optimal probability choice, a subject should enter the right or left arm on each trial. Explain why this is true.

16. In a study of group dynamics among business executives, R is the outcome where an executive's rank holds great influence and I is the outcome where employees are directly influenced by an executive's decision. State the following probabilities in words.

    (a) $p(R)$

    (b) $p(I)$

    (c) $p(R \cap I)$

    (d) $p(R \cup I)$

17. In a proposed program of research, L is an effect that will be detected in a population, and E is an effect that exists in a population. State the following probabilities in words.

    (a) $p(L)$

    (b) $p(E)$

    (c) $p(L / E)$

    (d) $p(L \cap E)$

18. A psychologist determines that the probability of relapse in her clinic is $p = .12$. Assuming independent outcomes, what is the probability that two of her patients relapse?

19. The probability that a student in college will "experiment" with drugs is $p = .31$. The probability that a college student will not experiment with drugs is $q = .69$.

    (a) What type of relationship do these probabilities have?

    (b) A student heads off to college. What is the probability that the student experiments with drugs or does not experiment with drugs?

20. A psychologist states that there is a 5% chance ($p = .05$) that his decision will be wrong. Assuming complementary outcomes, what is the probability that his decision will be correct?

21. The probability that a student passes a class is $p(P) = .59$. The probability that a student studied for a class is $p(S) = .53$. The probability that a student passes a class given that he or she studied for the class is $p(P / S) = .89$. What is the probability that a student studied for the class, given that he or she passed the class ($p(S / P)$)? *Hint:* Use Bayes' theorem.

22. The probability that a participant is happy is $p(H) = .63$. The probability that a participant is wealthy is $p(W) = .25$. The probability that a participant is happy given that he or she is wealthy is $p(H / W) = .50$. What is the probability that a participant is wealthy, given that he or she is happy ($p(W / H)$)? *Hint:* Use Bayes' theorem.

23. The probability that a student will attend class is $p = .84$. The probability that a student will skip class is $p = .16$. The probability that a student will both attend and skip class is $p = 1.00$. Explain why the last probability must be false.

24. The probability that a teenager will fall in love is $p = .72$. The probability that a student will play a sport is $p = .55$. The probability that a student will fall in love and play a sport is $p = .60$. Explain why the last probability must be false.

25. The relative frequency distribution of the number of phobias reported by a hypothetical sample of 500 college students is given as follows.

0–2	0.49
3–5	0.28
6–8	0.11
9–11	0.09
12–14	0.03

(a) What is the probability that a college student expresses fewer than three phobias?

(b) What is the probability that a college student expresses more than eight phobias?

(c) What is the probability that a college student has between 3 and 11 phobias?

26. The following is an incomplete probability distribution for a given random variable, x. What is the probability for the blank cell?

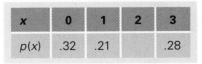

x	0	1	2	3
$p(x)$	.32	.21		.28

27. The following is an inaccurate probability distribution for a given random variable, x. State two errors with this probability distribution.

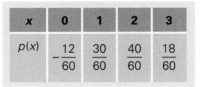

x	0	1	2	3
$p(x)$	$-\dfrac{12}{60}$	$\dfrac{30}{60}$	$\dfrac{40}{60}$	$\dfrac{18}{60}$

28. The following is a hypothetical probability distribution of the number of dreams recalled (per night) among students during a final exam week. How many dreams should we expect a student to recall during final exam week? *Hint:* Compute the expected value of this probability distribution.

Number of Dreams Recalled	0	1	2	3	4
$p(x)$	0.22	0.11	0.24	0.31	0.12

29. Suppose a researcher is interested in the number of good versus bad dreams that students have during final exam week. The researcher states that $p = .62$ that a student will have a bad dream during final exam week.

(a) What type of probability distribution is appropriate for these data?

(b) Assuming complementary outcomes, what is the probability (q) that a student will have a good dream?

(c) If a professor has 50 students in his class, then how many students should he expect to have bad dreams during final exam week?

30. A researcher is interested in whether allowing employees to wear casual clothing will increase the likelihood that employees come to work on time. She observes that the probability of an employee coming to work on time on "casual days" is $p = .92$, whereas the probability of an employee coming to work on time on any other day is $p = .84$. If the business has 200 employees, (a) how many employees should we expect to come to work on time on casual days? (b) How many should we expect to come to work on time on any other day?

Problems in Research

31. **Probability of first marriage among women.** In 2002, the Centers for Disease Control and Prevention (CDC) reported that 8%

of women married for the first time by their 18th birthday, 25% married by their 20th birthday, and 76% married by their 30th birthday. Based on these data, what is the probability that in a family with two daughters, the first *and* second daughter will be married by

(a) 18 years of age?

(b) 20 years of age?

(c) 30 years of age?

32. **Genetic susceptibility and schizophrenia.** Gottesman and Bertelsen (1989) showed that genetically identical twins, where one expresses schizophrenia (a disorder of thought) and the other shows no evidence of the disorder, have the same likelihood of passing the disease to their offspring. The probability of either twin passing the disease to their offspring was $p = .17$. Based on this result, and assuming independent outcomes, what is the probability that a schizophrenic twin with three children has all offspring with schizophrenia?

33. **Penalty kicks to the left in professional soccer.** Bar-eli, Azar, Ritov, Keidar-Levin, and Schein (2007) analyzed 286 penalty kicks among professional soccer players. They recorded the direction that the ball was kicked (left, center, right) and the direction that the goalie went to block the kick (left, center, right). The table shows the results of their study.

		Jump direction			
		Left	Center	Right	Total
	Left	54	1	37	92
Kick direction	Center	41	10	31	82
	Right	46	7	59	112
	Total	141	18	127	286

Based on this table, (a) what is the probability that the ball was kicked to the left? (b) What is the probability that the ball was kicked left and the goalie jumped left? (c) What is the probability that the goalie jumped to the left, given that the ball was kicked to the left? *Note:* This is now a conditional probability statement.

34. **Penalty kicks to the right in professional soccer.** Based on the same table given in Question 31, (a) what is the probability that the ball was kicked to the right? (b) What is the probability that the ball was kicked right and the goalie jumped right? (c) What is the probability that the goalie jumped to the right, given that the ball was kicked to the right? *Note:* This is now a conditional probability statement.

35. **Presenting bets as a probability or relative frequency.** Tunney (2006) was interested in various probability relationships. Specifically, he was interested in how the presentation of probabilities (either as a probability or as a frequency) influenced participant choices. The following is an example of how he presented bets for frequency and probability. Both statements say the same thing for each bet but in different ways.

Example bets for frequency and probability formats

	Format	
	Probability	**Frequency**
P-bet	$p = .95$ to win £3.50, and $p = .05$ to lose £1.00	95 tickets in every 100 will win you £3.50, the other 5 tickets will lose you £1.00
£-bet	$p = .40$ to win £11.00, and $p = .60$ to lose £2.50	40 tickets in every 100 will win you £11.00, the other 60 tickets will lose you £2.50

Based on this table, (a) what is the mathematical expectation for winning the P-bet? (b) What is the mathematical expectation for winning the £-bet? (c) Based on the mathematical expectation of making P-bets and £-bets, if you had to make one bet, which one should you make? Explain.

NOTE: Answers for even numbers are in Appendix C.

Probability and Normal Distributions

LEARNING OBJECTIVES

After reading this chapter, you should be able to:

1. Identify eight characteristics of the normal distribution.

2. Define the standard normal distribution and the standard normal transformation.

3. Locate proportions of area under any normal curve above the mean, below the mean, and between two scores.

4. Locate scores in a normal distribution with a given probability.

5. Compute a binomial probability using the normal approximation.

6. Convert raw scores to standard *z*-scores using SPSS.

CHAPTER 6

6.1 THE NORMAL DISTRIBUTION IN BEHAVIORAL SCIENCE

When researchers study behavior, they find that in many physical, behavioral, and social measurement studies, the data are normally distributed. Many behaviors are distributed about normally, with very few people at the extremes of behavior relative to the general population. For example, most people express some tendency toward aggression, a few express almost no aggression, and a few express an abnormally high level of aggression. Most people have some level of faith, a few are atheists, and a few are extremists in their faith.

In Chapter 5, we introduced probability as the frequency of times an outcome is likely to occur, divided by the total number of possible outcomes. Because most behavior is approximately normally distributed, we can use the empirical rule (introduced in Chapter 4) to determine the probability of obtaining a particular outcome in a research study. We know, for example, that scores closer to the mean are more probable or likely than scores further from the mean. In this chapter, we extend the concepts of probability to cover situations where we locate probabilities for scores in a **normal distribution.** In Chapter 7, we will extend the concepts of normal distributions covered in this chapter to introduce *sampling distributions*.

NOTE: The behavioral data that researchers measure often tend to approximate a normal distribution.

DEFINITION

The **normal distribution,** also called the **symmetrical**, **Gaussian**, or **bell-shaped distribution**, is a theoretical distribution with data that are symmetrically distributed around the mean, the median, and the mode.

6.2 CHARACTERISTICS OF THE NORMAL DISTRIBUTION

In 1733, Abraham de Moivre introduced the normal distribution, first discussed in Chapter 3, as a mathematical approximation to the binomial distribution, although de Moivre's 1733 work was not widely recognized until the accomplished statistician Karl Pearson rediscovered it in 1924. The shape of the curve in a normal distribution can drop suddenly at the tails, or the tails can be stretched out. Figure 6.1 shows two examples of normal distributions. Notice that normal distributions can vary in appearance. So what exactly makes a set of data normally distributed? In this section, we introduce eight characteristics that make a set of data normally distributed:

1. **The normal distribution is mathematically defined.** The shape of a normal distribution is specified by an equation relating each score (distributed along the *x*-axis) with each frequency (distributed along the *y*-axis):

$$Y = \left(\frac{1}{\sigma\sqrt{2\pi}} e^{-\frac{1}{2}\left(\frac{x-\mu}{\sigma}\right)^2} \right).$$

It is not necessary to memorize this formula. It is important to understand that rarely do behavioral data fall exactly within the limits of this formula. When we say

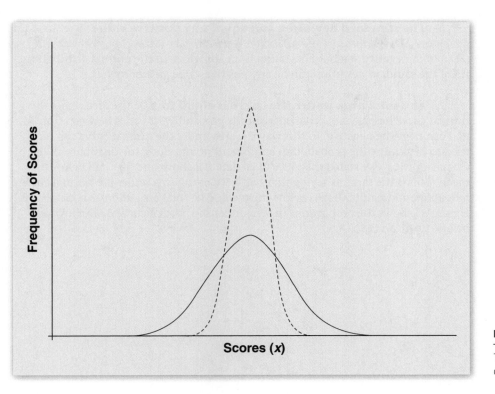

FIGURE 6.1

Two examples of the many shapes of a normal distribution.

that data are normally distributed, we mean that the data approximate a normal distribution. The normal distribution is so exact that it is simply impractical to think that behavior can fit exactly within the limits defined by this formula.

2. **The normal distribution is theoretical.** This characteristic follows from the first in that it emphasizes that data can be normally distributed in theory—although rarely do we observe behaviors that are exactly normally distributed. Instead, behavioral data typically approximate a normal distribution. As you will see in this chapter, we can still use the normal distribution to describe behavior so long as the behaviors being described are approximately normally distributed.

NOTE: Most behavioral data approximate a normal distribution. Rarely are behavioral data exactly normally distributed.

3. **The mean, median, and mode are all located at the 50th percentile.** In a normal distribution, the mean, the median, and the mode are the same value at the center of the distribution. So half the data (50%) in a normal distribution fall above the mean, the median, and the mode, and half the data (50%) fall below each measure.

4. **The normal distribution is symmetrical.** The normal distribution is symmetrical in that the distribution of data above the mean is the same as the distribution of data below the mean. If you fold a normal curve in half, both sides of the curve would exactly overlap.

NOTE: In a normal distribution, 50% of all data fall above the mean, the median, and the mode, and 50% fall below these measures.

5. **The mean can equal any value.** The normal distribution can be defined by its mean and standard deviation. The mean of a normal distribution can equal any number from positive infinity ($+\infty$) to negative infinity ($-\infty$):

$$-\infty \leq M \leq +\infty$$

6. **The standard deviation can equal any positive value.** The standard deviation (*SD*) is a measure of variability. Data can vary (*SD* > 0) or not vary (*SD* = 0). A negative standard deviation is meaningless. In the normal distribution, then, the standard deviation can be any positive value greater than 0.

NOTE: In a normal distribution, the mean can equal any value between +∞ and −∞; the standard deviation can equal any positive value greater than 0.

7. **The total area under the curve is equal to 1.0.** The area under the normal curve has the same characteristics as probability: It varies between 0 and 1 and can never be negative. In this way the area under the normal curve can be used to determine the probabilities at different points along the distribution. In Characteristic 3, we stated that 50% of all data fall above and 50% fall below the mean. This is the same as saying that half (.50) of the area under the normal curve falls above and half (.50) falls below the mean. The total area, then, is equal to 1.0. Figure 6.2 shows the proportions of area under the normal curve 3 *SD* above and below the mean (±3 *SD*).

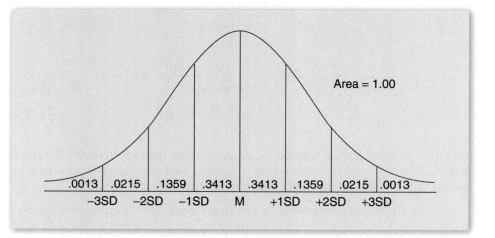

FIGURE 6.2

The proportion of area within each standard deviation of the mean. The total area is equal to 1.00.

NOTE: Proportions of area under a normal curve are used to determine the probabilities for normally distributed data.

NOTE: The tails of a normal distribution never touch the x-axis, so it is possible to observe outliers in a normally distributed data set.

8. **The tails of a normal distribution are asymptotic.** In a normal distribution, the tails are asymptotic, meaning that the tails of the distribution are always approaching the *x*-axis but never touch it. That is, as you travel away from the mean along the curve, the tails in a normal distribution always approach the *x*-axis but never touch it. Because the tails of the normal distribution go out to infinity, this characteristic allows for the possibility of outliers (or scores far from the mean) in a data set.

6.3 RESEARCH IN FOCUS: THE STATISTICAL NORM

Researchers often use the word *normal* to describe behavior in a study but with little qualification for what exactly constitutes normal behavior. Researchers studying the links between obesity and sleep duration have stated that short sleepers are at a higher risk of obesity compared to normal sleepers (see Horne, 2008; Lumeng et al., 2007), and researchers studying middle school–aged children claim to measure normal changes that occur during the school year (see Evans, Langberg, Raggi,

Allen, & Buvinger, 2005). What do researchers mean when they say that sleeping or change is normal?

Statistically speaking, normal behavior is defined by the statistical norm, which is data that fall within about 2 *SD* of the mean in a normal distribution. Figure 6.3 shows that about 95% of all data fall within 2 *SD* of the mean in a normal distribution—these data are normal only inasmuch as they fall close to the mean. Data that are more than 2 *SD* from the mean are characteristic of less than 5% of data in that distribution—these data are not normal only inasmuch as they fall far from the mean.

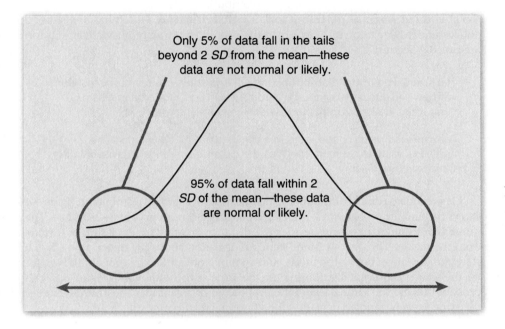

Only 5% of data fall in the tails beyond 2 *SD* from the mean—these data are not normal or likely.

95% of data fall within 2 *SD* of the mean—these data are normal or likely.

FIGURE 6.3

The statistical norm. Behavioral data that fall within 2 *SD* of the mean are regarded as normal because these data fall near the mean. Behavioral data that fall outside of 2 *SD* from the mean are regarded as abnormal because these data fall far from the mean in a normal distribution.

 **LEARNING CHECK 1**

1. All of the following characteristics are true about a normal distribution, except:
   a. The mean can be any positive or negative number.
   b. The variance can be any positive number.
   c. The shape of the normal distribution is symmetrical.
   d. The tails of a normal distribution touch the *x*-axis at 3 *SD* from the mean.

2. A normal distribution has a mean equal to 5. What is the value of the median and mode in this distribution?

3. The area under a normal curve ranges between 0 and 1 and can never be negative. What type of statistic also has these same characteristics?

4. What term describes behavior that falls within 2 *SD* of the mean in a normal distribution?

Answers: 1. (d); 2. Median = 5, mode = 5; 3. Probability; 4. Statistical norm.

6.4 THE STANDARD NORMAL DISTRIBUTION

In a normal distribution, the mean can be any positive or negative number, and the standard deviation can be any positive number (see Characteristics 5 and 6). For this reason, we could combine values of the mean and standard deviation to construct an infinite number of normal distributions. To find the probability of a score in each and every one of these normal curves would be quite overwhelming.

As an alternative, statisticians found the area under one normal curve, called the "standard," and stated a formula to convert all other normal distributions to this standard. As stated in Characteristic 7, the area under the normal curve is a probability at different points along the distribution. The "standard" curve is called the **standard normal distribution** or **z-distribution,** which has a mean of 0 and a standard deviation of 1. Scores on the *x*-axis in a standard normal distribution are called **z-scores.**

NOTE: The standard normal distribution is one of the infinite normal distributions— it has a mean of 0 and variance of 1.

DEFINITION

The **standard normal distribution**, or **z-distribution**, is a normal distribution with a mean equal to 0 and a standard deviation equal to 1. The standard normal distribution is distributed in *z*-score units along the *x*-axis.

A **z-score** is a value on the *x*-axis of a standard normal distribution. The numerical value of a *z*-score specifies the distance or standard deviation of a value from the mean.

The standard normal distribution is one example of a normal distribution. Figure 6.4 shows the area, or probabilities, under the standard normal curve at each *z*-score. The numerical value of a *z*-score specifies the distance or standard deviation of a value from the mean. (Thus, *z* = +1 is one standard deviation above the mean, *z* = −1 is one standard deviation below the mean, and so on.) Notice that the probabilities given for the standard normal distribution are the same as those shown in Figure 6.2. The probabilities are the same because the proportion of area under the normal curve is the same at each standard deviation for all normal distributions.

FIGURE 6.4

The proportion of total area (total area = 1.0) under the standard normal curve. Again, the standard normal distribution is one example of a normal distribution. Hence, the areas in this figure are identical to those given in Figure 6.2.

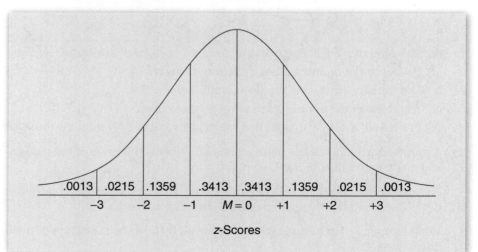

Because we know the probabilities under a standard normal curve, we need to convert all other normal distributions to this standard. By doing so, we can find the probabilities of scores in any normal distribution using probabilities listed for the standard normal distribution. To convert any normal distribution to a standard normal distribution, we compute the **standard normal transformation,** or **z-transformation.** The formula for the z-transformation is

$$z = \frac{x - \mu}{\sigma} \text{ for a population of scores, or}$$

$$z = \frac{x - M}{SD} \text{ for a sample of scores.}$$

The **standard normal transformation** or **z-transformation** is a formula used to convert any normal distribution with any mean and any variance to a standard normal distribution with a mean equal to 0 and a standard deviation equal to 1.

DEFINITION

NOTE: The z-transformation formula converts any normal distribution to the standard normal distribution with a mean equal to 0 and variance equal to 1.

We use the z-transformation to locate where a score in any normal distribution would be in the standard normal distribution. To illustrate, we will compute a z-transformation in Example 6.1 and ask a more conceptual question in Example 6.2.

A researcher measures the farthest distance (in feet) that students moved from a podium during a class presentation. The data were normally distributed with $M = 12$ and $SD = 2$. What is the z-score for $x = 14$ feet?

EXAMPLE 6.1

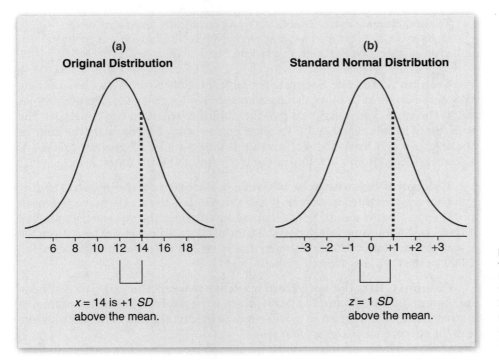

(a)
Original Distribution

6 8 10 12 14 16 18

$x = 14$ is +1 *SD*
above the mean.

(b)
Standard Normal Distribution

−3 −2 −1 0 +1 +2 +3

$z = 1$ *SD*
above the mean.

FIGURE 6.5

Computing the z-transformation for a sample with $M = 12$ and $SD = 2$. A score of $x = 14$ in the original distribution is located at $z = 1.0$ in a standard normal distribution, or 1 *SD* above the mean.

Because $M = 12$ and $SD = 2$, we can find the z-score for $x = 14$ by substituting these values into the z-transformation formula:

$$z = \frac{14 - 12}{2} = 1.00.$$

Figure 6.5A shows the original normal distribution of scores (x) with $M = 12$ and $SD = 2$. Notice that in Figure 6.5b, a score of $x = 14$ in the original distribution is exactly one z-score, or one standard deviation, above the mean in a standard normal distribution.

EXAMPLE 6.2

Suppose we want to determine the z-score for the mean of a normal distribution. The z-transformation for the mean of any normal distribution will always equal what z-score value?

NOTE: The mean in any normal distribution corresponds to a z-score equal to 0.

The mean is always at the center of a normal distribution. If you substitute the mean for x in the z-transformation, the solution will always be 0. In other words, when $M = x$, the solution for the z-transformation is 0.

6.5 THE UNIT NORMAL TABLE: A BRIEF INTRODUCTION

The proportion of area under the standard normal distribution is given in the **unit normal table,** or **z-table,** in Table B.1 in Appendix B. A portion of the table is shown in Table 6.1. The unit normal table has three columns: A, B, and C. This section will familiarize you with each column in the table.

DEFINITION

The **unit normal table** or **z-table** is a type of probability distribution table displaying a list of z-scores and the corresponding probabilities (or proportions of area) associated with each z-score listed.

Column A lists the z-scores. The table lists only positive z-scores, meaning that only z-scores at or above the mean are listed in the table. For negative z-scores below the mean, you must know that the normal distribution is symmetrical. The areas listed in columns B and C for each z-score below the mean are the same as those for z-scores listed above the mean in the unit normal table. In column A, z-scores are listed from $z = 0$ at the mean to $z = 4.00$ above the mean.

Column B lists the area between a z-score and the mean. The first value for the area listed in column B is .0000, which is the area between the mean ($z = 0$) and $z = 0$ (the mean). Notice that the area between the mean and a z-score of 1.00 is .3413—the same value given in Figure 6.4. As a z-score moves away from the mean, the proportion of area between that score and the mean increases closer to .5000, or the total area above the mean.

Column C lists the area from a z-score toward the tail. The first value for the area listed in column C is .5000, which is the total area above the mean. As a z-score increases and therefore moves closer to the tail, the area between that score and the tail decreases closer to .0000.

TABLE 6.1 A portion of the unit normal table in Table B.1 in Appendix B.

(A)	(B)	(C)
z	Area Between Mean and z	Area Beyond z in Tail
0.00	.0000	.5000
0.01	.0040	.4960
0.02	.0080	.4920
0.03	.0120	.4880
0.04	.0160	.4840
0.05	.0199	.4801
0.06	.0239	.4761
0.07	.0279	.4721
0.08	.0319	.4681
0.09	.0359	.4641
0.10	.0398	.4602
0.11	.0438	.4562
0.12	.0478	.4522
0.13	.0517	.4483
0.14	.0557	.4443

Source: Based on J. E. Freund, *Modern Elementary Statistics* (11th edition). Pearson Prentice Hall, 2004.

Keep in mind that the normal distribution is used to determine the probability of a certain outcome in relation to all other outcomes. For example, to describe data that are normally distributed, we ask questions about observing scores greater than . . . , less than . . . , among the top or bottom --% . . . , or the likelihood of scoring between a range of values. In each case, we are interested in the probability of an outcome in relation to all other normally distributed outcomes. Finding the area, and therefore probability, of any value in a normal distribution is introduced in Section 6.6.

NOTE: To estimate probabilities under the normal curve, we determine the probability of a certain outcome in relation to all other outcomes.

LEARNING CHECK 2

1. A set of data is normally distributed with a mean equal to 10 and a standard deviation equal to 3. Compute a *z*-transformation for each of the following scores in this normal distribution:

   (a) −2   (b) 10   (c) 3   (d) 16   (e) 0

2. Identify the column in the unit normal table for each of the following:

   (a) z-scores are listed in which column?

   (b) The area from a z-score toward the tail is listed in which column?

   (c) The area between a z-score and the mean is listed in which column?

3. Complete the following sentence: The normal distribution is used to determine the probability of a certain outcome _____ to all other outcomes.

Answers: 1. (a) $z = \dfrac{-2-10}{3} = -4.00$, (b) $z = \dfrac{10-10}{3} = 0$, (c) $z = \dfrac{3-10}{3} = -2.33$, (d) $z = \dfrac{16-10}{3} = 2.00$, (e) $z = \dfrac{0-10}{3} = -3.33$. 2. (a) Column A, (b) column C, (c) column B; 3. In relation or relative.

6.6 LOCATING PROPORTIONS

The area at each z-score is given as a proportion in the unit normal table. Hence, we can use the unit normal table to locate the proportion or probability of a score in a normal distribution. To locate the proportion, and therefore the probability, of scores in any normal distribution, we follow two steps:

Step 1: Transform a raw score (x) into a z-score.

Step 2: Locate the corresponding proportion for the z-score in the unit normal table.

In Examples 6.3 and 6.4, we will follow these steps to locate the proportion associated with scores above the mean. In Examples 6.5 and 6.6, we will follow these steps to locate the proportion associated with scores below the mean. In Example 6.7, we will follow these steps to locate the proportion between two scores. In each example, we will show the normal curve and shade the region under the curve that we are locating.

LOCATING PROPORTIONS ABOVE THE MEAN

EXAMPLE 6.3

A sample of scores is normally distributed with $M = 8$ and $SD = 2$. What is the probability of obtaining a score greater than 12?

Figure 6.6 shows the normal curve for this distribution. The shaded region in Figure 6.6 represents the proportion, or probability, of obtaining a score greater than 12. We apply the two steps to find the proportion associated with this shaded region.

Step 1: To transform a raw score (x) to a z-score, we compute a z-transformation. In this example, $x = 12$. The z-transformation is

$$z = \frac{12-8}{2} = \frac{4}{2} = 2.00.$$

A score equal to 12 in the distribution illustrated in Figure 6.6 is located 2.00 z-scores (or 2 SD) above the mean in a standard normal distribution.

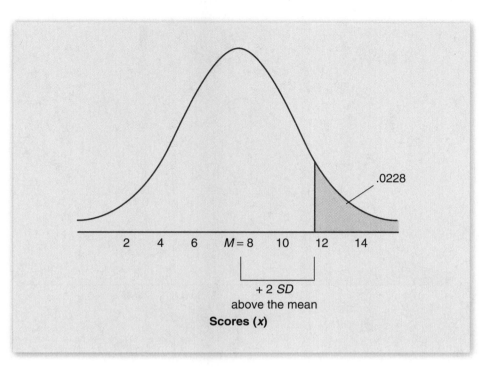

.0228

2   4   6   *M* = 8   10   12   14

+ 2 *SD*
above the mean
Scores (*x*)

FIGURE 6.6

A normal distribution with *M* = 8
and *SD* = 2. The shaded region
shows scores that are at or above
12 in this distribution.

Step 2: In this example, we are looking for the proportion from $z = +2.00$ toward the tail. To locate the proportion, look in column A in Table B1 in Appendix B for a z-score equal to 2.00. The proportion toward the tail is listed in column C. The proportion greater than 12 in the original distribution is

$$p = .0228.$$

The probability is $p = .0228$ of obtaining a score greater than 12.

NOTE: For normally distributed data, we use the unit normal table to find the probability of obtaining an outcome in relation to all other outcomes.

A local business is concerned that employees are staying on their lunch breaks longer than they are allowed. To test this, a researcher records the time (in minutes) that a sample of employees stayed on their lunch break beyond the time allotted. She reports that employees took a mean time of 5.2 ± 1.6 ($M \pm SD$) minutes beyond the time allotted. Assuming these data are normally distributed, what is the probability that employees spent less than 6 minutes beyond the time allotted at lunch?

EXAMPLE 6.4

Figure 6.7 shows the distribution of times. The shaded regions in Figure 6.7 represent the proportion, or probability, of obtaining a time less than 6 minutes. We apply the two steps to find the proportion associated with the shaded region.

Step 1: To transform a raw score (*x*) to a z-score, we compute a z-transformation. In this example, $x = 6$. The z-transformation is

$$z = \frac{6 - 5.2}{1.6} = \frac{0.8}{1.6} = 0.50.$$

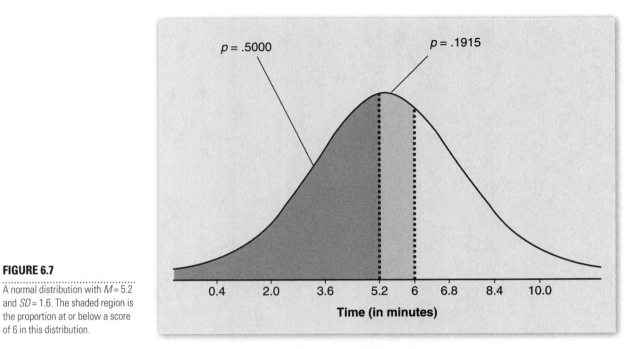

FIGURE 6.7

A normal distribution with $M = 5.2$ and $SD = 1.6$. The shaded region is the proportion at or below a score of 6 in this distribution.

In the distribution shown in Figure 6.7, a time equal to 6 minutes is located 0.50 z-scores, or half a standard deviation, above the mean in a standard normal distribution.

Step 2: In this example, we are looking for the proportion from $z = .50$ to the mean, and then we will add .5000, which is the total proportion of area below the mean. To locate the proportion, we look in column A in Table B.1 in Appendix B for a z-score equal to 0.50. The proportion from $z = .50$ to the mean given in column B is $p = .1915$. Add .1915 to the proportion below the mean ($p = .5000$) to find the total proportion:

NOTE: The total area is .5000 above the mean and .5000 below the mean in a normal distribution.

$$p = .1915 + .5000 = .6915.$$

The probability is $p = .6915$ that employees spent less than 6 minutes beyond the time allotted at lunch.

LOCATING PROPORTIONS BELOW THE MEAN

EXAMPLE 6.5

Kausch, Loreen, and Douglas (2006) reported that participants with a history of physical trauma had high scores on an impulsivity test. The participants scored 20.9 ± 8.1 ($M \pm SD$) on the Barratt cognitive impulsivity test, where higher scores indicate greater impulsivity. Assuming these data are normally distributed, what is the probability that participants scored less than 15 on this test?

Figure 6.8 is a normal curve showing this distribution of scores. The shaded region in Figure 6.8 is the proportion, or probability, of scores less than 15 on this test. We follow the two steps to find the proportion associated with the shaded region.

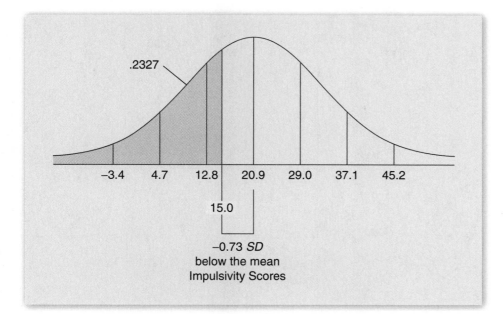

FIGURE 6.8

A normal distribution with
$M = 20.9$ and $SD = 8.1$. The shaded
region is the proportion at or
below a score of 15 in this
distribution.

Step 1: To transform a raw score (x) to a z-score, we compute a z-transformation. In this example, $x = 15$. The z-transformation is

$$z = \frac{15 - 20.9}{8.1} = -\frac{5.9}{8.1} = -0.73.$$

In the distribution shown in Figure 6.8, a score equal to 15 is located 0.73 z-scores, or standard deviations, below the mean in a standard normal distribution. The negative sign indicates that the z-score is located below the mean.

Step 2: In this example, we are looking for the proportion toward the lower tail. To locate the proportion, we look in column A in Table B.1 in Appendix B. We find $z = 0.73$ in the table. Again, the normal distribution is symmetrical. A proportion given for a positive z-score will be the same for a corresponding negative z-score. The proportion for a z-score of 0.73 toward the lower tail is listed in column C. The proportion is

$$p = .2327.$$

Hence, the probability is $p = .2327$ that a participant scored less than 15 on this test.

NOTE: In the standard normal distribution, z-scores above the mean are positive; z-scores below the mean are negative.

In the study by Kausch and colleagues (2006), participants with a history of physical trauma scored high on the Barratt impulsivity test, with scores equal to 20.9 ± 8.1 ($M \pm SD$). Assuming these data are normally distributed, what is the probability that participants scored greater than 10 on this impulsivity test?

EXAMPLE 6.6

The shaded regions in Figure 6.9 reflect the proportion, or probability, of a score greater than 10 on this test. We follow the two steps to find the proportion associated with the shaded regions.

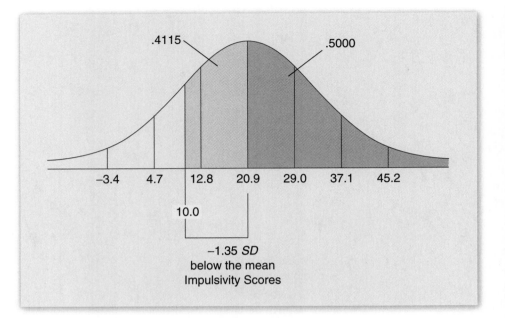

FIGURE 6.9

A normal distribution with $M = 20.9$ and $SD = 8.1$. The shaded region is the proportion at or above a score of 10 in this distribution.

Step 1: To transform a raw score (x) to a z-score, we compute a z-transformation. In this example, $x = 10$. The z-transformation is

$$z = \frac{10 - 20.9}{8.1} = -\frac{10.9}{8.1} = -1.35.$$

In the distribution shown in Figure 6.9, a score equal to 10 is located 1.35 z-scores, or standard deviations, below the mean in a standard normal distribution.

Step 2: In this example, we are looking for the proportion from $z = -1.35$ to the mean, and then we will add .5000, which is the total proportion of area above the mean. To locate the proportion, search in column A in Table B.1 in Appendix B for a z-score equal to 1.35. (Remember that a proportion given for a positive z-score is the same for a corresponding negative z-score.) The proportion given in column B is $p = .4115$. Add .4115 to the proportion of area above the mean ($p = .5000$) to find the proportion:

$$p = .4115 + .5000 = .9115.$$

NOTE: Because the normal distribution is symmetrical, probabilities associated with positive z-scores are the same for corresponding negative z-scores.

The probability is $p = .9115$ that a participant scored greater than 10 on this test.

LOCATING PROPORTIONS BETWEEN TWO VALUES

EXAMPLE 6.7

Spinks and colleagues (2007) had a group of participants complete a Full Scale IQ (FSIQ) test for intelligence. Mean scores on this test were 107.3 ± 13.1 ($M \pm SD$). Assuming these data are normally distributed, what is the probability that participants in this study had an FSIQ score between 94.2 and 120.4?

Figure 6.10 is a normal curve showing this distribution. The shaded regions in Figure 6.10 are the proportions, or probability, associated with scores between 94.2 and 120.4 on this test. To find the proportion in the shaded regions, we apply the two steps for each score, x:

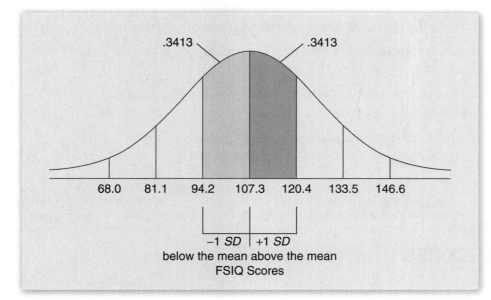

FIGURE 6.10.

A normal distribution with $M = 107.3$ and $SD = 13.1$. The shaded region is between $x = 94.2$ and $x = 120.4$ in this distribution.

Step 1 for $x = 94.2$: To transform a raw score (x) to a z-score, we compute a z-transformation. In this example, $x = 94.2$. The z-transformation is

$$z = \frac{94.2 - 107.3}{13.1} = -\frac{13.1}{13.1} = -1.00.$$

In the distribution shown in Figure 6.10, a score equal to 94.2 is located 1.00 z-score, or one standard deviation, below the mean in a standard normal distribution.

Step 2 for $x = 94.2$: Find the z-score 1.00 in column A of Table B.1 in Appendix B, and then look in column B for the proportion between −1.00 and the mean: $p = .3413$.

To find the total proportion between the two scores, we will add .3413 to the proportion associated with the second score $(x = 120.4)$.

Step 1 for $x = 120.4$: Compute the z-transformation for $x = 120.4$:

$$z = \frac{120.4 - 107.3}{13.1} = \frac{13.1}{13.1} = 1.00.$$

A score equal to 120.4 in the distribution illustrated in Figure 6.10 is located 1.00 z-score above the mean in a standard normal distribution.

Step 2 for $x = 120.4$: The proportion between the mean and a z-score of 1.00 is the same as that for −1.00: $p = .3413$. The total proportion between 94.2 and 120.4 is the sum of the proportion for each score:

$$p = .3413 + .3413 = .6826.$$

The probability is $p = .6826$ that a participant scored between 94.2 and 120.4 on the FSIQ test.

LEARNING CHECK 3

1. State the two steps for locating proportions under the normal curve.

2. Find the probability of a score at or above the following *z*-scores:
   (a) 1.23   (b) –2.50   (c) 0.50

3. Find the probability of a score at or below the following *z*-scores:
   (a) 0.08   (b) –1.00   (c) 2.90

4. Find the probability of a score between the following *z*-scores:
   (a) The mean and 1.40   (b) –1.00 and 1.00   (c) .60 and 1.20

Answers: 1. Step 1: transform a raw score (*x*) into a *z*-score, and Step 2: locate the corresponding probability for that *z*-score in the unit normal table; 2. (a) *p* = .1093, (b) *p* = .9938, (c) *p* = .3085; 3. (a) *p* = .5319, (b) *p* = .1587, (c) *p* = .9981; 4. (a) *p* = .4192, (b) *p* = .6826, (c) *p* = .1592.

6.7 LOCATING SCORES

In a normal distribution, we can also find the scores that fall within a given proportion, or percentile, using the unit normal table. Finding scores in a given percentile can be useful in certain situations, such as when instructors grade "on a curve" with, say, the top 10% earning As. In this example, the unit normal table can be used to determine which scores will receive an A, that is, which scores fall in the top 10%. To find scores in a given proportion, we follow two steps:

NOTE: The unit normal table can be used to locate scores that fall within a given proportion or percentile.

Step 1: Locate a *z*-score associated with a given proportion in the unit normal table.

Step 2: Transform the *z*-score into a raw score (*x*).

In Examples 6.8 and 6.9, we will apply these steps to locate scores that fall within a given proportion in a normal distribution. In each example, we will show the normal distribution and shade the proportion under the curve that we are given.

EXAMPLE 6.8

In the study by Spinks and colleagues (2007), given in Example 6.7, mean scores on the Full Scale IQ test were 107.3 ± 13.1 ($M \pm SD$). Assuming these data are normally distributed, what is the minimum score needed to be in the top 10% of this distribution of intelligence scores on the FSIQ test?

Figure 6.11 shows this distribution of scores. The shaded region in Figure 6.11 is the top 10% ($p = .1000$) of scores—we need to find the cutoff or lowest score, *x*, in this shaded region. We will apply the two steps to locate the cutoff score for the top 10% of data:

Step 1: The top 10% of scores is the same as $p = .1000$ toward the tail. To locate the *z*-score associated with this proportion, we look for $p = .1000$ in column C of the unit normal table in Table B.1 in Appendix B. The *z*-score is $z = 1.28$. A *z*-score equal to 1.28 is the cutoff for the top 10% of data.

Step 2: We need to determine which score, *x*, in the distribution shown in Figure 6.11 corresponds to a *z*-score equal to 1.28. Because $z = 1.28$, we can substitute this value into the *z*-transformation formula:

$$1.28 = \frac{x - 107.3}{13.1}.$$

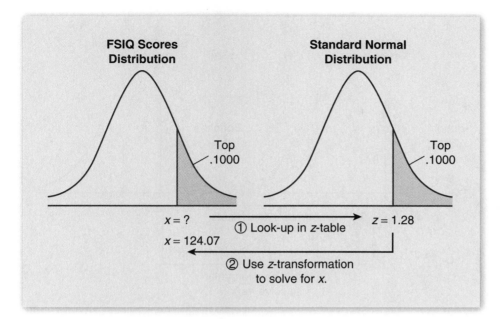

FIGURE 6.11

A Full Scale IQ score greater than 124.07 represents the top 10% of intelligence scores in this distribution. Steps 1 and 2 show the method used to locate scores that fall within a given area of a normal curve.

First, multiply both sides of the equation times 13.1 to eliminate the fraction:

$$(13.1)1.28 = \left(\frac{x - 107.3}{13.1} \right)(13.1)$$

$$16.77 = x - 107.3.$$

To find the solution for x, add 107.3 to each side of the equation:

$$124.07 = x.$$

A score of 124.07 on the FSIQ test is the cutoff for the lowest score in the top 10% of scores in this distribution.

Let's use the same data from Example 6.7, where participants completed a Full Scale IQ (FSIQ) test for intelligence with mean scores equal to 107.3 ± 13.1 ($M \pm SD$). Suppose participants scoring in the bottom 25th percentile on this test were disqualified from participating in the study. What was the cutoff score that disqualified a participant from participating in this study?

EXAMPLE 6.9

Figure 6.12 shows this distribution. The shaded region in Figure 6.12 is the bottom 25% ($p = .2500$). We need to find the cutoff score, x, for this shaded region. We follow the two steps to locate the cutoff score that falls in the bottom 25%.

Step 1: The bottom 25% of scores is $p = .2500$ toward the tail. To locate the z-score associated with this proportion, we look for $p = .2500$ in column C of the unit normal table in Table B.1 in Appendix B. Because $p = .2500$ falls between a z-score of 0.67 and 0.68 in the table, we compute the average of the two z-scores: $z = 0.675$. Keep in mind that this z-score is actually negative because it is located below the mean. A z-score equal to –0.675 is the cutoff for the bottom 25% of data in this distribution.

NOTE: The unit normal table can be used to locate scores in a given proportion for data that are normally distributed.

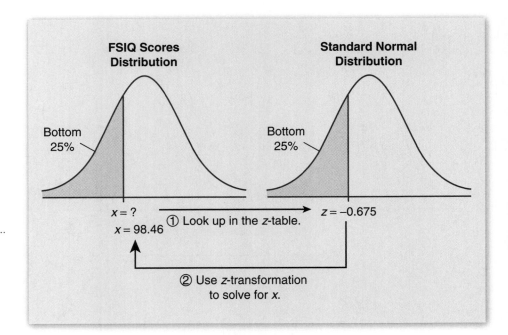

FIGURE 6.12

······································

A Full Scale IQ score less than 98.46 represents the bottom 25% of intelligence scores in this distribution. Steps 1 and 2 show the method used to locate scores that fall within a given area of a normal curve.

Step 2: We need to determine which score, x, in the distribution shown in Figure 6.12 corresponds to a z-score equal to -0.675. Because $z = -0.675$, we substitute this value into the z-transformation formula:

$$-0.675 = \frac{x - 107.3}{13.1}.$$

First, multiply both sides of the equation times 13.1 to eliminate the fraction:

$$(13.1)(-0.675) = \left(\frac{x - 107.3}{13.1}\right)(13.1)$$

$$-8.84 = x - 107.3.$$

To find the solution for x, add 107.3 to each side of the equation.

NOTE: The unit normal table allows us to locate raw scores, x, and determine probabilities, p, for data that are normally distributed.

$$98.46 = x.$$

A score equal to 98.46 on the FSIQ test is the cutoff for the bottom 25% of scores in this distribution.

LEARNING CHECK 4

1. State the two steps for locating scores in a given proportion of data.

2. What are the z-scores associated with the following probabilities toward the tail in a normal distribution?

   (a) .4013   (b) .3050   (c) .0250   (d) .0505

3. State the *z*-score that most closely approximates the following probabilities:

   (a) Top 10% of scores

   (b) Bottom 10% of scores

   (c) Top 50% of scores

Answers: 1. Step 1: locate the z-score associated with a given proportion in the unit normal table, and Step 2: transform the z-score into a raw score (x); 2. (a) z = 0.25, (b) z = 0.51, (c) z = 1.96, (d) z = 1.64; 3. (a) z ≈ 1.28, (b) z ≈ −1.28, (c) z = 0.

SPSS IN FOCUS: CONVERTING RAW SCORES TO STANDARD *Z*-SCORES   6.8

SPSS can be used to compute a *z*-transformation for a given data set. To demonstrate how SPSS does this, suppose you observe a SAT remedial tutoring course with 16 students who plan to retake the standardized exam. Table 6.2 gives the first-attempt SAT scores for the 16 students. We will use SPSS to convert these data into *z*-scores.

TABLE 6.2   The first-attempt SAT scores for 16 students.

500	950	780	800
750	880	800	680
600	990	800	550
900	560	450	600

1. Click on the **variable view** tab and enter *SAT* in the **name column.** We will enter whole numbers, so reduce the value to 0 in the **decimals column.**

2. In the **data view** tab, enter the 16 values in the column labeled *SAT.*

   Go to the **menu bar** and click **Analyze,** then **Descriptive Statistics** and **Descriptives,** to display a dialog box.

3. In the **dialog box,** select *SAT* and click the arrow to move it into the **Variable(s)** box. Select the "Save standardized values as variables" box, shown in the left side of Figure 6.13.

4. Select **Paste** and then **Run.**

SPSS will create two outputs. First, it will create the output table shown in Table 6.3. The output table contains the sample size, the minimum and maximum score, the mean, and the standard deviation. Second, SPSS creates an additional column of *z*-scores in the data view tab, shown in the right side of Figure 6.13. The added column is labeled with Z and then your variable name. In this example, we named the variable SAT, so the column is labeled ZSAT. Each *z*-score in the ZSAT column is the number of standard deviations that the corresponding score in the original SAT column is from the mean.

TABLE 6.3 SPSS output table.

Descriptive Statistics

	N	Minimum	Maximum	Mean	Std. Deviation
SAT	16	450	990	724.38	166.011
Valid N (listwise)	16				

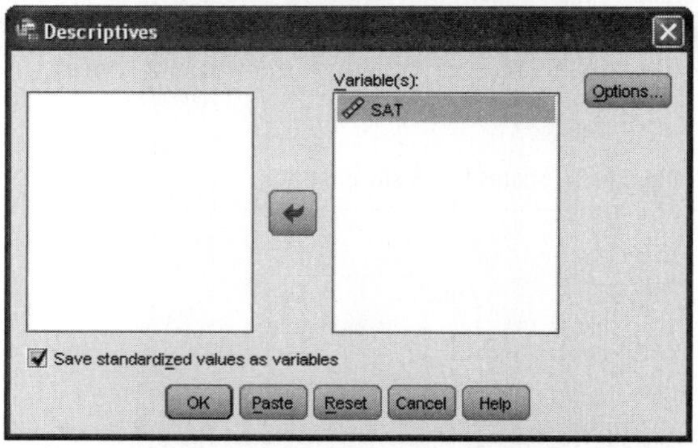

FIGURE 6.13

The dialog box for Step 3 (left side) and the data view with the ZSAT column listing z-scores for each of the 16 SAT scores (right side).

SAT	ZSAT
500	-1.35157
750	.15436
600	-.74920
900	1.05791
950	1.35910
880	.93744
990	1.60005
560	-.99015
780	.33507
800	.45554
800	.45554
450	-1.65275
800	.45554
680	-.26730
550	-1.05038
600	-.74920

MAKING SENSE: Standard Deviation and the Normal Distribution

Keep in mind that the standard deviation is very informative, particularly for normally distributed data. To illustrate, consider that when students get an exam grade back, they often compare their grade to others in the class. Suppose, for example, that two professors give an exam, where the top 10% of scores receive an A grade. You take the exam given by Professor 1 and receive an 80 on the exam. In Figure 6.14, (a) shows that grades for that exam were 76 ± 2.0 ($M \pm SD$).

You then ask your friend how he did on Professor 2's exam and find that your friend scored an 86 on the same exam. In Figure 6.14, (b) shows that grades for that exam were 76 ± 8.0 ($M \pm SD$).

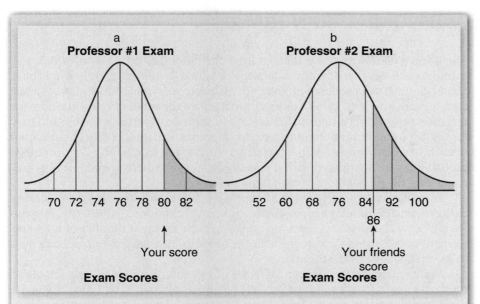

a
Professor #1 Exam

70 72 74 76 78 80 82

↑
Your score

Exam Scores

b
Professor #2 Exam

52 60 68 76 84 92 100

86

↑
Your friends
score

Exam Scores

FIGURE 6.14
....
A distribution of exam scores with your grade on Professor 1's exam (a) and your friend's grade on Professor 2's exam (b). $M = 76$ in both distributions, but the standard deviations are different.

NOTE: *To find the probabilities of scores in a normal distribution, you must know the mean and standard deviation in that distribution.*

Because the mean grade is the same in both distributions, you may conclude that your friend performed better on the exam than you did, but you'd be wrong. To see why, let's follow the steps to locate the cutoff score for earning an A on the exam, which is the top 10% of scores in each distribution.

The lowest score you can get and still receive an A on Professor 1's exam is the following:

Step 1: The top 10% of scores is $p = .1000$ toward the tail located in column C in the unit normal table. The z-score associated with $p = .1000$ is $z = 1.28$.

Step 2: Substitute 1.28 for z in the z-transformation formula and solve for x:

$$1.28 = \frac{x - 76}{2}.$$

$x - 76 = 2.56$ (multiply both sides times 2).
$x = 78.56$ (solve for x).

Your score on Professor 1's exam was an 80. Your score is in the top 10%; you earned an A on the exam.

The lowest score you can get and still receive an A on Professor 2's exam is the following:

Step 1: We already located this z-score. The z-score associated with the top 10% is $z = 1.28$.

Step 2: Substitute 1.28 for z in the z-transformation equation and solve for x:

$$1.28 = \frac{x - 76}{8}.$$

$x - 76 = 10.24$ (multiply both sides times 8).
$x = 86.24$ (solve for x).

Your friend's score on Professor 2's exam was an 86. This score is just outside the top 10%; your friend did not earn an A on the exam. Therefore, your 80 is an A, and your friend's 86 is not, even though the mean was the same in both classes. The mean tells you only the average outcome—the standard deviation tells you the distribution of all other outcomes. Your score was lower than your friend's score, but you outperformed a larger percentage of your classmates than your friend did. The standard deviation is important because it gives you information about how your score compares relative to all other scores.

6.9 GOING FROM BINOMIAL TO NORMAL

NOTE: A binomial probability distribution is distributed with $\mu = np$ and $\sigma = \sqrt{npq}$.

The normal distribution was derived from the binomial distribution, which was introduced in Chapter 5. A binomial variable is one that takes on only two values. Some binomial values occur naturally; for instance, sex is male and female, or a fair coin is heads and tails. Other binomial variables are the result of categorization; for instance, height can be categorized as tall and short or self-esteem as high and low. The distribution of random outcomes for binomial variables is called a binomial probability distribution, which was also introduced in Chapter 5. Binominal probabilities are distributed with $\mu = np$ and $\sigma = \sqrt{npq}$, where n = sample size, and p and q are the probabilities of each binomial outcome.

From the work of Abraham de Moivre in the 1700s, we know that the outcomes for a binomial distribution approximate a normal distribution. To illustrate, suppose we select two participants from a population with an equal number of men and women. Let's construct a histogram for the binomial distribution for selecting men to see the shape of the distribution.

In this example, the random variable, *x*, is the number of men. In a sample of two participants, there are three possible outcomes for *x:* 0, 1, or 2 men. Table 6.4 displays the sample space (Table a) and the corresponding relative frequency distribution (Table b) for selecting men in this population. The binomial data given in Table 6.4 are converted to a histogram in Figure 6.15. Notice that the shape of this binomial probability distribution appears approximately normal in shape.

TABLE 6.4 The sample space (a) and relative frequency distribution (b) for selecting men from a population with an equal number of men and women.

x	Description	
0	Woman	Woman
1	Man	Woman
	Woman	Man
2	Man	Man

(a)

x	Relative Frequency
0	0.25
1	0.50
2	0.25

(b)

If we increase the sample size, say, to four participants, the binomial probability distribution more clearly approximates a normal distribution. The random variable, *x*, in this example is still the number of men. In a sample of four participants, there are five possible outcomes for *x:* 0, 1, 2, 3, or 4 men could be selected. Table 6.5 displays the relative frequency distribution for selecting men in this example. The binomial data given in Table 6.5 are converted to a histogram in Figure 6.16. Notice that the shape of this binomial probability distribution is approximately normal.

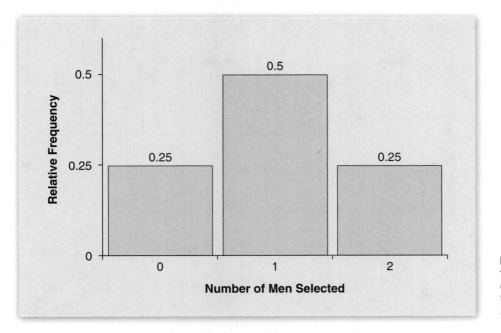

FIGURE 6.15

A histogram for the relative frequency of selecting men when $n = 2$.

TABLE 6.5 The relative frequency distribution for selecting men when $n = 4$.

x	f(x)
0	0.06
1	0.25
2	0.38
3	0.25
4	0.06

NOTE: *The binomial distribution approximates a normal distribution. The larger n is, the more closely it approximates a normal distribution.*

For a binomial distribution, so long as $n \geq 2$, the binomial distribution will approximate a normal distribution. The larger the sample size (n), the more closely a binomial distribution will approximate a normal distribution. When $n = \infty$, a binomial distribution is, in theory, a perfect normal distribution.

All binomial data sets that researchers work with are less than infinite (∞) of course. So when we work with binomial data, we can use the normal distribution to approximate the probabilities of certain outcomes. Using the same notation introduced in Chapter 5, when both np and nq are greater than 10, the normal distribution can be used to estimate probabilities for binomial data. To illustrate, we will use this criterion in Example 6.10.

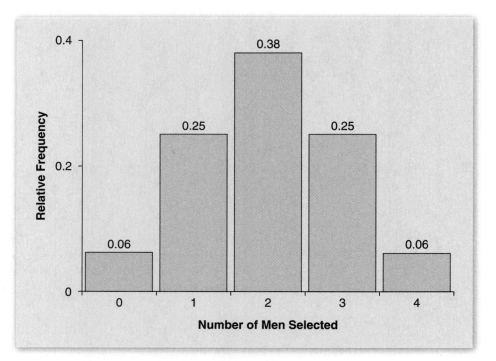

FIGURE 6.16

A histogram for the relative frequency of selecting men when $n = 4$.

EXAMPLE 6.10

Harrell and Karim (2008) conducted a study testing gender differences in alcohol consumption in a sample of 266 women and 140 men. Can these researchers use the normal distribution to estimate binomial probabilities for gender in this sample?

If both np and nq are greater than 10, then they can use the normal distribution to estimate binomial probabilities for gender. If we assign the probability of selecting a woman as p and the probability of selecting a man as q, then the probability of selecting a woman is

$$p = \frac{266}{406} = 0.66.$$

The probability of selecting a man is

$$p = \frac{140}{406} = 0.34.$$

The sample size, n, is 406 adults. We can compute np and nq by substituting n, p, and q into each calculation:

$$np = 406(0.66) = 267.96;$$
$$nq = 406(0.34) = 138.04.$$

Because the solution to both formulas is greater than 10, the normal distribution can be used to estimate binomial probabilities in this sample.

LEARNING CHECK 5

1. A probability distribution for binomial outcomes approximates the shape of what type of distribution?

2. True or false: The larger is the sample size, the more closely a binomial probability distribution will approximate a normal distribution.

3. To use the normal approximation for the binomial distribution, *np* and *nq* must be equal to at least what value?

Answers: 1. A normal distribution; 2. True; 3. Both must equal at least 10.

THE NORMAL APPROXIMATION TO
THE BINOMIAL DISTRIBUTION 6.10

Assuming that *np* and *nq* are greater than 10, we can approximate binomial probabilities using the standard normal distribution. To use the normal approximation to estimate probabilities in a binomial distribution, we use five steps:

Step 1: Check for normality.

Step 2: Compute the mean and standard deviation.

Step 3: Find the real limits.

Step 4: Locate the *z*-score for each real limit.

Step 5: Find the proportion located within the real limits.

We will work through these five steps in Example 6.11 to see how probabilities in a normal distribution can be used to estimate the probability of a binomial outcome.

NOTE: For a binomial distribution where np *and* nq *are greater than 10, the normal distribution can be used to approximate the probability of any given outcome.*

Suppose we want to estimate the probability of selecting 30 men in a sample of 50 participants from a population with an equal number of men and women. Follow the five steps to use the normal approximation to estimate probabilities for this binomial distribution.

EXAMPLE 6.11

We'll verify the answer we get using the five steps by comparing it to the exact binomial probability of selecting 30 men in a sample of 50 participants. That probability is $p = .0419$.

Step 1: Check for normality. We first want to determine whether we can use the normal distribution to estimate probabilities for gender. In this example, $n = 50$, $p = .50$, and $q = .50$, where $n =$ the total number of participants, $p =$ probability of selecting a man, and $q =$ the probability of selecting a woman. We can use the normal approximation because the calculations are greater than 10:

$$np = 50(0.50) = 25;$$
$$nq = 50(0.50) = 25.$$

Because the solution for both formulas is greater than 10, we can use the normal approximation to estimate binomial probabilities. Go to Step 2.

Step 2: Compute the mean and standard deviation. Again, a binominal probability distribution is distributed with $\mu = np$ and $\sigma = \sqrt{npq}$. The mean of this binomial distribution is

$$\mu = np = 50(.50) = 25.$$

The standard deviation of this binomial distribution is

$$\sigma = \sqrt{npq} = \sqrt{50(.50)(.50)} = 3.54.$$

This binomial distribution is approximately normally distributed with a mean of 25 and a standard deviation of 3.54. Go to Step 3.

Step 3: Find the real limits. We need to define the limits around 30, within which we can isolate the proportion of area under the normal curve that gives us the probability of selecting exactly 30 participants. The limits are called **real limits,** and for the discrete value 30, are 30 ± 0.5. Hence, in the normal distribution, the probability of sampling 30 men is the proportion under the normal curve between 29.5 and 30.5, which is shaded in Figure 6.17.

DEFINITION

The **real limits** of the outcome of a binomial variable are the upper and lower values within which the probability of obtaining that outcome is contained. The real limits for a binomial outcome, x, is $x \pm 0.5$.

Step 4: Locate the z-score for each real limit. In this example, the first real limit is $x = 29.5$. The z-transformation is

$$z = \frac{29.5 - 25}{3.54} = \frac{4.5}{3.54} = 1.27.$$

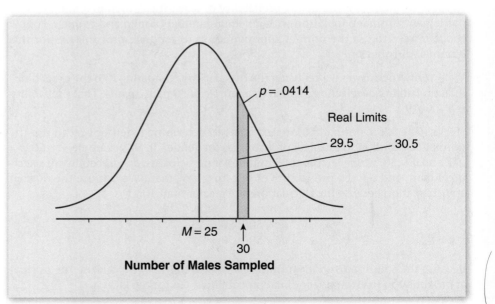

FIGURE 6.17

The normal approximation to the binomial distribution. The real limits for 30 (the discrete value) determine the binomial probability of its occurrence.

In this example, the second real limit is $x = 30.5$. The z-transformation is

$$z = \frac{30.5 - 25}{3.54} = \frac{5.5}{3.54} = 1.55.$$

Step 5: Find the proportion located within the real limits. There are many ways we can do this. We will look up the proportion toward the tail in column C of the unit normal table in Table B.1 in Appendix B.

The proportion toward the tail for $x = 29.5$ is $p = .1020$. The proportion toward the tail for $x = 30.5$ is $p = .0606$.

The difference between these two proportions gives you the proportion, or probability, between $x = 29.5$ and $x = 30.5$. The difference is the overlapping proportion contained within the real limits:

$$p = .1020 - .0606 = .0414.$$

We estimate that the probability of sampling 30 men in a sample of 50 is $p = .0414$. Recall that the exact binomial probability of selecting 30 men is $p = .0419$. The difference between our estimate and the actual probability is only .0005, making the estimate we computed a close approximation of the actual binomial probability.

LEARNING CHECK 6

1. What are the real limits for the following outcomes of a binomial variable?

   (a) 2   (b) −5   (c) 0

2. A binomial probability distribution is distributed with a mean equal to 8 and a standard deviation equal to 2. If the real limits of a binomial outcome are 9.5 and 10.5, then what is the normal approximation for the probability, p, of obtaining this binomial outcome?

Answers: 1. (a) Real limits: 1.5 to 2.5, (b) Real limits: −4.5 to −5.5, (c) Real limits: −0.5 to 0.5; 2. $p = .121$.

CHAPTER SUMMARY ORGANIZED BY LEARNING OBJECTIVE

LO 1: Identify eight characteristics of the normal distribution.

The **normal distribution** is a theoretical distribution with data that are symmetrically distributed around the mean, the median, and the mode.

Eight characteristics of a normal distribution are as follows:

1. The normal distribution is mathematically defined.

2. The normal distribution is theoretical.

3. The mean, the median, and the mode are all located at the 50th percentile.

4. The normal distribution is symmetrical.

5. The mean can equal any value.

6. The standard deviation can equal any positive value.

7. The total area under the curve is equal to 1.00.

8. The tails of a normal distribution are asymptotic.

LO 2: Define the standard normal distribution and the standard normal transformation.

- The **standard normal distribution,** or **z-distribution,** is a normal distribution with a mean equal to 0 and a standard deviation equal to 1. The standard normal distribution is distributed in z-score units along the x-axis.
- The **standard normal transformation,** or **z-transformation,** is an equation that converts any normal distribution with any mean and any positive standard deviation into a standard normal distribution with a mean equal to 0 and a standard deviation equal to 1:

$$\text{For a population: } z = \frac{x - \mu}{\sigma}.$$

$$\text{For a sample: } z = \frac{x - M}{SD}.$$

- The probabilities of **z-scores** in a standard normal distribution are listed in the **unit normal table** in Table B.1 in Appendix B.

LO 3: Locate proportions of area under any normal curve above the mean, below the mean, and between two scores.

- To locate the proportion, and therefore probabilities, for scores in any normal distribution, we follow two steps:

  Step 1: Transform a raw score (x) into a z-score.

  Step 2: Locate the corresponding proportion for the z-score in the unit normal table.

LO 4: Locate scores in a distribution with a given probability.

- To locate scores that fall within a given proportion, or probability, we follow two steps:

  Step 1: Locate a z-score associated with a given proportion in the unit normal table.

  Step 2: Transform the z-score into a raw score (x).

LO 5: Compute a binomial probability using the normal approximation.

- It is appropriate to use the normal distribution to approximate or estimate binomial probabilities when $np > 10$ and $nq > 10$.
- To use the normal approximation to estimate probabilities in a binomial distribution, follow five steps:

  Step 1: Check for normality.

  Step 2: Compute the mean and standard deviation.

  Step 3: Find the **real limits.**

  Step 4: Locate the z-score for each real limit.

  Step 5: Find the proportion located within the real limits.

SPSS LO 6: Convert raw scores to standard z-scores using SPSS.

- SPSS can be used to convert raw scores to standard z-scores. After entering the data for each variable, raw scores are converted to standard z-scores using the **Analyze,**

Descriptive Statistics, and **Descriptives** options in the menu bar. These actions will allow you to select the "Save standardized values as variables" option to convert raw scores to standard z-scores (for more details, see Section 6.8).

KEY TERMS

bell-shaped distribution	standard normal distribution	z-distribution
Gaussian distribution	standard normal transformation	z-scores
normal distribution	symmetrical distribution	z-table
real limits	unit normal table	z-transformation

END-OF-CHAPTER PROBLEMS

Factual Problems

1. Define normal distribution.

2. Why is the normal distribution applied to behavioral research?

3. State eight characteristics of the normal distribution.

4. What are the values of the mean and the standard deviation in the standard normal distribution?

5. What is a z-score?

6. State the standard normal transformation formula in words.

7. What are two steps to locate proportions under the normal curve?

8. What are two steps to locate scores with a given proportion?

9. What type of distribution does the binomial distribution approximate?

10. The values of np and nq must equal at least what value for the normal approximation to be used as an estimate for binomial probabilities?

Concepts and Application Problems

11. Using the unit normal table, find the proportion under the standard normal curve that lies to the right of:

(a) $z = 1.00$

(b) $z = -1.05$

(c) $z = 0$

(d) $z = -2.80$

(e) $z = 1.96$

12. Using the unit normal table, find the proportion under the standard normal curve that lies to the left of:

(a) $z = 0.50$

(b) $z = -1.32$

(c) $z = 0$

(d) $z = -1.96$

(e) $z = -0.10$

13. Using the unit normal table, find the proportion under the standard normal curve that lies between:

(a) The mean and $z = 1.96$

(b) The mean and $z = 0$

(c) $z = -1.50$ and $z = 1.50$

(d) $z = -0.30$ and $z = -0.10$

(e) $z = 1.00$ and $z = 2.00$

14. State whether the first area is bigger, the second area is bigger, or the two areas are equal in each of the following situations:

(a) The area to the left of $z = 1.00$ or the area to the right of $z = -1.00$

(b) The area to the left of $z = 1.00$ or the area to the left of $z = -1.00$

(c) The area between the mean and $z = 1.20$ or the area to the right of $z = 0.80$

(d) The area to the left of the mean or the area between $z = \pm 1.00$

(e) The area to the right of $z = 1.65$ or the area to the right of $z = -1.65$

15. An athletics coach states that the distribution of player run times (in seconds) for a 100-meter dash are normally distributed with a mean equal to 0.12 and a standard deviation equal to 0.02 seconds. What percentage of players on the team runs the 100-meter dash in faster than 0.14 seconds?

16. State the z-score that is the cutoff for:
    (a) The top 5% of scores
    (b) The bottom 2.5% of scores
    (c) The top 69.5% of scores
    (d) The top 50% of scores
    (e) The bottom 50% of scores

17. A sample of final exam scores is normally distributed with a mean equal to 20 and a variance equal to 25.
    (a) What percentage of scores are between 15 and 25?
    (b) What raw score is the cutoff for the top 10% of scores?
    (c) What is the proportion below 13?
    (d) What is the probability of a score less than 27?

18. A college administrator states that the average high school GPA for incoming freshman students is normally distributed with a mean equal to 3.30 and a standard deviation equal to 0.20. If students with a GPA in the top 10% will be offered a scholarship, then what is the minimum GPA required to receive the scholarship?

19. A set of data is normally distributed with a mean of 3.5 and a standard deviation of 0.6. State whether the first area is bigger, the second area is bigger, or the two areas are equal

in each of the following situations for these data:
    (a) The area above the mean or the area below the mean
    (b) The area between 2.9 and 4.1 or the area between 3.5 and 4.7
    (c) The area between the mean and 3.5 or the area above 5.3
    (d) The area below 3.6 or the area above 3.4
    (e) The area between 4.1 and 4.7 or the area between 2.9 and 3.5

20. A set of scores measuring aggression is normally distributed with a mean equal to 23 and a standard deviation equal to 2.5. Find the proportion:
    (a) To the left of $x = 19.0$
    (b) To the right of $x = 25.5$
    (c) Between the mean and $x = 19.0$
    (d) To the left of $x = 25.5$
    (e) To the right of $x = 19.0$

21. A normal distribution has a mean equal to 45. What is the standard deviation of this normal distribution if 2.5% of the proportion under the curve lies to the right of $x = 50.88$?

22. A normal distribution has a mean equal to 10. What is the standard deviation of this normal distribution if the cutoff for the bottom 5% is $x = 12.47$?

23. A normal distribution has a standard deviation equal to 32. What is the mean of this normal distribution if the probability of scoring above $x = 200$ is .0228?

24. A normal distribution has a standard deviation equal to 10. What is the mean of this normal distribution if the probability of scoring below $x = 10$ is .5000?

25. According to national data, about 10% of American college students earn a graduate degree. Using this estimate, what is the probability that

exactly 25 undergraduates in a random sample of 200 students will earn a college degree? *Hint:* Use the normal approximation to the binomial distribution, where $p = .10$ and $q = .90$.

Problems in Research

26. **The inaccuracy of lie detection.** Maureen O'Sullivan (2007) stated that research on expert lie detection is "based on three assumptions: 1) Lie detection is an ability that can be measured; 2) This ability is distributed like many other abilities (i.e., normally); 3) Therefore, only a very few people will be highly accurate" (p. 118). How does this researcher know that very few people will be highly accurate at lie detection?

27. **Body image satisfaction among men and women.** McCabe, Ricciardelli, and James (2007) recruited 107 men and 151 women to complete a series of surveys pertaining to factors such as body image and body satisfaction. Using the Body Image Satisfaction scale, where higher scores indicate greater satisfaction, they found that men scored 19.10 ± 4.55 ($M \pm SD$), whereas women scored 16.84 ± 5.66 ($M \pm SD$) on this scale. Assuming these data are normally distributed,

    (a) What is the *z*-score for 19.10 in the sample of data for men?

    (b) What is the *z*-score for 16.84 in the sample of data for women?

    (c) Why are these *z*-scores the same value?

28. **Visual sequential memory and poor spellers.** Holmes, Malone, and Redenbach (2008) found that good readers and good spellers correctly read 93.8 ± 2.9 ($M \pm SD$) words from a spelling list. On the other hand, average readers and poor spellers correctly read 84.8 ± 3.0 ($M \pm SD$) words from the same spelling list. Assuming these data are normally distributed,

    (a) What percentage of participants correctly read at least 90 words in the good readers and good spellers group?

    (b) What percentage of participants correctly read at least 90 words in the average readers and poor spellers group?

29. **Preferences for specific body parts: The eyes.** Montoya (2007) asked 56 men and 82 women to rate 21 different body parts on a scale of 1 (*no opinion*) to 5 (*very desirable*). They found that men and women rated the eyes similarly, with an average rating of about 3.77 ± 1.23 ($M \pm SD$). Assuming these data are normally distributed,

    (a) What percentage of participants rated the eyes at least a 5 (*very desirable*)?

    (b) What percentage rated the eyes at most a 1 (*no opinion*)?

30. **Getting infants to eat their vegetables.** Mennella, Kennedy, and Beauchamp (2006) showed that infants fed a bitter-tasting hydrolysate formula consumed less (in grams) of a vegetable mixture, 64.8 ± 9.6 ($M \pm SD$), compared to infants fed a milk-based formula, 101.0 ± 12.1 ($M \pm SD$). Assuming these data are normally distributed,

    (a) What percentage of hydrolysate formula-fed infants consumed between 86.8 and 101.0 grams of the vegetable mixture?

    (b) What percentage of milk-based formula-fed infants consumed between 86.8 and 101.0 grams of the vegetable mixture?

31. **Judging the humorousness of "lawyer" jokes.** Stillman, Baumeister, and DeWall (2007) conducted a study where participants listened to a variety of jokes. To determine how funny the jokes were, the researchers asked a group of 86 undergraduates to rate the jokes on a scale from 1 (*very unfunny*) to 21 (*very funny*). Participants rated a "lawyer joke" as one of the funniest jokes, with a rating of 14.48 ± 4.38 ($M \pm SD$). Assuming that these data are normally distributed,

    (a) What was the rating that marks the cutoff for the top 10% of participant ratings for this joke?

(b) How many of the 86 undergraduates gave the joke a rating of at least 10?

32. **Judging the humorousness of "muffin" jokes.** In the same jokes rating study by Stillman and colleagues (2007), participants also rated a "muffin joke" as funny, with a rating of 14.93 ± 5.65 ($M \pm SD$). Assuming that these data are normally distributed,

(a) What was the rating that marks the cutoff for the top 10% of participant ratings for this joke?

(b) How many of the 86 undergraduates gave the joke a rating of at least 10?

NOTE: Answers for even numbers are in Appendix C

Probability and Sampling Distributions

LEARNING OBJECTIVES

After reading this chapter, you should be able to:

1. Define *sampling distribution*.

2. Compare theoretical and experimental sampling strategies.

3. Identify three characteristics of the sampling distribution of the sample mean.

4. Calculate the mean and standard error of a sampling distribution of the sample mean and draw the shape of this distribution.

5. Identify three characteristics of the sampling distribution of the sample variance.

6. Explain the relationship between standard error, standard deviation, and sample size.

7. Compute *z*-transformations for the sampling distribution of the sample mean.

8. Summarize the standard error of the mean in APA format.

9. Compute the estimate for the standard error of the mean using SPSS.

7.1 SELECTING SAMPLES FROM POPULATIONS

In Chapter 6, we computed the probability of obtaining any score in a normal distribution by converting the scores in a normal distribution to z-scores and then using the unit normal table to locate the probability of each z-score. We can apply these same steps to inferential statistics—specifically in situations in which we select samples from populations. The use of z-scores and the normal distribution in this chapter lays the theoretical foundation for our use of inferential statistics in Chapters 8 to 18.

INFERENTIAL STATISTICS AND SAMPLING DISTRIBUTIONS

In inferential statistics, researchers select a sample or portion of data from a much larger population. They then measure a sample statistic they are interested in, such as the mean or variance in a sample. But they do not measure a sample mean, for example, to learn about the mean in that sample. Instead, they select a sample mean to learn more about the mean in a population. As illustrated in Figure 7.1,

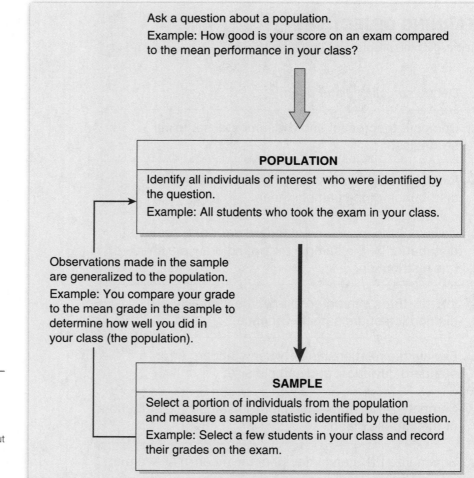

FIGURE 7.1

Selecting samples from populations. In inferential statistics, researchers use the sample statistics they measure in a sample to make inferences about the characteristics, or population parameters, in a population of interest.

you may ask a few students (the sample) how they scored on an exam to compare your score to theirs. You do this, though, to learn more about how you did in the entire class (the population), not just compared to only those few students. In a similar way, researchers select samples to learn more about populations.

When researchers measure sample statistics such as the mean and variance, they do so to estimate the value of the mean and variance in a population. But how well do sample statistics, such as the sample mean and sample variance, estimate the value of population parameters, such as the population mean and population variance? What is the probability that a sample statistic will be smaller, larger, or exactly equal to the value of a population parameter? These questions can be answered, in part, by applying our knowledge of normal distributions from Chapter 6.

In this chapter, we compare the mean and variance in a sample to the mean and variance in a small hypothetical population. We make this comparison by constructing a **sampling distribution,** which is a distribution of the mean and variance for all possible samples of a given size from a population. We can then compare the statistics we obtain in the samples to the value of the mean and variance in the hypothetical population. By doing so, we will answer the two questions asked in the previous paragraph.

NOTE: Researchers measure a mean and variance in some sample to gauge the value of the mean and variance in a population.

> A **sampling distribution** is a distribution of all sample means or sample variances that could be obtained in samples of a given size from the same population.

DEFINITION

SAMPLING AND CONDITIONAL PROBABILITIES

To avoid bias, researchers use a random procedure to select a sample from a given population. For samples to be selected at random, all individuals in a population must have an equal chance of being selected—so the probability of selecting each participant must be the same.

To illustrate the requirements for random sampling, suppose you place eight squares face down on a desk in front of you. Two squares are marked A, two are marked B, two are marked C, and two are marked D. To select two squares at random, we must ensure that each square has the same probability of being selected. The most common sampling method in behavioral research is **sampling without replacement,** meaning that after we select a square, we do not replace that square before selecting a second square. Let's find the probability of selecting a square marked A on the first draw and a square marked A on the second draw using this sampling method.

> **Sampling without replacement** is a method of sampling where each participant or item selected is not replaced before the next selection. This method of sampling is the most common method used in behavioral research.

DEFINITION

First draw: The probability of selecting a square marked A is the number of squares marked A divided by the total number of squares on the desk:

$$p(\text{square marked A on first draw}) = \frac{2}{8} = .25.$$

Second draw: We do not replace the square marked A. If we selected a square marked A on the first draw, then only seven squares remain, one of which is marked A.

NOTE: Sampling without replacement means that the probability of each selection is conditional. The probabilities of each selection are not the same.

The probability of selecting a square marked A is the number of squares marked A divided by the total number of squares remaining on the desk:

$$p(\text{square marked A on second draw}) = \frac{1}{7} = .14.$$

Using the typical sampling method in behavioral science, we find that the probabilities of each selection are not the same because we did not replace each selection. To ensure that each individual or item has the same probability of being selected, we can use **sampling with replacement**, in which each individual or item is replaced after each selection.

DEFINITION

Sampling with replacement is a method of sampling where each participant or item selected is replaced before the next selection. Replacing before the next selection ensures that the probability for each selection is the same. This method of sampling is used in the development of statistical theory.

Although sampling with replacement is a more random sampling method, it is typically not necessary in behavioral research because the populations of interest are large. In a population of 100 women, for example, the probability of selecting the first woman is $p = \frac{1}{100} = .01$. The probability of selecting the second woman if we sample without replacement is $p = \frac{1}{99} = .01$. When we round to the hundredths place, these probabilities are the same because the total number of individuals in the population is so large. As the population size increases, the differences in probabilities become minimal. Therefore, with large populations, random samples can be selected, even when we use a sampling without replacement method.

LEARNING CHECK 1

1. A researcher uses a sample _____ to make inferences about the value of a population _____ of interest.

2. Which method for sampling is associated with equal probabilities for each selection, even with small sample sizes?

3. The number of left-handed people in a hypothetical population of 25 students is 8. What is the probability of selecting 2 left-handed people from this population when:
   a. Sampling *with* replacement?
   b. Sampling *without* replacement?

4. Which sampling method is the most commonly used in behavioral research?

Answers: 1. statistic, parameter; 2. Sampling with replacement; 3. (a) $\frac{8}{25} \times \frac{8}{25} = .10$, (b) $\frac{8}{25} \times \frac{7}{24} = .09$; 4. Sampling without replacement.

SELECTING A SAMPLE: WHO'S IN AND WHO'S OUT? 7.2

Once we identify a population of interest, we need to determine a **sample design** for selecting samples from the population. A sample design is a plan for how individuals will be selected from a population of interest. There are many appropriate sample designs, and all of them address the following two questions:

1. Does the order of selecting participants matter?

2. Do we replace each selection before the next draw?

A **sample design** is a specific plan or protocol for how individuals will be selected or sampled from a population of interest.

DEFINITION

The first question determines how often people in a population can be selected. Both questions determine the number of samples of a given size that can be selected from a given population. Answering both questions leads to two strategies for sampling, which we describe in this section. One strategy, called theoretical sampling, is that used in the development of statistical theory. The second strategy, called experimental sampling, is the most common strategy used in behavioral research. Figure 7.2 shows how we can apply each strategy.

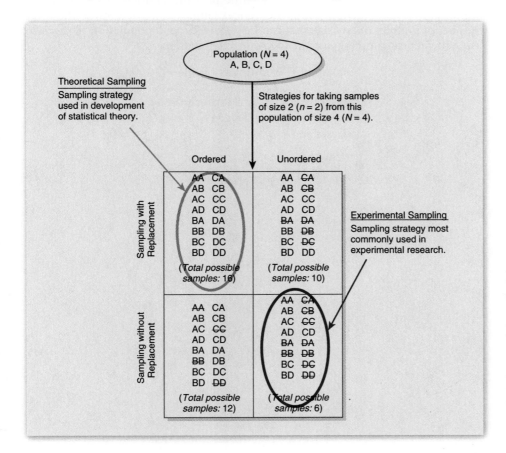

FIGURE 7.2

The effect of replacement and order changes on the many possible samples that can be drawn from a given population. In this example, all possible samples of size 2 ($n = 2$) are taken from this population of size 4 ($N = 4$). Notice that theoretical sampling allows for the most possible samples (16), whereas experimental sampling allows for the fewest possible samples (6).

SAMPLING STRATEGY: THE BASIS FOR STATISTICAL THEORY

We defined statistics in Chapter 1 as a branch of mathematics used to summarize, analyze, and interpret a group of numbers or observations. This branch of mathematics is based on theoretical proofs that show how statistical methods can be used to describe and interpret observations. Theoretical sampling, then, is used in the development of the theories that have led to statistics as a branch of mathematics.

To develop theories of sampling, statisticians answered "yes" to both questions stated above. To select samples from populations, the order of selecting people mattered, and each person selected was replaced before selecting again. To illustrate, suppose we select as many samples of two participants as possible from a population of three individuals (A, B, and C). In theoretical sampling:

NOTE: In theoretical sampling, the order of selecting individuals matters, and each individual selected is replaced before sampling again.

1. Order matters. If two participants (A and B) are selected from a population, then selecting Participant A first, then B, differs from selecting Participant B first, then A. Each of these samples is regarded as a different possible sample that can be selected from this population.

2. We sample with replacement. This means that a sample of Participant A and then Participant A again is a possible sample because we replaced Participant A before making the second selection.

Table 7.1 shows that we can select nine possible samples of size 2 from a population of three people using theoretical sampling. To determine the total number of samples of any size that can be selected from a population of any size using theoretical sampling, use the following computation:

$$\text{Total number of samples possible} = N^n.$$

TABLE 7.1 Total number of samples of size 2 ($n = 2$) from a population of size 3 ($N = 3$) using theoretical sampling.

Total Possible Samples ($n = 2$)
AA
AB
AC
BA
BB
BC
CA
CB
CC

Let's verify the results shown in Table 7.1, in which we had samples of two participants ($n = 2$) from a population of three people ($N = 3$). If we substitute these values into the computation, we obtain

$$N^n = 3^2 = 9 \text{ samples.}$$

We use this computation for a larger population and larger sample size in Example 7.1.

A researcher selects a sample of size 3 ($n = 3$) from a population of size 10 ($N = 10$). How many possible samples of size 3 can be selected using theoretical sampling?

EXAMPLE 7.1

To find the answer, we substitute the sample size (n) and population size (N) into the computation. The total number of samples possible using theoretical sampling is $N^n = 10^3 = 1,000$ samples.

SAMPLING STRATEGY: MOST USED IN BEHAVIORAL RESEARCH

In practice, however, we select diverse samples. For most studies in behavioral science, order does not matter because we do not care about the order in which participants are selected. Also, we usually do not want to select the same person twice for the same study, and so we sample without replacement. Experimental sampling, then, is the strategy used by the experimenters who engage in behavioral research.

To illustrate the sampling strategy used in behavioral research, suppose we select as many samples of two participants as possible from a population of three people (A, B, and C). In experimental sampling:

1. Order does not matter. If two participants, A and B, are selected from a population, then selecting Participant A first, then B, is the same as selecting Participant B first, then A. These samples are counted as one sample and not as separate samples. In the example given in Figure 7.2, this was one criterion by which samples were crossed out for experimental sampling.

2. We sample without replacement. This means that the same participant can never be sampled twice. So samples of AA, BB, and CC from the population in this example are not possible. In the example given in Figure 7.2, this was the second criterion by which samples were crossed out for experimental sampling.

NOTE: In experimental sampling, the order of selecting individuals does not matter, and each individual selected is not replaced before selecting again.

Table 7.2 shows that three different samples are possible if we select samples of size 2 from a population of size 3 using experimental sampling. To determine the total number of samples of any size that can be selected from a population of any size using experimental sampling, use the following computation:

$$\text{Total number of samples possible} = \frac{N!}{n!(N-n)!}.$$

TABLE 7.2 Total number of samples of size 2 ($n = 2$) from a population of size 3 ($N = 3$) using experimental sampling.

Total Possible Samples ($n = 2$)
AB
AC
CB

Let's use this computation to verify the results in Table 7.2 in which we selected as many samples of size two ($n = 2$) from a population of three individuals ($N = 3$):

$$\frac{N!}{n!(N-n)!} = \frac{3!}{2!(3-2)!} = \frac{3 \times 2 \times 1}{2 \times 1 \times 1} = 3.$$

We use this computation for a larger population and larger sample size in Example 7.2.

EXAMPLE 7.2

In Example 7.1, a researcher selected a sample of size 3 ($n = 3$) from a population of size 10 ($N = 10$). Using this same example, how many possible samples of size 3 can be selected using the experimental sampling strategy?

To find the answer, we substitute the sample size (n) and population size (N) into the computation. The total number of samples possible is

$$\frac{N!}{n!(N-n)!} = \frac{10!}{3!(10-3)!} = \frac{10 \times 9 \times 8 \times 7 \times 6 \times 5 \times 4 \times 3 \times 2 \times 1}{3 \times 2 \times 1 \times 7 \times 6 \times 5 \times 4 \times 3 \times 2 \times 1} = 120.$$

LEARNING CHECK 2

1. State the two criteria for theoretical sampling.

2. A researcher draws a sample of size 4 ($n = 4$) from a population of size 50 ($N = 50$). How many possible samples of this size can the researcher draw using theoretical sampling?

3. State the two criteria for experimental sampling.

4. A researcher draws a sample of size 2 ($n = 2$) from a population of size 5 ($N = 5$). How many possible samples of this size can the researcher draw using experimental sampling?

Answers: 1. Order matters and we sample with replacement; 2. $50^4 = 6,250,000$ possible samples; 3. Order does not matter and we sample without replacement; 4. $\frac{5 \times 4 \times 3 \times 2 \times 1}{2 \times 1 \times 3 \times 2 \times 1} = 10$ possible samples.

SAMPLING DISTRIBUTIONS: THE MEAN   7.3

In behavioral research, we often measure a sample mean to estimate the value of a population mean. To determine how well a sample mean estimates a population mean, we need to identify a population of interest and then determine the distribution of the sample means for all possible samples of a given size that can be selected from that population—thus, we need to construct a sampling distribution.

Because statisticians used theoretical sampling to learn about the characteristics of the mean, we also will use this sampling strategy to select samples from a population. We can use the sampling distribution we construct in this section to see how well a sample mean estimates the value of a population mean.

To construct a sampling distribution, let's identify a hypothetical population of three people ($N = 3$) who took a psychological assessment. Person A scored an 8, Person B scored a 5, and Person C scored a 2 on this assessment. Because we know all three scores in this population, we can identify the mean in this population (we will identify the variance in Section 7.4). Then we can construct a sampling distribution of the mean to determine how the sample means we could select from this population compare to the population mean we calculated.

The population mean for $N = 3$: The population mean (μ) is computed by summing all scores in the population, then dividing by the population size:

$$\mu = \frac{8+5+2}{3} = 5.0.$$

To find the sampling distribution for $n = 2$, we use the possible samples from Table 7.1, which lists all the possible samples of size 2 that can be drawn from a population of three people using theoretical sampling. These nine samples are repeated in Table 7.3 along with the scores and sample means we would have measured in those samples using the assessment scores we listed for each person.

TABLE 7.3   The participants, individual scores, and sample means for each possible sample of size 2 from a population of size 3.

Participants Sampled ($n = 2$)	Scores for Each Participant	Sample Mean for Each Sample (M)
A,A	8,8	8.0
A,B	8,5	6.5
A,C	8,2	5.0
B,A	5,8	6.5
B,B	5,5	5.0
B,C	5,2	3.5
C,A	2,8	5.0
C,B	2,5	3.5
C,C	2,2	2.0
$N^n = 9$ samples		$\Sigma M = 45$
		$\mu_M = \dfrac{45}{9} = 5.0$

In the last column in Table 7.3, ΣM is the sum of the sample means. The average sample mean (μ_M) is computed by dividing the sum of the sample means (ΣM) by the total number of samples summed (nine samples). Using the data in this table, we will find that the sample mean is related to the population mean in three ways: The sample mean is an unbiased estimator, follows the central limit theorem, and has a minimum variance.

UNBIASED ESTIMATOR

A sample mean is an **unbiased estimator** when the sample mean we obtain in a randomly selected sample equals the value of the population mean on average. We know that the population mean in our hypothetical example is equal to 5.0. The mean of the sampling distribution of sample means is the sum of the sample means we could select (ΣM) divided by the total number of samples summed:

$$\mu_M = \frac{45}{9} = 5.0 \, .$$

DEFINITION

A sample statistic is an **unbiased estimator** if its value equals the value of the population parameter on average. The sample mean is an unbiased estimator because it equals the population mean on average.

NOTE: The sample mean is an unbiased estimator of the value of the population mean.

On average, we can expect the sample mean from a randomly selected sample to be equal to the population mean. The sample mean, then, is an unbiased estimator of the value of the population mean. In statistical terms, $M = \mu$, on average. We can state this as a rule for the sample mean:

$$\text{When } M = \frac{\sum x}{n}, \text{ then } M = \mu \text{ on average.}$$

CENTRAL LIMIT THEOREM

We know that on average, the sample mean is equal to the population mean. But what about all other possible values of the sample mean that we could obtain? We can distribute all other possible sample means by listing the value of each possible sample mean on the x-axis and the frequency of times it occurs on the y-axis of a graph. Figure 7.3(b) shows that the sampling distribution of sample means selected from this population is normally distributed, and this will always be the case regardless of the distribution of scores in the population. Notice in Figure 7.3(a) that the frequency of scores in the original population is nonmodal. Although the population of scores is not normally distributed, the sampling distribution of the sample means selected from this population is normally distributed. This outcome is described by the **central limit theorem.**

NOTE: The central limit theorem explains that the shape of a sampling distribution of sample means tends toward a normal distribution, regardless of the distribution in the population.

DEFINITION

The **central limit theorem** explains that regardless of the distribution of scores in a population, the sampling distribution of sample means selected from that population will be approximately normally distributed.

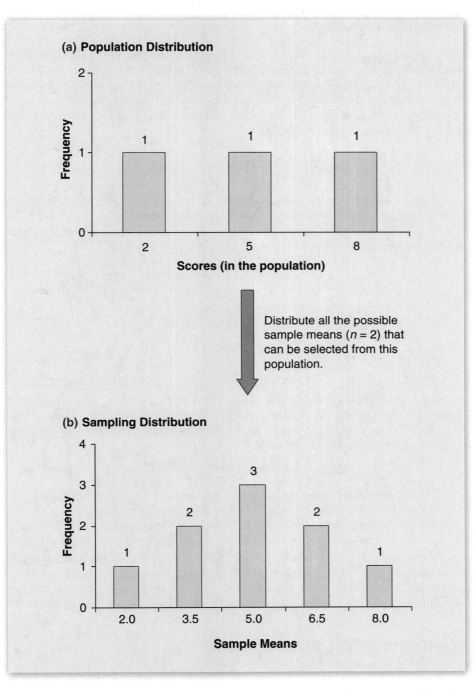

FIGURE 7.3

The central limit theorem. The hypothetical population has a nonmodal distribution (a), yet the sampling distribution of possible sample means ($n = 2$) is approximately normally distributed (b).

The central limit theorem has an important implication: It means that the probability distribution for obtaining a sample mean from a population is normally distributed. From the empirical rule, then, we know that at least 95% of all possible sample means we could select from a population are within two standard deviations (*SD*) of the population mean.

MINIMUM VARIANCE

The variance of a normal distribution can be any positive number, and defining the variance can give us an idea of how far the value of a sample mean can deviate from the value of the population mean. To compute the variance, we use the same formula that was introduced in Chapter 4 except that we use the notation for a sampling distribution. The formula for the variance of the sampling distribution of the sample means (symbolized as σ_M^2) is

$$\sigma_M^2 = \sum \frac{(M - \mu_M)^2}{N^n}.$$

In this formula, M is the sample mean in each possible sample, μ_M is the mean of the sampling distribution (this equals the population mean, $\mu_M = 5$), and N^n is the total number of possible samples that can be selected (nine possible samples). The variance when the population mean is $\mu_M = 5$ and $N^n = 9$ is

$$\sigma_M^2 = \frac{(2-5)^2}{9} + \frac{(3.5-5)^2}{9} + \frac{(3.5-5)^2}{9} + \frac{(5-5)^2}{9} + \frac{(5-5)^2}{9} +$$
$$\frac{(5-5)^2}{9} + \frac{(6.5-5)^2}{9} + \frac{(6.5-5)^2}{9} + \frac{(8-5)^2}{9}$$

$$= \frac{27}{9} = 3.0.$$

The variance equals 3.0. The standard deviation of a sampling distribution is called the **standard error of the mean** (*SEM* or σ_M), or simply the **standard error** (*SE*). The standard error tells us how far possible sample means deviate from the value of the population mean. To compute the standard error, we take the square root of the variance:

$$\sigma_M = \sqrt{\sigma_M^2} = \sqrt{3.0} = 1.73.$$

The **standard error of the mean**, or **standard error**, is the standard deviation of a sampling distribution of sample means. It is the standard error or distance that sample mean values deviate from the value of the population mean.

NOTE: The standard error of the mean is the standard deviation of the sampling distribution of sample means.

The value 1.73 is the smallest possible value we could obtain for standard error. If we used any other value for the mean, other than the population mean ($\mu = 5$), to compute standard error, then the solution would be larger. In this way, all other possible values for the sample mean vary minimally from the population mean.

OVERVIEW OF THE SAMPLE MEAN

In all, three characteristics of the sample mean make it a good estimate of the value of the population mean:

1. The sample mean is an unbiased estimator. On average, the sample mean will equal the value of the population mean.

2. A distribution of sample means follows the central limit theorem. That is, regardless of the shape of the distribution in a population, the distribution

of sample means selected from the population will be approximately normally distributed.

3. A distribution of sample means has minimum variance. The sampling distribution of sample means will vary minimally from the value of the population mean.

LEARNING CHECK 6

1. If a random sample is selected from a population with a mean equal to 15, then what can we expect the value of the sample mean to be on average?

2. An _____ is any sample statistic obtained from a randomly selected sample that equals, on average, the value of its respective population parameter.

3. Suppose a population consists of a positively skewed distribution of scores. If we select samples of size 10 from this population, what shape can we expect the sampling distribution of sample means to be for this sample size?

4. What is the standard error of the mean (σ_M) when the variance of the sampling distribution of sample means (σ_M^2) is equal to (a) 4, (b) 144, and (c) 1,225?

5. The _____ states that regardless of the distribution of scores in a population, the sampling distribution of sample means selected from that population will be approximately normally distributed.

Answers: 1. $\mu_M = 15$; 2. Unbiased estimator; 3. Normally distributed; 4. (a) $\sqrt{4} = 2$, (b) $\sqrt{144} = 12$, (c) $\sqrt{1,225} = 35$; 5. central limit theorem.

SAMPLING DISTRIBUTIONS: THE VARIANCE   7.4

In Section 7.3, we distributed all the possible samples of size 2 that we could select from a population of size 3 using theoretical sampling. We found that we could select any one of nine samples, and we computed the mean for each sample. In this section, we will use the same example, except we will distribute the variance for each of the nine possible samples.

In Chapter 4, we introduced two formulas for variance: a population variance and a sample variance. We apply both formulas to the hypothetical population of three individuals ($N = 3$) who took a psychological assessment. Again, in this population, Person A scored an 8, Person B scored a 5, and Person C scored a 2. Because we know all three scores in this population, we can compute the variance in this population. Then we can construct a sampling distribution of the variance to determine how the sample variances we could select from this population compare to the value of the population variance we calculated.

The population variance for $N = 3$: The population variance (σ^2) is the sum of the squared deviation of scores from their mean (SS), divided by the population size (N):

$$\sigma^2 = \frac{(8-5)^2 + (5-5)^2 + (2-5)^2}{3} = 6.0.$$

The sampling distribution for $n = 2$: In Table 7.1, we listed all the possible samples of size 2 that can be drawn from a population of three individuals using theoretical sampling. Table 7.4 lists these nine samples, with the scores and sample variances that we would have measured in each of those samples. Using the data in this table, we will find that the sample variance is related to the population variance in three ways depending on how the variance is calculated (either dividing *SS* by *n* or dividing *SS* by (*n* – 1)).

TABLE 7.4   The participants, individual scores, and samples variances for each possible sample of size 2 from a population of size 3.

Participants Sampled (*n* = 2)	Scores for Each Participant	Sample Variance for Each Sample $\left(\frac{SS}{n-1}\right)$
A,A	8,8	0
A,B	8,5	4.50
A,C	8,2	18.00
B,A	5,8	4.50
B,B	5,5	0
B,C	5,2	4.50
C,A	2,8	18.00
C,B	2,5	4.50
C,C	2,2	0
$N^n = 9$ samples		$\sum s^2 = 54$
		$\mu_{s^2} = \dfrac{54}{9} = 6.0$

UNBIASED ESTIMATOR

A sample variance is an unbiased estimator when the sample variance we obtain in a randomly selected sample equals, on average, the value of the population variance. We know that the population variance in the hypothetical example is equal to 6.0. The mean of the sampling distribution of sample variances is the sum of the sample variances we could select $\left(\sum s^2\right)$, divided by the total number of samples summed:

$$\mu_{s^2} = \frac{54}{9} = 6.0.$$

NOTE: On average, the sample variance is equal to the population variance when we divide SS by df. *This makes the sample variance an unbiased estimator of the population variance.*

On average, we can expect the sample variance from a randomly selected sample to equal the population variance when we divide *SS* by *df* (note: the degrees of freedom, *df,* for variance is *n* – 1). The sample variance, then, is an unbiased estimator of the value of the population variance. In statistical terms, $s^2 = \sigma^2$ on average. We can state this as a rule for the sample variance:

$$\text{When } s^2 = \frac{SS}{n-1} \text{ or } \frac{SS}{df}, \text{ then } s^2 = \sigma^2 \text{ on average.}$$

If we divided SS by n, the result would be that we underestimate the population variance on average, which would make the sample variance a biased estimator of the population variance when we divide SS by n. Only when we divide SS by df will the sample variance be an unbiased estimator of the population variance. For this reason, we divide SS by the df for sample variance to compute sample variance.

SKEWED DISTRIBUTION RULE

We know that the sample variance is equal to the population variance, on average, when we divide SS by df. But what about all other possible outcomes we could obtain in the samples we select? We can distribute all other possible outcomes by listing the value of each possible sample variance on the x-axis and the frequency of times it occurs on the y-axis of a graph. Figure 7.4 shows that the sampling distribution of the sample variance selected from this population is positively skewed. This result demonstrates the skewed distribution rule: The distribution of sample variances will be approximately positively skewed, regardless of the distribution of scores in a population.

NOTE: The sampling distribution of sample variances tends toward a positively skewed distribution, regardless of the distribution in the population.

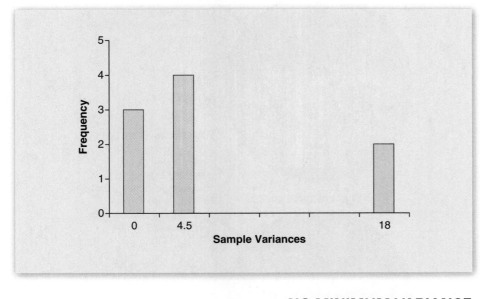

FIGURE 7.4

The skewed distribution rule.
The sampling distribution of sample variances tends toward a positively skewed distribution, regardless of the shape of the distribution in the population.

NO MINIMUM VARIANCE

The variance of a skewed distribution can be any positive number. Defining the variance can give us an idea of how far the value of a sample variance can deviate from the population variance. When we divide SS by df to compute variance, however, we find that the sample variance does not vary minimally from the population variance. That is, when we select a sample variance that doesn't equal the population variance, its value can be quite far from the actual value of the population variance that we are trying to estimate, particularly for smaller sample sizes.

NOTE: Although the sample variance equals the population variance on average, the distribution of all other sample variances can vary far from the population variance when we divide SS by df.

The distribution of sample variances is minimal only when we divide *SS* by *n*. Statisticians generally agree that it is better for the sample variance we measure to be unbiased (i.e., to be equal on average to the population variance) than for a distribution of sample variances to vary minimally from the population variance. For this reason, the sample variance is calculated by dividing *SS* by *df*. This reasoning is described further in the Making Sense section.

MAKING SENSE: Minimum Variance Versus Unbiased Estimator

In terms of measuring sample variance, the question is whether it is more important that the sample variance is unbiased (we divide *SS* by *df*) or that it minimally varies from the population variance (we divide *SS* by *n*). To find the best answer, imagine you are playing a game of darts. Let the bull's-eye on the dartboard represent the population variance and the darts being thrown represent the sample variance (see Figure 7.5). There are two teams. Team Unbiased Estimator hits the bull's-eye on average but otherwise is all over the dartboard. Team Minimum Variance hits below the bull's-eye on average, but it throws many darts closely grouped around the bull's-eye. Which team would you rather play for? Statisticians choose Team Unbiased Estimator.

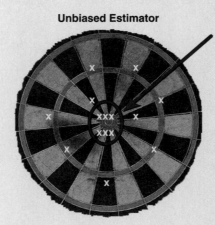

Unbiased Estimator

Darts hit the bull's-eye on average—similar to how the sample variance equals the population variance on average when we divide *SS* by *df*.

Darts fail to hit the bull's-eye on average, but they are grouped closer together—similar to how the sample variance varies minimally from the population variance when we divide *SS* by *n*.

Minimum Variance

FIGURE 7.5

An analogy for an unbiased estimator (top dartboard) and minimum variance (bottom dartboard). The bull's-eye represents the population variance, and the darts being thrown (indicated with an x) represent a sample variance that could be selected from a given population.

Ultimately, researchers measure sample statistics to learn more about parameters in a given population. The primary use of sample statistics is to estimate the value of population parameters. This estimate must be unbiased, and so we divide *SS* by *df* to compute the sample variance. From the statistician's perspective, when it comes to playing darts, if you are hitting the bull's-eye on average, then you're playing with the best strategy. *

OVERVIEW OF THE SAMPLE VARIANCE

In all, the sample variance is a good estimate of the value of the population variance because it is unbiased. The characteristics of the sample variance are as follows:

1. The sample variance is an unbiased estimator. On average, we can expect the sample variance to equal the population variance when we divide *SS* by *df*, where *df* = (*n* – 1).

2. A distribution of sample variances follows the skewed distribution rule. Regardless of the shape of the distribution in a population, the distribution of sample variances selected from the population will be approximately positively skewed.

3. A distribution of sample variances has no minimum variance. The sampling distribution of sample variances will not vary minimally from the value of the population variance when we divide *SS* by *df*.

1. If a random sample is selected from a population with a variance equal to 12, then what can we expect the value for the sample variance will equal on average when we divide *SS* by *df*?

2. What is the shape of the sampling distribution of sample variances when the population distribution is normally distributed?

3. Is it more important for the sample variance to be an unbiased estimator of the population variance or to vary minimally from the value of the population variance?

✔ **LEARNING CHECK 4**

Answers: 1. (a) $\mu_{s^2} = 12$; 2. (a) Positively skewed; 3. It is more important for the sample variance to be an unbiased estimator.

THE STANDARD ERROR OF THE MEAN 7.5

In Section 7.3, we introduced that the standard error of the mean is the standard deviation of a sampling distribution of sample means. In the example of a hypothetical population with a mean of 5, we found that the variance of the sampling distribution of sample means was equal to $\sigma_M^2 = 3.0$. The standard error of the mean was equal to the square root of the variance, or $\sigma_M = 1.73$. In this section, we introduce a new formula to find the variance $\left(\sigma_M^2\right)$ and standard error $\left(\sigma_M\right)$ of a sampling distribution of sample means.

To compute the variance of the sampling distribution of sample means, divide the population variance $\left(\sigma^2\right)$ by the sample size (n). If we substitute the population variance (6) and sample size (2) from the original example into the formula, we find that the variance of the sampling distribution of sample means is equal to

$$\sigma_M^2 = \frac{\sigma^2}{n} = \frac{6}{2} = 3.0.$$

This is the same value we computed in Section 7.3 for the variance of the sampling distribution of sample means. The standard error of the mean is the square root of the variance. We can write the shortcut formula as

$$\sigma_M = \sqrt{\frac{\sigma^2}{n}} = \frac{\sigma}{\sqrt{n}}.$$

NOTE: To compute the standard error of the mean, divide the population standard deviation by the square root of the sample size.

If we take the square root of the variance, we obtain the same value we computed in Section 7.3 for the standard error of the mean:

$$\sigma_M = \sqrt{3.0} = 1.73.$$

Researchers fully understand that when they select a sample, the mean they measure will not always be equal to the population mean. They understand that two random samples selected from the same population can produce different estimates of the same population mean, which is called **sampling error.** The standard error of the mean is a numeric measure of sampling error, with larger values indicating greater sampling error or greater differences that can exist from one sample to the next.

DEFINITION

Sampling error is the extent to which sample means selected from the same population differ from one another. This difference, which occurs by chance, is measured by the standard error of the mean.

In Example 7.3, we will apply the characteristics of the sample mean to distribute the mean and standard error of a sampling distribution.

EXAMPLE 7.3

Participants in a random sample of 100 college students (the population) are asked to state the number of hours they spend studying during finals week. The mean study time in this population is equal to 20 hours per week, with a standard deviation equal to 15 hours per week. Construct a sampling distribution of the mean.

To construct the sampling distribution, we must (1) identify the mean of the sampling distribution, (2) compute the standard error of the mean, and (3) distribute the possible sample means 3 *SEM* above and below the mean.

Because the sample mean is an unbiased estimator of the population mean, the mean of the sampling distribution is equal to the population mean. The mean of this sampling distribution is equal to 20. The standard error is the population standard deviation divided by the square root of the sample size:

$$\sigma_M = \frac{\sigma}{\sqrt{n}} = \frac{15}{\sqrt{100}} = 1.50.$$

The sampling distribution of the sample mean for a sample of size 100 from this population is normally distributed with a mean equal to 20 and a standard error equal to 1.50. We know the sampling distribution is normally distributed because of the central limit theorem. Figure 7.6 shows this sampling distribution. From the empirical rule, we know that at least 95% of all sample means will be within 3 hours of the value of the population mean ($\mu = 20$). In other words, at least 95% of the sample means we could select from this population will be between $M = 17$ hours and $M = 23$ hours.

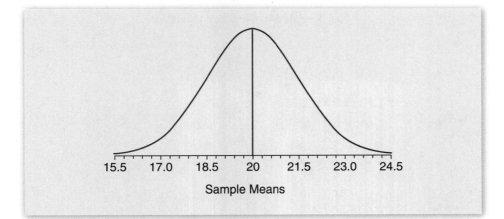

FIGURE 7.6

The sampling distribution of sample means for samples of size 100 selected from a population with a mean of 20 and standard deviation of 15.

FACTORS THAT DECREASE STANDARD ERROR   7.6

The standard error can increase or decrease depending on the sample size and the value of the population standard deviation. First, as the population standard deviation (σ) decreases, standard error decreases. That is, the less scores in a population deviate from the population mean, the less possible sample means will deviate from the population mean. Suppose, for example, that we select samples of size 2 ($n = 2$) from one of five populations having a population standard deviation equal to $\sigma_1 = 4$, $\sigma_2 = 9$, $\sigma_3 = 16$, $\sigma_4 = 25$, and $\sigma_5 = 81$. Figure 7.7 shows that the standard error decreases as the population standard deviation decreases.

NOTE: The larger the standard deviation in the population, the larger the standard error.

Second, as the sample size increases (n), standard error decreases. The larger the sample, the more data you collect, and the closer your estimate of the population mean will be. Suppose, for example, that we select samples of size 4 ($n = 4$), 9 ($n = 9$), 16 ($n = 16$), 25 ($n = 25$), and 81 ($n = 81$) from a single population with a standard deviation equal to s = 4. Figure 7.8 shows that the standard error decreases as the sample size increases. This result is called the **law of large numbers.**

NOTE: The law of large numbers explains that the larger the sample size, the smaller the standard error.

The **law of large numbers** states that increasing the number of observations or sample size in a study will decrease the standard error. Hence, larger samples are associated with closer estimates of the population mean on average.

DEFINITION

FIGURE 7.7

As the standard deviation in the population increases, the standard error of the mean (*SEM*), or the distance that sample means deviate from the population mean, also increases.

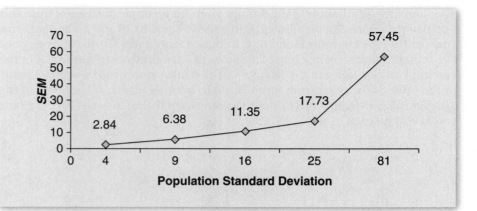

FIGURE 7.8

The law of large numbers. As the sample size increases, the standard error of the mean (*SEM*) decreases, so sample means deviate closer to the population mean as sample size increases.

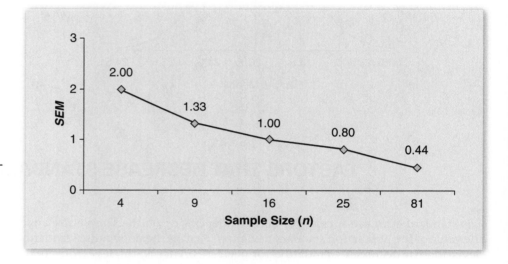

7.7 SPSS IN FOCUS: ESTIMATING THE STANDARD ERROR OF THE MEAN

Researchers rarely know the value of the population standard deviation, which is in the numerator of the formula for standard error. It is more common to estimate the standard error by substituting the sample standard deviation in place of the population standard deviation in the formula for standard error. SPSS makes this substitution to compute an estimate of standard error. The formula, which is discussed further in Chapter 9, is

$$s_M = \frac{s}{\sqrt{n}}.$$

SPSS is designed to estimate the standard error using this formula. Let's suppose that we measure the individual reaction times (in seconds) for a team of 10 firefighters to respond to an emergency call. The reaction times are 93, 66, 30, 44, 20, 100, 35, 58, 70, and 81. Let's use SPSS to estimate the standard error of these data:

1. Click on the **variable view** tab and enter *reaction* in the **name column.** We will enter whole numbers, so reduce the value to 0 in the **decimals column.**

2. Click on the **data view** tab and enter the 10 values in the column labeled *reaction.*

3. Go to the **menu bar** and click **Analyze,** then **Descriptive Statistics** and **Descriptives,** to display a dialog box.

4. In the **dialog box,** select the *reaction* variable and click the arrow to move it into the box labeled **Variable(s):** to the right. Click the **Options . . .** tab to bring up a new dialog box.

5. In the new dialog box, shown in Figure 7.9, select **S.E. mean** in the **Dispersion** box and click continue.

6. Select **Paste,** and click the **Run** command.

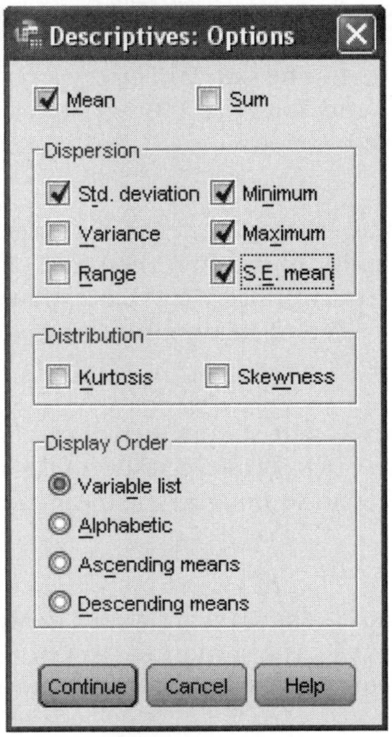

FIGURE 7.9

The SPSS dialog box in Step 5.

The SPSS output table, shown in Table 7.5, gives the value for the standard error as 8.596. We can double-check that the value of standard error is correct because the SPSS output table also gives us the value of the sample standard deviation and sample size. When we enter these values into the formula for standard error, we obtain the same result given in the table:

$$\text{Standard error} = \frac{s}{\sqrt{n}} = \frac{27.183}{\sqrt{10}} \approx 8.596.$$

TABLE 7.5   The SPSS output table. The standard error of the mean is circled in the table.

The value of standard error

	N	Minimum	Maximum	Mean		Std. Deviation
	Statistic	Statistic	Statistic	Statistic	Std. Error	Statistic
reaction	10	20	100	59.70	8.596	27.183
Valid N (listwise)	10					

Descriptive Statistics

7.8   APA IN FOCUS: REPORTING THE STANDARD ERROR

The standard error of the mean is often reported in research journals using the American Psychological Association (APA) guidelines. The *Publication Manual of the American Psychological Association* (APA, 2009) recommends any combination of three ways to report the standard error: in the text, in a table, or in a graph.

Reporting* SEM *in the text.   The standard error can be reported directly in the text. For example, Powers and Young (2008) reported the effects of alcohol consumption on general health as follows:

> Consistent alcohol intake showed mean scores for general health of moderate drinkers were significantly better than that of non-drinkers [mean difference = 4.3, standard error (SE) = 0.61], occasional drinkers (mean difference = 3.1, SE = 0.52) and heavy drinkers (mean difference = 2.1, SE = 1.00). (p. 424)

Reporting* SEM *in a table.   The standard error can be reported in a table. For example, the standard error can be displayed as *M ± SEM,* as shown in Table 7.6. The table provides a concise way to summarize the mean and standard error of many measures.

Reporting* SEM *in a graph.   The standard error can also be reported in a graph. The standard error is displayed as a vertical bar extending above and below each mean plot, as shown in Figure 7.10, or mean bar, as shown in Figure 7.11.

TABLE 7.6   Mean characteristics of female participants included in a dietary health study. Means are given plus and minus *SEM*.

Characteristics	Participants	
	Lean	Obese
Age (years)	30.6 ± 1.7	29.2 ± 1.7
Height (m)	1.63 ± 0.01	1.68 ± 0.01
Weight (kg)	60.4 ± 1.2	94.9 ± 2.5
Body mass index (kg/m²)	22.7 ± 0.4	33.5 ± 0.7
Body fat (%)	22.5 ± 0.9	33.8 ± 0.7
Waist circumference (cm)	71.6 ± 1.0	97.3 ± 2.0

Source: Adapted from Rolls and Roe (2002).

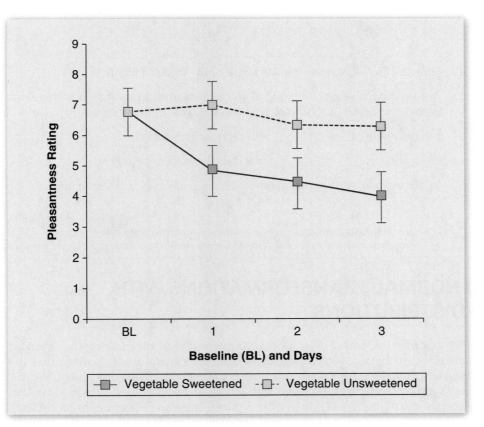

FIGURE 7.10

Using error bars in a line graph. Mean pleasantness ratings over days for vegetables that were sweetened (solid line) or unsweetened (dashed line). Lower ratings reflect greater liking. Vertical lines represent *SEM*.

Source: Adapted from Capaldi and Privitera (2008).

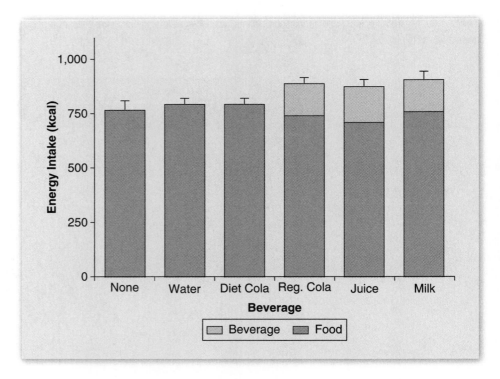

FIGURE 7.11

Using error bars in a bar graph. Mean energy intake in a lunch. Vertical lines represent *SEM*.

Source: Adapted from DellaValle, Roe, and Rolls (2005).

 **LEARNING CHECK 5**

1. State the formula for the standard error of the mean in words.

2. A psychologist selects a sample of 36 children from a population with a standard deviation of 12. Compute the standard error for this example.

3. Increasing the _____ will decrease standard error.

4. Decreasing the _____ will decrease standard error.

5. What are three ways that the standard error is reported in research journals?

Answers: 1. The standard error is the standard deviation divided by the square root of the sample size; 2. $\sigma_M = \frac{12}{\sqrt{36}} = 2.0$; 3. Sample size; 4. Population standard deviation; 5. The standard error is reported in the text of an article, in tables, or in graphs.

7.9 STANDARD NORMAL TRANSFORMATIONS WITH SAMPLING DISTRIBUTIONS

We can find the probability of obtaining any sample mean using the standard normal distribution because we know from the central limit theorem that the sampling distribution of the mean is approximately normally distributed. We can convert any sampling distribution with any mean and standard error to a standard normal distribution by applying the *z*-transformation. Using the notation for a sampling distribution, the *z*-transformation can be stated as

$$z = \frac{M - \mu_M}{\sigma_M}.$$

Because the mean of the sampling distribution of the mean, μ_M, equals the population mean, μ, we can also write the z-transformation as

$$z = \frac{M - \mu}{\sigma_M}.$$

To locate the proportion, and therefore the probability, of selecting sample means in any sampling distribution, we follow two steps:

Step 1: Transform a sample mean (M) into a z-score.

Step 2: Locate the corresponding proportion for the z-score in the unit normal table.

In Example 7.4, we follow these steps to locate the probability of obtaining a sample mean from a given population.

NOTE: The z-transformation is used to determine the likelihood of measuring a particular sample mean, from a population with a given mean and variance.

Templer and Tomeo (2002) measured scores obtained on the Graduate Record Examination (GRE) General Test from 1994 to 1997. They reported the mean and standard deviation of all scores on the exam during this period. Table 7.7 lists the mean and standard deviation for this population of scores on each section (verbal, quantitative, and analytic) of the GRE General Test. Suppose we select a sample of 100 college students. Using the population parameters listed in Table 7.7, what is the probability of selecting a sample of students who took the GRE General Test with a mean of 570 or better on the verbal, quantitative, and analytical sections of the test?

EXAMPLE 7.4

TABLE 7.7 The mean and standard deviation for a population of GRE scores.

GRE Section	μ	σ
Verbal	474	114
Quantitative	558	139
Analytical	547	130

Source: Adapted from Templer and Tomeo (2002).

Let's apply the steps to find the proportion under the normal curve for each section of the GRE General Test.

Verbal section. To compute the z-transformation, we need to know M, μ, and σ_M:

1. M is the sample mean: $M = 570$.

2. μ is the mean of the population, which is also the mean of the sampling distribution of sample means: $\mu = \mu_M = 474$.

3. σ_M is the standard error and is calculated as $\frac{\sigma}{\sqrt{n}} = \frac{114}{\sqrt{100}} = 11.40$.

Step 1: To transform a sample mean (M) to a z-score, we compute a z-transformation. In this example, $M = 570$. The z-transformation is

$$z = \frac{570 - 474}{11.40} = 8.42.$$

Step 2: In the unit normal table, we find that a z-score equal to 8.42 is so far away from the mean that it is not even listed in the table. The probability of selecting a sample mean greater than 570 in this population is close to 0.

Quantitative section. To compute the z-transformation, we again need to know M, μ, and σ_M:

1. M is the sample mean: $M = 570$.

2. μ is the mean of the population, which is also the mean of the sampling distribution of sample means: $\mu = \mu_M = 558$.

3. σ_M is the standard error and is calculated as $\dfrac{\sigma}{\sqrt{n}} = \dfrac{139}{\sqrt{100}} = 13.90$.

Step 1: To transform a sample mean (M) to a z-score, we compute a z-transformation. In this example, $M = 570$. The z-transformation is

$$z = \frac{570 - 558}{13.90} = 0.86.$$

Step 2: In the unit normal table, the probability of selecting a sample mean greater than 570 toward the tail is $p = .1949$.

Analytical section. To compute the z-transformation, we again need to know M, μ, and σ_M:

1. M is the sample mean: $M = 570$.

2. μ is the mean of the population, which is also the mean of the sampling distribution of sample means: $\mu = \mu_M = 547$.

3. σ_M is the standard error and is calculated as $\dfrac{\sigma}{\sqrt{n}} = \dfrac{130}{\sqrt{100}} = 13.0$.

Step 1: To transform a sample mean (M) to a z-score, we compute a z-transformation. In this example, $M = 570$. The z-transformation is

$$z = \frac{570 - 547}{13.0} = 1.77.$$

Step 2: In the unit normal table, the probability of selecting a sample mean greater than 570 toward the tail is $p = .0384$.

In this example, the probability of selecting a sample mean greater than 570 is basically zero on the verbal section, slightly more probable ($p = .0384$) on the analytical section, and most probable ($p = .1949$) on the quantitative section. We can use the z-transformation to locate the probability of obtaining any sample mean because the sampling distribution of the mean is always normally distributed.

LEARNING CHECK 6

1. What formula is used to find the probability of obtaining a sample mean from a given population?

2. Compute a z-transformation to find the z-score, given the following measures: $\mu = 5$, $\sigma_M = 1.5$, and $M = 8$.

3. Explain the following statement in words: $\mu_M = \mu$.

Answers: 1. The standard normal transformation or z-transformation; 2. $z = \dfrac{8-5}{1.5} = 2.00$; 3. The mean of the sampling distribution of the mean is equal to the value of the population mean.

CHAPTER SUMMARY ORGANIZED BY LEARNING OBJECTIVE

LO 1: Define *sampling distribution.*

- A **sampling distribution** is a distribution of all sample means or sample variances that could be obtained in samples of a given size from the same population.

LO 2: Compare theoretical and experimental sampling strategies.

- The theoretical sampling strategy is a sampling method in which we sample with replacement and the order in which a participant is selected matters.
- **Sampling with replacement** is a method of sampling in which each participant or item selected is replaced before the next draw.
- The experimental sampling strategy is a sampling method in which we sample without replacement and the order in which a participant is selected does not matter.
- **Sampling without replacement** is a method of sampling in which each participant or item selected is not replaced before the next draw.

LO 3–4: Identify three characteristics of the sampling distribution of the sample mean; calculate the mean and standard error of a sampling distribution of the sample mean and draw the shape of this distribution.

- The sample mean has the following three characteristics:
  a. The sample mean is an **unbiased estimator.** On average, we can expect the sample mean to equal the value of the population mean.
  b. A distribution of sample means follows the **central limit theorem.** Regardless of the shape of the distribution in a population, the distribution of sample means selected from the population will be approximately normally distributed.
  c. A distribution of sample means has minimum variance. The sampling distribution of the mean will vary minimally from the value of the population mean.

- The variance of the sampling distribution of sample means equals the population variance divided by the sample size:

$$\sigma_M^2 = \frac{\sigma^2}{n}.$$

- The **standard error of the mean** is the standard deviation of the sampling distribution of the sample means. It is the square root of the variance:

$$\sigma_M = \sqrt{\sigma_M^2} = \sqrt{\frac{\sigma^2}{n}} = \frac{\sigma}{\sqrt{n}}.$$

LO 5: Identify three characteristics of the sampling distribution of the sample variance.

- The sample variance has the following characteristics:
  a. The sample variance is an unbiased estimator. On average, we can expect the sample variance to equal the value of the population variance when we divide *SS* by *df.*
  b. A distribution of sample variances follows the skewed distribution rule. Regardless of the shape of the distribution in a population, the distribution of sample variances selected from the population will be approximately positively skewed.
  c. A distribution of sample variances has no minimum variance, meaning that this distribution will not vary minimally from the value of the population variance when we divide *SS* by *df.*

LO 6: Explain the relationship between standard error, standard deviation, and sample size.

- As the population standard deviation increases (σ), standard error increases. Hence, the farther scores in a population deviate from the mean in a population, the farther possible samples means can deviate from the value of the population mean.
- As the sample size increases (*n*), standard error decreases. Hence, the more data you

collect, the closer your estimate of the value of the population mean. This relationship is explained by the **law of large numbers.**

LO 7: Compute z-transformations for a sampling distribution of the sample mean.

- Using the notation for sample means, the z-transformation formula can be stated as:

$$z = \frac{M - \mu_M}{\sigma_M} \text{ or } z = \frac{M - \mu}{\sigma_M}.$$

- To locate the proportion of area, and therefore probabilities, of sample means in any sampling distribution, we follow two steps:

  Step 1: Transform a sample mean (M) into a z-score.

  Step 2: Locate the corresponding proportion for the z-score in the unit normal table.

APA LO 8: Summarize the standard error of the mean in APA format.

- The standard error is most often reported in the text, in a table, or in a graph. When data are reported in the text or in a table, they are usually reported with the value of the mean. In a graph, the standard error is displayed as a vertical bar extending above and below each mean plot or mean bar.

SPSS LO 9: Compute the estimate for the standard error of the mean using SPSS.

- SPSS can be used to compute an estimate of the standard error of the mean. An estimate for the standard error is computed using the **Analyze, Descriptive Statistics,** and **Descriptives** options in the menu bar. These actions will bring up a dialog box that will allow you to identify your variable, select **Options,** and choose the **S.E mean** option to compute an estimate of the standard error (for more details, see Section 7.7).

KEY TERMS

central limit theorem	sampling error	standard error of the mean
law of large numbers	sampling with replacement	unbiased estimator
sample design	sampling without replacement	
sampling distribution	standard error	

END-OF-CHAPTER PROBLEMS

Factual Problems

1. What is a sampling distribution?

2. Explain how conditional probabilities are related to sampling without replacement.

3. Distinguish between sampling where order matters and order does not matter.

4. Distinguish between sampling with replacement and sampling without replacement.

5. The sample mean is an unbiased estimator of the population mean. Explain this statement.

6. Define the central limit theorem.

7. Explain why the following statement is true: $\mu = \mu_M$.

8. The sample variance is an unbiased estimator of the population variance when we divide SS by df. What does this mean?

9. The sampling distribution of sample variances approximates the shape of what type of distribution?

10. To measure sample variance, is it more important that the sample variance be unbiased or vary minimally from a population variance?

11. What does the standard error measure?

12. How would the standard error change if (a) the population standard deviation increased and (b) the sample size increased?

Concepts and Application Problems

13. A statistics instructor wants to measure the effectiveness of his teaching skills in a class of 102 students ($N = 102$). He selects students by waiting at the door to the classroom prior to his lecture and pulling aside every third student to give him or her a questionnaire.

    (a) Is this sample design an example of random sampling? Explain.

    (b) Assuming that all students attend his class that day, how many students will he select to complete the questionnaire?

14. A local high school is interested in studying how teacher perceptions of students, as being intelligent or not, affect the success of freshman students in the classroom. The school creates an Excel spreadsheet listing all freshmen students in alphabetical order and places their names into one of two columns. All students listed in the second column are selected to participate in this study. Is this sample design an example of random sampling? Explain.

15. A clinical psychologist is the primary therapist for 12 patients. She randomly selects a sample of 3 patients to be in her study. How many different samples of this size can be selected from this population of 12 patients using (a) theoretical sampling and (b) experimental sampling?

16. Using the theoretical sampling strategy, how many samples of size 4 ($n = 4$) can be drawn from a population of size:

    (a) $N = 5$ (b) $N = 8$ (c) $N = 16$ (d) $N = 50$

17. Using the experimental sampling strategy, how many samples of size 3 ($n = 3$) can be drawn from a population of size:

    (a) $N = 5$ (b) $N = 6$ (c) $N = 7$ (d) $N = 8$

18. The sample mean is an unbiased estimator of the population mean. What do we expect the sample mean to be equal to when the population mean is equal to:

    (a) $\mu = 8$ (b) $\mu = 0$ (c) $\mu = -20$

    (d) $\mu = \infty$ (e) $\mu = -\infty$ (f) $\mu = .03$

19. Using the central limit theorem, what is the distribution of sample means when the population distribution is:

    (a) rectangular (b) normally distributed

    (c) positively skewed (d) nonmodal

    (e) multimodal (f) negatively skewed

20. State whether each of the following statements concerning the sample mean is true or false.

    (a) The value of the sample mean equals the population mean on average.

    (b) The value of the sample mean can vary from sample to sample.

    (c) There is more than a 5% probability of selecting a sample mean that is farther than 2 *SEM* from the population mean.

    (d) The sampling distribution of sample means is approximately normally distributed.

21. Using the skewed distribution rule, what is the distribution of sample variances when the population distribution is:

    (a) rectangular (b) normally distributed

    (c) positively skewed (d) nonmodal

    (e) multimodal (f) negatively skewed

22. State whether each of the following statements concerning the sample variance is true or false.

    (a) The value of the sample variance is an unbiased estimator of the population variance when dividing *SS* by *df*.

    (b) The value of the sample variance will vary minimally from the population variance when dividing *SS* by *df*.

    (c) It is more important that the sample variance be an unbiased estimator than vary minimally from the population variance.

    (d) The sampling distribution of sample variances is approximately normally distributed.

23. A population is normally distributed with a mean of 56 and a standard deviation of 12.

    (a) What is the mean of the sampling distribution (μ_M) for this population?

    (b) If a sample of 36 participants is selected from this population, what is the standard error of the mean (σ_M)?

    (c) Sketch the shape of this distribution with $M \pm 3$ *SEM*.

24. A population is normally distributed with a mean of –30 and a standard deviation of 4.

    (a) What is the mean of the sampling distribution (μ_M) for this population?

    (b) If a sample of 16 participants is selected from this population, what is the standard error of the mean (σ_M)?

    (c) Sketch the shape of this distribution with $M \pm 3$ *SEM*.

25. A population of scores is normally distributed with a standard deviation equal to 7. State whether the standard error will increase, decrease, or remain unchanged if the value of the population standard deviation is changed to:

    (a) $\sigma = 10$ (b) $\sigma = 2$ (c) $\sigma = \dfrac{28}{4}$
    (d) $\sigma = \dfrac{4}{20}$ (e) $\sigma = 7.5$ (f) $\sigma = 0$

26. A sample of 26 scores is selected from a normally distributed population. State whether the standard error will increase or decrease if the sample size is changed to:

    (a) $n = 36$ (b) $n = 5$ (c) $n = 28$ (d) $n = 25$

Problems in Research

27. **Sampling from the population.** Conners, Epstein, Angold, and Klaric (2003) selected a random sample of 816 children from a population of 17,117 children who lived in western North Carolina.

    (a) How many possible samples of 816 children are possible from this population of 17,117 using theoretical sampling?

    (b) Would more samples be possible if the researchers used experimental sampling?

28. **Classroom assessment: Sampling and the population.** Ryan (2006) reported about the effectiveness of an assignment given to students during a statistics class. The in-class assignment was aimed at helping students understand sampling distributions. In this study, participants selected 120 samples of size 3 from a population of 5 scores (0, 0, 0, 3, and 6) using the theoretical sampling strategy.

    (a) How many possible samples can be drawn from this population?

    (b) What is the population mean?

    (c) What is the population standard deviation?

29. **Classroom assessment: Central limit theorem.** In the Ryan (2006) study described in Question 28, participants selected 120 samples of size 3 from a population of 5 scores (0, 0, 0, 3, and 6) using theoretical sampling. Based on this example,

    (a) What is the shape of the population distribution? *Hint:* Graph the frequency distribution of the population of scores: 0, 0, 0, 3, and 6.

    (b) What is the shape of the sampling distribution of sample means? *Hint:* You do not need calculations to answer this question.

30. **Classroom assessment: Standard error.** In the Ryan (2006) study described in Question 28, participants selected 120 samples of size 3 from a population of 5 scores (0, 0, 0, 3, and 6) using theoretical sampling. Ryan (2006) reported the mean and standard error for the theoretical sampling distribution listed in the following table. Compute the formula for standard error to confirm the value of the standard error shown in the table.

	Theoretical Sampling Distribution
Mean	1.80
Standard error	1.39

31. **Child-directed and teacher-directed play behavior.** Gmitrova and Gmitrov (2004) conducted a study in which playtime among children was directed by another child (child directed) or by a teacher (teacher directed). In their study, they reported that "the average number of children participating in 'teacher-directed' and 'child-directed' play was 15.8 ± 3.0 and 14.9 ± 3.07 [mean ± standard error], respectively" (p. 270). Assuming these data are normally distributed, use the steps to conduct a z-transformation to determine the following probabilities:

    (a) What is the probability of selecting a sample mean between 14 and 18 for the group with teacher-directed play?

    (b) What is the probability of selecting a sample mean between 14 and 18 for the group with child-directed play?

32. **Variability in sampling.** Wild (2006) stated, "The main priority with sampling distributions is to get across the idea that estimates and other statistics change every time we do a new study" (p. 19). Explain what the researcher meant in this statement.

NOTE: Answers for even numbers are in Appendix C.

PART

III

Making Inferences About One or Two Means

Introduction to Hypothesis Testing

LEARNING OBJECTIVES

After reading this chapter, you should be able to:

1 Identify the four steps of hypothesis testing.

2 Define null hypothesis, alternative hypothesis, level of significance, test statistic, *p* value, and statistical significance.

3 Define Type I error and Type II error, and identify the type of error that researchers control.

4 Calculate the one-independent sample *z*-test and interpret the results.

5 Distinguish between a one-tailed and a two-tailed test, and explain why a Type III error is possible only with one-tailed tests.

6 Explain what effect size measures and compute a Cohen's *d* for the one-independent sample *z*-test.

7 Define *power* and identify six factors that influence power.

8 Summarize the results of a one-independent sample *z*-test in American Psychological Association (APA) format.

CHAPTER 8

8.1   INFERENTIAL STATISTICS AND HYPOTHESIS TESTING

We use inferential statistics because it allows us to measure behavior in samples to learn more about the behavior in populations that are often too large or inaccessible. We use samples because we know how they are related to populations. For example, suppose the average score on a standardized exam in a given population is 1,000. In Chapter 7, we showed that the sample mean as an unbiased estimator of the population mean—if we selected a random sample from a population, then on average the value of the sample mean will equal the population mean. In our example, if we select a random sample from this population with a mean of 1,000, then, on average, the value of a sample mean will equal 1,000. On the basis of the central limit theorem, we know that the probability of selecting any other sample mean value from this population is normally distributed.

In behavioral research, we select samples to learn more about populations of interest to us. In terms of the mean, we measure a sample mean to learn more about the mean in a population. Therefore, we will use the sample mean to describe the population mean. We begin by stating the value of a population mean, and then we select a sample and measure the mean in that sample. On average, the value of the sample mean will equal the population mean. The larger the difference or discrepancy between the sample mean and population mean, the less likely it is that we could have selected that sample mean, if the value of the population mean is correct. This type of experimental situation, using the example of standardized exam scores, is illustrated in Figure 8.1.

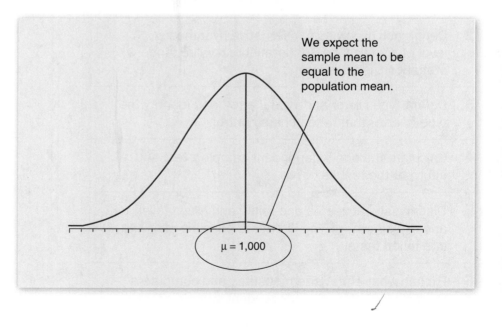

FIGURE 8.1

The sampling distribution for a population with a mean equal to 1,000. If 1,000 is the correct population mean, then the sample mean will equal 1,000, on average, with outcomes farther from the population mean being less and less likely to occur.

The method in which we select samples to learn more about characteristics in a given population is called **hypothesis testing**. Hypothesis testing is really a systematic way to test claims or ideas about a group or population. To illustrate, suppose we read an article stating that children in the United States watch an average of 3 hours of TV per week. To test whether this claim is true, we record the time (in hours) that a group of 20 American children (the sample), among all children in the United States (the population), watch TV. The mean we measure for these 20 children is a sample mean. We can then compare the sample mean we select to the population mean stated in the article.

> **Hypothesis testing** or **significance testing** is a method for testing a claim or hypothesis about a parameter in a population, using data measured in a sample. In this method, we test some hypothesis by determining the likelihood that a sample statistic could have been selected, if the hypothesis regarding the population parameter were true.

DEFINITION

The method of hypothesis testing can be summarized in four steps. We describe each of these four steps in greater detail in Section 8.2.

1. To begin, we identify a hypothesis or claim that we feel should be tested. For example, we might want to test the claim that the mean number of hours that children in the United States watch TV is 3 hours.

2. We select a criterion upon which we decide that the claim being tested is true or not. For example, the claim is that children watch 3 hours of TV per week. Most samples we select should have a mean close to or equal to 3 hours if the claim we are testing is true. So at what point do we decide that the discrepancy between the sample mean and 3 is so big that the claim we are testing is likely not true? We answer this question in this step of hypothesis testing.

3. Select a random sample from the population and measure the sample mean. For example, we could select 20 children and measure the mean time (in hours) that they watch TV per week.

4. Compare what we observe in the sample to what we expect to observe if the claim we are testing is true. We expect the sample mean to be around 3 hours. If the discrepancy between the sample mean and population mean is small, then we will likely decide that the claim we are testing is indeed true. If the discrepancy is too large, then we will likely decide to reject the claim as being not true.

NOTE: Hypothesis testing is the method of testing whether claims or hypotheses regarding a population are likely to be true.

---

1. On average, what do we expect the sample mean to be equal to?

2. True or false: Researchers select a sample from a population to learn more about characteristics in that sample.

LEARNING CHECK 1

8.2 FOUR STEPS TO HYPOTHESIS TESTING

The goal of hypothesis testing is to determine the likelihood that a population parameter, such as the mean, is likely to be true. In this section, we describe the four steps of hypothesis testing that were briefly introduced in Section 8.1:

Step 1: State the hypotheses.

Step 2: Set the criteria for a decision.

Step 3: Compute the test statistic.

Step 4: Make a decision.

Step 1: State the hypotheses. We begin by stating the value of a population mean in a **null hypothesis,** which we presume is true. For the children watching TV example, we state the null hypothesis that children in the United States watch an average of 3 hours of TV per week. This is a starting point so that we can decide whether this is likely to be true, similar to the presumption of innocence in a courtroom. When a defendant is on trial, the jury starts by assuming that the defendant is innocent. The basis of the decision is to determine whether this assumption is true. Likewise, in hypothesis testing, we start by assuming that the hypothesis or claim we are testing is true. This is stated in the null hypothesis. The basis of the decision is to determine whether this assumption is likely to be true.

DEFINITION

The **null hypothesis (H_0),** stated as the **null**, is a statement about a population parameter, such as the population mean, that is assumed to be true.

The null hypothesis is a starting point. We will test whether the value stated in the null hypothesis is likely to be true.

Keep in mind that the only reason we are testing the null hypothesis is because we think it is wrong. We state what we think is wrong about the null hypothesis in an **alternative hypothesis.** For the children watching TV example, we may have reason to believe that children watch more than (>) or less than (<) 3 hours of TV per week. When we are uncertain of the direction, we can state that the value in the null hypothesis is not equal to (≠) 3 hours.

NOTE: In hypothesis testing, we conduct a study to test whether the null hypothesis is likely to be true.

In a courtroom, the defendant is assumed to be innocent (this is the null hypothesis so to speak), so the burden is on a prosecutor to conduct a trial to show evidence that the defendant is not innocent. In a similar way, we assume the null hypothesis is true, placing the burden on the researcher to conduct a study to show evidence that the null hypothesis is unlikely to be true. Regardless, we always make a decision about the null hypothesis (that it is likely or unlikely to be true). The alternative hypothesis is needed for Step 2.

DEFINITION

An **alternative hypothesis (H_1)** is a statement that directly contradicts a null hypothesis by stating that that the actual value of a population parameter is less than, greater than, or not equal to the value stated in the null hypothesis.

The alternative hypothesis states what we think is wrong about the null hypothesis, which is needed for Step 2.

MAKING SENSE: Testing the Null Hypothesis

A decision made in hypothesis testing centers on the null hypothesis. This means two things in terms of making a decision:

1. Decisions are made about the null hypothesis. Using the courtroom analogy, a jury decides whether a defendant is guilty or not guilty. The jury does not make a decision of guilty or *innocent* because the defendant is assumed to be innocent. All evidence presented in a trial is to show that a defendant is guilty. The evidence either shows guilt (decision: guilty) or does not (decision: not guilty). In a similar way, the null hypothesis is assumed to be correct. A researcher conducts a study showing evidence that this assumption is unlikely (we reject the null hypothesis) or fails to do so (we retain the null hypothesis).

2. The bias is to do nothing. Using the courtroom analogy, for the same reason the courts would rather let the guilty go free than send the innocent to prison, researchers would rather do nothing (accept previous notions of truth stated by a null hypothesis) than make statements that are not correct. For this reason, we assume the null hypothesis is correct, thereby placing the burden on the researcher to demonstrate that the null hypothesis is not likely to be correct.

Step 2: Set the criteria for a decision. To set the criteria for a decision, we state the **level of significance** for a test. This is similar to the criterion that jurors use in a criminal trial. Jurors decide whether the evidence presented shows guilt *beyond a reasonable doubt* (this is the criterion). Likewise, in hypothesis testing, we collect data to show that the null hypothesis is not true, based on the likelihood of selecting a sample mean from a population (the likelihood is the criterion). The likelihood or level of significance is typically set at 5% in behavioral research studies. When the probability of obtaining a sample mean is less than 5% if the null hypothesis were true, then we conclude that the sample we selected is too unlikely and so we reject the null hypothesis.

Level of significance, or significance level, refers to a criterion of judgment upon which a decision is made regarding the value stated in a null hypothesis. The criterion is based on the probability of obtaining a statistic measured in a sample if the value stated in the null hypothesis were true.

In behavioral science, the criterion or level of significance is typically set at 5%. When the probability of obtaining a sample mean is less than 5% if the null hypothesis were true, then we reject the value stated in the null hypothesis.

DEFINITION

The alternative hypothesis establishes where to place the level of significance. Remember that the sample mean will equal the population mean on average if the null hypothesis is true. All other possible values of the sample mean are normally distributed (central limit theorem). The empirical rule tells us that at least 95% of all sample means fall within about 2 standard deviations (*SD*) of the population mean, meaning that there is less than a 5% probability of obtaining a sample mean that is

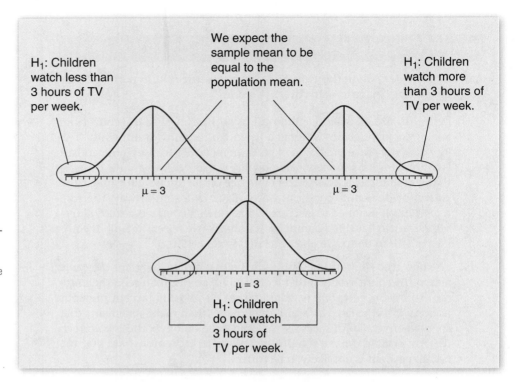

FIGURE 8.2

The alternative hypothesis determines whether to place the level of significance in one or both tails of a sampling distribution. Sample means that fall in the tails are unlikely to occur (less than a 5% probability) if the value stated for a population mean in the null hypothesis is true.

beyond 2 *SD* from the population mean. For the children watching TV example, we can look for the probability of obtaining a sample mean beyond 2 *SD* in the upper tail (greater than 3), the lower tail (less than 3), or both tails (not equal to 3). Figure 8.2 shows that the alternative hypothesis is used to determine which tail or tails to place the level of significance for a hypothesis test.

NOTE: The level of significance in hypothesis testing is the criterion we use to decide whether the value stated in the null hypothesis is likely to be true.

Step 3: Compute the test statistic. Suppose we measure a sample mean equal to 4 hours per week that children watch TV. To make a decision, we need to evaluate how likely this sample outcome is, if the population mean stated by the null hypothesis (3 hours per week) is true. We use a **test statistic** to determine this likelihood. Specifically, a test statistic tells us how far, or how many standard deviations, a sample mean is from the population mean. The larger the value of the test statistic, the farther the distance, or number of standard deviations, a sample mean is from the population mean stated in the null hypothesis. The value of the test statistic is used to make a decision in Step 4.

DEFINITION

The **test statistic** is a mathematical formula that allows researchers to determine the likelihood of obtaining sample outcomes if the null hypothesis were true. The value of the test statistic is used to make a decision regarding the null hypothesis.

NOTE: We use the value of the test statistic to make a decision regarding the null hypothesis.

Step 4: Make a decision. We use the value of the test statistic to make a decision about the null hypothesis. The decision is based on the probability of obtaining a sample mean, given that the value stated in the null hypothesis is true. If the probability of obtaining a sample mean is less than 5% when the null hypothesis is true, then the decision is to reject the null hypothesis. If the probability of obtaining a sample mean is greater than 5% when the null hypothesis is true, then the decision is to retain the null hypothesis. In sum, there are two decisions a researcher can make:

1. Reject the null hypothesis. The sample mean is associated with a low probability of occurrence when the null hypothesis is true.

2. Retain the null hypothesis. The sample mean is associated with a high probability of occurrence when the null hypothesis is true.

The probability of obtaining a sample mean, given that the value stated in the null hypothesis is true, is stated by the **p value.** The p value is a probability: It varies between 0 and 1 and can never be negative. In Step 2, we stated the criterion or probability of obtaining a sample mean at which point we will decide to reject the value stated in the null hypothesis, which is typically set at 5% in behavioral research. To make a decision, we compare the p value to the criterion we set in Step 2.

DEFINITION

A **p value** is the probability of obtaining a sample outcome, given that the value stated in the null hypothesis is true. The p value for obtaining a sample outcome is compared to the level of significance.

Significance, or **statistical significance**, describes a decision made concerning a value stated in the null hypothesis. When the null hypothesis is rejected, we reach significance. When the null hypothesis is retained, we fail to reach significance.

NOTE: Researchers make decisions regarding the null hypothesis. The decision can be to retain the null (p > .05) or reject the null (p < .05).

When the p value is less than 5% ($p < .05$), we reject the null hypothesis. We will refer to $p < .05$ as the criterion for deciding to reject the null hypothesis, although note that when $p = .05$, the decision is also to reject the null hypothesis. When the p value is greater than 5% ($p > .05$), we retain the null hypothesis. The decision to reject or retain the null hypothesis is called **significance.** When the p value is less than .05, we reach significance; the decision is to reject the null hypothesis. When the p value is greater than .05, we fail to reach significance; the decision is to retain the null hypothesis. Figure 8.3 shows the four steps of hypothesis testing.

 **LEARNING CHECK 2**

1. State the four steps of hypothesis testing.

2. The decision in hypothesis testing is to retain or reject which hypothesis: the null or alternative hypothesis?

3. The criterion or level of significance in behavioral research is typically set at what probability value?

4. A test statistic is associated with a p value less than .05 or 5%. What is the decision for this hypothesis test?

5. If the null hypothesis is rejected, then did we reach significance?

Answers: 1. Step 1: State the hypotheses. Step 2: Set the criteria for a decision. Step 3: Compute the test statistic. Step 4: Make a decision; 2. Null; 3. The level of significance is typically set at .05; 4. Reject the null; 5. Yes.

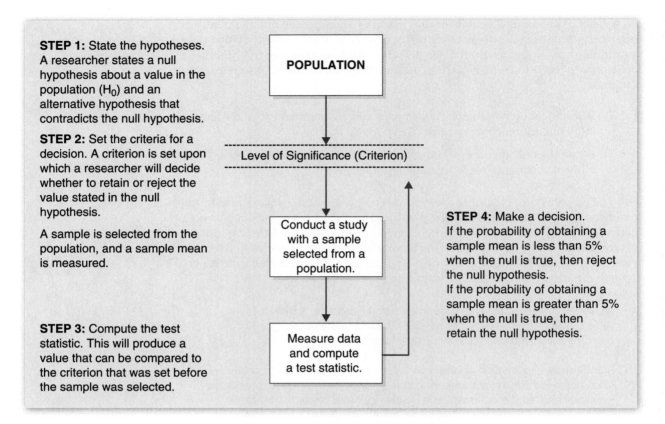

STEP 1: State the hypotheses. A researcher states a null hypothesis about a value in the population (H_0) and an alternative hypothesis that contradicts the null hypothesis.

STEP 2: Set the criteria for a decision. A criterion is set upon which a researcher will decide whether to retain or reject the value stated in the null hypothesis.

A sample is selected from the population, and a sample mean is measured.

STEP 3: Compute the test statistic. This will produce a value that can be compared to the criterion that was set before the sample was selected.

POPULATION

Level of Significance (Criterion)

Conduct a study with a sample selected from a population.

Measure data and compute a test statistic.

STEP 4: Make a decision. If the probability of obtaining a sample mean is less than 5% when the null is true, then reject the null hypothesis. If the probability of obtaining a sample mean is greater than 5% when the null is true, then retain the null hypothesis.

FIGURE 8.3

A summary of hypothesis testing.

8.3 HYPOTHESIS TESTING AND SAMPLING DISTRIBUTIONS

The logic of hypothesis testing is rooted in an understanding of the sampling distribution of the mean. In Chapter 7, we showed three characteristics of the mean, two of which are particularly relevant in this section:

1. The sample mean is an unbiased estimator of the population mean. On average, a randomly selected sample will have a mean equal to that in the population. In hypothesis testing, we begin by stating the null hypothesis. We expect that, if the null hypothesis is true, then a random sample selected from a given population will have a sample mean equal to the value stated in the null hypothesis.

2. Regardless of the distribution in the population, the sampling distribution of the sample mean is normally distributed. Hence, the probabilities of all other possible sample means we could select are normally distributed. Using this distribution, we can therefore state an alternative hypothesis to locate the probability of obtaining sample means with less than a 5% chance of being selected if the value stated in the null hypothesis is true. Figure 8.2 shows that we can identify sample mean outcomes in one or both tails.

To locate the probability of obtaining a sample mean in a sampling distribution, we must know (1) the population mean and (2) the standard error of the mean (*SEM;* introduced in Chapter 7). Each value is entered in the test statistic formula computed in Step 3, thereby allowing us to make a decision in Step 4. To review, Table 8.1 displays the notations used to describe populations, samples, and sampling distributions. Table 8.2 summarizes the characteristics of each type of distribution.

TABLE 8.1 A review of the notation used for the mean, variance, and standard deviation in population, sample, and sampling distributions.

Characteristic	Population	Sample	Sampling Distribution
Mean	μ	M or $\bar{X}$	$\mu_M = \mu$
Variance	σ^2	s^2 or SD^2	$\sigma_M^2 = \dfrac{\sigma^2}{n}$
Standard deviation	σ	s or SD	$\sigma_M = \dfrac{\sigma}{\sqrt{n}}$

TABLE 8.2 A review of the key differences between population, sample, and sampling distributions.

	Population Distribution	Sample Distribution	Distribution of Sample Means
What is it?	Scores of all persons in a population	Scores of a select portion of persons from the population	All possible sample means that can be drawn, given a certain sample size
Is it accessible?	Typically, no	Yes	Yes
What is the shape?	Could be any shape	Could be any shape	Normally distributed

LEARNING CHECK 3

1. For the following statement, write increases or decreases as an answer. The likelihood that we reject the null hypothesis (increases or decreases):

   a. The closer the value of a sample mean is to the value stated by the null hypothesis?

   b. The further the value of a sample mean is from the value stated in the null hypothesis?

2. A researcher selects a sample of 49 students to test the null hypothesis that the average student exercises 90 minutes per week. What is the mean for the sampling distribution for this population of interest if the null hypothesis is true?

8.4   MAKING A DECISION: TYPES OF ERROR

In Step 4, we decide whether to retain or reject the null hypothesis. Because we are observing a sample and not an entire population, it is possible that a conclusion may be wrong. Table 8.3 shows that there are four decision alternatives regarding the truth and falsity of the decision we make about a null hypothesis:

1. The decision to retain the null hypothesis could be correct.

2. The decision to retain the null hypothesis could be incorrect.

3. The decision to reject the null hypothesis could be correct.

4. The decision to reject the null hypothesis could be incorrect.

TABLE 8.3   Four outcomes for making a decision. The decision can be either correct (correctly reject or retain null) or wrong (incorrectly reject or retain null).

		Decision	
		Retain the Null	**Reject the Null**
Truth in the Population	True	CORRECT $1-\alpha$	TYPE I ERROR α
	False	TYPE II ERROR β	CORRECT $1-\beta$ POWER

We investigate each decision alternative in this section. Because we will observe a sample, and not a population, it is impossible to know for sure the truth in the population. So for the sake of illustration, we will assume we know this. This assumption is labeled as truth in the population in Table 8.3. In this section, we will introduce each decision alternative.

DECISION: RETAIN THE NULL HYPOTHESIS

When we decide to retain the null hypothesis, we can be correct or incorrect. The correct decision is to retain a true null hypothesis. This decision is called a null result or null finding. This is usually an uninteresting decision because the decision is to retain what we already assumed: that the value stated in the null hypothesis is correct. For this reason, null results alone are rarely published in behavioral research.

NOTE: A Type II error, or beta (β) error, is the probability of incorrectly retaining the null hypothesis.

The incorrect decision is to retain a false null hypothesis. This decision is an example of a **Type II error, or β error.** With each test we make, there is always some probability that the decision could be a Type II error. In this decision, we decide to retain previous notions of truth that are in fact false. While it's an error, we still did nothing; we retained the null hypothesis. We can always go back and conduct more studies.

Type II error, or **beta (β) error**, is the probability of retaining a null hypothesis that is actually false.

DEFINITION

DECISION: REJECT THE NULL HYPOTHESIS

When we decide to reject the null hypothesis, we can be correct or incorrect. The incorrect decision is to reject a true null hypothesis. This decision is an example of a **Type I error.** With each test we make, there is always some probability that our decision is a Type I error. A researcher who makes this error decides to reject previous notions of truth that are in fact true. Making this type of error is analogous to finding an innocent person guilty. To minimize this error, we place the burden on the researcher to demonstrate evidence that the null hypothesis is indeed false. To demonstrate evidence that leads to a decision to reject the null hypothesis, the research must reach significance ($p < .05$).

Type I error is the probability of rejecting a null hypothesis that is actually true. Researchers directly control for the probability of committing this type of error.

An **alpha (α) level** is the level of significance or criterion for a hypothesis test. It is the largest probability of committing a Type I error that we will allow and still decide to reject the null hypothesis.

DEFINITION

Because we assume the null hypothesis is true, we control for Type I error by stating a level of significance. The level we set, called the **alpha level** (symbolized as α), is the largest probability of committing a Type I error that we will allow and still decide to reject the null hypothesis. This criterion is usually set at .05 ($α = .05$), and we compare the alpha level to the p value. When the probability of a Type I error is less than 5% ($p < .05$), we decide to reject the null hypothesis; otherwise, we retain the null hypothesis.

NOTE: Researchers directly control for the probability of a Type I error by stating an alpha (α) level.

The correct decision is to reject a false null hypothesis. In other words, we decide that the null hypothesis is false when it is indeed false. This decision is called the **power** of the decision-making process because it is the decision we aim for. Remember that we are only testing the null hypothesis because we think it is wrong. Deciding to reject a false null hypothesis, then, is the power, inasmuch as we learn the most about populations when we accurately reject false notions of truth. This decision is the most published result in behavioral research.

NOTE: The power in hypothesis testing is the probability of correctly rejecting the value stated in the null hypothesis.

The **power** in hypothesis testing is the probability of rejecting a false null hypothesis. Specifically, it is the probability that a randomly selected sample will show that the null hypothesis is false when the null hypothesis is indeed false.

DEFINITION

✔ **LEARNING CHECK 4**

1. What type of error do we directly control?

2. What type of error is associated with decisions to retain the null?

3. What type of error is associated with decisions to reject the null?

4. State the two correct decisions that a researcher can make.

8.5 TESTING A RESEARCH HYPOTHESIS: EXAMPLES USING THE *Z*-TEST

The test statistic in Step 3 converts the sampling distribution we observe into a standard normal distribution, thereby allowing us to make a decision in Step 4. The test statistic we use depends largely on what we know about the population. When we know the mean and standard deviation in a single population, we can use the **one–independent sample z-test**, which we will use in this section to illustrate the four steps of hypothesis testing.

DEFINITION

The **one–independent sample z-test** is a statistical procedure used to test hypotheses concerning the mean in a single population with a known variance.

NOTE: The z-test is used to test hypotheses about a population mean when the population variance is known.

Recall that we can state one of three alternative hypotheses: A population mean is greater than (>), less than (<), or not equal (≠) to the value stated in a null hypothesis. The alternative hypothesis determines which tail of a sampling distribution to place the level of significance, as illustrated in Figure 8.2. In this section, we will use an example for each type of alternative hypothesis.

NONDIRECTIONAL, TWO-TAILED HYPOTHESIS TESTS (H$_1$: ≠)

NOTE: Nondirectional tests are used to test hypotheses when we are interested in any alternative from the null hypothesis.

In Example 8.1, we will use the z-test for a **nondirectional**, or **two-tailed test**, where the alternative hypothesis is stated as *not equal to* (≠) the null hypothesis. For this test, we will place the level of significance in both tails of the sampling distribution. We are therefore interested in any alternative from the null hypothesis. This is the most common alternative hypothesis tested in behavioral science.

DEFINITION

Nondirectional tests, or **two-tailed tests**, are hypothesis tests where the alternative hypothesis is stated as *not equal to* (≠). The researcher is interested in any alternative from the null hypothesis.

EXAMPLE 8.1

Templer and Tomeo (2002) reported that the population mean score on the quantitative portion of the Graduate Record Examination (GRE) General Test for students taking the exam between 1994 and 1997 was 558 ± 139 ($\mu \pm \sigma$). Suppose we select a sample of 100 participants ($n = 100$). We record a sample mean equal to 585 ($M = 585$). Compute the one–independent sample z-test for whether we will retain the null hypothesis ($\mu = 558$) at a .05 level of significance ($\alpha = .05$).

Step 1: State the hypotheses. The population mean is 558, and we are testing whether the null hypothesis is (=) or is not (≠) correct:

H_0: $\mu = 558$ Mean test scores are equal to 558 in the population.

H_1: $\mu \neq 558$ Mean test scores are not equal to 558 in the population.

Step 2: Set the criteria for a decision. The level of significance is .05, which makes the alpha level $\alpha = .05$. To locate the probability of obtaining a sample mean from a given population, we use the standard normal distribution. We will locate the z scores in a standard normal distribution that are the cutoffs, or **critical values,** for sample mean values with less than a 5% probability of occurrence if the value stated in the null hypothesis ($\mu = 558$) is true.

A **critical value** is a cutoff value that defines the boundaries beyond which less than 5% of sample means can be obtained if the null hypothesis is true. Sample means obtained beyond a critical value will result in a decision to reject the null hypothesis.

DEFINITION

In a nondirectional two-tailed test, we divide the alpha value in half so that an equal proportion of area is placed in the upper and lower tail. Table 8.4 gives the critical values for one- and two-tailed tests at a .05, .01, and .001 level of significance. Figure 8.4 displays a graph with the critical values for Example 8.1 shown. In this example $\alpha = .05$, so we split this probability in half:

$$\text{Splitting } \alpha \text{ in half: } \frac{\alpha}{2} = \frac{.05}{2} = .0250 \text{ in each tail.}$$

TABLE 8.4 Critical values for one- and two-tailed tests at three commonly used levels of significance.

Level of Significance (α)	Type of Test	
	One-Tailed	**Two-Tailed**
0.05	+1.645 or −1.645	±1.96
0.01	+2.33 or −2.33	±2.58
0.001	+3.09 or −3.09	±3.30

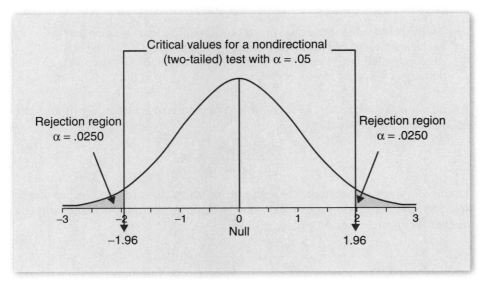

FIGURE 8.4

The critical values (±1.96) for a nondirectional (two-tailed) test with a .05 level of significance.

NOTE: For two-tailed tests, the alpha is split in half and placed in each tail of a standard normal distribution.

NOTE: A critical value marks the cutoff for the rejection region.

To locate the critical values, we use the unit normal table given in Table B.1 in Appendix B and look up the proportion .0250 toward the tail in column C. This value, .0250, is listed for a z-score equal to $z = 1.96$. This is the critical value for the upper tail of the standard normal distribution. Because the normal distribution is symmetrical, the critical value in the bottom tail will be the same distance below the mean, or $z = -1.96$. The regions beyond the critical values, displayed in Figure 8.4, are called the **rejection regions.** If the value of the test statistic falls in these regions, then the decision is to reject the null hypothesis; otherwise, we retain the null hypothesis.

DEFINITION

The **rejection region** is the region beyond a critical value in a hypothesis test. When the value of a test statistic is in the rejection region, we decide to reject the null hypothesis; otherwise, we retain the null hypothesis.

Step 3: Compute the test statistic. Step 2 sets the stage for making a decision because the criterion is set. The probability is less than 5% that we will obtain a sample mean that is at least 1.96 standard deviations above or below the value of the population mean stated in the null hypothesis. In this step, we will compute a test statistic to determine whether the sample mean we selected is beyond or within the critical values we stated in Step 2.

The test statistic for a one–independent sample z-test is called the **z-statistic.** The z-statistic converts any sampling distribution into a standard normal distribution. The z-statistic is therefore a z-transformation. The solution of the formula gives the number of standard deviations, or z-scores, that a sample mean falls above or below the population mean stated in the null hypothesis. We can then compare the value of the z-statistic, called the **obtained value,** to the critical values we determined in Step 2. The z-statistic formula is the sample mean minus the population mean stated in the null hypothesis, divided by the standard error of the mean:

$$\textbf{z-statistic: } z_{obt} = \frac{M - \mu}{\sigma_M}, \text{ where } \sigma_M = \frac{\sigma}{\sqrt{n}}.$$

DEFINITION

The **z-statistic** is an inferential statistic used to determine the number of standard deviations in a standard normal distribution that a sample mean deviates from the population mean stated in the null hypothesis.

The **obtained value** is the value of a test statistic. This value is compared to the critical value(s) of a hypothesis test to make a decision. When the obtained value exceeds a critical value, we decide to reject the null hypothesis; otherwise, we retain the null hypothesis.

NOTE: The z-statistic measures the number of standard deviations, or z-scores, that a sample mean falls above or below the population mean stated in the null hypothesis.

To calculate the z-statistic, first compute the standard error (σ_M), which is the denominator for the z-statistic:

$$\sigma_M = \frac{\sigma}{\sqrt{n}} = \frac{139}{\sqrt{100}} = 13.9.$$

Then compute the z-statistic by substituting the values of the sample mean, $M = 585$; the population mean stated by the null hypothesis, $\mu = 558$; and the standard error we just calculated, $\sigma_M = 13.9$:

$$z_{obt} = \frac{M - \mu}{\sigma_M} = \frac{585 - 558}{13.9} = 1.94.$$

Step 4: Make a decision. To make a decision, we compare the obtained value to the critical values. We reject the null hypothesis if the obtained value exceeds a critical value. Figure 8.5 shows that the obtained value ($z_{obt} = 1.94$) is less than the critical value; it does not fall in the rejection region. The decision is to retain the null hypothesis.

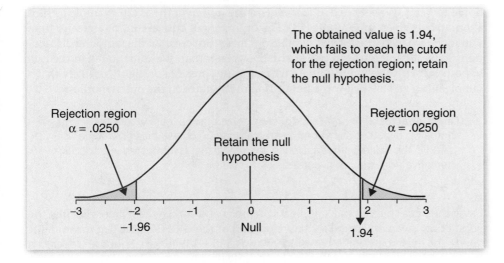

The obtained value is 1.94, which fails to reach the cutoff for the rejection region; retain the null hypothesis.

FIGURE 8.5

Since the obtained value fails to reach the rejection region (it is within the critical values of ± 1.96), we decide to retain the null hypothesis.

The probability of obtaining $z_{obt} = 1.94$ is stated by the p value. To locate the p value or probability of obtaining the z-statistic, we refer to the unit normal table in Table B.1 in Appendix B. Look for a z-score equal to 1.94 in column A, then locate the probability toward the tail in column C. The value is .0262. Finally, multiply the value given in column C times the number of tails for alpha. Because this is a two-tailed test, we multiply .0262 times 2: $p = (.0262) \times 2$ tails $= .0524$. Table 8.5 summarizes how to determine the p value for one- and two-tailed tests. (We will compute one-tailed tests in Examples 8.2 and 8.3.)

TABLE 8.5 To find the p value for the z-statistic, find its probability (toward the tail) in the unit normal table and multiply this probability times the number of tails for alpha.

	One-Tailed Test	**Two-Tailed Test**
Number of tails	1	2
Probability	p	p
p value calculation	$1p$	$2p$

We found in Example 8.1 that if the null hypothesis were true, then $p = .0524$ that we could have selected this sample mean from this population. The criteria we set in Step 2 was that the probability must be less than 5% that we obtain a sample mean, if the null hypothesis were true. Because p is greater than 5%, we decide to retain the null hypothesis. We conclude that the mean score on the GRE General Test in this population is 558 (the value stated in the null hypothesis).

DIRECTIONAL, UPPER-TAIL CRITICAL HYPOTHESIS TESTS (H$_1$: >)

NOTE: An upper tail critical test is conducted when it is not possible or highly unlikely that a sample mean will fall below the population mean stated in the null hypothesis.

In Example 8.2, we will use the z-test for a **directional,** or **one-tailed test,** where the alternative hypothesis is stated as *greater than* (>) the null hypothesis. A directional test can also be stated as *less than* (<) the null hypothesis (an example for this alternative is given in Example 8.3). For an upper tail critical test, or a greater than statement, we place the level of significance in the upper tail of the sampling distribution. So we are interested in any alternative greater than the value stated in the null hypothesis. This test is appropriate when it is not possible or highly unlikely that a sample mean will fall below the population mean stated in the null hypothesis.

DEFINITION

Directional tests, or **one-tailed tests**, are hypothesis tests where the alternative hypothesis is stated as greater than (>) or less than (<) a value stated in the null hypothesis. Hence, the researcher is interested in a specific alternative from the null hypothesis.

EXAMPLE 8.2

Using the same study from Example 8.1, Templer and Tomeo (2002) reported that the population mean on the quantitative portion of the GRE General Test for students taking the exam between 1994 and 1997 was 558 ± 139 ($\mu \pm \sigma$). Suppose we select a sample of 100 students enrolled in an elite private school ($n = 100$). We hypothesize that students at this elite school will score higher than the general population. We record a sample mean equal to 585 ($M = 585$), same as measured in Example 8.1. Compute the one–independent sample z-test at a .05 level of significance.

Step 1: State the hypotheses. The population mean is 558, and we are testing whether the alternative is greater than (>) this value:

H$_0$: $\mu = 558$ Mean test scores are equal to 558 in the population of students at the elite school.

H$_1$: $\mu > 558$ Mean test scores are greater than 558 in the population of students at the elite school.

Step 2: Set the criteria for a decision. The level of significance is .05, which makes the alpha level $\alpha = .05$. To determine the critical value for an upper tail critical test, we locate the probability .0500 toward the tail in column C in the unit normal table. The z-score associated with this probability is between $z = 1.64$ and $z = 1.65$. The average of these z-scores is $z = 1.645$. This is the critical value or cutoff for the rejection region. Figure 8.6 shows that for this test, we place all the value of alpha in the upper tail of the standard normal distribution.

NOTE: For one-tailed tests, the alpha level is placed in a single tail of a distribution. For upper tail critical tests, the alpha level is placed above the mean in the upper tail.

Step 3: Compute the test statistic. Step 2 sets the stage for making a decision because the criterion is set. The probability is less than 5% that we will obtain a sample mean that is at least 1.645 standard deviations above the value of the population mean stated in the null hypothesis. In this step, we will compute a test statistic to determine whether or not the sample mean we selected is beyond the critical value we stated in Step 2.

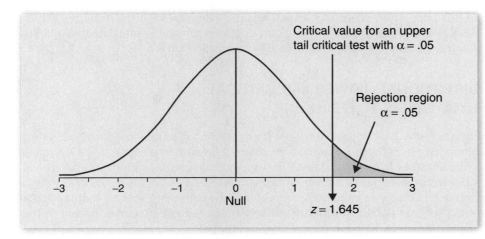

FIGURE 8.6

The critical value (1.645) for a directional (upper tail critical) hypothesis test at a .05 level of significance. When the test statistic exceeds 1.645, we reject the null hypothesis; otherwise, we retain the null hypothesis.

The test statistic does not change from that in Example 8.1. We are testing the same population, and we measured the same value of the sample mean. We changed only the location of the rejection region in Step 2. The z-statistic is the same computation as that shown in Example 8.1:

$$z_{obt} = \frac{M - \mu}{\sigma_M} = \frac{585 - 558}{13.9} = 1.94.$$

Step 4: Make a decision. To make a decision, we compare the obtained value to the critical value. We reject the null hypothesis if the obtained value exceeds the critical value. Figure 8.7 shows that the obtained value ($z_{obt} = 1.94$) is greater than the critical value; it falls in the rejection region. The decision is to reject the null hypothesis. The p value for this test is .0262 ($p = .0262$). We do not double the p value for one-tailed tests.

We found in Example 8.2 that if the null hypothesis were true, then $p = .0262$ and that we could have selected this sample mean from this population. The criteria we set in Step 2 was that the probability must be less than 5% that we obtain a sample mean, if the null hypothesis were true. Since p is less than 5%, we decide to reject the null hypothesis. We decide that the mean score on the GRE General Test

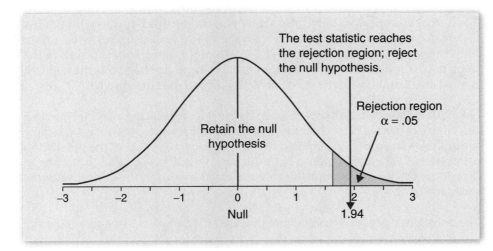

FIGURE 8.7

Since the obtained value reaches the rejection region, we decide to reject the null hypothesis.

in this population is not 558, which was the value stated in the null hypothesis. Also, notice that we made two different decisions using the same data in Examples 8.1 and 8.2. This outcome is explained further in Section 8.6.

DIRECTIONAL, LOWER TAIL CRITICAL HYPOTHESIS TESTS (H$_1$: <)

NOTE: A lower tail critical test is conducted when it is not possible or highly unlikely that a sample mean will fall above the population mean stated in the null hypothesis.

In Example 8.3, we will use the z-test for a directional, or one-tailed test, where the alternative hypothesis is stated as *less than* (<) the null hypothesis. For a lower tail critical test, or a less than statement, we place the level of significance or critical value in the lower tail of the sampling distribution. So we are interested in any alternative less than the value stated in the null hypothesis. This test is appropriate when it is not possible or highly unlikely that a sample mean will fall above the population mean stated in the null hypothesis.

EXAMPLE 8.3

Using the same study from Example 8.1, Templer and Tomeo (2002) reported that the population mean on the quantitative portion of the GRE General Test for those taking the exam between 1994 and 1997 was 558 ± 139 ($\mu \pm \sigma$). Suppose we select a sample of 100 students enrolled in a school with low funding and resources ($n = 100$). We hypothesize that students at this school will score lower than the general population. We record a sample mean equal to 585 ($M = 585$), same as measured in Examples 8.1 and 8.2. Compute the one–independent sample z-test at a .05 level of significance.

Step 1: State the hypotheses. The population mean is 558, and we are testing whether the alternative is less than (<) this value:

> H$_0$: $\mu = 558$ Mean test scores are equal to 558 in the population at this school.

> H$_1$: $\mu < 558$ Mean test scores are less than 558 in the population at this school.

NOTE: For one-tailed tests, the alpha level is placed in a single tail of the distribution. For lower tail critical tests, the alpha is placed below the mean in the lower tail.

Step 2: Set the criteria for a decision. The level of significance is .05, which makes the alpha level $\alpha = .05$. To determine the critical value for a lower tail critical test, we locate the probability .0500 toward the tail in column C in the unit normal table. The z-score associated with this probability is again $z = 1.645$. Because this test is a lower tail critical test, we place the critical value the same distance below the mean: The critical value for this test is $z = -1.645$. All of the alpha level is placed in the lower tail of the distribution beyond the critical value. Figure 8.8 shows the standard normal distribution, with the rejection region beyond the critical value.

Step 3: Compute the test statistic. Step 2 sets the stage for making a decision because the criterion is set. The probability is less than 5% that we will obtain a sample mean that is at least 1.645 standard deviations below the value of the population mean stated in the null hypothesis. In this step, we will compute a test statistic to determine whether the sample mean we selected is beyond the critical value we stated in Step 2.

The test statistic does not change from that used in Example 8.1. We are testing the same population, and we measured the same value of the sample mean. We changed

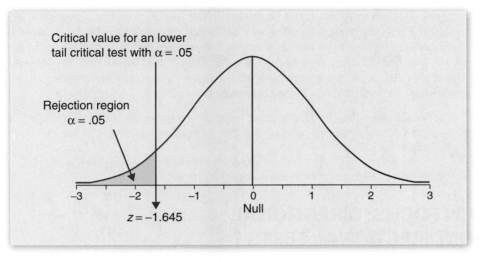

Critical value for an lower tail critical test with $\alpha = .05$

Rejection region
$\alpha = .05$

$z = -1.645$

Null

FIGURE 8.8

The critical value (-1.645) for a directional (lower tail critical) test at a .05 level of significance. When the test statistic is less than -1.645, we reject the null hypothesis; otherwise, we retain the null hypothesis.

only the location of the rejection region in Step 2. The z-statistic is the same computation as that shown in Example 8.1:

$$z_{obt} = \frac{M - \mu}{\sigma_M} = \frac{585 - 558}{13.9} = 1.94.$$

Step 4: Make a decision. To make a decision, we compare the obtained value to the critical value. We reject the null hypothesis if the obtained value exceeds the critical value. Figure 8.9 shows that the obtained value ($z_{obt} = +1.94$) does not exceed the critical value. Instead, the value we obtained is located in the opposite tail. The decision is to retain the null hypothesis.

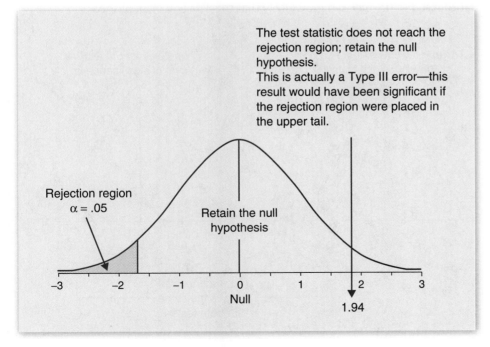

The test statistic does not reach the rejection region; retain the null hypothesis.
This is actually a Type III error—this result would have been significant if the rejection region were placed in the upper tail.

Rejection region
$\alpha = .05$

Retain the null hypothesis

Null

1.94

FIGURE 8.9

Since the obtained value does not reach the rejection region, we decide to retain the null hypothesis.

NOTE: A Type III error occurs when the rejection region is located in the wrong tail. This type of error is only possible for one-tailed tests.

The decision in Example 8.3 was to retain the null hypothesis, although if we placed the rejection region in the upper tail (as we did in Example 8.2), we would have decided to reject the null hypothesis. We anticipated that scores would be worse, and instead, they were better than the value stated in the null hypothesis. When we fail to reject the null hypothesis because we placed the rejection region in the wrong tail, we commit a **Type III error** (Kaiser, 1960).

DEFINITION

A **Type III error** occurs with one-tailed tests, where the researcher decides to retain the null hypothesis because the rejection region was located in the wrong tail.

The "wrong tail" refers to the opposite tail from where a difference was observed and would have otherwise been significant.

8.6   RESEARCH IN FOCUS: DIRECTIONAL VERSUS NONDIRECTIONAL TESTS

Kruger and Savitsky (2006) conducted a study in which they performed two tests on the same data. They completed an upper-tail critical test at $\alpha = .05$ and a two-tailed test at $\alpha = .10$. A shown in Figure 8.10, these are similar tests, except in the upper-tail test, all the alpha level is placed in the upper tail, and in the two-tailed test, the alpha level is split so that .05 is placed in each tail. When the researchers showed these results to a group of participants, they found that participants were more persuaded by a significant result when it was described as a one-tailed test, $p < .05$, than when it was described as a two-tailed test, $p < .10$. This was interesting because the two results were identical— both tests were associated with the same critical value in the upper tail.

Most editors of peer-reviewed journals in behavioral research will not publish the results of a study where the level of significance is greater than .05. Although the two-tailed test, $p < .10$, was significant, it is unlikely that the results would be published in a peer-reviewed scientific journal. Reporting the same results as a one-tailed test, $p < .05$, makes it more likely that the data will be published.

FIGURE 8.10

When $\alpha = .05$, all of that value is placed in the upper tail for an upper tail critical test. The two-tailed equivalent would require a test with $\alpha = .10$, such that .05 is placed in each tail.

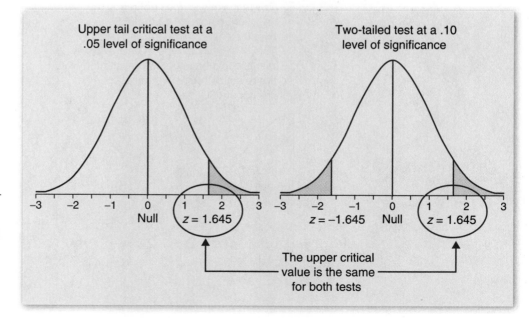

The two-tailed test is more conservative; it makes it more difficult to reject the null hypothesis. It also eliminates the possibility of committing a Type III error. The one-tailed test, though, is associated with greater power. If the value stated in the null hypothesis is false, then a one-tailed test will make it easier to detect this (i.e., lead to a decision to reject the null hypothesis). Because the one-tailed test makes it easier to reject the null hypothesis, it is important that we justify that an outcome can occur in only one direction. Justifying that an outcome can occur in only one direction is difficult for much of the data that behavioral researchers measure. For this reason, most studies in behavioral research are two-tailed tests.

NOTE: *Two-tailed tests are more conservative and eliminate the possibility of committing a Type III error. One-tailed tests are associated with more power, assuming the value stated in the null hypothesis is wrong.*

LEARNING CHECK 5

1. Is the following set of hypotheses appropriate for a directional or a nondirectional hypothesis test?
   $H_0: \mu = 35$
   $H_1: \mu \neq 35$

2. A researcher conducts a one–independent sample z-test. The z-statistic for the upper tail critical test at a .05 level of significance was $z_{obt} = 1.84$. What is the decision for this test?

3. A researcher conducts a hypothesis test and finds that the probability of selecting the sample mean is $p = .0689$ if the value stated in the null hypothesis is true. What is the decision for a hypothesis test at a .05 level of significance?

4. Which type of test, one-tailed or two-tailed, is associated with greater power to detect an effect when the null hypothesis is false?

Answers: 1. A nondirectional (two-tailed) hypothesis test; 2. Reject the null; 3. Retain the null; 4. One-tailed tests.

MEASURING THE SIZE OF AN EFFECT: COHEN'S *d*   8.7

A decision to reject the null hypothesis means that an effect is significant. For a one-sample test, an **effect** is the difference between a sample mean and the population mean stated in the null hypothesis. In Example 8.2, we found a significant effect, meaning that the sample mean, $M = 585$, was significantly larger than the value stated in the null hypothesis, $\mu = 558$. Hypothesis testing identifies whether an effect exists in a population. When a sample mean is likely to occur if the null hypothesis were true ($p > .05$), we decide that an effect doesn't exist in a population; the effect is insignificant. When a sample mean is unlikely to occur if the null hypothesis were true ($p < .05$), we decide that an effect does exist in a population; the effect is significant. Hypothesis testing does not, however, inform us of how big the effect is.

To determine the size of an effect, we compute **effect size.** There are two ways to calculate the size of an effect. We can determine

1. how far scores shifted in the population.

2. the percent of variance that can be explained by a given variable.

DEFINITION

For a single sample, an **effect** is the difference between a sample mean and the population mean stated in the null hypothesis. In hypothesis testing, an effect is insignificant when we retain the null hypothesis; an effect is significant when we reject the null hypothesis.

Effect size is a statistical measure of the size of an effect in a population, which allows researchers to describe how far scores shifted in the population, or the percent of variance that can be explained by a given variable.

NOTE: Cohen's d is a measure of the number of standard deviations an effect is shifted above or below the population mean stated by the null hypothesis.

Effect size is most meaningfully reported with significant effects when the decision was to reject the null hypothesis. If an effect is not significant, as in instances when we retain the null hypothesis, then we are concluding that an effect does not exist in a population. It makes little sense to compute the size of an effect that we just concluded doesn't exist. In this section, we describe how far scores shifted in the population using a measure of effect size called Cohen's *d*.

Cohen's *d* measures the number of standard deviations an effect shifted above or below the population mean stated by the null hypothesis. The formula for Cohen's *d* replaces the standard error in the denominator of the test statistic with the population standard deviation (J. Cohen, 1988):

$$\text{Cohen's } d = \frac{M - \mu}{\sigma}.$$

The value of Cohen's *d* is zero when there is no difference between two means and increases as the differences get larger. To interpret values of *d*, we refer to **Cohen's effect size conventions** outlined in Table 8.6. The sign of *d* indicates the direction of the shift. When values of *d* are positive, an effect shifted above the population mean; when values of *d* are negative, an effect shifted below the population mean.

NOTE: Hypothesis testing determines whether an effect exists in a population. Effect size measures the size of an observed effect from small to large.

TABLE 8.6   Cohen's effect size conventions.

Description of Effect	Effect Size (*d*)
Small	$d < 0.2$
Medium	$0.2 < d < 0.8$
Large	$d < 0.8$

DEFINITION

Cohen's *d* is a measure of effect size in terms of the number of standard deviations that mean scores shifted above or below the population mean stated by the null hypothesis. The larger the value of *d*, the larger the effect in the population.

Cohen's effect size conventions are standard rules for identifying small, medium, and large effects based on typical findings in behavioral research.

In Example 8.4, we will compute effect size for the research study in Examples 8.1 to 8.3. Because we tested the same population and measured the same sample mean in each example, the effect size estimate will be the same for all examples.

In Examples 8.1 to 8.3, we used data given by Templer and Tomeo (2002). They reported that the population mean on the quantitative portion of the GRE General Test for those taking the exam between 1994 and 1997 was 558 ± 139 ($\mu \pm \sigma$). In each example, the mean test score in the sample was 585 ($M = 585$). What is the effect size for this test using Cohen's d?

EXAMPLE 8.4

The numerator for Cohen's d is the difference between the sample mean ($M = 585$) and the population mean ($\mu = 558$). The denominator is the population standard deviation ($\sigma = 139$):

$$d = \frac{M - \mu}{\sigma} = \frac{27}{139} = 0.19.$$

We conclude that the observed effect shifted 0.19 standard deviations above the mean in the population. This way of interpreting effect size is illustrated in Figure 8.11. We are stating that students in the elite school scored 0.19 standard deviations higher, on average, than students in the general population. This interpretation is most meaningfully reported with Example 8.2 because we decided to reject the null hypothesis using this example. Table 8.7 compares the basic characteristics of hypothesis testing and effect size.

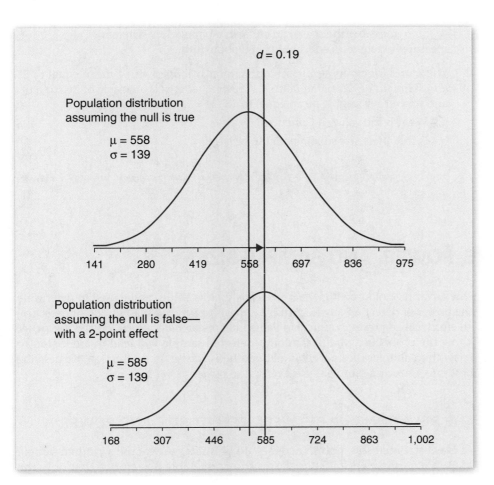

FIGURE 8.11

Effect size. Cohen's d estimates the size of an effect in the population. A 27-point effect shifted the distribution of scores in the population by 0.19 standard deviations.

TABLE 8.7 Distinguishing characteristics for significance testing and effect size.

	Hypothesis (Significance) Testing	Effect Size (Cohen's *d*)
Value being measured?	*p* value	*d*
What type of distribution is the test based upon?	Sampling distribution	Population distribution
What does the test measure?	The probability of obtaining a measured sample mean	The size of a measured effect in the population
What can be inferred from the test?	Whether the null hypothesis is true or false	Whether the size of an effect is small to large
Can this test stand alone in research reports?	Yes, the test statistic can be reported without an effect size	No, effect size is almost always reported with a test statistic

✔ **LEARNING CHECK 6**

1. _____ measures the size of an effect in a population, whereas _____ measures whether an effect exists in a population.

2. The scores for a population are normally distributed with a mean equal to 25 and standard deviation equal to 6. A researcher selects a sample of 36 students and measures a sample mean equal to 23 (*M* = 23). For this example,
   a. What is the value of Cohen's *d*?
   b. Is this effect size small, medium, or large?

Answers: 1. Effect size, hypothesis or significance testing; 2. (a) $d = \dfrac{23-25}{6} = -0.33$, (b) Medium effect size.

8.8 EFFECT SIZE, POWER, AND SAMPLE SIZE

One advantage of knowing effect size, *d*, is that its value can be used to determine the power of detecting an effect in hypothesis testing. The likelihood of detecting an effect, called power, is critical in behavioral research because it lets the researcher know the probability that a randomly selected sample will lead to a decision to reject the null hypothesis, if the null hypothesis is false. In this section, we describe how effect size and sample size are related to power.

THE RELATIONSHIP BETWEEN EFFECT SIZE AND POWER

As effect size increases, power increases. To illustrate, we will use a random sample of quiz scores in two statistics classes shown in Table 8.8. Notice that only the standard deviation differs between these populations. Using the values given in Table 8.8, we already have enough information to compute effect size:

TABLE 8.8 Characteristics for two hypothetical populations of quiz scores.

Class 1	Class 2
$M_1 = 40$	$M_2 = 40$
$\mu_1 = 38$	$\mu_2 = 38$
$\sigma_1 = 10$	$\sigma_2 = 2$

$$\text{Effect size for Class 1}: d = \frac{M - \mu}{\sigma} = \frac{40 - 38}{10} = 0.20.$$

$$\text{Effect size for Class 2}: d = \frac{M - \mu}{\sigma} = \frac{40 - 38}{2} = 1.00.$$

The numerator for each effect size estimate is the same. The mean difference between the sample mean and the population mean is 2 points. Although there is a 2-point effect in both Class 1 and Class 2, Class 2 is associated with a much larger effect size in the population because the standard deviation is smaller. Because a larger effect size is associated with greater power, we should find that it is easier to detect the 2-point effect in Class 2. To determine whether this is true, suppose we select a sample of 30 students ($n = 30$) from each class and measure the same sample mean value that is listed in Table 8.8. Let's determine the power of each test when we conduct an upper-tail critical test at a .05 level of significance.

To determine the power, we will first construct the sampling distribution for each class, with a mean equal to the population mean and standard error equal to $\frac{\sigma}{\sqrt{n}}$:

$$\text{Sampling distribution for Class 1: Mean: } \mu_M = 38$$
$$\text{Standard error: } \frac{\sigma}{\sqrt{n}} = \frac{10}{\sqrt{30}} = 1.82$$

$$\text{Sampling distribution for Class 2: Mean: } \mu_M = 38$$
$$\text{Standard error: } \frac{\sigma}{\sqrt{n}} = \frac{2}{\sqrt{30}} = 0.37$$

If the null hypothesis is true, then the sampling distribution of the mean for alpha (α), the type of error associated with a true null hypothesis, will have a mean equal to 38. We can now determine the smallest value of the sample mean that is the cutoff for the rejection region, where we decide to reject that the true population mean is 38. For an upper tail critical test using a .05 level of significance, the critical value is 1.645. We can use this value to compute a z transformation to determine what sample mean value is 1.645 standard deviations above 38 in a sampling distribution for samples of size 30:

$$\text{Cutoff for } \alpha \text{ (Class 1): } 1.645 = \frac{M - 38}{1.82}$$

$$M = 40.99$$

$$\text{Cutoff for } \alpha \text{ (Class 2): } 1.645 = \frac{M - 38}{0.37}$$

$$M = 38.61$$

If we obtain a sample mean equal to 40.99 or higher in Class 1, then we will reject the null hypothesis. If we obtain a sample mean equal to 38.61 or higher in Class 2, then we will reject the null hypothesis. To determine the power for this test, we assume that the sample mean we selected (M = 40) is the true population mean—we are therefore assuming that the null hypothesis is false. We are asking the following question: If we are correct and there is a 2-point effect, then what is the probability that we will detect the effect? In other words, what is the probability that a sample randomly selected from this population will lead to a decision to reject the null hypothesis?

If the null hypothesis is false, then the sampling distribution of the mean for β, the type of error associated with a false null hypothesis, will have a mean equal to 40. This is what we believe is the true population mean, and this is the only change; we do not change the standard error. Figure 8.12 shows the sampling distribution for Class 1, and Figure 8.13 shows the sampling distribution for Class 2, assuming the null hypothesis is correct (top graph) and assuming the 2-point effect exists (bottom graph).

NOTE: As the size of an effect increases, the power to detect the effect also increases.

FIGURE 8.12

Small effect size and low power for Class 1. In this example, when alpha is .05, the critical value or cutoff for alpha is 40.99. When α = .05, notice that only about 29% of samples will detect this effect (the power). So even if the researcher is correct, and the null is false (with a 2-point effect), only about 29% of the samples he or she selects at random will result in a decision to reject the null hypothesis.

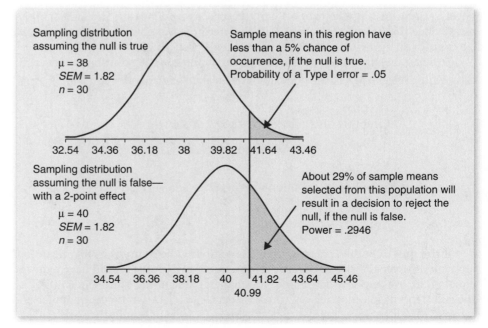

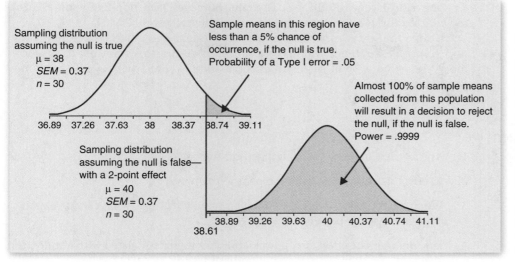

Sampling distribution
assuming the null is true
μ = 38
SEM = 0.37
n = 30

Sample means in this region have
less than a 5% chance of
occurrence, if the null is true.
Probability of a Type I error = .05

36.89   37.26   37.63   38   38.37   38.74   39.11

Sampling distribution
assuming the null is false—
with a 2-point effect
μ = 40
SEM = 0.37
n = 30

Almost 100% of sample means
collected from this population
will result in a decision to reject
the null, if the null is false.
Power = .9999

38.89   39.26   39.63   40   40.37   40.74   41.11
38.61

FIGURE 8.13

Large effect size and high power for Class 2. In this example, when alpha is .05, the critical value or cutoff for alpha is 38.61. When α = .05, notice that practically any sample will detect this effect (the power). So if the researcher is correct, and the null is false (with a 2-point effect), nearly 100% of the samples he or she selects at random will result in a decision to reject the null hypothesis.

If we are correct, and the 2-point effect exists, then we are much more likely to detect the effect in Class 2 for *n* = 30. Class 1 has a small effect size (*d* = .20). Even if we are correct, and a 2-point effect does exist in this population, then of all the samples of size 30 we could select from this population, only about 29% (power = .2946) of those samples will show the effect (i.e., lead to a decision to reject the null). The probability of correctly rejecting the null hypothesis (power) is low.

Class 2 has a large effect size (*d* = 1.00). If we are correct, and a 2-point effect does exist in this population, then of all the samples of size 30 we could select from this population, nearly 100% (power = .9999) of those samples will show the effect (i.e., lead to a decision to reject the null). The probability of correctly rejecting the null hypothesis (power) is high.

THE RELATIONSHIP BETWEEN SAMPLE SIZE AND POWER

To overcome low effect size, we can increase the sample size. Increasing sample size decreases standard error, thereby increasing power. To illustrate, let's compute the test statistic for the one-tailed significance test for Class 1, which had a small effect size. The data for Class 1 are given in Table 8.8 for a sample of 30 participants. The test statistic for Class 1 when *n* = 30 is

$$z_{obt} = \frac{M - \mu}{\dfrac{\sigma}{\sqrt{n}}} = \frac{40 - 38}{\dfrac{10}{\sqrt{30}}} = 1.10.$$

For a one-tailed test that is upper-tail critical, the critical value is 1.645. The value of the test statistic (+1.10) does not exceed the critical value (+1.645), so we retain the null hypothesis.

Increase the sample size to *n* = 100. The test statistic for Class 1 when *n* = 100 is

$$z_{obt} = \frac{M - \mu}{\dfrac{\sigma}{\sqrt{n}}} = \frac{40 - 38}{\dfrac{10}{\sqrt{100}}} = 2.00.$$

NOTE: Increasing the sample size increases power by reducing the standard error, thereby increasing the value of the test statistic in hypothesis testing.

The critical value is still 1.645. The value of the test statistic (+2.00) now exceeds the critical value (+1.645), so we reject the null hypothesis.

Notice that increasing the sample size alone led to a decision to reject the null hypothesis. Hence, increasing sample size increases power: It makes it more likely that we will detect an effect, assuming that an effect exists in some population.

LEARNING CHECK 7

1. As effect size increases, what happens to the power?

2. As effect size decreases, what happens to the power?

3. When a population is associated with a small effect size, what can a researcher do to increase the power of the study?

4. True or false: The effect size, power, and sample size associated with a study can affect the decisions we make in hypothesis testing.

Answers: 1. Power increases; 2. Power decreases; 3. Increase the sample size (n); 4. True.

8.9 ADDITIONAL FACTORS THAT INCREASE POWER

The power is the likelihood of detecting an effect. Behavioral research often requires a great deal of time and money to select, observe, measure, and analyze data. And the institutions that supply the funding for research studies want to know that they are spending their money wisely and that researchers conduct studies that will show results. Consequently, to receive a research grant, researchers are often required to state the likelihood that they will detect the effect they are studying, assuming they are correct. In other words, researchers must disclose the power of their study.

The typical standard for power is .80. Researchers try to make sure that at least 80% of the samples they select will show an effect when an effect exists in a population. In Section 8.8, we showed that increasing effect size and sample size increases power. In this section, we introduce four additional factors that influence power.

INCREASING POWER: INCREASE EFFECT SIZE, SAMPLE SIZE, AND ALPHA

NOTE: To increase power: increase effect size, sample size, and alpha; decrease beta, population standard deviation, and standard error.

Increasing effect size, sample size, and the alpha level will increase power. Section 8.8 showed that increasing effect size and sample size increases power; here we discuss increasing alpha. The alpha level is the probability of a Type I error; it is the rejection region for a hypothesis test. The larger the rejection region, the greater the likelihood of rejecting the null hypothesis, and the greater the power will be. This was illustrated by the difference in the decisions made for Examples 8.1 and 8.2. Increasing the size of the rejection region in the upper tail in Example 8.2 increased the power to detect the 27-point effect. This is why one-tailed tests are more powerful than two-tailed tests: They increase alpha in the direction that an effect is expected to occur, thereby increasing the power to detect an effect.

INCREASING POWER: DECREASE BETA, STANDARD DEVIATION (σ), AND STANDARD ERROR

Decreasing three factors can increase power. Decreasing beta error (β) increases power. In Table 8.3, β is given as the probability of a Type II error, and $1 - \beta$ is given as the power. So the lower β is, the greater the solution will be for $1 - \beta$. For example, say $\beta = .20$. In this case, $1 - \beta = (1 - .20) = .80$. If we decreased β, say, to $\beta = .10$, the power will increase: $1 - \beta = (1 - .10) = .90$. Hence, decreasing beta error increases power.

Decreasing the population standard deviation (σ) and standard error (σ_M) will also increase power. The population standard deviation is the numerator for computing standard error. Decreasing the population standard deviation will decrease the standard error, thereby increasing the value of the test statistic. To illustrate, suppose that we select a sample from a population of students with quiz scores equal to 10 ± 8 ($\mu \pm \sigma$). We select a sample of 16 students from this population and measure a sample mean equal to 12. In this example, the standard error is

$$\sigma_M = \frac{\sigma}{\sqrt{n}} = \frac{8}{\sqrt{16}} = 2.0.$$

To compute the z-statistic, we subtract the sample mean from the population mean and divide by the standard error:

$$z_{obt} = \frac{M - \mu}{\sigma_M} = \frac{12 - 10}{2} = 1.00.$$

An obtained value equal to 1.00 does not exceed the critical value for a one-tailed test (critical value = 1.645) or a two-tailed test (critical values = ±1.96). The decision is to retain the null hypothesis.

If the population standard deviation is smaller, the standard error will be smaller, thereby making the value of the test statistic larger. Suppose, for example, that we reduce the population standard deviation to 4. The standard error in this example is now

$$\sigma_M = \frac{\sigma}{\sqrt{n}} = \frac{4}{\sqrt{16}} = 1.0.$$

To compute the z-statistic, we subtract the sample mean from the population mean and divide by this smaller standard error:

$$z_{obt} = \frac{M - \mu}{\sigma_M} = \frac{12 - 10}{1} = 2.00.$$

An obtained value equal to 2.00 does exceed the critical value for a one-tailed test (critical value = 1.645) and a two-tailed test (critical values = ±1.96). Now the decision is to reject the null hypothesis. Assuming that an effect exists in the population, decreasing the population standard deviation decreases standard error and increases the power to detect an effect. Table 8.9 lists each factor that increases power.

TABLE 8.9 A summary of factors that increase power—the probability of rejecting a false null hypothesis.

To increase power:	
Increase	**Decrease**
d (Effect size)	β (Type II error)
n (Sample size)	σ (Standard deviation)
α (Type I error)	σ_M (Standard error)

8.10 SPSS IN FOCUS: A PREVIEW FOR CHAPTERS 9 TO 18

As discussed in Section 8.5, it is rare that we know the value of the population variance, so the z-test is not a common hypothesis test. It is so uncommon that SPSS can't be used to compute this test statistic, although it can be used to compute all other test statistics described in this book. For each analysis, SPSS provides output analyses that indicate the significance of a hypothesis test and the information needed to compute effect size and even power. SPSS statistical software can be used to compute nearly any statistic or measure used in behavioral research. For this reason, most researchers use SPSS software to analyze their data.

8.11 APA IN FOCUS: REPORTING THE TEST STATISTIC AND EFFECT SIZE

To report the results of a z-test, we report the test statistic, p value, and effect size of a hypothesis test. Here is how we could report the significant result for the z-statistic in Example 8.2:

> Test scores for students in the elite school were significantly higher than the standard performance of test takers, $z = 1.94$, $p < .03$.

Notice that when we report a result, we do not state that we reject or retain the null hypothesis. Instead, we report whether a result is significant (the decision was to reject the null hypothesis) or not significant (the decision was to retain the null hypothesis). Also, you are not required to report the exact p value, although it is recommended. An alternative is to report it in terms of the closest value to the hundredths or thousandths place that its value is less than. In this example, we stated $p < .03$ for a p value actually equal to .0262.

Finally, it is often necessary to include a figure or table to illustrate a significant effect and the effect size associated with it. For example, we could describe the effect size in one additional sentence supported by the following figure (Figure 8.14):

> As shown in Figure 8.14, students in the elite school scored an average of 27 points higher on the exam compared to the general population ($d = .19$).

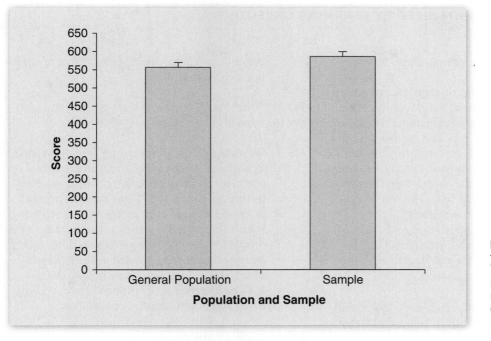

FIGURE 8.14

The mean Graduate Record Examination (GRE) General Test scores in the sample and in the general population. Error bars indicate *SEM*.

In two sentences and a figure, we reported the value of the test statistic, *p* value, effect size, and the mean test scores. The error bars indicate the standard error of the mean for this study.

CHAPTER SUMMARY ORGANIZED BY LEARNING OBJECTIVE

LO 1: Identify the four steps of hypothesis testing.

- **Hypothesis testing,** or **significance testing,** a method of testing a claim or hypothesis about a parameter in a population, using data measured in a sample. In this method, we test some hypothesis by determining the likelihood that a sample statistic could have been selected, if the hypothesis regarding the population parameter were true. The four steps of hypothesis testing are as follows:
  - Step 1: State the hypotheses.
  - Step 2: Set the criteria for a decision.
  - Step 3: Compute the test statistic.
  - Step 4: Make a decision.

LO 2: Define null hypothesis, alternative hypothesis, level of significance, test statistic, p value, and statistical significance.

- The **null hypothesis (H_0),** stated as the **null,** is a statement about a population parameter, such as the population mean, that is assumed to be true.
- An **alternative hypothesis (H_1)** is a statement that directly contradicts a null hypothesis by stating that the actual value of a population parameter, such as the mean, is less than, greater than, or not equal to the value stated in the null hypothesis.
- **Level of significance** refers to a criterion of judgment upon which a decision is made regarding the value stated in a null hypothesis.
- The **test statistic** is a mathematical formula that allows researchers to determine the likelihood or probability of obtaining sample outcomes if the null hypothesis were true. The value of a test statistic can be used to make inferences concerning the value of population parameters stated in the null hypothesis.
- A **p value** is the probability of obtaining a sample outcome, given that the value stated in the null hypothesis is true. The p value of a sample outcome is compared to the level of significance.
- **Significance,** or **statistical significance,** describes a decision made concerning a value stated in the null hypothesis. When a null hypothesis is rejected, a result is significant.

When a null hypothesis is retained, a result is not significant.

LO 3: Define Type I error and Type II error, and identify the type of error that researchers control.

- We can decide to retain or reject the null hypothesis, and this decision can be correct or incorrect. Two types of errors in hypothesis testing are called Type I and Type II errors.
- A **Type I error** is the probability of rejecting a null hypothesis that is actually true. The probability of this type of error is determined by the researcher and stated as the level of significance or alpha level for a hypothesis test.
- A **Type II error** is the probability of retaining a null hypothesis that is actually false.

LO 4: Calculate the one–independent sample z-test and interpret the results.

- The **one–independent sample z-test** is a statistical procedure used to test hypotheses concerning the mean in a single population with a known variance. The test statistic for this hypothesis test is

$$z_{obt} = \frac{M - \mu}{\sigma_M}, \text{where } \sigma_M = \frac{\sigma}{\sqrt{n}}.$$

- **Critical values,** which mark the cutoffs for the **rejection region,** can be identified for any level of significance. The value of the test statistic is compared to the critical values. When the value of a test statistic exceeds a critical value, we reject the null hypothesis; otherwise, we retain the null hypothesis.

LO 5: Distinguish between a one-tailed and two-tailed test, and explain why a Type III error is possible only with one-tailed tests.

- **Nondirectional (two-tailed) tests** are hypothesis tests where the alternative hypothesis is stated as *not equal to* ($\neq$). So we are interested in any alternative from the null hypothesis.
- **Directional (one-tailed) tests** are hypothesis tests where the alternative hypothesis is

stated as *greater than* (>) or *less than* (<) some value. So we are interested in a specific alternative from the null hypothesis.

- A **Type III error** occurs for one-tailed tests where a result would have been significant in one tail, but the researcher retains the null hypothesis because the rejection region was placed in the wrong or opposite tail.

LO 6: Explain what effect size measures and compute a Cohen's *d* for the one–independent sample *z*-test.

- **Effect size** is a statistical measure of the size of an observed effect in a population, which allows researchers to describe how far scores shifted in the population, or the percent of variance that can be explained by a given variable.
- **Cohen's *d*** is used to measure how far scores shifted in a population and is computed using the following formula:

$$\text{Cohen's } d = \frac{M - \mu}{\sigma}.$$

- To interpret the size of an effect, we refer to **Cohen's effect size conventions,** which are standard rules for identifying small, medium, and large effects based on typical findings in behavioral research.

LO 7: Define *power* and identify six factors that influence power.

- The **power** in hypothesis testing is the probability that a randomly selected sample will show that the null hypothesis is false when the null hypothesis is in fact false.
- To increase the power of detecting an effect in a given population:
  a. Increase effect size (*d*), sample size (*n*), and alpha (α).
  b. Decrease beta error (β), population standard deviation (σ), and standard error (σ$_M$).

APA LO 8: Summarize the results of a one–independent sample *z*-test in American Psychological Association (APA) format.

- To report the results of a *z*-test, we report the test statistic, *p* value, and effect size of a hypothesis test. In addition, a figure or table is usually provided to summarize the means and standard error or standard deviation measured in a study.

KEY TERMS

alpha (α) level
alternative hypothesis (H$_1$)
beta (β) error
Cohen's *d*
Cohen's effect size conventions
critical values
directional tests
effect
effect size
hypothesis

hypothesis testing
level of significance
nondirectional (two-tailed) tests
null
null hypothesis (H$_0$)
obtained value
one–independent sample *z*-test
one-tailed test
power
p value

rejection region
significance
significance testing
statistical significance
test statistic
Type I error
Type II error
Type III error
z-statistic

END-OF-CHAPTER PROBLEMS

Factual Problems

1. State the four steps of hypothesis testing.

2. What are two decisions that a researcher makes in hypothesis testing?

3. What is a Type I error (α)?

4. What is a Type II error (β)?

5. What is the power in hypothesis testing?

6. What are the critical values for a one–independent sample nondirectional (two-tailed) *z*-test at a .05 level of significance?

7. Explain why a one-tailed test is associated with greater power than a two-tailed test.

8. How are the rejection region, the probability of a Type I error, the level of significance, and the alpha level related?

9. Alpha (α) is used to measure the error for decisions concerning true null hypotheses. What is beta (β) error used to measure?

10. What three factors can be increased to increase power?

11. What three factors can be decreased to increase power?

12. Distinguish between the significance of a result and the size of an effect.

Concepts and Application Problems

13. Explain why the following statement is true: The population standard deviation is always larger than the standard error when the sample size is greater than one ($n > 1$).

14. A researcher conducts a hypothesis test and concludes that his hypothesis is correct. Explain why this conclusion is never an appropriate decision in hypothesis testing.

15. The weight (in pounds) for a population of school-aged children is normally distributed with a mean equal to 135 ± 20 pounds ($\mu \pm \sigma$). Suppose we select a sample of 100 children ($n = 100$) to test whether children in this population are gaining weight at a .05 level of significance.
    (a) What are the null and alternative hypotheses?
    (b) What is the critical value for this test?
    (c) What is the mean of the sampling distribution?
    (d) What is the standard error of the mean for the sampling distribution?

16. A researcher selects a sample of 30 participants and makes the decision to retain the null hypothesis. She conducts the same study testing the same hypothesis with a sample of 300 participants and makes the decision to reject the null hypothesis. Give a likely explanation for why the two samples led to different decisions.

17. A researcher conducts a one–independent sample z-test and makes the decision to reject the null hypothesis. Another researcher selects a larger sample from the same population, obtains the same sample mean, and makes the decision to retain the null hypothesis using the same hypothesis test. Is this possible? Explain.

18. Determine the level of significance for a hypothesis test in each of the following populations given the specified standard error and critical values. *Hint:* Refer to the values given in Table 8.4:
    (a) $\mu = 100$, $\sigma_M = 8$, critical values: 84.32 and 115.68
    (b) $\mu = 100$, $\sigma_M = 6$, critical value: 113.98
    (c) $\mu = 100$, $\sigma_M = 4$, critical value: 86.8

19. For each p value stated below, (1) What is the decision for each if $\alpha = .05$? (2) What is the decision for each if $\alpha = .01$?
    (a) $p = .1000$
    (b) $p = .0250$
    (c) $p = .0050$
    (d) $p = .0001$

20. For each obtained value stated below, (1) What is the decision for each if $\alpha = .05$ (one-tailed test, upper tail critical)? (2) What is the decision for each if $\alpha = .01$ (two-tailed test)?
    (a) $z_{obt} = 2.10$
    (b) $z_{obt} = 1.70$
    (c) $z_{obt} = 2.75$
    (d) $z_{obt} = -3.30$

21. Will each of the following increase, decrease, or have no effect on the value of a test statistic for the one–independent sample z-test?
    (a) The sample size is increased.
    (b) The population variance is decreased.
    (c) The sample variance is doubled.
    (d) The difference between the sample mean and population mean is decreased.

22. The police chief selects a sample of 49 local police officers from a population of officers with a mean physical fitness rating of 72 ± 7.0 ($\mu \pm \sigma$) on a 100-point physical endurance rating scale. He measures a sample mean physical fitness rating on

this scale equal to 74. He conducts a one–independent sample z-test to determine whether physical endurance increased at a .05 level of significance.

(a) State the value of the test statistic and whether to retain or reject the null hypothesis.

(b) Compute effect size using Cohen's d.

23. A cheerleading squad received a mean rating (out of 100 possible points) of 75 ± 12 ($\mu \pm \sigma$) in competitions over the previous three seasons. The same cheerleading squad performed in 36 local competitions this season with a mean rating equal to 78 in competitions. Suppose we conduct a one–independent sample z-test to determine whether mean ratings increased this season (compared to the previous three seasons) at a .05 level of significance.

(a) State the value of the test statistic and whether to retain or reject the null hypothesis.

(b) Compute effect size using Cohen's d.

24. A local school reports that its average GPA is 2.66 ± 0.40 ($\mu \pm \sigma$). The school announces that it will be introducing a new program designed to improve GPA scores at the school. What is the effect size (d) for this program if it is expected to improve GPA by:

(a) .05 points?

(b) .10 points?

(c) .40 points?

25. Will each of the following increase, decrease, or have no effect on the value of Cohen's d?

(a) The sample size is decreased.

(b) The population variance is increased.

(c) The sample variance is reduced.

(d) The difference between the sample and population mean is increased.

26. State whether the effect size for a 1-point effect ($M - \mu = 1$) is small, medium, or large given the following population variances:

(a) $\sigma = 1$

(b) $\sigma = 2$

(c) $\sigma = 4$

(d) $\sigma = 6$

27. As α increases, so does the power to detect an effect. Why, then, do we restrict α from being larger than .05?

28. Will increasing sample size (n) and decreasing the population standard deviation (σ) increase or decrease the value of standard error? Will this increase or decrease power?

Problems in Research

29. **Directional vs. nondirectional hypothesis testing.** In an article reviewing directional and nondirectional tests, Leventhal (1999) stated the following hypotheses concerning the difference between two population means.

A	B
$\mu 1 - \mu 2 = 0$	$\mu 1 - \mu 2 = 0$
$\mu 1 - \mu 2 > 0$	$\mu 1 - \mu 2 \neq 0$

(a) Which did he identify as nondirectional?

(b) Which did he identify as directional?

30. **The one-tailed tests.** In their book *Common Errors in Statistics (and How to Avoid Them)*, Good and Hardin (2003) wrote, "No one will know whether your [one-tailed] hypothesis was conceived before you started or only after you'd examined the data" (p. 347). Why do the authors state this as a concern for one-tailed tests?

31. **The hopes of a researcher.** Hayne Reese (1999) wrote, "The standard method of statistical inference involves testing a null hypothesis that the researcher usually hopes to reject" (p. 39). Why does the researcher usually hope to reject the null hypothesis?

32. **Describing the z-test.** In an article describing hypothesis testing with small sample sizes, Collins and Morris (2008) provided the following description for a z-test: "Z is considered significant if the difference is more than roughly two standard deviations above or below zero (or more

precisely, $|Z| > 1.96$)" (p. 464). Based on this description,

(a) Are the authors referring to critical values for a one- or two-tailed z-test?

(b) What alpha level are the authors referring to?

33. **Sample size and power.** Collins and Morris (2008) simulated selecting thousands of samples and analyzed the results using many different test statistics. With regard to the power for these samples, they reported that "generally speaking, all tests became more powerful as sample size increased" (p. 468). How did increasing the sample size in this study increase power?

34. **Describing hypothesis testing.** Blouin and Riopelle (2004) made the following statement concerning how scientists select test statistics: "[This] test is the norm for conducting a test of H_0, when . . . the population(s) are normal with known variance(s)" (p. 78). Based on this description, what test statistic are they describing as the norm? How do you know this?

Testing Means

Independent Sample *t*-Tests

LEARNING OBJECTIVES

After reading this chapter, you should be able to:

1. Explain why a *t*-distribution is associated with $n - 1$ degrees of freedom and describe the information that is conveyed by the *t*-statistic.

2. Calculate the degrees of freedom for a one– and two–independent sample *t*-test and locate critical values in the *t*-table.

3. Identify the assumptions for the one–independent sample *t*-test.

4. Compute a one–independent sample *t*-test and interpret the results.

5. Compute effect size and proportion of variance for a one–independent sample *t*-test.

6. Identify the assumptions for the two–independent sample *t*-test.

7. Compute a two–independent sample *t*-test and interpret the results.

8. Compute effect size and proportion of variance for a two–independent sample *t*-test.

9. Summarize the results of a one–independent sample and a two–independent sample *t*-test in APA format.

10. Compute a one–independent sample and a two–independent sample *t*-test using SPSS.

9.1 GOING FROM Z TO T

In Chapter 8, in the discussion of hypothesis testing, we introduced the one–independent sample z-test. To compute the test statistic for a one–independent sample z-test, we must know the value of the population variance. However, in behavioral science, it is rare that we know the variance of a population, which makes it impossible to compute the z-statistic:

$$z_{obt} = \frac{M - \mu}{\sigma_M}, \text{ where } \sigma_M = \frac{\sigma}{\sqrt{n}}.$$

To compute this z-statistic formula, we need to know the population standard deviation, which requires that we know the variance. If we don't know the population variance, then we can't compute the value for z. We need an alternative test statistic that can be computed when the population variance is unknown.

An alternative to the z-statistic was proposed by William Sealy Gosset, a scientist working with the Guinness Brewing Company to improve brewing processes in the early 1900s. He proposed substituting the population variance with the sample variance in the formula for standard error. When this substitution is made, the formula for error is called the **estimated standard error (s_M)**:

$$\text{Estimated standard error: } s_M = \sqrt{\frac{s^2}{n}} = \frac{SD}{\sqrt{n}}.$$

DEFINITION

The **estimated standard error** is an estimate of the standard deviation of a sampling distribution of sample means selected from a population with an unknown variance. It is an estimate of the standard error or standard distance that sample means deviate from the value of the population mean stated in the null hypothesis.

The substitution is possible because, as explained in Chapter 7, the sample variance is an unbiased estimator of the population variance: On average, the sample variance equals the population variance. Hence, we are able to make this substitution because, on average, the sample variance equals the population variance. Gosset did just this and introduced an alternative test statistic for one–independent sample when the population variance in unknown. The formula is known as the **t-statistic:**

$$t_{obt} = \frac{M - \mu}{s_M}, \text{where } s_M = \frac{SD}{\sqrt{n}}.$$

DEFINITION

The **t-statistic**, known as **t-observed** or **t-obtained**, is an inferential statistic used to determine the number of standard deviations in a t-distribution that a sample mean deviates from the mean value or mean difference stated in the null hypothesis.

Gosset showed that substituting the sample variance for the population variance led to a new sampling distribution known as the **t-distribution.** In Figure 9.1, you can see how similar the t-distribution is to the normal distribution. The difference is that the *t*-distribution has greater variability in the tails because the sample variance is not always equal to the population variance. Sometimes the estimate for variance is too large; sometimes the estimate is too small. This leads to a larger probability of obtaining sample means further from the population mean. Otherwise, the *t*-distribution shares all the same characteristics as the normal distribution: It is symmetrical and asymptotic, and its mean, median, and mode are all located at the center of the distribution.

The ***t*-distribution**, or **Student's *t***, is a normal-like distribution with greater variability in the tails because the sample variance is substituted for the population variance to estimate the standard error in this distribution.

DEFINITION

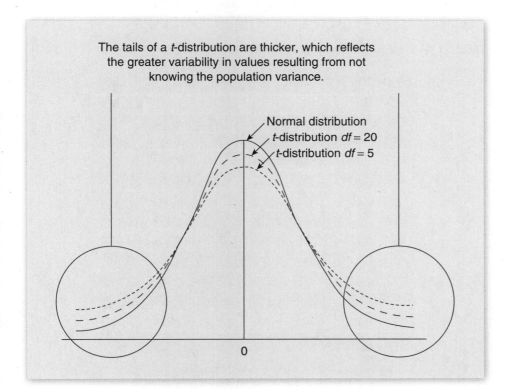

The tails of a *t*-distribution are thicker, which reflects the greater variability in values resulting from not knowing the population variance.

Normal distribution
t-distribution *df* = 20
t-distribution *df* = 5

0

FIGURE 9.1

A normal distribution and two *t*-distributions. Notice that the tails in a normal distribution approach the *x*-axis faster; otherwise, these distributions share the same characteristics.

THE DEGREES OF FREEDOM 9.2

The *t*-distribution is associated with **degrees of freedom (*df*).** In Chapter 4, we stated that the degrees of freedom for sample variance equal $n - 1$. As the sample size increased, the degrees of freedom of the sample variance increased. The *t*-distribution is a sampling distribution where the estimated standard error is computed using the sample variance in the formula. As sample size increases, the sample variance more closely approximates the population variance. The result is that there is less variability in the tails as sample size increases. So the shape of the *t*-distribution changes (the tails approach the *x*-axis faster) as the sample size is increased. Each changing *t*-distribution is associated with the same degrees of freedom as for sample variance: $df = n - 1$.

DEFINITION

The **degrees of freedom (df)** for a *t*-distribution are equal to the degrees of freedom of the sample variance: $n - 1$. As the degrees of freedom of the sample variance increase, the shape of the corresponding *t*-distribution changes—the probability of outcomes in the tails becomes less likely, and the tails approach the *x*-axis faster.

9.3 READING THE *T*-TABLE

NOTE: The degrees of freedom for a t-distribution are equal to the degrees of freedom for sample variance: n – 1.

To locate probabilities and critical values in a *t*-distribution, we use a *t*-table, such as Table 9.1, which reproduces part of Table B.2 in Appendix B. In the *t*-table, there are six columns of values listing alpha levels for one-tailed tests (top heading) and two-tailed tests (lower heading). The rows show the degrees of freedom (*df*) for a *t*-distribution.

TABLE 9.1   A portion of the *t*-table adapted from Table B.2 in Appendix B.

df	Proportion in One Tail					
	0.25	0.10	0.05	0.25	0.01	0.005
	Proportion in Two Tails Combined					
	0.50	0.20	0.10	0.05	0.02	0.01
1	1.000	3.078	6.314	12.706	31.821	63.657
2	0.816	1.886	2.920	4.303	6.965	9.925
3	0.765	1.638	2.353	3.182	4.541	5.841
4	0.741	1.533	2.132	2.776	3.747	4.604
5	0.727	1.476	2.015	2.571	3.365	4.032
6	0.718	1.440	1.943	2.447	3.143	3.707
7	0.711	1.415	1.895	2.365	2.998	3.499
8	0.706	1.397	1.86o	2.306	2.896	3.355
9	0.703	1.383	1.833	2.282	2.821	3.250
10	0.700	1.372	1.812	2.228	2.764	3.169

Source: Table III of R.A. Fisher and F. Yates, *Statistical Tables for Biological, Agricultural and Medical Research, 6th ed.* London: Longman Group Ltd., 1974 (previously published by Oliver and Boyd Ltd., Edinburgh). Adapted and reprinted with permission of the Addison Wesley Longman.

To use this table, you need to know the sample size (*n*), alpha level (a), and the location of the rejection region (in one or both tails). For example, if we select a sample of 11 students, then $n = 11$, and *df* equals 10 ($n - 1 = 10$). To find the *t*-distribution with 10 degrees of freedom, we look for 10 listed in the rows. The critical values for this distribution at a .05 alpha level or level of significance appear in the column with that probability listed: For a one-tailed test, the critical value is 1.812 for an upper tail critical test and –1.812 for a lower tail critical test. For a two-tailed test, the critical values are ±2.228. Each critical value identifies the cutoff for the rejection region, beyond which the decision will be to reject the null hypothesis for a hypothesis test.

NOTE: The t-table lists critical values for six levels of significance for one- and two-tailed tests.

Keep in mind that a *t*-distribution is an estimate of a normal distribution. The larger the sample size, the more closely a *t*-distribution estimates a normal distribution. When the sample size is so large that it equals the population size, we describe the sample size as infinite. In this case, the *t*-distribution is a normal distribution. You can see this in the *t*-table in Appendix B. The critical values at a .05 level of significance are ±1.96 for a two-tailed *t*-test with infinite (∞) degrees of freedom and 1.645 (upper tail critical) or –1.645 (lower tail critical) for a one-tailed test. These are the same critical values listed in the unit normal table for a .05 level of significance.

In terms of the null hypothesis, in a small sample, there is a greater probability of obtaining sample means that are further from the value stated in the null hypothesis. As sample size increases, the probability of obtaining sample means that are further from the value stated in the null hypothesis becomes less likely. The result is that critical values get smaller as sample size increases.

LEARNING CHECK 1

1. Requires population variance to be known, which is rare

1. What is the main limitation of the *z*-test in behavioral research?

2. The __*t*-test__ is a normal-like distribution with greater variability in the tails because the sample variance is substituted for the population variance to estimate the standard error in this distribution.

3. How does increasing sample size affect the estimate of the population variance?

4. What is the calculation for the degrees of freedom of a *t*-distribution?

5. What are the degrees of freedom for each of the following samples?
   a. $n = 12$ b. $n = 22$ c. $n = 5$ d. $n = 30$
      df = 11   df = 21   df = 4   df = 29

6. Assuming $\alpha = .05$, what is the critical value in each of the following tests?
   a. $df = 10$, two-tailed test   ± 2.228
   b. $df = 30$, one-tailed test (lower tail critical)   – 1.697
   c. $df = \infty$, two-tailed test   ± 1.960
   d. $df = 15$, one-tailed test (upper tail critical)   1.753

Answers: 1. It requires that the population variance is known, and behavioral researchers rarely know the value of the population variance; 2. *t*-distribution; 3. Increasing sample size generally results in the sample variance being a closer estimate of the population variance; 4. $n - 1$; 5. (a) $df = 11$, (b) $df = 21$, (c) $df = 4$, (d) $df = 29$; 6. (a) ±2.228, (b) –1.697, (c) ±1.96, (d) 1.753.

ONE–INDEPENDENT SAMPLE *T*-TEST   9.4

In this section, we compute the alternative for a one—independent sample *z*-test, called the **one–independent sample *t*-test.** This test is used to test hypotheses concerning a single group mean selected from a population with an unknown variance. Table 9.2 summarizes the differences and similarities between the *z*-test and *t*-test. To compute the one–independent sample *t*-test, we make three assumptions:

DEFINITION

The **one–independent sample *t*-test** is a statistical procedure used to test hypotheses concerning the mean in a single population with an unknown variance.

1. *Normality*. We assume that data in the population being sampled are normally distributed. This assumption is particularly important for small samples. In larger samples ($n > 30$), the standard error is smaller, and this assumption becomes less critical as a result.

TABLE 9.2 The differences and similarities between the *z*-test and *t*-test.

	z-Test	**t-Test**
What is the obtained value?	*z*-statistic, *p* value	*t*-statistic, *p* value
What distribution is used to locate the probability of obtaining a sample mean?	Normal distribution	*t*-distribution
What is the denominator of the test statistic?	Standard error	Estimated standard error
Do we know the population variance?	Yes, the population variance is known.	No, the sample variance is used to estimate the population variance.
Are degrees of freedom required for this test?	No, the population variance is known.	Yes, the degrees of freedom for a *t*-test are equal to the degrees of freedom for sample variance: $n - 1$.
What does the test measure?	The probability of obtaining a measured sample mean	
What can be inferred from the test?	Whether the null hypothesis should be retained or rejected	

2. *Random sampling.* We assume that the data we measure were obtained from a sample that was selected using a random sampling procedure. It is considered inappropriate to conduct hypothesis tests with nonrandom samples.

3. *Independence.* We assume that the probabilities of each measured outcome in a study are independent. Outcomes are independent when the probability of one outcome has no effect on the probability of another outcome. Using random sampling usually satisfies this assumption.

NOTE: Three assumptions for a one–independent sample t-test are normality, random sampling, and independence.

In Example 9.1, we will compute the one–independent sample *t*-test using the four steps to hypothesis testing introduced in Chapter 8.

EXAMPLE 9.1

Albert, Salvi, Saracco, Bogetto, and Maina (2007) studied relatives of patients with obsessive-compulsive disorder (OCD). As part of their study, they recorded the social functioning of relatives using a 36-item short-form health survey (SF-36), where scores ranged from 0 (*worst possible health*) to 100 (*best possible health*). They cited that the mean score for social functioning in the population of interest was 77.43. Suppose that researchers selected a sample of 61 relatives and recorded a mean social functioning score equal to 61.91 ± 23.29 (*M ± SD*). Test whether the mean score in this sample significantly differs from that in the general population at a .05 level of significance.

Step 1: State the hypotheses. The population mean is 77.43, and we are testing whether (=) or not (≠) the population mean differs from the sample mean:

H_0: μ = 77.43   The mean social functioning score in the population is _(null)_ equal to 77.43.

H_1: μ ≠ 77.43   The mean social functioning score in the population is _(alternative)_ not equal to 77.43.

Step 2: Set the criteria for making a decision. The level of significance for this test is .05. We are computing a two-tailed test with $n - 1$ degrees of freedom. With $n = 61$, the degrees of freedom for this test are 60: 61 – 1 = 60. To locate the critical values, we find 60 listed in the rows of Table B.2 in Appendix B and go across to the column for .05 in two-tails combined. The critical values are ±2.000. Figure 9.2 shows the *t*-distribution, with rejection regions beyond the critical values.

NOTE: The t-*table lists critical values for* t-*distributions with various degrees of freedom.*

We will compare the value of the test statistic with these critical values. If the value of the test statistic is beyond a critical value (either greater than +2.000 or less than –2.000), then there is less than a 5% chance we could have obtained that outcome if the null hypothesis were correct, so we reject the null hypothesis; otherwise, we retain the null hypothesis.

Step 3: Compute the test statistic. In this example, we measured a sample mean equal to 61.91 and the null hypothesis is μ = 77.43. To find the *t*-statistic, we first compute the estimated standard error. To compute the estimated standard error, which is the denominator for the *t*-statistic, we divide the sample standard deviation (*SD*) by the square root of the sample size (*n*). In this example, *SD* = 23.29, and *n* = 61:

$$s_M = \frac{SD}{\sqrt{n}} = \frac{23.29}{\sqrt{61}} = 2.98.$$

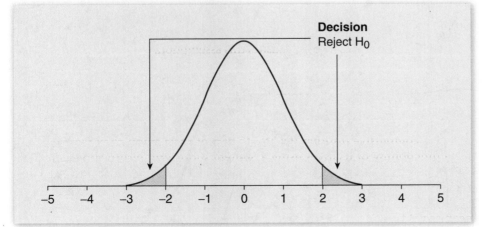

FIGURE 9.2

The shaded regions represent the rejection regions with critical values equal to ±2.000. If the value of the test statistic falls in the shaded region, we reject the null hypothesis; otherwise, we retain the null hypothesis.

Find the *t*-statistic by substituting the values for the sample mean, *M* = 61.91; the population mean stated in the null hypothesis, $\mu = 77.43$; and the estimated standard error we just calculated, $s_M = 2.98$:

$$t_{obt} = \frac{M - \mu}{s_M} = \frac{61.91 - 77.43}{2.98} = -5.21.$$

NOTE: The test statistic for a one–independent sample t-test is the difference between the sample mean and population mean stated by the null hypothesis, divided by the estimated standard error.

Step 4: Make a decision. To decide to reject or retain the null hypothesis, we compare the obtained value to the critical values. Figure 9.3 shows that the obtained value $(t_{obt} = -5.21)$ falls beyond the critical value in the lower tail; it falls in the rejection region. The decision is to reject the null hypothesis. This is the same decision Albert and colleagues (2007) made in their study. If the result were reported in a research journal, it would look something like this:

Social functioning scores among relatives of patients with OCD (*M* = 61.91) were significantly lower than scores in the general population, *t*(60) = −5.21, *p* < .05.

✔ **LEARNING CHECK 2**

1. What are the three assumptions of the one–independent sample *t*-test?
2. Researchers record the number of errors on some behavioral task for 15 participants. They report a sample mean equal to 6 ± 1 (*M* ± *SD*). What is the critical value for a two-tailed test with α = .01?
3. Using the same study described in Question 2, what is the decision if the following values for the test statistic are obtained?
   (a) 2.558   (b) 1.602   (c) 2.999   (d) −3.404

Answers: 1. Normality, random sampling, and independence; 2. ± 2.977; 3. (a) Retain the null hypothesis, (b) Retain the null hypothesis, (c) Reject the null hypothesis, (d) Reject the null hypothesis.

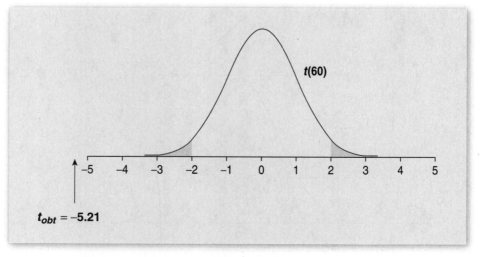

FIGURE 9.3

The value of the test statistic falls in the rejection region. Therefore, we reject the null hypothesis.

EFFECT SIZE FOR THE ONE–INDEPENDENT SAMPLE *T*-TEST   9.5

↱identifies

As described in Chapter 8, hypothesis testing identities whether or not an effect exists in a population. When we decide to retain the null hypothesis, we conclude that an effect doesn't exist in the population. When we decide to reject the null hypothesis, we conclude that an effect does exist in the population. However, hypothesis testing does not tell us how large the effect is.

In Example 9.1, we concluded that mean social functioning scores among relatives of patients with OCD are significantly lower than those in the general population. To determine how big the effect is, we compute effect size, which gives an estimate of the size of the effect in the population. We can select from three measures of effect size for the one–independent sample *t*-test: estimated Cohen's *d* and two measures of proportion of variance (eta-squared and omega-squared).

ESTIMATED COHEN'S *d*

The estimate of effect size that is most often used with a *t*-test is the **estimated Cohen's d.** The Cohen's *d* measure introduced with the *z*-test in Chapter 8 placed the population standard deviation in the denominator of the formula. When the population standard deviation is unknown, we substitute it with the sample standard deviation because it gives an unbiased estimate of the population standard deviation. The estimated Cohen's *d* formula is

$$d = \frac{M - \mu}{SD}.$$

An **estimated Cohen's d** is a measure of effect size in terms of the number of standard deviations that mean scores shift above or below the population mean stated by the null hypothesis. The larger the value of estimated Cohen's *d*, the larger the effect in the population.

DEFINITION

↰ $d = \dfrac{61.91 - 77.43}{23.29}$

In Example 9.1, $M = 61.91$, $\mu = 77.43$, and $SD = 23.29$. The estimated Cohen's *d* for Example 9.1 is

$$d = \frac{61.91 - 77.43}{23.29} = -0.67.$$

We conclude that being a relative of a patient with OCD reduces mean social functioning 0.67 standard deviations below the mean in the general population. The effect size conventions given in Table 8.8 (Chapter 8) and in the first column of Table 9.3 show that this is a medium effect size. We could report this measure with the significant *t*-test in Example 9.1 by stating,

Social functioning scores among relatives of patients with OCD ($M = 61.91$) were significantly lower than scores in the general population, $t(60) = -5.21$, $p < .05$ ($d = -0.67$).

NOTE: The sample standard deviation is used to estimate the population standard deviation in the estimated Cohen's d formula.

PROPORTION OF VARIANCE

Another measure of effect size is to estimate the **proportion of variance** that can be accounted for by some **treatment.** A treatment, which is any unique characteristic of a sample or any unique way that a researcher treats a sample, can change the value of a dependent variable. A treatment is associated with variability in a study. Proportion of variance estimates how much of the variability in a dependent variable can be accounted for by the treatment. In the proportion of variance formula, the variability explained by a treatment is divided by the total variability observed:

$$\text{Proportion of variance} = \frac{\text{variability explained}}{\text{total variability}}.$$

<table>
<tr><td>DEFINITION</td><td>The proportion of variance is a measure of effect size in terms of the proportion or percent of variability in a dependent variable that can be explained or accounted for by a treatment.

In hypothesis testing, a treatment is any unique characteristic of a sample or any unique way that a researcher treats a sample.</td></tr>
</table>

In Example 9.1, we found that relatives of patients with OCD had significantly lower social functioning scores. The unique characteristic of the sample in this study was that the participants were relatives of patients with OCD. The variable we measured (i.e., the dependent variable) was social functioning scores. Measuring proportion of variance determines how much of the variability in the dependent variable (social functioning scores) can be explained by the treatment (the fact that the participants were relatives of patients with OCD). We introduce two measures for proportion of variance: eta-squared $\left(\eta^2\right)$ and omega-squared $\left(\omega^2\right)$.

Eta-Squared $\left(\eta^2\right)$

Eta-squared is a measure of proportion of variance that can be expressed in a single formula based on the result of a *t*-test:

$$\eta^2 = \frac{t^2}{t^2 + df}.$$

In this formula, *t* is the value of the *t*-statistic and *df* is the degrees of freedom. In this example $t_{obt} = -5.21$ and $df = 60$. To find variance, we square the standard deviation. In the eta-squared formula, we square the value of *t* to find the variance. The proportion of variance for the data in Example 9.1 is

$$\eta^2 = \frac{(-5.21)^2}{(-5.21)^2 + 60} = 0.31.$$

We conclude that 31% of the variability in social functioning (the dependent variable) can be explained by the fact that participants were relatives of patients with OCD (the treatment). We could report this measure with the significant *t*-test in Example 9.1 by stating,

Social functioning scores among relatives of patients with OCD ($M = 61.91$) were significantly lower than scores in the general population, $t(60) = -5.21$, $p < .05$ $\left(\eta^2 = 0.31 \right)$.

The second column in Table 9.3 displays guidelines for interpreting a small, medium, and large effect for η^2. Using this table, we find that $\eta^2 = 0.31$ is a large effect. When we used estimated Cohen's *d*, we concluded that it was a medium effect size. This discrepancy is partly due to eta-squared being biased. Although eta-squared is a popular measure of proportion of variance, it tends to overestimate the proportion of variance explained by a treatment. To correct for this bias, many researchers use a modified eta-squared formula, called omega-squared.

NOTE: Eta-squared tends to overestimate the size of an effect in a population. Omega-squared corrects for this bias.

TABLE 9.3   The size of an effect using estimated Cohen's *d* and two measures of proportion of variance.

Description of Effect	*d*	η^2	ω^2
Trivial	—	$\eta^2 < .01$	$\omega^2 < .01$
Small	$d < 0.2$	$.01 < \eta^2 < .09$	$.01 < \omega^2 < .09$
Medium	$0.2 < d < 0.8$	$.10 < \eta^2 < .25$	$.10 < \omega^2 < .25$
Large	$d > 0.8$	$\eta^2 > 0.25$	$\omega^2 > 0.25$

Omega-Squared (ω^2)

Omega-squared is also the variability explained by a treatment, divided by the total variability observed. The change in the formula of proportion of variance is that 1 is subtracted from t^2 in the numerator:

$$\omega^2 = \frac{t^2 - 1}{t^2 + df}.$$

Subtracting 1 in the numerator reduces the estimate of effect size. Hence, omega-squared will always give a smaller or more conservative estimate of effect size, making it less biased than eta-squared. Using the omega-squared formula, the proportion of variance for the data in Example 9.1 is

$$\omega^2 = \frac{(-5.21)^2 - 1}{(-5.21)^2 + 60} = 0.30.$$

We conclude that 30% of the variability in social functioning (the dependent variable) can be explained by the fact that participants were relatives of patients with OCD (the treatment). In the last column in Table 9.3, we find that the value of omega-squared, while smaller than eta-squared, is also a large effect size. We could report this measure with the significant *t*-test in Example 9.1 by stating,

Social functioning scores among relatives of patients with OCD ($M = 61.91$) were significantly lower than scores in the general population, $t(60) = -5.21$, $p < .05$ $\left(\omega^2 = 0.30\right)$.

LEARNING CHECK 3

1. An estimated Cohen's *d* substitutes which value in the formula to estimate the population standard deviation?

2. A researcher compares the mean grade point average (GPA) of college students with a full-time job to in the mean GPA of the general population of college students. In this example, identify (a) the dependent variable and (b) the treatment.

3. State whether each of the following values for estimated Cohen's *d* has a small, medium, or large effect size.

   a. 0.40   b. 1.20   c. 0.05   d. 0.10

4. A researcher reports that a sample of workers with high-stress careers slept significantly less than workers in the general population, $t(48) = 2.36$, $p < .05$. Compute eta-squared for this one–independent sample *t*-test.

5. What measure, eta-squared or omega-squared, gives a more conservative or smaller estimate of proportion of variance?

Answers: 1. Sample standard deviation; 2. (a) GPA, (b) Having a full-time job; 3. (a) Medium, (b) Large, (c) Small, (d) Small; 4. $\eta^2 = .10$; 5. Omega-squared.

9.6 SPSS IN FOCUS: ONE–INDEPENDENT SAMPLE *T*-TEST

SPSS can be used to compute the one–independent sample *t*-test, as demonstrated in Example 9.2.

EXAMPLE 9.2

In the place preference paradigm (PPP), rats are placed in a cage where they receive reinforcement in one side (food pellets, for example) but not the other side of the cage. The researcher then measures the amount of time rats spend in the side of the cage that they received reinforcement. In a 10-minute test, we assume that there is no preference when rats spend half their time in each location: 5 minutes in each side. Suppose a researcher measures the time (in minutes) that 12 rats spend in the reinforced side of a cage. The times measured were 7, 5, 8, 6, 8, 7, 9, 10, 3, 7, 6, and 9. Let's test whether the rats showed a place preference using a .05 level of significance ($\alpha = .05$)

1. Click on the **variable view** tab and enter *preference* in the **name column.** We will enter whole numbers for this variable, so reduce the value in the **decimals column** to 0.

2. Click on the **data view** tab and enter the 12 values in the column labeled *preference.*

3. Go to the **menu bar** and click **Analyze,** then **Compare Means,** and **One-Sample T Test** to display the dialog box shown in Figure 9.4.

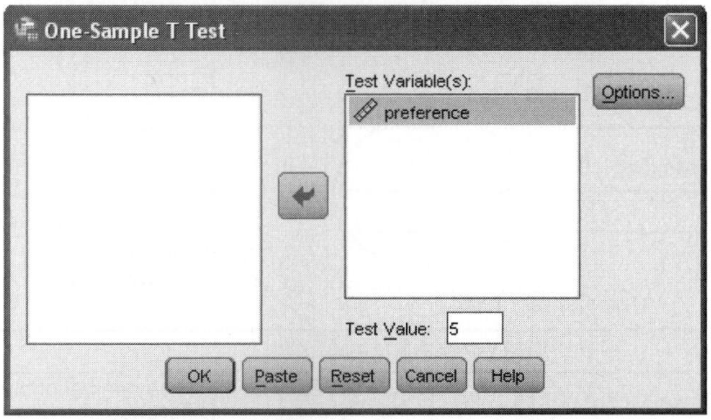

FIGURE 9.4

SPSS dialog box for Steps 3 to 5.

4. In the **dialog box,** select the variable *preference* and click the arrow in the middle to move this variable to the **Test Variable(s):** box.

5. The **Test Value:** box is set with a default value equal to 0. The value in this box is the value of the null hypothesis. In our example, we assume the rats will spend 5 minutes in each side of the cage when there is no preference, which is the null hypothesis. Type the value *5* in the **Test Value:** box.

6. Select **Paste** and click the **Run** command.

In Table 9.4, the top table displays the sample size, the sample mean, the sample standard deviation, and the estimated standard error. The bottom table displays the obtained value for *t*, degrees of freedom, *p* value, the mean difference between the sample mean and the test value, and confidence intervals (confidence intervals will be described in Chapter 11).

Although SPSS does not compute effect size, notice that the output provides all the information needed to compute effect size:

$$\text{Effect size: Estimated Cohen's } d = \frac{2.083}{1.929} = 1.08 \text{ (large effect size)}.$$

$$\text{Proportion of variance: } \eta^2 = \frac{(3.742)^2}{(3.742)^2 + 11} = 0.56 \text{ (large proportion of variance)}.$$

$$\omega^2 = \frac{(3.742)^2 - 1}{(3.742)^2 + 11} = 0.52 \text{ (large proportion of variance)}.$$

TWO–INDEPENDENT SAMPLE *T*-TEST 9.7

Many studies in the behavioral sciences test for differences between two groups or populations. Studies may examine differences in multitasking between men and

TABLE 9.4 SPSS output table.

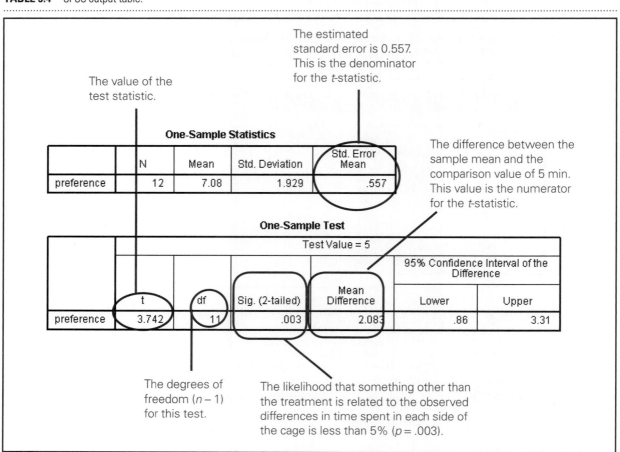

The value of the test statistic.

The estimated standard error is 0.557. This is the denominator for the *t*-statistic.

The difference between the sample mean and the comparison value of 5 min. This value is the numerator for the *t*-statistic.

One-Sample Statistics

	N	Mean	Std. Deviation	Std. Error Mean
preference	12	7.08	1.929	.557

One-Sample Test

	Test Value = 5					
					95% Confidence Interval of the Difference	
	t	df	Sig. (2-tailed)	Mean Difference	Lower	Upper
preference	3.742	11	.003	2.083	.86	3.31

The degrees of freedom (*n* – 1) for this test.

The likelihood that something other than the treatment is related to the observed differences in time spent in each side of the cage is less than 5% (*p* = .003).

women, differences in forgiveness between pet owners and non–pet owners, or differences in recall between participants randomly assigned to observe one of two teaching methods. In each study, researchers measure two means (one mean in each group) and then compare differences between groups. The **two–independent sample *t*-test** is used to compare the difference between two population means.

DEFINITION

The **two–independent sample *t*-test** is a statistical procedure used to test hypotheses concerning the difference between two population means, where the variance in one or both populations is unknown.

In terms of the null hypothesis, we state the mean difference that we expect in the population and compare it to the difference we observe between the two sample means in our sample. Table 9.5 shows two ways to state the difference between two means in a population. For a two–independent sample *t*-test concerning two population means, we make four assumptions:

1. *Normality.* We assume that data in each population being sampled from are normally distributed. This assumption is particularly important for small samples because the standard error is typically much larger. In larger sample

TABLE 9.5 Two ways to state that there is no difference between two population means.

Statement	Meaning
$\mu_1 - \mu_2 = 0$ $\mu_1 = \mu_2$	There is no difference between two population means.

sizes ($n > 30$), the standard error is smaller, and this assumption becomes less critical as a result.

2. *Random sampling.* We assume that the data we measure were obtained from samples that were selected using a random sampling procedure. It is generally considered inappropriate to conduct hypothesis tests with nonrandom samples.

3. *Independence.* We assume that the probabilities for each measured outcome in a study are independent. Outcomes are independent when the probability of one outcome has no effect on the probability of another outcome. Using random sampling usually satisfies this assumption.

4. *Equal variances.* We assume that the variance in each population is equal to each other. This assumption is usually satisfied so long as the larger sample variance is not greater than two times that of the smaller:

$$\frac{\text{larger } s^2}{\text{smaller } s^2} < 2.$$

NOTE: Four assumptions for a two–independent sample t-test are normality, random sampling, independence, and equal variances.

Example 9.3 demonstrates how to compute the two–independent sample *t*-test using the four steps of hypothesis testing.

Orathinkal, Vansteenwegen, and Burggraeve (2008) hypothesized that heterosexual married adults in their first marriage would have more positive perceptions of forgiveness than would remarried adults. To measure forgiveness, participants completed the Positive Perception of Forgiveness (PPF) scale, where higher scores indicate more positive perceptions of forgiveness. Table 9.6 lists data that are similar to those reported by the authors of this study. The sample we use is smaller so that we can look up critical values in the *t*-table. With these data, test if first-marriage adults will be more forgiving (i.e., score higher on the PPF scale) than remarried adults will be using a .05 level of significance.

EXAMPLE 9.3

Step 1: State the hypotheses. The null states that there is no difference, and the alternative hypothesis states that the difference is greater than zero (>):

$H_0 : \mu_1 - \mu_2 = 0$ Mean PPF scores do not differ for first-marriage and remarried adults.

$H_1 : \mu_1 - \mu_2 > 0$ Mean PPF scores are larger for first-marriage than for remarried adults.

TABLE 9.6   The sample size, mean, variance, and standard deviation for the study in Example 9.3.

First-Marriage Adults	Remarried Adults
$n_1 = 26$	$n_2 = 16$
$M_1 = 34.72$	$M_2 = 31.74$
$s_1^2 = 29.16$ $SD_1 = 5.40$	$s_2^2 = 27.98$ $SD_2 = 5.29$

Step 2: Set the criteria for a decision. The level of significance for this test is .05. Because the alternative hypothesis is a greater than statement, we are computing a one-tailed test that is upper tail critical. We will place the rejection region in the upper tail. The degrees of freedom for each sample are $n - 1$. To find the degrees of freedom for two samples, we add the degrees of freedom in each sample. This can be found using one of three methods:

NOTE: We add the degrees of freedom for each sample to find the degrees of freedom for a two–independent sample t-test.

Method 1: df for two–independent sample t-test $= df_1 + df_2$.

Method 2: df for two–independent sample t-test $= (n_1 - 1) + (n_2 - 1)$.

Method 3: df for two–independent sample t-test $= N - 2$.

As summarized in Table 9.7, we can add the degrees of freedom for each sample using the first two methods. In the third method, N is the total sample size across both samples, and we subtract 2 from this value. Each method will produce the same result for degrees of freedom. When we add the degrees of freedom for each sample in Example 9.3, we find that df is $n - 1 = 25$ for first-marriage adults and $n - 1 = 15$ for remarried adults. The degrees of freedom for the test are the sum of these values:

$$df = 25 + 15 = 40.$$

Locate 40 degrees of freedom in the far-left column in the t-table in Table B.2 in Appendix B. Move across the column to find the critical value for a .05 proportion in one tail. The critical value for this upper tail test is +1.684. The rejection region beyond this critical value is shown in the t-distribution in Figure 9.5.

We will compare the value of the test statistic with this critical value. If the value of the test statistic is beyond the critical value (is greater than or equal to 1.684), then there is less than a 5% chance that we could have obtained that outcome if the null hypothesis were correct, so we reject the null hypothesis; otherwise, we retain the null hypothesis.

TABLE 9.7 Computing the degrees of freedom for a *t*-test. Because a sample variance is computed for each sample, each sample has its own degrees of freedom. The sum of the *df* is the value you look up in the *t*-table for the critical value(s) of a *t*-test.

Type of *t*-Test	Sample 1		Sample 2	Total *df*
One–independent sample *t*-test	$(n-1)$	+	—	$(n-1)$
Two–independent sample *t*-test	$(n-1)$	+	$(n-1)$	$(n-1)+(n-1)$

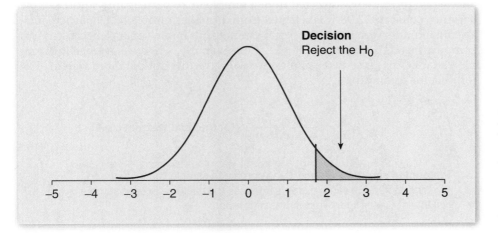

Decision
Reject the H_0

FIGURE 9.5

The shaded region shows the rejection region with a critical value equal to 1.684. If the value of the test statistic falls in the shaded region, we reject the null hypothesis; otherwise, we retain the null hypothesis.

Step 3: Compute the test statistic. In this example, we measured two sample means: 34.72 and 31.74. The difference between these sample means is 2.98. We will compute the test statistic to determine how many standard deviations a mean difference equal to 2.98 is from a mean difference equal to 0 stated in the null hypothesis.

In the formula for a two–independent sample *t*-test, we subtract the mean difference between the sample means $(M_1 - M_2 = 2.98)$ from the mean difference stated in the null $(\mu_1 - \mu_2 = 0)$. We then divide this difference by the overall standard error in both samples, called the **estimated standard error for the difference** $(s_{M_1 - M_2})$ which is computed using the following formula:

$$s_{M_1 - M_2} = \sqrt{\frac{s_p^2}{n_1} + \frac{s_p^2}{n_2}}.$$

DEFINITION

The **estimated standard error for the difference ($s_{M_1-M_2}$)** is an estimate of the standard deviation of a sampling distribution of mean differences between two sample means. It is an estimate of the standard error or standard distance that mean differences can be expected to deviate from the mean difference stated in the null hypothesis.

NOTE: The two–independent sample t-test measures the number of standard deviations in a t-distribution that a mean difference between two samples deviates from the mean difference stated in the null hypothesis.

Hence, the *t*-statistic for a two–independent sample *t*-test is

$$t_{obt} = \frac{(M_1 - M_2) - (\mu_1 - \mu_2)}{s_{M_1-M_2}}.$$

To find the estimated standard error for the difference in the denominator, we need to compute s_p^2, which is the **pooled sample variance.** A pooled sample variance is the mean sample variance for two samples. When the sample size is unequal, the variance is a weighted mean. Table 9.6 shows that a sample variance equal to 29.16 was selected from a sample of 26 participants, and a sample variance equal to 27.98 was selected from a smaller sample of 16 participants. The first sample variance is the better estimate of sample variance because it was computed using a larger sample size. Consequently, when we average the sample variances of these two samples, we will give this sample more weight. The formula for computing s_p^2 is

$$s_p^2 = \frac{s_1^2(df_1) + s_2^2(df_2)}{df_1 + df_2} \quad \text{(for unequal sample sizes).}$$

DEFINITION

The **pooled sample variance** is the combined sample variance of two samples. When the sample size is unequal, the variance in each sample is weighted by its respective degrees of freedom.

The degrees of freedom are the weights in the formula. When we have equal sample sizes, we don't have to weight each sample variance by multiplying it times its respective degrees of freedom. We discuss the effect of sample size further in the Making Sense section. For equal sample sizes, we can compute the pooled sample variance by adding the two sample variances and dividing by 2:

$$s_p^2 = \frac{s_1^2 + s_2^2}{2} \quad \text{(for equal sample sizes).}$$

MAKING SENSE: The Pooled Sample Variance

When we have equal sample sizes, we don't have to weight the sample variances with their degrees of freedom. We compute an arithmetic mean of the two sample variances. To illustrate, suppose we have two samples with the size and variance listed in Table 9.8. Notice both samples are the same size and therefore have the same degrees of freedom: Both samples have 19 degrees of freedom. If we substitute the values for *s* and *df* into the formula for unequal sample sizes, we obtain

$$s_p^2 = \frac{s_1^2(df_1) + s_2^2(df_2)}{df_1 + df_2} = \frac{12(19) + 18(19)}{19 + 19} = 15.$$

TABLE 9.8 The sample size and variance for two hypothetical samples.

Samples	
1	**2**
$n_1 = 20$	$n_2 = 20$
$s_1^2 = 12$	$s_2^2 = 18$

Notice that the value for the pooled sample variance is the middle value between the two sample variances (12 and 18) when the sample sizes are equal. If we substitute the values for *s* and *df* into the formula for equal sample sizes, we will obtain the same value for the pooled sample variance:

$$s_p^2 = \frac{s_1^2 + s_2^2}{2} = \frac{12 + 18}{2} = 15.$$

Both formulas for pooled sample variance produce the same result when $n_1 = n_2$. Only when the sample sizes are unequal is it necessary to weight each sample variance by its respective degrees of freedom.

To compute the test statistic, we (1) compute the pooled sample variance, (2) compute the estimated standard error for the difference, and (3) compute the test statistic for the two–independent sample *t*-test. For reference, Table 9.9 lists the values needed in each step.

1. Compute the pooled sample variance. We substitute the sample variance and degrees of freedom of each sample into the following formula:

$$s_p^2 = \frac{29.16(25) + 27.98(15)}{25 + 15} = 28.72.$$

2. Compute the estimated standard error for the difference. We substitute the pooled sample variance and sample size into the following formula:

$$s_{M_1-M_2} = \sqrt{\frac{s_p^2}{n_1} + \frac{s_p^2}{n_2}} = \sqrt{\frac{28.72}{26} + \frac{28.72}{16}} = 1.70.$$

TABLE 9.9 Data from Example 9.3 needed to compute the *t*-statistic. Except for *df*, these values are also listed in Table 9.6.

First-Marriage Sample	Remarriage Sample
$n_1 = 26$	$n_2 = 16$
$df_1 = 25$	$df_2 = 15$
$M_1 = 34.72$	$M_2 = 31.74$
$s_1^2 = 29.16$	$s_2^2 = 27.98$

3. Compute the test statistic for the two–independent sample *t*-test. We substitute the mean difference we observed (34.72 – 31.74 = 2.98), the mean difference stated by the null hypothesis $(\mu_1 - \mu_2 = 0)$, and the estimated standard error for the difference $\left(s_{M_1-M_2} = 1.70\right)$ into the test statistic formula:

$$t_{obt} = \frac{(M_1 - M_2) - (\mu_1 - \mu_2)}{s_{M_1-M_2}} = \frac{2.98 - 0}{1.70} = 1.753.$$

Step 4: Make a decision. To decide whether to reject or retain the null hypothesis, we compare the obtained value to the critical value. Figure 9.6 shows that the obtained value $(t_{obt} = 1.753)$ is greater than the critical value; it falls in the rejection region. The decision is to reject the null hypothesis. This is the same decision Orathinkal and colleagues (2008) made in their study. If the result were reported in a research journal, it would look something like this:

As expected, first-marriage adults expressed more positive perceptions of forgiveness (*M* = 34.72) compared to remarried adults (*M* = 31.74), *t*(40) = 1.753, *p* < .05.

FIGURE 9.6

The value of the test statistic falls in the rejection region. Therefore, we reject the null hypothesis.

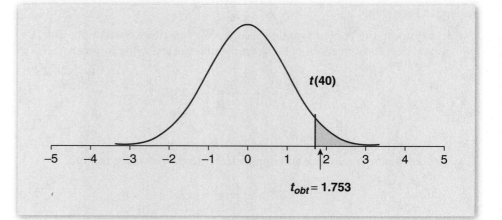

1. What are the four assumptions for the one–independent sample *t*-test?

2. What value is placed in the denominator for the two–independent sample *t*-test?

3. A researcher measures the time it takes 13 men and 15 women to complete multiple tasks in a study. She compares the mean difference between men and women using the two–independent sample *t*-test. What is the critical value for this test if she conducts a two-tailed test at a .05 level of significance?

4. Using the same example as in Question 3, what is the researcher's decision if she reports the following values for the test statistic?

    a. 2.558   b. 1.602   c. 2.042   d. –2.500

Answers: 1. Normality, random sampling, independence, and equal variances; 2. The estimated standard error for the difference; 3. ±2.056; 4. (a) Reject null, (b) Retain null, (c) Retain null, (d) Reject null.

EFFECT SIZE FOR THE TWO–INDEPENDENT SAMPLE *T*-TEST 9.8

Hypothesis testing is used to identify whether an effect exists in one or more populations of interest. When we reject the null hypothesis, we conclude that an effect does exist in the population, which was the decision in Example 9.3: A difference in PPF scores for first-marriage and remarried adults exists between these populations of adults. We can compute effect size to determine how large this effect or mean difference is. We can select from three measures of effect size for the two–independent sample *t*-test: estimated Cohen's *d* and the same two measures of proportion of variance (eta-squared and omega-squared).

ESTIMATED COHEN'S *d*

As stated in Section 9.5, the estimated Cohen's *d* is most often used with the *t*-test. When the estimated Cohen's *d* is used with the two–independent sample *t*-test, we place the difference between two sample means in the numerator and the **pooled sample standard deviation** (or square root of the pooled sample variance) in the denominator. The pooled sample standard deviation is an estimate for the pooled or mean standard deviation for the difference between two population means. The formula for estimated Cohen's *d* for the two–independent sample *t*-test is

$$\text{Estimate Cohen's } d : \frac{M_1 - M_2}{\sqrt{s_p^2}}.$$

NOTE: The pooled sample standard deviation is used as an unbiased estimate for the standard deviation of the difference between two population means in the formula for estimated Cohen's d.

The **pooled sample standard deviation** $\left(\sqrt{s_p^2}\right)$ is the combined sample standard deviation of two samples. It is computed by taking the square root of the pooled sample variance. This measure estimates the standard deviation for the difference between two population means.

DEFINITION

In Example 9.3, $M_1 = 34.72 = 34.72$, $M_2 = 31.74$, and $\sqrt{s_p^2} = \sqrt{28.72} = 5.36$. The estimated Cohen's *d* for Example 9.3 is

$$d = \frac{34.72 - 31.74}{5.36} = 0.56.$$

We conclude that being in a first-marriage increases PPF scores in the population by 0.56 standard deviations compared with remarried adults. The effect size conventions given in Table 8.8 (Chapter 8) and in Table 9.3 show that this is a medium effect size. We could report this measure with the significant t-test in Example 9.3 by stating,

> As expected, first-marriage adults expressed more positive perceptions of forgiveness ($M = 34.72$) compared to remarried adults ($M = 31.74$), $t(40) = 1.753$, $p < .05$ ($d = 0.56$).

PROPORTION OF VARIANCE

Another measure of effect size is proportion of variance, which estimates the proportion of variance in a dependent variable that can be explained by some treatment. In Example 9.3, this measure can describe the proportion of variance in PPF scores that can be explained by whether participants were in their first marriage or remarried. Two measures of proportion of variance for the two–independent sample t-test are eta-squared and omega-squared. These measures are computed the same for all t-tests.

Eta-Squared (η^2)

Eta-squared is one measure of proportion of variance that can be expressed in a single formula based on the result of a t-test:

$$\eta^2 = \frac{t^2}{t^2 + df}.$$

In Example 9.3, the test statistic $t = 1.753$ and $df = 40$. The proportion of variance for Example 9.3 is

$$\eta^2 = \frac{(1.753)^2}{(1.753)^2 + 40} = 0.07.$$

We conclude that 7% of the variability in PPF scores can be explained by whether participants were in their first marriage or remarried. Based on the effect size conventions listed in Table 9.3, this is a small effect size. We could report this measure with the significant t-test in Example 9.3 by stating,

NOTE: Proportion of variance is calculated using the same formula for one– and two–independent sample t-tests.

> As predicted, first-marriage adults expressed more positive perceptions of forgiveness ($M = 34.72$) compared to remarried adults ($M = 31.74$), $t(40) = 1.753$, $p < .05$ $\left(\eta^2 = 0.07\right)$.

Omega-Squared (ω^2)

Same as described in Section 9.5, we compute omega-squared by subtracting 1 from t^2 in the numerator of the eta-squared formula. This makes the estimate of effect size smaller than eta-squared, thereby making omega-squared a less biased measure. Using the omega-squared formula, the proportion of variance for Example 9.3 is

$$\omega^2 = \frac{t^2 - 1}{t^2 + df} = \frac{(1.753)^2 - 1}{(1.753)^2 + 40} = 0.05.$$

We conclude that 5% of the variability in PPF scores can be explained by whether participants were in their first marriage or remarried. The effect size conventions listed in Table 9.3 show that this is again a small effect size. We could report this measure with the significant *t*-test in Example 9.3 by stating,

As predicted, first-marriage adults expressed more positive perceptions of forgiveness ($M = 34.72$) compared to remarried adults ($M = 31.74$), $t(40) = 1.753$, $p < .05$ $\left(\omega^2 = 0.05\right)$.

In sum, eta-squared and omega-squared estimated a small effect size, whereas estimated Cohen's *d* estimated a medium effect size for the data in Example 9.3. While different measures of effect size do not always make the same estimates, there is little consensus as to which is the superior measure. Each measure is regarded as an acceptable estimate of effect size in the published scientific literature.

LEARNING CHECK 5

1. What is the denominator for computing an estimated Cohen's *d* for a two–independent sample *t*-test?

2. If the difference between two means is 4, then what will the estimated Cohen's *d* value be with a pooled sample standard deviation of:

   a. 4   b. 8   c. 16   d. 40

3. The value of the test statistic for a two–independent sample *t*-test is 2.400. Using eta-squared, what is the proportion of variance when the degrees of freedom are 30?

4. Using the sample example in Question 3, what is the proportion of variance using omega-squared?

Answers: 1. The pooled sample standard deviation; 2. (a) $\frac{4}{4} = 1.00$ (large effect size), (b) $\frac{4}{8} = 0.50$ (medium effect size), (c) $\frac{4}{16} = 0.25$ (medium effect size), (d) $\frac{4}{40} = 0.10$ (small effect size); 3. $\eta^2 = \frac{(2.400)^2}{(2.400)^2 + 30} = 0.16$ (medium effect); 4. $\omega^2 = \frac{(2.400)^2 - 1}{(2.400)^2 + 30} = 0.13$ (medium effect).

SPSS IN FOCUS: TWO–INDEPENDENT SAMPLE *T*-TEST   9.9

SPSS can be used to compute the two-independent sample *t*-test, as demonstrated in Example 9.4.

In a study on the likeability of comedians, 10 participants were randomly assigned to observe either a humorous comedian or one who was not humorous. After observing a comedian, participants rated how likable the comedian was on a 7-point scale from 1 (*not likable at all*) to 7 (*very likable*). The ratings are given in Table 9.10.

EXAMPLE 9.4

1. Click on the **variable view** tab and enter *groups* in the **name column.** In the second row, enter *ratings* in the **name column.** We will enter whole numbers, so reduce the value in the **decimals column** to 0.

TABLE 9.10 Ratings given by participants for humorous and nonhumorous comedians in two hypothetical samples.

Ratings for Humorous Comedian ($n = 5$)	Rating for Nonhumorous Comedian ($n = 5$)
8	2
6	3
7	4
4	5
5	1

2. In the row labeled *groups,* click on the small gray box with three dots in the **Values** column. In the **dialog box,** enter *1* in the value cell and *humorous* in the label cell, and then click **add.** Then enter *2* in the value cell and *nonhumorous* in the label cell, and then click *add.* Select **OK.**

3. Click on the **data view** tab. In the *groups* column, enter *1* in the first five cells, then *2* in the next five cells. In the *ratings* column, enter the participant ratings in the cells that correspond with the codes for each group listed in the first column.

4. Go to the **menu bar** and click **Analyze,** then **Compare Means,** and **Independent-Samples T Test** to display the dialog box shown in Figure 9.7.

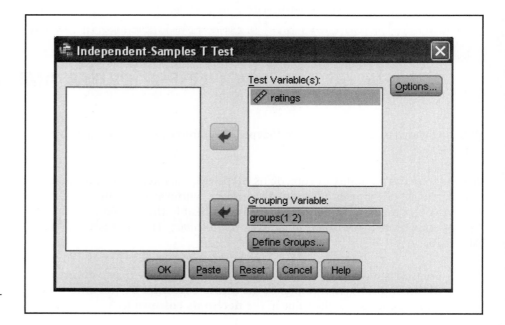

FIGURE 9.7

SPSS dialog box for Steps 4 to 6.

5. Using the arrows, select *ratings* and move it into the **Test Variable(s):** box; select *groups* and move it into the **Grouping Variable:** box. Two question marks will appear in the **Grouping Variable** box.

6. To define the groups, click **Define Groups . . .** to bring up a new dialog box. Enter *1* in the **Group 1:** box, and enter *2* in the **Group 2:** box, and then click **Continue**. Now a 1 and 2 will appear in the Grouping Variable box instead of question marks.

7. Select **Paste** and click the **Run** command.

Table 9.11 shows the output. The top table displays the sample size, mean, standard deviation, and standard error for both groups. The bottom table displays a summary for the *t*-test. The effect size is not given; again, you need to use the data given in the output tables to compute effect size. Also, notice that the bottom table gives you the numerator and denominator for the *t*-test. If we substitute the values in the SPSS output table into the formula, we will obtain the value of the test statistic:

$$t_{obs} = \frac{\text{Mean Difference}}{\text{Std. Error Difference}} = \frac{3.00}{1.00} = 3.00.$$

TABLE 9.11   SPSS output table.

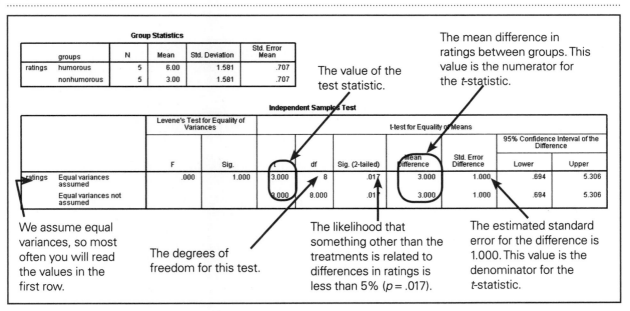

APA IN FOCUS: REPORTING THE *T*-STATISTIC AND EFFECT SIZE   9.10

When reporting the results of a *t*-test, we include the value of the test statistic, degrees of freedom, *p* value, and effect size. In addition, a figure or table is often used to summarize the means and standard error or standard deviations measured in the study. While this information can be included in the written results of the study, it is often more concise to do so in a table or figure.

Many scientific journals will not publish the results of a study without the standard deviations or estimated standard errors reported with a t-test. It is your choice whether to summarize these values in a figure, a table, or the written report, but they must be reported. Reporting a Cohen's d, eta-squared (η^2), and omega-squared (ω^2) are all acceptable measures of effect size, although Cohen's d is the most often used to report effect size with the t-test.

CHAPTER SUMMARY ORGANIZED BY LEARNING OBJECTIVE

LO 1: Explain why a *t*-distribution is associated with $n - 1$ degrees of freedom and describe the information that is conveyed by the *t*-statistic.

- The **t-distribution** is a normal-like distribution with greater variability in the tails because the sample variance is substituted for the population variance to estimate the standard error in this distribution.

- The *t*-distribution is a sampling distribution for *t*-statistic values that are computed using the sample variance to estimate the population variance in the formula. As sample size increases, the sample variance more closely estimates the population variance. The result is that there is less variability in the tails of a *t*-distribution as the sample size increases. Each *t*-distribution is associated with the same degrees of freedom as sample variance: $df = n - 1$.

- The **t-statistic** is an inferential statistic used to determine the number of standard deviations in a *t*-distribution that a sample mean deviates from the mean value or mean difference stated in the null hypothesis.

LO 2: Calculate the degrees of freedom for a one– and two–independent sample *t*-test and locate critical values in the *t*-table.

- The **degrees of freedom** for a *t*-distribution are equal to the degrees of freedom for sample variance: $n - 1$. As the degrees of freedom increase, the tails of the corresponding *t*-distribution change, and the probability of sample outcomes in the tails become less likely.

- The degrees of freedom for a one–independent sample *t*-test are $(n - 1)$; the degrees of freedom for a two–independent sample *t*-test are $(n_1 - 1) + (n_2 - 1)$.

LO 3–4: Identify the assumptions for the one–independent sample *t*-test; compute a one–independent sample *t*-test and interpret the results.

- We compute a one–independent sample *t*-test concerning a single population mean from a population with an unknown variance. We make three assumptions for this test: normality, random sampling, and independence.

- The larger the value of the test statistic, the less likely a sample mean is to occur if the null hypothesis were true, and the more likely we are to reject the null hypothesis. The test statistic for a **one–independent sample *t*-test** is the difference between the sample mean and population mean, divided by the estimated standard error:

$$t_{obt} = \frac{M - \mu}{s_M}, \text{ where } s_M = \sqrt{\frac{s^2}{n}}.$$

- The **estimated standard error** (s_M) is an estimate of the standard deviation of a sampling distribution of sample means. It is an estimate of the standard error or standard distance that sample means can be expected to deviate from the value of the population mean stated in the null hypothesis.

LO 5: Compute effect size and proportion of variance for a one–independent sample *t*-test.

- Effect size measures the size of an observed difference in a population. For the one–independent sample *t*-test, this measure estimates how far, or how many standard deviations, an effect shifts in a population. The formula for estimated Cohen's *d* is

$$d = \frac{M - \mu}{SD}.$$

- **Proportion of variance** is a measure of effect size in terms of the proportion or percent of variability in a dependent variable that can be explained by a treatment. In hypothesis testing, a **treatment** is considered as any unique characteristic of a sample or any unique way that a researcher treats a sample. Two measures of proportion of variance are computed the same for all *t*-tests:

Using eta-squared: $\eta^2 = \dfrac{t^2}{t^2 + df}$.

Using omega-squared: $\omega^2 = \dfrac{t^2 - 1}{t^2 + df}$.

LO 6–7: Identify the assumptions for the two–independent sample *t*-test; compute a two–independent sample *t*-test and interpret the results.

- We compute a two–independent sample *t*-test concerning two population means from one or two populations with unknown variances. We make four assumptions for this test: normality, random sampling, independence, and equal variances.
- The larger the value of the test statistic, the less likely a sample mean is to occur if the null hypothesis were true, and the more likely we are to reject the null hypothesis. The test statistic for a **two–independent sample *t*-test** is the mean difference between two samples minus the mean difference stated in the null hypothesis, divided by the estimated standard error for the difference:

$$t_{obt} = \frac{(M_1 - M_2) - (\mu_1 - \mu_2)}{s_{M_1 - M_2}}, \text{ where}$$

$$s_{M_1 - M_2} = \sqrt{\frac{s_p^2}{n_1} + \frac{s_p^2}{n_2}} \text{ and } s_p^2 = \frac{s_1^2(df_1) + s_2^2(df_2)}{df_1 + df_2}.$$

- The **estimated standard error for the difference** is an estimate of the standard deviation of a sampling distribution of mean differences between two sample means. It is an estimate of the standard error or distance that mean differences can deviate from the mean difference stated in the null hypothesis.

LO 8: Compute effect size and proportion of variance for a two–independent sample *t*-test.

- **Estimated Cohen's *d*** can be used to estimate effect size for the two–independent sample *t*-test. This measure estimates how far, or how many standard deviations, an observed

mean difference is shifted in one or two populations. The formula for estimated Cohen's *d* is

$$\frac{M_1 - M_2}{\sqrt{s_p^2}}.$$

- The computation and interpretation of **proportion of variance** are the same for all *t*-tests.

APA LO 9: Summarize the results of a one–independent sample and a two–independent sample *t*-test in APA format.

- To report the results of a one– and two–independent sample *t*-test, state the test statistic, degree of freedom, *p* value, and effect size. In addition, a figure or table is often used to summarize the means and standard error or standard deviations measured in a study. While this information can be included in the written report, it is often more concise to do so in a table or figure.

SPSS LO 10: Compute a one–independent sample and a two–independent sample *t*-test using SPSS.

- SPSS can be used to compute a one–independent sample *t*-test. The one–independent sample *t*-test is computed using the **Analyze, Compare Means,** and **One-Sample T Test** options in the menu bar. These actions will display a dialog box that allows you to identify the variable, enter the comparison or null hypothesis value for the test, and run the test (for more details, see Section 9.6).
- SPSS can be used to compute a two–independent sample *t*-test. The two–independent sample *t*-test is computed using the **Analyze, Compare Means,** and **Independent-Samples T Test** options in the menu bar. These actions will display a dialog box that allows you to identify the groups and run the test (for more details, see Section 9.9).

KEY TERMS

degrees of freedom (*df*)	pooled sample standard deviation	*t*-observed
estimated Cohen's *d*		*t*-obtained
estimated standard error	pooled sample variance	treatment
estimated standard error for the difference	proportion of variance	*t*-statistic
	Student's *t*	two–independent sample *t*-test
one–independent sample *t*-test	*t*-distribution	

END-OF-CHAPTER PROBLEMS

Factual Problems

1. What is the main limitation of the z-test? Name the alternative to the z-test that does not have this limitation.

2. The sample variance is used in the formula for standard error when the population variance is not known. Why is it appropriate to substitute the sample variance for the population variance?

3. How does the shape of a *t*-distribution change as the sample size increases? Explain.

4. Why are the degrees of freedom for the *t*-distribution and the degrees of freedom for sample variance the same?

5. Name the two *t*-tests used in hypothesis testing for independent samples.

6. Name three measures used to estimate effect size for one– and two–independent sample *t*-tests.

7. Name two measures of proportion of variance. Which measure is the most conservative?

8. What value is used to estimate the population standard deviation of the difference between two means in the formula for estimated Cohen's *d?*

9. What measure of effect size is most often reported with the *t*-test?

10. What values must be included in an APA summary of the results of a *t*-test?

Concepts and Application Problems

11. In the following studies, state whether you would use a one–independent or two–independent sample *t*-test.

    (a) A study measuring differences in attitudes about morality among Democrats and Republicans

    (b) A study testing whether night-shift workers sleep the recommended 8 hours per day

    (c) An experiment measuring differences in brain activity among rats placed on either a continuous or intermittent reward schedule

12. The values listed below are the obtained values for a *t*-statistic. (1) What is your decision for each if $df = 30$ and $\alpha = .05$ for a two-tailed test? (2) What is your decision for each if $df = 30$, and we change to $\alpha = .01$ for an upper tail critical test?

    (a) $t_{obt} = 2.050$

    (b) $t_{obt} = 1.680$

    (c) $t_{obt} = 2.834$

    (d) $t_{obt} = -3.030$

13. Will each of the following increase, decrease, or have no effect on the value of the test statistic in a one–independent sample *t*-test?

    (a) The sample size is increased.

    (b) The level of significance is reduced from .05 to .01.

    (c) The sample variance is doubled.

    (d) The difference between the sample and population mean increased.

14. State the critical values for a one–independent sample *t*-test given the following conditions:

    (a) Two-tailed test, $\alpha = .05$, $n = 12$

    (b) One-tailed test, lower tail critical, $\alpha = .01$, $df = 15$

    (c) Two-tailed test, $a = .01$, $df = 26$

    (d) One-tailed test, upper tail critical, $\alpha = .05$, $n = 30$

15. State the total degrees of freedom for the following *t*-tests:

    (a) $n = 12$ for a one–independent sample *t*-test

    (b) $df_1 = 12$, $n_2 = 19$ for a two–independent sample *t*-test

    (c) Critical value = 1.645 for a one-tailed test, $\alpha = .05$

    (d) Critical value = 63.657 for a two-tailed test, $\alpha = .01$

16. Will each of the following increase, decrease, or have no effect on the value of the test statistic for a two–independent sample *t*-test?

    (a) The total sample size is increased.

    (b) The level of significance is reduced from .05 to .01.

    (c) The pooled sample variance is doubled.

17. A schoolteacher is concerned that her students watch more TV than the average American child. She reads that according to the American Academy of Pediatrics (AAP), the average American child watches 4 hours of TV per day ($\mu = 4.0$ hours). She records the number of hours of TV each of her six students watch per day. The times (in hours) are 4.4, 2.5, 5.5, 2.8, 4.8, and 4.0.

    (a) Test the hypothesis that her students watch more TV than the average American child using a .05 level of significance and a one–independent sample t-test. State the value of the test statistic and the decision to retain or reject the null hypothesis.

    (b) Compute effect size using estimated Cohen's d.

18. A psychology department secretary notices that the average number of student complaints the department receives per week is 1.4 ($\mu = 1.4$). He notices that the department has made some poor policy changes recently and wants to see if the number of complaints that the department receives has increased. He records the following number of complaints that came in per week for 8 weeks: 2, 4, 3, 5, 4, 1, 1, and 4.

    (a) Test his hypothesis that the number of complaints has increased using a .05 level of significance and a one–independent sample t-test. State the value for the test statistic and the decision to retain or reject the null hypothesis.

    (b) Compute effect size using estimated Cohen's d.

19. While researching lifestyle changes to improve heart health, you come across a research article reporting that the average American consumes about 2,700 calories per day ($\mu = 2,700$). You come across another article that refutes this, stating that a sample of Americans consumed significantly less than this mean standard on average, $t(50) = 2.993$, $p < .05$ ($\eta^2 = 0.15$). Assuming this test was a one–independent sample t-test, answer the following questions:

    (a) Is this a significant effect?

    (b) What is the proportion of variance for this effect?

20. In a study on the likeability of comedians, 10 participants observed one of two comedians (one who was humorous and another who was not humorous) and rated how likable these comedians were on a 7-point scale from 1 (*not likable at all*) to 7 (*very likable*). The ratings by each participant are given below.

Ratings for Humorous Comedian ($n = 5$)	Rating for Non-humorous Comedian ($n = 5$)
8	2
6	3
7	4
4	5
5	1

    (a) Test whether or not likeability ratings differ between groups using a .05 level of significance. State the value of the test statistic and the decision to retain or reject the null hypothesis.

    (b) Compute effect size using estimated Cohen's d.

21. To demonstrate flavor aversion learning (that is, learning to dislike a flavor that is associated with becoming sick), researchers gave one group of laboratory rats an injection of lithium chloride immediately following consumption of saccharin-flavored water. Lithium chloride makes rats feel sick. A second control group was not made sick after drinking the flavored water. The next day, both groups were allowed to drink saccharin-flavored water. The amounts consumed (in milliliters) for both groups during this test are given below.

Amount Consumed by Rats That Were Made Sick ($n = 4$)	Amount Consumed by Control Rats ($n = 4$)
4	7
5	12
1	8
3	11

(a) Test whether or not consumption of saccharin-flavored water differed between groups using a .05 level of significance. State the value of the test statistic and the decision to retain or reject the null hypothesis.

(b) Compute effect size using eta-squared (η^2).

22. A social psychologist records the number of outbursts in a sample of different classrooms at a local school. Based on the statement below, what are the sample size, decision (retain or reject the null hypothesis), and effect size in this study?

    The number of outbursts among students at this local school ($M = 3$) were significantly less than that in the general population, $t(39) = 4.19$, $p < .05$ ($d = 0.25$).

23. A researcher records the number of words recalled by students presented a list of words for one minute. In one group, students were presented the list of words in color; for a second group, the same words were presented in black and white. An equal number of students were in each group. Based on the statement below, state the sample size in each group, the decision (to retain or reject the null hypothesis), and the effect size in this study.

    Participants recalled significantly more words when the words were presented in color ($M = 12.4$ words) versus black and white ($M = 10.9$ words), $t(48) = 2.009$, $p < .05$ ($d = 0.18$).

24. Using Cohen's *d,* state whether a 3-point treatment effect ($M_1 - M_2 = 3$) is small, medium, or large for a one–independent sample *t*-test, given the following values for the sample standard deviation:

    (a) $SD = 3$ (b) $SD = 6$ (c) $SD = 12$ (d) $SD = 24$

25. Using Cohen's *d,* state whether a 3-point treatment effect ($M_1 - M_2 = 3$) is small, medium, or large for a two–independent sample *t*-test, given the following values for the pooled sample variance:

    (a) $s_p^2 = 9$ (b) $s_p^2 = 36$
    (c) $s_p^2 = 144$ (d) $s_p^2 = 576$

Problems in Research

26. **Estimating the population variance.** In an article comparing the *t*-test with the *z*-test, Arthur Riopelle (2003) demonstrated that as the sample size increased from 10 to 200 participants, the sample variance more closely estimated the population variance. Knowing this, how will increasing the sample size change the shape of the *t*-distribution?

27. **Estimating effect size.** Yuan and Maxwell (2005) investigated how the power of a study influences the decisions researchers make in an experiment. In their introduction concerning effect size, they stated that "the exact true effect size is generally unknown even after the experiment. But one can estimate the effect size . . . [and] when the sample size is large, the estimated effect size is near the true effect size" (p. 141).

    (a) Why is the exact true effect size generally unknown even after the experiment? Explain.

    (b) How does increasing the sample size improve our estimate of effect size when we use estimated Cohen's *d?*

28. **General motor skills of children with a developmental disorder.** Lopata, Hamm, Volker, and Sowinski (2007) studied the general motor and visual skills of children with a neurological developmental disorder. They gave 17 children with the disorder ($n = 17$) the Bruininks-Oseretsky Test of Motor Proficiency, where higher scores indicate better skills. Children in this study scored 30.4 ± 14.9 ($M \pm SD$) points on this test. They compared mean scores in the sample with scores from the general normative population ($\mu = 50$). Test whether or not scores in this sample differed from the general normative population using a .05 level of significance. State the value of the test statistic and the decision to retain or reject the null hypothesis.

29. **Mental health among relatives of patients with OCD.** In Example 9.1, we examined a study completed by Albert and colleagues (2007). In this study, they assessed various health and psychological measures for relatives of patients with obsessive-compulsive disorder (OCD). As part of this study, they measured mental health in 26 male relatives of patients with OCD. They

compared the mean scores with those of the normative male population ($\mu = 71.29$). In this study, men scored 59.54 ± 19.31 ($M \pm SD$) on this mental health test.

(a) Test whether men in this sample scored at the normative level for the population, using a .05 level of significance. State the value of the test statistic and the decision to retain or reject the null hypothesis.

(b) Compute the estimated Cohen's d for this test.

30. **Preferences for general health.** Montoya (2007) asked a group of 56 men and 82 women to rate their preference for the physical characteristics of partners. One question asked the participants to rate general fitness on a 5-point Likert scale from 1 (*no opinion*) to 5 (*very desirable*). They reported that women ($M = 2.79$) rated general fitness as a significantly more desirable trait as compared to men ($M = 2.47$), $t(136) = -2.45$, $p < .05$.

(a) Compute the proportion of variance using omega-squared.

(b) Suppose the pooled sample standard deviation for this test is 0.74. Using this value, compute estimated Cohen's d.

31. **Racial stereotypes among nonminorities.** Hentges, Meier, and Bartsch (2007) measured racial stereotypes in a sample of 42 nonminority participants. Suppose that 20 participants rated the first type of commercial, and a separate group of 22 rated the second. The following table lists the sample mean and variance in their responses for each type of commercial.

Sample	Liking of Commercial 1 With Racial Stereotypes	Liking of Commercial 1 Without Racial Stereotypes
Mean	3.15	3.39
Variance	0.34	0.23

Test the null hypothesis that there is no difference in ratings between these two types of commercials, using a two-tailed test ($\alpha = .05$). State the value of the test statistic and the decision to retain or reject the null hypothesis.

32. **Global IQ and shaken baby syndrome.** As part of a larger study, Stipanicic, Nolin, Fortin, and Gobeil (2008) compared Global IQ scores in a sample of 11 children ($n_1 = 11$) with shaken baby syndrome (SBS) to 11 children without the syndrome ($n_2 = 11$). Global IQ scores were 86.36 ± 15.16 ($M \pm SD$) for children with SBS and 104.09 ± 12.10 ($M \pm SD$) for children without SBS.

(a) Test whether or not mean scores differed between groups, using a .05 level of significance. State the value of the test statistic and the decision to retain or reject the null hypothesis.

(b) Compute effect size using estimated Cohen's d.

(c) Compute effect size using eta-squared.

NOTE: Answers for even numbers are in Appendix C.

Testing Means

Related Samples
t-Test

LEARNING OBJECTIVES

After reading this chapter, you should be able to:

1. Describe two types of research designs used when we select related samples.

2. Explain why difference scores are computed for the related samples *t*-test.

3. Calculate the degrees of freedom for a related samples *t*-test and locate critical values in the *t*-table.

4. Identify the assumptions for the related samples *t*-test.

5. Compute a related samples *t*-test and interpret the results.

6. Compute effect size and proportion of variance for a related samples *t*-test.

7. State three advantages for selecting related samples.

8. Summarize the results of a related samples *t*-test in APA format.

9. Compute a related samples *t*-test using SPSS.

chapter 10

10.1 RELATED AND INDEPENDENT SAMPLES

In Chapters 8 and 9, we introduced hypothesis tests for **independent samples.** An independent sample is one in which participants in each sample are unrelated and are observed in only one sample. There are two ways that we can collect two independent samples: We can select a sample from two different populations, or we can select a sample from a single population and randomly assign participants to two groups or conditions. In the one– and two–independent sample *t*-tests introduced in Chapter 9, we assumed that the samples we selected were independent.

DEFINITION

In an **independent sample,** participants are unrelated in that they are observed once in only one group. To collect independent samples, participants are selected from different populations or selected from a single population and randomly assigned to different groups.

In some studies, the sample we select is not independent. Such a sample is called a **related** or **dependent sample.** A related sample is one where the participants in each group are observed in more than one treatment or matched on common characteristics. In this chapter, we introduce how to select related samples and compute the test statistic for analyzing data measured in related samples. Two research designs are associated with selecting related samples: the repeated measures design and matched-pairs design. While both research designs are computed the same, the way in which the data are collected is not. Each research design is described in this section.

DEFINITION

In a **related sample**, also called a **dependent sample**, participants in each group or sample are related. Participants can be related in two ways: They are observed in more than one group (repeated measures design), or they are matched, experimentally or naturally, based on the common characteristics or traits that they share (matched-pairs design).

REPEATED MEASURES DESIGN

The most common related samples design is the **repeated measures design,** in which each participant is observed repeatedly. Table 10.1 shows a situation with two treatments. In a repeated measures design, each participant (n_1, n_2, etc.) is

TABLE 10.1 In a repeated measures design with two treatments, *n* participants are observed two times.

Treatment 1		Treatment 2
n_1	–	n_1
n_2	–	n_2
n_3	–	n_3
n_4	–	n_4
n_5	–	n_5

observed twice (once in each treatment). We can create repeated measures by using a pre-post design or a within-subjects design.

DEFINITION

The **repeated measures design** is a research design in which the same participants are observed in each treatment. Two types of repeated measures designs are the pre-post design and the within-subjects design.

Using the **pre-post design,** we measure a dependent variable for participants observed before (pre) and after (post) some treatment. For example, we could measure athletic performance (the dependent variable) in a sample of athletes before and after a training camp. We can compare the difference in athletic performance before and after the camp. This type of repeated measures design is limited to observing participants at two times (i.e., before and after a treatment).

Using the **within-subjects design,** we observe participants across many treatments but not necessarily before and after some treatment. For two samples, we may measure student grades in each of two psychology classes with the same instructor. In this case, we observed participants twice, or in each class, but not before and after some treatment. Any time the same participants are observed in each group, either pre-post or within-subjects, we are using the repeated measures design to select related samples.

NOTE: Two types of designs for selecting related samples are the repeated measures and the matched-pairs designs.

The **pre-post design** is a type of repeated measures design in which researchers measure a dependent variable for participants before (pre) and following (post) some treatment.

DEFINITION

The **within-subjects design** is a type of repeated measures design where researchers observe the same participants across many treatments but not necessarily before and after a treatment.

NOTE: In a repeated measures design, the same participants are observed in each treatment. Two types of repeated measures designs are the pre-post and within-subjects designs.

MATCHED-PAIRS DESIGN

The matched-pairs design is also used to study related samples. In the **matched-pairs design,** participants are selected and then matched, experimentally or naturally, based on the common characteristics or traits that they share. The matched-pairs design is limited to observing two groups, where pairs of participants are matched. Using this design, Table 10.2 shows a situation with two treatments. In a matched-pairs design, different, yet matched, participants (n_1, n_2, etc.) are observed in each treatment, and scores from each matched pair of participants are compared.

DEFINITION

The **matched-pairs design**, also called the **matched-subjects design** or **matched-samples design**, is a research design in which participants are selected and then matched, experimentally or naturally, based on the common characteristics or traits that they share.

Matching through experimental manipulation is typical for experiments in which the researcher manipulates the traits or characteristics used to match the participants.

Matching through natural occurrence is typical for quasi-experiments in which participants are matched based on their preexisting traits or characteristics.

NOTE: In a matched-pairs design, participants are matched on based on the characteristics that they share. Matched-pairs can be obtained either experimentally or through natural occurrence.

There are two ways we can obtain matched pairs: experimental manipulation or natural occurrence. Matching through experimental manipulation is typical for

TABLE 10.2 In a matched-pairs design, n pairs are matched and observed one time.

Treatment 1		Treatment 2
n_1	–	n_2
n_3	–	n_4
n_5	–	n_6
n_7	–	n_8
n_9	–	n_{10}

research studies in which the researcher manipulates the traits or characteristics upon which participants are matched. We can match pairs of participants on any number of variables, including their level of intelligence, their personality type, their eating habits, their level of education, or their sleep patterns. We could measure these characteristics and then match participants. For example, we could measure intelligence, then match the two participants scoring the highest, the two participants scoring the next highest, and so on. Matching through experimental manipulation requires that we measure some trait or characteristic first, before we match participants into pairs.

Matching through natural occurrence is typical for quasi-experiments in which participants are matched based on preexisting traits of the participants. The preexisting traits are typically biological or physiological in nature. For example, we could match participants based on genetics (e.g., biological twins) or family affiliation (e.g., brothers, sisters, or cousins). Each trait or characteristic is inherent to the participant. There is no need to measure this in order to pair participants. Instead, the participants are already matched naturally. Pairs of identical twins or brothers, for example, are paired together naturally. One member of each pair is assigned to a group or a treatment, and differences between pairs of scores are compared. Any time participants are matched on the common traits that they share, either experimentally or through natural occurrence, we are using the matched-pairs design to select related samples. Figure 10.1 summarizes the designs used with related samples.

LEARNING CHECK 1

1. How do related samples differ from independent samples?

2. Name two types of repeated measures designs.

3. Distinguish between the repeated measures design and the matched-pairs design.

4. A researcher records the amount of computer use (in hours per day) in a sample of students, then matches the students based on their amount of computer use. Is this an example of matching through experimental manipulation or matching through natural occurrence?

Answers: 1. In related samples, participants are related either because they are observed more than once or matched on common traits. In independent samples, participants are not related because different participants are observed in each group. 2. Pre-post design and within-subjects design; 3. Each participant is observed at least two times in the repeated measures design. In the matched-pairs design, each pair of participants is matched and observed one time. 4. Matching through experimental manipulation.

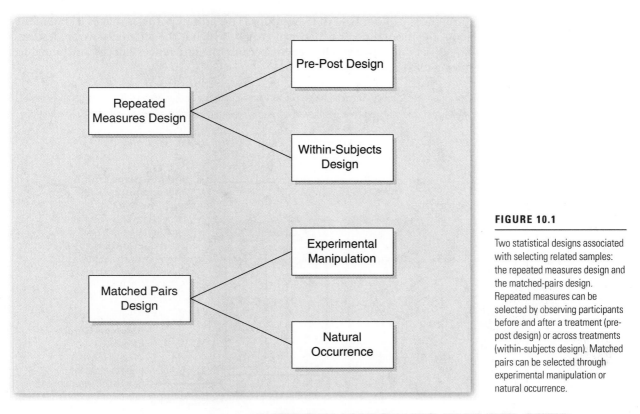

FIGURE 10.1

Two statistical designs associated with selecting related samples: the repeated measures design and the matched-pairs design. Repeated measures can be selected by observing participants before and after a treatment (pre-post design) or across treatments (within-subjects design). Matched pairs can be selected through experimental manipulation or natural occurrence.

INTRODUCTION TO THE RELATED SAMPLES *T*-TEST 10.2

When we select two related samples, we can compare differences using the **related samples *t*-test.** To test the null hypothesis, we state the mean difference between pairs of scores in the population and compare this to the difference we observe between pairs of scores in our sample. This test is different from the two–independent sample *t*-test in that we subtract the pairs of scores first to obtain the **difference score** of each participant; then we compute the test statistic.

> The **related samples *t*-test** is a statistical procedure used to test hypotheses concerning two related samples selected from populations in which the variance in one or both populations is unknown.
>
> A **difference score** is a score or value obtained by subtracting two scores. In a related samples *t*-test, difference scores are obtained prior to computing the test statistic.

DEFINITION

There is a good reason for subtracting each pair of scores before computing the test statistic using a related samples *t*-test: It eliminates the source of error associated with observing different participants in each group or treatment. When we select related samples, we observe the same, or matched, participants in each group, not different participants. So we can eliminate this source of error.

Consider the hypothetical data shown in Table 10.3 for four participants (A, B, C, and D) observed in two groups (Q and Z). Table 10.3 identifies three places where differences can occur with two groups. The null hypothesis makes a statement about the mean difference between groups, which is the difference we are testing. Any other difference is called **error** because the differences can't be attributed to having different groups.

TABLE 10.3   A hypothetical set of data of four participants. There are three places where differences occur. Mean differences (the between-groups effect) are the differences we are testing. The other two places where differences occur are regarded as errors in that they have nothing to do with having different groups.

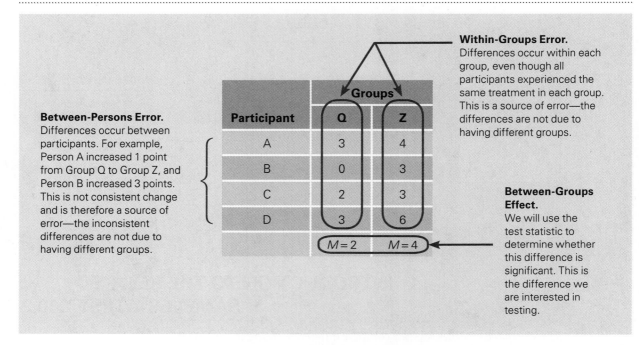

Within-Groups Error. Differences occur within each group, even though all participants experienced the same treatment in each group. This is a source of error—the differences are not due to having different groups.

Between-Persons Error. Differences occur between participants. For example, Person A increased 1 point from Group Q to Group Z, and Person B increased 3 points. This is not consistent change and is therefore a source of error—the inconsistent differences are not due to having different groups.

Between-Groups Effect. We will use the test statistic to determine whether this difference is significant. This is the difference we are interested in testing.

| | Groups | |
Participant	Q	Z
A	3	4
B	0	3
C	2	3
D	3	6
	$M = 2$	$M = 4$

TABLE 10.4   A hypothetical set of data of the same four participants in Table 10.3. Notice that when we subtract paired scores, only one source of error remains (within-groups error). The between-persons error is eliminated when the same or matched participants are observed in each group.

Within-Groups Error. Differences occur within the column of difference scores, even though all participants experienced the same pair of groups. This is a source of error—these differences are not due to having different groups.

Participant	Difference Scores (Q – Z)
A	−1
B	−3
C	−1
D	−3
	$M = -2$

Mean difference score.

DEFINITION

For a *t*-test, the term **error** refers to any unexplained difference that cannot be attributed to, or caused by, having different treatments. The standard error of the mean is used to measure the error or unexplained differences in a statistical design.

As shown in Table 10.4, when we reduce pairs of scores to a single column of difference scores, we eliminate the between-persons error that was illustrated in Table 10.3. Between-persons error is associated with differences associated with observing different participants in each group or treatment. However, using the related samples design we observe the same (or matched) participants in each group, not different participants, so we can eliminate this source of error before computing the test statistic. Error in a study is measured by the estimate of standard error. Eliminating between-persons error makes the total value of error smaller, thereby reducing standard error. In Chapter 8, we showed that reducing standard error increases the power of detecting an effect. This is the reason we compute difference scores prior to computing the test statistic: It reduces standard error, thereby increasing the power to detect an effect.

NOTE: Computing difference scores prior to computing the test statistic reduces error by eliminating one possible source of error, thereby increasing the power of a hypothesis test.

THE TEST STATISTIC

The test statistic for a related samples *t*-test is similar to the other test statistics introduced in Chapters 8 and 9. Mean differences are placed in the numerator, and the estimate of standard error is placed in the denominator. For a related samples *t*-test, in the numerator, we subtract the mean difference in two related samples (M_D) from the mean difference stated in the null hypothesis (μ_D):

$$M_D - \mu_D$$

The estimate of standard error is placed in the denominator of the test statistic for a related samples *t*-test. The standard error for a distribution of mean difference scores, called the **estimated standard error for difference scores** (s_{MD}), is computed using the following formula:

$$s_{MD} = \sqrt{\frac{s_D^2}{n_D}} = \frac{s_D}{\sqrt{n_D}}.$$

The **estimated standard error for difference scores (s_{MD})** is an estimate of the standard deviation of a sampling distribution of mean difference scores. It is an estimate of the standard error or standard distance that the mean difference scores deviate from the mean difference score stated in the null hypothesis.

DEFINITION

By placing mean differences in the numerator and the estimated standard error for difference scores in the denominator, we obtain the formula for the test statistic for a related samples *t*-test:

$$t_{obt} = \frac{M_D - \mu_D}{s_{MD}}.$$

The test statistic for a related samples *t*-test estimates the number of standard deviations in a *t*-distribution that a sample mean difference falls from the population mean difference stated in the null hypothesis. The larger the value of the test statistic, the less likely a sample mean difference could occur if the null hypothesis were true, thereby making it more likely that we will decide to reject the null hypothesis.

DEGREES OF FREEDOM

NOTE: The degrees of freedom for the related samples t-test equal the number of difference scores minus 1 ($n_D - 1$).

To compute the test statistic, we first reduce each pair of scores to one column of difference scores. Hence, the degrees of freedom for the related samples *t*-test equal the number of difference scores minus 1: $df = (n_D - 1)$.

ASSUMPTIONS

NOTE: Two assumptions for a related samples t-test are normality and independence within groups.

There are two assumptions we make to compute the related samples *t*-test:

1. *Normality.* We assume that data in the population of difference scores are normally distributed. Again, this assumption is most important for small sample sizes. With larger samples ($n > 30$), the standard error is small, and this assumption becomes less critical as a result.

2. *Independence within groups.* The samples are related or matched between groups. However, we must assume that difference scores were obtained from different individuals within each group or treatment.

✔ **LEARNING CHECK 2**

1. Why do we subtract pairs of scores (computing difference scores) before computing the test statistic for a related samples *t*-test?

2. What is the value for the degrees of freedom for each example listed below?
   a. A study comparing 10 matched pairs of scores
   b. A study involving 18 participants observed two times

3. What is in the denominator of the test statistic for the related samples *t*-test?

4. What do we assume to compute a related samples *t*-test?

Answers: 1. Computing difference scores eliminates the between-persons error, thereby increasing the power of the test; 2. (a) $df = 9$, (b) $df = 17$; 3. Estimated standard error for difference scores; 4. Normality and independence within groups.

10.3 RELATED SAMPLES *T*-TEST: REPEATED MEASURES DESIGN

Two designs associated with selecting related samples are the repeated measures design and the matched-pairs design. In Example 10.1, we will compute the related samples *t*-test for a study using the repeated measures design. In Example 10.2 (in Section 10.5), we compute a study using the matched-pairs design.

Students often "go over their minutes" for allotted cell phone use in a given month. Suppose we hypothesize that one reason is that when students are at home, they still use their cell phone, possibly out of habit, and not their home phone. To test this hypothesis, we measure the time in minutes that a sample of eight popular adolescent students spent talking on a cell phone and a home phone at their home over a 2-day period. Table 10.5 lists the results of this study with the difference scores given. Test whether or not these times differ using a .05 level of significance.

EXAMPLE 10.1

TABLE 10.5 The time spent (in minutes) talking on two types of phones in a hypothetical sample of eight participants. Difference scores are given in the last column.

Participants	Talking Time On		Difference Scores
	Cell Phone	Home Phone	
1	220	210	(220 − 210) = 10
2	245	220	(245 − 220) = 25
3	215	195	(215 − 195) = 20
4	260	265	(260 − 265) = −5
5	300	275	(300 − 275) = 25
6	280	290	(280 − 290) = −10
7	250	220	(250 − 220) = 30
8	310	285	(310 − 285) = 25

Step 1: State the hypotheses. Because we are testing whether (=) or not (≠) a difference exists, the null hypothesis states that there is no mean difference, and the alternative hypothesis states that there is a mean difference:

$H_0: \mu_D = 0$ There is no mean difference in time spent talking on a cell phone versus home phone.

$H_1: \mu_D \neq 0$ There is a mean difference in time spent talking on a cell phone versus home phone.

NOTE: The null and the hypotheses alternative make statements about a population of mean difference scores.

Step 2: Set the criteria for a decision. The level of significance for this test is .05. This is a two-tailed test for the mean difference between two related samples. The degrees of freedom for this test are $df = 8 - 1 = 7$. We locate 7 degrees of freedom in the far-left column of the *t*-table in Table B.2 in Appendix B. Move across to the column to find the critical values for a .05 proportion in two tails. The critical values for this test are ±2.365. Figure 10.2 shows the *t*-distribution and the rejection regions beyond these critical values.

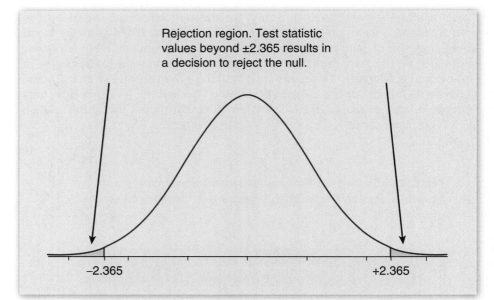

FIGURE 10.2

The shaded areas show the rejection regions. The critical value cutoffs are ±2.365. If the value of the test statistic falls in the shaded area, then we choose to reject the null hypothesis; otherwise, we retain the null hypothesis.

We will compare the value of the test statistic to these critical values. If the value of the test statistic falls beyond either critical value (falls beyond ±2.365), then there is less than a 5% chance we could have obtained that outcome if the null hypothesis were correct, so we reject the null hypothesis; otherwise, we retain the null hypothesis.

Step 3: Compute the test statistic. To compute the test statistic, we (1) compute the mean, variance, and standard deviation of difference scores; (2) compute the estimated standard error for difference scores; then (3) compute the test statistic.

(1) Compute the mean, variance, and standard deviation for difference scores. Keep in mind that the sign (negative or positive) of difference scores matters when we compute the mean and standard deviation. To compute the mean, sum the difference scores ($\sum D$) and divide by number of difference scores summed (n_D):

$$\text{Mean}: M_D = \frac{\sum D}{n_D} = \frac{120}{8} = 15.$$

To compute the variance, we will use the shortcut method. Table 10.6 shows the calculations for computing D and D^2:

$$\text{Variance}: s_D^2 = \frac{SS}{n_D - 1}, \text{where } SS = \sum D^2 - \frac{\left(\sum D\right)^2}{n_D}.$$

$$SS = 3400 - \frac{(120)^2}{8} = 1600.$$

$$s_D^2 = \frac{1600}{8-1} = 228.57.$$

TABLE 10.6 Calculations for the variance of difference scores. The first column lists the same difference scores as those in the last column of Table 10.5.

D	D²
10	100
25	625
20	400
−5	25
25	625
−10	100
30	900
25	625
$\sum D = 120$	$\sum D^2 = 3400$

To compute the standard deviation, we take the square root of the variance:

$$\text{Standard deviation}: s_D = \sqrt{s_D^2} = \sqrt{228.57} = 15.12.$$

(2) To compute the estimated standard error for difference scores (s_{MD}), we substitute 15.12 for s_D and 8 for n_D:

$$s_{MD} = \frac{s_D}{\sqrt{n_D}} = \frac{15.12}{\sqrt{8}} = 5.35.$$

NOTE: The mean difference and the estimated standard error for difference scores are entered in the formula for a related samples t-test.

(3) Compute the test statistic. We substitute 15 for M_D, 0 for μ_D (this is the value stated in the null hypothesis), and 5.35 for s_{MD}:

$$t_{obt} = \frac{M_D - \mu_D}{s_{MD}} = \frac{15 - 0}{5.35} = 2.804.$$

Step 4: Make a decision. To make a decision, we compare the obtained value to the critical value. We reject the null hypothesis if the obtained value exceeds the critical value. Figure 10.3 shows that the obtained value ($t_{obt} = 2.804$) exceeds the upper

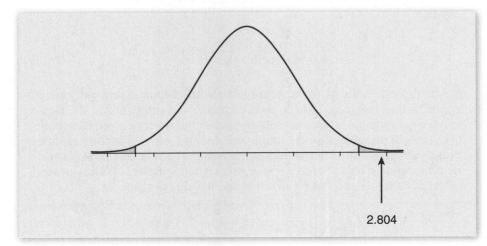

2.804

FIGURE 10.3

The test statistic falls in the rejection region (it is beyond the critical value). Hence, we reject the null hypothesis.

critical value; it falls in the rejection region. The decision is to reject the null hypothesis. If we were to report this result in a research journal, it would look something like this:

> Popular adolescent participants spent significantly more time talking on a cell phone compared to time spent talking on a home phone, $t(7) = 2.804$, $p < .05$.

MAKING SENSE: Increasing Power by Reducing Error

As illustrated in Table 10.3, there are three places where scores can differ: Two are attributed to error (within-groups and between-persons), and one is tested by the null hypothesis (between-groups). When we compute difference scores, we eliminate one of the sources of error (i.e., between-persons error), thereby increasing the power of a related samples t-test compared to the two–independent sample t-test. To see how this increases power, let's take another look at Example 10.1.

In Example 10.1, the null hypothesis was that the mean difference equals 0, and we computed the following test statistic:

$$t_{obt} = \frac{\text{mean difference}}{\text{estimate for error}} = \frac{15}{5.35} = 2.804, p < .05.$$

The test statistic reached significance; we decided to reject the null hypothesis. Now, let's suppose that different participants were assigned to each group and we obtained the same data shown in Table 10.5. In this case, we would compute the two–independent sample t-test, and we would not reduce the scores in each group to one column of difference scores.

When we do not reduce the two columns (cell phone and home phone use) to one column, this leaves between-persons error and should make our estimate of standard error in the denominator of the test statistic larger. When we compute the two–independent sample t-test, the mean difference is still 15, but our estimate for standard error will be larger. When we analyze these data using the test statistic for the two–independent sample t-test, we obtain

$$t_{obt} = \frac{\text{mean difference}}{\text{estimate for error}} = \frac{15}{18.10} = 0.829, p > .05.$$

Notice that the estimate for standard error in the denominator was indeed larger. In this case, our decision would change as a result. Using the two–independent sample t-test, we would not detect the effect or mean difference between cell phone and home phone use. Instead, we decide to retain the null hypothesis. All other things being equal, the related samples t-test reduces standard error. For this reason, the related samples t-test has greater power to detect an effect or mean difference between two groups.

1. What is the test statistic for a related samples *t*-test with a mean difference equal to 5 and an estimated standard error for difference scores equal to:

   a. 2.5   b. 5.0   c. 10.0

2. The test statistic for a related samples *t*-test is +2.100. Using a .05 level of significance, would you retain or reject the null hypothesis when:

   a. *df* = 10, two-tailed test

   b. *df* = 30, one-tailed test (upper tail critical)

   c. *df* = 20, two-tailed test

   d. *df* = 40, one-tailed test (lower tail critical)

3. How does computing difference scores increase the power of a related samples *t*-test as compared to a two–independent sample *t*-test?

Answers: 1. (a) $t_{obt} = \frac{5}{2.5} = 2.000$, (b) $t_{obt} = \frac{5}{5} = 1.000$, (c) $t_{obt} = \frac{5}{10} = 0.500$; 2. (a) Retain the null, (b) Reject the null, (c) Retain the null, (d) Reject the null; 3. Computing difference scores eliminates between-persons error, thereby reducing the estimate for standard error in the denominator.

SPSS IN FOCUS: THE RELATED SAMPLES *T*-TEST 10.4

In Example 10.1, we tested whether eight popular adolescents spent more time talking on a cell phone or a home phone at their home during a 2-day period. We used a two-tailed test at a .05 level of significance and decided to reject the null hypothesis: Popular adolescents spent significantly more time talking on a cell phone than on a home phone, $t(7) = 2.804$, $p < .05$. Let's confirm this result using SPSS.

1. Click on the **variable view** tab and enter *cell* in the **name column.** In the second row, enter *home* in the name column. We will enter whole numbers, so reduce the value in the **decimals column** to 0.

2. Click on the **data view** tab. Enter the data in each column same as shown in Table 10.7.

TABLE 10.7 Data view in SPSS for Step 2.

cell	home
220	210
245	220
215	195
260	265
300	275
280	290
250	220
310	285

3. Go to the **menu bar** and click **Analyze,** then **Compare Means,** and **Paired-Samples T Test** to display the dialog box shown in Figure 10.4.

4. In the **dialog box,** select *cell* and *home* in the left box and move them to the right box using the arrow in the middle. The variables should be side by side in the box to the right.

5. Select **Paste** and click the **Run** command.

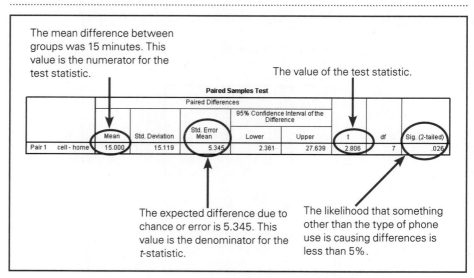

FIGURE 10.4

SPSS dialog box for Steps 3 and 4.

Notice that the calculations we made match the results displayed in the output table shown in Table 10.8. These same step-by-step directions for using SPSS can be used to compute the repeated measures design (shown in this section) and the matched-pairs design. Finally, note that SPSS gives the confidence intervals for this test in the output table (confidence intervals are described in Chapter 11).

TABLE 10.8 The SPSS output table.

The mean difference between groups was 15 minutes. This value is the numerator for the test statistic.

The value of the test statistic.

Paired Samples Test

		Paired Differences							
					95% Confidence Interval of the Difference				
		Mean	Std. Deviation	Std. Error Mean	Lower	Upper	t	df	Sig. (2-tailed)
Pair 1	cell - home	15.000	15.119	5.345	2.361	27.639	2.806	7	.026

The expected difference due to chance or error is 5.345. This value is the denominator for the *t*-statistic.

The likelihood that something other than the type of phone use is causing differences is less than 5%.

RELATED SAMPLES *T*-TEST: 10.5
MATCHED-PAIRS DESIGN

In Example 10.1, we computed the related samples *t*-test for the repeated measures design. In Example 10.2, we will compute the related samples *t*-test for the matched-pairs design.

Psychologists tested whether older or younger twins are more or less introverted. They used McCroskey's introversion scale to measure the personality trait introversion in a sample of seven pairs of identical twins. Scores on this scale range from 12 to 60, with higher scores indicating greater introversion. Table 10.9 displays the data for this hypothetical study with the difference scores given. Test the null hypothesis that the mean difference in introversion scores between older and younger twins is zero, using a two-tailed test at a .05 level of significance.

EXAMPLE 10.2

TABLE 10.9 Introversion scores for a hypothetical sample of identical twins.

Pairs of Twins		
Older	**Younger**	**Difference Scores**
34	40	$(34 - 40) = -6$
22	19	$(22 - 19) = 3$
43	35	$(43 - 35) = 8$
44	30	$(44 - 30) = 14$
35	50	$(35 - 50) = -15$
32	32	$(32 - 32) = 0$
29	26	$(29 - 26) = 3$

Step 1: State the hypotheses. The null hypothesis states that there is no mean difference (=), and the alternative hypothesis states that there is a mean difference (≠):

$H_0: \mu_D = 0$ There is no mean difference in introversion scores between identical twins.

$H_1: \mu_D \neq 0$ There is a mean difference in introversion scores between identical twins.

Step 2: Set the criteria for a decision. The level of significance for this test is .05. This is a two-tailed test for the mean difference between two related samples. The degrees of freedom for this test are $df = 7 - 1 = 6$. We locate 6 degrees of freedom with a .05 proportion in two tails in the *t*-table in Table B2 in Appendix B. The critical values for this test are ±2.447. Figure 10.5 shows the *t*-distribution, with rejection region beyond the critical values.

We will compare the value of the test statistic to these critical values. If the value of the test statistic falls beyond either critical value (falls beyond ±2.447), then there is less than a 5% chance we could have obtained that outcome if the null hypothesis

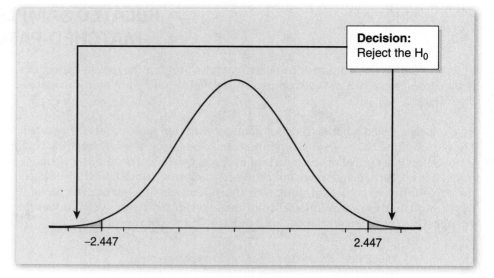

FIGURE 10.5

The shaded areas show the rejection region. The *t*-critical cutoff is ±2.447. If the value of the test statistic falls in the shaded region, then we reject the null hypothesis; otherwise, we retain the null hypothesis.

NOTE: The related samples t-test is computed the same for a repeated measures design and a matched-pairs design.

were correct, so we reject the null hypothesis; otherwise, we retain the null hypothesis.

Step 3: Compute the test statistic. To compute the test statistic, we again (1) compute the mean, variance, and standard deviation for difference scores; (2) compute the estimated standard error for difference scores; then (3) compute the test statistic.

(1) Compute the mean, variance, and standard deviation for difference scores. Again, keep in mind that the sign (negative or positive) of difference scores matters when we compute the mean and standard deviation. To compute the mean, we sum the difference scores (ΣD) and divide by the number of difference scores summed (n_D):

$$\text{Mean}: M_D = \frac{\sum D}{n_D} = \frac{7}{7} = 1.$$

To compute the variance, we will use the shortcut method. Table 10.10 shows the calculations for computing D and D^2:

$$\text{Variance}: s_D^2 = \frac{SS}{n_D - 1}, \text{where } SS = \sum D^2 - \frac{\left(\sum D\right)^2}{n_D}.$$

$$SS = 539 - \frac{(7)^2}{7} = 532.$$

$$s_D^2 = \frac{532}{7 - 1} = 88.67.$$

TABLE 10.10 Calculations for the variance of difference scores. The first column lists the same difference scores as those in the last column of Table 10.9.

D	D²
−6	36
3	9
8	64
14	196
−15	225
0	0
3	9
$\sum D = 7$	$\sum D^2 = 539$

To compute the standard deviation, we take the square root of the variance:

$$\text{Standard deviation: } s_D = \sqrt{s_D^2} = \sqrt{88.67} = 9.42.$$

(2) To compute the estimated standard error for difference scores (s_{MD}), we substitute 9.42 for s_D and 7 for n_D:

$$s_{MD} = \frac{s_D}{\sqrt{n_D}} = \frac{9.42}{\sqrt{7}} = 3.55.$$

(3) Compute the test statistic. We substitute 1 for M_D, 0 for μ_D (this is the value stated in the null hypothesis), and 3.55 for s_{MD}:

$$t_{obt} = \frac{M_D - \mu_D}{s_{MD}} = \frac{1 - 0}{3.55} = 0.282.$$

Step 4: Make a decision. To make a decision, we compare the obtained value to the critical value. Figure 10.6 shows that the obtained value ($t_{obt} = 0.282$) does not exceed a critical value; it is not in the rejection region. The decision is to retain the null hypothesis. If we were to report this result in a research journal, it would look something like this:

There were no significant differences in introversion scores between older and younger identical twins, $t(6) = 0.282$, $p > .05$.

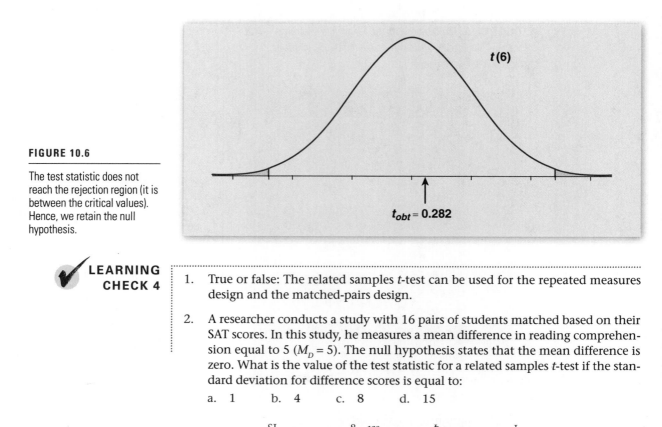

FIGURE 10.6

The test statistic does not reach the rejection region (it is between the critical values). Hence, we retain the null hypothesis.

LEARNING CHECK 4

1. True or false: The related samples t-test can be used for the repeated measures design and the matched-pairs design.

2. A researcher conducts a study with 16 pairs of students matched based on their SAT scores. In this study, he measures a mean difference in reading comprehension equal to 5 ($M_D = 5$). The null hypothesis states that the mean difference is zero. What is the value of the test statistic for a related samples t-test if the standard deviation for difference scores is equal to:

   a. 1   b. 4   c. 8   d. 15

Answers: 1. True; 2. (a) $t_{obt} = \frac{5}{1} = 5.000$, (b) $t_{obt} = \frac{5}{4} = 1.250$, (c) $t_{obt} = \frac{5}{8} = 0.625$, (d) $t_{obt} = \frac{5}{15} = 0.333$

10.6 MEASURING EFFECT SIZE FOR THE RELATED SAMPLES T-TEST

Hypothesis testing identifies whether or not an effect exists. In Example 10.1, we concluded that an effect does exist: The mean difference in cell phone and home phone use was significant; we rejected the null hypothesis. The size of this effect is determined by measures of effect size. We will compute effect size for Example 10.2 because the decision was to reject the null hypothesis for that hypothesis test. There are three measures of effect size for the related-samples t-test: estimated Cohen's d, eta-squared, and omega-squared.

ESTIMATED COHEN'S d

NOTE: The standard deviation of difference scores is used to estimate the population standard deviation in the formula for Cohen's d.

An estimated Cohen's d is the most common measure of effect size used with the t-test. For two related samples, d measures the number of standard deviations that mean difference scores shifted above or below the population mean difference stated in the null hypothesis. The larger the value of d, the larger the effect in the population. To compute estimated Cohen's d with two related samples, we place the mean difference between two samples in the numerator and the standard deviation of the difference scores to estimate the population standard deviation in the denominator:

$$\text{Estimated Cohen's } d = \frac{M_D}{s_D}.$$

In Example 10.1, the mean difference was $M_D = 15$, and the standard deviation of difference scores was $s_D = 15.12$. The estimated Cohen's d is

$$d = \frac{15}{15.12} = 0.99.$$

We conclude that time spent talking on a cell phone is 0.99 standard deviations longer than on a home phone in the population. The effect size conventions listed in Table 8.8 (Chapter 8) and Table 9.3 (Chapter 9) show that this is a large effect size ($d > 0.8$). We could report this measure with the significant t-test in Example 10.1 by stating,

> Popular adolescent participants spent significantly more time talking on a cell phone compared to time spent talking on a home phone, $t(7) = 2.804$, $p < .05$ ($d = 0.99$).

PROPORTION OF VARIANCE

Another measure of effect size is proportion of variance. Specifically, this is an estimate of the proportion of variance in a dependent variable that can be explained by a treatment. In Example 10.1, we can measure the proportion of variance in time spent talking (the dependent variable) that can be explained by whether participants used a cell phone or home phone (the treatment). Two measures of proportion of variance for the related samples t-test are eta-squared and omega-squared. The calculations are the same as those for the one– and two–independent sample t-tests.

NOTE: *Proportion of variance is computed the same for all* t-*tests.*

In Example 10.1, we found that participants spent significantly more time talking on a cell phone than on a home phone, $t(7) = 2.804$, $p < .05$. To compute eta-squared, we substitute $t = 2.804$ and $df = 7$:

$$\eta^2 = \frac{t^2}{t^2 + df} = \frac{(2.804)^2}{(2.804)^2 + 7} = 0.53.$$

Using eta-squared, we conclude that 53% of the variability in time spent talking can be explained by the type of phone used (home phone vs. cell phone).

Again, eta-squared tends to overestimate the size of an effect. To correct for this, we can compute omega-squared. To compute omega-squared, we subtract 1 from t^2 in the numerator of the eta-squared formula, thereby reducing the value of the proportion of variance. To compute omega-squared, we again substitute $t = 2.804$ and $df = 7$:

$$\omega^2 = \frac{t^2 - 1}{t^2 + df} = \frac{(2.804)^2 - 1}{(2.804)^2 + 7} = 0.46.$$

Using omega-squared, we conclude that 46% of the variability in time spent talking can be explained by the type of phone used (home phone vs. cell phone). The effect size conventions listed in Table 9.3 (Chapter 9) show that both measures of proportion of variance estimate a large effect size in the population. We would report only one measure in a research journal. Using omega-squared, we could report this measure with the significant t-test in Example 10.1 by stating,

> Adolescent participants spent significantly more time talking on a cell phone compared to time spent talking on a home phone, $t(7) = 2.804$, $p < .05$ ($\omega^2 = 0.46$).

 **LEARNING CHECK 5**

1. What is the denominator for the estimated Cohen's d when used with the related samples t-test?

2. The mean difference between two related samples is 4.00. What is the value for

an estimated Cohen's *d* if a sample standard deviation for the difference scores in this example is equal to (a) 4 and (b) 40?

3. A psychologist reports that the value of the test statistic for two related samples is 2.400. If the degrees of freedom are 20, then what is the value for eta-squared? Is this is small, medium, or large effect size?

4. Using the same data as in Question 3, what is the proportion of variance explained using omega-squared? Is this is small, medium, or large effect size?

Answers: 1. The standard deviation for the difference scores; 2. (a) $d = \frac{4}{4} = 1.00$, (b) $d = \frac{4}{40} = 0.10$; 3. $\eta^2 = \frac{(2.400)^2}{(2.400)^2 + 20} = 0.22$ (medium effect size); 4. $\omega^2 = \frac{(2.400)^2 - 1}{(2.400)^2 + 20} = 0.18$ (medium effect size).

10.7 ADVANTAGES FOR SELECTING RELATED SAMPLES

Selecting related samples has many advantages and disadvantages. Because most of the disadvantages pertain specifically to a repeated measures design and not a matched-pairs design, we introduce only the advantages that pertain to both designs. There are three key advantages for selecting related samples compared to selecting independent samples in behavioral research:

1. Selecting related samples can be more practical. It is more practical in that selecting related samples may provide a better way to test your hypotheses. This is especially true for research areas in learning and development in which researchers must observe changes in behavior or development over time or between matched pairs of participants. For example, it can be more practical to observe the behavior of the same participants before and after some treatment (repeated measures) or to compare how well participants of similar ability master some task (matched samples).

2. Selecting related samples minimizes standard error. Computing difference scores prior to computing the test statistic eliminates the between-persons source of error, which reduces the estimate of standard error. Using the same data, this makes the test statistic for the related samples *t*-test larger than that for the two–independent sample *t*-test.

3. Selecting related samples increases power. It follows from the second advantage that reducing the estimate for standard error will increase the value of the test statistic. Using the same data, a related samples *t*-test is more likely than a two–independent sample *t*-test to result in a decision to reject the null hypothesis. Hence, the related samples *t*-test is associated with greater power to detect an effect.

10.8 APA IN FOCUS: REPORTING THE *T*-STATISTIC AND EFFECT SIZE FOR RELATED SAMPLES

To summarize a related samples *t*-test, we report the test statistic, degrees of freedom, and *p* value. In addition, we summarize the means and standard error or standard deviations measured in the study in a figure or table or in the main text. When reporting results, though, it is not necessary to identify the type of *t*-test computed. The type of *t*-test that was used is typically reported in a data analysis section that precedes the results section, where the statistics are reported.

CHAPTER SUMMARY ORGANIZED BY LEARNING OBJECTIVE

LO 1: Describe two types of research designs used when we select related samples.

- In a **related sample,** participants in each group are related. There are two ways for participants to be related: They are observed in more than one group (repeated measures design), or they are matched, experimentally or naturally, based on the common characteristics or traits that they share (matched-pairs design).
- The **repeated measures design** is a research design in which the same participants are observed in each treatment. Two types of repeated measures designs are the pre-post design and the within-subjects design.
- The **matched-pairs design** is a research design in which participants are selected, then matched, experimentally or naturally, based on the common characteristics or traits that they share.

LO 2: Explain why difference scores are computed for the related samples *t*-test.

- To test the null hypothesis, we state the mean difference between pairs of scores in the population and compare this to the difference between pairs of scores in a sample. A related samples *t*-test is different from a two–independent sample *t*-test in that we subtract the pairs of scores first and then compute the test statistic. The differences between pairs of scores are called **difference scores.**
- Computing difference scores eliminates between-persons error. This error is associated with differences associated with observing different participants in each group or treatment. Because we observe the same (or matched) participants in each treatment, not different participants, we can eliminate this source of error before computing the test statistic. Removing this error reduces the value of the estimate of standard error, which increases the power to detect an effect.

LO 3–5: Calculate the degrees of freedom for a related samples *t*-test and locate critical values in the *t*-table; identify the assumptions for the related samples *t*-test; compute a related samples *t*-test and interpret the results.

- The **related samples *t*-test** is a statistical procedure used to test hypotheses concerning two related samples selected from related populations in which the variance in one or both populations is unknown.
- The degrees of freedom for a related samples *t*-test is the number of difference scores minus 1: $df = (n_D - 1)$.
- To compute a related samples *t*-test, we assume normality and independence within groups. The test statistic for a related samples *t*-test concerning the difference between two related samples is as follows:

$$t_{obt} = \frac{M_D - \mu_D}{s_{MD}}, \text{ where } s_{MD} = \frac{s_D}{\sqrt{n_D}}.$$

LO 6: Compute effect size and proportion of variance for a related samples *t*-test.

- Estimated Cohen's *d* is the most popular estimate of effect size used with the *t*-test. It is a measure of effect size in terms of the number of standard deviations that mean difference scores shifted above or below the population mean stated in the null hypothesis. To compute estimated Cohen's *d* with two related samples, divide the mean difference (M_D) between two samples by the standard deviation of the difference scores (s_D):

$$\text{Estimated Cohen's } d = \frac{M_D}{s_D}.$$

- Another measure of effect size is proportion of variance. Specifically, this is an estimate of the proportion of variance in the dependent variable that can be explained by some treatment. Two measures of proportion of variance for the related samples *t*-test are eta-squared and omega-squared. These measures are computed the same for all *t*-tests:

$$\text{Using eta-squared: } \eta^2 = \frac{t^2}{t^2 + df}.$$

$$\text{Using omega-squared: } \omega^2 = \frac{t^2 - 1}{t^2 + df}.$$

LO 7: State three advantages for selecting related samples.

- Three advantages for selecting related samples are that selecting related samples (1) can be more practical, (2) minimizes standard error, and (3) increases power.

APA LO 8: Summarize the results of a related samples *t*-test in APA format.

- To report the results of a related samples *t*-test, state the test statistic, the degrees of freedom, the *p* value, and the effect size. In addition, summarize the means and the standard error or the standard deviations measured in the study

in a figure or a table or in the text. Finally, note that the type of *t*-test computed is reported in a data analysis section that precedes the results section, where the statistics are reported.

SPSS LO 9: Compute a related samples *t*-test using SPSS.

- SPSS can be used to compute a related samples *t*-test. The related samples *t*-test is computed using the **Analyze, Compare Means,** and **Paired-Samples T Test** options in the menu bar. These actions will display a dialog box that allows you to identify the groups and run the test (for more details, see Section 10.4).

KEY TERMS

dependent sample
difference scores
error
estimated standard error for
    difference scores

independent sample
matched-pairs design
matched-samples design
matched-subjects design
pre-post design

related sample
related samples *t*-test
repeated measures design
within-subjects design

END-OF-CHAPTER PROBLEMS

Factual Problems

1. Distinguish between selecting related samples and independent samples.

2. Name two research designs in which related samples are selected.

3. Name and define two repeated measures designs.

4. State two ways for matching pairs of participants using the matched-pairs research design.

5. State three advantages for using related samples in behavioral research.

6. Describe in words what the degrees of freedom are for a related samples *t*-test.

7. Define difference scores. How does using difference scores increase the power of a related samples *t*-test?

8. How does computing difference scores change the value of the estimate of standard error in the

denominator of the test statistic for a related samples *t*-test?

9. What are the assumptions for a related samples *t*-test?

10. Is the related samples *t*-test computed differently for a repeated measures design and a matched-pairs design? Explain.

11. Describe in words the formula of an estimated Cohen's *d* for two related samples.

12. What information is provided when you report the results of a related samples *t*-test?

Concepts and Application Problems

13. For each example, state whether the one–independent, the two–independent, or the related samples *t*-test is most appropriate. If it is a related samples *t*-test, indicate whether the test is a repeated measures design or a matched-pairs design.

(a) A professor tests whether students sitting in the front row score higher than students sitting in the back row.

(b) A researcher matches right-handed and left-handed siblings to test whether right-handed siblings express greater emotional intelligence than left-handed siblings.

(c) A graduate student selects a sample of 25 participants to test whether the average time students attend to some task is greater than 30 minutes.

(d) A principal at a local school wants to know how much students gain from being in an honors class. He gives students in an honors English class a test prior to the school year and again at the end of the school year to measure how much students learned during the year.

14. State the degrees of freedom and the type of test (repeated measures or matched pairs) for the following examples of measures for a related samples *t*-test:

(a) The difference in coping ability in a sample of 20 brothers and sisters paired based on their relatedness

(b) The difference in comprehension before and after an experimental training seminar in a sample of 30 students

(c) The difference in relationship satisfaction in a sample of 25 pairs of married couples

(d) The difference in athletic performance at the beginning and end of an athletic season for 12 athletes

15. What are the difference scores for the following list of scores for participants observed at two times?

Time 1	Time 2
4	8
3	2
5	7
4	6
6	3

16. Using the data listed in Question 15,

(a) Compute the mean difference (M_D), standard deviation (s_D), and standard error for the difference scores (s_{MD}).

(b) Sketch a graph of the distribution of mean difference scores ($M_D \pm s_D$).

(c) Sketch a graph of the sampling distribution of mean difference scores ($M_D \pm s_{MD}$).

17. Would each of the following increase, decrease, or have no effect on the value of the test statistic for a related samples *t*-test?

(a) The sample size is increased.

(b) The level of significance is reduced from .05 to .01.

(c) The estimated standard error for difference scores is doubled.

(d) The mean difference is decreased.

18. What is the value of the test statistic for a related samples *t*-test given the following measurements?

(a) $n_D = 16$, $M_D = 4$, and $s_D = 8$

(b) $M_D = 4$ and $s_{MD} = 8$

(c) $n_D = 64$, $M_D = 8$, and $s_D = 16$

(d) $M_D = 8$ and $s_{MD} = 16$

19. A statistics tutor wants to assess whether her remedial tutoring has been effective for her five students. She decides to conduct a related samples *t*-test and records the following grades for students prior to and after receiving her tutoring.

Tutoring	
Before	**After**
2.4	3.0
2.5	2.8
3.0	3.5
2.9	3.1
2.7	3.5

(a) Test whether or not her tutoring is effective at a .05 level of significance. State the value of the test statistic and the decision to retain or reject the null hypothesis.

(b) Compute effect size using estimated Cohen's *d*.

20. Published reports indicate that a brain region called the nucleus accumbens (NAC) is involved in interval timing, which is the perception of time in the seconds to minutes range. To test this, researchers investigated whether removing the NAC interferes with rats' ability to time the presentation of a liquid reward. Using a conditioning procedure, the researchers had rats press a lever for a reward that was delivered after 16 seconds. The time that rats responded the most (peak responding) was recorded before and after removing the NAC. The following is the peak responding time for eight rats before and after surgery to remove the NAC.

Peak Interval Timing	
Before NAC Surgery	**After NAC Surgery**
15	20
14	26
16	20
16	18
17	25
18	21
15	18
16	23

(a) Test whether or not the difference in peak responding changed at a .05 level of significance (two-tailed test). State the value of the test statistic and the decision to retain or reject the null hypothesis.

(b) Compute effect size using estimated Cohen's d.

21. A psychologist wants to know whether wives and husbands who both serve in a foreign war have similar levels of satisfaction in their marriage. To test this, six married couples currently serving in a foreign war were asked how satisfied they are with their spouse on a 7-point scale ranging from 1 (*not satisfied at all*) to 7 (*very satisfied*). The following are the responses from husband and wife pairs.

Married Couples	
Wife	**Husband**
7	5
4	6
7	5
7	6
7	5
6	5

(a) Test whether or not mean ratings differ at a .05 level of significance. State the value of the test statistic and the decision to retain or reject the null hypothesis.

(b) Compute effect size using eta-squared.

22. A health psychologist noticed that the siblings of his obese patients are often not overweight. He hypothesized that the normal-weight siblings consume fewer daily calories than the obese patients. To test this, she compared the daily caloric intake of 20 obese patients to a respective normal-weight sibling. The following are the calories consumed for each sibling pair.

Normal-Weight Sibling	Overweight Sibling
1,600	2,000
1,800	2,400
2,100	2,000
1,800	3,000
2,400	2,400
2,800	1,900
1,900	2,600
2,300	2,450
2,000	2,000
2,050	1,950

(a) Test whether or not obese patients consumed significantly more calories than their normal-weight siblings at a .05 level of significance. State the value of the test statistic and the decision to retain or reject the null hypothesis.

(b) Compute effect size using omega-squared.

(c) Did this test support her hypothesis? Explain.

23. State whether each of the following related samples *t*-tests is significant for a two-tailed test at a .05 level of significance.

 (a) $t(30) = 3.220$

 (b) $t(18) = 2.034$

 (c) $t(12) = 2.346$

 (d) $t(60) = 1.985$

24. A researcher develops an advertisement aimed at increasing how much the public trusts some federal organization. She asks participants to rate their level of trust for the organization before and after viewing an advertisement. Higher ratings indicate greater trust. From the following findings reported in APA format, interpret these results by stating the research design used (repeated measures or matched pairs), the sample size, the decision, and the effect size.

 Participants rated the federal organization as significantly more trustworthy (M_D = +4 points) after viewing the advertisement, $t(119) = 4.021, p < .05, d = 0.88$.

25. A researcher records the amount of time (in minutes) that parent-child pairs spent on social networking sites to test whether they show any generational differences. From the following findings reported in APA format, interpret these results by stating the research design used (repeated measures or matched pairs), sample size, decision, and effect size.

 Parents spent significantly less time on social networking sites compared to their children ($M_D = -42$ minutes), $t(29) = 4.021, p < .05, d = 0.49$.

26. Would each of the following increase, decrease, or have no effect on the value of estimated Cohen's *d* for the related samples *t*-test?

 (a) The sample standard deviation for difference scores is increased.

 (b) The estimated standard error for difference scores is increased.

 (c) The mean difference is increased.

Problems in Research

27. **Self-assessment skills.** McDonald (2002) conducted a series of matched-pairs designs for a variety of self-assessment measures. She computed a related samples *t*-test to compare gender differences (male-female) using measures of achievement (Ac), autonomy (Au), and understanding (Un), among other measures. The mean difference and the estimated standard error for difference scores are given in the following table for three variables. If the null hypothesis states that the mean difference is 0, then what is the value of the test statistic for a related samples *t*-test for each variable listed in the table?

Variable	Mean Difference	Standard Error of Difference
Ac	−0.49	0.16
Au	−0.03	0.13
Un	−0.20	0.17

28. **Liking for a vanilla milkshake.** Naleid and colleagues (2008) asked how the interaction of the ingredients corn oil and sucrose enhanced liking for vanilla milkshakes. To test this, rats responded on a lever to gain access to sucrose alone and to gain access to sucrose mixed with corn oil. The researchers hypothesized that rats would work harder (respond with a higher rate of lever pressing) for the mixture compared with sucrose alone. They found that adding 1.4% corn oil to a 12.5% sucrose solution enhanced liking (increased responding on the lever) compared to 12.5% sucrose alone, $p < .01$.

 (a) Is this a repeated measures design or a matched-pairs design?

 (b) Did these authors find support for their hypothesis?

29. **Posttraumatic stress disorder (PTSD) following 9/11.** Levitt, Malta, Martin, Davis, and Cloitre (2007) evaluated the effectiveness of cognitive behavioral therapy (CBT) for treating PTSD and related symptoms for survivors of the 9/11 terrorist attacks on the World Trade Center (WTC). They used a pretest-posttest design to see if CBT was successful at reducing the symptoms of PTSD and related symptoms of depression. They used the Modified PTSD Symptom Scale Self-Report (MPSS-SR) questionnaire to measure symptoms of PTSD and the Beck Depression Inventory (BDI) self-report questionnaire to measure symptoms of depression. For both questionnaires, lower scores indicated fewer symptoms. The authors reported the following results:

Pre- to post treatment t-tests for the WTC sample revealed significant decreases in scores on the MPSS-SR, ($t(37) = 12.74$, $p < .01$); as well as on the BDI ($t(34) = 7.36$, $p < .01$). (p. 1427)

(a) Was this a repeated measures design or a matched-pairs design?

(b) Which questionnaire (MPSS-SR or BDI) was completed by more participants?

(c) Did the authors find support for their hypothesis? Explain.

30. **Teacher perceptions of children with cancer.** Liang, Chiang, Chien, and Yeh (2007) tested whether teachers for children with cancer (case) perceived these children similarly compared to a group of healthy children (control). They measured a variety of social factors, including social withdrawal, somatic complaints, and other social problems. The following table summarizes many of their results using the related samples t-test.

| Measures | Mean (*SD*) | | *t* | *p* Value |
	Case	Control		
Withdrawn	0.32 (2.58)	0.15 (1.45)	3.52	<.01
Somatic complaints	0.19 (2.22)	0.06 (1.24)	3.85	<.001
Social problems	0.26 (3.34)	0.08 (1.32)	4.31	<.001

(a) Is this a repeated measures design or a matched-pairs design?

(b) Interpret the results displayed in the table. Do teachers perceive children with cancer as having more social problems than their peers?

31 **Parent perceptions of children with cancer.** Liang and colleagues (2007) also tested whether parents of children with cancer (case) perceived these children similarly compared to a group of healthy children (control). They measured the same social factors listed in the table for Question 30. The following table summarizes many of their results using the related samples t-test. Interpret the results displayed in the table. Do parents perceive children with cancer as having more social problems than their peers?

| Measures | Mean (*SD*) | | *p* Value |
	Case	Control	
Withdrawn	0.22 (1.77)	0.24 (1.82)	<.05
Somatic complaints	0.32 (1.97)	0.19 (2.22)	>.05
Social problems	0.21 (1.70)	0.30 (1.93)	<.05

32. **The psychological contract.** Bellou (2007) tested how well employees adjust to organizational change in terms of the *psychological contract*. This contract refers to employees' belief that their on-the-job performance while employed will be fairly recognized. She tested employees working in a merged or acquired organization who had also worked at the premerger organization for at least 6 months. Employees completed a 5-point scale for a variety of measures (both pre- and postmerger), with higher scores indicating more positive perceptions. She measured a variety of factors, including beliefs concerning opportunity to promote, high pay, and pay according to performance. Pre- and postmerger scores were compared using a related samples t-test. The results are given in the following table.

| | Limited coping with changes | | | | | |
| | Pre-M&A Organization | | Post-M&A Organization | | | |
	Mean	*SD*	Mean	*SD*	*t*	*p*
Opportunity to promote	2.34	1.18	1.92	1.09	3.65	0.000
High pay	2.48	1.19	1.95	1.02	5.50	0.000
Pay according to performance	2.66	1.25	1.99	1.19	5.61	0.000

(a) What is the decision for each measure?

(b) The sample size for this study was 255 employees. Compute proportion of variance for each measure using omega-squared.

NOTE: Answers for even numbers are in Appendix C.

Estimation and Confidence Intervals

LEARNING OBJECTIVES

After reading this chapter, you should be able to:

1. Describe the process of estimation and identify two types of estimation.

2. Distinguish between significance testing and estimation.

3. Compute confidence intervals for the one–independent sample z-test.

4. Compute confidence intervals for the one–independent sample t-test.

5. Compute confidence intervals for the two–independent sample t-test.

6. Compute confidence intervals for the related samples t-test.

7. Distinguish between the certainty and precision of an interval estimate.

8. Summarize confidence intervals for the z-test and t-tests in APA format.

9. Compute confidence intervals for the one–independent, the two–independent, and the related samples t-tests using SPSS.

11.1 POINT ESTIMATION AND INTERVAL ESTIMATION

Using hypothesis testing in Chapters 8 to 10, we stated a null hypothesis regarding the value of the mean or mean difference in a population. We then computed a test statistic to determine the probability of obtaining a sample outcome if the null hypothesis were true. When the probability of obtaining the sample outcome was less than 5% if the null hypothesis were true, we rejected the null hypothesis; otherwise, the decision was to retain the null hypothesis. The goal in hypothesis testing was to learn more about the value of a mean or a mean difference in a population of interest by deciding whether to retain or reject the null hypothesis.

We can also learn more about the mean or mean difference in a population without ever stating a null hypothesis. An alternative approach requires only that we set limits for the population parameter within which it is likely to be contained. The goal of this alternative approach, called **estimation,** is the same as that in hypothesis testing—to learn more about the value of a mean or mean difference in a population of interest. To use estimation, we select a sample, measure a sample mean or mean difference, and then use that sample mean or mean difference to estimate the value of a population parameter. While the processes of hypothesis testing and estimation are different, the goal or result is the same, as shown in Figure 11.1. Table 11.1 contrasts the processes of hypothesis testing and estimation.

DEFINITION

Estimation is a statistical procedure in which a sample statistic is used to estimate the value of an unknown population parameter. Two types of estimation are point estimation and interval estimation.

Estimation does not require that we state a null hypothesis and decide whether it should be rejected. We use estimation to measure the mean or mean difference in a sample, as we did in hypothesis testing, but instead of making a decision regarding

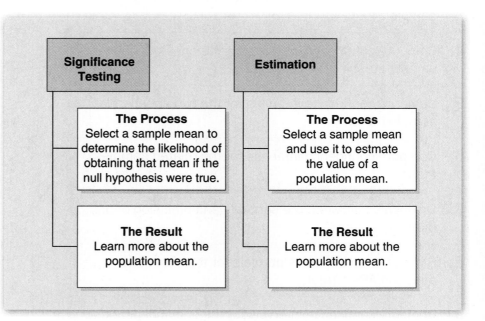

FIGURE 11.1

The process and results of hypothesis or significance testing and estimation. The processes are different, but the result is the same.

TABLE 11.1 The characteristics of hypothesis testing and estimation.

	Significance Testing	Point/Interval Estimation
Do we know the population mean?	Yes—it is stated in the null hypothesis.	No—we are trying to estimate it.
What is the process used to determine?	The likelihood of obtaining a sample mean	The value of a population mean
What is learned?	Whether the population mean is correct	The range of values within which the population mean is likely to be contained
What is decision?	To retain or reject the null hypothesis.	The population mean is estimated—there is no decision per se.

a null hypothesis, we estimate the limits within which the population mean or mean difference is likely to be contained.

The use of estimation is common in the popular media. For example, you may read that the average family in the United States has 2.3 children or that the average child in the United States watches 4 hours of television per day. In each of these applications of estimation, researchers reported an estimate of the population mean based on the value of the sample mean measured in a large sample. When the value of a sample mean is used to estimate the value of a population mean, we call this a **point estimate.**

> **Point estimation** is a statistical procedure that involves the use of a sample statistic (e.g., a sample mean) to estimate a population parameter (e.g., a population mean).

DEFINITION

The advantage of using point estimation is that the point estimate, or sample mean, is an unbiased estimator—that is, the sample mean will equal the population mean on average. The disadvantage of using point estimation is that we have no way of knowing for sure whether a sample mean equals the population mean. For this reason, researchers often report the sample mean (a point estimate) and an interval within which a population mean is likely to be contained (an **interval estimate**). An interval estimate, called the **confidence interval,** is stated within a given **level of confidence,** which is the likelihood that an interval contains an unknown population mean. The characteristics of point estimation and interval estimation described in this chapter are identified in Table 11.2.

NOTE: A point estimate is a sample mean or a sample mean difference. The sample mean is used to estimate the population mean.

NOTE: An interval estimate is the interval or range of values within which an unknown population mean is likely to be contained.

> **Interval estimation** is a statistical procedure in which a sample of data is used to find the interval or range of possible values within which a population parameter is likely to be contained.

DEFINITION

Level of confidence is the probability or likelihood that an interval estimate will contain an unknown population parameter (e.g., a population mean).

A **confidence interval (CI)** is the interval or range of possible values within which an unknown population parameter is likely to be contained.

The **confidence limits** or **confidence boundaries** are the upper and lower boundaries of a confidence interval given within a specified level of confidence.

TABLE 11.2 The characteristics of point estimation and interval estimation.

	Point Estimate	Interval Estimate
What is it estimating?	The population mean	The population mean
How is the population mean estimated?	The sample mean is used to estimate the population mean.	A range of values is used within which the population mean is likely to be contained.
How precise is it?	Very precise; it states an exact estimate of the population mean.	Less precise; it identifies a range of means, any one of which could be equal to the population mean.

Interval estimates are reported as a point estimate ± interval estimate. For example, you may read that 53% ± 3% of Americans believe that evolution is true, 34% ± 3% believe in ghosts, or 38% ± 3% believe that professional athletes are good role models for children. The ±3%, called the *margin of error*, is added to and subtracted from the point estimate to find the **confidence limits** or **confidence boundaries** of an interval estimate. If we add and subtract 3% from each point estimate, we find that we can be confident that 50% to 56% of Americans believe evolution is true, 31% to 37% believe in ghosts, and 35% to 41% believe that professional athletes are good role models for children, on average. Exactly how confident we are depends on the level of confidence. Determining the level of confidence and using estimation is described in Section 11.2.

11.2 THE PROCESS OF ESTIMATION

Using estimation, we use the sample mean as a point estimate and the standard error to determine the interval estimate. The standard error is used to find the range of sample means within which the population mean is likely to be contained. For example, suppose we selected a sample of 100 participants and measured $M = 4$ and $SD = 5$. The point estimate is $M = 4$. To find the interval estimate, we must compute standard error, then add and subtract this value from the point estimate.

In this example, the sampling distribution is a distribution of all possible sample means of size 100 we could have selected from a given population. We can substitute $SD = 5$ and $n = 100$ into the formula of standard error:

$$s_M = \frac{SD}{\sqrt{n}} = \frac{5}{\sqrt{100}} = 0.50.$$

The sampling distribution is shown in Figure 11.2. The point estimate, or sample mean, is the mean of the sampling distribution. From the empirical rule, we know that at least 68% of all possible sample means fall within the first standard error of the mean. If we add and subtract one standard error (±0.50) from the sample mean, we find that the true population mean is between 3.5 and 4.5 at a 68% level of confidence—this is the level of confidence because at least 68% of all possible sample means are contained with this range or interval. Figure 11.2 shows the 68% level of confidence in this example.

NOTE: The interval estimate is computed using the standard error of a sampling distribution.

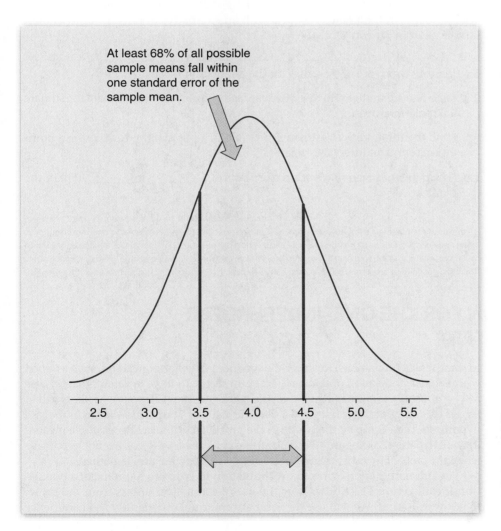

At least 68% of all possible sample means fall within one standard error of the sample mean.

FIGURE 11.2

The sampling distribution for samples of size 100 with $M = 4$ and $SE = 0.5$ (left graph). The 68% confidence interval for this sampling distribution is identified in the figure.

In all, we follow three steps to estimate the value of a population mean using a point estimate and interval estimate:

Step 1: Compute the sample mean and standard error.

Step 2: Choose the level of confidence and find the critical values at that level of confidence.

Step 3: Compute the estimation formula to find the confidence limits.

Remember that a point estimate is a sample mean, and an interval estimate uses the standard error to find the confidence limits within which a population mean is likely to be contained. We can therefore state the estimate of a population mean as follows:

Population Mean = Point Estimate ± Interval Estimate.

NOTE: A population mean is estimated as a point estimate plus or minus an interval estimate.

In this chapter, we will use the three steps of estimation as alternatives to the *z*-test and *t*-tests taught in Chapters 8 to 10. For each example, we will compute a point and interval estimate. We begin with an alternative to the one–independent sample *z*-test in Section 11.3.

 **LEARNING CHECK 1**

1. Identify two types of estimates for the population mean.

2. State one advantage and one disadvantage of using a point estimate to estimate a population mean.

3. State the three steps to estimate the value of a population mean using a point estimate and an interval estimate.

4. A population mean falls within the limits of a _____ ± _____. (Fill in the blanks).

Answers: 1. Point estimate, interval estimate; 2. The advantage is that the point estimate is an unbiased estimator of the population mean. The disadvantage is that we have no way of knowing for sure whether a sample mean equals the population mean; 3. Step 1: Compute the sample mean and the standard error. Step 2: Choose the level of confidence and find the critical values at that level of confidence. Step 3: Compute the estimation formula to find the confidence limits; 4. Point estimate, interval estimate.

11.3 ESTIMATION FOR THE ONE–INDEPENDENT SAMPLE *Z*-TEST

In some research situations, we know the variance in a single population, such as when we measure a population of standardized exam scores. In these research situations, we can compute the one–independent sample *z*-test taught in Chapter 8. As illustrated in Figure 11.3, in hypothesis testing, we state the value of a population mean in the null hypothesis, then compare that value to the probability of selecting a sample mean if the null hypothesis were true. At a .05 level of significance, we reject the null hypothesis when the probability is less than 5%; otherwise, we retain the null hypothesis.

An alternative approach is to use estimation to estimate the value of a population mean. Figure 11.4 shows how the use of estimation differs from the use of hypothesis testing. We will use the estimation formula to identify the confidence

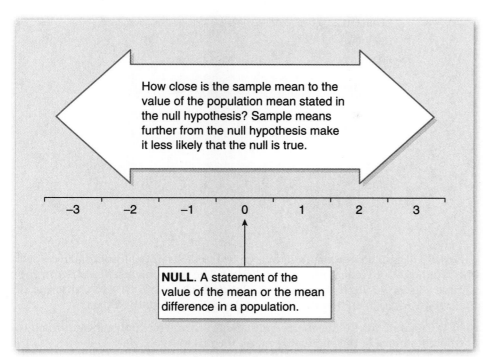

FIGURE 11.3

Hypothesis testing. In hypothesis testing, we state a value for the population mean in the null hypothesis, then collect samples to determine the likelihood that this hypothesis is correct.

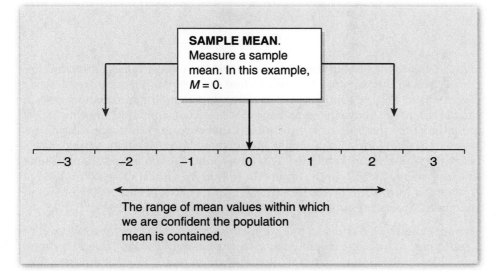

FIGURE 11.4

Estimation. In estimation, we measure a sample mean and standard error to determine a range of mean values within which we can be confident some fixed but unknown population mean is contained.

limits within which the true population mean is likely to be contained. Table 11.3 summarizes the notation used in the estimation formula for the z-test.

In Example 11.1, we use the three steps to compute the estimation formula for the one–independent sample z-test. The estimation formula is as follows:

$$M \pm z(\sigma_M).$$

NOTE: We use estimation to learn more about an unknown population mean by identifying the confidence limits within which the true population mean is likely to be contained.

TABLE 11.3 Expressions used in the estimation of populations with a known variance.

Symbols	Meanings
M	Sample mean
μ	Population mean
σ_M	Standard error of the mean

EXAMPLE 11.1

Zwick and Sklar (2005) studied a sample of 100 students in California and recorded their high school grade point average (GPA). The mean high school GPA in the sample was $M = 2.90$. If the mean population high school GPA in California is $2.78 \pm 0.61 (\mu \pm \sigma)$, then find the 90% confidence interval for these data.

Step 1: Compute the sample mean and standard error. The sample mean, which is the point estimate of the population mean, is equal to $M = 2.90$.

The standard error is the population standard deviation ($\sigma = 0.61$) divided by the square root of the sample size ($n = 100$):

$$\sigma_M = \frac{\sigma}{\sqrt{n}} = \frac{0.61}{\sqrt{100}} = 0.061.$$

Step 2: Choose the level of confidence and find the critical values at that level of confidence. In this example, we want to find the 90% confidence interval, so we choose a 90% level of confidence. Remember, in a sampling distribution, 50% of sample means fall above the sample mean we selected, and 50% fall below it. We are looking for the 90% of sample means that surround the sample mean we selected, meaning the 45% of sample means above and the 45% of sample means below the sample mean we selected. This leaves only 5% of sample means remaining in the upper tail and 5% in the lower tail. To find the critical value at this level of confidence, we look in the z-table in Table B.1, Appendix B. Find .0500 (or 5%) in column C. The z-score associated with 5% toward the tails is $z = 1.645$.

This is the same as a critical value we used for a two-tailed test at a .10 level of significance, or for a one-tailed test at a .05 level of significance. Table 11.4 shows how different levels of confidence using estimation match up with different two-tailed alpha levels using hypothesis testing.

Step 3: Compute the estimation formula to find the confidence limits for a 90% confidence interval. Because we are estimating the mean in a single population with a known variance, we use the $M \pm z(\sigma_M)$ estimation formula.

To compute the formula, multiply z times the standard error:

$$z(\sigma_M) = 1.645 \ (.061) = 0.10.$$

TABLE 11.4 Levels of significance in hypothesis testing and the corresponding levels of confidence in estimation.

Level of Confidence	Alpha Level (two-tailed)
99%	0.01
95%	0.05
90%	0.10
80%	0.20

Add 0.10 to the sample mean to find the **upper confidence limit:**

$$M + z(\sigma_M) = 2.90 + 0.10 = 3.00.$$

The **upper confidence limit** is the largest possible value of a population parameter in a confidence interval with a specified level of confidence.

DEFINITION

Subtract 0.10 from the sample mean to find the **lower confidence limit:**

$$M - z(\sigma_M) = 2.90 - 0.10 = 2.80.$$

The **lower confidence limit** is the smallest possible value of a population parameter in a confidence interval with a specified level of confidence.

DEFINITION

As shown in Figure 11.5, the 90% confidence interval in this population is between 2.80 and 3.00. We can estimate within a 90% level of confidence that the mean high school GPA in this population is between 2.80 and 3.00. We are 90% confident that the population mean falls within this range of GPAs because 90% of all sample

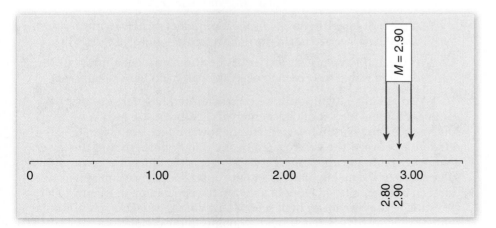

FIGURE 11.5

In Example 11.1, the 90% confidence interval was 2.80 to 3.00.

means we could have selected from this population fall within the range of sample means we specified.

Notice that we are not making a decision using estimation, other than to state confidence limits for a 90% confidence interval. In hypothesis testing, we selected a sample to decide whether or not to reject the null hypothesis. However, using estimation, we select a sample to identify the interval or range of possible values for an unknown population mean. The larger the level of confidence, the more confident we are that the true population mean is contained within the confidence interval we identified.

MAKING SENSE: Estimation, Significance, and Effect Size

In Example 11.1, the average high school GPA in the population was $\mu = 2.78$. This value would have been the null hypothesis using a hypothesis test ($\mu = 2.78$). Notice in Figure 11.6 that this value is outside the limits of the 90% confidence interval we identified in Example 11.1.

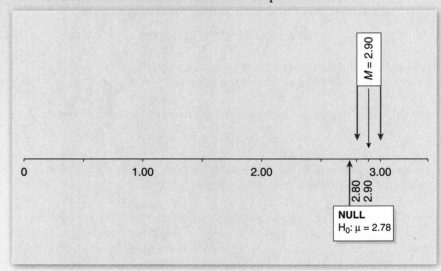

FIGURE 11.6

Estimation and the null. In Example 11.1, the 90% confidence interval does not contain the value of what would have been the null hypothesis.

NOTE: When the null hypothesis of a population mean is outside a confidence interval, this indicates a significant effect in the population.

In terms of the decisions we make in hypothesis testing,

1. if the null hypothesis were inside a confidence interval, the decision would have been to retain the null hypothesis (not significant).

2. if the null hypothesis were outside the confidence interval, the decision would have been to reject the null hypothesis (significant).

When a result is significant, we can then interpret effect size using the confidence limits for a confidence interval. The effect size for a confidence interval is a range or interval, where the lower effect size estimate is the difference between the value stated in the null hypothesis and the lower confidence limit; the upper effect size estimate is the difference between the value stated in the null hypothesis and the upper confidence limit. Effect size can then be interpreted in terms of a shift in the population. In Example 11.1, we estimate that the mean high school GPA among students in California shifted or increased between .02 and .22 points in the population.

LEARNING CHECK 2

1. What is the two-tailed level of significance that corresponds with the following levels of confidence?

   a. 99% CI   b. 95% CI   c. 90% CI   d. 80% CI

2. What is $z(\sigma_M)$ for a 95% confidence interval given the following data for a one–independent sample z-test?

   a. $n = 16$, $\sigma = 40$ b. $\sigma_M = 5$

3. If the sample mean is equal to 80, then what are the upper and lower confidence limits for (a) and (b) from Question 2?

Answers: 1. (a) .01, (b) .05, (c) .10, (d) .20; 2. (a) $z(\sigma_M) = (1.96) * \dfrac{40}{\sqrt{16}} = 19.6$, (b) $z(\sigma_M) = (1.96) * 5 = 9.8$; 3. (a) 95% CI = 60.4 to 99.6, (b) 95% CI = 70.2 to 89.8.

ESTIMATION FOR THE ONE–INDEPENDENT SAMPLE *T*-TEST   11.4

In most research situations, we do not know the value of the population variance. In these situations, we use the *t*-test to make hypothesis tests concerning one and two samples. The one– and two–independent sample *t*-tests were introduced in Chapter 9; the related samples *t*-test was introduced in Chapter 10.

We can also use estimation as an alternative to each *t*-test. We will use the estimation formula to identify the confidence limits within which the true population mean or mean difference is likely to be contained. Table 11.5 summarizes the notation used in the estimation formula for each *t*-test. The estimation formulas for the one–independent, two–independent, and related samples *t*-tests are as follows:

NOTE: The estimation formula for a t-test is used when we estimate the mean or the mean difference in populations with an unknown variance.

Estimation formula for the one–independent sample *t*-test: $M \pm t(s_M)$.

Estimation formula for the two–independent sample *t*-test: $M_1 - M_2 \pm t(s_{M_1 - M_2})$.

Estimation formula for the related samples *t*-test: $M_D \pm t(s_{MD})$.

In Example 11.2, we use the three steps to compute the estimation formula for the one–independent sample *t*-test. Example 11.2 is the same as that given in Example 9.2 in the SPSS in Focus section (see Chapter 9, Section 9.6). Using the same example will allow us to compare the results in Example 11.2 to the results of the one–independent sample *t*-test we computed in Example 9.2.

EXAMPLE 11.2

In the place preference paradigm (PPP), rats are placed in a cage where they receive reinforcement in one side (food pellets, for example) but not the other side of the cage. The researcher then measures the amount of time 12 rats spend in the side of the cage that they received reinforcement during a 10-minute test. The times measured in this study were 7.08 ± 0.557 $(M \pm s_M)$ minutes in the reinforced side of the cage. Find the 95% confidence interval for these data.

Step 1: Compute the sample mean and the estimated standard error. The sample mean, which is the point estimate of the population mean, is equal to $M = 7.08$.

The estimated standard error, s_M, is equal to 0.557.

TABLE 11.5 Expressions used in the estimation of populations with unknown variance. An asterisk (*) indicates expressions used only for related samples.

Symbols	Meanings
M	Sample mean
μ	Population mean
M_D	Mean difference*
s_M	Estimated standard error of the mean
$s_{M_1-M_2}$	Estimated standard error for the difference
s_{MD}	Estimated standard error for the difference scores*

Step 2: Choose the level of confidence and find the critical values at that level of confidence. In this example, we want to find the 95% confidence interval, so we choose a 95% level of confidence. Remember, in a sampling distribution, 50% of sample means fall above the sample mean we selected, and 50% fall below it. We are looking for the 95% of sample means that surround the sample mean we selected. Referring to Table 11.4, we find that a 95% CI corresponds to a two-tailed test at a .05 level of significance. To find the critical value at this level of confidence, we look in the t-table in Table B2, Appendix B. The degrees of freedom are 11 ($df = n - 1$ for a one-independent sample). The upper critical value for the interval estimate is $t = 2.201$.

Step 3: Compute the estimation formula to find the confidence limits for a 95% confidence interval. Because we are estimating the mean in a single population with an unknown variance, we use the $M \pm t(s_M)$ estimation formula.

To compute the formula, multiply t times the estimated standard error:

$$t(s_M) = 2.201(.557) = 1.23.$$

Add 1.23 to the sample mean to find the upper confidence limit:

$$M + t(s_M) = 7.08 + 1.23 = 8.31.$$

Subtract 1.23 from the sample mean to find the lower confidence limit:

$$M - t(s_M) = 7.08 - 1.23 = 5.85.$$

As shown in Figure 11.7, the 95% confidence interval in this population is between 5.85 minutes and 8.31 minutes. We can estimate within a 95% level of confidence that the mean preference or time subjects spent in the reinforced side of the cage

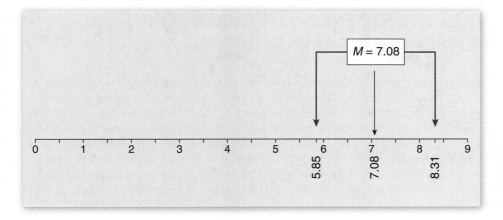

FIGURE 11.7

In Example 11.2, the 95% confidence interval was 5.85 to 8.31.

was between 5.85 minutes and 8.31 minutes in the population. We are 95% confident that the population mean falls within this range because 95% of all sample means we could have selected from this population fall within the range of sample means we specified.

We can also determine the decision we would have made using hypothesis testing. In Example 11.2, we assumed that there was no side preference when rats spent the same amount of time in each side of the cage during a 10-minute test. So the null hypothesis was $\mu = 5$ minutes in each side. Because 5 minutes does not fall within the 95% CI of 5.85 to 8.31, we would have decided to reject the null hypothesis using hypothesis testing, which was the decision we made in Chapter 9. We can also estimate the effect size of this result. As shown in Figure 11.8, we estimate that the preference or added time spent in the reinforced side of the cage is between 0.85 minutes and 3.31 minutes in the population.

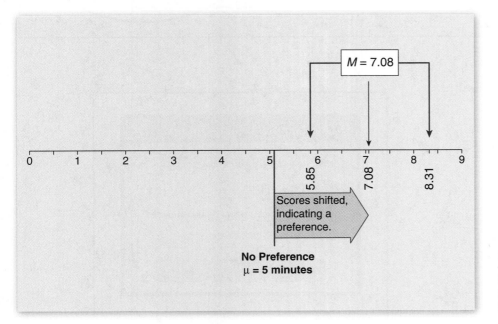

FIGURE 11.8

In Example 11.2, the effect size is between 0.85 minutes to 3.31 minutes in the population.

11.5 SPSS IN FOCUS: CONFIDENCE INTERVALS FOR THE ONE–INDEPENDENT SAMPLE *T*-TEST

Using the example in Chapter 9, we computed a one–independent sample *t*-test for Example 11.2 using SPSS. Table 11.6 shows the SPSS output table for that test, which was originally given in Table 9.4 in Chapter 9. The table lists the 95% confidence interval for the place preference we observed. To change the confidence interval, follow the steps for computing the one–independent sample *t*-test given in Chapter 9, and select **Options** in the dialog box in Steps 3 to 5. This action will display an additional dialog box, shown in Figure 11.9, which allows you to choose any level of confidence. By default, SPSS gives a 95% confidence interval with the *t*-test.

TABLE 11.6 SPSS output table. Confidence intervals are circled in the bottom table.

One-Sample Statistics

	N	Mean	Std. Deviation	Std. Error Mean
preference	12	7.08	1.929	.557

One-Sample Test

	Test Value = 5					
					95% Confidence Interval of the Difference	
	t	df	Sig. (2-tailed)	Mean Difference	Lower	Upper
preference	3.742	11	.003	2.083	.86	3.31

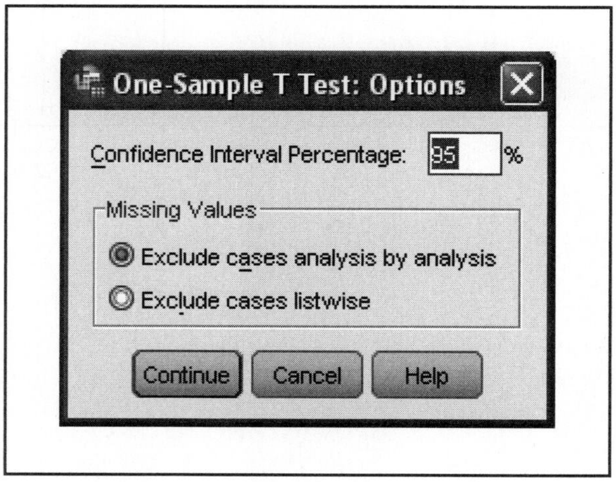

FIGURE 11.9

The SPSS dialog box for selecting any level of confidence.

Notice that the lower and upper confidence limits (circled in Table 11.6) in the SPSS output do not match those we computed. This is because we computed confidence intervals for the actual scores, or the actual times that rats spent in the reinforced side of the cage. SPSS, however, computes the confidence interval for the mean difference between what we observed and what we expected. What we expect is stated in the null hypothesis that rats will spend 5 minutes in each side of the cage.

The SPSS output, then, gives the effect size for the confidence intervals. The mean times in Example 11.2 shifted between 0.85 minutes and 3.31 minutes from the expected outcome that rats would spend 5 minutes in the reinforced side of the cage. These values, 0.85 and 3.31, are the confidence limits displayed in the SPSS output table, give or take a rounding error.

LEARNING CHECK 3

1. State the estimation formula for a one–independent sample *t*-test.

2. A researcher measures $M = 3.406$, $SD = 4.0$ in one sample of 16 participants. What is the 95% CI (confidence interval) for these data using the estimation formula for a one–independent sample *t*-test?

3. A researcher notes that the null hypothesis of $\mu = 6$ is not contained within the 95% confidence interval. Based on this result, would the decision have been to retain or reject the null hypothesis using hypothesis testing?

Answers: 1. $M \pm t(s_M)$; 2. The 95% CI is between 1.275 and 5.537; 3. Reject the null hypothesis.

ESTIMATION FOR THE TWO–INDEPENDENT SAMPLE *T*-TEST 11.6

The estimation formula can be used for a two–independent sample *t*-test. The estimation formula for two independent samples is used to identify the confidence limits within which the difference between two population means is contained. As stated in Section 11.4, the point estimate for a two–independent sample *t*-test is $M_1 - M_2$, and the interval estimate is $t\left(s_{M_1-M_2}\right)$.

In Example 11.3, we use the three steps to compute the estimation formula for the two–independent sample *t*-test. Example 11.3 is the same as that given in Example 9.4 in the SPSS in Focus section (see Chapter 9, Section 9.9). Using the same example will allow us to compare the results in Example 11.3 to the results of the two–independent sample *t*-test we computed in Example 9.4.

NOTE: The point estimate for the difference between two population means is $M_1 - M_2$; the interval estimate is $t(s_{M_1} - s_{M_2})$.

EXAMPLE 11.3

In a study on the likeability of comedians, 10 participants were randomly assigned to observe either a humorous comedian or one that was not humorous. After observing a comedian, participants rated how likable the comedian was on a 7-point scale from 1 (*not likable at all*) to 7 (*very likable*). Ratings were $M_1 = 6.0$ for the humorous comedian and $M_2 = 3.0$ for the nonhumorous comedian. If the estimated standard error for the difference, $s_{M_1-M_2}$, is equal to 1.0, then find the 95% confidence interval for these data.

Step 1: Compute the sample mean and standard error. The difference between the two sample means is $M_1 - M_2 = 3.0$. Therefore, the mean difference, which is the point estimate of the population mean difference, is equal to 3.0.

The estimated standard error for the difference, $s_{M_1-M_2}$, is equal to 1.0.

Step 2: Choose the level of confidence and find the critical values at that level of confidence. In this example, we want to find the 95% confidence interval, so we choose a 95% level of confidence. Remember, in a sampling distribution, 50% of the differences between two sample means fall above the mean difference we selected in our sample, and 50% fall below it. We are looking for the 95% of differences between two sample means that surround the mean difference we measured in our sample. Referring to Table 11.4, we find that a 95% CI corresponds to a two-tailed test at a .05 level of significance. To find the critical value at this level of confidence, we look in the t-table in Table B.2, Appendix B. The degrees of freedom are 8 ($df = n - 2$ for two-independent samples). The upper critical value for the interval estimate is $t = 2.306$.

Step 3: Compute the estimation formula to find the confidence limits for a 95% confidence interval. Because we are estimating the difference between two sample means in the population with an unknown variance, we use the $M_1 - M_2 \pm t\left(s_{M_1 - M_2}\right)$ estimation formula.

To compute the formula, multiply t times the estimated standard error for the difference:

$$t\left(s_{M_1 - M_2}\right) = 2.306 \ (1) = 2.306.$$

Add 2.306 to the sample mean difference to find the upper confidence limit:

$$\left(M_1 - M_2\right) + t\left(s_{M_1 - M_2}\right) = 3 + 2.306 = 5.306.$$

Subtract 2.306 from the sample mean difference to find the lower confidence limit:

$$\left(M_1 - M_2\right) - t\left(s_{M_1 - M_2}\right) = 3 - 2.306 = 0.694.$$

As shown in Figure 11.10, the 95% confidence interval in this population is between 0.694 and 5.306 points. We can estimate within a 95% level of confidence that humorous comedians are rated between 0.694 and 5.306 points more likable compared to ratings of nonhumorous comedians. We are 95% confident that the mean difference in the population falls within this range because 95% of all sample mean differences we could have selected from this population fall within the range of sample mean differences we specified.

FIGURE 11.10

In Example 11.3, the 95% confidence interval was 0.694 to 5.306.

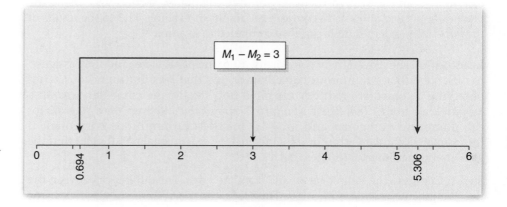

We can also determine the decision we would have made using hypothesis testing. In Example 11.3, the null hypothesis was a mean difference of 0 in the likability ratings of humorous and nonhumorous comedians in the population. Because a mean difference of 0 does not fall within the 95% CI of 0.694 to 5.306, we would have decided to reject the null hypothesis using hypothesis testing, which was the decision we made in Chapter 9. We can also estimate the effect size of this result. We estimate that mean likability ratings are between 0.694 and 5.306 points higher in humorous versus nonhumorous populations of comedians.

SPSS IN FOCUS: CONFIDENCE INTERVALS FOR THE TWO–INDEPENDENT SAMPLE *T*-TEST 11.7

Using the example in Chapter 9, we computed a two–independent sample *t*-test for Example 11.3 using SPSS. Table 11.7 shows the SPSS output table for that test, which was originally given in Table 9.11 in Chapter 9. The table lists the 95% confidence interval for the mean difference in likability ratings. To change the confidence interval, follow the steps for computing the two–independent sample *t*-test given in Chapter 9, and select **Options** in the dialog box in Steps 4 to 6. This action will display an additional dialog box, shown in Figure 11.11, which allows you to choose any level of confidence. By default, SPSS gives a 95% confidence interval with the *t*-test.

We can determine the effect size of the confidence interval using the confidence limits given in the SPSS output table. The lower and upper confidence limits (circled in Table 11.7) in the SPSS output match those we already computed. Using these 95% confidence limits, we again conclude that mean likability ratings are between 0.694 and 5.306 points higher in humorous versus nonhumorous populations of comedians.

TABLE 11.7 SPSS output table. Confidence intervals are circled in the bottom table. Read the first row labeled "equal variances assumed" in the bottom table.

Group Statistics

	groups	N	Mean	Std. Deviation	Std. Error Mean
ratings	humorous	5	6.00	1.581	.707
	nonhumorous	5	3.00	1.581	.707

Independent Samples Test

		Levene's Test for Equality of Variances		t-test for Equality of Means					95% Confidence Interval of the Difference	
		F	Sig.	t	df	Sig. (2-tailed)	Mean Difference	Std. Error Difference	Lower	Upper
ratings	Equal variances assumed	.000	1.000	3.000	8	.017	3.000	1.000	.694	5.306
	Equal variances not assumed			3.000	8.000	.017	3.000	1.000	.694	5.306

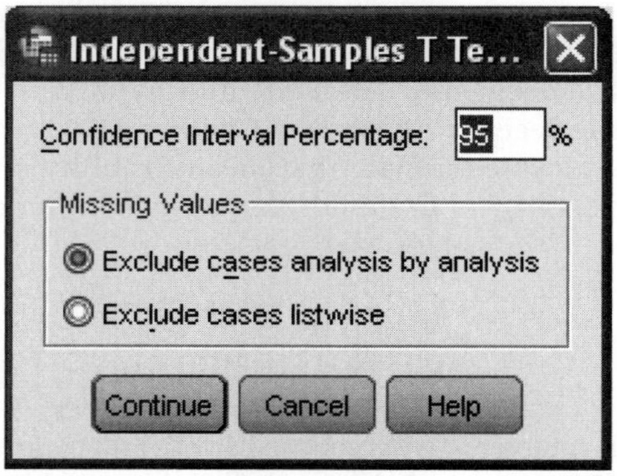

FIGURE 11.11

The SPSS dialog box for selecting any level of confidence.

11.8 ESTIMATION FOR THE RELATED SAMPLES T-TEST

The estimation formula can be used for a related samples *t*-test. The estimation formula for two related samples is used to identify the confidence limits within which the mean difference between two related populations is likely to be contained. As stated in Section 11.4, the point estimate for a related samples *t*-test is M_D, and the interval estimate is $t(s_{MD})$.

NOTE: The point estimate for the mean difference between two related populations is M_D; the interval estimate is $t(s_{MD})$.

In Example 11.4, we use the three steps to compute the estimation formula for the related samples *t*-test. Example 11.4 is the same as that given in Example 10.1 in Chapter 10. Using the same example will allow us to compare the results in Example 11.4 to the results of the related samples *t*-test we computed in Example 10.1.

EXAMPLE 11.4

Students often "go over their minutes" for allotted cell phone use in a given month. Suppose we believe that one reason is that when students are at home, they still use their cell phone more than their home phone. To estimate the difference in time spent talking, we measure the time in minutes that a sample of eight popular adolescent students spent talking on a cell phone and home phone at their home over a 2-day period. In this study, we compute a sample mean difference of $M_D = 15$. If the estimated standard error for the difference scores, s_{MD}, is 5.345, then find the 95% confidence interval for these data.

Step 1: Compute the sample mean and standard error. The mean difference, which is the point estimate of the population mean difference, is equal to $M_D = 15$.

The estimated standard error for difference scores, s_{MD}, is equal to 5.345.

Step 2: Choose the level of confidence and find the critical values at that level of confidence. In this example, we want to find the 95% confidence interval, so we choose a 95% level of confidence. Remember, in a sampling distribution, 50% of the mean differences fall above the mean difference we selected in our sample, and 50% fall below it. We are looking for the 95% of mean differences that surround the mean difference we selected in our sample. Referring to Table 11.4, we find that a

95% CI corresponds to a two-tailed test at a .05 level of significance. To find the critical value at this level of confidence, we look in the t-table in Table B.2, Appendix B. The degrees of freedom are 7 ($df = n_D - 1$ for two related samples). The critical value for the interval estimate is $t = 2.365$.

Step 3: Compute the estimation formula to find the confidence limits for a 95% confidence interval. Because we are estimating the mean difference between two related samples from a population with an unknown variance, we use the $M_D \pm t(s_{MD})$ estimation formula.

To compute the formula, multiply t times the estimated standard error for difference scores:

$$t(s_{MD}) = 2.365(5.345) = 12.64.$$

Add 12.64 to the sample mean difference to find the upper confidence limit:

$$M_D + t(s_{MD}) = 15 + 12.64 = 27.64.$$

Subtract 12.64 from the sample mean difference to find the lower confidence limit:

$$M_D - t(s_{MD}) = 15 - 12.64 = 2.36.$$

As shown in Figure 11.12, the 95% confidence interval in this population is between 2.36 minutes and 27.64 minutes. We can estimate within a 95% level of confidence that the mean difference in time that popular adolescents spent talking is between 2.36 and 27.64 minutes longer on a cell phone than on a home phone during a 2-day period at their home. We are 95% confident that the mean difference in the population falls within this range because 95% of all sample mean differences we could have selected from this population fall within the range of sample mean differences we specified.

We can also determine the decision we would have made using hypothesis testing. In Example 11.4, the null hypothesis was a mean difference of 0 in the time spent talking on a cell phone and home phone. Because a mean difference of 0 does not fall within the 95% CI of 2.36 to 27.64, we would have decided to reject the null hypothesis, which was the decision we made in Chapter 10. We can also estimate the effect size of this result. We estimate that over a 2-day period, the population of popular adolescents talks between 2.36 minutes and 27.64 minutes more on a cell phone than on a home phone at their home.

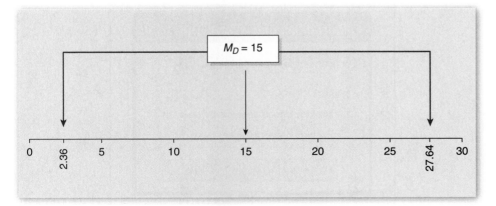

FIGURE 11.12

In Example 11.4, the 95% confidence interval was 2.36 to 27.64.

11.9 SPSS IN FOCUS: CONFIDENCE INTERVALS FOR THE RELATED SAMPLES *T*-TEST

Using the example in Chapter 10, we computed a related samples *t*-test for Example 11.4 using SPSS. Table 11.8 shows the SPSS output table for that test, which was originally given in Table 10.8 in Chapter 10. The table lists the 95% confidence interval for the mean difference in time spent talking. To change the confidence interval, follow the steps for computing the related samples *t*-test given in Chapter 10, and select **Options** in the dialog box in Steps 3 to 4. This action will display an additional dialog box, shown in Figure 11.13, which allows you to choose any level of confidence. By default, SPSS gives a 95% confidence interval with the *t*-test.

We can determine the effect size of the confidence interval using the confidence limits given in the SPSS output table. The lower and upper confidence limits (circled in Table 11.8) in the SPSS output match those we already computed. Using these 95% confidence limits, we again conclude that, over a 2-day period, the population of popular adolescents talks between 2.36 minutes and 27.64 minutes more on a cell phone than on a home phone at their home.

TABLE 11.8 SPSS output table. Confidence intervals are circled in the table.

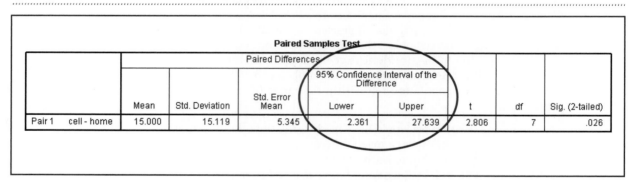

Paired Samples Test

		Paired Differences							
					95% Confidence Interval of the Difference				
		Mean	Std. Deviation	Std. Error Mean	Lower	Upper	t	df	Sig. (2-tailed)
Pair 1	cell - home	15.000	15.119	5.345	2.361	27.639	2.806	7	.026

FIGURE 11.13

The SPSS dialog box for selecting any level of confidence.

1. State the estimation formula for a related samples *t*-test.

2. What is $t\left(s_{MD}\right)$ for a 95% confidence interval given that $n_D = 4$ and $s_D = 8$?

3. If the sample mean is 30 for the data given in Question 2, then what are the upper and lower confidence limits in Question 2?

4. Based on your answers in Questions 2 and 3, if the null hypothesis were $\mu_D = 20$, then would we decide to retain or reject the null hypothesis using a hypothesis test?

Answers: 1. $M_D \pm t\left(s_{MD}\right)$; 2. $t\left(s_{MD}\right) = 3.182 \times \dfrac{8}{\sqrt{4}} = 12.728$; 3. 95% CI = 17.272 to 42.728; 4. Retain the null hypothesis because 20 falls within the limits of the confidence interval.

CHARACTERISTICS OF ESTIMATION: PRECISION AND CERTAINTY 11.10

In this chapter, we described the use of estimation as a way of learning about a mean or mean difference in some population of interest. Using estimation, we do not make decisions about whether or not the value of a population parameter should be retained or rejected. Instead, we measure statistics in a sample to estimate the limits within which we can be confident that the mean or mean difference in a population is likely contained.

When we use estimation to find the confidence interval, we typically refer to the precision and the certainty of the interval. The *precision* of an estimate is determined by the range of the confidence interval: The smaller the range of the interval, the more precise the estimate. The *certainty* of an estimate is determined by the level of confidence: The larger the level of confidence, the more certain the estimate. Therefore, we can use the following rules to determine the precision and certainty of a confidence interval:

1. Decreasing the level of confidence increases the precision of an estimate.

2. Increasing the level of confidence increases the certainty of an estimate.

To illustrate these rules, we will compute an interval estimate for the data in Example 11.4 at an 80% and a 95% level of confidence. The upper and lower confidence limits at each level of confidence are given in Figure 11.14. Rule 1 indicates that the smaller the level of confidence, the more precise the estimate. The 80% confidence interval is the smaller level of confidence. This estimate is more precise because it estimates the narrowest range within which the mean difference in the population is likely to be contained.

NOTE: The more certain an estimate is the less precise it is.

Rule 2 indicates that the larger the level of confidence, the more certain the estimate. The 95% confidence interval is the larger level of confidence. This estimate is associated with greater certainty because we are 95%, compared to 80%, confident that the population mean difference is contained within the confidence interval specified. These rules lead to an important conclusion regarding the precision and certainty of a confidence interval: To be more certain that an interval contains a population parameter, we must give up precision. This is usually a sacrifice most researchers are willing to make. Most studies report a 95% or 99% CI in published scientific research journals.

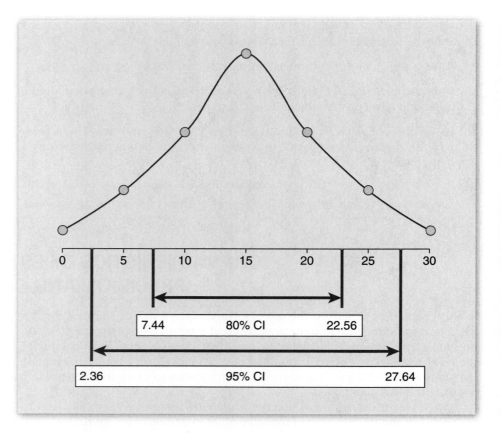

FIGURE 11.14

The 80% and 95% confidence intervals for the related samples data in Example 11.4. Notice that the lower the level of confidence, the more precise the estimate, but the less certain we are that the confidence interval contains the true population mean.

 **LEARNING CHECK 5**

1. Name two rules for the precision and certainty of a confidence interval.

2. What is the difference between the precision and certainty of a confidence interval?

Answers: 1. Decreasing the level of confidence increases the precision of an estimate, and increasing the level of confidence increases the certainty of an estimate; 2. The precision of an estimate is determined by the range of the confidence interval, whereas the certainty of an estimate is determined by the level of confidence.

11.1 APA IN FOCUS: REPORTING CONFIDENCE INTERVALS

To report estimation in scientific journals, we state the level of confidence, point estimate, and interval estimate of each confidence interval. For example, we could report the confidence interval in Example 11.2 as follows:

> The mean time rats spent in the reinforced side of the cage was 7.08 minutes (95% confidence interval [CI] 5.85–8.31).

We can also report the point estimate with the interval estimate given in brackets. For example, we could report the confidence interval in Example 11.3 as follows:

> Humorous comedians were rated as more likable compared to those who were nonhumorous (mean [95% CI] = 3.0 [0.694–5.306]).

These examples provide a concise summary of the confidence intervals we computed in this chapter. In addition, we can summarize the sample means, the standard error, and the standard deviations in a figure or table or in the main text.

CHAPTER SUMMARY ORGANIZED BY LEARNING OBJECTIVE

LO 1: Describe the process of estimation and identify two types of estimation.

- **Estimation** is a statistical procedure in which a sample statistic is used to estimate the value of an unknown population parameter. Two types of estimation are point estimation and interval estimation.
- **Point estimation** is a statistical procedure that involves the use of a sample statistic (e.g., a sample mean) to estimate a population parameter (e.g., a population mean).
- **Interval estimation** is a statistical procedure in which a sample of data is used to find the interval or range of possible values within which a population parameter is likely to be contained.
- In research studies that use estimation, we report the sample mean (a point estimate) and the interval within which a population mean is likely to be contained (an interval estimate).

LO 2: Distinguish between significance testing and estimation.

- Estimation does not require that we state a null hypothesis and decide whether or not it should be rejected. We use estimation to measure the mean or mean difference in a sample, as we did in hypothesis testing, but instead of making a decision regarding a null hypothesis, we estimate the limits within which the population mean or mean difference is likely to be contained.
- The decision for a hypothesis test can be determined by comparing the value stated in the null hypothesis to the confidence limits for a confidence interval. When the value stated in the null hypothesis is outside the confidence limits, the decision would be to reject the null hypothesis. When the value stated in the null hypothesis is inside the confidence limits, the decision would be to retain the null hypothesis.
- The effect size of a confidence interval can be determined when the value stated in the null hypothesis is outside the confidence limits. The effect size is a range in which the lower effect size estimate is the difference between the value stated in the null hypothesis and the lower confidence limit; the upper effect size

estimate is the difference between the value stated in the null hypothesis and the upper confidence limit. The effect size for a confidence interval is interpreted in terms of a shift in the population.

LO 3–6: Compute confidence intervals for the one–independent sample z-test, the one–independent sample t-test, the two–independent sample t-test, and the related samples t-test.

- The three steps to estimation are the following:
  Step 1: Compute the sample mean and standard error.
  Step 2: Choose the level of confidence and find the critical values at that level of confidence.
  Step 3: Compute the estimation formula to find the confidence limits.
- The estimation formula for the one–independent sample z is $M \pm z(\sigma_M)$.
- The estimation formula for each t-test is as follows:
  One–independent sample t: $M \pm t(s_M)$
  Two–independent sample t: $M_1 - M_2 \pm t\left(s_{M_1 - M_2}\right)$
  Related samples t: $M_D \pm t\left(s_{MD}\right)$

LO 7: Distinguish between the certainty and precision of an interval estimate.

- The precision of an estimate is determined by the range of the confidence interval. The certainty of an estimate is determined by the level of confidence.
- To be more certain that an interval contains a population parameter, we must generally give up precision by increasing the size of the interval.

APA LO 8: Summarize confidence intervals for the z-test and t-tests in APA format.

- To report confidence intervals in scientific journals, state the level of confidence, point estimate, and interval estimate of the confidence interval. In addition, the sample means, the standard error, and the standard deviations can be summarized in a figure or table or in the main text.

SPSS LO 9: Compute confidence intervals for the one–independent, the two–independent, and the related samples t-tests using SPSS.

- To compute the confidence interval for a one-sample *t*-test, follow the steps for computing the one–independent sample *t*-test given in Chapter 9, and select **Options** in the dialog box in Steps 3 to 5. This action will display an additional dialog box that will allow you to choose any level of confidence (for more details, see Sections 11.5).
- To compute the confidence interval for a two-sample *t*-test, follow the steps for computing the two–independent sample *t*-test given in Chapter 9, and select **Options** in the dialog box in Steps 4 to 6. This action will display an additional dialog box that will allow you to choose any level of confidence (for more details, see Section 11.7).
- To compute the confidence interval for a related samples *t*-test, follow the steps for computing the related samples *t*-test given in Chapter 10, and select **Options** in the dialog box in Steps 3 to 4. This action will display an additional dialog box that will allow you to choose any level of confidence (for more details, see Section 11.9).

KEY TERMS

confidence boundaries
confidence interval (CI)
confidence limits

estimation
interval estimation
level of confidence

lower confidence limit
point estimation
upper confidence limit

END-OF-CHAPTER PROBLEMS

Factual Problems

1. Explain how estimation differs from hypothesis testing in terms of making decisions regarding the null hypothesis.

2. Explain how the process of estimation is different from hypothesis testing.

3. Define point estimation and interval estimation.

4. What are an advantage and a disadvantage of using only the sample mean to estimate the population mean?

5. Who determines the level of confidence for an interval estimate?

6. What level of confidence is associated with a two-tailed hypothesis test at a .05 level of significance?

7. Explain how to determine the effect size of an outcome based on the limits stated for a confidence interval.

8. What are the three steps to compute an estimation formula?

9. What is the estimation formula for a one–independent sample *z*-test?

10. What is the estimation formula for each type of *t*-test?

11. As the level of confidence decreases, what happens to the certainty of an interval estimate?

12. Is the point estimate or interval estimate a more precise estimate of the population mean?

Concepts and Application Problems

13. Using the following information, the estimation formula for which type of hypothesis test was computed?

    (a) The estimated standard error for the difference was computed.

    (b) The estimated standard error for difference scores was computed.

    (c) The estimated standard error was computed.

    (d) The standard error was computed.

14. State which estimation formula should be computed for each of the following hypotheses concerning a population with an unknown variance:

    (a) A neuroscientist measures the mean difference in symptoms of depression before and after a drug treatment.

(b) A forensic psychologist has jurors read a vignette about an alleged crime committed by either a Black or a White defendant. Participants in each group rate the culpability of the defendant.

(c) A cognitive psychologist places a group of participants in front of a computer and asks them to press a key 90 seconds following a prompt to begin timing. She tests how closely (in seconds) their key presses are to the 90-second interval.

15. Researchers report a 95% CI = 1.56 to 5.77. What would the decision be for a hypothesis test if the null hypothesis were:

(a) $\mu = 0$

(b) $\mu = 3$

(c) $\mu = 6$

16. What is the decision for a hypothesis test if the null hypothesis were:

(a) Within the confidence interval

(b) Outside the confidence interval

17. True or false for (a) and (b): It is appropriate to state the effect size based on a confidence interval when a null hypothesis is:

(a) Within the confidence interval

(b) Outside the confidence interval

18. A researcher compared the time (in seconds) that children in two classrooms remained seated during a behavioral task. The null hypothesis is that the two classrooms will not differ. She reports a 95% CI = −2.1 to 32.6 seconds. What would the decision have been for a hypothesis test?

19. Will each of the following increase, decrease, or have no effect on the precision of a confidence interval?

(a) The sample size is increased.

(b) The level of confidence is decreased.

(c) The standard error is increased.

(d) The population size is increased.

20. What are the upper and lower limits of a 95% confidence interval given the following estimation formulas?

(a) 12 ± 2.3

(b) $94 \pm (2.228)\dfrac{24}{\sqrt{64}}$

(c) $\dfrac{20}{5} \pm (1.96)(0.75)$

21. A group of students enroll in a behavioral statistics course taught by one of two professors. The mean grade in Professor G's class is 80% (95% CI = 72%–88%), and the mean grade in Professor P's class is 76% (95% CI = 68%–82%).

(a) Is one confidence interval more precise? Explain.

(b) Is one confidence interval associated with greater certainty? Explain.

22. Teachers employed at a learning center developed a teaching program to improve scores on a standardized exam. The teachers select a sample of 36 participants and measure a sample mean equal to 510 from a population with a standard deviation equal to 114.

(a) Find the confidence limits at a 90% CI for this one-independent sample. *Note:* The population variance is known.

(b) If the null hypothesis states that scores in the population equal 474, then what would the decision be for an upper tail critical hypothesis test at a .05 level of significance?

23. Listening to music has long been thought to enhance intelligence, especially during infancy and childhood. To test whether this is true, a researcher records the number of hours that eight high-performing students listened to music per day for 1 week. The data are listed in the table.

Music Listening Per Day (in hours)
4.2
4.8
5.0
3.8
4.2
5.5
4.1
4.4

(a) Find the confidence limits at a 95% CI for this one–independent sample.

(b) Suppose the null hypothesis states that students listen to 3.5 hours of music per day. What would the decision be for a two-tailed hypothesis test at a .05 level of significance?

24. An instructor implements a new teaching strategy in the classroom by using a teaching strategy to teach a sample of six students. After the instruction, he gives each student a test out of 100 possible points to test their recall. The scores are listed in the table.

Score on the Exam
65
73
77
70
68
67

(a) Find the confidence limits at a 90% CI for this one–independent sample.

(b) If the mean grade in the entire class is $\mu = 75$ points, then did the new teaching strategy improve grades compared to the mean grade in the entire class (the population)?

25. To save money, a local charity organization wants to target its mailing requests for donations to individuals who are most supportive of its cause. They ask a sample of 5 men and 5 women to rate the importance of their cause on a scale from 1 (*not important at all*) to 7 (*very important*). The ratings for men were $M_1 = 6.4$. The ratings for women were $M_2 = 5.3$. If the estimated standard error for the difference $\left(s_{M_1-M_2}\right)$ is equal to 0.25, then:

(a) Find the confidence limits at an 80% CI for these two–independent samples.

(b) Can we conclude that men or women are more supportive to their cause? Explain.

26. Nonverbal communication (e.g., the use of hand gestures) is a common form of human expression. Some researchers believe it may even help people make quicker decisions. To test this belief, a team of researchers conducted a study where they recorded the time it took 12 college students to count scattered dots on a computer screen. Half ($n = 6$) the students pointed to the dots as they counted (Group Gesture); the other half ($n = 6$) were told not to point as they counted (Group No Gesture). The table lists the time it took students in each group to correctly count the dots (in seconds).

Speed of Counting (in seconds)	
Group Gesture	Group No Gesture
22	32
16	27
18	24
14	31
26	29
18	31

(a) Find the confidence limits at a 99% CI for these two–independent samples.

(b) Can we conclude that using hand gestures to count the dots resulted in quicker counting? Explain.

27. An instructor believes that students do not retain as much information from a lecture on a Friday compared to a Monday. To test this belief, the instructor teaches a small sample of college students some preselected material from a single topic on statistics on a Friday and on a Monday. All students received a test on the material. The differences in exam scores for material taught on Friday minus Monday are listed in the following table.

Difference Scores (Friday – Monday)
+3.4
−1.6
+4.4
+6.3
+1.0

(a) Find the confidence limits at a 95% CI for these related samples.

(b) Can we conclude that students retained more of the material taught in the Friday class?

28. A researcher hypothesizes that children will eat more of foods wrapped in familiar packaging than the same foods wrapped in plain packaging. To test this hypothesis, she records the number of bites that 24 children take of a food given to them wrapped in fast-food packaging versus plain packaging. If the mean difference (fast-food packaging minus plain packaging) is $M_D = 12$, and $s_{MD} = 2.4$, then:

(a) Find the confidence limits at a 95% CI for these related samples.

(b) Can we conclude that wrapping foods in familiar packaging increases the number of bites that children took compared to plain packaging?

Problems in Research

29. **The width (or precision) of confidence intervals.** Sanchez-Meca and Marin-Martinez (2008) noted in their article that "using the *t*-distribution produces CIs that are wider then those of the standard normal distribution" (p. 34). Explain why this statement is true.

30. **Confidence intervals, significance, and effect size.** Guang Yong Zou (2007) noted in an article that confidence intervals "encompass significance tests and provide an estimate of the magnitude of the effect" (p. 399). What does "the magnitude of the effect" refer to in this citation?

31. **Fatalism among teens in the United States.** Jamieson and Romer (2008) evaluated children's beliefs concerning life expectancy in a diverse sample of American children. In their study, they reported at a 95% CI that "approximately 1 out of every 15 youth interviewed (6.7%[5.9%, 7.5%]) responded that they agreed they would not live much past the age of 30" (p. 154).

(a) What is the point estimate and interval estimate for these data?

(b) If these researchers computed an 80% CI, how would this change the precision and certainty of their estimate?

32. **Substance abuse risk and bipolar disorder.** Wilens and colleagues (2008) studied the association between bipolar disorder and substance abuse. In their study, they reported at a 95% CI that "bipolar disorder was associated with an age-adjusted risk for . . . alcohol abuse (7.66[2.20 26.7]), drug abuse (18.5[2.46 139.10]), dependence (12.1[1.54 95.50]) . . . and cigarette smoking (12.3[2.83 53.69])" (p. 188).

(a) Which risk factor was associated with the least variability?

(b) Which risk factor was associated with the most variability?

33. **The 95% confidence interval.** To clarify the kind of information conveyed by a level of confidence, Thompson (2007) stated, "CIs are extremely useful because they convey not only our point estimate, but also, via the width of the intervals, something about the precision of our estimates" (p. 427). What is the name of the estimate that conveys the width of the intervals?

NOTE: Answers for even numbers are in Appendix C.

Making Inferences About the Variability of Two or More Means

Analysis of Variance

One-Way Between-Subjects Design

LEARNING OBJECTIVES

After reading this chapter, you should be able to:

1. Define the one-way between-subjects ANOVA and identify each source of variation in this statistical procedure.

2. Calculate the degrees of freedom for the one-way between-subjects ANOVA and locate critical values in the F-table.

3. Identify the assumptions for the one-way between-subjects ANOVA.

4. Compute the one-way between-subjects ANOVA and interpret the results.

5. Compute Fisher's LSD and Tukey's HSD post hoc tests and identify which test is most powerful.

6. Compute proportion of variance for the one-way between-subjects ANOVA.

7. Summarize the results of the one-way between-subjects ANOVA in APA format.

8. Compute the one-way between-subjects ANOVA and select an appropriate post hoc test using SPSS.

12.1 INCREASING *K*: A SHIFT TO ANALYZING VARIANCE

In hypothesis testing, we are often interested in more than two groups. An analysis of variance (ANOVA) is a test used when we observe more than two groups in a study. The *t*-tests, though, are limited in that they can only be used to test for differences between one or two groups. The reason we need to change statistical tests is because more pairs of group means can differ as the number of groups increases. To illustrate, consider the following example.

Many studies suggest that college students tend to buy cheaper foods, regardless of the healthfulness of those foods. To test this, suppose we place a buffet of foods on a table where half the foods are healthy and half are unhealthy. One group of participants is assigned to Group Pricey. Participants in this group choose from foods at a table where the healthy foods are high priced. A second group of participants is assigned to Group Cheap. Participants in this group choose from the same foods at a table, except that the healthy foods are low priced. We record the total calories chosen and hypothesize that participants in Group Cheap will chose a lower calorie meal because the healthier foods had lower prices.

This example is a research situation in which we compute the two–independent samples *t*-test because we observed two groups. When the differences observed between these two groups are unlikely to occur if the null hypothesis were true, then we decide to reject the null hypothesis; otherwise, we retain the null hypothesis. Figure 12.1a

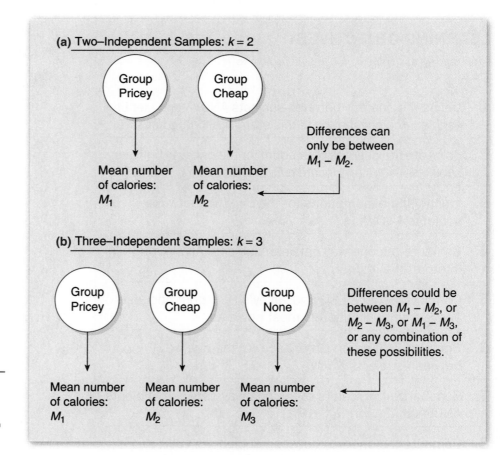

FIGURE 12.1

Group differences when $k = 2$ (a) and $k = 3$ (b). When the number of groups increases, so does the number of pairs of group means that can differ.

illustrates that when we decide to reject the null hypothesis, we conclude that one mean is different from the other in the population. We can make this conclusion when we limit the number of groups or **levels of the factor,** symbolized as k, to two.

The **levels of the factor**, symbolized as k, are the number of groups or different ways that an independent or quasi-independent variable is observed.

DEFINITION

But most research studies, particularly experiments, include some sort of control group for the sake of making a comparison. For example, suppose we want to compare choices in the two groups to another group where no foods are priced and we call this control Group None. We can assign participants to Group None and have them choose from the same foods as Group Pricey and Group Cheap, except none of the foods have prices. In Figure 12.1, (b) shows that there are now three pairs of groups that can be different, and it is not clear which differences are significant. When many pairs of group means can differ, we analyze the variance of group means using a test called an **analysis of variance (ANOVA)**. This is one of the most popular hypothesis tests used in behavioral science. Chapters 12 to 14 introduce many versions of this test.

An **analysis of variance (ANOVA)**, also called the *F*-test, is a statistical procedure used to test hypotheses for one or more factors concerning the variance among two or more group means ($k \geq 2$), where the variance in one or more populations is unknown.

DEFINITION

In this chapter, we explain what the one-way between-subjects design is and introduce the methods used to select samples and state research hypotheses. Although the steps to hypothesis testing using an ANOVA are the same as those described in Chapters 8 to 10, the test statistic and calculation of degrees of freedom in an ANOVA differ. Once we learn to calculate them, we're ready to work with an example of an ANOVA test, the topic of Section 12.5. The remainder of the chapter evaluates the results of the ANOVA test, particularly when we reject the null hypothesis and seek to find the pairs of groups that are significantly different.

NOTE: An analysis of variance measures the variance among two or more group means.

AN INTRODUCTION TO ANALYSIS OF VARIANCE 12.2

Like the *t*-tests, an ANOVA is a statistical procedure used when we measure interval or ratio scale data. The type of ANOVA we use to analyze data depends on (1) the number of factors being tested and (2) how the participants are observed across the levels of each factor. In this section, we explain how these two criteria help us to identify each type of ANOVA test.

IDENTIFYING THE TYPE OF ANOVA

In this chapter, we introduce the most basic type of ANOVA, called the **one-way between-subjects ANOVA.** The "one-way" in the name of this hypothesis test refers to the number of factors being tested in the study. In a one-way ANOVA, we test one factor. If we tested two factors, we would call the test a two-way ANOVA. If three factors, then it would be a three-way ANOVA, and so on.

The word *subjects* in the name of this hypothesis test refers to the design that describes how participants are observed—whether the same or different participants are observed. When the same participants are observed across the levels of a factor, we use the within-subjects design (the within-subjects design was defined in Chapter 10). For example, to see whether students preferred celery or carrots as a healthy snack, we could use the same group and subject them to two treatments (e.g., the celery first and then the carrots). When different participants are observed at each level of a factor, we use the **between-subjects design.** For example, to see whether students preferred celery or carrots as a healthy snack, we could use two groups and give one group the celery and the second group the carrots.

NOTE: In a one-way between-subjects ANOVA, different participants are observed at each level of one factor.

DEFINITION

A **one-way between-subjects ANOVA** is a statistical procedure used to test hypotheses for one factor with two or more levels concerning the variance among group means. This test is used when different participants are observed at each level of a factor and the variance in any one population is unknown.

Between-subjects design is a research design in which we select independent samples, meaning that different participants are observed at each level of a factor.

TWO WAYS TO SELECT INDEPENDENT SAMPLES

In this chapter, we will introduce the one-way between-subjects ANOVA. Recall that *between-subjects* refers to the selection of independent samples, meaning that different participants are observed in each group. Figure 12.2 shows two ways to select two or more groups in a between-subjects ANOVA, such that different participants are observed in each group. Each way to select independent samples is described in this section.

The first way, shown in Figure 12.2a, is to select a sample from two or more populations. This type of sampling is commonly used to conduct quasi-experiments. A quasi-experiment, described in Chapter 1, is a study that does not have a comparison group and/or includes a factor that is preexisting. When a factor is preexisting, we cannot manipulate or create the differences in the levels of that factor; instead, the differences already exist. For example, suppose we hypothesize that students who pay for their own college education, without financial assistance, will study more. We record the time spent studying in a sample of students who, prior to the study, were paying their tuition with or without financial assistance. Referring to Figure 12.2a, Population 1 consists of students who pay for their education with financial assistance; Population 2 consists of students who pay for their college education without financial assistance. Each sample is selected from a different population; hence, each sample constitutes a different group. The factor is the type of financial assistance, and this factor has two preexisting levels (yes, no).

The second way to select independent samples, shown in Figure 12.2b, is to select one sample from the same population and randomly assign participants in the sample to two or more groups. This type of sampling is commonly used in experiments. An experiment, described in Chapter 1, is a study that includes randomization, manipulation, and a comparison group. The only way to achieve an experiment is to randomly assign participants selected from a single population to different groups. For example, suppose we hypothesize that paying students for earning higher grades will improve their performance on an exam. To test this, we

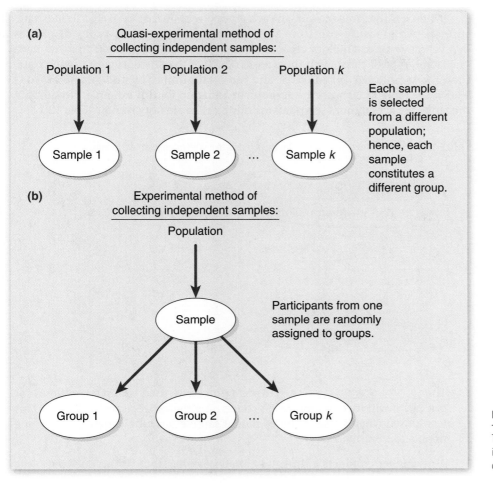

FIGURE 12.2

Two methods for selecting independent samples from one (a) or more (b) populations.

could select a group of students and have them study a word list and test their recall. In one group, participants are paid for better scores, and in a second group, participants are not paid. Referring to Figure 12.2b, the population would be college students, from which one sample was selected and randomly assigned to be paid (Group 1) or not paid (Group 2) for earning grades. The factor is payment, and this factor has two randomly assigned levels (paid, not paid).

NOTE: A one-way between-subjects ANOVA can be used when samples are selected from one or more populations.

CHANGES IN NOTATION

The notation used to identify the sample size for an ANOVA is different from the notation we used to describe sample size with the *t*-tests. For the ANOVA, *n* represents the number of participants per group (not sample size), and *N* represents the number of total participants in a study (not population size).

NOTE: For an ANOVA, k is the number of groups, n is the number of participants per group, and N is the total number of participants in a study.

$$n = \text{number of participants per group}$$
$$N = \text{number of total participants in a study}$$

When n is the same or equal in each group, we state that $k \times n = N$. To illustrate, suppose we measure the time spent talking during three types of classes (a psychology class, a biology class, and a sociology class). In this example, we have one factor (type of class), with three levels ($k = 3$). If five students were in each class, then the sample size (n) equals 5, and the total number of students observed is $3 \times 5 = 15$. Table 12.1 shows the appropriate notation for this example. (To simplify the table, the actual times spent talking during class are not given in Table 12.1.)

TABLE 12.1 The notation of *N*, *n*, and *k* in a hypothesis test with more than two groups.

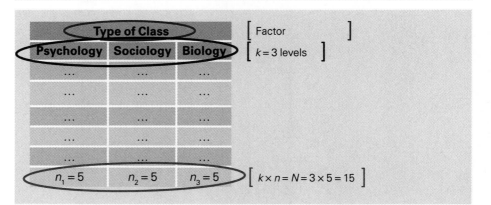

LEARNING CHECK 1

1. The _____ is a statistical procedure used to test hypotheses for one factor with two or more levels concerning the variance among means. This test is used when we select independent samples and the variance in any one population is unknown.

2. A researcher conducts a three-way analysis of variance. What does *three-way* indicate?

3. A researcher conducts a between-subjects ANOVA. What does *between-subjects* indicate?

4. What is the total sample size for each example, assuming that *n* is equal in each group?

   a. $k = 4$, $n = 12$ b. $k = 3$, $n = 8$ c. $N = 28$

Answers: 1. One-way between-subjects ANOVA; 2. The ANOVA has three factors; 3. Different participants are observed in each group; 4. (a) $4 \times 12 = 48$, (b) $3 \times 8 = 24$, (c) 28.

12.3 SOURCES OF VARIATION AND THE TEST STATISTIC

A one-way ANOVA is used to analyze the variance of two or more levels of one factor. Each level of a factor is a group. We conduct an ANOVA test to determine if the means in each group significantly vary. The larger the differences are between group means, the larger the variance will be. If group means are equal, then the variance of group means is equal to 0 (the means do not vary). The larger the differences between the group means, the larger the variance of group means will be. This variance is placed in the numerator of the test statistic, just as mean differences between groups were placed in the numerator for the *t*-tests.

However, the variance of group means, called **between-groups variation,** is only one **source of variation.** Another source of variation can be attributed to error or any unexplained variation that cannot be attributed to, or caused by, having different groups. The variation attributed to error or chance, called **within-groups variation,** is similar to the estimate of standard error we computed with the *t*-tests. This variance is placed in the denominator of the test statistic, just as our estimate of standard error was placed in the denominator for the *t*-tests. This makes the general form of the test statistic, F_{obt}, for a one-way between-subjects ANOVA:

$$F_{obt} = \frac{\text{variance attributed to group differences}}{\text{variance attributed to chance}}.$$

DEFINITION

A **source of variation** is any variation that can be measured in a study. In the one-way between-subjects ANOVA, there are two sources of variation: variation attributed to differences between group means and variation attributed to error.

Between-groups variation is the variation attributed to mean differences between groups.

Within-groups variation is the variation attributed to mean differences within each group. This source of variation cannot be attributed to or caused by having different groups and is therefore called error variation.

To compute variance, values in the numerator and denominator must be some positive value. In other words, scores can vary (variance is greater than 0) or not vary (variance is equal to 0). The computations for variance are more involved with an ANOVA, but we are nonetheless computing variances: one in the numerator and one in the denominator. Specially, the portion of the total variance attributed to differences between groups is placed in the numerator, and the portion attributed to error is placed in the denominator.

To illustrate the sources of variation, suppose we again measure the time (in minutes) spent talking during three types of classes (a psychology class, biology class, and sociology class). Table 12.2 presents the same study shown in Table 12.1 but includes hypothetical data. The between-groups variation reflects the differences between group means. The within-groups variation reflects the differences in times (in minutes) within each group. The within-groups variation is regarded as error because students in the psychology class, for example, did not all talk the same amount of time. Although they were in the same group or class, their scores were not all the same, so this variability had nothing to do with differences between groups.

In Chapter 7, we explained that the sampling distribution of the sample variance is positively skewed. Likewise, the distribution of possible outcomes for the test statistic of an analysis of variance (ANOVA) is positively skewed. The distribution, called the ***F*-distribution,** is derived from a sampling distribution of

NOTE: There are two sources of variation in a one-way between-subjects ANOVA: one attributed to differences between-groups and one associated with observing different participants in each group (within-groups).

TABLE 12.2 Between-groups and within-groups variability for the one-way between-subjects ANOVA. Between-groups variability is attributed to differences between group means. Within-groups variability is attributed to variability that has nothing to do with having different groups.

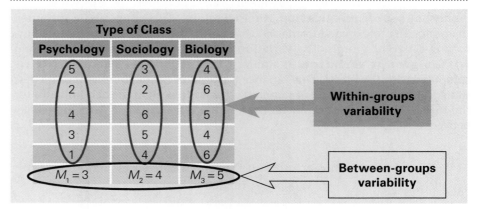

F-ratios and is illustrated in Figure 12.3. An F-ratio reflects the between-groups variance. When group means are the same, the F-ratio is equal to 0. The larger the differences between group means, the larger the F-ratio becomes. The test statistic is used to determine how large or disproportionate the differences are between group means compared to the variance we would expect to occur by chance.

DEFINITION

An **F-distribution** is a positively skewed distribution derived from a sampling distribution of F-ratios.

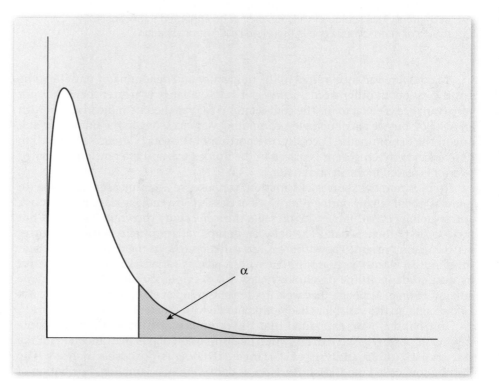

FIGURE 12.3

The F-distribution. The rejection region or alpha level (α) is placed in the upper tail of an F-distribution because values farther from 0 indicate outcomes that are less likely to occur if the null hypothesis were true.

The variances measured in an ANOVA test are computed as mean squares. A mean square is a variance. The two terms mean the same thing; they are synonyms. The formula for the test statistic, called the **F-statistic,** is the variance between groups, or **mean square between groups** (MS_{BG}), divided by the variance within groups, or **mean square within groups.** Mean square within groups is more commonly called **mean square error** (MS_E). The formula for the test statistic is

$$F_{obt} = \frac{MS_{BG}}{MS_E} \text{ or } \frac{\text{variance between groups}}{\text{variance within groups}}.$$

NOTE: The test statistic for an ANOVA measures the variance attributed to the mean differences between groups (MS_{BG}) divided by the variance attributed to error (MS_E).

DEFINITION

The **F-statistic,** or **F-obtained (F_{obt}),** is the test statistic for an ANOVA. It is computed as mean square (or variance) between groups divided by the mean square (or variance) within groups.

Mean square between groups (MS_{BG}) is the variance attributed to differences between group means. It is the numerator for the test statistic.

Mean square error (MS_E), or **mean square within groups,** is the variance attributed to differences within each group. It is the denominator for the test statistic.

DEGREES OF FREEDOM 12.4

For the *t*-tests, we used degrees of freedom to find the critical values for the hypothesis test. Similarly, we use degrees of freedom to find the critical values for an ANOVA. The critical value for an ANOVA is the cutoff value for the rejection region, same as it was for the *t*-tests. The degrees of freedom for a one-way between-subjects ANOVA is $N - 1$. These are the same as the degrees of freedom for sample variance. However, there are two sources of variation for the one-way between-subjects ANOVA. For this reason, we must split the total degrees of freedom ($N - 1$) into two parts: one for each source of variation.

The variance in the numerator is attributed to differences between group means. The degrees of freedom for this variance is called the **degrees of freedom numerator** or **degrees of freedom between groups.** The degrees of freedom for this variance is the number of groups (k) minus 1:

$$df_{BG} = k - 1.$$

The **degrees of freedom between groups** or **degrees of freedom numerator** are the degrees of freedom associated with the variance of the group means in the numerator of the test statistic. It is equal to the number of groups (k) minus 1.

The variance in the denominator is attributed to error. The degrees of freedom for this variance is called the **degrees of freedom error, degrees of freedom within groups,** or **degrees of freedom denominator.** The degrees of freedom for this variance is the total sample size (N) minus the number of groups (k):

$$df_E = N - k.$$

DEFINITION

The **degrees of freedom error (df_E), degrees of freedom within groups**, or **degrees of freedom denominator** are the degrees of freedom associated with the error variance in the denominator. It is equal to the total sample size (N) minus the number of groups (k).

The reason for the reference to numerator and denominator for degrees of freedom is because there are two sets of degrees of freedom: one for the variance between groups and one for error variance. The degrees of freedom numerator is associated with between-groups variation, and the degrees of freedom denominator is associated with the error variation. This is shown here:

$$F_{obt} = \frac{\text{variance between groups}}{\text{variance within groups}} \xleftarrow{\text{degrees of freedom}} \frac{k-1}{N-k}.$$

Let's calculate the degrees of freedom using the data in Table 12.2. In this hypothetical study, we had one factor (type of class) with three levels (psychology, sociology, biology): $k = 3$. We observed five students in each class ($n = 5$) for a total of 15 participants in the study ($N = 15$). Because $N = 15$, the total degrees of freedom for this test should sum to 14 ($N - 1 = 14$). The degrees of freedom between groups in the numerator is $k - 1$:

$$df_{BG} = 3 - 1 = 2.$$

The degrees of freedom error in the denominator is $N - k$:

$$df_E = 15 - 3 = 12.$$

When we state the degrees of freedom for an ANOVA, we always state the degrees of freedom between groups, then the degrees of freedom error. For this study, then, we have an ANOVA with 2 and 12 degrees of freedom. These degrees of freedom sum to 14, which equals $N - 1$.

The number of groups (k) and sample size (per group, n, and total, N) are used to compute degrees of freedom, so changing any one of the degrees of freedom will change the shape of the F-distribution. As the value for k, N, or n increases, so also will the total degrees of freedom. As the total degrees of freedom increase, the F-distribution becomes less skewed, meaning that the tails of the F-distribution pull closer to the y-axis. In terms of the critical values for an ANOVA, as degrees of freedom increase, the critical values get smaller. Smaller critical values are associated with greater power. Hence, as the degrees of freedom increase, the power to detect an effect also increases.

To locate the critical values for an ANOVA, we use an F-table, such as that given in Table B.3 in Appendix B. The F-table in Appendix B lists the critical values at a .05 and .01 level of significance; the values in boldface are for a .01 level of significance. Table 12.3 shows a portion of the F-table. To use the table, locate the degrees of freedom numerator listed in the columns and then

TABLE 12.3 A portion of the F-table given in Table B.3 in Appendix B. The degrees of freedom numerator are listed in the columns; the degrees of freedom denominators are listed in the rows.

		Degrees of Freedom Numerator			
		1	**2**	**3**	**4**
Degrees of Freedom Denominator	**1**	161 **4052**	200 **5000**	216 **5403**	225 **5625**
	2	18.51 **98.49**	19.00 **99.00**	19.16 **99.17**	19.25 **99.25**
	3	10.13 **34.12**	9.55 **30.92**	9.28 **29.46**	9.12 **28.71**
	4	7.71 **21.20**	6.94 **18.00**	6.59 **16.69**	6.39 **15.98**
	5	6.61 **16.26**	5.79 **13.27**	5.41 **12.06**	5.19 **11.39**
	6	5.99 **13.74**	5.14 **10.92**	4.76 **9.78**	4.53 **9.15**
	7	5.59 **13.74**	4.74 **9.55**	4.35 **8.45**	4.12 **7.85**
	8	5.32 **11.26**	4.46 **8.65**	4.07 **7.59**	3.84 **7.01**
	9	5.12 **10.56**	4.26 **8.02**	3.86 **6.99**	3.63 **6.42**
	10	4.96 **10.04**	4.10 **7.56**	3.71 **6.55**	3.48 **5.99**
	11	4.84 **9.65**	3.98 **7.20**	3.59 **6.22**	3.36 **5.67**
	12	4.75 **9.33**	3.89 **6.93**	3.49 **5.95**	3.26 **5.41**

the degrees of freedom denominator listed down the rows. The critical value is the entry found at the intersection of the two degrees of freedom. For a one-way ANOVA with 2 and 12 degrees of freedom at a .05 level of significance, the critical value is 3.89.

Keep in mind that the F-distribution is positive skewed. It begins at 0 and is skewed toward positive values. So the critical value for all F-tests is placed in the upper tail. Negative outcomes are not possible in an F-distribution.

LEARNING CHECK 2

1. The value of the test statistic for the one-way between-subjects ANOVA can be:
   a. Any positive number
   b. Any negative number
   c. Both a and b

2. Name the source of variation in the numerator and the source of variance in the denominator of the test statistic for the one-way between-subjects ANOVA.

3. True or false: The power of an ANOVA test increases as the sample size increases.

4. A researcher computes an analysis of variance with 4 and 12 degrees of freedom. What is the critical value for this test at a .05 level of significance?

Answers: 1. a; 2. Between-groups variation is in the numerator and within-groups variation is in the denominator; 3. True; 4. 3.26.

12.5 THE ONE-WAY BETWEEN-SUBJECTS ANOVA

NOTE: The null hypothesis for an analysis of variance states that group means in the population do not vary; the alternative states that group means in the population do vary.

In this section, we will compute the one-way between-subjects ANOVA. We compute this test when we compare two or more group means, in which different participants are observed in each group. The null hypothesis states that group means do not vary in the population:

$$H_0: \sigma_\mu^2 = 0.$$

The alternative hypothesis states that group means in the population do vary:

$$H_1: \sigma_\mu^2 > 0.$$

In terms of variance, group means either vary ($\sigma_\mu^2 > 0$) or do not vary ($\sigma_\mu^2 = 0.$). A negative variance is meaningless. For this reason, the alternative hypothesis is always a greater than statement. There are four assumptions we must make to compute the one-way between-subjects ANOVA:

1. *Normality.* We assume that data in the population or populations being sampled from are normally distributed. This assumption is particularly important for small sample sizes. In larger samples, the overall variance is reduced, and this assumption becomes less critical as a result.

2. *Random sampling.* We assume that the data we measure were obtained from a sample that was selected using a random sampling procedure. It is generally considered inappropriate to conduct hypothesis tests with nonrandom samples.

3. *Independence.* We assume that the probabilities of each measured outcome in a study are independent or equal. Using random sampling usually satisfies this assumption.

NOTE: Four assumptions for a one-way between-subjects ANOVA are normality, random sampling, independence, and homogeneity of variance.

4. *Homogeneity of variance.* We assume that the variance in each population is equal to each other. Violating this assumption can inflate the value of the variance in the numerator of the test statistic, thereby increasing the likelihood of committing a Type I error (incorrectly rejecting the null hypothesis).

Also, an analysis of variance is used to measure variability across groups. Because we compute variance across groups, the sample size (*n*) must be equal in each group—it is necessary that the same number of scores are averaged in each group. Most researchers plan for equal samples by making sure that the same number of participants is observed in each group. Sometimes this is too difficult or impractical to accomplish. In these circumstances, the best alternative is to increase the sample size to minimize problems associated with averaging a different number of scores in each group.

In Example 12.1, we will follow the four steps in hypothesis testing to compute a one-way between-subjects ANOVA.

A psychologist wants to determine whether having a job interferes with student academic performance. She measures academic performance as a grade point average (GPA) score on the 4.0 GPA scale, where higher scores indicate better performance. She selects a sample of 30 students—10 did not work, 10 worked part-time, and 10 worked full-time during the previous semester—and records their GPA. The data for this hypothetical study are given in Table 12.4. Conduct an analysis of variance at a .05 level of significance.

EXAMPLE 12.1

TABLE 12.4   The grade point average (GPA) of students who did not work, worked part-time, or worked full-time during a semester that grades were recorded.

Work Status			
No Work	**Part-Time**	**Full-Time**	$k = 3$
3.40	3.50	2.90	
3.20	3.60	3.00	
3.00	2.70	2.60	
3.00	3.50	3.30	
3.50	3.80	3.70	
3.80	2.90	2.70	
3.60	3.40	2.40	
4.00	3.20	2.50	
3.90	3.30	3.30	
2.90	3.10	3.40	
$n_1 = 10$	$n_2 = 10$	$n_3 = 10$	$N = k \times n = 30$

Step 1: State the hypotheses. The null hypothesis states that group means in the population do not vary (=); the alternative hypothesis states that group means in the population do vary (>):

$H_0: \sigma_\mu^2 = 0$ Mean GPA scores do not vary between groups in the student population.

$H_0: \sigma_\mu^2 > 0$ Mean GPA scores vary between groups in the student population.

Step 2: Set the criteria for a decision. The level of significance for this test is .05. The degrees of freedom between groups is $k - 1$:

$$df_{BG} = 3 - 1 = 2.$$

The degrees of freedom error is $N - k$:

$$df_E = 30 - 3 = 27.$$

To locate the critical value for an ANOVA with 2 and 27 degrees of freedom, find where 2 and 27 intersect in Table B3 in Appendix B. The critical value for this test is 3.35. Figure 12.4 shows where this critical value falls in an F-distribution. The region in the upper tail is the rejection region for this test.

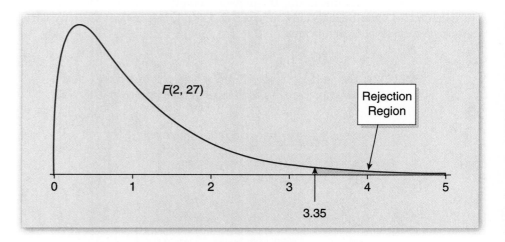

FIGURE 12.4

The F-distribution with 2 and 27 degrees of freedom. The alpha level (α) is placed in the upper tail at or above 3.35.

NOTE: The rejection region is always located in the upper tail of the F-distribution, so the critical value is always positive.

We will compare the value of the test statistic with this critical value. If the value of the test statistic falls beyond the critical value (greater than 3.35), then we reject the null hypothesis; otherwise, we retain the null hypothesis.

Step 3: Compute the test statistic. We compute the F-statistic to determine whether a significant amount of the total variance in a study is attributed to differences between group means relative to variance attributed to error. The test statistic is the variance between groups (MS_{BG}) divided by error variance (MS_E):

$$F_{obt} = \frac{MS_{BG}}{MS_E}.$$

There are many different ways to compute a mean square. We will describe this analysis in four stages: preliminary calculations, intermediate calculations, compute the sum of squares, and complete the F-table.

Stage 1: Preliminary calculations: Find Σx, G, Σx^2, Σx_T^2, n, and k. These preliminary calculations are shown in Table 12.5. Each calculation made in the table is described here.

TABLE 12.5 Preliminary calculations for the one-way between-subjects analysis of variance in Example 12.1.

	Work Status		
No Work	**Part-Time**	**Full-Time**	← **k = 3**
3.40	3.50	2.90	
3.20	3.60	3.00	
3.00	2.70	2.60	
3.00	3.50	3.30	
3.50	3.80	3.70	
3.80	2.90	2.70	
3.60	3.40	2.40	
4.00	3.20	2.50	
3.90	3.30	3.30	
2.90	3.10	3.40	
$n_1 = 10$	$n_2 = 10$	$n_3 = 10$	$N = 30$
$\Sigma x_1 = 34.30$	$\Sigma x_2 = 33.00$	$\Sigma x_3 = 29.80$	$\Sigma x_T = 97.10$
$\Sigma x_1^2 = 119.07$	$\Sigma x_2^2 = 109.90$	$\Sigma x_3^2 = 90.50$	$\Sigma x_T^2 = 319.47$

1. Find k and n. We have three groups, $k = 3$, and 10 participants are in each group, $n = 10$.

2. Find Σx and G. Sum the scores in each group: Σx. The grand total (Σx_T) is the sum of scores in all groups combined.

3. Find Σx^2 and Σx_T^2. Square each score, and then sum the squared scores in each group: Σx^2. The sum of the squared scores in all groups combined is Σx_T^2.

Stage 2: Compute intermediate calculations: Find [1], [2], and [3]. In Stage 1, we computed the values needed to make calculations in Stage 2. There are three calculations in Stage 2:

First, we compute a correction factor by squaring the grand total (Σx_T) and dividing by the total sample size (N):

$$[1] \quad \frac{\left(\sum x_T\right)^2}{N} = \frac{(97.10)^2}{30} = 314.28.$$

Second, we divide the sum of squared scores in each group by the sample size in each group:

$$[2] \quad \sum \frac{x^2}{n} = \frac{(34.30)^2}{10} + \frac{(33.00)^2}{10} + \frac{(29.80)^2}{10} = 315.35.$$

Third, we restate the sum of the squared scores in all groups combined:

$$[3] \sum x_T^2 = 319.47.$$

NOTE: In Stage 3, we compute the numerator (SS) for the variance between and within groups.

We can use these values to compute sum of squares (*SS*) for each source of variation in the ANOVA. *SS* is the numerator for variance (see Chapter 4). Hence, the calculations we make in Stage 3 will give us the numerator in the formula for variance for each source of variation.

Stage 3: Compute the sum of squares (*SS*) for each source of variation.

The **sum of squares between groups** (SS_{BG}) is the difference between Calculation [2] and Calculation [1] in Stage 2:

$$SS_{BG} = [2] - [1] = 315.35 - 314.28 = 1.07.$$

The **sum of squares total** (SS_T) is the difference between Calculation [3] and Calculation [1] in Stage 2:

$$SS_T = [3] - [1] = = 319.47 - 314.28 = 5.19.$$

The **sum of squares error** (SS_E) is the sum of squares total minus the sum of squares between groups:

$$SS_E = SS_T = SS_{BG} = 5.19 - 1.07 = 4.12.$$

DEFINITION

Sum of squares between groups (SS_{BG}) is the sum of squares attributed to variability between groups.

Sum of squares total (SS_T) is the overall sum of squares across all groups.

Sum of squares within groups, or **sum of squares error (SS_E)**, is the sum of squares attributed to variability within each group.

Stage 4: Complete the *F*-table. The *F*-table lists the sum of squares (*SS*), degrees of freedom (*df*), mean squares (*MS*), and the value of the test statistic. The calculations in the table are described below and are listed in Table 12.6. Table 12.7 is the completed *F*-table.

TABLE 12.6 An *F*-table with the formulas for completing the table.

Source of Variation	SS	df	MS	F_{obt}
Between groups	1.07	$k - 1 = 2$	$\dfrac{SS_{BG}}{df_{BG}}$	$\dfrac{MS_{BG}}{MS_E}$
Within groups (error)	4.12	$N - k = 27$	$\dfrac{SS_E}{df_E}$	
Total	5.19	$N - 1 = 29$		

The first column of values in the *F*-table lists the sum of squares (we computed *SS* in Stage 3). The second column lists the degrees of freedom (we computed *df* in Stage 2). We will use these values to compute the mean squares for the test statistic. The formula for variance is *SS* divided by *df*, so we divide across each row to compute each mean square.

To compute the variance or mean square between groups, we divide SS_{BG} by df_{BG}:

$$MS_{BG} = \frac{SS_{BG}}{df_{BG}} = \frac{1.07}{2} = 0.535.$$

Likewise, to compute the variance or mean square error, we divide SS_E by df_E:

$$MS_E = \frac{SS_E}{df_E} = \frac{4.12}{27} = 0.152.$$

The formula for the test statistic is mean square between groups (0.535) divided by mean square error (0.152):

$$F_{obt} = \frac{MS_{BG}}{MS_E} = \frac{0.535}{0.152} = 3.52.$$

TABLE 12.7 The completed *F*-table for Example 12.1. An asterisk (*) next to the *F*-statistic indicates significance or a decision to reject the null hypothesis.

Source of Variation	SS	df	MS	F_{obt}
Between groups	1.07	2	0.535	3.52*
Within groups (error)	4.12	27	0.152	
Total	5.19	29		

NOTE: The mean squares for each source of variation are computed by dividing SS by df for each source of variation.

Step 4: Make a decision. To make a decision, we compare the obtained value to the critical value. As shown in Figure 12.5, the obtained value (3.52) is greater than the critical value (3.35); it falls in the rejection region. The decision is to reject the null hypothesis.

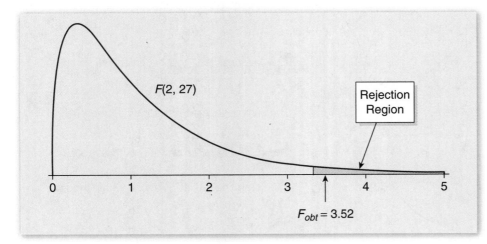

FIGURE 12.5

The test statistic, F_{obt}, reaches the rejection region, so we choose to reject the null hypothesis. At least one pair of group means significantly differs.

TABLE 12.8 The steps used to compute a one-way between-subjects ANOVA.

Steps for Computing a One-Way Between-Subjects ANOVA		
Terminology	**Statement**	**Meaning**
Step 1: State the hypotheses		
Null hypothesis	$\sigma_\mu^2 = 0$	Population means do not vary.
Alternative hypothesis	$\sigma_\mu^2 > 0$	Population means do vary.
Step 2: Set the criteria for a decision		
Degrees of freedom between groups	$df_{BG} = k - 1$	The number of groups minus 1
Degrees of freedom error	$df_E = N - k$	The number of total participants minus the number of groups
Degrees of freedom total	$df_T = N - 1$	The number of total participants minus 1
Step 3: Compute test statistic		
STAGE 1		
Groups	k	The number of groups or levels of a factor
Participants	n, N	The number of participants per group (n) and overall (N)
Grand total	$\sum x_T$	The sum of all scores in a study
Total sum of squared scores	$\sum x_T^2$	The sum of all scores individually squared in a study
STAGE 2		
[1]	$\dfrac{\left(\sum x_T\right)^2}{N}$	The correction factor
[2]	$\sum \dfrac{x^2}{n}$	The "uncorrected" variation between groups
[3]	$\sum x_T^2$	The "uncorrected" total variation in a study
STAGE 3		
Sum of squares between groups	$SS_{BG} = [2] - [1]$	The sum of squared deviations between groups
Sum of squares total	$SS_T = [3] - [1]$	The sum of squared deviations in all groups
Sum of squares error	$SS_T = SS_T - SS_{BG}$	The sum of squared deviations within groups (error)

Steps for Computing a One-Way Between-Subjects ANOVA		
Terminology	**Statement**	**Meaning**
STAGE 4		
Mean square between groups	$MS_{BG} = \dfrac{SS_{BG}}{df_{BG}}$	The variance between groups. This is the numerator for the test statistic.
Mean square error	$MS_E = \dfrac{SS_E}{df_E}$	The variance within groups (error). This is the denominator for the F-statistic.
F-statistic formula	$F_{obt} = \dfrac{MS_{BG}}{MS_E}$	The obtained value of the test statistic for an ANOVA
Step 4: Make a decision		
Decision criterion	—	When $F_{obt} < F_{crit}$, retain the null. When $F_{obt} \geq F_{crit}$, reject the null.

Table 12.8 summarizes the procedures used to compute a one-way between-subjects ANOVA. If we were to report the result for Example 12.1 in a research journal, it would look something like this:

> The one-way analysis of variance showed that academic performance (measured on a 4.0 GPA scale) varied depending on whether students did not work, worked part-time, or worked full-time during the semester, $F(2, 27) = 3.52$, $p < .05$.

MAKING SENSE: Mean Squares and Variance

To compute a variance, or mean square, we compute sum of squares (SS), which is the numerator for sample variance, and degrees of freedom (df), which is the denominator for sample variance:

$$\text{Sample variance} = \frac{SS}{df}.$$

For an ANOVA, the formula is the same. To find the variance or mean square attributed to differences between groups, we divide SS_{BG} by df_{BG}. To find the variance or mean square attributed to error, we divide SS_E by df_E. The procedures for computing SS and df for an ANOVA may be a bit different, but the formula for variance is still the same. Computing a mean square is the same as computing a variance:

$$MS = \frac{SS}{df} \text{ for between-groups and error variance.}$$

The test statistic for an ANOVA, then, is a ratio used to determine whether the variance attributed to differences between groups (MS_{BG}) is significantly larger than the variance attributed to error (MS_E).

12.6 WHAT IS THE NEXT STEP?

When the decision is to retain the null hypothesis for an ANOVA, we stop the analysis. No pairs of group means are significantly different. As shown in Figure 12.6, following a decision to retain the null hypothesis, we stop, start over, think of an alternative study, and begin again.

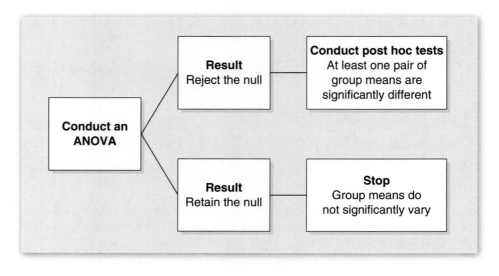

FIGURE 12.6

Following an ANOVA. A decision chart for when to compute post hoc tests.

NOTE: *When the ANOVA is significant, conduct post hoc tests to determine which pair or pairs of group means significantly differ. When the ANOVA is not significant, stop; no group means significantly differ.*

The decision in Example 12.1 was to reject the null hypothesis: The test was significant. A significant ANOVA indicates that at least one pair of group means significantly differs. However, this test does not tell us which pairs of means differ. To determine which pairs differ, we compute **post hoc tests** or "after-the-fact" tests. These tests analyze differences for all possible pairs of group means, called **pairwise comparisons.** With only two groups ($k = 2$), post hoc tests are not needed because only one pair of group means can be compared. With more than two groups ($k > 2$), multiple comparisons must be made, and so post hoc tests are necessary.

Pairwise comparisons are still necessary for Example 12.1, which means that our calculations are not yet complete. We still need to determine which pair or pairs of group means significantly differ. Figure 12.6 displays a decision chart for determining when it is appropriate to compute post hoc tests. In Section 12.7, we describe various procedures for performing post hoc tests.

DEFINITION

A **post hoc test** is a statistical procedure computed following a significant ANOVA to determine which pair or pairs of group means significantly differ. These tests are necessary when $k > 2$ because multiple comparisons are needed. When $k = 2$, the two means must significantly differ; this is the only comparison.

A **pairwise comparison** is a statistical comparison for the difference between two group means. A post hoc test evaluates all possible pairwise comparisons for an ANOVA with any number of groups.

1. State the four assumptions for the one-way between-subjects ANOVA.

2. What is the alternative hypothesis for the one-way between-subjects ANOVA?

3. Given the following computations, compute SS_T: $\Sigma x_T = 70$, $N = 25$, $\Sigma x_T^2 = 220$.

4. If $SS_{BG} = 40$ in a one-way between-subjects ANOVA with five groups, what is the numerator of the F-statistic?

5. Make a decision given the following values for the F-statistic in a test with 3 and 20 degrees of freedom.

   a. $F_{obt} = 3.05$ b. $F_{obt} = 4.00$ c. $F_{obt} = 5.35$

6. A mean square is the same as what descriptive statistic?

Answers: 1. Normality, random sampling, independence, and homogeneity of variance; 2. Group means vary in the population ($\sigma_\mu^2 > 0$); 3. $SS_T = 220 - 196 = 24$; 4. $MS_{BG} = \dfrac{40}{4} = 10$; 5. (a) Retain the null hypothesis, (b) Reject the null hypothesis, (c) Reject the null hypothesis; 6. Variance.

POST HOC COMPARISONS 12.7

All post hoc tests begin by making pairwise comparisons for each pair of group means. The mean GPAs in the three groups in Example 12.1 are 3.43 (Group No Work), 3.30 (Group Part-Time), and 2.98 (Group Full-Time). A post hoc test will determine if the differences between pairs of group means are significantly different. In Example 12.1, there are three possible pairwise comparisons:

Comparison 1:   No work and full-time: 3.43 – 2.98 = 0.45.

Comparison 2:   Part-time and full-time: 3.30 – 2.98 = 0.32.

Comparison 3:   No work and part-time: 3.43 – 3.30 = 0.13.

All post hoc tests are aimed at making sure that no matter how many tests we compute, the overall likelihood of committing a Type I error is .05. In other words, all post hoc tests control for **experimentwise alpha,** which is the overall alpha level for multiple tests conducted on the same data.

NOTE: Experimentwise alpha is the alpha level stated for multiple tests conducted on the same data.

> **Experimentwise alpha** is the alpha level, or overall probability of committing a Type I error when multiple tests are conducted on the same data.

DEFINITION

In Example 12.1, we state an experimentwise alpha equal to .05 for all tests. Post hoc tests are used to control for experimentwise alpha, thereby making the overall alpha or probability of a Type I error for all pairwise comparisons or tests equal to .05. Figure 12.7 lists five tests used to control for experimentwise alpha. The tests in the figure are listed from most conservative (associated with the least power) to most liberal (associated with the greatest power).

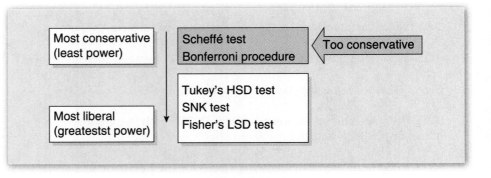

For a between-subjects test, the two most conservative tests are the Scheffé test and the Bonferroni procedure. For a between-subjects design, both post hoc tests tend to be too conservative—in a way, these post hoc tests do too good of a job of controlling for experimentwise alpha. However, the Bonferroni procedure is only too conservative when the number of pairwise comparisons is greater than three. Because we are making three pairwise comparisons in Example 12.1, this procedure would not be too conservative in this case.

The remaining three post hoc tests are Fisher's least significant difference (LSD), Studentized Newman-Keuls (SNK), and Tukey's honestly significant difference (HSD) tests. Each test has drawbacks as well, although all tend to have a better balance between making it too easy (too liberal) or too difficult (too conservative) to reject the null hypothesis. In this section, we will describe the most conservative (Tukey's HSD) and the most liberal (Fisher's LSD) of these post hoc tests. To compute each post hoc test, follow three steps (only Step 2 is different for each test):

Step 1: Compute the test statistic for each pair of group means.

Step 2: Compute the critical value for each pairwise comparison.

Step 3: Make a decision to retain or reject the null hypothesis.

Step 1: Compute the test statistic for each pair of group means. We compute a test statistic for each pairwise comparison. The test statistic for each pairwise comparison is the difference between the largest and the smallest group mean. We compute the test statistic the same for both post hoc tests. The test statistic for each comparison is as follows:

Comparison 1: 3.43 − 2.98 = 0.45

Comparison 2: 3.30 − 2.98 = 0.32

Comparison 3: 3.43 − 3.30 = 0.13

We will compare the value of the test statistic we computed in Step 1 with the critical value we will compute in Step 2. In Step 3, we make a decision. The decision for each pairwise comparison is to retain or reject the null hypothesis. The null hypothesis is that there is no mean difference between two groups. The alternative hypothesis is that there is a mean difference between two groups. When the test statistic is larger than the critical value, we reject the null hypothesis; otherwise, we retain the null hypothesis.

FISHER'S LEAST SIGNIFICANT DIFFERENCE (LSD) TEST

Fisher's LSD test, also called the protected t-test, is the most liberal post hoc test allowed in published research studies. It has the lowest critical values acceptable, which increases the power to detect an effect or mean difference between two groups. Also, this test does not require that the number of participants in each group is equal. We computed the test statistic for each pairwise comparison in Step 1. Here, we will compute the critical value (Step 2) and make a decision (Step 3).

NOTE: Fisher's LSD is the most liberal acceptable post hoc test. This test is associated with the greatest power to detect an effect in the population.

Step 2: Compute the critical value for each pairwise comparison. The critical value is computed using the following statistic:

$$\text{Fisher's LSD: } t_\alpha \sqrt{MS_E\left(\frac{1}{n_1}+\frac{1}{n_2}\right)}.$$

In this formula, t_α is the critical value for a two-tailed t-test at a .05 level of significance. The degrees of freedom are df_E from Table 12.7: $df_E = 27$. To locate the critical value, we find 27 in the t-table in Table B.2 in Appendix B and look under the proportion in two tails column: $t(27) = 2.052$. In Table 12.7, $MS_E = 0.152$, and we know that $n = 10$ per group. Substitute these values into the Fisher's LSD formula. The critical value for this test is

$$2.052\sqrt{0.152\left(\frac{1}{10}+\frac{1}{10}\right)} = 0.36.$$

Step 3: Make a decision to retain or reject the null hypothesis. The value 0.36 is the critical value for each pairwise comparison. For each comparison, we decide that the two groups are significantly different if the test statistic is larger than the critical value we computed. The decision for each comparison is given below (an asterisk is included to indicate significance where appropriate):

Comparison 1: No work and full-time: $3.43 - 2.98 = 0.45*$ (reject the null hypothesis; this value is larger than 0.36)

Comparison 2: Part-time and full-time: $3.30 - 2.98 = 0.32$ (retain the null hypothesis; this value is less than 0.36)

Comparison 3: No work and part-time: $3.43 - 3.30 = 0.13$ (retain the null hypothesis; this value is less than 0.36).

We conclude that working full-time is associated with significantly lower GPA scores compared to those who do not work at all. This was the only significant difference. If we were to report this result in a research journal, it would look something like this:

The one-way analysis of variance reached significance, $F(2, 27) = 3.52$, $p < .05$, with semester GPA scores being significantly lower among students working full-time compared to those who did not work during the semester (Fisher LSD, $p < .05$). Otherwise, no significant differences were evident ($p > .05$).

TUKEY'S HONESTLY SIGNIFICANT DIFFERENCE (HSD) TEST

An alternative post hoc test is Tukey's HSD test. This test is more conservative than Fisher's LSD test in that the critical values are larger for each pairwise comparison. We computed the test statistic for each pairwise comparison in Step 1. Again, Step 1 is the same for Fisher's LSD and Tukey's HSD tests. Here, we will compute the critical value (Step 2) and make a decision (Step 3).

Step 2: Compute the critical value for each pairwise comparison. The critical value is computed using the following statistic:

$$\text{Tukey's HSD} : q_\alpha \sqrt{\frac{MS_E}{n}}.$$

In this formula, q is the **studentized range statistic.** We must find this value in the studentized range statistic table in Table B.4 in Appendix B. Table 12.9 shows a portion of this table. To locate values for q in Table B.4, we need to know df_E and the real range (r). For Tukey's HSD test, the real range, r, is equal to the number of groups, k, in a study. In Example 12.1, we observed three groups; therefore, $r = 3$.

TABLE 12.9 A portion of the studentized range statistic table in Table B.4 in Appendix B.

df_E	Range 2	Range 3	Range 4	Range 5
6	3.46	4.34	4.90	5.30
	5.24	6.32	7.02	7.55
7	3.34	4.17	4.68	5.06
	4.95	5.91	6.54	7.00
8	3.26	4.05	4.53	4.89
	4.75	5.64	6.21	6.63
9	3.20	3.95	4.42	4.76
	4.60	5.43	5.95	6.34
10	3.15	3.88	4.33	4.66
	4.48	5.27	5.77	6.14
11	3.11	3.82	4.27	4.59
	4.38	5.16	5.63	5.98
12	3.08	3.78	4.20	4.51
	4.32	5.05	5.50	5.84

The **studentized range statistic (*q*)** is a statistic used to determine critical values for comparing pairs of means at a given range. This statistic is used in the formula to find the critical value for Tukey's HSD post hoc test.

DEFINITION

In Table B.4, we go across to 3 in the columns and down to 27 (the value for df_E) in the rows. Because 27 is not in the table, the most conservative rule is to use the next smallest value, which is 26 in the table. We use the q value at 3 and 26: $q = 3.52$. For this test, $MS_E = 0.152$ and $n = 10$, and the critical value for Tukey's HSD is

$$3.52\sqrt{\frac{0.152}{10}} = 0.43.$$

Step 3: Make a decision to retain or reject the null hypothesis. The value 0.43 is the critical value for each pairwise comparison. For each comparison, we decide that the two groups are significantly different if the test statistic is larger than the critical value we computed. The decision for each comparison is given below (an asterisk is included to indicate significance where appropriate):

Comparison 1: No work and full-time: 3.43 − 2.98 = 0.45* (reject the null hypothesis; this value is larger than 0.43)

Comparison 2: Part-time and full-time: 3.30 − 2.98 = 0.32 (retain the null hypothesis; this value is less than 0.43)

Comparison 3: No work and part-time: 3.43 − 3.30 = 0.13 (retain the null hypothesis; this value is less than 0.43)

We conclude that working full-time is associated with significantly lower GPA scores compared to not working at all. This was the only significant difference. Both post hoc tests produced the same result. If we were to report this result in a research journal, it would look something like this:

The one-way analysis of variance reached significance, $F(2, 27) = 3.52$, $p < .05$, with semester GPA scores being significantly lower among students working full-time compared to those who did not work during the semester (Tukey's HSD, $p < .05$). Otherwise, no significant differences were evident ($p > .05$).

In Example 12.1, an SNK test and Bonferroni procedure would have found the same result as the two post hoc tests introduced in this chapter. However, be cautious when using the Bonferroni procedure because as k increases, this post hoc procedure becomes too conservative for a between-subjects design. If we had computed a Scheffé test, we would have retained the null hypothesis for all pairwise comparisons. Deciding that all pairwise comparisons are not significant is unacceptable. A fair post hoc test must show that at least one pair of group means significantly differs following a significant ANOVA. Otherwise, the post hoc test is too conservative.

✓ LEARNING CHECK 4

1. All post hoc tests compute critical values that control for what value?

2. Place each test in order from most conservative to most liberal: Tukey's HSD, Fisher's LSD.

3. The following is an ANOVA summary table for a significant result ($p < .05$):

	SS	df	MS	F_{obt}
Between groups	66.08	2	33.04	3.815
Error	181.88	21	8.66	
Total	247.96	23		

If the means in each group were 4.00 (Group A), 6.63 (Group B), and 8.00 (Group C), then which pairs of groups are significantly different using the following tests:

a. Fisher's LSD

b. Tukey's HSD

Answers: 1. Experimentwise alpha; 2. Tukey's HSD and Fisher's LSD; 3. (a) Only Group A and Group C significantly differ; (b) Only Group A and Group C significantly differ.

12.8 SPSS IN FOCUS: THE ONE-WAY BETWEEN-SUBJECTS ANOVA

There are two commands for computing a one-way between-subjects ANOVA using SPSS—the One-Way ANOVA and the GLM Univariate commands. We will use both commands to analyze Example 12.1. Using the data given in Table 12.4, we will confirm our conclusion using the **One-Way ANOVA** command:

1. Click on the **variable view** tab and enter *groups* in the **name column.** Go to the **decimals column** for this row only and reduce the value to 0 (we use only whole numbers to code groups). To label the groups, click on the small gray box with three dots in the **values column** to display a **dialog box.** In the **dialog box,** enter *1* in the value cell and *No work* in the label cell, and then click **add;** enter *2* in the value cell and *Part-time* in the label cell, and then click **add;** enter *3* in the value cell and *Full-time* in the label cell, and then click **add.** Click **OK.**

2. Still in the **variable view,** enter *gpa* in the name column in the second row. We will list GPA scores to the tenths place, so go to the **decimals column** for this row only and reduce the value to 1.

3. Click on the **data view** tab. In the *groups* column, enter *1* down the first 10 cells, *2* down the next 10 cells, and *3* down the next 10 cells. These values (1, 2, and 3) are the codes for each group. In the *gpa* column, enter the GPA scores in the cells that correspond with the codes for each group listed in the first column.

4. Go to the **menu bar** and click **Analyze,** then **Compare Means,** and **One-Way ANOVA** to display the dialog box shown in Figure 12.8.

5. Using the appropriate arrows, move *groups* into the **Factor:** box to identify the groups. Move *gpa* into the **Dependent List:** box.

6. Click the **Post Hoc** option to display the new dialog box shown in Figure 12.9. Notice that every post hoc test discussed in Section 12.7 is an option in SPSS. Select Fisher's LSD and Tukey's HSD (this differs from the Tukey-b option) and click **Continue.**

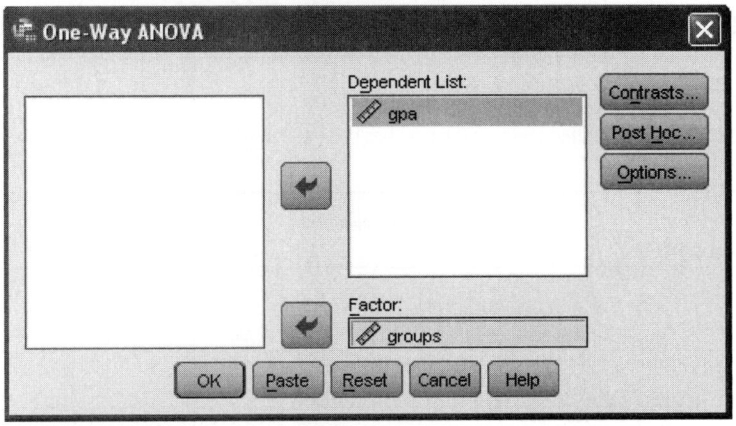

FIGURE 12.8

Dialog box for Steps 4 to 5.

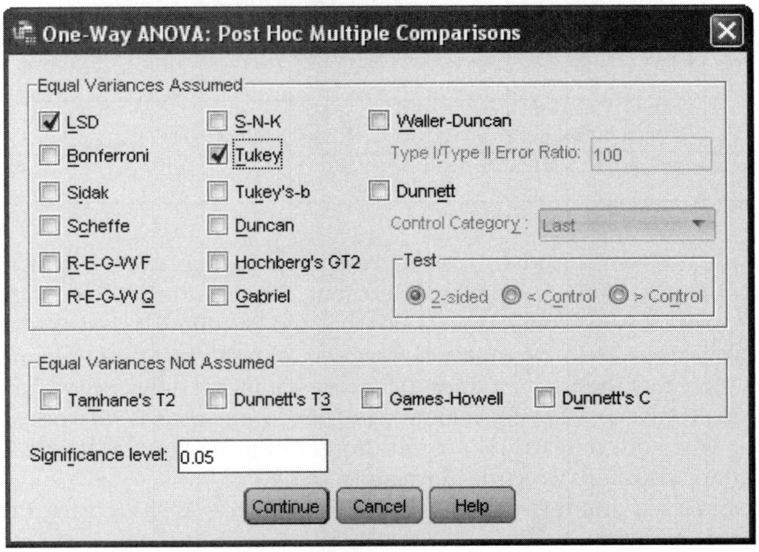

FIGURE 12.9

Dialog box for Step 6.

7. Select **Paste** and click the **Run** command.

Notice that the ANOVA table, shown in Table 12.10, is the same as the one we computed for Example 12.1. In addition, SPSS gives with the exact p value for this test in the last column. Table 12.11 displays the SPSS output for the post hoc tests.

TABLE 12.10 The SPSS output *F*-table using the One-Way ANOVA command.

ANOVA

gpa

	Sum of Squares	df	Mean Square	F	Sig.
Between Groups	1.073	2	.536	3.517	.044
Within Groups	4.117	27	.152		
Total	5.190	29			

TABLE 12.11 The SPSS output table for the post hoc comparisons using Tukey's HSD and Fisher's LSD.

Multiple Comparisons

Dependent Variable:gpa

	(I) groups	(J) groups	Mean Difference (I-J)	Std. Error	Sig.	95% Confidence Interval Lower Bound	95% Confidence Interval Upper Bound
Tukey HSD	No work	Part-time	.1300	.1746	.740	-.303	.563
		Full-time	.4500*	.1746	.040	.017	.883
	Part-time	No work	-.1300	.1746	.740	-.563	.303
		Full-time	.3200	.1746	.178	-.113	.753
	Full-time	No work	-.4500*	.1746	.040	-.883	-.017
		Part-time	-.3200	.1746	.178	-.753	.113
LSD	No work	Part-time	.1300	.1746	.463	-.228	.488
		Full-time	.4500*	.1746	.016	.092	.808
	Part-time	No work	-.1300	.1746	.463	-.488	.228
		Full-time	.3200	.1746	.078	-.038	.678
	Full-time	No work	-.4500*	.1746	.016	-.808	-.092
		Part-time	-.3200	.1746	.078	-.678	.038

*. The mean difference is significant at the 0.05 level.

The post hoc comparisons in Table 12.11 label each group. At the top, you see No work with Part-time; Full-time is placed next to it. You read the table as comparisons across the rows. The first comparison is No work and Part-time. If there is no asterisk next to the value given in the **mean difference** column, then those two means do not differ (note that the *p* value, which indicates a significant difference when smaller than .05, is also given in the **Sig.** column). The next comparison is No work and Full-time. This post hoc comparison is significant, as indicated by the asterisk, which confirms the conclusions we made in Example 12.1.

We can also compute the one-way between-subjects ANOVA using the **GLM Univariate** command:

1. Follow Steps 1 to 3 from the steps given for the One-Way ANOVA command.

2. Go to the **menu bar** and click **Analyze,** then **General Linear Model,** and **Univariate** to display the dialog box shown in Figure 12.10.

3. Using the appropriate arrows, move *groups* into the **Fixed Factor(s):** box to identify the groups. Move *gpa* into the **Dependent Variable:** box.

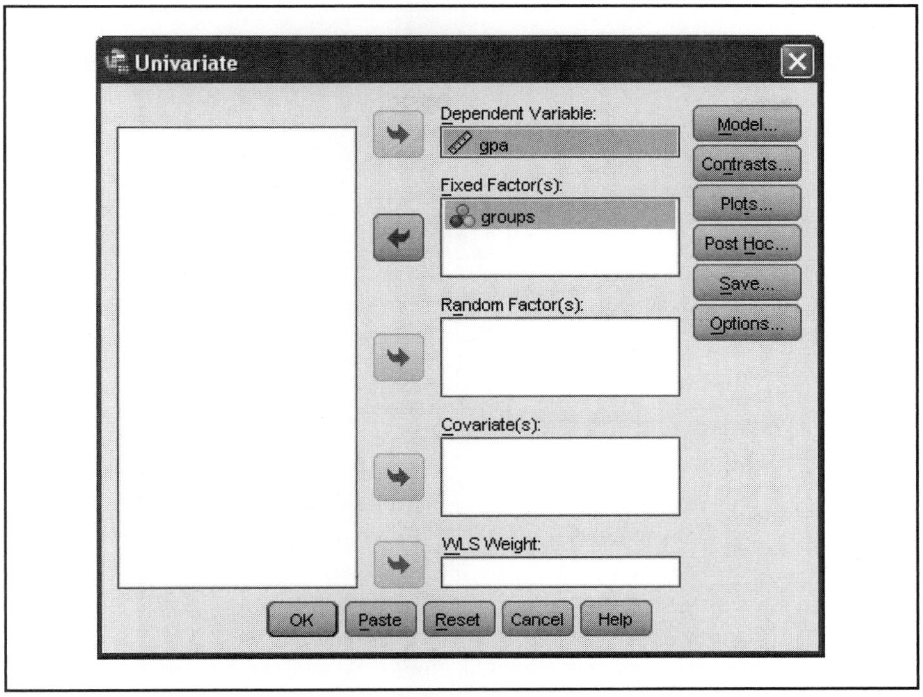

FIGURE 12.10

Dialog box for Steps 2 to 3.

4. Select the **Post Hoc** option to display a new dialog box that will allow you to select a post hoc test. You can also select **Options** to display the new dialog box shown in Figure 12.11. Select **Observed power** and click **Continue.**

5. Select **Paste** and click the **Run** command.

The ANOVA table, shown in Table 12.12, is a bit more detailed than the ANOVA table in Table 12.10. To read Table 12.12, read only the rows labeled groups (between-group variation), error, and corrected total—ignore the rest of the table. The values in this table are again the same as those we computed for Example 12.1.

The advantage of using the **GLM Univariate** command is that it allows you to compute the **observed power.** In the last column we find the observed power is .606, meaning that if these results reflect a true effect in the population, then we can expect to detect the effect in about 61% of the samples we select from this population.

Observed power is a type of post hoc or retrospective power analysis that is used to estimate the likelihood of detecting a population effect, assuming that the observed results in a study reflect a true effect in the population.

Be aware that there is a lot of criticism for estimating power this way (for a detailed review, see Hoenig & Heisey, 2001).

DEFINITION

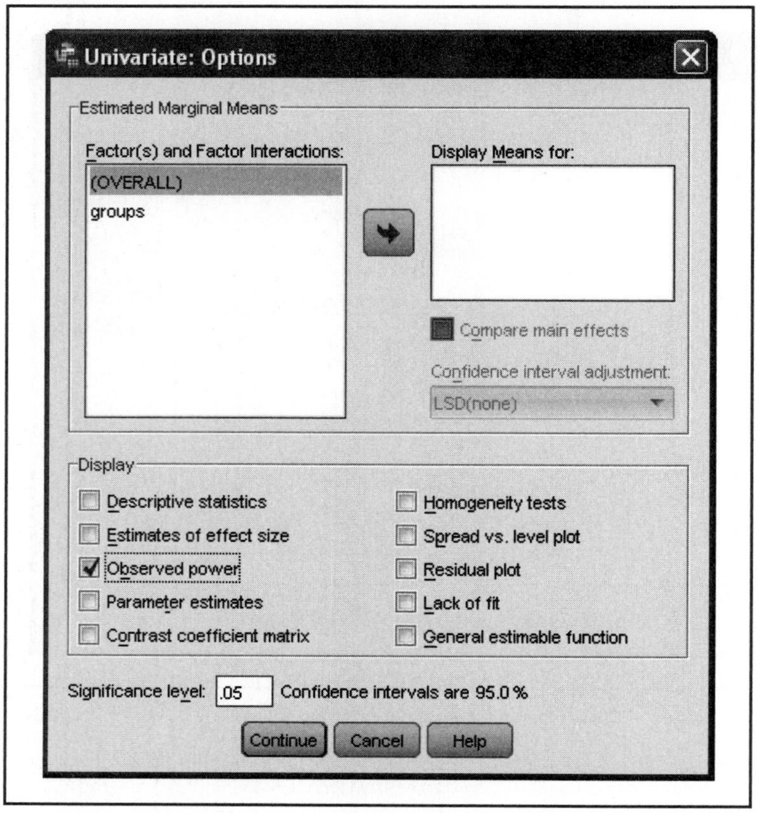

FIGURE 12.11

Dialog box for Steps 4.

TABLE 12.12 The SPSS output *F*-table using the GLM Univariate command.

Tests of Between-Subjects Effects

Dependent Variable:gpa

Source	Type III Sum of Squares	df	Mean Square	F	Sig.	Noncent. Parameter	Observed Power[b]
Corrected Model	1.073[a]	2	.536	3.517	.044	7.035	.606
Intercept	314.280	1	314.280	2061.105	.000	2061.105	1.000
groups	1.073	2	.536	3.517	.044	7.035	.606
Error	4.117	27	.152				
Total	319.470	30					
Corrected Total	5.190	29					

a. R Squared = .207 (Adjusted R Squared = .148)
b. Computed using alpha = .05

These middle two rows and the last row give a summary of the one-way between-subjects ANOVA, similar to the ANOVA table given in Table 12.10.

MEASURING EFFECT SIZE   12.9

An ANOVA determines whether group means significantly vary in the population. In Example 12.1, we concluded that mean GPA scores significantly varied by the type of work status (no work, part-time, full-time). We can also determine the size of this variance in the population by computing the measure of effect size, called proportion of variance.

Proportion of variance estimates how much of the variability in the dependent variable can be accounted for by the levels of the factor. In Example 12.1, the dependent variable is GPA scores, and the levels of the factor or work status are no work, part-time, and full-time. Proportion of variance will measure how much variability in GPA scores can be accounted for by work status. The two measures of proportion of variance are eta-squared (η^2 or R^2) and omega-squared (ω^2).

ETA-SQUARED (η^2 OR R^2)

One measure for effect size is eta-squared. When this measure is used with the ANOVA, the symbol R^2 may be used instead of η^2. Eta-squared is computed as the sum of squares between groups divided by the sum of squares total:

$$R^2 = \eta^2 = \frac{SS_{BG}}{SS_T}.$$

In Example 12.1, Table 12.7 shows that $SS_{BG} = 1.07$ and $SS_T = 5.19$. The value for eta-squared is

$$\eta^2 = \frac{1.07}{5.19} = 0.21.$$

We conclude that 21% of the variability in GPA scores can be explained by the work status of students. Based on the effect size conventions listed in Table 9.3 in Chapter 9, this is a medium effect size and is the same value listed at the bottom of the SPSS output table in Table 12.12 for R-squared (in the table this value is equal to .207, and we have rounded up). Here is how we might report eta-squared with the significant result:

NOTE: Eta-squared is often reported as R^2 for an analysis of variance test.

> The one-way analysis of variance showed that semester GPA scores varied depending on the work status of students, $F(2, 27) = 3.52$, $p < .05$ ($R^2 = 0.21$).

As for the *t*-test, eta-squared is biased in that it tends to overestimate the proportion of variance explained by the levels of a factor. To correct for the overestimate, we can use omega-squared to estimate proportion of variance.

OMEGA-SQUARED (ω^2)

Omega-squared is also a measure of the variability explained by the levels of a factor, divided by the total variability observed. This estimate has two advantages over eta-squared:

1. It corrects for the size of error by including MS_E in the formula.

2. It corrects for the number of groups by including the degrees of freedom between groups (df_{BG}) in the formula.

The formula for omega-squared is

$$\omega^2 = \frac{SS_{BG} - df_{BG}(MS_E)}{SS_T + MS_E}.$$

In Example 12.1, Table 12.7 shows that $SS_{BG} = 1.07$, $df_{BG} = 2$, $MS_E = 0.152$, and $SS_T = 5.19$. The value for omega-squared is:

$$\omega^2 = \frac{1.07 - 2(0.152)}{5.19 + 0.152} = 0.14.$$

NOTE: Omega-squared corrects for the number of groups and the size of error in an analysis of variance test.

We conclude that 14% of the variability in GPA scores can be explained by the work status of students. This is a smaller estimate than eta-squared but still a medium effect size. Here is how we might report omega-squared with the significant result:

The one-way analysis of variance showed that semester GPA scores varied depending on the work status of students, $F(2, 27) = 3.52$, $p < .05$ ($\omega^2 = 0.14$).

Again, different measures of effect size do not give us the same estimates, and there is little consensus as to which is the superior measure. This lack of consensus is something to be aware of when reading reports of effect size in scientific journals.

LEARNING CHECK 5

1. Compute effect size for this significant one-way between-subjects ANOVA using η^2 and ω^2.

	SS	df	MS	F
Between groups	66.08	2	33.04	3.815
Error	181.88	21	8.66	
Total	247.96	23		

2. Does eta-squared or omega-squared give a larger estimate of proportion of variance for the same data?

Answers: 1. $\eta^2 = \frac{66.08}{247.96} = 0.27$ (large effect), $\omega^2 = \frac{66.08 - 2(8.66)}{247.96 + 8.66} = 0.19$ (medium effect); 2. Eta-squared.

APA IN FOCUS: REPORTING THE *F*-STATISTIC, SIGNIFICANCE, AND EFFECT SIZE 12.10

To summarize the results of a one-way between-subjects ANOVA test, we report the test statistic, the degrees of freedom, and the *p* value. You should also report the effect size for significant analyses. You can summarize the means, standard error, or standard deviations measured in a study in a figure or a table or in the main text of the article. To report the results of a post hoc test, identify which post hoc test you computed and the *p* value for significant results. For example the following is an appropriate full summary for the results we stated for Example 12.1, using omega-squared as the estimate for effect size and Tukey's HSD as the post hoc test:

> The one-way analysis of variance reached significance, $F(2, 27) = 3.52$, $p < .05$ ($\omega^2 = .14$), with semester GPA scores being significantly lower among students working full-time compared to those who did not work during the semester (Tukey HSD, $p < .05$). Otherwise, no significant differences were evident ($p > .05$).

We summarized all our work in only two sentences. In addition, you will also want to include a figure or table summarizing the means and standard error or standard deviations in each group.

CHAPTER SUMMARY ORGANIZED BY LEARNING OBJECTIVE

LO 1: Define the one-way between-subjects ANOVA and identify each source of variation in this statistical procedure.

- An **analysis of variance (ANOVA),** also called an **F-test,** is a statistical procedure used to test hypotheses for one or more factors concerning the variance among two or more group means, where the variance in one or more populations is unknown.
- The **one-way between-subjects ANOVA** is a statistical procedure used to test hypotheses for one factor with two or more levels concerning the variance among means. This test is used when different participants are observed in each group and the variance in any one population is unknown.
- A **source of variation** is any variation that can be measured in a study. In the one-way between-subjects ANOVA, there are two sources of variation: variation attributed to differences between group means and variation attributed to error.
- **Between-groups variation** is variance attributed to differences between group means.
- **Within-groups variation** is variance attributed to differences within each group. This is a source of error because it is variability that is not associated with mean differences between groups.

LO 2: Calculate the degrees of freedom for the one-way between-subjects ANOVA and locate critical values in the *F*-table.

- The degrees of freedom for a one-way between-subjects ANOVA are the following:
  - **Degrees of freedom between groups** is the degrees of freedom for the variance of the group means. It is equal to the number of groups minus 1: $df_{BG} = k - 1$.
  - **Degrees of freedom within groups** or **degrees of freedom error** is the degrees of freedom for the variance attributed to error. It is equal to the total sample size minus the number of groups: $df_E = N - k$.

LO 3–4: Identify the assumptions for the one-way between-subjects ANOVA; compute the one-way between-subjects ANOVA and interpret the results.

- Four assumptions for the one-way between-subjects ANOVA are normality, random sampling, independence, and homogeneity of variance.
- The test statistic for the one-way ANOVA is $F_{obt} = \dfrac{MS_{BG}}{MS_E}$. The test statistic is computed as the mean square (or variance) between groups divided by the mean square (or variance) within groups.
- The steps for conducting a one-way between-subjects ANOVA are as follows:
  - Step 1: State the hypotheses.
  - Step 2: Set the criteria for a decision.
  - Step 3: Compute the test statistic.
    - Stage 1: Preliminary calculations.
    - Stage 2: Compute intermediate calculations.
    - Stage 3: Compute the *SS* for each source of variation.
    - Stage 4: Complete the *F*-table.
  - Step 4: Make a decision.

LO 5: Compute Fisher's LSD and Tukey's HSD post hoc tests, and identify which test is most powerful.

- A **post hoc test** is a statistical procedure computed following a significant ANOVA to determine which pair or pairs of group means significantly differ. These tests are necessary when $k > 2$ because multiple comparisons are needed. When $k = 2$, the two means must significantly differ; this is the only comparison.
- A **pairwise comparison** is a statistical comparison for the difference between two group means. A post hoc test evaluates all possible pairwise comparisons for an ANOVA with any number of groups.
- To compute Fisher's LSD and Tukey's HSD post hoc tests, follow three steps (only Step 2 is different for each test):
  Step 1: Compute the test statistic for each pair of group means.

Step 2: Compute the critical value for each pairwise comparison.

Step 3: Make a decision to retain or reject the null hypothesis.

- All post hoc tests control for experimentwise alpha when multiple pairwise comparisons are made on the same data. The formulas used to compute the critical values for each post hoc test are listed here from the most to least powerful:

$$\text{Fisher's LSD: } t_\alpha \sqrt{MS_E \left(\frac{1}{n_1} + \frac{1}{n_2} \right)}$$

$$\text{Tukey's HSD: } q_\alpha \sqrt{\frac{MS_E}{n}}$$

LO 6: Compute proportion of variance for the one-way between-subjects ANOVA.

- Proportion of variance estimates how much of the variability in the dependent variable can be accounted for by the levels of the factor. Two measures of proportion of variance are eta-squared (η^2 or R^2) and omega-squared (ω^2). The formula for each measure is

$$R^2 = \eta^2 = \frac{SS_{BG}}{SS_T} ;$$

$$\omega^2 = \frac{SS_{BG} - df_{BG}(MS_E)}{SS_T + MS_E} .$$

APA LO 7: Summarize the results of the one-way between-subjects ANOVA in APA format.

- To summarize a one-way between-subjects ANOVA test, we report the test statistic, degrees of freedom, and p value. You should also report the effect size for significant analyses. The means and standard error or standard deviations measured in a study can be summarized in a figure or table or in the main text. To report the results of a post hoc test, you must identify which post hoc test you computed and the p value for significant results.

SPSS LO 8: Compute the one-way between-subjects ANOVA and select an appropriate post hoc test using SPSS.

- SPSS can be used to compute the one-way between-subjects ANOVA. The one-way between-subjects ANOVA test is computed using one of two commands:
  o Using the **One-Way ANOVA** command: select the **Analyze, Compare Means,** and **One-Way ANOVA** options in the menu bar. These actions will display a dialog box that allows you to identify the variables, choose an appropriate post hoc test, and run the analysis (for more details, see Section 12.8).
  o Using the **GLM Univariate** command: select the **Analyze, General Linear Model,** and **Univariate** options in the menu bar. These actions will display a dialog box that allows you to identify the variables, choose an appropriate post hoc test, measure observed power, and run the analysis (for more details, see Section 12.8).

KEY TERMS

analysis of variance (ANOVA)
between-groups variation
between-subjects design
degrees of freedom
    between groups
degrees of freedom denominator
degrees of freedom error
degrees of freedom numerator
degrees of freedom
    within groups

experimentwise alpha
F-distribution
F-obtained
F-statistic
F-test
levels of the factor
mean square between groups
mean square error
mean square within groups
observed power

one-way between-subjects ANOVA
pairwise comparisons
post hoc tests
source of variation
sum of squares between groups
sum of squares error
sum of squares total
sum of squares within groups
studentized range statistic (q)
within-group variation

END-OF-CHAPTER PROBLEMS

Factual Problems

1. Suppose you conduct a one-way between-subjects ANOVA. Explain the meaning of the terms *one-way* and *between-subjects*.

2. Can an analysis of variance (ANOVA) be used when participants are selected from a single population? Explain.

3. A researcher conducts a one-way ANOVA in which one independent variable has four levels. How many different groups are in this study?

4. Name two sources of variation in the one-way between-subjects ANOVA.

5. State in words the null hypothesis for a one-way between-subjects ANOVA.

6. A mean square is the same as what type of descriptive statistic?

7. Define the following terms:
   (a) Sum of squares between groups
   (b) Sum of squares error
   (c) Mean square between groups
   (d) Mean square error

8. A researcher rejects the null hypothesis for a one-way between-subjects ANOVA, where $k = 4$. What is the next step in the analysis?

9. Define experimentwise alpha. What type of tests control for experimentwise alpha?

10. Which post hoc test, a Fisher's LSD or a Tukey's HSD, has the most power to detect an effect?

11. Are post hoc tests necessary following a significant ANOVA testing one independent variable with two levels ($k = 2$)? Explain.

12. Name two measures of the proportion of variance. Which measure is a more conservative estimate of effect size?

Concepts and Application Problems

13. State the degrees of freedom error in each of the following tests.

(a) A researcher tests how nervous public speakers get in front of a small, medium, or large audience. Ten participants are randomly assigned to each group.

(b) A consultant measures job satisfaction in a sample of 15 supervisors, 15 managers, or 15 executives at a local firm.

(c) A high school counselor has 12 students in each of four classes rate how much they like their teacher.

14. State the factor and the number of levels for the factor in each of the following tests.

(a) A marine biologist measures the effectiveness of mating displays among tortoises in one of six environmental conditions.

(b) A neuropsychologist measures the behavioral response to electrical stimulation in one of five brain regions.

(c) A sociologist records the number of children born in a local village for each season (spring, summer, fall, and winter) in a single year.

(d) A social psychologist has participants rate the likability of a person described as having one of three types of leadership styles (autocratic, bureaucratic, or democratic).

15. What is the decision at a .05 level of significance for each of the following tests? *Hint:* Find the critical value for each test; then make a decision.
    (a) $F(3, 26) = 3.00$
    (b) $F(5, 20) = 2.54$
    (c) $F(2, 12) = 3.81$
    (d) $F(4, 30) = 2.72$

16. State whether a post hoc test is necessary for each of the following results. Explain your answer for each result.
    (a) $F(1, 18) = 6.29, p < .05$
    (b) $F(4, 55) = 3.98, p < .05$
    (c) $F(2, 33) = 2.03, p > .05$

17. A researcher records the following data for each of four groups. Can an F-statistic be computed for these data? Explain your answer.

Group A	Group B	Group C	Group D
3	8	2	5
3	8	2	5
3	8	2	5
3	8	2	5

18. A researcher records the following data for each of three groups. What is the value of the F-statistic? Explain your answer.

Group A	Group B	Group C
8	9	12
4	6	0
7	1	12
5	8	0

19. State three errors in the following APA-style summary for the outcome of a one-way between-subjects ANOVA:

A one-way analysis of variance showed that women scored significantly higher on a test for emotional intelligence compared to men in this sample, $F(2, 18) = 2.87$, $p < .05$ ($\eta^2 = -0.19$).

20. A researcher recorded the calories burned by subjects during a 10-minute treadmill exercise. All participants had televisions located in front of them while exercising. In one group, the television played music videos. In a second group, the television played a news channel. In a third group, the television was turned off. Based on the following description in APA format, state the value of k, n, and N, and interpret the effect size as small, medium, or large.

A one-way analysis of variance reached significance, $F(2, 57) = 4.26$, $p < .05$ ($\omega^2 = 0.11$), with participants watching the music video

burning significantly more calories compared to participants watching the news channel or those watching no television (LSD, $p < .05$). Otherwise, no significant differences were evident ($p > .05$).

21. A researcher measures job satisfaction among married, single, and divorced employees to determine whether marital status can influence job satisfaction. Based on the following description in APA format, state the value for k, N, and n.

A one-way analysis of variance showed that job satisfaction did not vary by marital status, $F(2, 33) = 1.41$, $p > .05$.

22. The following is an incomplete F-table summarizing the results of a study of the variance of reaction times during a training exercise in a sample of 14 ($n = 14$) highly experienced, moderately experienced, and inexperienced athletes.

Source of Variation	SS	df	MS	F
Between groups				
Within groups (error)	50			
Total	80			

(a) Complete the F-table.
(b) Compute eta-squared (η^2).
(c) Is the decision to retain or reject the null hypothesis?

23. The following is an incomplete F-table summarizing the results of a study of the variance of life satisfaction scores among unemployed, retired, part-time, and full-time employees.

Source of Variation	SS	df	MS	F
Between groups			16	
Within groups (error)		36		
Total	128			

(a) Complete the F-table.

(b) Compute omega-squared (ω^2).

(c) Is the decision to retain or reject the null hypothesis?

24. To test whether animal subjects consume the same amounts of sweet-tasting solutions, a researcher has 10 subjects ($n = 10$) consume one of three sweet-tasting solutions ($k = 3$): sucrose, saccharin, or polycose. The amount consumed (in milliliters) of each solution is given in the table.

Type of Sweet Taste Solution		
Sucrose	Saccharin	Polycose
12	6	12
10	7	9
9	9	10
8	8	13
10	4	11
6	6	9
8	11	6
7	8	8
11	10	10
10	7	11

(a) Complete the F-table.

(b) Compute Tukey's HSD post hoc test and interpret the results.

25. Iconic memory is a type of memory that holds visual information for about half a second (0.5 seconds). To demonstrate this type of memory, participants were shown three rows of four letters for 50 milliseconds. They were then asked to recall as many letters as possible, with a 0-, 0.5-, or 1.0-second delay before responding. Researchers hypothesized that longer delays would result in poorer recall. The number of letters correctly recalled is given in the table.

Delay Before Recall		
0	0.5	1
12	8	4
11	4	4
6	10	2
10	6	5
8	3	7
7	5	2

(a) Complete the F-table.

(b) Compute Tukey's HSD post hoc test and interpret the results.

26. To test whether arousal or stress levels increase as the difficulty of a task increases, 10 participants ($n = 10$) were asked to complete an easy, typical, or difficult task. Their galvanic skin response (GSR) was recorded. A GSR measures the electrical signals of the skin in units called microSiemens (μS), with higher signals indicating greater arousal or stress. The data for each task are given in the table.

Difficulty of Task		
Easy	Typical	Difficult
2.6	5.6	9.0
3.9	4.5	5.6
3.4	3.7	3.5
1.2	2.0	7.8
2.1	3.3	6.4
1.2	4.6	7.5
1.8	3.1	4.4
2.2	2.0	3.8

(a) Complete the *F*-table.

(b) Compute Fisher's LSD post hoc test and interpret the results.

27. To test whether students in a higher grade level will be less disruptive in class, a school psychologist records the number of documented interruptions during one day of classes from nine local high schools. The sample consisted of nine ($n = 9$) freshman, sophomore, junior, and senior high school classes. The data for each high school class are given in the table.

High School Class			
Freshman	**Sophomore**	**Junior**	**Senior**
1	4	0	2
2	2	3	4
4	5	6	3
0	3	4	5
5	1	5	4
1	0	3	2
4	0	0	3
2	4	4	4
3	1	5	2

(a) Complete the *F*-table.

(b) Is it necessary to compute a post hoc test? Explain.

28. State whether each of the following will increase or decrease the power of a one-way between-subjects ANOVA.

(a) The effect size increases.

(b) Mean square error decreases.

(c) Mean square between groups decreases.

(d) The sample size decreases.

Problems in Research

29. **Characteristics of employment.** Bonache (2005) tested how positive perceptions of certain job characteristics varied among three types of employees: expatriates (employees working outside their country of origin), repatriates (employees returning to work in their country of origin), and domestics (employees with no international experience). The following table summarizes the results of the study. For which job characteristics did the groups (or types of employees) significantly vary?

Job Characteristics	**F**	***p* Value**
Autonomy	4.14	.016
Responsibility	4.58	.011
Pay satisfaction	1.16	.315
Promotion	17.81	.001

30. **Pairwise comparisons, effect size, and significance.** Volker (2006) stated the following in an article describing recommendations for the use of effect size in school psychology research: "Report at least one measure of effect size for each major [pairwise] comparison . . . it is probably best to report only effect size results for comparisons that are statistically significant" (p. 670). Explain why it is not necessary to report effect size estimates for results that are not significant.

31. **Life satisfaction among sport coaches.** Drakou, Kambitsis, Charachousou, and Tzetzis (2006) tested differences in life satisfaction among sport coaches. They tested differences by gender, age, marital status, and education. The results of each *F*-test in the following table are similar to the way in which the data were given in their article.

Independent Variables	Life Satisfaction			
	M	SD	F	p
Gender			0.68	.409
Men	3.99	0.51		
Women	3.94	0.49		
Age			3.04	.029
20s	3.85	0.42		
30s	4.03	0.52		
40s	3.97	0.57		
50s	4.02	0.50		
Marital status			12.46	.000
Single	3.85	0.48		
Married	4.10	0.50		
Divorced	4.00	0.35		
Education			0.82	.536
High school	3.92	0.48		
Postsecondary	3.85	0.54		
University degree	4.00	0.51		
Masters	4.00	0.59		

(a) Which factors were significant at a .05 level of significance?

(b) State the number of levels for each factor.

32. **Academic achievement in mathematics.** Okpala, Bell, and Tuprah (2007) evaluated student achievement in mathematics at one of two schools: public middle schools of choice and traditional public middle schools. The following is an incomplete F-table summarizing their data. Complete the F-table and state the decision for this test.

Source of Variation	SS	df	MS	F
Between groups	1,134.91			14.87*
Within groups (error)		46	76.34	
Total	4,646.42	47		

33. **Computer anxiety and usage frequency.** Using a rating scale, Tekinarslan (2008) measured computer anxiety among university students who use the computer very often, often, sometimes, and seldom. Below are the results of the one-way ANOVA.

Source of Variation	SS	df	MS	F
Between groups	1,959.79	3	653.26	21.16*
Within groups (error)	3,148.61	102	30.86	
Total	5,108.41	105		

(a) What are the values for N and k?

(b) Was the sample size, n, equal in each group? Explain.

34. **Computer anxiety and usage level.** Using a rating scale, Tekinarslan (2008) measured computer anxiety among university students who were beginners, intermediate, or advanced computer users. Below are the results of the one-way ANOVA. Complete the F-table and state the decision to retain or reject the null hypothesis for this test.

Source of Variation	SS	df	MS	F
Between groups	2,472.57	2		
Within groups (error)		103		
Total	5,108.41	105		

NOTE: Answers for even numbers are in Appendix C)

Analysis of Variance

One-Way Within-Subjects Design

LEARNING OBJECTIVES

After reading this chapter, you should be able to:

1. Define the one-way within-subjects ANOVA and identify each source of variation in this statistical procedure.

2. Calculate the degrees of freedom for the one-way within-subjects ANOVA and locate critical values in the F-table.

3. Identify the assumptions for the one-way within-subjects ANOVA.

4. Compute the one-way within-subjects ANOVA and interpret the results.

5. Compute the Bonferroni procedure and explain why it is appropriate to use following a significant one-way within-subjects ANOVA.

6. Compute proportion of variance for the one-way within-subjects ANOVA.

7. Explain how the consistency of changes in the dependent variable across groups influences the power of a one-way within-subjects ANOVA.

8. Summarize the results of the one-way within-subjects ANOVA in APA format.

9. Compute the one-way within-subjects ANOVA and select an appropriate post hoc test using SPSS.

13.1 OBSERVING THE SAME PARTICIPANTS ACROSS GROUPS

The one-way between-subjects analysis of variance (ANOVA), introduced in Chapter 12, is a hypothesis test computed when different participants are assigned to each level of one factor with two or more levels. However, many research studies require that we observe the same participants at each level of one factor with two or more levels. These types of research studies use the within-subjects design (see Chapter 10 for a discussion of study designs).

As an example in which a within-subjects design is needed, suppose a researcher wants to compare troop morale during each month of a 6-month military deployment. The goal of such a study may be to better understand the conditions that cause morale to change over time. One practical way to conduct this study would be to have the same group of soldiers complete an identical survey each month to gauge the soldiers' current level of morale. The factor is time in months, and the number of levels is 6 months. Notice that the same, and not different, soldiers are observed across time. In this study design, we will compare the morale of the same soldiers each month, which is a within-subjects design. For this reason, we use an ANOVA for the within-subjects design.

THE ONE-WAY WITHIN-SUBJECTS ANOVA

When the same participants are observed across two or more levels of one factor, we use the **one-way within-subjects ANOVA** to analyze the data. The term *one-way* indicates that we are testing one factor. The term *within-subjects* indicates that the same participants are observed in each group. Hence, for a one-way within-subjects ANOVA, n participants are each observed k times. Suppose that in the study of troop morale, 20 soldiers were observed six times. In that case, $n = 20$ and $k = 6$.

DEFINITION

NOTE: *The one-way within-subjects ANOVA is used to analyze data for situations where the same participants are observed across two or more levels of one factor.*

A **one-way within-subjects ANOVA** is a statistical procedure used to test hypotheses for one factor with two or more levels concerning the variance among group means. This test is used when the same participants are observed at each level of a factor and the variance in any one population is unknown.

SELECTING RELATED SAMPLES: THE WITHIN-SUBJECTS DESIGN

A within-subjects design is used when the same participants are observed at each level of the factor. As illustrated in Figure 13.1, participants are typically selected from a single population and then observed across the levels of one factor.

13.2 SOURCES OF VARIATION AND THE TEST STATISTIC

In this chapter, we use the one-way within-subjects ANOVA to conduct a hypothesis test. We use the same test statistic for any one-way ANOVA. Whether we observe different (between-subjects) or the same (within-subjects) participants in each group, we must analyze the variance of two or more group means. The test statistic

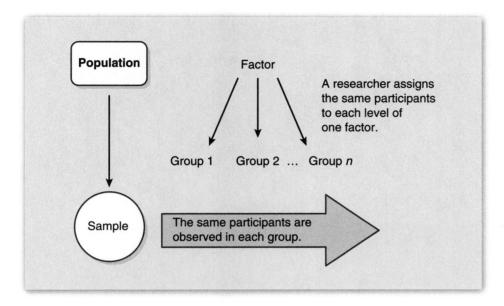

FIGURE 13.1

The within-subjects design. One sample of participants is selected from the population, and participants are observed in each group or at each level of the factor.

is still the variance between groups divided by the variance within groups (or error). We will compute variance as a mean square (*MS*), same as we did in Chapter 12. The test statistic has the general form:

$$F_{obt} = \frac{MS_{BG}}{MS_E} = \frac{\text{variance between groups}}{\text{variance within groups}}.$$

To work with this test statistic, we again have to locate the sources of variation (introduced in this section), and need to determine the degrees of freedom (in Section 13.3). The number of sources of variation and the calculations of the degrees of freedom are slightly different for the within-subjects design compared to the between-subjects design. As illustrated in Figure 13.2, the three sources of variation in the one-way within-subjects ANOVA are between-groups, within-groups, and between-persons variation.

BETWEEN-GROUPS VARIATION

In the one-way within-subjects ANOVA, we still compute the variance of group means. The variation of group means is called between-groups variation, as illustrated in Table 13.1 for Groups A, B, and C. This variance, or mean square, is computed and placed as the numerator of the test statistic for the one-way within-subjects ANOVA, just as it was using the one-way between-subjects ANOVA (see Chapter 12).

ERROR VARIATION

Two sources of variation also are measured but can't be attributed to having different groups: the between-persons variation and the within-groups variation. We call

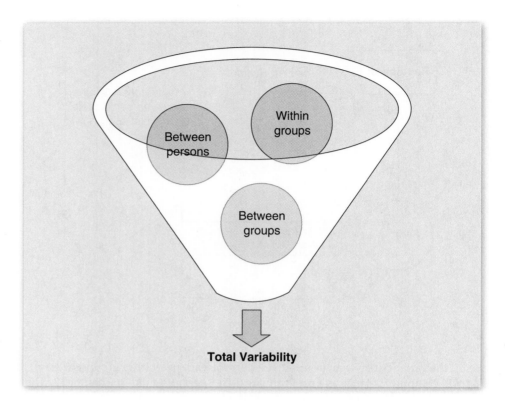

FIGURE 13.2

The total variability measured in the one-way within-subjects ANOVA.

NOTE: There are two sources of error in the one-way within-subjects ANOVA: one associated with observing different participants in each group (within groups) and one associated with observing the same participants across groups (between persons).

these sources of variation "error" because they have nothing to do with mean differences between groups. Each source of error is also shown in Table 13.1.

The **between-persons variation** is associated with the differences between person means averaged across groups. When different participants are observed in each group (between subjects), individual differences, or the unique characteristics of participants in each group, may systematically vary across groups. In the between-subjects design, then, this is an important source of error to account for. However, in a within-subjects design, the same, not different, participants are observed in each group. Hence, the individual differences in participant characteristics are the same in each group—because the same participants are observed in each group. In a within-subjects design, then, we can assume that any differences in the characteristics of participants across groups are the same. For this reason, between-persons variation can be measured and then removed from the error term in the denominator of the test statistic.

DEFINITION

The **between-persons variation** is the variance attributed to the differences between person means averaged across groups. Using a within-subjects design, the same participants are observed across groups, so this source of variation is removed from the error term in the denominator of the test statistic for the one-way within-subjects ANOVA.

The remaining source of error is within-groups variation. While the same participants are observed in each group, different participants are still observed within each group. This source of variation is measured, and its value is placed in the

TABLE 13.1   Three sources of variability in a within-subjects design: between groups, between persons, and within groups. The between-persons source of variation is calculated and then removed from the denominator of the test statistic.

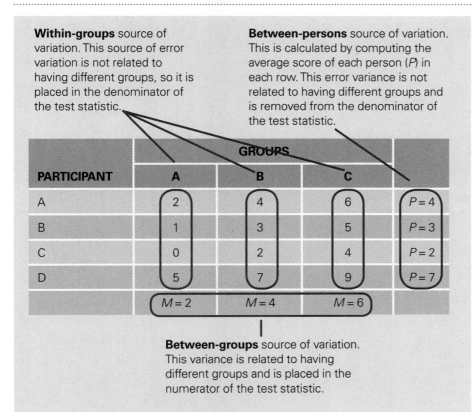

Within-groups source of variation. This source of error variation is not related to having different groups, so it is placed in the denominator of the test statistic.

Between-persons source of variation. This is calculated by computing the average score of each person (P) in each row. This error variance is not related to having different groups and is removed from the denominator of the test statistic.

PARTICIPANT	GROUPS			
	A	B	C	
A	2	4	6	$P = 4$
B	1	3	5	$P = 3$
C	0	2	4	$P = 2$
D	5	7	9	$P = 7$
	$M = 2$	$M = 4$	$M = 6$	

Between-groups source of variation. This variance is related to having different groups and is placed in the numerator of the test statistic.

denominator of the test statistic. Table 13.1 shows where to identify each source of variation in a table. Again, one source of variation is attributed to differences between groups, and two are associated with error variation, as shown in Figure 13.3.

Although we have two sources of error in a within-subjects design, this does not mean that we have more error variation in this design compared to the between-subjects design. Think of error variation as a pie with two slices. In the between-subjects design, we measure the whole pie and place it all in the denominator of the test statistic. In the within-subjects design, we cut this same pie into two slices and then remove the between-persons slice. The remaining slice is placed in the denominator of the test statistic.

To illustrate further, suppose we measure 24 units of error variation in an analysis of variance with Groups A, B, and C. If different participants are observed in each group (between subjects), then all 24 units are attributed to a single source of error: the within-groups error. If the same participants are observed across groups (within subjects), then the 24 units are divided into two sources of error: within groups and between persons. As shown in Figure 13.4, the total error variation is the same; the difference is that we split the pie into two slices in a within-subjects design.

NOTE: A within-subjects design does not have more error variation. Instead, the error variation is split, and the between-persons variation is removed as a source of error from the denominator of the test statistic.

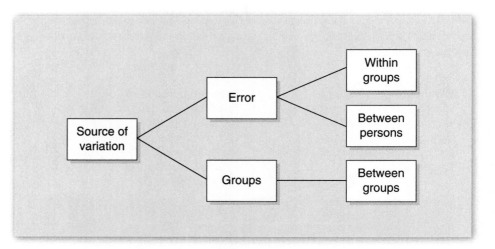

FIGURE 13.3

A flowchart for the different sources of variation measured using the within-subjects design.

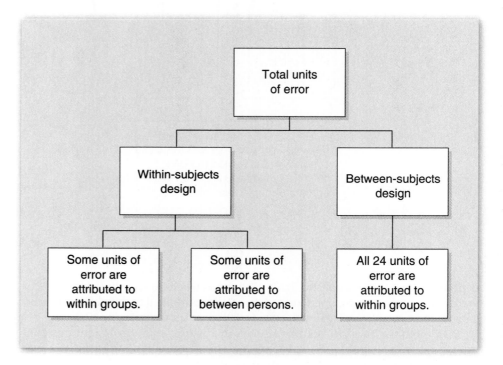

FIGURE 13.4

A flowchart of error variability measured using the within-subjects versus the between-subjects design.

MAKING SENSE: Sources of Error

In the within-subjects design, we have two sources of error: between-persons variation and within-groups variation. The term *error* is used to refer to any source of variation that is not attributed to the different groups. The goal of a statistical test is to separate the variation attributed to having different groups from all other sources of variation (collectively called *error*). Error, of course, is not literally an error or mistake. Instead, it is any source of variation that is not attributed to having different groups.

DEGREES OF FREEDOM 13.3

We will use degrees of freedom to find the critical values for an ANOVA, same as we did for the between-subjects design in Chapter 12. The total degrees of freedom for the one-way within-subjects ANOVA are $(k \times n) - 1$, where k is the number of groups and n is the number of participants per group. However, there are three sources of variation in the one-way within-subjects ANOVA, so we must split the total degrees of freedom into three parts: one for each source of variation.

NOTE: Each source of variation in the one-way within-subjects ANOVA is associated with degrees of freedom.

The degrees of freedom between groups, df_{BG}, are the number of levels of the factor, or the number of groups (k), minus 1:

$$df_{BG} = k - 1.$$

The **degrees of freedom between persons,** df_{BP}, are the number of participants per group (n) minus 1:

$$df_{BP} = n - 1.$$

The **degrees of freedom between persons (df_{BP})** are the degrees of freedom associated with the variance of person means averaged across groups. It is equal to the number of participants (n) minus 1.

DEFINITION

The degrees of freedom within groups or error, df_E, is equal to the degrees of freedom between groups ($k - 1$) times the degrees of freedom between persons ($n - 1$):

$$df_E = (k - 1)(n - 1).$$

LEARNING CHECK 1

1. How are participants observed using the within-subjects design?

2. State the three sources of variation in the one-way within-subjects ANOVA.

3. Which source of error is removed from the denominator of the test statistic in the one-way within-subjects ANOVA?

4. A neuropsychologist measured brainwave patterns in a group of 10 patients exposed to four different groups. Find the degrees of freedom:

   a. Between groups

   b. Between persons

   c. Within groups (error)

Answers: 1. Using the within-subjects design, the same participants are observed across groups. 2. Between groups, between persons, and within groups; 3. Between-persons variation; 4. $df_{BG} = 3$, $df_{BP} = 9$, and $df_E = 27$.

THE ONE-WAY WITHIN-SUBJECTS ANOVA 13.4

In this section, we will compute the one-way within-subjects ANOVA. We compute this test when we compare two or more group means, in which the same participants are observed in each group. The null hypothesis states that group means do not vary in the population:

$$H_0 : \sigma_\mu^2 = 0.$$

The alternative hypothesis states that group means in the population do vary:

$$H_1: \sigma_\mu^2 > 0.$$

We must make four assumptions to compute the one-way within-subjects ANOVA:

1. *Normality.* We assume that data in the population or populations being sampled from are normally distributed. This assumption is particularly important for small sample sizes. In larger samples, the overall variance of sample outcomes is reduced, and this assumption becomes less critical as a result.

2. *Independence within groups.* The same participants are observed between groups. Within each group, different participants are observed. For this reason, we make the assumption that participants are independently observed within groups but not between groups.

3. *Homogeneity of variance.* We assume that the variance in each population is equal to each other.

4. *Homogeneity of covariance.* We assume that participant scores in each group are related because the same participants are observed across or between groups. The reasons for this assumption are rather complex and beyond the scope of this book.

Together, the assumptions of homogeneity of variance and homogeneity of covariance are called *sphericity*. Note that if we violate the assumption of sphericity, then the value of the variance in the numerator of the test statistic can be inflated, which can increase the likelihood of committing a Type I error (or incorrectly rejecting the null hypothesis).

In Example 13.1, we will follow the four steps in hypothesis testing to compute the one-way within-subjects ANOVA.

EXAMPLE 13.1

A researcher wants to determine which of three advertisements is most likely to encourage teens not to smoke. To assess the impact of each advertisement, she asks a sample of teenagers to view each ad and to rate the ad's effectiveness on a scale from 1 (*not at all effective*) to 7 (*very effective*). One ad uses words only (a no-cues condition). A second ad uses a generic abstract picture (generic-cues condition). A third ad shows a picture of a teenager smoking and coughing (smoking-related-cues condition). Using the data listed in Table 13.2, conduct the one-way within-subjects ANOVA at a .05 level of significance.

Step 1: State the hypotheses. The null hypothesis states that group means in the population do not vary (=); the alternative hypothesis states that group means in the population do vary (>):

$H_0: \sigma_\mu^2 = 0$ Mean ratings for each advertisement do not vary in the population.

$H_1: \sigma_\mu^2 > 0$ Mean ratings for each advertisement do vary in the population.

TABLE 13.2   The results of a within-subjects study in which participants rated the effectiveness of three different types of ads in Example 13.1.

Person	Cues		
	No Cues	**Generic Cues**	**Smoking-Related Cues**
A	2	5	5
B	3	5	6
C	1	4	5
D	4	5	7
E	4	3	6
F	5	4	7
G	2	2	6

Step 2: Set the criteria for a decision. The level of significance for this test is .05. The degrees of freedom between groups are $k - 1$:

$$df_{BG} = 3 - 1 = 2.$$

The degrees of freedom between persons are $n - 1$:

$$df_{BP} = 7 - 1 = 6.$$

The degrees of freedom error is $(k - 1)(n - 1)$:

$$df_E = 2 \times 6 = 12.$$

The test statistic is the variance between groups (MS_{BG}) divided by the variance attributed to error (MS_E). The corresponding degrees of freedom for the test statistic are the degrees of freedom numerator or between groups $(df_{BG} = 2)$ and the degrees of freedom denominator or error $(df_E = 12)$:

$$F_{obt} = \frac{MS_{BG}}{MS_E} \xleftarrow{\textit{Degrees of freedom}} \frac{df_{BG}}{df_E}.$$

Hence, we are locating the critical value for an ANOVA with 2 and 12 degrees of freedom. To locate the critical value, find the intersection where each degree of freedom intersects in Table B.3 in Appendix B. The critical value for this test is 3.89. As explained in Chapter 12, we use the F-distribution to make decisions about a null hypothesis using an ANOVA test. The *F*-distribution is positively skewed, and the rejection region for an ANOVA test is always located in the upper tail of this distribution. The critical value and rejection region for Example 13.1 are shown in Figure 13.5.

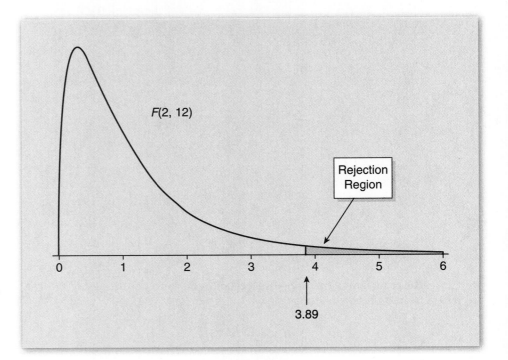

FIGURE 13.5

An *F*-distribution with 2 and 12 degrees of freedom. The rejection region is placed in the upper tail at or above 3.89.

We will compare the test statistic with this critical value. If the value of the test statistic falls beyond the critical value (greater than 3.89), then we reject the null hypothesis; otherwise, we retain the null hypothesis.

Step 3: Compute the test statistic. We compute the *F*-statistic to determine whether a significant portion of the total variance in a study is attributed to the differences between group means relative to the variance attributed to error. The test statistic is the same as that used for the between-subjects design in Chapter 12:

NOTE: The rejection region is always placed in the upper tail of the F-*distribution for an ANOVA.*

$$F_{obt} = \frac{MS_{BG}}{MS_E}.$$

There are many ways to compute a mean square. We will describe this analysis in four stages, as we did in Chapter 12: preliminary calculations, intermediate calculations, compute the sum of squares, and complete the *F*-table.

Stage 1: Preliminary calculations—find $\sum x$, $\sum x_T$, $\sum x^2$, $\sum x_T^2$, $\sum P$, n, and k. These preliminary calculations are shown in Table 13.3. Each calculation made in the table is the same as those described in Chapter 12, except that we also sum the person scores. Each calculation is described here.

TABLE 13.3 Preliminary calculations for the one-way within-subjects ANOVA in Example 13.1.

Person	Cues			$\sum P$
	No Cues	Generic Cues	Smoking-Related Cues	
A	2	5	5	12
B	3	5	6	14
C	1	4	5	10
D	4	5	7	16
E	4	3	6	13
F	5	4	7	16
G	2	2	6	10
	$\sum x_1 = 21$	$\sum x_2 = 28$	$\sum x_3 = 42$	$\sum x_T = 91$
	$\sum x_1^2 = 75$	$\sum x_2^2 = 120$	$\sum x_3^2 = 256$	$\sum x_T^2 = 451$

1. Find k and n. In this study, seven participants ($n = 7$) are observed across three groups ($k = 3$).

2. Find $\sum x$ and $\sum x_T$. Sum the scores in each group: $\sum x$. The grand total $\left(\sum x_T\right)$ is the sum of scores in all groups combined.

3. Find $\sum x^2$ and $\sum x_T^2$. Square each score, and then sum the squared scores in each group: $\sum x^2$. The sum of the squared scores in all groups combined is $\sum x_T^2$.

4. Find $\sum P$. Sum across the rows for each person. The sum of person scores is $2 + 5 + 5 = 12$ for Person A, $3 + 5 + 6 = 14$ for Person B, and so on. The total of these scores equals the grand total $\left(\sum P = \sum x_T = 91\right)$.

Stage 2: Compute intermediate calculations—find [1], [2], [3], and [4]. In Stage 1, we computed the values needed to make calculations in Stage 2. There are four calculations in Stage 2 (the first three calculations are the same as those described in Chapter 12).

First, we compute a correction factor by squaring the grand total $\left(\sum x_T\right)$ and dividing by the total number of observations ($k \times n$):

$$[1] \quad \frac{\left(\sum x_T\right)^2}{k \times n} = \frac{(91)^2}{3 \times 7} = 394.33.$$

Second, we divide the sum of squared scores in each group by the sample size for each group:

$$[2] \quad \sum \frac{x^2}{n} = \frac{(21)^2}{7} + \frac{(28)^2}{7} + \frac{(42)^2}{7} = 427.$$

Third, we restate the sum of the squared scores in all groups combined:

$$[3] \quad \sum x_T^2 = 451.$$

Fourth, we divide the sum of squared person scores by the number of groups:

$$[4] \quad \sum \frac{P^2}{k} = \frac{12^2}{3} + \frac{14^2}{3} \ldots + \frac{16^2}{3} + \frac{10^2}{3} = 407.$$

We can use these values to compute the sum of squares (SS) for each source of variation in the ANOVA. Remember that SS is the numerator for variance (see Chapter 4). The calculations we make in Stage 3 will give us the numerator in the formula for variance, or SS, for each source of variation.

NOTE: In Stage 3, we compute SS for the variance between groups, between persons, and within groups.

Stage 3: Compute the sums of squares (SS) for each source of variation.

The sum of squares between groups (SS_{BG}) is the difference between Calculation [2] and Calculation [1] in Stage 2:

$$SS_{BG} = [2] - [1] = 427 - 394.33 = 32.67.$$

The sum of squares total (SS_T) is the difference between Calculation [3] and Calculation [1] in Stage 2:

$$SS_T = [3] - [1] = 451 - 394.33 = 56.67.$$

NOTE: Calculations of SS between persons is unique to the one-way within-subjects ANOVA. All remaining calculations of SS are the same as those computed using the one-way between-subjects ANOVA in Chapter 12.

The **sum of squares between persons** (SS_{BP}) is the difference between Calculation [4] and Calculation [1] in Stage 2:

$$SS_{BP} = [4] - [1] = 407 - 394.33 = 12.67.$$

The sum of squares within groups, called the sum of squares error (SS_E), is the sum of squares total minus the sum of squares between groups and between persons:

$$SS_E = SS_T - SS_{BG} - SS_{BP} = 56.67 - 32.67 - 12.67 = 11.33.$$

DEFINITION

The **sum of squares between persons (SS_{BP})** is the sum of squares attributed to variability in participant scores across groups.

Stage 4: Complete the F-table. The F-table lists the sum of squares (SS), the degrees of freedom (df), the mean squares (MS), and the value of the test statistic. The calculations in the F-table are described here and listed in Table 13.4. Table 13.5 is the completed F-table.

TABLE 13.4   The *F*-table with the formulas for completing the table given.

Source of Variation	SS	df	MS	F_{obt}
Between groups	32.67	$k - 1 = 2$	$\dfrac{SS_{BG}}{df_{BG}}$	$\dfrac{MS_{BG}}{MS_E}$
Between persons	12.67	$n - 1 = 6$	$\dfrac{SS_{BP}}{df_{BP}}$	
Within groups (error)	11.33	$(k-1)(n-1) = 12$	$\dfrac{SS_E}{df_E}$	
Total	56.67	$(kn) - 1 = 20$		

The first column of values in the *F*-table lists the sum of squares (we computed these in Stage 3). The second column lists the degrees of freedom (we computed these in Stage 2). We will use these values to compute the mean squares for the test statistic. The formula for variance is *SS* divided by *df,* so we divide across each row to compute each mean square.

To compute the variance or mean square between groups, we divide SS_{BG} by df_{BG}:

$$MS_{BG} = \frac{SS_{BG}}{df_{BG}} = \frac{32.67}{2} = 16.34.$$

To compute the variance or **mean square between persons,** which is the variance attributed to differences between persons across groups, we divide SS_{BP} by df_{BP} :

$$MS_{BP} = \frac{SS_{BP}}{df_{BP}} = \frac{12.67}{6} = 2.11.$$

Mean square between persons (MS_{BP}) is a measure of the variance attributed to differences in scores between persons.

DEFINITION

To compute the variance or mean square error, we divide SS_E by df_E:

$$MS_E = \frac{SS_E}{df_E} = \frac{11.33}{12} = 0.94.$$

The formula for the test statistic is mean square between groups (16.34) divided by mean square error (0.94):

$$F_{obt} = \frac{MS_{BG}}{MS_E} = \frac{16.34}{0.94} = 17.38.$$

NOTE: The mean squares for each source of variation are computed by dividing SS by df for each source of variation.

TABLE 13.5 The completed *F*-table for Example 13.1. The asterisk (*) indicates significance.

Source of Variation	SS	df	MS	F_{obt}
Between groups	32.67	2	16.34	17.38*
Between persons	12.67	6	2.11	
Within groups (error)	11.33	12	0.94	
Total	56.67	20		

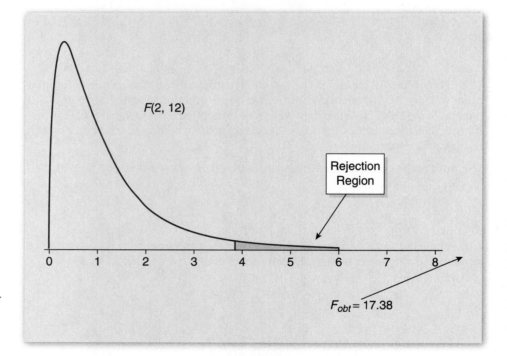

FIGURE 13.6

The test statistic reaches the rejection region, so we decide to reject the null hypothesis.

Step 4: Make a decision. To make a decision, we compare the obtained value to the critical value. As shown in Figure 13.6, the obtained value (17.38) is greater than the critical value (3.89); it falls well into the rejection region. The decision is to reject the null hypothesis.

Table 13.6 summarizes the procedures used to compute a one-way within-subjects ANOVA. If we were to report the result for Example 13.1 in a research journal, it would look something like this:

> A one-way analysis of variance showed that ratings of effectiveness for one of three advertisements significantly varied, $F(2, 12) = 17.38$, $p < .05$.

TABLE 13.6 The steps used to compute a one-way within-subjects ANOVA.

Steps for Computing a One-Way Within-Subjects ANOVA		
Terminology	**Formula**	**Meaning**
Step 1: State the hypotheses		
Null hypothesis	$\sigma_\mu^2 = 0$	Population means do not vary.
Alternative hypothesis	$\sigma_\mu^2 > 0$	Population means do vary.
Step 2: Set the criteria for a decision		
Degrees of freedom between groups	$df_{BG} = k - 1$	The number of groups minus 1
Degrees of freedom between persons	$df_{BP} = n - 1$	The number of participants per group minus 1
Degrees of freedom error	$df_E = (k - 1)(n - 1)$	The degrees of freedom between groups times the degrees of freedom between persons
Degrees of freedom total	$df_T = (kn) - 1$	The number of groups times the number participants, minus 1.
Step 3: Compute test statistic		
STAGE 1		
Groups	k	The number of groups or levels of a factor
Participants	n	The number of participants per group (n)
Grand total	$\sum x_T$	The sum of all scores in a study
Sum of person scores	$\sum P$	The sum of scores for each person
Sum of squared scores	$\sum x_T^2$	The sum of all scores individually squared in a study

(Continued)

(Continued)

STAGE 2		
[1]	$\dfrac{\left(\sum x_T\right)^2}{k \times n}$	The correction factor
[2]	$\sum \dfrac{x^2}{n}$	The "uncorrected" between-groups variation
[3]	$\sum x_T^2$	The "uncorrected" total variation in a study
[4]	$\sum \dfrac{P^2}{k}$	The "uncorrected" between-persons variation
STAGE 3		
Sum of squares between groups	$SS_{BG} = [2] - [1]$	The sum of squared deviations between groups.
Sum of squares between persons	$SS_{BP} = [4] - [1]$	The sum of squared deviations between persons
Sum of squares total	$SS_T = [3] - [1]$	The sum of squared deviations in all groups
Sum of squares error	$SS_E = SS_T - SS_{BG} - SS_{BP}$	The sum of squared deviations within each group
STAGE 4		
Mean square between groups	$MS_{BG} = \dfrac{SS_{BG}}{df_{BG}}$	The variance between groups. This is the numerator for the test statistic.
Mean square between persons	$MS_{BP} = \dfrac{SS_{BP}}{df_{BP}}$	The variance between persons averaged across groups
Mean square error	$MS_E = \dfrac{SS_E}{df_E}$	The variance within groups. This is the denominator for the test statistic.
F-statistic formula	$F_{obt} = \dfrac{MS_{BG}}{MS_E}$	The obtained value of the test statistic for an ANOVA
Step 4: Make a decision		
Decision criterion	—	When $F_{obt} < F_{crit}$, retain the null. When $F_{obt} \geq F_{crit}$, reject the null.

> **MAKING SENSE:** Mean Squares and Variance
>
> To compute a variance, or mean square, we compute sum of squares (SS), which is the numerator for sample variance, and degrees of freedom (df), which is the denominator for sample variance:
>
> $$\text{Sample variance} = \frac{SS}{df}.$$
>
> For an ANOVA, the numerator for the test statistic is the variance between groups (SS_{BG} divided by df_{BG}), and the denominator for the test statistic is the variance attributed to error (SS_E divided by df_E). Each mean square is equal to the formula for sample variance:
>
> $$MS = \frac{SS}{df} \text{ for between groups, between persons, and error variance}$$
>
> The test statistic for an ANOVA, then, is a ratio used to determine whether the variance attributed to differences between groups (MS_{BG}) is significantly larger than the variance attributed to error (MS_E).

LEARNING CHECK 2

1. State the four assumptions for the one-way within-subjects ANOVA.

2. What is the null hypothesis for the one-way within-subjects ANOVA?

3. Given the following values, compute the F-statistic: $SS_{BG} = 10$, $SS_E = 25$, $df_{BG} = 2$, $df_E = 25$.

4. Make a decision given the following test statistic values for a one-way within-subjects ANOVA with 4 and 30 degrees of freedom.

   a. $F_{obt} = 2.50$ b. $F_{obt} = 2.80$ c. $F_{obt} = 4.00$

POST HOC COMPARISONS: BONFERRONI PROCEDURE   13.5

In Example 13.1, we decided to reject the null hypothesis: At least one pair of group means significantly differs. Because we have more than two groups, we need to make multiple pairwise comparisons using a post hoc test to determine which pair or pairs of group means significantly differ. The post hoc test analyzes differences for all possible pairs of group means or pairwise comparisons. Mean ratings in Example 13.1 are 3.0 (Group No Cue), 4.0 (Group Generic Cue), and 6.0 (Group Smoking-Related Cue). In Example 13.1, then, there are three possible pairwise comparisons:

Comparison 1:   Generic Cue and No Cue: $4.0 - 3.0 = 1.0$.

Comparison 2:   Smoking-Related Cue and Generic Cue: $6.0 - 4.0 = 2.0$.

Comparison 3:   Smoking-Related Cue and No Cue: $6.0 - 3.0 = 3.0$.

All post hoc tests ensure that no matter how many tests we compute, the overall likelihood of committing a Type I error is .05. In other words, all post hoc tests control for experimentwise alpha (see Chapter 12), which is the overall alpha level for multiple tests conducted on the same data. Of the post hoc tests introduced in Chapter 12, the Bonferroni procedure is best adapted for use following a significant one-way within-subjects ANOVA. However, keep in mind that this procedure gets too conservative as *k* increases. With a larger number of comparisons, more specialized tests beyond the scope of this book, such as trend analysis, are recommended.

NOTE: Post hoc tests are computed following a significant one-way ANOVA to determine which pair or pairs of group means significantly differ.

In this section, we will use the Bonferroni procedure to determine which pair or pairs of group means significantly differ. The Bonferroni procedure adjusts the alpha level, or probability of committing a Type I error, for each test. The alpha level for each test is called **testwise alpha.** We find testwise alpha such that the experimentwise alpha, or alpha level for all tests, equals .05. To find testwise alpha, we divide experimentwise alpha by the total number of pairwise comparisons made:

$$\text{Testwise alpha} = \frac{\text{experimentwise alpha}}{\text{total number of pairwise comparisons}}.$$

DEFINITION

Testwise alpha is the alpha level, or probability of committing a Type I error, for each test or pairwise comparison made on the same data.

To use the Bonferroni procedure following a significant one-way within-subjects ANOVA, we follow two steps:

Step 1: Calculate the testwise alpha and find the critical values.

Step 2: Compute a related samples *t*-test for each pairwise comparison and make a decision to retain or reject the null hypothesis.

The decision for each pairwise comparison is to retain or reject the null hypothesis. The null hypothesis is that there is no mean difference between two groups. The alternative hypothesis is that there is a mean difference between two groups. When the test statistic is larger than the critical value, we reject the null hypothesis; otherwise, we retain the null hypothesis.

NOTE: The Bonferroni procedure is an appropriate post hoc test with the one-way within-subjects ANOVA because the related samples t-tests are computed on the data.

The related samples *t*-test is used with the within-subjects design because it is an appropriate test that is adapted for situations where the same participants are observed in each group (see Chapter 10 for a discussion of research designs). For this reason, the Bonferroni procedure is an appropriate post hoc test to use following a significant one-way within-subjects ANOVA. Let's follow the two steps to compute the Bonferroni procedure for Example 13.1.

Step 1: Calculate the testwise alpha and find the critical values. We set an experimentwise alpha for all tests, which in Example 13.1 is .05. To find the testwise alpha, we divide .05 by the number of pairwise comparisons we will make. In Example 13.1 we will make three pairwise comparisons, so the testwise alpha is

$$\frac{.05}{3} = .016 \text{ or} \approx .02.$$

The alpha level, or level of significance, for each pairwise comparison is .02. This will ensure that the overall experimentwise alpha remains .05. We will compute a

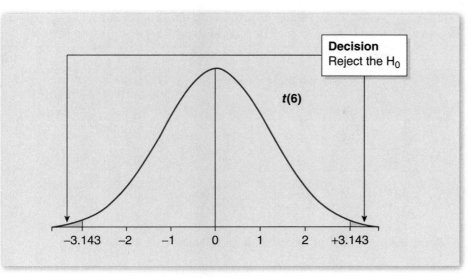

FIGURE 13.7

The shaded region shows the rejection region with the cutoff for the rejection region being ±3.143. For each pairwise comparison, if the value of the test statistic falls in the shaded region, we reject the null hypothesis; otherwise, we retain the null hypothesis.

related samples *t*-test in Step 2. To find the critical value for this *t*-test, we look in the *t*-table in Table B.2 in Appendix B, as we did in Chapter 10. All post hoc tests should be two-tailed tests, with the degrees of freedom for each test equal to $n - 1 = 6$. The critical value for a *t*-test with 6 degrees of freedom at a .02 level of significance is ±3.143.

Remember that for this post hoc test, we are computing a related samples *t*-test for each pair of group means. For the *t*-test, we use a *t*-distribution (described in Chapter 9), as shown in Figure 13.7 with the critical values and rejection region shown.

Step 2: Compute a related samples *t*-test for each pairwise comparison and make a decision to retain or reject the null hypothesis. The test statistic for the related samples *t*-test, introduced in Chapter 10, is the mean difference between groups (M_D) divided by an estimate for standard error (s_{MD}):

$$t_{obt} = \frac{M_D}{s_{MD}}.$$

Table 13.7 shows the mean difference and the estimated standard error for difference scores for each pairwise comparison. (The discussion of performing these calculations is given in Chapter 10, Section 10.3.) With the values given in Table 13.7, let's compute each related samples *t*-test and make a decision for each pairwise comparison.

Comparison 1: Generic Cue and No Cue: 4.0 − 3.0 = 1.0:

$$t_{obt} = \frac{-1.0}{0.655} = -1.527.$$

Decision: Because −1.527 does not exceed the critical value (±3.143), we retain the null hypothesis. Mean ratings for the ads do not significantly differ between these two groups.

TABLE 13.7 The mean difference and the estimated standard error for difference scores for each pairwise comparison. The means by group were no cues (3.0), generic cues (4.0), and smoking-related cues (6.0).

Comparison	Pairwise Comparisons		Mean Difference (M_D)	Standard Error (s_{MD})
	Mean 1	Mean 2		
#1	3.0	4.0	−1.000	0.655
#2	4.0	6.0	−2.000	0.535
#3	3.0	6.0	−3.000	0.309

Comparison 2: Smoking-Related Cue and Generic Cue: 6.0 − 4.0 = 2.0:

$$t_{obt} = \frac{-2.0}{0.535} = -3.738.$$

Decision: Because −3.738 exceeds the critical value (±3.143), we reject the null hypothesis. Mean ratings significantly differ between these two groups.

Comparison 3: Smoking-Related Cue and No Cue: 6.0 − 3.0 = 3.0:

$$t_{obt} = \frac{-3.0}{0.309} = -9.709.$$

Decision: Because −9.709 exceeds the critical value (±3.143), we reject the null hypothesis. Mean ratings significantly differ between these two groups.

In sum, Comparison 2 and Comparison 3 were significant. If we were to report these results in a research journal, it would look something like this:

> A one-way analysis of variance showed that ratings of effectiveness for one of three advertisements significantly varied, $F(2, 12) = 17.38$, $p < .05$. Using the Bonferroni procedure, related samples t-tests showed that ratings of effectiveness were significantly greater for the ad with smoking-related cues compared to the ad with generic cues and the ad with no cues ($p < .05$). Otherwise, no significant differences were evident ($p > .05$).

 **LEARNING CHECK 3**

1. What is testwise alpha for each of six tests with an experimentwise alpha equal to .05?

2. Why is the Bonferroni procedure an appropriate post hoc test following a significant one-way within-subjects ANOVA?

3. What are the two steps for using the Bonferroni procedure following a significant one-way within-subjects ANOVA?

Answers: 1. Testwise alpha = .008; 2. Because a related samples t-test is used to make pairwise comparisons. The related samples t-test is adapted for situations where the same participants are observed in each group; 3. Step 1: Calculate the testwise alpha and find the critical value. Step 2: Compute a related samples t-test for each pairwise comparison and make a decision to retain or reject the null hypothesis.

SPSS IN FOCUS: THE ONE-WAY WITHIN-SUBJECTS ANOVA 13.6

In Example 13.1, we concluded that ratings of the effectiveness for one of three advertisements significantly varied, $F(2, 12) = 17.38$, $p < .05$. A Bonferroni procedure showed that participants rated the effectiveness of an ad with smoking-related cues higher compared to ads with no cues and compared to ads with generic cues. We will use SPSS to confirm the calculations we computed in Example 13.1.

1. Click on the **variable view** tab and enter *nocue* in the **name column;** enter *gencue* in the name column below it; enter *smokecue* in the name column below that. We will enter whole numbers, so reduce the value in the **decimals column** to 0 in each row.

2. Click on the **data view** tab. Enter the data for each group in the appropriate column, as shown in the background of Figure 13.8.

3. Go to the **menu bar** and click **Analyze,** then **General Linear Model,** and **Repeated Measures** to display the dialog box shown in Figure 13.9.

4. In the **Within-Subject Factor Name** box, label the within-subjects factor. Enter *cues* in this box. Because this factor has three levels, enter *3* in the **Number of Levels** box. These actions will illuminate the **Add** option. Click **Add,** then **Define** to display a new dialog box.

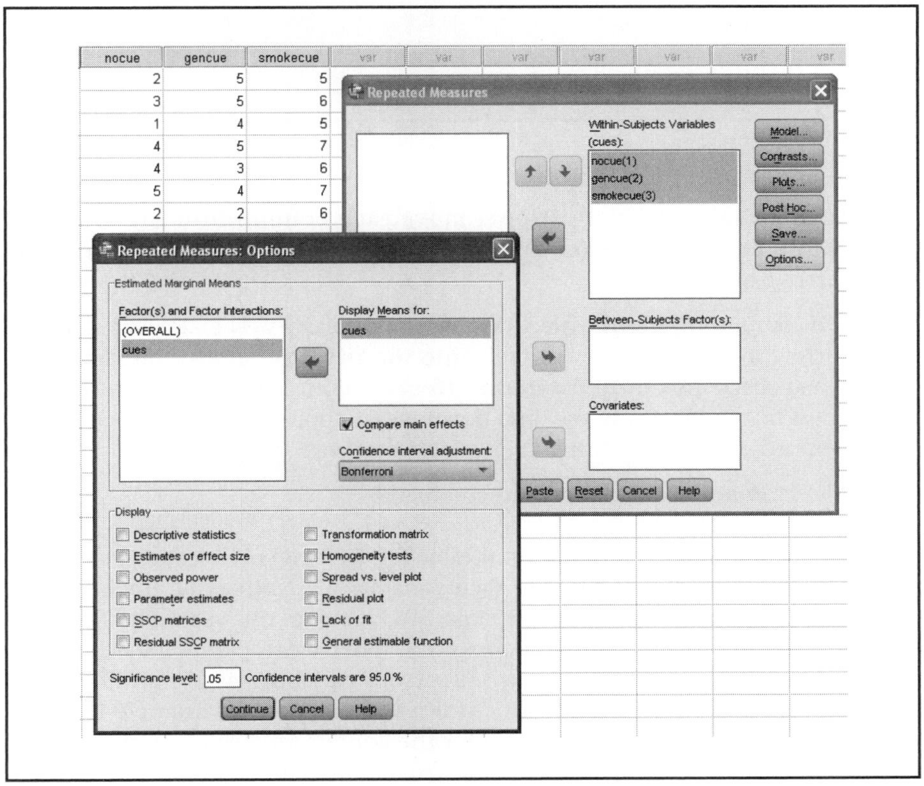

FIGURE 13.8

The SPSS data view with data entry in each cell for Step 2 given (left background). Also shown is the dialog box for Step 5 (right) and the dialog box for Step 6 (front).

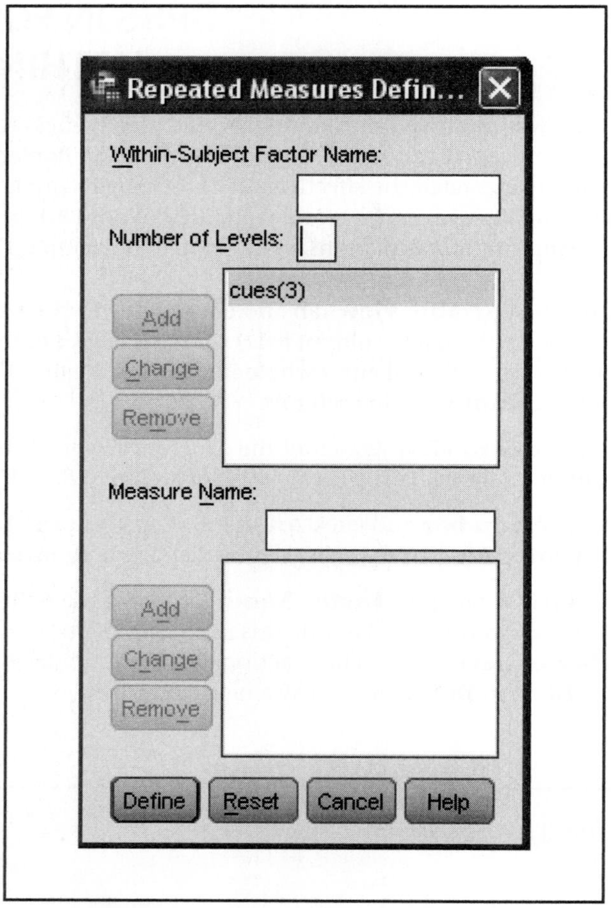

FIGURE 13.9

Dialog box for Steps 3 to 4.

5. Using the appropriate arrows, move each column into the **Within-Subjects Variables (cues)** box. Figure 13.8 shows the dialog boxes for Steps 5 and 6.

6. To compute effect size, select **Options** to display a new dialog box. Use the arrow to move the *cues* variable into the **Display Means for:** box, and then check the **Compare main effects** option. Select **Bonferroni** as the post hoc test by using the drop-down menu under the **Confidence interval adjustment** heading, then select **continue.**

7. Select **Paste** and click the **Run** command.

Table 13.8 displays the SPSS output table for the ANOVA. Because we assume sphericity, read only the first row in each variable cell. Notice that the between-persons variability is not given in this table. SPSS removes this variability from the error term, leaving only the within-groups error. When we read only the first row in each cell and recognize that the between-persons variability is not given, we see that Table 13.8 is identical to Table 13.5, which we computed for Example 13.1.

Table 13.9 displays the SPSS output for the Bonferroni post hoc test. This display is similar to that for the post hoc test we computed using SPSS in Chapter 12.

TABLE 13.8 SPSS output *F*-table. Because we assume sphericity, read only the top row for cues and error(cues) to find the values needed in this table.

Tests of Within-Subjects Effects

Measure:MEASURE_1

Source		Type III Sum of Squares	df	Mean Square	F	Sig.
cues	Sphericity Assumed	32.667	2	16.333	17.294	.000
	Greenhouse-Geisser	32.667	1.323	24.698	17.294	.002
	Huynh-Feldt	32.667	1.552	21.050	17.294	.001
	Lower-bound	32.667	1.000	32.667	17.294	.006
Error(cues)	Sphericity Assumed	11.333	12	.944		
	Greenhouse-Geisser	11.333	7.936	1.428		
	Huynh-Feldt	11.333	9.311	1.217		
	Lower-bound	11.333	6.000	1.889		

TABLE 13.9 SSPSS output table for post hoc comparisons using the Bonferroni procedure.

Pairwise Comparisons

Measure:MEASURE_1

(I) cues	(J) cues	Mean Difference (I-J)	Std. Error	Sig.[a]	95% Confidence Interval for Difference[a]	
					Lower Bound	Upper Bound
1	2	-1.000	.655	.532	-3.152	1.152
	3	-3.000[*]	.309	.000	-4.015	-1.985
2	1	1.000	.655	.532	-1.152	3.152
	3	-2.000[*]	.535	.029	-3.757	-.243
3	1	3.000[*]	.309	.000	1.985	4.015
	2	2.000[*]	.535	.029	.243	3.757

Based on estimated marginal means

a. Adjustment for multiple comparisons: Bonferroni.
*. The mean difference is significant at the .05 level.

An asterisk in the **Mean Difference** column indicates significance, and the *p* values for each pairwise comparison are given in the **Sig.** column. The display in Table 13.9 confirms the results we obtained for Example 13.1.

13.7 MEASURING EFFECT SIZE

An ANOVA determines whether group means significantly vary in the population. In Example 13.1, we concluded that there was an effect—mean ratings significantly varied by the type of ad (no cues, generic cues, smoking-related cues). We can also determine the size of this effect in the population using a measure of effect size called proportion of variance.

Proportion of variance measures how much of the variability in the dependent variable can be accounted for by the levels of the factor. In Example 13.1, the dependent variable was ratings of effectiveness, and the levels of the factor or type of ad were no cue, generic cue, and smoking-related cue. A proportion of variance will measure how much of the variability in ratings of effectiveness can be accounted for by the different types of ads.

NOTE: Partial measures of proportion of variance are used to estimate the effect size for the one-way within-subjects ANOVA.

For a within-subjects design, the two measures of proportion of variance are partial eta-squared $\left(\eta_P^2\right)$ and partial omega-squared $\left(\omega_P^2\right)$. Using a partial proportion of variance, we remove or partial out the between-persons variation before calculating the proportion of variance. We do this because the between-persons variation was removed from the denominator of the test statistic for the one-way within-subjects ANOVA. In this section, we will describe both measures of proportion of variance: partial eta-squared and partial omega-squared.

PARTIAL ETA-SQUARED (η_P^2)

In Chapter 12, we introduced eta-squared as being equal to the sum of squares between groups divided by the sum of squares total. To compute partial eta-squared, we remove the sum of squares between persons from the sum of squares total in the denominator.

There are two ways we can remove the sum of squares between persons. We can subtract the sum of squares between persons from the sum of squares total:

$$\eta_P^2 = \frac{SS_{BG}}{SS_T - SS_{BP}},$$

or we can add the sum of squares between groups and sum of squares error. This will leave the sum of squares between persons out of the denominator:

$$\eta_P^2 = \frac{SS_{BG}}{SS_{BG} + SS_E}.$$

In Example 13.1, Table 13.5 shows that $SS_{BG} = 32.67$ and $SS_T - SS_{BP} = 44$. The value of partial eta-squared using either formula is

$$\eta_P^2 = \frac{32.67}{44} = 0.74.$$

We conclude that 74% of the variability in ratings can be explained by the type of ad being rated. Using the effect size conventions listed in Table 9.3 in Chapter 9, we determine that this is a large effect size. Here is how we might report partial eta-squared with the significant result:

A one-way analysis of variance showed that ratings of effectiveness for one of the three advertisements significantly varied, $F(2, 12) = 17.38$, $p < .05$ $\left(\eta_P^2 = 0.74\right)$.

NOTE: The formulas for partial eta-squared and partial omega-squared have between-persons variation removed or partial out of the denominator.

PARTIAL OMEGA-SQUARED (ω_P^2)

Partial eta-squared tends to overestimate effect size. A more conservative measure of effect size is partial omega-squared. This estimate has two advantages over partial eta-squared:

1. It corrects for the size of error by including MS_E in the formula.

2. It corrects for the number of groups by including the degrees of freedom between groups $\left(df_{BG}\right)$ in the formula.

To compute partial omega-squared, we remove the sum of squares between persons from the sum of squares total in the denominator of the omega-squared formula, same as we did for partial eta-squared. There are two ways we can remove this sum of squares. We can subtract the sum of squares between persons from the sum of squares total in the denominator:

$$\omega_P^2 = \frac{SS_{BG} - df_{BG}(MS_E)}{(SS_T - SS_{BP}) + MS_E},$$

or we can add the sum of squares between groups and sum of squares error. This will leave the sum of squares between persons out of the denominator:

$$\omega_P^2 = \frac{SS_{BG} - df_{BG}(MS_E)}{(SS_{BG} + SS_E) + MS_E}.$$

In Example 13.1, Table 13.5 shows that $SS_{BG} = 32.67$, $df_{BG} = 2$, $MS_E = 0.94$, and $SS_T - SS_{BP} = 44$. The value for partial omega-squared using either formula is

$$\omega_P^2 = \frac{32.67 - 2(0.94)}{44 + 0.94} = 0.69.$$

We conclude that 69% of the variability in ratings can be explained by the type of ad being rated. Using the effect size conventions given in Table 9.3 in Chapter 9, we determine that this is a large effect size. Here is how we might report partial omega-squared with the significant result:

A one-way analysis of variance showed that ratings of effectiveness for one of the three advertisements significantly varied, $F(2, 12) = 17.38$, $p < .05$ $\left(\omega_P^2 = 0.69\right)$.

Notice that to compute a partial proportion of variance, we remove the between-persons variation, thereby making the denominator smaller. Therefore, using the same data, partial measures of proportion of variance (partial eta-squared and partial omega-squared) will be larger than the measures used with the between-subjects design (eta-squared and omega-squared). These relationships can be represented as

$$\eta_P^2 > \eta^2 \text{ and } \omega_P^2 > \omega^2.$$

LEARNING CHECK 4

1. The following are the results for a one-way within-subjects ANOVA. Compute effect size for this test using η_p^2 and ω_p^2.

Source of Variation	SS	df	MS	F_{obt}
Between groups	4.50	2	2.25	4.50
Between persons	8.25	3	2.75	
Within groups (error)	3.00	6	0.50	
Total	15.75	11		

2. Which estimate (partial eta-squared or partial omega-squared) gives a larger estimate of proportion of variance?

Answers: 1. $\eta_p^2 = \dfrac{4.50}{7.50} = 0.60$, $\omega_p^2 = \dfrac{4.50 - 2(0.25)}{7.5 + 0.25} = 0.52$; 2. Partial eta-squared.

13.8 THE WITHIN-SUBJECTS DESIGN: CONSISTENCY AND POWER

The within-subjects design is associated with more power to detect an effect than the between-subjects design because we remove some of the error in the denominator of the test statistic. However, the increased power for a within-subjects design is only true when responding between groups is consistent. In this section, we show how consistency can influence the power of the within-subjects and between-subjects designs.

Eliminating the between-persons error makes the denominator of a test statistic smaller and the value of a test statistic larger. In the related samples t-test, we reduced two columns of scores to one column of difference scores. In the one-way within-subjects ANOVA, we measured the between-persons variation and then subtracted it from the error term in the denominator. Both strategies ultimately reduced the error term in the denominator, thereby increasing the power of the test.

However, for the ANOVA, we also adjust the degrees of freedom. So subtracting the between-persons variation will not always increase the power of a one-way within-subjects ANOVA. Instead, the power of the one-way within-subjects ANOVA is largely based on the assumption that observing the same participants across groups will result in more consistent responding, or changes in the dependent variable, between groups. We will use two hypothetical data sets in Example 13.2 to see how consistency influences the power of the one-way within-subjects ANOVA.

EXAMPLE 13.2

Table 13.10 shows the results of two hypothetical studies measuring lever pressing in rats. In each study, a group of four rats pressed a lever to receive a small, medium, or large reward. Rats were run on successive trials, and the number of lever presses on a given trial were recorded. In both hypothetical studies, the group means were identical. We will compare the data for each hypothetical study. If consistency influences power, then we will find that more consistent changes in the dependent variable between groups are associated with increased power, or a greater likelihood of rejecting the null hypothesis for the one-way within-subjects ANOVA.

TABLE 13.10 The data measured in Study 1 (top) and Study 2 (bottom). Note that the group means are the same in both studies.

Study 1 (Consistent Responding)			
Reward Size			
Subject	Small	Medium	Large
A	2	3	4
B	1	2	3
C	3	4	5
D	0	2	4
Means:	1.50	2.75	4.0

Study 2 (Inconsistent Responding)			
Reward Size			
Subject	Small	Medium	Large
A	2	2	4
B	3	3	3
C	1	4	4
D	0	2	5
Means:	1.50	2.75	4.0

Between-subjects design: If we observed different subjects in each group, then each study would be a between-subjects design, and we would use a one-way between-subjects ANOVA. In the between-subjects design, we place all of the error term in the denominator, so both studies would give the same value for error variance in the *F*-table. Table 13.11 shows the results of the one-way between-subjects ANOVA, which would apply to both studies. For both studies, we decide to reject the null hypothesis; the variance between groups is significant.

If we assume that these results reflect a true effect in the population, then the observed power of each study is 0.72. We expect 72% of the samples we select to detect this effect and show a significant result using the between-subjects design. How does this power compare to the power of the within-subjects design? We will answer this question here.

Within-subjects design (high consistency): If we observed the same subjects in each group, then each study would be a within-subjects design, and we would compute a one-way within-subjects ANOVA. For both studies, the variance attributed to having different groups is the same because the group means are the same. The variance in

TABLE 13.11 Between-subjects design. The completed *F*-table for Study 1 and Study 2 using a one-way between-subjects ANOVA. Both studies will result in the same *F*-table because the individual scores and the group means are the same for each group. Values for within-groups error are given in bold.

Source of Variation	SS	df	MS	F_{obt}
Between groups	12.50	2	6.25	5.79*
Within groups (error)	**9.75**	**9**	**1.08**	
Total	22.25	11		

the numerator, then, will be the same for both studies. However, the value of each measure of error variation (between persons and within groups) will depend on the consistency of subject responses in each group.

Consistency refers to the extent to which the dependent variable (number of lever presses in this example) changes in an identifiable or predictable pattern across groups. Let's look at Study 1. Table 13.10 shows that responses in Study 1 always increased as the reward increased. Subject A increased from 2 to 3 to 4; Subject D from 0 to 2 to 4. There is high consistency in subject responses across groups. When changes in the dependent variable are consistent across groups, most of the error variation is attributed to the between-persons source of variation, as shown in Figure 13.10. Table 13.12 shows that the one-way within-subjects ANOVA for Study 1 will result in a very large value of the test statistic. The decision in Study 1 is to reject the null hypothesis; the variance between groups is significant.

If we assume that the decision for Study 1 reflects a true effect in the population, then the observed power of this study is 0.99. The power increased compared to an analysis using the between-subjects design. We now expect 99% of the samples we select to detect this effect and show a significant result. The within-subjects design

FIGURE 13.10

Error variation for Study 1 using a within-subjects design. When there is consistent responding, most of the error variation is attributed to the between-persons source of variation.

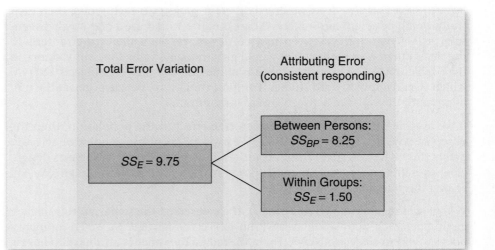

TABLE 13.12 Within-subjects design (high consistency). The completed *F*-table for Study 1 using a one-way within-subjects ANOVA. Notice that *SS* within groups is small because most of the variation attributed to error was attributed to between-persons variation. Values for within-groups error are given in bold.

Source of Variation	SS	df	MS	F_{obt}
Between groups	12.50	2	6.25	25.00*
Between persons	8.25	3	2.75	
Within groups (error)	**1.50**	**6**	**0.25**	
Total	22.25	11		

is more powerful than the between-subjects design when changes in the dependent variable are consistent across groups.

Within-subjects design (low consistency): Suppose we also compute the one-way within-subjects ANOVA for Study 2. In Study 2, changes in the dependent variable are not consistent. For example, Subject D increased from 0 to 2 to 5, but Subject B showed no change. Because the group means are the same as those in Study 1, the numerator will be the same. However, when changes in the dependent variable are not consistent across groups, most of the error variation is attributed to the within-groups source of error (see Figure 13.11). Table 13.13 shows that the one-way within-subjects ANOVA for Study 2 will result in a much smaller value of the test statistic compared to the test statistic we computed in Study 1. The decision in Study 2 is to retain the null hypothesis; the variance between groups is not significant.

If we assume that the decision in Study 2 reflects a true effect in the population, then the observed power of this study is 0.51. We now expect only 51% of our samples to detect this effect and show a significant result. The test for Study 2 is now less powerful than the one-way between-subjects ANOVA we first computed.

NOTE: The within-subjects design is more powerful than the between-subjects design when changes in the dependent variable are consistent across groups.

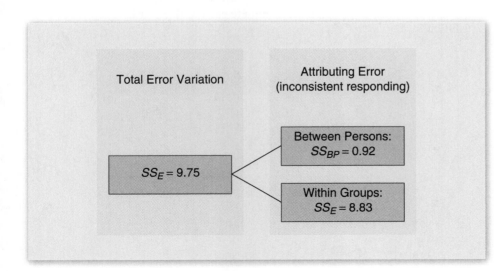

Total Error Variation

Attributing Error (inconsistent responding)

$SS_E = 9.75$

Between Persons: $SS_{BP} = 0.92$

Within Groups: $SS_E = 8.83$

FIGURE 13.11

Error variation for Study 2 using a within-subjects design. When there is inconsistent responding, most of the error variation is attributed to the within-groups or error source of variation.

TABLE 13.13 Within-subjects design (low consistency). The completed F-table for Study 2 using a one-way within-subjects ANOVA. Notice that the SS within groups is larger because most of the variation attributed to error was attributed to this source of variation. Values for within-groups error are given in bold.

Source of Variation	SS	df	MS	F_{obt}
Between groups	12.50	2	6.25	4.25
Between persons	0.92	3	0.31	
Within groups (error)	**8.83**	**6**	**1.47**	
Total	22.25	11		

Hence, when changes in the dependent variable across groups are not consistent, the within-subjects design can actually be less powerful than the between-subjects design.

The power of a within-subjects design depends on the consistency of changes in the dependent variable because both the sum of squares and the degrees of freedom for error are reduced. Unless we remove a large amount of variation from the within groups error term, we could actually end up with a larger mean square error in the denominator, making the within-subjects design less powerful than the between-subjects design. In all, we can state the following rules for the power of the one-way within-subjects ANOVA:

1. As SS_{BP} increases, power increases.

2. As SS_E decreases, power increases.

3. As MS_E decreases, power increases.

LEARNING CHECK 5

1. The following table lists data from a hypothetical study measuring the time (in seconds) it takes participants to complete each of three tasks (easy, moderate, difficult).

Easy	Moderate	Difficult
9	14	15
7	9	17
10	12	16
6	8	9
7	8	13

a. Are changes in the dependent variable consistent? Explain.

b. Is this within-subjects design associated with high power? Explain.

2. What three values increase the power of a one-way within-subjects ANOVA?

Answers: 1. (a) Yes, the dependent variable increases for each participant across groups. (b) Yes, consistent changes in the dependent variable indicate that most of the error will be attributed to the between persons source of variation. This will increase the value of the test statistic, thereby increasing power or the likelihood of detecting an effect. 2. To increase power: increase SS_{BP}, and decrease SS_E and MS_E.

APA IN FOCUS: REPORTING THE *F*-STATISTIC, SIGNIFICANCE, AND EFFECT SIZE   13.9

To summarize a one-way within-subjects ANOVA, we report the test statistic, the degrees of freedom, and the *p* value. The effect size for significant analyses should also be reported. The means and standard error or standard deviations measured in a study can be summarized in a figure or table or in the main text. To report the results of a post hoc test, identify which post hoc test was computed and the *p* value for significant results. For example, here is an APA summary of the results in Example 13.1, using partial omega-squared as the estimate of effect size and a Bonferroni procedure as the post hoc test:

A one-way analysis of variance showed that ratings of effectiveness for one of three advertisements significantly varied, $F(2, 12) = 17.38$, $p < .05$ $\left(\omega_P^2 = 0.69\right)$. Using the Bonferroni procedure, related samples *t*-tests showed that ratings of effectiveness were significantly greater for the ad with smoking-related cues compared to the ad with generic cues and the ad with no cues ($p < .05$). Otherwise, no significant differences were evident ($p > .05$). The means and standard deviations for each group are shown in Table 13.14.

It is not required to identify whether an ANOVA test was a between-subjects or a within-subjects analysis when reporting statistical results. This information is usually provided in a data analysis section or in a procedures section of a published study; both sections precede the results section where the statistics are reported.

TABLE 13.14   The means and the standard deviations for each type of ad in Example 13.1.

Type of Ad	M	SD
No cue	3.0	1.41
Generic cue	4.0	1.15
Smoking-related cue	6.0	0.82

CHAPTER SUMMARY ORGANIZED BY LEARNING OBJECTIVE

LO 1: Define the one-way within-subjects ANOVA and identify each source of variation in this design.

- The **one-way within-subjects ANOVA** is a statistical procedure used to test hypotheses for one factor with two or more levels concerning the variance among group means. This test is used when the same participants are observed in each group.
- In the one-way within-subjects ANOVA, we measure three sources of variation: between-groups, within-groups, and between-persons variation. The between-groups and within-groups sources of variation are the same as those described in Chapter 12.
- **Between-persons variation** is the variance attributed to differences between person means averaged across groups. Because the same participants are observed across groups, this source of variation is removed from the error term in the denominator of the test statistic.

LO 2: Calculate the degrees of freedom for the one-way within-subjects ANOVA and locate critical values in the *F*-table.

- The degrees of freedom for a one-way within-subjects ANOVA are as follows:
  - The degrees of freedom between groups are the degrees of freedom associated with the variance of group means: $df_{BG} = k - 1$.
  - The **degrees of freedom between persons** are the degrees of freedom associated with the variance of person means averaged across groups: $df_{BP} = n - 1$.
  - The degrees of freedom error is the variance associated with differences within each group: $df_E = (k - 1)(n - 1)$.

LO 3–4: Identify the assumptions for the one-way within-subjects ANOVA; compute the one-way within-subjects ANOVA and interpret the results.

- Four assumptions for the one-way within-subjects ANOVA are normality, independence within groups, homogeneity of variance, and homogeneity of covariance.
- The test statistic for the one-way ANOVA is $F_{obt} = \dfrac{MS_{BG}}{MS_E}$.

- The steps to conduct a one-way within-subjects ANOVA are as follows:
  Step 1: State the hypotheses.
  Step 2: Set the criteria for a decision.
  Step 3: Compute the test statistic.
    Stage 1: Preliminary calculations.
    Stage 2: Compute intermediate calculations.
    Stage 3: Compute SS for each source of variation.
    Stage 4: Complete the *F*-table.
  Step 4: Make a decision.

LO 5: Compute the Bonferroni procedure and explain why it is appropriate to use following a significant one-way within-subjects ANOVA.

- A Bonferroni procedure is used to control for testwise alpha, which is the alpha level, or the probability of committing a Type I error, for each pairwise comparison made on the same data. The calculation for testwise alpha is

$$\frac{\text{experimentwise alpha}}{\text{total number of pairwise comparisons}}.$$

- The Bonferroni procedure is appropriate following a significant one-way within-subjects ANOVA because we can use the related samples *t*-test, which is adapted for situations where the same participants are observed in each group. We follow two steps to complete the Bonferroni procedure using related samples *t*-tests:
  Step 1: Calculate the testwise alpha and find the critical values.
  Step 2: Compute a related samples *t*-test for each pairwise comparison and make a decision to retain or reject the null hypothesis.

LO 6: Compute proportion of variance for the one-way within-subjects ANOVA.

- Proportion of variance measures how much of the variability in the dependent variable can be accounted for by the levels of the factor. Two measures of proportion of variance using the within-subjects design are partial eta-squared $\left(\eta_P^2\right)$ and partial omega-squared $\left(\omega_P^2\right)$. To compute each measure, we partial out the between-persons variation before computing effect size. The formula for each estimate is

$$\eta_P^2 = \frac{SS_{BG}}{SS_T - SS_{BP}} \quad \text{or} \quad \eta_P^2 = \frac{SS_{BG}}{SS_{BG} + SS_E}.$$

$$\omega_P^2 = \frac{SS_{BG} - df_{BG}(MS_E)}{(SS_T - SS_{BP}) + MS_E} \quad \text{or} \quad \omega_P^2 = \frac{SS_{BG} - df_{BG}(MS_E)}{(SS_{BG} + SS_E) + MS_E}.$$

LO 7: Explain how the consistency of changes in the dependent variable across groups influences the power of a one-way within-subjects ANOVA.

- Consistency refers to the extent to which the dependent measure changes in an identifiable or predictable pattern across groups. As consistency increases, the power to detect an effect also increases. Increased consistency increases the value of SS_{BP} and decreases the value of SS_E and MS_E.

APA LO 8: Summarize the results of the one-way within-subjects ANOVA in APA format.

- To summarize the one-way within-subjects ANOVA, we report the test statistic, the degrees of freedom, and the p value. The effect size for significant analyses should also be reported. The means and the standard error or standard deviations measured in a study can be summarized in a figure or table or in the main text. To report the results of a post hoc test, identify which post hoc test was computed and the p value for significant results.

SPSS LO 9: Compute the one-way within-subjects ANOVA and select an appropriate post hoc test using SPSS.

- SPSS can be used to compute the one-way within-subjects ANOVA. The one-way within-subjects ANOVA is computed using the **Analyze, General Linear Model,** and **Repeated Measures** options in the menu bar. These actions will display a dialog box that allows you to identify the variables, choose an appropriate post hoc test, and run the analysis (for more details, see Section 13.6).

KEY TERMS

between-persons variation	mean square between persons	sum of squares between persons
degrees of freedom between persons	one-way within-subjects ANOVA	testwise alpha

End-of-Chapter Problems

Factual Problems

1. When it is appropriate to compute the one-way within-subjects ANOVA?

2. Name three sources of variation in the one-way within-subjects ANOVA. Which source of variation is associated with variance between group means?

3. Which source of error is included in the F-table for the one-way within-subjects ANOVA but not for the one-way between-subjects ANOVA?

4. How many participants are observed in a one-way within-subjects ANOVA if $n = 12$ and $k = 4$?

5. Explain why the between-persons variation is removed from the denominator of the test statistic for the one-way within-subjects ANOVA.

6. What is the value of the test statistic when the within-groups variation is equal to 0? Explain.

7. Define the following terms:
   (a) Degrees of freedom between persons
   (b) Sum of squares between persons
   (c) Mean square between persons

8. Define testwise alpha. Name the post hoc procedure used to determine the testwise alpha for multiple pairwise comparisons.

9. Explain why the Bonferroni procedure is an appropriate post hoc test for making pairwise comparisons following a significant one-way within-subjects ANOVA.

10. What value do we remove from the formula for partial eta-squared and partial omega-squared?

11. Which measure (partial eta-squared or partial omega-squared) is the more conservative estimate of proportion of variance?

12. If the consistency of changes in the dependent variable across groups increases, then how does the power of the within-subjects design change?

Concepts and Application Problems

13. State whether the following situations describe a between-subjects design or a within-subjects design.

    (a) A biopsychologist tests the time course for the release of a neurohormone before, during, and following a task thought to cause its release.

    (b) A sport psychologist compares mental functioning in a sample of athletes in four different sports.

    (c) A college professor compares the average class grade for students in each of three sections of a statistics course.

    (d) A behavioral psychologist allows a sample of children to play with four toys of various colors and has them rate how much they like playing with each toy. The psychologist compares mean ratings for each toy.

14. Each of the following examples describes situations where we can use the one-way within-subjects ANOVA. State the degrees of freedom between groups and the degrees of freedom error for each situation.

    (a) A sample of 21 expert chess players rated the effectiveness of six different playing strategies.

    (b) A developmental psychologist measures the amount of time 10 infants spend near their respective mother in three novel social contexts.

    (c) A researcher records the cellular response to four unique environmental stimuli in a sample of nine participants exposed to each stimulus.

    (d) An experimental psychologist compares scores on four measures related to addiction (impulsiveness, attention, inhibition, and discounting) in a sample of 21 people who use drugs.

15. Given the following information for the one-way within-subjects ANOVA, state the number of participants observed in each group.

    (a) $df_{BP} = 12$ (b) $df_{BG} = 4$, $df_E = 20$

    (c) $k = 3$, $n = 12$

16. A researcher reports that intake of junk food among college participants 1 week before, during, and after finals week significantly varied, $F(2, 38) = 6.21$, $p < .05$. Based on the results, state the number of participants observed in this study.

17. Researcher A observes a sample of 10 subjects four times and decides to retain the null hypothesis. Researcher B also observes a sample of 10 subjects four times, obtains the same group means, but decides to reject the null hypothesis. Is this possible? If so, explain why.

18. Two researchers independently observe three groups of participants and report the follow scores for each group. For which set of data will the value of the F-statistic be undefined (meaning that the variance in the denominator will equal 0)? Explain.

    Researcher 1 data:

Group A	Group B	Group C
3	3	3
7	7	7
2	2	2
4	4	4
9	9	9

    Researcher 2 data:

Group A	Group B	Group C
4	8	6
4	8	6
4	8	6
4	8	6
4	8	6

19. A researcher records the following data for each of three groups. What is the value of the F-statistic? Explain your answer.

Group A	Group B	Group C
10	13	11
4	5	11
12	9	9
5	10	2
9	3	7

20. A researcher is interested in how perceptions of global warming influence consumer spending. He collects a sample of 10 environmentalists with strong perceptions of global warming and has them report how much they spend on a variety of "typical" items. These items were categorized as detrimental, safe, or helpful to the environment. The following is a F-table for this hypothetical study using the one-way within-subjects ANOVA.

Source of Variation	SS	df	MS	F_{obt}
Between groups			198	
Between persons	234			
Within groups (error)				
Total	1,278	29		

(a) Complete the F-table and make a decision to retain or reject the null hypothesis.
(b) Compute effect size using partial eta-squared: η_P^2.

21. A child psychologist treats four children who are afraid of snakes with a behavioral modification procedure called systematic desensitization. In this procedure, children were slowly introduced to a snake over four treatment sessions. Children rated how fearful they are of the snake before the first session (baseline) and following each treatment session. Higher ratings indicated greater fear. The hypothetical data are listed in the table.

	Sessions				
Baseline	1	2	3	4
7	7	5	4	3
7	6	6	4	4
6	6	7	7	3
7	7	5	4	3

(a) Complete the F-table.
(b) Compute a Bonferroni procedure and interpret the results.

22. In a study on attention and performance of memory tasks, six participants attended a 1-hour lecture on a topic chosen at random. Following this lecture, they received a survey testing their knowledge of the topics covered. After each 15-minute interval of the lecture, participants were asked 10 questions concerning facts covered. The table lists the number of incorrect answers recorded in each interval in this hypothetical study.

15-Minute Intervals			
First	Second	Third	Last
1	5	4	0
0	4	3	2
2	7	7	1
2	5	4	2
3	3	7	1
0	4	5	1

(a) Complete the F-table.
(b) Compute a Bonferroni procedure and interpret the results.

23. A study investigated the effects of physical fatigue on the performance of professional tennis players. Researchers measured the number of unforced errors committed by a random sample of 12 professional tennis players during the first three sets of a match. They hypothesized that increased fatigue would be associated with a greater number of errors. The following is an F-table for this hypothetical study using the one-way within-subjects ANOVA.

Source of Variation	SS	df	MS	F_{obt}
Between groups			12	
Between persons			3	
Within groups (error)	55			
Total				

(a) Complete the F-table and make a decision to retain or reject the null hypothesis.

(b) Estimate effect size using partial omega-squared: ω_P^2.

24. A group of clinicians who are members of the U.S. military are concerned with the morale of troops serving in war regions. They hypothesize that the number of tours a soldier has served significantly affects morale. To test this hypothesis, they select a sample of eight soldiers who served three tours in war regions and asked them to rate their morale during each tour they served in. Lower ratings indicate lower morale. The table lists the hypothetical results of this study. Complete the F-table and make a decision to retain or reject the null hypothesis.

Number of War Tours		
First	Second	Third
6	5	4
5	4	5
7	6	3
6	7	7
5	7	6
6	6	7
7	7	7
7	6	7

25. Air traffic controllers perform the vital function of regulating the traffic of passenger planes. Frequently, air traffic controllers work long hours with little sleep. Researchers wanted to test their ability to make basic decisions as they become increasingly sleep deprived. To test their abilities, a sample of 10 air traffic controllers is selected and given a decision-making skills test following 12-hour, 24-hour, and 48-hour sleep deprivation. Higher scores indicate better decision-making skills. The table lists the hypothetical results of this study.

Sleep Deprivation		
12 Hours	24 Hours	48 Hours
21	16	15
17	20	19
32	21	20
25	19	12
21	13	14
19	19	13

(a) Complete the F-table.

(b) Compute a Bonferroni procedure and interpret the results.

26. An administrator notices that high school students tend to be more disruptive in classes with a substitute teacher. To test this, the administrator records the number of student outbursts during a class of 10 students with their assigned teacher and a substitute teacher. The following is an ANOVA summary table for the results of this hypothetical study. Complete the F-table and make a decision to retain or reject the null hypothesis.

Source of Variation	SS	df	MS	F_{obt}
Between groups			30	2.00
Between persons		9	3	
Within groups (error)		9		
Total	192	19		

CHAPTER 13: ANALYSIS OF VARIANCE: ONE-WAY WITHIN-SUBJECTS DESIGN **423**

27. Some studies show that people who think they are intoxicated will show signs of intoxication, even if they did not consume alcohol. To test whether this is true, researchers had a group of five adults consume nonalcoholic drinks, which they were told contained alcohol. The participants completed a standard driving test before drinking and then after one nonalcoholic drink and after five nonalcoholic drinks. A standard driving test was conducted in a school parking lot where the participants had to maneuver through traffic cones. The number of cones knocked over during each test was recorded. The following table lists the data for this hypothetical study.

Driving Test		
Before Drinking	**After One Drink**	**After Five Drinks**
0	0	3
0	1	2
1	2	3
3	2	5
0	1	0

(a) Complete the F-table.

(b) Compute a Bonferroni procedure and interpret the results.

Problems in Research

28. **Assumptions of independence and significance.** Wainwright, Leatherdale, and Dublin (2007) evaluated the advantages and disadvantages of using an ANOVA to analyze data with animal models. They explained that animal pups are often raised or clustered together. In terms of the assumptions for an ANOVA, they state,

An analysis that is based on individual pups without taking this clustering into account is likely to over-estimate the statistical significance of any observed effect. Similar concerns apply to [within-subjects] analyses, where the errors in an individual over time are likely to be [related], violating statistical assumptions of independence. (p. 665)

Explain why housing rat pups in clusters might violate the assumption of independence for a within-subjects design.

29. **Importance of subject area.** Guan, McBride, and Xiang (2005) tested the attitudes of teachers regarding four subject areas: (1) motor skill development (MS), physical fitness/health (PA), self-actualization and personal growth (SA), and social development (SD). Teachers rated each subject area on a scale ranging from 1 (*extremely important*) to 5 (*not important*). The following table lists a portion of the data similar to results reported by the authors.

Subject Area			
MS	**PA**	**SA**	**SD**
2	2	2	2
2	1	2	3
3	2	2	3
2	2	2	2
3	2	1	2
2	2	2	2
2	2	1	3

(a) Explain why the one-way within-subjects ANOVA is an appropriate statistical test for these data.

(b) Complete the F-table and make a decision to retain or reject the null hypothesis.

30. **Social power in the classroom.** Elias (2007) asked students about the appropriateness of various types of social power used by professors in the classroom. They asked a group of participants to complete a survey where higher scores indicated more appropriate ratings for the use of a type of social power. They found that students rated informational power (student complies because instructor gave logical explanation) and expert power (compliance because the instructor is considered to have superior knowledge) as the most appropriate for professors to use in the classroom:

A [within-subjects] ANOVA indicated that informational power and expert power were rated as being the most appropriate individual bases of power for professors to use, $F(10, 81) - 49.00$, $p < .001$, $\eta^2 = .86$. (p. 2540)

(a) The authors found that two types of power were rated as the most appropriate for professors to use in the classroom. In all, how many types of power did participants in this study rate?

(b) Is their estimate for effect size appropriate? Explain.

31. **Frequency of binge eating with treatment.** Wilfley and colleagues (2008) tested whether the antiobesity drug sibutramine would be an effective treatment for people with binge eating disorder. They measured the frequency of binge eating every 2 weeks for 24 weeks during treatment. The following table lists a portion of the data similar to results reported by the authors for the frequency of binge eating over the first 8 weeks of the drug treatment.

Frequency of Binge Eating				
Baseline	Week 2	Week 4	Week 6	Week 8
4	1	0	0	1
6	4	2	0	0
3	0	1	1	0
1	1	0	1	1
2	2	1	1	1
5	1	2	2	2

(a) Complete the F-table and make a decision to retain or reject the null hypothesis.

(b) Use the Bonferroni procedure to make the post hoc test. In which week do we first see significant differences compared to baseline?

32. **Frequency of binge eating without treatment.** Wilfley and colleagues (2008) also ran a control group in their binge eating disorder treatment study. A control group received a placebo (a fake drug that has no physiological effect) instead of the antiobesity drug sibutramine. The authors measured the frequency of binge eating every 2 weeks for 24 weeks for this control group as well. The following table lists a portion of the data similar to results reported by the authors for the frequency of binge eating over the first 8 weeks for participants in the control group.

Frequency of Binge Eating				
Baseline	Week 2	Week 4	Week 6	Week 8
4	3	2	2	2
5	4	4	2	3
3	1	2	1	1
2	2	3	1	1
2	0	0	0	0
5	1	1	0	0

(a) Complete the F-table and make a decision to retain or reject the null hypothesis.

(b) Contrast your answer to the results obtaining in Question 31. Why are the results with the control group interesting?

NOTE: Answers for even numbers are in Appendix C.

Analysis of Variance

Two-Way Between-Subjects Factorial Design

CHAPTER

14

LEARNING OBJECTIVES

After reading this chapter, you should be able to:

1. Describe how the complexity of the two-way ANOVA differs from that of the *t*-tests and the one-way ANOVA.

2. List the three types of research designs for the two-way ANOVA.

3. Define and explain the following terms: *cells*, *main effect*, and *interaction*.

4. Identify the assumptions and list the order of interpretation for outcomes in the two-way between-subjects ANOVA.

5. Calculate the degrees of freedom for the two-way between-subjects ANOVA and locate critical values in the *F*-table.

6. Compute the two-way between-subjects ANOVA and interpret the results.

7. Identify when it is appropriate to compute simple main effect tests and analyze a significant interaction.

8. Compute proportion of variance for the two-way between-subjects ANOVA.

9. Summarize the results of the two-way between-subjects ANOVA in APA format.

10. Compute the two-way between-subjects ANOVA using SPSS.

14.1 OBSERVING TWO FACTORS AT THE SAME TIME

To this point, the complexity of statistical design has varied in two ways:

1. We changed the levels of one factor. In Chapters 9 and 10, we described tests for differences between one and two groups or levels of one factor. In Chapters 12 and 13, we described tests for the variance of more than two groups or levels of one factor.

2. We changed how participants were observed. In Chapters 9 and 12, we described tests in which different participants were observed in each group or at each level of one factor (between-subjects design). In Chapters 10 and 13, we described tests in which the same participants were observed in each group or across the levels of one factor (within-subjects design).

In each statistical design, we included the levels of a single factor. In this chapter, we describe a new way to change the complexity of design by adding a second factor that will be observed in the same study. In behavioral science, there are two common reasons we include a second factor in a design.

First, a hypothesis may require that we observe two factors. Suppose, for example, we state that the higher the difficulty level of a book, the less students will comprehend when there is highlighting in the book. This hypothesis identifies two factors: the presence of highlighting (yes, no) and book difficulty (easy, difficult). To test this hypothesis, then, we must observe the levels of both factors at the same time. The structure of this design is illustrated in Table 14.1. If we measure comprehension as a test score, then on the basis of our hypothesis, we can expect scores to be lowest in the group with a difficult book that has highlighting in it.

Second, we need to control for threats to validity. Broadly defined, *validity* is the extent to which we demonstrate the effect we claim to be demonstrating. For example, suppose we claim that the more positive a teacher is with students, the

TABLE 14.1 The structure of a study that combines the levels of two factors. The hypothesis predicts that participants reading the difficult book with highlighting in it (Group Difficult, Yes) will have the lowest scores.

| | | Highlighting | |
		No	Yes
	Easy	Group Easy, No	Group Easy, Yes
Book Difficulty	Difficult	Group Difficult, No	Group Difficult, Yes

If the hypothesis is correct, then we expect this group to have the lowest test scores.

more students will like their teacher. To test this claim, we could randomly assign a sample of teachers to interact positively or negatively with students in a classroom setting, then have students rate how much they like the teacher.

One possible threat to validity in this study is the subject being taught. Maybe ratings reflect the subject taught and not the teacher. We could control for this possibility by adding the subject taught as a factor in the study. Suppose we tested the hypothesis using a sample that consisted of biology and psychology teachers. As illustrated in Table 14.2, we can include the subject taught as a second factor. On the basis of our hypothesis, we expect the type of interaction (positive, negative) and not the subject taught (biology, psychology) to be associated with differences in ratings. We included subject taught as a factor only to eliminate it as a possible threat to the validity of our claim.

TABLE 14.2   The structure of a study that combines the levels of two factors. On the basis of the hypothesis, we expect the type of interaction (positive, negative) and not the subject taught (biology, psychology) to be associated with differences in ratings.

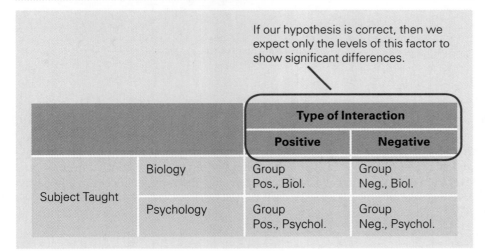

NEW TERMINOLOGY AND NOTATION 14.2

When the levels of two factors are combined, we use the **two-way ANOVA** to analyze the data, and this also leads to new terminology. The new terminology and notation for the two-way ANOVA is described in this section.

The **two-way ANOVA** is a statistical procedure used to test hypotheses concerning the variance of groups created by combining the levels of two factors. This test is used when the variance in any one population is unknown.

DEFINITION

NOTE: When the levels of two factors are combined, we use the two-way ANOVA to analyze the data.

In a two-way ANOVA, each factor is identified with a letter in alphabetical order: Factor A, then Factor B. Separating the factors with a multiplication sign and listing only the letters can simplify this notation. For example, we can state a two-way ANOVA as an A × B ANOVA. You read the multiplication sign as a "by" statement; we read this test as an "A by B" ANOVA.

More common is to identify the levels of each factor numerically. For example, if we measure how quickly (in seconds) subjects respond to a stimulus that varies in size (small, medium, large) and color (bright, dark), we might designate Factor A as size and Factor B as color. Factor A has three levels (small, medium, large), and Factor B has 2 levels (bright, dark). Using the levels of each factor, we can state this test as a 3 × 2 (read "3 by 2") ANOVA. Each number represents the levels of each factor. Table 14.3 shows the structure for this hypothetical study.

TABLE 14.3 A 3 × 2 ANOVA. Each cell is a combination of levels of each factor. For example, the combination of Factor A Level 2 (medium) with Factor B Level 1 (light) is A_2B_1.

		Factor A (Size)		
		1 (Small)	2 (Medium)	3 (Large)
Factor B (Color)	1 (Light)	A_1B_1	A_2B_1	A_3B_1
	2 (Dark)	A_1B_2	A_2B_2	A_3B_2

We often arrange the data for a two-way ANOVA in a table, and when we do, there is special notation to indicate each entry. The levels of Factor A are symbolized as p, and the levels of Factor B are symbolized as q. The combination of one level from each factor is called a **cell.** To calculate the number of cells in a two-way ANOVA, we multiply the levels of each factor:

$$\text{Total number of cells} = pq.$$

The number of cells is the number of groups in a study. In other words, each combination of one level from each factor creates a new group. In the 3 × 2 ANOVA example shown in Table 14.3, the number of cells is $pq = 3 \times 2 = 6$; there are six groups in this study. In this chapter, we introduce only **complete factorial designs,** where each level of each factor is combined. For example, if subjects were not observed in cell A_2B_1 shown in Table 14.3, then the ANOVA would not be a complete factorial design. In this book, we do not cover situations in which some cells are empty. These situations require statistical procedures beyond the scope of this book.

NOTE: Each cell is a group created by the unique combination of one level from each factor. Hence, the total number of cells (pq) is equal to the total number of groups in a study.

DEFINITION

A **cell** is the combination of one level from each factor. Each cell is a group in a research study.

A **complete factorial design** is a research design where each level of one factor is combined or crossed with each level of the other factor, with participants observed in each cell or combination or levels.

DESIGNS FOR THE TWO-WAY ANOVA 14.3

In a two-way ANOVA, we can observe the same or different participants in each group or cell. When different participants are observed at each level of one factor, we call the factor a **between-subjects factor.** When we observe the same participants across the levels of one factor, we call the factor a **within-subjects factor.** In all, there are three types of designs using the two-way ANOVA, depending on whether we have between-subjects or within-subjects factors in a study. The three types of designs, which we discuss in this section, are the following:

1. The 2-between, or between-subjects design

2. The 1-between 1-within, or mixed design

3. The 2-within, or within-subjects design

DEFINITION

A **between-subjects factor** is a type of factor where different participants are observed at each level of the factor.

A **within-subjects factor** is a type of factor where the same participants are observed across the levels of the factor.

2-BETWEEN OR BETWEEN-SUBJECTS DESIGN

When we combine the levels of two between-subjects factors, we are using the **2-between or between-subjects design.** In this design, different participants are observed in each cell or at each level of a factor. For example, suppose we measure decision-making skills in a sample of military veterans from three branches of the armed services (Factor A) who hold different ranks (Factor B). Table 14.4 shows the structure of this 3×2 between-subjects ANOVA with five participants ($n = 5$) observed in each cell.

DEFINITION

A **2-between or between-subjects design** is a research design for a two-way ANOVA in which different participants are observed in each cell or group.

For a two-way ANOVA, n is the number of participants per cell or group, and N is the total number of participants in a study. Using the between-subjects design, we can determine the total number of participants (N) in the study by multiplying n times the number of levels of each factor (pq):

Total number of participants: $N = npq$.

In this example, $n = 5$, $p = 3$, and $q = 2$. The total number of participants using this between-subjects design is

$$N = 5 \times 3 \times 2 = 30.$$

NOTE: A between-subjects design for a two-way ANOVA is used when different participants are observed in each cell or group.

TABLE 14.4 A between-subjects two-way ANOVA with two between-subjects factors, where 5 participants are observed in each cell. In this study, $n = 5$ participants per cell and $N = 30$ total participants.

		Branch of Service		
		Army	Navy	Marines
Type of Rank	Enlisted	$n = 5$	$n = 5$	$n = 5$
	Officer	$n = 5$	$n = 5$	$n = 5$

$N = 30$

1-BETWEEN 1-WITHIN OR MIXED DESIGN

When we combine the levels of one between-subjects factor and one within-subjects factor, we are using the **1-between 1-within or mixed design.** In this design, different participants are observed at each level of the between-subjects factor and the same participants are observed across the levels of the within-subjects factor. For example, suppose we record the number of times that students at different class levels (Factor A) seek advice from different authority figures (Factor B). Table 14.5 shows the structure of this 4×2 mixed ANOVA with five participants ($n = 5$) observed in a given cell or group.

DEFINITION

A **1-between 1-within or mixed design** is a research design for a two-way ANOVA in which different participants are observed at each level of the between-subjects factor and the same participants are observed across the levels of the within-subjects factor.

TABLE 14.5 A mixed two-way ANOVA with one between-subjects factor (class level) and one within-subjects factor (authority figure). Five participants are observed at each level of the between-subjects factor; then the same participants in each group are observed at each level of the within-subjects factor. The vertical ellipses indicate that the same participants are observed in that cell. In this study, $n = 5$ and $N = 20$ total participants observed two times.

		Class Level			
		Freshman	Sophomore	Junior	Senior
Authority Figure	Parent	$n = 5$	$n = 5$	$n = 5$	$n = 5$
	Teacher	⋮	⋮	⋮	⋮

$N = 20$

In this example, Factor A (class level) is a between-subjects factor. Each student is at a different class level. Factor B (authority figure) is a within-subjects factor. We record the number of times that students seek advice from each type of authority figure. Hence, five students at each class level are observed two times.

NOTE: A mixed design for a two-way ANOVA is used when we combine the levels of one between-subjects factor and one within-subjects factor.

Using a mixed design, we can determine the total number of participants (N) in a study by multiplying n times the number of levels of the between-subjects factor. Factor A is the between-subjects factor in this example, so we multiple $n = 5$ times $p = 4$ class levels. The total number of participants using this mixed design is

$$N = 5 \times 4 = 20.$$

2-WITHIN OR WITHIN-SUBJECTS DESIGN

When we combine the levels of two within-subjects factors, we are using the **2-within or within-subjects design.** In this design, the same participants are observed in each cell or group. For example, in a taste perception study, suppose we measure the amount consumed (in milliliters) of a solution mixed with different concentrations of sugar (Factor A) and different flavors (Factor B). Table 14.6 shows the structure of this 3×2 between-subjects ANOVA with five participants ($n = 5$) observed in each cell or group.

A **2-within or within-subjects design** is a research design for the two-way ANOVA in which the same participants are observed in each cell or group.

DEFINITION

NOTE: A within-subjects design for a two-way ANOVA is used when the same participants are observed in each cell or group.

If participants consumed each flavor–sugar mixture, then the same participants were observed in each cell or group. Using a within-subjects design, $n = N$ because n participants are observed pq times. Hence, in this study, $n = 5$ participants consumed six ($pq = 2 \times 3 = 6$) flavor–sugar mixtures.

TABLE 14.6 A within-subjects two-way ANOVA with two within-subjects factors, where 5 participants are observed in each cell. Each participant will taste each flavor-sugar combination. The ellipses indicate that the same participants are observed in all groups or cells. In this study, $n = N = 5$ participants each observed 6 times (once in each cell or group).

		Sweet Taste Concentration		
		2%	5%	10%
Flavor	Orange	$n = 5$	...	...
	Banana	...	...	...
				$N = 5$

LEARNING CHECK 1

1. State two reasons for including two or more factors in the same study.

2. A researcher measures stress in a group of participants who travel different distances to work (none, short, or long commute) from different demographic areas (urban, rural). In this example:

   a. State the number of factors.

   b. State the number of levels of each factor.

3. A researcher conducts a 3 × 2 ANOVA with 15 participants observed in each cell or group. How many participants are needed to conduct this study if he or she conducts a:

   a. Between-subjects factorial design

   b. Within-subjects factorial design

   c. Mixed factorial design in which the first factor is a within-subjects factor

   d. Mixed factorial design in which the second factor is a within-subjects factor

Answers: 1. The hypothesis requires the observation of two factors and to control for threats to validity; 2. (a) Distance of commute and demographic area, (b) the levels of each factor are 3 (distance of commute) and 2 (demographic area); 3. (a) 90 participants, (b) 15 participants, (c) 30 participants, (d) 45 participants.

14.4 DESCRIBING VARIABILITY: MAIN EFFECTS AND INTERACTIONS

In this chapter, we introduce an analysis of variance using the 2-between or between-subjects factorial design called the **two-way between-subjects ANOVA.** When we combine the levels of two factors in which different participants are observed in each cell, four sources of variation can be measured: One source is error variation, and three sources are between-groups variation, which is variation associated with having different groups. We make a hypothesis test to analyze each between-groups variation, same as we did for the one-way ANOVA. Each source of variation, the *F*-statistic for each, and each hypothesis test are introduced in this section.

DEFINITION

A **two-way between-subjects ANOVA** is a statistical procedure used to test hypotheses concerning the combination of levels of two factors using the 2-between or between-subjects design.

SOURCES OF VARIABILITY

Figure 14.1 identifies four sources of variation that arise when we combine the levels of two factors and observe different participants in each cell or combination of levels. One source of variation is associated with differences attributed to error, which is variation that has nothing to do with differences associated with having different groups. The other three sources of variation are associated with differences between group means for each factor and for the combination of levels of each factor. Each source of variation for the two-way between-subjects ANOVA is described in this section.

One source of variation is associated with differences in participant scores within each group (located in the cells of a table summary). This variation, called *within-groups variation,* is also called error because it can't be attributed to differences between group means. This is the same error variation measured for the *t*-tests and

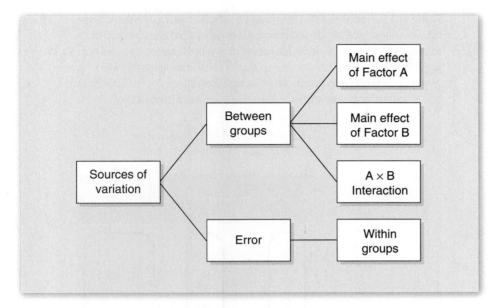

FIGURE 14.1

The different sources of variation present in the two-way between-subjects ANOVA. There are three sources of variation between groups and one source of error (within groups).

one-way ANOVAs. Table 14.7 shows that this source of variation is located in the cells of a table summary for a 2 × 2 between-subjects ANOVA with $n = 5$ participants in each group. Because participants in each cell experience the same treatment, differences in participant scores in each cell or group can't be attributed to differences between group means. As we did for the *t*-tests and one-way ANOVAs, this source of error is placed in the denominator of the test statistic. The test statistic for the two-way between-subjects ANOVA follows the same general form used for the one-way ANOVAs:

$$F_{obt} = \frac{\text{variance between groups}}{\text{error variance}}.$$

Three between-groups sources of variation, or three ways that group means can be compared are also shown in Table 14.7. Each set of group means is a source of variation that can be measured. We can measure the variation of group means across the levels of Factor A (the column means in Table 14.7) and across the levels of Factor B (the row means in Table 14.7). These sources of variation are called **main effects,** and each is a source of between-groups variation:

1. Main effect of Factor A

2. Main effect of Factor B

A **main effect** is a source of variation associated with mean differences across the levels of a single factor.

In the two-way ANOVA, there are two factors and therefore two main effects: one for Factor A and one for Factor B.

DEFINITION

Notice also that we can compute the mean at each combination of levels for each factor or in each cell. The third between-groups variation is associated with the variance of group means in each cell (the cell means in Table 14.7). This source of variation is called an **interaction,** and this is the third source of between-groups variation:

3. The interaction of Factors A × B

TABLE 14.7 A crosstabulation illustrating the sources of variability in the two-way between-subjects ANOVA. The within groups (or error) variation is associated with differences within each cell, which has nothing to do with differences attributed to having different groups. The other three sources of variation are associated with differences between group means: one for Factor A (main effect), one for Factor B (main effect), and one for the combination of levels for Factors A and B (interaction).

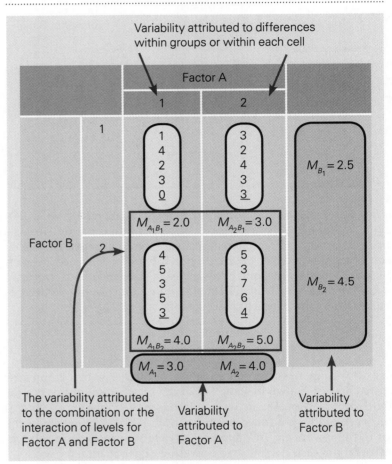

An **interaction** is a source of variation associated with the variance of group means across the combination of levels of two factors. It is a measure of how cell means at each level of one factor change across the levels of a second factor.

NOTE: There are four sources of variation in a two-way between-subjects ANOVA: two main effects, one interaction, and error (within groups).

In an analysis of variance, we want to decide whether group means significantly vary. In the two-way between-subjects ANOVA, there are three ways that the group means can vary (in the rows, columns, and cells). Therefore, we must compute three hypothesis tests: one for each source of between-groups variation. We make two main effect tests (one for Factor A and one for Factor B) and one interaction test (one for the combination of levels for Factors A and B). The within-groups (or error) variation is the denominator for each test. The test statistic for each test is described here.

TESTING MAIN EFFECTS

The hypothesis test for each main effect (one for Factor A and one for Factor B) determines whether group means significantly vary across the levels of a single factor. In a table summary, such as that given in Table 14.7, we compare the variance of row and column means. To compute the test statistic for a main effect, we place the between-groups variance for one factor in the numerator and the error variance in the denominator. We again measure the variance as a mean square (*MS*), same as we did for the one-way ANOVAs. The test statistic for the main effect of Factor A is

$$F_A = \frac{\text{variance of group means for Factor A}}{\text{variance attributed to error}} = \frac{MS_A}{MS_E}.$$

The test statistic for the main effect of Factor B is

$$F_B = \frac{\text{variance of group means for Factor B}}{\text{variance attributed to error}} = \frac{MS_B}{MS_E}.$$

A significant main effect indicates that group means significantly vary across the levels of one factor, independent of the second factor. To illustrate, suppose the data in Table 14.7 are quiz scores, where Factor A is whether students studied for a quiz (no, yes), and Factor B is their class attendance (high, low). Table 14.8 identifies each main effect and shows how each would be interpreted, if significant. Notice that we interpret a significant main effect similar to the interpretation of significant results using the one-way ANOVA.

NOTE: A main effect reflects differences between row and column means in a table summary.

TABLE 14.8 Main effects. The main effect for each factor reflects the difference between the row and column totals in the table. There are two main effects (one for Factor A and one for Factor B) in a two-way ANOVA.

Main effect of Factor A. If significant, we state that students who studied earned higher quiz scores, regardless of their class attendance.

Main effect of Factor B. If significant, we state that students with high attendance earned higher quiz scores, regardless of whether they studied for the quiz.

TESTING THE INTERACTION

The hypothesis test for the combination of levels of two factors is called an A × B interaction test, where each letter (A and B) refers to each factor. The interaction test determines whether group means at each level of one factor significantly change across the levels of a second factor. In a table summary, such as that given in Table 14.7, we compare the variance of cell means.

NOTE: The interaction reflects differences between cell means in a table summary.

To compute the test statistic for an interaction, we place the between-groups variance for the combination of levels for two factors (the cell means) in the numerator and the error variance in the denominator. We again measure the variance as a mean square (*MS*). The test statistic for the A × B interaction test is

$$F_{A \times B} = \frac{\text{variance of cell means}}{\text{variance attributed to error}} = \frac{MS_{A \times B}}{MS_E}.$$

TABLE 14.9 Interaction. A significant interaction indicates that at least one pair of cell means are significantly different. For the interaction in a two-way ANOVA, we analyze cell or group means inside the table.

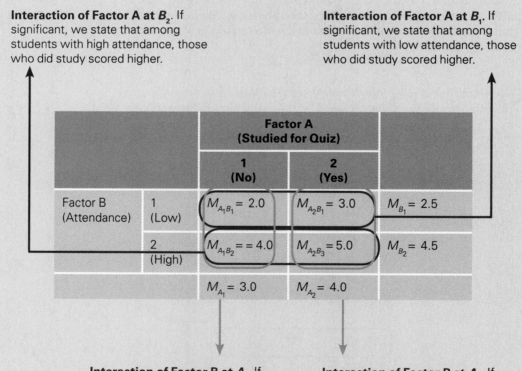

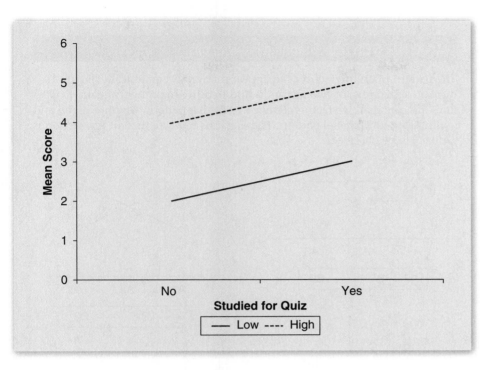

FIGURE 14.2

The cell means from the study in Tables 14.8 and 14.9. The graph indicates that an interaction is unlikely because these lines are parallel.

A significant interaction indicates that group means across the levels for one factor significantly vary depending on which level of the second factor you look at. To illustrate this interpretation, let's go back again to the quiz scores study, where Factor A is whether students studied for a quiz (yes, no) and Factor B is class attendance (high, low). Table 14.9 identifies four ways to interpret the A × B interaction. For each interpretation, we look across the levels of one factor at each level of the second factor. Which interpretation we use to describe the interaction depends largely on how we want to describe the data.

The pattern of an interaction can be obvious when it is graphed. To graph an interaction, we plot the cell means for each combination of factors. Figure 14.2 shows a graph of the cells means for the studying and class attendance example. There are two ways to interpret this graph:

1. When the two lines are parallel, this indicates that a significant interaction is not likely.

2. When the two lines touch or cross, this indicates that there is a possible significant interaction.

The pattern in Figure 14.2 shows that an interaction between class attendance and studying is unlikely. Parallel lines indicate that changes across the levels of both factors are constant. When the lines are not parallel, this indicates that changes are not constant; instead, changes in group means across the levels of one factor vary at each level of the second factor. The two-way ANOVA is used to determine whether these changes are significant.

MAKING SENSE: Graphing Interactions

The pattern of an interaction can appear many ways graphically. Figure 14.3 displays six graphs for two factors, A and B, using hypothetical data. Parallel lines indicate that two factors change in a similar pattern. Graphs (a), (b), and (c) illustrate this parallel pattern. These graphs indicate that an interaction is unlikely to be observed.

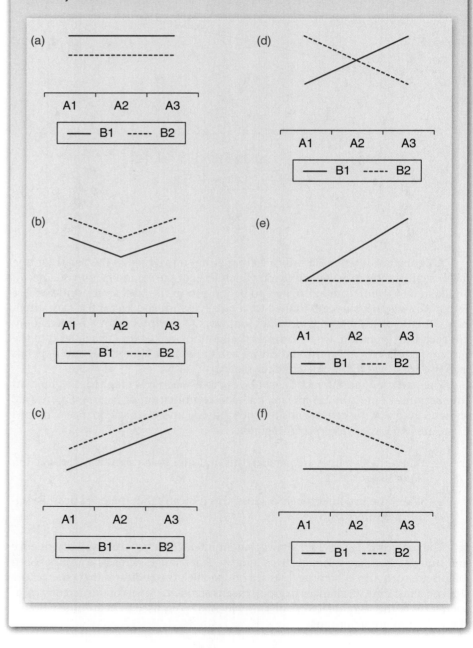

FIGURE 14.3

Six hypothetical results for two factors (A and B). Possible interactions are evident in Graphs (d), (e), and (f).

On the other hand, Graphs (d), (e), and (f) illustrate patterns where the lines touch or cross. When looking at a graph, imagine that the lines extend beyond the limits of the graph. For example, notice that Graph (f) has two lines that don't touch or cross. But if the lines continued, they would eventually cross. Hence, Graph (f) is an example of a pattern where the lines touch or cross. When the distance between two lines changes, or is not parallel, this indicates that an interaction is possible. However, keep in mind that data do always follow simple patterns. The graphical displays of interactions described here can be used as a general rule. It is not possible, however, to know for sure if an interaction is significant until we analyze the data statistically.

NOTE: When two lines are not parallel, meaning that they touch or cross, this indicates that an interaction is possible.

OUTCOMES AND ORDER OF INTERPRETATION

We compute three hypothesis tests in the two-way between-subjects ANOVA, and each hypothesis test is an independent test. Any combination of these three tests could be significant when we compute the two-way between-subjects ANOVA. In all, there are eight possible outcomes we could obtain:

1. All three hypothesis tests are not significant.

2. Significant main effect of Factor A only

3. Significant main effect of Factor B only

4. Significant main effect of Factor A and Factor B

5. Significant A × B interaction only

6. Significant main effect of Factor A and an A × B interaction

7. Significant main effect of Factor B and an A × B interaction

8. All three hypothesis tests are significant.

A significant interaction identifies the mean differences that can't necessarily be explained by a main effect alone. A significant main effect shows that group means vary across the levels of one factor. A significant interaction, however, is more specific. The interaction shows that group means significantly vary across the levels of one factor, depending on which level of the second factor you look at. Therefore, we always analyze a significant interaction first, before analyzing significant main effects. Hence, if we obtain outcomes 6 to 8 from the list above, then examine the interaction first.

NOTE: A significant interaction is analyzed first, before analyzing significant main effects, if any.

1. What are the three sources of between-groups variation in the two-way between-subjects ANOVA?

2. What is the denominator for each hypothesis test in the two-way between-subjects ANOVA?

LEARNING CHECK 2

3. What is the pattern in a graph that indicates that a significant interaction is possible?

4. A researcher computes the two-way between-subjects ANOVA and the results show a significant main effect and a significant interaction. Which significant result should the researcher analyze first?

Answers: 1. Factor A (main effect), Factor B (main effect), and the combination of levels for Factors A and B (A × B interaction); 2. Variance attributed to error or, specifically, mean square error; 3. A pattern where two lines are not parallel; instead, the lines touch or cross; 4. The significant interaction.

14.5 THE TWO-WAY BETWEEN-SUBJECTS ANOVA

In this section, we will compute the two-way between-subjects ANOVA. We use the two-way between-subjects ANOVA when we combine the levels of two factors using the 2-between or between-subjects design. We must make four assumptions to compute the two-way between-subjects ANOVA:

1. *Normality.* We assume that data in the population or populations being sampled from are normally distributed. This assumption is particularly important for small sample sizes. In larger samples, the overall variance is reduced, and this assumption becomes less critical as a result.

2. *Random sampling.* We assume that the data we measure were obtained from a sample that was selected using a random sampling procedure. It is generally considered inappropriate to conduct hypothesis tests with nonrandom samples.

3. *Independence.* We assume that the probabilities of each measured outcome in a study are independent or equal. Using random sampling usually satisfies this assumption.

4. *Homogeneity of variance.* We assume that the variance in each population is equal to each other. Violating this assumption can increase the likelihood of committing a Type I error.

In Example 14.1, we will follow the four steps in hypothesis testing to compute a two-way between-subjects ANOVA.

EXAMPLE 14.1

The more sugar people consume (increased exposure), the more they tend to like sugary foods. A researcher hypothesizes that a person's level of sugar exposure can interfere or distract him or her during a computer task when food is present. To test this, the researcher uses a survey to categorize participants by their level of exposure to sugars (low, moderate, high exposure). All participants complete a computer task at a table with a buffet of sugary foods (buffet present) or a stack of papers (buffet absent) on the table. Slower times to complete the computer task indicate greater interference or distraction. Table 14.10 gives the hypothetical data for this example. Compute the two-way between-subjects ANOVA using a .05 level of significance.

Let's start by graphing the interaction. The graph in Figure 14.4 plots the six cell means given in Table 14.10. When we distribute Factor A (exposure to sugar) on the x-axis and then plot the cell means, we find that the two lines touch or cross. This pattern indicates that the interaction could be significant. The only way to know

TABLE 14.10   Example 14.1. The data for a 3 × 2 ANOVA that gives the times (in seconds) it took 36 participants (n = 6 per cell) to complete a computer task. Cell means are given in each cell.

		Exposure to Sugars (Factor A)		
		Low	**Moderate**	**High**
Buffet of Sugary Foods (Factor B)	Absent	8 7 9 10 12 8 $M = 9$	10 12 15 8 6 9 $M = 10$	13 9 11 8 13 12 $M = 11$
	Present	5 8 5 6 5 7 $M = 6$	15 10 8 9 7 11 $M = 10$	15 12 15 16 12 14 $M = 14$

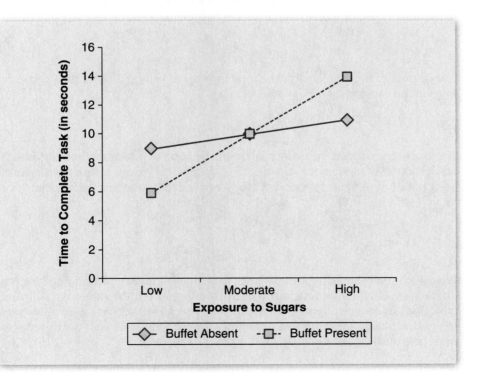

FIGURE 14.4

The cell means in Example 14.1. The lines in the graph cross, indicating that a significant interaction is possible between exposure to sugar and the buffet.

for sure is to compute a two-way between-subjects ANOVA for these data. We begin by stating our hypotheses.

Step 1: State the hypotheses. The null hypothesis states that the group means for exposure to sugar (main effect), buffet (main effect), and both factors combined (interaction) do not vary (=) in the population; the alternative hypothesis states that the group means do vary (>) in the population:

NOTE: The null hypothesis for a two-way ANOVA states that group means do not vary in the population for each factor and for both factors combined.

H_0: $\sigma^2_{\mu's} = 0$ Mean times to complete the computer task do not vary by exposure to sugar, buffet, and/or the combination of these two factors.

H_1: $\sigma^2_{\mu's} > 0$ Mean times to complete the computer task do vary by exposure to sugar, buffet, and/or the combination of these two factors)

Step 2: Set the criteria for a decision. The level of significance for this test is .05. We must compute the degrees of freedom to find the critical values for each hypothesis test. There are four sources of variation in the two-way between-subjects ANOVA, and we compute degrees of freedom for each source of variation.

The degrees of freedom for Factor A (exposure) are $p - 1$:

$$df_A = 3 - 1 = 2.$$

The degrees of freedom for Factor B (buffet) are $q - 1$:

$$df_B = 2 - 1 = 1.$$

To compute the degrees of freedom for the A × B interaction, we multiply the degrees of freedom for Factor A times the degrees of freedom for Factor B, or $(p - 1)(q - 1)$:

$$df_{A \times B} = 2(1) = 2.$$

The degrees of freedom error is the total number of cells (pq) times the degrees of freedom for each cell ($n - 1$), or $pq(n - 1)$.

$$df_E = (3)(2)(6 - 1) = 30.$$

The total degrees of freedom are equal to the total number of participants, minus 1, which are the degrees of freedom for variance: $N - 1$, or $(npq) - 1$. We can add up the degrees of freedom we just computed or calculate $(npq) - 1$ to find the total degrees of freedom:

$$df_T = 2 + 1 + 2 + 30 = 35.$$

$$df_T = (6 \times 3 \times 2) - 1 = 35.$$

We will compute three hypothesis tests: one for each main effect and one for the interaction. Each hypothesis test requires a different critical value. We will find critical values for each hypothesis test in Step 4 because it will be easier to see why the critical values are computed differently for each test if we wait until Step 4 to find the critical values.

Step 3: Compute the test statistic. For each hypothesis test, we compute the F-statistic. The F-statistic can be used to determine whether group means for Factor A (exposure), Factor B (buffet), or the combination of Factors A and B significantly vary relatively more than the variance attributed to error. We compute the test statistic for each hypothesis test using a four-stage process, similar to that used for the one-way ANOVAs.

TABLE 14.11   STAGE 1. Preliminary calculations for the two-way between-subjects ANOVA in Example 14.1.

		Exposure to Sugars (Factor A)			
		Low	**Moderate**	**High**	
Buffet of Sugary Foods (Factor B)	Absent	$\sum x = 54$ $\sum x^2 = 502$	$\sum x = 60$ $\sum x^2 = 650$	$\sum x = 66$ $\sum x^2 = 748$	$\sum x = 180$
	Present	$\sum x = 36$ $\sum x^2 = 224$	$\sum x = 60$ $\sum x^2 = 640$	$\sum x = 84$ $\sum x^2 = 1,190$	$\sum x = 180$
		$\sum x = 90$	$\sum x = 120$	$\sum x = 150$	$\sum x_T = 360$ $\sum x_T^2 = 3,954$

Stage 1: Preliminary calculations: Find $\sum x$ in each cell and across each row and column, $\sum x_T, \sum x^2$ in each cell, $\sum x_T^2, n, p,$ and q. These preliminary calculations are shown in Table 14.11. Each calculation made in the table is described here.

1. Find $n, p,$ and q. The number of participants per cell is $n = 6$. Exposure to sugars is Factor A, and the buffet is Factor B. Hence, $p = 3$ (the levels of Factor A), and $q = 2$ (the levels of Factor B). The total number of participants in this study is therefore $npq = 36$ participants.

2. Find $\sum x$ and $\sum x_T$. Sum the scores (Σx) in each cell. Sum the row and the column totals by adding across the rows and columns, respectively. The grand total $\left(\sum x_T \right)$ is the sum of the cell totals. The sum of the cell totals, the row totals, and the column totals will each equal the grand total.

3. Find $\sum x^2$ and $\sum x_T^2$ total. Square each score, then sum the squared scores in each cell. For example, in the top left cell (low exposure, buffet absent), we sum $8^2 + 7^2 + 9^2 + 10^2 + 12^2 + 8^2 = 502$. The sum of the squared scores across cells is equal to the total sum of squared scores: $\sum x_T^2$.

Stage 2: Compute intermediate calculations: Find [1], [2], [3], [4], and [5].

In Stage 1, we computed the values needed to make calculations in Stage 2. We will use the values we compute in Stage 2 to find the sum of squares for each source of variation in Stage 3. There are five calculations in Stage 2:

First we compute a correction factor by squaring the grand total $\left(\sum x_T\right)$ and dividing by the total sample size (npq):

$$[1] \quad \frac{\left(\sum x_T\right)^2}{npq} = \frac{(360)^2}{36} = 3,600.$$

Second, we restate the sum of the squared scores in all cells:

$$[2] \quad \sum x_T^2 = 3,954.$$

Third, we calculate variation attributed to Factor A (exposure) by dividing the sum of squared scores in each column total (A) by the number of scores summed in each column (nq):

$$[3] \quad \frac{\sum A^2}{nq} = \frac{90^2 + 120^2 + 150^2}{6 \times 2} = 3,750.$$

Fourth, we calculate variation attributed to Factor B (buffet) by dividing the sum of squared scores in each row total (B) by the number of scores summed in each row (np):

$$[4] \quad \frac{\sum B^2}{np} = \frac{180^2 + 180^2}{6 \times 3} = 3,600.$$

Last, we calculate variation attributed to the interaction (Exposure × Buffet) by dividing the sum of squared scores in each cell total (AB) by the number of scores in each cell (n).

$$[5] \quad \frac{\sum AB^2}{n} = \frac{54^2 + 60^2 + 66^2 + 36^2 + 60^2 + 84^2}{6} = 3,804.$$

Stage 3: Compute the sums of squares (SS) for each source of variation. SS is the numerator for the variance. We will compute the variance (a mean square) for each main effect, the interaction, error, and the total. So we compute SS for each source of variation and SS total.

The sum of squares for Factor A $\left(SS_A\right)$ is the difference between Calculation [3] and Calculation [1] in Stage 2:

$$SS_A = [3] - [1] = 3,750 - 3,600 = 150.$$

The sum of squares for Factor B $\left(SS_B\right)$ is the difference between Calculation [4] and Calculation [1] in Stage 2:

$$SS_B = [4] - [1] = 3,600 - 3,600 = 0.$$

The sum of squares for the A × B interaction $(SS_{A\times B})$ is Calculation [5] minus Calculation [1] in Stage 2, minus the sum of squares for Factors A and B:

$$SS_{A\times B} = [5] - [1] - SS_A - SS_B = 3,804 - 3,600 - 150 - 0 = 54.$$

The sum of squares error (SS_E) is the difference between Calculation [2] and Calculation [5] in Stage 2:

$$SS_E = [2] - [5] = 3,954 - 3,804 = 150.$$

The sum of squares total (SS_T) is the difference between Calculation [2] and Calculation [1] in Stage 2:

$$SS_T = [2] - [1] = 3,954 - 3,600 = 354.$$

Stage 4: Complete the *F*-table. The *F*-table lists *SS, df, MS,* and the test statistic value for each hypothesis test. The calculations in the *F*-table are described here and listed in Table 14.12.

The first column of values in the *F*-table lists the sum of squares (we computed these in Stage 3). The second column lists the degrees of freedom (we computed these in Stage 2). We will use these values to compute the mean square (or variance) for each source of variation. The formula for variance is *SS* divided by *df*, so we divide across each row to compute each mean square.

TABLE 14.12 The F-table for a two-way between-subjects ANOVA, with formulas for completing the table given. Notice that mean square error (MS_E) is the denominator for each hypothesis test.

Source of Variation	SS	df	MS	F
Factor A (Exposure)	150	$p-1$	$\dfrac{SS_A}{df_A}$	$F_A = \dfrac{MS_A}{MS_E}$
Factor B (Buffet)	0	$q-1$	$\dfrac{SS_B}{df_B}$	$F_B = \dfrac{MS_B}{MS_E}$
A × B (Exposure × Buffet)	54	$(p-1)(q-1)$	$\dfrac{SS_{A\times B}}{df_{A\times B}}$	$F_{A\times B} = \dfrac{MS_{A\times B}}{MS_E}$
Error (within groups)	150	$pq(n-1)$	$\dfrac{SS_E}{df_E}$	
Total	354	$npq-1$		

The variance or mean square for Factor A is

$$MS_A = \frac{SS_A}{df_A} = \frac{150}{2} = 75.$$

The variance or mean square for Factor B is

$$MS_B = \frac{SS_B}{df_B} = \frac{0}{1} = 0.$$

The variance or mean square for the A × B interaction is

$$MS_{A\times B} = \frac{SS_{A\times B}}{df_{A\times B}} = \frac{54}{2} = 27.$$

NOTE: A mean square is the same as a variance. It is SS divided by df for each source of variation.

The variance or mean square for error is

$$MS_E = \frac{SS_E}{df_E} = \frac{150}{30} = 5.$$

The test statistic is basically the same as that for the one-way ANOVAs: It is the mean square between groups divided by the mean square error. For a two-way between-subjects ANOVA, we compute a different hypothesis test for each source of between-groups variation: one for each main effect and one for the interaction.

The test statistic for Factor A (exposure) is

$$F_A = \frac{MS_A}{MS_E} = \frac{75}{5} = 15.00.$$

To find the critical value, we need to know the degrees of freedom for Factor A and for error. The degrees of freedom numerator (for Factor A) is 2. The degrees of freedom denominator (for error) is 30. We locate the critical value in Table B.3 in Appendix B. At a .05 level of significance, the critical value associated with 2 and 30 degrees of freedom is

Critical value: $F(2, 30) = 3.32$.

The test statistic for Factor B (buffet) is

$$F_B = \frac{MS_B}{MS_E} = \frac{0}{5} = 0.$$

To find the critical value, we need to know the degrees of freedom for Factor B and for error. The degrees of freedom numerator (for Factor B) is 1. The degrees of freedom denominator (for error) doesn't change (30). At a .05 level of significance, the critical value associated with 1 and 30 degrees of freedom given in Table B.3 in Appendix B is

Critical value: $F(1, 30) = 4.17$.

The test statistic for the A × B (Exposure × Buffet) interaction is

$$F_{A\times B} = \frac{MS_{A\times B}}{MS_E} = \frac{27}{5} = 5.40.$$

To find the critical value, we need to know the degrees of freedom for the A × B interaction and for error. The degrees of freedom numerator (for the interaction) is 2. The degrees of freedom denominator (for error) doesn't change (30). At a .05 level of significance, the critical value associated with 2 and 30 degrees of freedom given in Table B.3 in Appendix B is

Critical value: $F(2, 30) = 3.32$.

Table 14.13 shows the completed *F*-table for Example 14.1. We can now make a decision for each hypothesis test in Step 4.

TABLE 14.13   The completed *F*-table for Example 14.1. An asterisk indicates significance at $p < .05$.

Source of Variation	SS	df	MS	F
Factor A (exposure)	150	2	75	15.0*
Factor B (buffet)	0	1	0	0
A × B (Exposure × Buffet)	54	2	27	5.4*
Error (within groups)	150	30	5	
Total	354	35		

Step 4: Make a decision. We will make a decision for each hypothesis test by comparing the value of the test statistic to the critical value.

Main effect of Factor A (exposure) is significant: $F_A = 15.00$ exceeds the critical value of 3.32; we reject the null hypothesis.

Main effect of Factor B (buffet) is not significant: $F_B = 0$ does not exceed the critical value of 4.17; we retain the null hypothesis.

The A × B interaction (Exposure × Buffet) is significant: $F_{A×B} = 5.40$ exceeds the critical value of 3.32; we reject the null hypothesis.

Table 14.14 summarizes the procedures used to compute the two-way between-subjects ANOVA. If we were to report the result for Example 14.1 in a research journal, it would look something like this:

> Using a two-way between-subjects ANOVA, a significant main effect of Exposure, $F(2, 30) = 15.00$, $p < .05$, and a significant Exposure × Buffet interaction, $F(2, 30) = 5.40$, $p < .05$, were evident. A main effect of buffet (present, absent) was not evident ($p = 1.00$).

This study is an example of outcome 6 in the list of eight possible outcomes given under the last subheading of Section 14.4. The significant interaction confirms the pattern we observed in Figure 14.4. We know from the interaction that one pair of the six cell means significantly differs. Now we have to determine which pairs of cell means differ. The interaction was significant, so analyzing this result is the next step.

TABLE 14.14 Summary of the process for the two-way between-subjects ANOVA.

Terminology	Formula	Meaning
Step 1: State the hypotheses		
Null hypotheses	$\sigma_A^2 = 0$	The levels of Factor A do not vary.
	$\sigma_B^2 = 0$	The levels of Factor B do not vary.
	$\sigma_{A \times B}^2 = 0$	Cell means do not vary.
Alternative hypotheses	$\sigma_A^2 > 0$	The levels of Factor A vary.
	$\sigma_B^2 > 0$	The levels of Factor B vary.
	$\sigma_{A \times B}^2 > 0$	Cell means vary.
Step 2: Set the criteria for a decision		
Degree of freedom for Factor A	$df_A = p - 1$	The levels of Factor A minus 1
Degrees of freedom for Factor B	$df_B = q - 1$	The levels of Factor B minus 1
Degrees of freedom for the A × B interaction	$df_{A \times B} = (p - 1)(q - 1)$	The df for Factor A times the df for Factor B
Degrees of freedom error (within groups)	$df_E = pq(n - 1)$	The total number of cells times the df within each cell
Degrees of freedom total	$df_T = npq - 1$	The total number of participants minus 1
Step 3: Compute the test statistic		
STAGE 1		
Levels of Factor A	p	Number of levels for Factor A
Levels of Factor B	q	Number of levels for Factor B
Total cells	pq	Total number of cells (or groups) in a study
Sample size	npq	Total sample size
Grand total	$\sum x_T$	The sum of all cell totals
Sum of squared scores	$\sum x_T^2$	The sum of all individually squared scores in each cell
STAGE 2		
[1]	$\dfrac{\left(\sum x_T \right)^2}{npq}$	The correction factor
[2]	$\sum x_T^2$	The "uncorrected" total variation in a study
[3]	$\dfrac{\sum A^2}{nq}$	The "uncorrected" variation attributed to Factor A

[4]	$\dfrac{\sum B^2}{np}$	The "uncorrected" variation attributed to Factor B
[5]	$\dfrac{\sum AB^2}{n}$	The "uncorrected" variation attributed to the A × B interaction
STAGE 3		
Sum of squares for Factor A	$SS_A = [3] - [1]$	The sum of the squared deviations for Factor A
Sum of squares for Factor B	$SS_B = [4] - [1]$	The sum of the squared deviations for Factor B
Sum of squares for the A × B interaction	$SS_{A \times B} = [5] - [1] - SS_A - SS_B$	The sum of the squared deviations for the A × B interaction
Sum of squares error (within groups)	$SS_E = [2] - [5]$	The sum of the squared deviations within each cell
Sum of squares total	$SS_T = [2] - [1]$	The sum of the squared deviations in all cells
STAGE 4		
Mean square for Factor A	$MS_A = \dfrac{SS_A}{df_A}$	The variance for Factor A.
Mean squared for Factor B	$MS_B = \dfrac{SS_B}{df_B}$	The variance for Factor B.
Mean square for the A × B interaction	$MS_{A \times B} = \dfrac{SS_{A \times B}}{df_{A \times B}}$	The variance for the combined levels of Factor A and Factor B
Mean square error (within groups)	$MS_E = \dfrac{SS_E}{df_E}$	The variance within each cell. This is the denominator for all three hypothesis tests.
Hypothesis test for Factor A	$F_A = \dfrac{MS_A}{MS_E}$	The test statistic for Factor A
Hypothesis test for Factor B	$F_B = \dfrac{MS_B}{MS_E}$	The test statistic for Factor B
Hypothesis test for the A × B interaction	$F_{A \times B} = \dfrac{MS_{A \times B}}{MS_E}$	The test statistic for the A × B interaction
Step 4: Make a decision		
General decision criterion	—	When $F_{obt} < F_{crit}$, retain null. When $F_{obt} \geq F_{crit}$, reject null.

LEARNING CHECK 3

1. State four assumptions of the two-way between-subjects ANOVA.

2. A researcher conducts a study to determine whether parents with different levels of self-esteem (low, high) and family size (1, 2, 3, 4, or 5 children) display different parenting styles. Six parents ($n = 6$ per cell) were observed using a between-subjects design. Based on the information given here and in the table, answer the following questions. Hint: First complete the F-table.

Source of Variation	SS	df	MS	F
Factor A (self-esteem)	18			
Factor B (family size)	30			
A × B (Self-Esteem × Family Size)	42			
Error (within treatments)	75			
Total	165			

   a. What are the degrees of freedom for the A × B interaction?

   b. What is the value of mean square error?

   c. What is the value for the test statistic for each main effect and for the interaction?

3. Make a decision for each hypothesis test in Question 2.

14.6 ANALYZING MAIN EFFECTS AND INTERACTIONS

When the decision is to retain the null hypothesis for all three hypothesis tests, then we stop: No pairs of group means significantly vary. However, when the decision is to reject the null hypothesis, then we must analyze the data further. If main effects are significant, then we conduct post hoc tests (same as those taught in Chapter 12). If the interaction is significant, we analyze the interaction first using **simple main effect tests.**

Simple main effect tests are hypothesis tests used to analyze a significant interaction by comparing mean differences or simple main effects for one factor at each level of a second factor. After we compute simple main effect tests, we can then compute post hoc tests for the significant simple main effects that we find. Figure 14.5 shows the steps for analyzing a significant two-way ANOVA. In this section, we describe how to compute and interpret simple main effect tests for a significant interaction.

DEFINITION

Simple main effect tests are hypothesis tests used to analyze a significant interaction by comparing the mean differences or simple main effects of one factor at each level of a second factor.

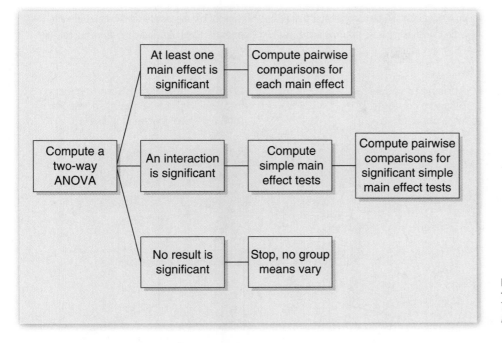

FIGURE 14.5

The steps following a two-way ANOVA.

INTERACTIONS: SIMPLE MAIN EFFECT TESTS

A significant interaction indicates that at least one pair of group means for the A × B interaction (in the cells of a table summary) significantly differs. To analyze the interaction, we first need to know what question we want to answer. We follow three steps to analyze the interaction:

NOTE: A significant interaction indicates that at least one pair of cell means significantly differs.

Step 1: Choose how to describe the data.

Step 2: Compute simple main effect tests.

Step 3: Compute pairwise comparisons.

Step 1: Choose how to describe the data. Table 14.15 shows two ways to interpret the interaction and five potential questions that can be asked. One way to interpret the interaction is to analyze the rows, leading to Q1 and Q2 in the table; the second way is to analyze the columns, leading to Q3, Q4, and Q5 in the table. We first choose which way we want to describe or interpret the data. Then we can make comparisons to answer the questions given in Table 14.15.

One way to interpret the interaction is to look in the table at how cell means for Factor A (exposure) change at each level of Factor B (buffet). This leads to two questions:

Q1: Does greater exposure to sugars interfere with completing a computer task when the buffet is absent?

Q2: Does greater exposure to sugars interfere with completing a computer task when the buffet is present?

TABLE 14.15 Analyzing the interaction. A significant interaction indicates that at least one pair of cell means are significantly different. There are two ways to analyze the A × B interaction. Analyzing across the rows addresses two questions (Q1 and Q2). Analyzing down the columns addresses three questions (Q3, Q4, and Q5) in this example.

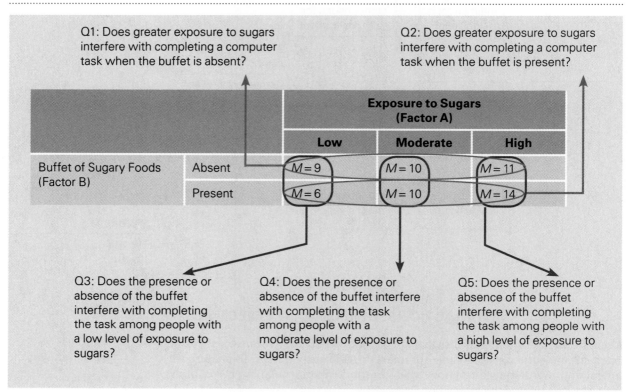

By limiting our comparisons to one level of Factor B (buffet) at a time, we can compare the cell means for Factor A (exposure). In other words, we can compare the cell means at each level of exposure when the buffet was absent (top row of cells in Table 14.15) and a separate comparison when the buffet was present (bottom row of cells in Table 14.15).

A second way to interpret the interaction is to look in the table at how the cell means for Factor B (buffet) change at each level of Factor A (exposure). This leads to three questions:

Q3: Does the presence or absence of the buffet interfere with completing the task among people with a low level of exposure to sugars?

Q4: Does the presence or absence of the buffet interfere with completing the task among people with a moderate level of exposure to sugars?

Q5: Does the presence or absence of the buffet interfere with completing the task among people with a high level of exposure to sugars?

By limiting our comparisons to one level of Factor A (exposure) at a time, we can compare the cell means for Factor B (buffet). In other words, we can compare the cell means at each level of buffet for persons with low exposure (left column of cells in Table 14.15), a separate comparison for persons with moderate exposure (middle column of cells in Table 14.15), and a separate comparison for persons with high exposure (right column of cells in Table 14.15).

NOTE: *There are many ways to analyze an interaction depending on the questions researchers want to answer.*

To decide whether we want to answer Q1 and Q2, or Q3, Q4, and Q5, we need to determine which questions best address the hypothesis. In the exposure and buffet study, we want to determine whether a buffet of foods interferes with completing a computer task when the buffet is present (sugary foods are placed on the desk) versus absent (stacks of papers are placed on the desk). We can determine this by answering Q1 and Q2, so let's choose to answer these two questions.

Step 2: Compute simple main effect tests. To answer Q1, we will compare the top row of cell means in Table 14.15 for the buffet-absent group. To answer Q2, we will compare the bottom row of cell means in Table 14.15 for the buffet-present group. We will answer Q1 first.

To answer Q1, we compare the top three cells in Table 14.15. Because different participants were assigned to each group or cell in this study, we can compute a one-way between-subjects ANOVA on these data—this is the simple main effect test we will use. Table 14.16 shows the data for the top row of cells (originally given in Table 14.10) and the *F*-table for the simple main effect test. On the basis of the results shown in the *F*-table, we decide to retain the null hypothesis. As expected, we conclude that a person's level of exposure to sugar does not interfere with the time it takes to complete a computer task when the buffet is absent.

TABLE 14.16   Simple main effect test for when the buffet was absent. The decision is to retain the null hypothesis. We decide that increased exposure to sugars does not interfere with completing the computer task when the buffet was absent (i.e., when stacks of paper were on the desk).

Exposure to Sugars		
Low	**Moderate**	**High**
8	10	13
7	12	9
9	15	11
10	8	8
12	6	13
8	9	12

Source of Variation	SS	df	MS	F
Between groups (exposure)	12	2	6.000	1.023
Error (within groups)	88	15	5.867	
Total	100	17		

To answer Q2, we compare the bottom three cells in Table 14.15. Because different participants were assigned to each group or cell in this study, we again compute a one-way between-subjects ANOVA on these data—this is the simple main effect test we use. Table 14.17 shows the data for the bottom row of cells (originally given in Table 14.10) and the F-table for the simple main effect test. On the basis of the results shown in the F-table, we decide to reject the null hypothesis. As expected, we conclude that a person's level of exposure to sugar interferes with the time it takes to complete a computer task when the buffet is present.

In Example 14.1, the researcher hypothesized that a person's level of sugar exposure can interfere or distract him or her during a computer task when food is present. We had participants with different levels of exposure to sugar complete a computer task with and without the buffet present. We measured the time it took participants to complete the computer task and used a two-way between-subjects ANOVA to analyze the data. The simple effect tests we just computed confirmed this original hypothesis: The time it took to complete the computer task significantly varied when the buffet was present but not when it was absent.

Step 3: Compute pairwise comparisons. In this step, we compute post hoc tests to analyze only the significant simple main effect tests we computed in Step 2. In this case, we will compare all possible pairs of cell means in the bottom row—to analyze the cell means for the significant simple main effect test for the buffet-present condition.

TABLE 14.17   Simple main effect test for when the buffet was present. The decision is to reject the null hypothesis. We decide that increased exposure to sugars interferes with the completion of a computer task when the buffet of sugary foods was present. An asterisk indicates signficance at $p < .05$.

Exposure to Sugars		
Low	Medium	High
5	15	15
8	10	12
5	8	15
6	9	16
5	7	12
7	11	14

Source of Variation	SS	df	MS	F
Between groups (exposure)	192	2	96.00	23.23*
Error (within groups)	62	15	4.133	
Total	254	17		

Step 3 is necessary only when we compare more than two cells. With two cells, only one pair of means can be compared; multiple pairwise comparisons are therefore unnecessary. In Example 14.1, multiple pairwise comparisons are necessary because we compare three cells or groups. The mean in each group in the bottom row of cells was $M = 6$ in the low-exposure group, $M = 10$ in the moderate-exposure group, and $M = 14$ in the high-exposure group.

In Chapter 12, we introduced two post hoc tests that can be used following a significant one-way between-subjects ANOVA. Because Tukey's honestly significant difference (HSD) is the more conservative post hoc test, let's use this test to compare each pair of cell means. For this post hoc test, the test statistic is the difference between each pair of group means. The critical value for each pairwise comparison is 3.05 (refer to Chapter 12 for a description of how to find the critical value using this post hoc test). Each pairwise comparison and the decision for each comparison are as follows:

NOTE: Making multiple pairwise comparisons in Step 3 is necessary only when we compare more than two cell means.

> Comparison 1: high exposure and low exposure: $14 - 6 = 8.0$ (reject the null hypothesis; this value is greater than 3.05).
>
> Comparison 2: moderate exposure and low exposure: $10 - 6 = 4.0$ (reject the null hypothesis; this value is greater than 3.05).
>
> Comparison 3: high exposure and moderate exposure: $14 - 10 = 4.0$ (reject the null hypothesis; this value is greater than 3.05).

The results show that every pairwise comparison is significant. Hence, the more exposure participants had with sugar, the slower they were to complete a computer task when the buffet was present but not absent. If we were to report the outcome for this analysis in a research journal, it would look something like this:

> A two-way between-subjects ANOVA showed a significant main effect of exposure, $F(2, 30) = 15.00$, $p < .05$, and a significant Exposure × Buffet interaction, $F(2, 30) = 5.40$, $p < .05$. Simple main effect tests showed that the more exposure participants had with sugars, the slower their times to complete the computer task when the buffet was present (Tukey HSD, $p < .05$) but not when it was absent (one-way ANOVA, $p > .05$).

MAIN EFFECTS: PAIRWISE COMPARISONS

If an interaction is significant, you must analyze the interaction. It may also be necessary to analyze significant main effects, in which case these analyses should also be reported. When the only significant effect is a main effect, you skip straight to Step 3 and compute pairwise comparisons. Keep in mind that in a table summary, the main effects are located outside the table—we compare the row or column means for a single factor, independent of the second factor. The sample size at each level of a single factor will be larger than the sample size per cell. In Example 14.1, a significant main effect of exposure was evident. Table 14.18 reorganizes the data for this test. Notice that $n = 12$ participants per group because participants in the buffet-absent and buffet-present cells were combined at each level of the exposure factor.

NOTE: When an interaction is not significant, we analyze each significant main effect by making pairwise comparisons for the row means, the column means, or both in a summary table.

TABLE 14.18 Data for analyzing the main effect. The data in this table are from Table 14.10. To analyze the significant main effect, the buffet absent and buffet present groups are combined at each level of exposure. Hence, $n = 12$ per group.

	Exposure to Sugars		
	Low	Moderate	High
Scores for when the buffet was absent	8	10	13
	7	12	9
	9	15	11
	10	8	8
	12	6	13
	8	9	12
Scores for when the buffet was present	5	15	15
	8	10	12
	5	8	15
	6	9	16
	5	7	12
	7	11	14
	$M = 7.5$	$M = 10$	$M = 12.5$

LEARNING CHECK 4

1. State the steps for analyzing an interaction.

2. Simple main effect tests compare mean differences or simple main effects of one factor at _____ of a second factor.

3. Which of the following is the next step to analyze a significant A × B interaction in a two-way between-subjects ANOVA?

   a. Compute simple main effect tests

   b. Compute pairwise comparisons

   c. Compute a two-way ANOVA

4. What is the next step for analyzing a significant main effect?

MEASURING EFFECT SIZE 14.7

We can compute effect size using proportion of variance for each effect tested using the two-way between-subjects ANOVA. Proportion of variance estimates how much of the variability in the dependent variable (time it took to complete the computer task) can be explained by each group (the two main effects and the interaction). Two measures of proportion of variance are eta-squared and omega-squared. In this section, we measure effect size for the significant results obtained in Example 14.1.

NOTE: Two measures of proportion of variance are eta-squared and omega-squared. These measures can be computed for each main effect and the interaction.

ETA-SQUARED (η^2 OR R^2)

Eta-squared can be computed for each main effect and the interaction. It is the sum of squares of the main effect or interaction divided by the sum of squares total. Based on the results given in Table 14.13, $SS_A = 150$ and $SS_T = 354$. The proportion of variance for Factor A is

$$\eta_A^2 = \frac{SS_A}{SS_T} = \frac{150}{354} = 0.43.$$

We conclude that 43% of the variability in the time it took to complete the computer task can be explained by the participants' level of exposure to sugars. To find the proportion of variance for the significant A × B interaction, we substitute the sum of squares for the interaction, $SS_{A \times B} = 54$, into the numerator of the formula:

$$\eta_{A \times B}^2 = \frac{SS_{A \times B}}{SS_T} = \frac{54}{354} = 0.15.$$

We conclude that 15% of the variability in the time it took to complete the computer task can be explained by the combination of the two factors. The proportion of variance for the interaction is less informative than for the main effects because a significant interaction must be analyzed further. For this reason, many researchers will analyze the interaction first and report an effect size only for the significant simple main effects.

OMEGA-SQUARED (ω^2)

Omega-squared can be computed for each main effect and the interaction. This measure is less biased than eta-squared in that it

NOTE: Omega-squared is a more conservative estimate for proportion of variance than eta-squared.

1. corrects for the size of error by including MS_E in the formula.
2. corrects for the number of groups by including the degrees of freedom for the main effect or interaction in the formula.

The formula for omega-squared is the same as that given in Chapter 12, except we substitute SS and df for each main effect or the interaction. The proportion of variance for Factor A is

$$\omega_A^2 = \frac{SS_A - df_A(MS_E)}{SS_T + MS_E} = \frac{150 - 2(5)}{354 + 5} = 0.39.$$

We conclude that 39% of the variability in the time it took to complete the computer task can be explained by the participants' level of exposure to sugars. The proportion of variance for the A × B interaction is

$$\omega^2_{A \times B} = \frac{SS_{A \times B} - df_{A \times B}(MS_E)}{SS_T + MS_E} = \frac{54 - 2(5)}{354 + 5} = 0.12.$$

We conclude that 12% of the variability in the time it took to complete the computer task can be explained by the combination of the two factors.

LEARNING CHECK 5

1. Using the data given in the following *F*-table:

Source of Variation	SS	df	MS	F
Factor A	12	1	12	4.0
Factor B	48	2	24	8.0
A × B	60	2	30	10.0
Error	90	30	3	
Total	210	35		

   a. Compute eta-squared for each hypothesis test.
   b. Compute omega-squared for each hypothesis test.

2. Which measure for proportion of variance is more conservative (eta-squared or omega-squared)?

Answers: 1. (a) $\eta^2_A = \frac{12}{210} = 0.06$, $\eta^2_B = \frac{48}{210} = 0.23$, $\eta^2_{A \times B} = \frac{60}{210} = 0.29$; (b) $\omega^2_A = \frac{12 - 1(3)}{210 + 3} = 0.04$, $\omega^2_B = \frac{48 - 2(3)}{210 + 3} = 0.20$, $\omega^2_{A \times B} = \frac{60 - 2(3)}{210 + 3} = 0.25$; 2. Omega-squared.

14.8 SPSS IN FOCUS: THE TWO-WAY BETWEEN-SUBJECTS ANOVA

In Example 14.1, we tested whether levels of exposure to sugars can interfere with the time it took participants to complete a computer task in the presence or absence of a buffet of sugary foods. We concluded that participants with more exposure to sugars took longer to complete the computer task when the buffet of sugary foods was present. Using the same data as in Example 14.1, we will use SPSS to confirm the calculations that we computed for these data.

1. Click on the **variable view** tab and enter *buffet* in the **name column;** enter *exposure* in the name column below it; enter *times* in the name column below that. We will enter whole numbers, so reduce the value in the **decimals column** to 0 in each row.

2. In the row named *buffet,* click on the small gray box with three dots in the **Values column.** In the **dialog box,** enter *1* in the value cell and *absent* in the label cell, and then click **add.** Then enter *2* in the value cell and *present* in the label cell, and then click add. Select **OK.**

3. In the row named *exposure,* follow the same directions stated in Step 2, except enter *1* for *low, 2* for *moderate,* and *3* for *high.*

4. Click on the **data view** tab. In the *buffet* column, enter *1* in the first 18 cells, then enter *2* in the next 18 cells.

5. In the *exposure* column, enter *1* in the first six cells, then enter 2 in the next six cells, then enter *3* in the next six cells. Repeat this: Enter *1* in the next six cells, enter *2* in the next six cells, and enter *3* in the next six cells. We have now set up the groups. For example, the first six cells read 1, 1; these codes identify the group with the buffet absent and low exposure to sugars.

6. In the *times* column, enter the data in the cells that correspond with the codes for each group listed in the first and second columns. A portion of the data view is shown in Table 14.19.

7. Go to the **menu bar** and click **Analyze,** then **General Linear Model,** and **Univariate** to display a dialog box.

TABLE 14.19   A partial display of the SPSS data view for Example 14.1.

buffet	exposure	times
1	1	8
1	1	7
1	1	9
1	1	10
1	1	12
1	1	8
1	2	10
1	2	12
1	2	15
1	2	8
1	2	6
1	2	9
1	3	13
1	3	9
1	3	11
1	3	8
1	3	13
1	3	12
2	1	5
2	1	8
2	1	5
2	1	6
2	1	5
2	1	7
2	2	15
2	2	10

TABLE 14.20 The output table for SPSS.

The first four rows and the last row circled here provide a summary for the two-way between-subjects ANOVA that is similar to the ANOVA table given in Table 14.13.

Tests of Between-Subjects Effects

Dependent Variable:times

Source	Type III Sum of Squares	df	Mean Square	F	Sig.	Noncent. Parameter	Observed Power[b]
Corrected Model	204.000[a]	5	40.800	8.160	.000	40.800	.998
Intercept	3600.000	1	3600.000	720.000	.000	720.000	1.000
buffet	.000	1	.000	.000	1.000	.000	.050
exposure	150.000	2	75.000	15.000	.000	30.000	.998
buffet * exposure	54.000	2	27.000	5.400	.010	10.800	.805
Error	150.000	30	5.000				
Total	3954.000	36					
Corrected Total	354.000	35					

a. R Squared = .576 (Adjusted R Squared = .506)
b. Computed using alpha = .05

8. Using the appropriate arrows, move *buffet* and *exposure* into the **Fixed Factor(s):** box. Move the dependent variable, *times,* into the **Dependent Variable:** box.

9. Click **Options** to display a new dialog box. In the **Factor(s) and Factor Interactions** box, move the two main effects and interaction into the **Display Means for** box by using the arrow. Click **Continue.**

10. Select **Post Hoc . . .** to display a new dialog box. Use the arrow to move both main effects in the **Factor(s)** box into the **Post Hoc Tests for** box. Select the Tukey box for the pairwise comparison for the main effects. (Note: SPSS does not perform simple effect tests by default. If you obtain a significant interaction, you will have to conduct these tests separately.) Select **Continue.**

11. Select **Paste** and click the **Run** command.

The SPSS output table, shown in Table 14.20, has many more rows than we included in the ANOVA table in Table 14.13. Referring to Table 14.20, read only the rows labeled *buffet, exposure, buffet*exposure, error,* and *corrected total*—ignore the rest. When we look only at those five rows, it now looks much like Table 14.13. These results confirm our conclusion that we have a Buffet × Exposure interaction and a main effect of exposure.

14.9 APA IN FOCUS: REPORTING MAIN EFFECTS, INTERACTIONS, AND EFFECT SIZE

To summarize any type of two-way ANOVA, we report the test statistic, the degrees of freedom, and the *p* value for each significant main effect and interaction. The effect size should also be reported for each significant hypothesis test and for the simple main effect tests. To report the results of a post hoc test, identify the name of the post hoc test used and the p value for the test. The means and standard error or standard deviations measured in a study can be summarized in a figure or table or in the main text. For example, here is an appropriate summary of the results obtained in Example 14.1, using eta-squared to estimate effect size and Tukey's HSD as the post hoc test:

> A two-way between-subjects ANOVA showed a significant main effect of exposure, $F(2, 30) = 15.00$, $p < .05$, and a significant Exposure × Buffet interaction, $F(2, 30) = 5.40$, $p < .05$. Simple main effect tests showed that the more exposure participants had with sugars, the slower their times to complete the computer task when the buffet was present (Tukey HSD, $p < .05$) but not when it was absent (one-way ANOVA, $p > .05$). Table 14.21 displays the means and standard deviations for each factor and the results for each hypothesis test.

In two sentences and a table, we summarized all of our work in this chapter: the test statistic, degrees of freedom, and p value for each test; effect size for both significant effects; post hoc tests; and the means and standard deviations for each group. In sum, this is a clear and concise summary for the two-way ANOVA.

TABLE 14.21   The mean (M) and standard deviation (SD) in seconds for each factor and interaction in Example 14.1. Results for each hypothesis test are also given. An asterisk indicates significance at $p < .05$.

Factor		M	SD	F	p Value
Buffet				0.00	1.000
	Absent	10.00	2.43		
	Present	10.00	3.87		
Exposure to sugars				15.00*	0.000
	Low	7.50	2.15		
	Moderate	10.00	2.86		
	High	12.50	2.39		
Buffet × Exposure				5.40*	0.010
Buffet absent	Low exposure	9.00	1.79		
	Moderate exposure	10.00	3.16		
	High exposure	11.00	2.10		
Buffet present	Low exposure	6.00	1.26		
	Moderate exposure	10.00	2.83		
	High exposure	14.00	1.67		

CHAPTER SUMMARY ORGANIZED BY LEARNING OBJECTIVE

LO 1: Describe how the complexity of the two-way ANOVA differs from that of the *t*-tests and one-way ANOVA.

- A two-way ANOVA is more complex in that the levels of two factors (not one factor) are observed in a single study. Like the *t*-tests and the one-way ANOVA, the two-way ANOVA can be used when different participants are observed in each group or at each level of one factor (between-subjects design), and when the same participants are observed in each group or across the levels of a factor (within-subjects design).

LO 2: List the three types of research designs for the two-way ANOVA.

- A **two-way ANOVA** is a statistical procedure used to test hypotheses concerning the variance of row, column, and cell means, where the levels of two factors are combined. This test is used when the variance in any one population is unknown.
- The three designs for a two-way ANOVA are as follows:

    1. **2-between or between-subjects design** is where different participants are observed in each cell or group.

    2. **1-between 1-within or mixed design** is where different participants are observed at each level of the between-subjects factor and the same participants are observed at each level of the within-subjects factor.

    3. **2-within or within-subjects design** is where the same participants are observed in each cell or group.

LO 3: Define and explain the following terms: cells, main effect, and interaction.

- A **cell** is the combination of one level from each factor. Each cell is a group in a study.
- A **main effect** is a source of variation associated with mean differences across the levels of a single factor.
- An **interaction** is a source of variation associated with the variance of group means across the combination of levels for two factors. It is a measure of how cell means at each level of one factor change across the levels of a second factor.

LO 4: Identify the assumptions and list the order of interpretation for outcomes in the two-way between-subjects ANOVA.

- Four assumptions for the two-way between-subjects ANOVA are normality, random sampling, independence, and homogeneity of variance.
- In the two-way between-subjects ANOVA, there are three sources of between-groups variation and one source of error variation:

    1. Between-groups variation is a measure of the variance of the group means. Three sources of between-groups variation are:
    Main effect of Factor A
    Main effect of Factor B
    Interaction of Factors A × B

    2. Within-groups (error) variation is a measure of the variance of scores in each group (or within the cells of a summary table). This source of error is the denominator for each hypothesis test.

- A significant interaction must be analyzed first using the two-way between-subjects ANOVA.

LO 5: Calculate the degrees of freedom for the two-way between-subjects ANOVA and locate critical values in the *F*-table.

- The degrees of freedom for a two-way between-subjects ANOVA are as follows:
    Degrees of freedom for Factor A: $df_A = p - 1$.
    Degrees of freedom for Factor B: $df_B = q - 1$.
    Degrees of freedom for the A × B interaction:
    $$df_{AXB} = (p-1)(q-1).$$
    Degrees of freedom error: $df_E = pq(n-1)$.
    Degrees of freedom total: $df_T = npq - 1$.
- To find the critical value for each hypothesis test, use the degrees of freedom for the factor or interaction that is being tested and the degrees of freedom error.

LO 6: Compute the two-way between-subjects ANOVA and interpret the results.

- The test statistic for each main effect and the interaction is

    Main effect for Factor A: $F_A = \dfrac{MS_A}{MS_E}$.

    Main effect for Factor B: $F_B = \dfrac{MS_B}{MS_E}$.

    A × B interaction: $F_{A \times B} = \dfrac{MS_{A \times B}}{MS_E}$.

- The steps for conducting a two-way between-subjects ANOVA are as follows:

  Step 1: State the hypotheses.
  Step 2: Set the criteria for a decision.
  Step 3: Compute the test statistic.
     Stage 1: Preliminary calculations.
     Stage 2: Compute intermediate calculations.
     Stage 3: Compute sums of squares (SS).
     Stage 4: Complete the F-table.
  Step 4: Make a decision.

LO 7: Identify when it is appropriate to compute simple main effect tests and analyze a significant interaction.

- Simple main effect tests are appropriate to analyze a significant interaction. If an interaction is significant, then the interaction is analyzed first. To analyze a significant interaction, follow three steps:

  Step 1: Choose how to describe the data.
  Step 2: Compute simple main effect tests.
  Step 3: Compute pairwise comparisons.

- **Simple main effect tests** are hypothesis tests used to analyze a significant interaction by comparing the mean differences or the simple main effects for one factor at each level of a second factor.

LO 8: Compute proportion of variance for the two-way between-subjects ANOVA.

- One measure of proportion of variance for the two-way between-subjects ANOVA is eta-squared:

$$\text{Factor A: } \eta_A^2 = \frac{SS_A}{SS_T}, \qquad \text{Factor B: } \eta_B^2 = \frac{SS_B}{SS_T},$$

$$\text{A} \times \text{B interaction: } \eta_{A\times B}^2 = \frac{SS_{A\times B}}{SS_T}.$$

- A second, more conservative measure, is omega-squared:

$$\text{Factor A: } \omega_A^2 = \frac{SS_A - df_A(MS_E)}{SS_T + MS_E},$$

$$\text{Factor B: } \omega_B^2 = \frac{SS_B - df_B(MS_E)}{SS_T + MS_E},$$

$$\text{A} \times \text{B interaction: } \omega_{A\times B}^2 = \frac{SS_{A\times B} - df_{A\times B}(MS_E)}{SS_T + MS_E}.$$

APA LO 9: Summarize the results of the two-way between-subjects ANOVA in APA format.

- To summarize any type of two-way ANOVA, we report the test statistic, the degrees of freedom, and the p value for each significant main effect and interaction. Effect size should also be reported for each significant hypothesis test and for the simple main effect tests. To report the results of a post hoc test, identify the name of post hoc test used and the p value for the test. Means and standard errors or standard deviations measured in a study can be summarized in a figure or a table or in the main text.

SPSS LO 10: Compute the two-way between-subjects ANOVA using SPSS.

- SPSS can be used to compute the two-way between-subjects ANOVA. The two-way between-subjects ANOVA is computed using the **Analyze, General Linear Model,** and **Univariate** options in the menu bar. These actions will display a dialog box that allows you to identify the variables, choose an appropriate post hoc test for the main effects, and run the analysis. SPSS does not perform simple main effect tests by default. If a significant interaction is obtained, then you must reorganize the data and conduct these tests separately (for more details, see Section 14.8).

KEY TERMS

1-between 1-within or mixed design
2-between or between-subjects design
2-within design or within-subjects design

between-subjects factor
cell
complete factorial design
interaction
main effect

simple main effect tests
two-way ANOVA
two-way between-subjects ANOVA
within-subjects factor

END-OF-CHAPTER PROBLEMS

Factual Problems

1. What is the difference between a one-way and two-way design?

2. Name three types of designs for the two-way ANOVA.

3. Define the following key terms:
   (a) Cell
   (b) Main effect
   (c) Interaction

4. Suppose you construct a table with cells, rows, and columns to summarize each factor in a two-way ANOVA.
   (a) Where are the main effects located in the table?
   (b) Where is the interaction located in the table?

5. When looking at a graph of an A × B interaction, describe the pattern that indicates that the interaction is possibly significant.

6. A researcher conducts a 3 × 3 between-subjects ANOVA with 15 participants assigned to each cell or group.
   (a) What is the total sample size in this study?
   (b) How many cells or groups are in this study?

7. State four assumptions for the two-way between-subjects ANOVA.

8. Which source of variation is placed in the denominator of the test statistic for each hypothesis test for the two-way between-subjects ANOVA?

9. Explain why the critical value can be different for each hypothesis test computed using the two-way between-subjects ANOVA.

10. A researcher obtains a significant interaction and a significant main effect. Which significant effect should the researcher analyze first? Explain.

11. What are the three steps used to analyze a significant interaction?

12. Which measure, eta-squared or omega-squared, is a more conservative estimate of proportion of variance?

Concepts and Application Problems

13. State whether each of the following is an example of a between-subjects, mixed, or within-subjects two-way ANOVA design.
    (a) A psychologist administers a small, medium, or large dose of a drug to a sample of mice (Factor A: drug dose) and measures reward-seeking behavior across three experimental trials (Factor B: trials).
    (b) An industrial organizational psychologist measures the GPA among men and women graduate students (Factor A: gender) with low, medium, or high leadership potential (Factor B: leadership potential).
    (c) A behavioral psychologist asks the same group of participants to rate the effectiveness of each of three marketing commercials (Factor A: commercials) for each of two products (Factor B: products).

14. A social scientist asks a sample of men and women to read a vignette describing an immoral act for reasons of preservation, protection, or self-gain. She measures moral reasoning among those sampled. Identify each factor and the levels of each factor in this example.

15. A psychotherapist asks a sample of violent and nonviolent criminals from impoverished, middle-class, and upper-class backgrounds to indicate how accountable they feel they are for their crimes. Identify each factor and the levels of each factor in this example.

16. The following table summarizes the cell, column, and row means for a 2 × 2 ANOVA.

		Factor A		
		A1	A2	
Factor B	B1	2	6	4
	B2	4	8	6
		3	7	

(a) Which means reflect a main effect for Factor A?

(b) Which means reflect a main effect for Factor B?

(c) Which means reflect the interaction between Factors A and B?

17. State the decision to retain or reject the null hypothesis for each of the following F-tests at a .05 level of significance.

   (a) $F(3, 24) = 3.29$

   (b) $F(2, 40) = 3.00$

   (c) $F(1, 120) = 4.00$

   (d) $F(2, 60) = 3.10$

18. A researcher reports a significant two-way between-subjects ANOVA, $F(3, 40) = 2.96$. State the decision to retain or reject the null hypothesis for this test.

19. If the value of the mean square for Factor A increases, will the value of the test statistic of Factor A increase or decrease?

20. If the value of mean square error increases, will the value of the test statistic increase or decrease?

21. For each of the following, state whether $F = 0$ for a main effect, the A × B interaction, or both.

   (a) Cell means are equal.

   (b) Row totals are equal.

   (c) Colum totals are equal.

22. To better understand eating patterns that might contribute to obesity, a researcher measures the average number of calories (per meal) consumed by shift workers (morning, afternoon, night) during two seasons (summer and winter). The hypothetical results are given in the following table.

		Shift		
		Morning	**Afternoon**	**Night**
Season	Summer	450	500	480
		500	490	660
		550	550	570
		650	700	510
	Winter	700	700	710
		550	500	630
		750	750	600
		500	600	650

(a) Complete the F-table and make a decision to retain or reject the null hypothesis for each hypothesis test.

(b) Explain why post hoc tests are not necessary.

23. Seasonal affective disorder (SAD) is a type of depression during seasons with less daylight (e.g., winter months). One therapy for SAD is phototherapy, which is increased exposure to light used to improve mood. A researcher tests this therapy by exposing a sample of SAD patients to different intensities of light (low, medium, high) in a light box, either in the morning or at night (these are the times thought to be most effective for light therapy). All participants rated their mood following this therapy on a scale from 1 (*poor mood*) to 9 (*improved mood*). The hypothetical results are given in the following table.

		Light Intensity		
		Low	**Medium**	**High**
Time of Day	Morning	5	5	7
		6	6	8
		4	4	6
		7	7	9
		5	9	5
		6	8	8
	Night	5	6	9
		8	8	7
		6	7	6
		7	5	8
		4	9	7
		3	8	6

(a) Complete the F-table and make a decision to retain or reject the null hypothesis for each hypothesis test.

(b) Compute Tukey's HSD to analyze the significant main effect. Summarize the results for this test using APA format.

24. Students (freshmen, sophomores, juniors, seniors) at a local college who were in the same

statistics class were given one of three tests (recall, recognition, or a mix of both). Test grades for each participant ($n = 10$) were recorded. Complete the F-table for this study.

Source of Variation	SS	df	MS	F
Exam		2	95	
Student class	60			
Exam × Student class	540			
Error				
Total	2,410			

25. To test the relationship between gender and ratings of a promiscuous partner, a group of men and women was given a vignette describing a person of the opposite sex who was in a dating relationship with one, two, or three partners. Participants rated how positively they felt about the individual described in the vignette, with higher ratings indicating more positive feelings.

Source of Variation	SS	df	MS	F
Gender	15			
Promiscuity				
Gender × Promiscuity	144			
Error	570	114		
Total	849			

(a) Complete the F-table and make a decision to retain or reject the null hypothesis for each hypothesis test.

(b) Based on the results you obtained, what is the next step?

26. A developmental psychologist placed children in a social situation in which they were either rewarded or punished (Factor A: consequence) by a parent, sibling, or stranger (Factor B: type of adult). Following this social situation, children were placed back in the same social situation, and the time it took them (in seconds) to engage in the punished or rewarded behavior was recorded.

The hypothetical results are given in the following table.

		Consequences	
		Reward	Punishment
Type of Adult	Parent	15	45
		16	43
		14	46
		13	50
	Sibling	22	41
		16	38
		19	49
		14	52
	Stranger	14	25
		15	29
		18	32
		23	39

(a) Complete the F-table and make a decision to retain or reject the null hypothesis for each hypothesis test.

(b) Compute simple main effect tests for the type of adult factor at each level of the consequences factor. Use Tukey's HSD to analyze the significant simple main effects. State your conclusions using APA format.

27. Recent studies show that conservative Republican political ideology is associated with greater overall life happiness than liberal Democratic ideology. One potential explanation for this is that conservatives are more likely than liberals to accept or rationalize the existence of inequalities as being fair and legitimate. To test this potential explanation, participants with conservative or liberal ideologies (Factor A: political ideology) who either rationalize or not (Factor B: rationalization) were asked to report their overall life satisfaction, where higher scores indicated greater life satisfaction. It was expected that conservatives who rationalize would report the greatest life satisfaction. The hypothetical results are given in the following table.

		Political Ideology	
		Conservative	Liberal
	Yes	9	7
		8	9
		12	8
		9	10
		10	11
		7	7
		9	5
		8	9
Rationalization	No	9	4
		10	6
		9	8
		11	7
		8	4
		9	5
		8	6
		7	5

(a) Complete the *F*-table and make a decision to retain or reject the null hypothesis for each hypothesis test.

(b) Compute simple main effect tests for the rationalization factor at each level of the political ideology factor. Use Tukey's HSD to analyze the significant simple main effects. State your conclusions using APA format.

28. Among other benefits, pets are thought to be great companions that increase satisfaction among pet owners, especially those who would otherwise live alone. A psychologist decides to test this notion. A sample of participants who live with others or alone (Factor A: living status) and own pets or don't (Factor B: pet owner status) were asked to indicate how satisfied they were with their living arrangements. It was expected that pet owners would report greater overall satisfaction than those who did not have pets. The hypothetical results are given in the following table.

		Pet Owner	
		Yes	No
	Yes	7	3
		6	4
		7	5
		6	5
Live Alone	No	6	4
		6	2
		7	5
		5	7

(a) Complete the *F*-table and make a decision to retain or reject the null hypothesis for each hypothesis test.

(b) Are post hoc tests necessary? Explain.

Problems in Research

29. **Denominators for the F-test.** B. H. Cohen (2002) stated that "the denominator of all three *F* ratios [for the two-way ANOVA] is the same" (p. 196). What is the denominator of test statistic for the two-way between-subjects ANOVA?

30. **Social power in the classroom.** Witt and Schrodt (2006) tested the relationship between nonverbal immediacy (behaviors that enhance closeness and nonverbal interaction with others) and technology. They tested whether teacher nonverbal immediacy (high, low) in classes with different levels of technology use (none, minimal, moderate, complete) would influence student perceptions of the teacher. They computed a 4×2 ANOVA to analyze the data. The table lists the cell means at each level of the two factors.

	No Technology	Minimal Technology	Moderate Technology	Complete Technology
High immediacy	58.66	71.89	69.45	50.83
Low immediacy	36.39	45.41	45.61	40.63

(a) Graph the cell means.

(b) Is a possible interaction evident? Explain.

31. **Self-construal and comparison standard.** Cheng and Lam (2007) noted that some people think of themselves independently of others (independent self-construal), whereas others think of themselves as being part of a larger group (interdependent self-construal). Also, people tend to evaluate themselves as being more positive when they compare themselves to others perceived to be below them (downward comparison), and they evaluate themselves as being less positive when they compare themselves to others perceived to be above them (upward comparison). To test whether there is a relationship between these two factors, the researchers computed a two-way between-subjects ANOVA. Participants rated their self-perception on a scale from 1 (*negative*) to 7 (*positive*). The following table describes the cell means at each level of the two factors.

Comparison Standard	Self-Construal	
	Independent	Interdependent
Upward	4.17	4.62
Downward	4.61	4.44

(a) Graph the cell means.

(b) Is a possible interaction evident? Explain.

32. **Rodent species and sociality.** Freitas, El-Hani, and da Rocha (2008) tested the hypothesis that rodent species (four different species) and sex (male, female) influence the level of affiliation acquired through social behavior. They measured the number of social behaviors exhibited by each rodent during a social encounter. As part of their study, they reported the following:

Hypothesis test was performed by means of a [factorial] two-way ANOVA. The test was able to detect significant differences only among species, not among sexes. (p. 389)

(a) Is a significant main effect or interaction evident in this study and, if so, for which factor?

(b) What is the appropriate next step?

33. **Spending time with the children.** Erkal, Copur, Dogan, and Safak (2007) studied how gender and gender roles influence the time parents spend with their children. In their study, they asked a sample of parents to report the amount of time they make accessible for their children. Women reported spending an average of 9.48 hours per week; men reported spending an average of 8.01 hours per week. The *F*-table summarizes the results of their study.

Source of Variation	SS	df	MS	F
Gender	191.93	1	191.93	9.34
Gender roles	11.90	3	3.97	0.19
Gender × Gender Roles	87.61	3	29.20	1.42
Error	12,163.98	592	20.55	
Total	12,455.42	599		

(a) Is a significant main effect or interaction evident in this study and, if so, for which factor?

(b) Referring to the group means given for gender, state the conclusion for this study.

34. **Emoticons (facial feedback) with e-learning.** Tung and Deng (2007) studied how emoticons (computerized facial expressions) and gender influenced intrinsic motivation to complete a computer task. Emoticons were used as feedback for responses during the task. These faces were either static (presented still for the duration of feedback) or dynamic (presented as a neutral face and changed to the expression corresponding to the feedback). The researchers conducted a 2×2 between-subjects ANOVA, with emoticon style (static, dynamic) and gender as the factors. The F-table gives the data reported in the study.

Source of Variation	SS	df	MS	F
Emoticon style	13.65	1	13.65	8.93
Gender	1.52	1	1.52	0.99
Emoticon Style × Gender	3.84	1	3.84	2.51
Error	258.57	169	1.53	
Total	277.58	172		

(a) Is a significant main effect or interaction evident in this study and, if so, for which factor?

(b) Are post hoc tests required? Explain.

NOTE: Answers for even numbers are in Appendix C.

PART

V

Making Inferences About Patterns, Frequencies, and Ordinal Data

Correlation

LEARNING OBJECTIVES

After reading this chapter, you should be able to:

1. Identify the direction and strength of a correlation between two factors.

2. Compute and interpret the Pearson correlation coefficient and test for significance.

3. Compute and interpret the coefficient of determination.

4. Define *homoscedasticity, linearity,* and *normality* and explain why each assumption is necessary to appropriately interpret a significant correlation coefficient.

5. Explain how causality, outliers, and restriction of range can limit the interpretation of a significant correlation coefficient.

6. Compute and interpret the Spearman correlation coefficient and test for significance.

7. Compute and interpret the point-biserial correlation coefficient and test for significance.

8. Compute and interpret the phi correlation coefficient and test for significance.

9. Convert the value of r to a t statistic and χ^2 statistic.

10. Summarize the results of a correlation coefficient in APA format.

11. Compute the Pearson, Spearman, point-biserial, and phi correlation coefficient using SPSS.

15.1 TREATING FACTORS AS DEPENDENT MEASURES

Beginning in Chapter 8, we described a variety of hypothesis tests. For each hypothesis test, we observed the levels of one factor, and in Chapter 14, we observed the combination of levels for two factors. Each level or combination of levels was a group, and in each group, we measured a dependent variable and analyzed differences between groups. Using this approach, suppose we observe students texting or not texting in class and compare differences in class performance (as an exam grade out of 100 points). In this example, illustrated in Figure 15.1a, the factor is texting (no, yes), and the dependent variable is class performance (an exam grade).

(a)

Texting	
No	Yes
76	82
98	64
88	88
82	85
80	90
73	54
80	66
69	82
75	87
89	62
$M = 81$	$M = 76$

We observe two levels of one factor (texting).

We compare mean differences in one dependent variable (exam grades) at each level of the factor.

(b)

Participant	Texting	Exam Grades
A	0	88
B	4	80
C	6	78
D	2	84
E	0	90
F	6	79
G	7	70
H	12	56
I	6	76
J	0	92

We measure two factors for each participant: texting (number of texts sent) and class performance (exam grade out of 100 points). We then compare how changes in the values of one factor are related to changes in the values of the second factor.

FIGURE 15.1

(a) The approach used in hypothesis testing in Chapters 8 to 14. (b) The correlational method. Instead of comparing mean differences for one dependent variable between groups, the correlational method compares the extent to which two measured factors are related.

An alternative method, called the correlational method, is to treat each factor like a dependent variable and measure the relationship between each variable. For example, we could measure texting during class (number of texts sent) and class performance (as an exam grade out of 100 points) for each student in a class. We could then test to see if there is a relationship between the pairs of scores for each participant. In this example, illustrated in Figure 15.1b, if the scores are related, then we would expect exam scores to decrease as the number of texts sent increases.

This type of analysis, using the correlational method, is introduced in this chapter. The statistics we use to measure correlations are called *correlation coefficients,* and we discuss four correlation coefficients in this chapter. Each coefficient is used for data measured on different scales of measurement in this chapter. The first coefficient introduced in this chapter is the Pearson correlation coefficient. The remaining three coefficients are derived from the Pearson correlation coefficient.

DESCRIBING A CORRELATION 15.2

A **correlation** can be used to (1) describe the pattern of change in the values of two factors and (2) determine whether the pattern observed in a sample is also present in the population from which the sample was selected. The pattern of change is described by the direction and strength of the relationship between two factors. In behavioral research, we mostly describe the linear (or straight-line) relationship between two factors. For this reason, this chapter focuses on linear relationships.

> A **correlation** is a statistical procedure used to describe the strength and direction of the linear relationship between two factors.

DEFINITION

THE DIRECTION OF A CORRELATION

The value of a correlation, measured by the **correlation coefficient (*r*),** ranges from –1.0 to +1.0. Values closer to ±1.0 indicate stronger correlations, meaning that a correlation coefficient of $r = -1.0$ is as strong as a correlation coefficient of $r = +1.0$. The sign of the correlation coefficient (– or +) indicates only the direction or slope of the correlation.

> The **correlation coefficient (*r*)** is used to measure the strength and direction of the linear relationship, or correlation, between two factors. The value of *r* ranges from –1.0 to +1.0.

DEFINITION

A **positive correlation** $(0 < r \leq +1.0)$ means that as the values of one factor increase, values of the second factor also increase; as the values of one factor decrease, values of the second factor also decrease. If two factors have values that change in the same direction, we can graph the correlation using a straight line. Figure 15.2 shows that values on the *y*-axis increase as values on the *x*-axis increase.

Figure 15.2a shows a *perfect* positive correlation, which occurs when each data point falls exactly on a straight line, although this is rare. More commonly, as shown in Figure 15.2b, a positive correlation is greater than 0 but less than 1.0, where the values of two factors change in the same direction, but not all data points fall exactly on a straight line.

DEFINITION

A **positive correlation** (0 < r ≤ + 1.0) is a positive value of r that indicates that the values of two factors change in the same direction: As the values of one factor increase, values of the second factor also increase; as the values of one factor decrease, values of the second factor also decrease.

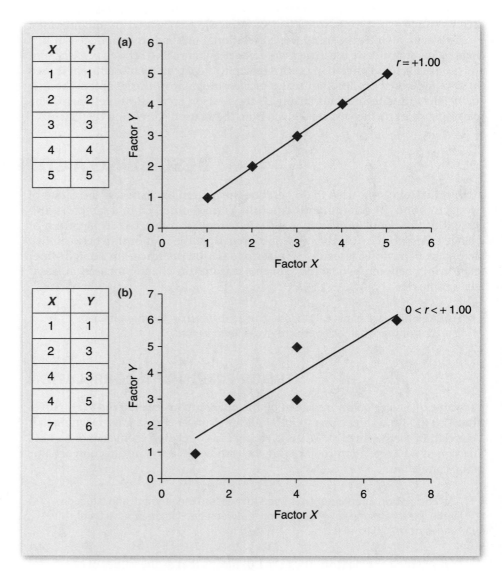

FIGURE 15.2

A perfect positive (a) and a positive (b) linear correlation. Both the table and scatter plot show the same data for (a) and (b).

NOTE: The sign of a correlation coefficient indicates the direction of the relationship between two measured factors: + indicates that two factors change in the same direction; – indicates that two factors change in opposite directions.

A **negative correlation** (−1.0 ≤ r < 0) means that as the values of one factor increase, values of the second factor decrease. If two factors have values that change in the opposite direction, we can graph the correlation using a straight line. Figure 15.3 shows that values on the *y*-axis decrease as values on the *x*-axis increase.

Figure 15.3a shows a *perfect* negative correlation, which occurs when each data point falls exactly on a straight line, although this is also rare. More commonly, as shown in Figure 15.3b, a negative correlation is greater than −1.0 but less than 0, where the values of two factors change in the opposite direction, but not all data points fall exactly on a straight line.

A **negative correlation** ($-1.0 \leq r < 0$) is a negative value of r that indicates that the values of two factors change in different directions, meaning that as the values of one factor increase, values of the second factor decrease.

DEFINITION

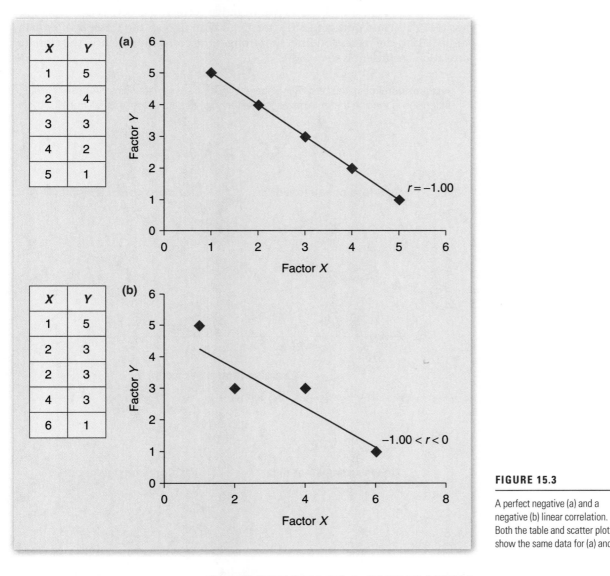

FIGURE 15.3

A perfect negative (a) and a negative (b) linear correlation. Both the table and scatter plot show the same data for (a) and (b).

THE STRENGTH OF A CORRELATION

A zero correlation ($r = 0$) means that there is no linear pattern or relationship between two factors. This outcome is rare because usually by mere chance, at least some values of one factor, X, will show some pattern or relationship with values of a second factor, Y. The closer a correlation coefficient is to $r = 0$, the weaker the correlation and the less likely that two factors are related; the closer a correlation coefficient is to $r = \pm 1.0$, the stronger the correlation and the more likely that two factors are related.

The strength of a correlation reflects how consistently scores for each factor change. When plotted in a graph, scores are more consistent the closer they fall to a **regression line,** or the straight line that best fits a set of data points. The best-fitting straight line minimizes the total distance of all data points that fall from it. Figure 15.4 shows two positive correlations between exercise (Factor X) and health (Factor Y), and Figure 15.5 shows two negative correlations between absences in class (Factor X) and quiz grades (Factor Y). In both figures, the closer a set of data points falls to the regression line, the stronger the correlation; hence, the closer a correlation coefficient is to $r = \pm 1.0$.

NOTE: The closer a set of data points fall to a regression line, the stronger the correlation (the closer a correlation is to r = ±1.0*).*

DEFINITION

A **regression line** is the best-fitting straight line to a set of data points. A best-fitting line is the line that minimizes the distance of all data points that fall from it.

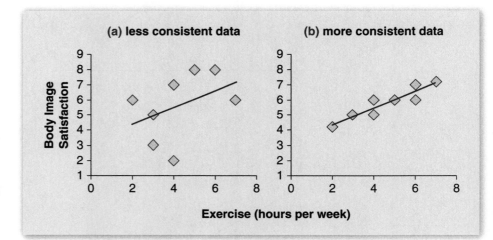

FIGURE 15.4

The consistency of scores for a positive correlation. Both figures show approximately the same regression line, but the data points in (b) are more consistent because they fall closer to the regression line than in (a).

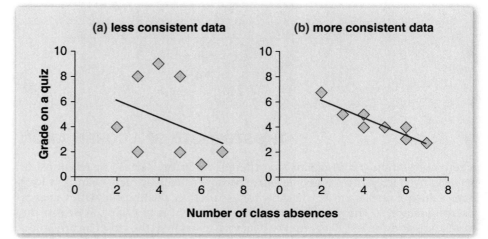

FIGURE 15.5

The consistency of scores for a negative correlation. Both figures show approximately the same regression line, but the data points in (b) are more consistent because they fall closer to the regression line than in (a).

1. A researcher records the number of school-aged children in the household and the stress levels of parents rated on a 7-point rating scale. Which method is appropriate for measuring the relationship between these two factors?

2. A researcher reports that the farther college students are from their parents, the more often they communicate with their parents (either by phone or e-mail). Is this an example of a positive or negative correlation?

3. An instructor reports that as the number of student interruptions during class decreases, student scores on in-class quizzes increase. Is this an example of a positive or negative correlation?

4. Which of the following indicates the strongest correlation?

   a. $r = -0.57$ b. $r = +0.78$ c. $r = -0.90$ d. $r = +0.88$

5. As data points fall closer to the regression line, how does the value of the correlation coefficient, r, change?

Answers: 1. The correlational method. 2. Positive correlation; 3. Negative correlation; 4. (c); 5. The correlation coefficient increases closer to $r = \pm1.0$.

PEARSON CORRELATION COEFFICIENT   15.3

The most commonly used formula for computing r is the **Pearson correlation coefficient**, or the Pearson product-moment correlation coefficient. The Pearson correlation coefficient is used to determine the strength and direction of the relationship between two factors on an interval or ratio scale of measurement. Recall from Chapter 6 that we located z-scores by computing a z-transformation on a set of data. In the same way, we can locate a sample of data points by converting them to z-scores and computing the following formula:

$$r = \frac{\sum(z_X z_Y)}{n-1}.$$

DEFINITION

The **Pearson (product-moment) correlation coefficient (r)** is used to measure the direction and strength of the linear relationship of two factors in which the data for both factors are measured on an interval or ratio scale of measurement.

Notice that the general form of this formula is similar to that for computing variance. This formula has the drawback of requiring that each score be transformed into a z-score, and consequently, an equivalent formula that uses raw scores is used more often to calculate the Pearson correlation coefficient. Writing this formula in terms of the sum of the squares gives us the following correlation coefficient:

$$r = \frac{SS_{XY}}{\sqrt{SS_X SS_Y}}.$$

NOTE: The Pearson correlation coefficient is the most popular correlation measure in the behavioral sciences.

To illustrate how we can use this formula to measure the distance that points fall from the regression line, consider the example, plotted in Figure 15.6, in which we seek to determine the relationship between the number of months that students attend college and the number of classes missed. Notice that some data points fall on the line and others fall some distance from the line. The correlation coefficient measures the variance in the distance that data points fall from the regression line.

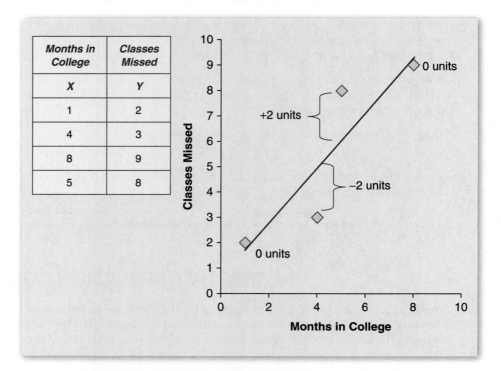

Months in College	Classes Missed
X	Y
1	2
4	3
8	9
5	8

FIGURE 15.6

A table and scatter plot showing the number of months that four students ($n = 4$) attended college and the number of classes they missed. The correlation coefficient (r) measures the distance, stated in units for this example, that data points fall from the regression line. Both the table and the scatter plot show the same data.

NOTE: The correlation coefficient measures the variance or distance that data points fall from the regression line.

The value in the numerator of the Pearson correlation coefficient reflects the extent to which values on the x-axis (X) and y-axis (Y) vary together. The extent to which the values of two factors vary together is called **covariance.** The extent to which values of X and Y vary independently, or separately, is placed in the denominator. The formula for r can be stated as follows:

$$r = \frac{\text{covariance of } X \text{ and } Y}{\text{variance of } X \text{ and } Y \text{ seperately}}.$$

DEFINITION

Covariance is the extent to which the values of two factors (X and Y) vary together. The closer data points fall to the regression line, the more that the values of two factors vary together.

The correlation coefficient r, measures the variance of X and the variance of Y, which constitutes the total variance that can be measured. The total variance is placed in the denominator of the formula for r. The covariance in the numerator is the amount or proportion of the total variance that is shared by X and Y. The larger the covariance, the closer data points will fall to the regression line. When all data points for X and Y fall exactly on a regression line, the covariance equals the total variance, making the formula for r equal to $+1.0$ or -1.0, depending on the direction of the relationship. The farther that data points fall from the regression line, the smaller the covariance will be compared to the total variance in the denominator, resulting in a value of r closer to 0.

MAKING SENSE: Understanding Covariance

If we conceptualize covariance as circles, as illustrated in Figure 15.7, then the variance of each factor (X and Y) would be contained within each circle. The two circles, then, contain the total measured variance. The covariance of X and Y reflects the extent to which the total variance or the two circles overlap. In terms of computing r, the overlap or covariance is placed in the numerator; the total variance contained within each circle is placed in the denominator. The more the two circles overlap, the more the covariance (in the numerator) will equal the independent variances contained within each circle (in the denominator)—and the closer r will be to ±1.0.

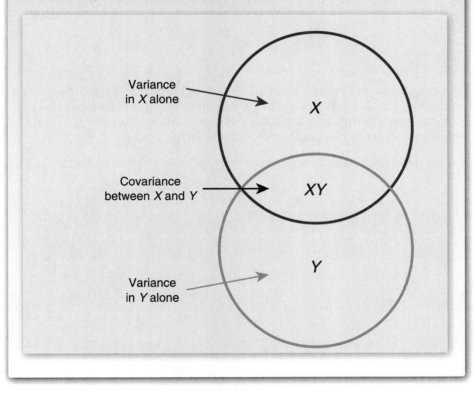

Variance in X alone

Covariance between X and Y

Variance in Y alone

X

XY

Y

FIGURE 15.7

Each circle represents the variance of a factor. The variance of two factors covary in as much as the two circles overlap. The more overlap or shared variance of two factors, the more the two factors are related.

In Example 15.1, we will compute the Pearson correlation coefficient for data measured on an interval or ratio scale of measurement, following these steps:

Step 1: Compute preliminary calculations.

Step 2: Compute the Pearson correlation coefficient (r).

A health psychologist measures the relationship between mood and eating. She measures mood using a 9-point rating scale, where higher ratings indicate better mood. She measures eating as the average number of daily calories that five participants consumed in the previous week. The results are listed in Figure 15.8. Find the Pearson correlation coefficient using these data.

EXAMPLE 15.1

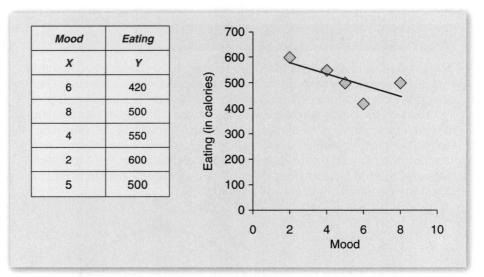

FIGURE 15.8

A table and scatter plot showing the relationship between mood and eating. The regression line is given in the scatter plot. Both the table and scatter plot show the same data.

Step 1: Compute preliminary calculations. We begin by making the preliminary calculations listed in Table 15.1. The signs (+ and −) of the values we measure for each factor are essential to making accurate computations. The goal is to find the sum of squares needed to complete the formula for r.

TABLE 15.1   Preliminary calculations in Step 1 of Example 15.1. The key values that are substituted into the formula for the Pearson correlation coefficient are circled.

Mood	Eating	Deviations Scores		Sum of Squares		
X	Y	$X - M_X$	$Y - M_Y$	$(X - M_X)(Y - M_Y)$	$(X - M_X)^2$	$(Y - M_Y)^2$
6	420	1	−94	−94	1	8,836
8	500	3	−14	−42	9	196
4	550	−1	36	−36	1	1,296
2	600	−3	86	−258	9	7,396
5	500	0	−14	0	0	196
$M_X = 5$	$M_Y = 514$			$SS_{XY} = -430$	$SS_X = 20$	$SS_Y = 17,920$

The sum of the products of deviations for X and Y

The sum of squares for X

The sum of squares for Y

1. Compute the average X and Y score. In Table 15.1, each column of X and Y scores was summed and then averaged. The result is that $M_X = 5$ and $M_Y = 514$.

2. Subtract each score from its respective mean. In the third column, each X score is subtracted from the mean for X (M_X); in the fourth column, each Y score is subtracted from the mean for Y (M_Y). Recall from Chapter 3 that

the sum of each column should be equal to 0. This is a way to check your work.

3. Multiply and sum the deviation scores for X and Y. Multiply across the rows in the third and fourth columns. The sum of these scores is the sum of squares for XY, also called the **sum of products (SP):**

$$SS_{XY} = -430.$$

The sum of products can be a negative value because positive and negative deviation values of X are multiplied times positive and negative deviation values of Y. Therefore, the sum of products determines whether a correlation coefficient is positive or negative.

> **Sum of products (SP)** is the sum of squares for two factors, X and Y. SP is the numerator for the Pearson correlation formula. To compute SP, we multiply the deviation of each X value times the deviation of each Y value.

DEFINITION

NOTE: The sum of products is an estimate of the sum of squares of XY. *The value of SP determines whether the direction of a correlation is positive or negative.*

4. Multiply and sum the deviation scores for X. Multiply the deviation scores of each X value in the third column times itself. The sum of these scores is the sum of squares of X:

$$SS_X = 20.$$

5. Multiply and sum the deviation scores for Y. Multiply the deviation scores for each Y value in the fourth column times itself. The sum of these scores is the sum of squares for Y:

$$SS_Y = 17{,}290.$$

Step 2: Compute the Pearson correlation coefficient (r). We computed each required computation in the formula. We now substitute these values into the formula to compute the Pearson correlation coefficient:

$$r = \frac{SS_{XY}}{\sqrt{SS_X SS_Y}} = \frac{-430}{\sqrt{20 \times 17{,}920}} = -0.718.$$

The Pearson correlation coefficient is $r = -0.718$. The sign of the correlation (–) indicates the direction of the relationship between mood and eating; the strength of the correlation is indicated by the value (0.718), with values closer to –1.0 and +1.0 indicating that mood and eating are more closely related.

EFFECT SIZE: THE COEFFICIENT OF DETERMINATION

A correlation coefficient ranges from –1 to +1, so it can be negative. To compute proportion of variance as an estimate of effect size, we square the correlation coefficient r. The value of r^2 or R^2 is called the **coefficient of determination.** The result of this calculation is a value between 0 and 1 that is mathematically equivalent to the value of eta-squared (η^2), which we computed for the t-tests and ANOVAs.

> The **coefficient of determination** (r^2 or R^2) is mathematically equivalent to eta-squared and is used to measure the proportion of variance of one factor (Y) that can be explained by known values of a second factor (X).

DEFINITION

In Example 15.1, we want to measure the proportion variance in ratings of mood that can be explained by the number of calories participants consumed in the previous week (eating). The coefficient of determination for the data in Example 15.1 is

$$r^2 = -(0.718)^2 = 0.516.$$

In terms of proportion of variance, we conclude that that about 52% of the variability in ratings of mood can be explained by the number of calories participants consumed the previous week.

NOTE: The coefficient of determination (r^2 or R^2) is mathematically equivalent to eta-squared (η^2).

HYPOTHESIS TESTING: TESTING FOR SIGNIFICANCE

We can also follow the steps to hypothesis testing to determine whether the correlation observed in a sample is present in the population from which the sample was selected. In Example 15.1, we will conduct a hypothesis test to determine whether the observed correlation between mood and eating ($r = -0.718$) in the sample we selected is also present in the population.

Step 1: State the hypotheses. To test for the significance of a correlation, the null hypothesis is that there is no relationship between two factors (a zero correlation) in the population. The alternative hypothesis is that there is a relationship between two factors (a positive or negative correlation) in the population. For a population, the correlation coefficient is symbolized by the Greek letter rho, ρ. We can therefore state the hypotheses for Example 15.1 as follows:

$H_0: \rho = 0$ (Mood is not related to eating in the population.)

$H_1: \rho \neq 0$ (Mood is related to eating in the population.)

NOTE: A hypothesis test is used to determine whether an observed correlation in a sample is present in a population of interest.

Step 2: Set the criteria for a decision. We will compute a two-tailed test at a .05 level of significance. The degrees of freedom are the number of scores that are free to vary for X and for Y. All X scores except one are free to vary, and all Y scores except one are free to vary. Hence, the degrees of freedom for a correlation are $n - 2$. In Example 15.1, $n = 5$; therefore, the degrees of freedom for this test are $5 - 2 = 3$.

To locate the critical value for this test, look in Table B.5 in Appendix B. Table 15.2 shows a portion of this table. The alpha levels for one-tailed and two-tailed tests are given in each column and the degrees of freedom in the rows. The critical values for this test are ±0.878. The probability is less than 5% that we will obtain a correlation stronger than $r = \pm0.878$ when $n = 5$. If r is stronger than or exceeds ±0.878, then we reject the null hypothesis; otherwise, we retain the null hypothesis.

Step 3: Compute the test statistic. The correlation coefficient r is the test statistic for the hypothesis test. We already measured this: $r = -0.718$.

Step 4: Make a decision. To decide whether to retain or reject the null hypothesis, we compare the value of the test statistic to the critical values. Because $r = -0.718$ does not exceed the critical values ($r = \pm0.878$), we retain the null hypothesis. We conclude that the correlation in our sample does not reflect a relationship between

TABLE 15.2   A portion of the Pearson correlation table in Table B.5 in Appendix B.

	Level of Significance for Two-Tailed Test			
$df = n - 2$	.10	.05	.02	.01
1	.988	.997	.9995	.9999
2	.900	.950	.980	.990
3	.805	.878	.934	.959
4	.729	.811	.882	.917
5	.669	.754	.833	.874
6	.622	.707	.789	.834
7	.582	.666	.750	.798
8	.549	.632	.716	.765
9	.521	.602	.685	.735
10	.497	.576	.658	.708

Source: Table VI of R. A. Fisher and F. Yates, *Statistical Tables for Biological, Agricultural and Medical Research, 6th ed.* London: Longman Group Ltd., 1974 (previously published by Oliver and Boyd Ltd., Edinburgh). Adapted and reprinted with permission of the Addison Wesley Longman.

mood and eating in the population. If we were to report this result in a research journal, it would look something like this:

> Using the Pearson correlation coefficient, we found a relationship between mood and eating was not significant, $r = -0.718$, $p > .05$.

SPSS IN FOCUS: PEARSON CORRELATION COEFFICIENT   15.4

In Example 15.1, we concluded that "a relationship between mood and eating was not significant, $r = -0.718$, $p > .05$," using the Pearson correlation coefficient. Let's confirm this conclusion using SPSS.

1. Click on the **variable view** tab and enter *mood* in the **name column;** enter *eating* in the name column below it. Reduce the value to 0 in the **decimals column** for both rows.

2. Click on the **data view** tab. Enter the data for mood in the first column; enter the data for eating in the second column.

3. Go to the **menu bar** and click **Analyze,** then **Correlate** and **Bivariate,** to display a dialog box.

4. Using the arrows, move both variables into the **Variables** box.

5. Select **Paste** and click the **Run** command.

TABLE 15.3 SPSS output table.

Correlations			mood	eating
mood	Pearson Correlation		1	-.718
	Sig. (2-tailed)			.172
	N		5	5
eating	Pearson Correlation		-.718	1
	Sig. (2-tailed)		.172	
	N		5	5

The SPSS output table, shown in Table 15.3, gives the results of a two-tailed test at a .05 level of significance. The SPSS output is set up in a matrix with mood and eating listed in the rows and columns. Each cell in the matrix gives the direction and strength of the correlation ($r = -0.718$ for mood and eating; this value will be shown with an asterisk for significant correlations), the significance ($p = .172$), and the sample size ($N = 5$). To find the coefficient of determination, square the correlation coefficient.

LEARNING CHECK 2

1. Name the correlation coefficient used to measure the strength and direction of the linear relationship of two factors on an interval or ratio scale of measurement.

2. Compute the Pearson correlation coefficient given the following data.
   a. $SS_{XY} = -53$, $SS_X = 58$, $SS_Y = 255.20$
   b. $SS_{XY} = 1448$, $SS_X = 2678.80$, $SS_Y = 896$
   c. $SS_{XY} = 3.8$, $SS_X = 5.2$, $SS_Y = 5.2$

3. State the coefficient of determination for (a) to (c) in Question 2.

4. State whether each of the following is significant for a study with a sample of 12 participants. Use a .05 level of significance and conduct a two-tailed test.
   a. $r = -0.55$ b. $r = +0.78$ c. $r = -0.60$ d. $r = +0.48$

Answers: 1. Pearson correlation coefficient; 2. (a) $r = -0.436$, (b) $r = +0.935$, (c) $r = +0.731$; 3. (a) $r^2 = (-0.436)^2 = 0.190$, (b) $r^2 = (0.935)^2 = 0.874$, (c) $r^2 = (0.731)^2 = 0.534$; 4. (a) Not significant, (b) Significant, (c) Significant, (d) Not significant.

15.5 ASSUMPTIONS OF TESTS FOR LINEAR CORRELATIONS

We make many assumptions to test for the significance of a linear correlation. These assumptions apply to any type of linear correlation and not just the Pearson correlation coefficient. Three key assumptions described in this section are homoscedasticity, linearity, and normality.

HOMOSCEDASTICITY

Homoscedasticity (pronounced "ho-mo-skee-das-ti-ci-ty") is the assumption of constant variance among data points. We assume that there is an equal ("homo") variance or scatter ("scedasticity") of data points dispersed along the regression line. Figure 15.9 shows an example in which this assumption is violated—in the figure, the variance of scores in Group B is obviously different from those in Group A. When the variance of data points from the regression line is not equal, the Pearson correlation coefficient (r) tends to underestimate the strength of a correlation.

Homoscedasticity is the assumption that there is an equal ("homo") variance or scatter ("scedasticity") of data points dispersed along the regression line.

DEFINITION

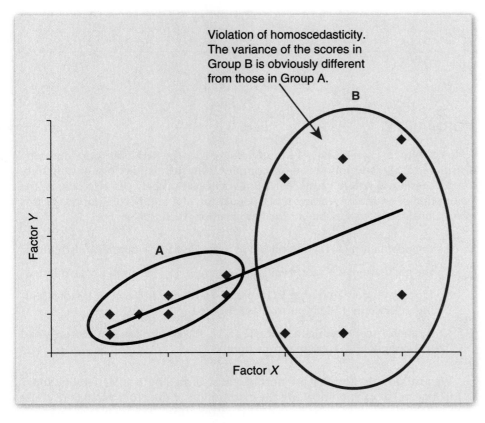

FIGURE 15.9

Violation of homoscedasticity. This population of scores shows a scatter of data points with unequal variances.

LINEARITY

Linearity is the assumption that the best way to describe the pattern of data is using a straight line. In truth, we could fit just about any set of data points to a best-fitting straight line, but the data may actually conform better to other shapes, such as curvilinear shapes. Figure 15.10 shows an example where the data are curvilinear. In this situation, a linear correlation should not be used to describe the data because the assumption of linearity is violated.

Linearity is the assumption that the best way to describe a pattern of data is using a straight line.

DEFINITION

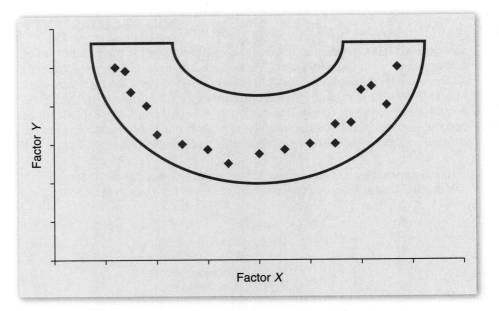

FIGURE 15.10

Violation of linearity. A population with a nonlinear relationship, which violates the assumption of linearity. In this example, the pattern is curvilinear.

NORMALITY

To test for linear correlations, we must assume that the data points are normally distributed. This assumption is more complex than the assumptions of normality for the *t*-tests and ANOVA tests. For a linear correlation between two factors, the assumption of normality requires that a population of X and Y scores for two factors forms a bivariate (two-variable) normal distribution, such that

1. the population of X scores (mood in Example 15.1) is normally distributed.

2. the population of Y scores (eating in Example 15.1) is normally distributed.

3. for each X score (mood in Example 15.1), the distribution of Y scores (eating in Example 15.1) is normally distributed.

4. for each Y score (eating in Example 15.1), the distribution of X scores (mood in Example 15.1) is normally distributed.

NOTE: To compute a correlation, we assume that the data points have equal variance (homoscedasticity), are best fit to a straight line (linearity), and are normally distributed (normality).

We assume that X and Y are normally distributed both in general (1 and 2 in the list) and at each point along the distribution of the other variable (3 and 4 in the list). To see the importance of this assumption, let's look at an extreme violation of it. Suppose we select a sample of six people and ask them how many fingers they have on their right and left hands. We record the following data displayed in Figure 15.11.

Notice that individuals with five fingers on their right hand also have five fingers on their left hand. The number of fingers on each hand is certainly related. However, in the scatter plot, only one data point is plotted because the data point for each person is the same (5, 5). As a result, the correlation coefficient will be a zero correlation: $r = 0$. This anomaly arises because of an extreme violation of the assumption of normality: All scores are the same and therefore are not normally distributed. In fact, these scores have no variance. Violating the assumption of normality can distort or bias the value of the correlation coefficient.

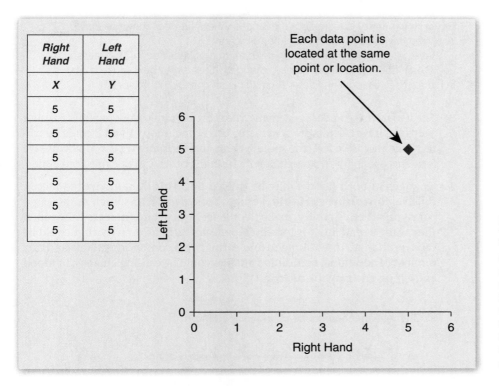

Right Hand	Left Hand
X	Y
5	5
5	5
5	5
5	5
5	5
5	5

Each data point is located at the same point or location.

FIGURE 15.11

Violation of normality. The table and the scatter plot showing the relationship between the number of fingers on the right and left hands of six people. In this example, the data points do not vary, which violates the assumption of normality. Both the table and scatter plot show the same data.

LIMITATIONS IN INTERPRETATION: CAUSALITY, OUTLIERS, AND RESTRICTION OF RANGE   15.6

Fundamental limitations using the correlational method require that a significant correlation be interpreted with caution. Among the many considerations for interpreting a significant correlation, in this section we consider causality, outliers, and restriction of range.

CAUSALITY

Using a correlational design, we do not manipulate an independent variable, and we certainly make no effort to control for other possible factors that may covary with the two variables we measured. For this reason, a significant correlation does not show that one factor causes changes in a second factor (causality). Instead, a significant correlation shows the direction and the strength of the relationship between two factors. Let's look at four possible interpretations for the correlation in Example 15.1, assuming that it was significant.

1. Decreases in how we feel (mood) can cause an increase in the amount we eat (eating). This possibility can't be ruled out.

2. Increases in the amount we eat (eating) can cause a decrease in how we feel (mood). So the direction of causality can be in the opposite direction. Hence, instead of changes in mood causing changes in eating, maybe changes in eating cause changes in mood. This possibility, called **reverse causality,** can't be ruled out either.

NOTE: Significant correlations show that two factors are related and not that one factor causes changes in a second factor

DEFINITION

Reverse causality is a problem that arises when the direction of causality between two factors can be in either direction.

Reverse causality occurs when the direction of causality for two factors, A and B, can't be determined. Hence, changes in Factor A could cause changes in Factor B, or changes in Factor B could cause changes in Factor A.

3. The two factors could be systematic, meaning that they work together to cause a change. If two factors are systematic, then conclusions 1 and 2 could be correct. The worse we feel, the more we eat, and the more we eat, the worse we feel. This possibility, that each factor causes the other, can't be ruled out either.

4. Changes in both factors may be caused by a third unanticipated factor, called a **confound variable.** Perhaps biological factors, such as increased parasympathetic activity, make people feel worse and increase how much they want to eat. So, it is increased parasympathetic activity that could be causing changes in both mood and eating. This confound variable and any number of additional confound variables could be causing changes in mood and eating and can't be ruled out either.

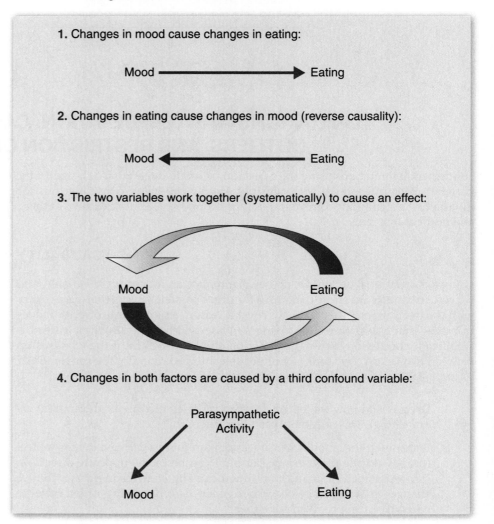

1. Changes in mood cause changes in eating:

Mood ⟶ Eating

2. Changes in eating cause changes in mood (reverse causality):

Mood ⟵ Eating

3. The two variables work together (systematically) to cause an effect:

Mood   Eating

4. Changes in both factors are caused by a third confound variable:

Parasympathetic Activity

Mood   Eating

FIGURE 15.12

Four potential explanations for a significant correlation. Because factors are measured, but not manipulated, using the correlational method, any one of these possibilities could explain a significant correlation.

DEFINITION

A **confound variable**, or third variable, is an unanticipated variable not accounted for in a research study that could be causing or associated with observed changes in one or more measured variables.

Figure 15.12 summarizes each possible explanation for an observed correlation between mood and eating. The correlational design can't distinguish between these four possible explanations. Instead, a significant correlation shows that two factors are related. It does not provide an explanation for how or why they are related.

OUTLIERS

In addition, outliers can obscure the relationship between two factors by altering the direction and the strength of an observed correlation. An outlier is a score that falls substantially above or below most other scores in a data set. Figure 15.13a shows data for the relationship between income and education without an outlier in the data. Figure 15.13b shows how an outlier, such as the income earned by a child movie star, changes the relationship between two factors. Notice in Figure 15.13 that the outlier changed both the direction and the strength of the correlation.

NOTE: Outliers can change the strength and direction of a correlation coefficient.

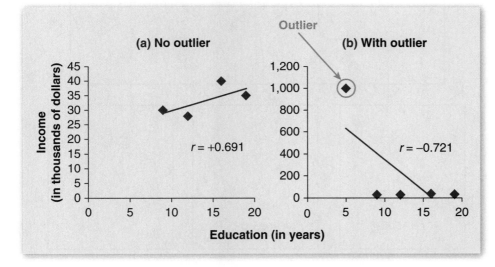

FIGURE 15.13

The effects of an outlier. (a) displays a typical correlation between income and education, with more education being associated with higher income. (b) shows the same data with an additional outlier of a child movie star who earns $1 million. The inclusion of this outlier changed both the direction and strength of the correlation.

RESTRICTION OF RANGE

When interpreting a correlation, it is also important to avoid making conclusions about relationships that fall beyond the range of data measured. The **restriction of range** problem occurs when the range of data measured in a sample is restricted or smaller than the range of data in the general population.

Figure 15.14 shows how the range of data measured in a sample can lead to erroneous conclusions about the relationship between two factors in a given population. In the figure, a positive correlation for a hypothetical population (top graph) and the correlations in three possible samples we could select from this population (smaller graphs below) are shown. Notice that, depending on the range of data measured, we could identify a positive, negative, or zero correlation from the same population, although the data in the population are actually positively correlated. To avoid the problem of restriction of range, the direction and the

NOTE: Do not describe a correlation beyond the range of data observed to avoid the problem of restriction of range.

strength of a significant correlation should only be generalized to a population within the limited range of measurements observed in the sample.

DEFINITION

Restriction of range is a problem that arises when the range of data for one or both correlated factors in a sample is limited or restricted, compared to the range of data in the population from which the sample was selected.

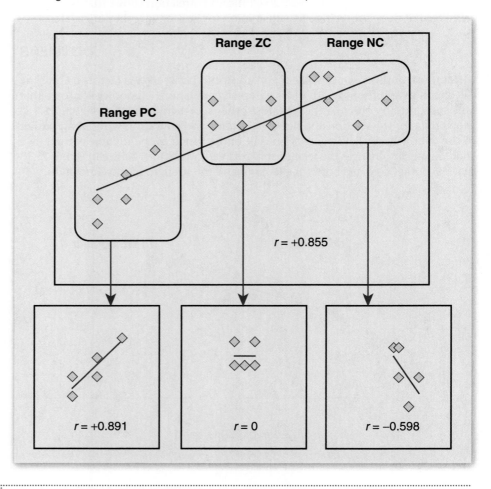

FIGURE 15.14

The effects of restriction of range. In this population, shown in the top graph, there is a positive correlation between two factors ($r = +0.855$). Also depicted are three possible samples we could select from this population. Range PC shows a positive correlation ($r = +0.891$), Range ZC shows a zero correlation ($r = 0$), and Range NC shows a negative correlation ($r = -0.598$)—all within the same population. Because different ranges of data within the same population can show very different patterns, correlations should never be interpreted beyond the range of data measured in a sample.

 **LEARNING CHECK 3**

1. State three assumptions of tests for linear correlations.

2. A researcher reports a significant positive correlation and concludes that spending more time writing a research paper will cause a better grade on the paper. Is this conclusion appropriate? Explain.

3. How can an outlier alter the relationship between two factors?

4. The range of data for one or both factors in a sample is limited, compared to the range of data in the population from which the sample was selected. What is this problem called?

Answers: 1. Homoscedasticity, linearity, and normality; 2. No, because a correlation does not demonstrate cause; 3. An outlier can change the direction and strength of a correlation; 4. Restriction of range.

ALTERNATIVE TO PEARSON *R*: SPEARMAN CORRELATION COEFFICIENT   15.7

The Pearson correlation coefficient is used to describe the relationship between two factors on an interval or ratio scale. The next few sections introduce alternative formulas for the correlation coefficient used to measure the relationship between two factors that are not both on an interval or ratio scale of measurement. Each of these new formulas was derived from the Pearson correlation coefficient, and therefore, the Pearson formula can be used to make each of the additional tests introduced in this chapter. The first of these alternative tests is the Spearman correlational coefficient.

In certain research situations, we want to determine the relationship between two ranked factors (ranks are an ordinal scale measurement). To measure the relationship between two ranked factors, we use the **Spearman rank-order correlation coefficient (r_s)**, or **Spearman's rho.** The formula for the Spearman correlation coefficient is

$$r_s = 1 - \frac{6\sum D^2}{n(n^2 - 1)}.$$

The **Spearman rank-order correlation coefficient (r_s)**, or **Spearman's rho**, is used to measure the direction and strength of the linear relationship of two ranked factors on an ordinal scale of measurement.

DEFINITION

In this formula, D is the difference between the ranks of Factor X and Factor Y, and n is the number of pairs of ranks. The Spearman formula produces a value between –1.0 and +1.0, same as for any correlation coefficient. We use the Spearman formula when we measure two ranked factors. If one or both factors are not ranked, then they must be transformed to ranks first to use this formula.

We will compute the Spearman correlation coefficient in Example 15.2 using ranked data. Once all data are ranked, we follow three steps:

Step 1: Average tied ranks.

Step 2: Compute preliminary calculations.

Step 3: Compute the Spearman correlation coefficient (r_s).

NOTE: The Spearman correlation coefficient is derived from the Pearson correlation coefficient for measuring the correlation between two ranked factors.

To measure motivation, an animal behavior psychologist ranked the time it took six mice that were deprived of food and water to complete two tasks: one reinforced with food (food task) and a second with water (water task). He ranked the mice based on their times, with the fastest time being ranked 1 and so on for each test. The researcher hypothesized that mice would finish at a similar rank for each test. Figure 15.15 displays the results of this hypothetical study.

EXAMPLE 15.2

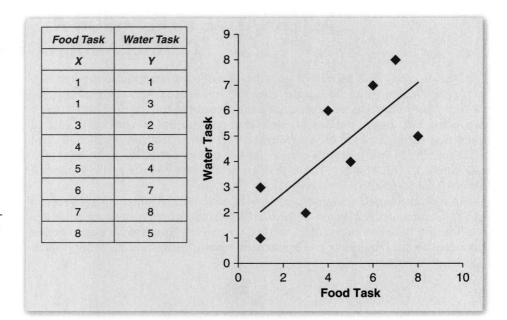

FIGURE 15.15

A table and a scatter plot showing the relationship in rankings for finishing times in a food task and water task. The regression line is given in the scatter plot. Both the table and scatter plot show the same data.

Step 1: Average tied ranks. Figure 15.15 shows the ranks in the order that mice completed each task. Notice that two mice tied for the fastest time on the food task. Tied ranks in the data will bias the correlation, and we must remove them by averaging the tied ranks using the following procedures:

1. Assume the ranks are in order. We treat the tied ranks as if they are not tied. In Example 15.2, we assume that one mouse finished first (rank 1) and another finished second (rank 2).

2. Compute the mean of the tied ranks. We average the tied ranks as if they are not tied. In Example 15.2, we add the ordered tied ranks and divide by the number of tied ranks added:

$$\frac{\text{sum of tied ranks}}{\text{number of tied ranks added}} = \frac{1+2}{2} = 1.5.$$

We will assign this average rank, 1.5, to both mice that finished first.

NOTE: Tied ranks can bias the correlation coefficient, so they must be averaged before computing the Spearman formula.

3. Shift the remaining ranks accordingly. In Example 15.2, we averaged the first two ranks, so ranks 1 and 2 are already recorded. The ranks for the remaining mice begin at Rank 3 and shift downward (the remaining ranks are already shifted in Figure 15.15).

Step 2: Compute preliminary calculations. Table 15.4 lists the adjusted ranks along with the preliminary calculations for computing the Spearman formula. The signs (+ and –) of the values for each factor are essential to making accurate computations. The calculations in Table 15.4, from left to right, are as follows:

TABLE 15.4 Preliminary calculations in Step 2 of Example 15.2. The key value that is substituted into the formula for the Spearman correlation coefficient is boxed.

Food Task	Water Task	D	D²
X	Y	(X – Y)	(X – Y)²
1.5	1	0.5	0.25
1.5	3	–1.5	2.25
3	2	1.0	1.00
4	6	–2.0	4.00
5	4	1.0	1.00
6	7	–1.0	1.00
7	8	–1.0	1.00
8	5	3.0	9.00
			$\Sigma D^2 = 19.50$

1. Subtract X and Y scores. The third column shows the difference (D) between each row of X and Y ranks.

2. Square and sum the deviation scores for X and Y. In the fourth column, each difference score is squared. The sum of the squared difference of ranks is the value of D^2:

$$\Sigma D^2 = 19.50.$$

Step 3: Compute the Spearman correlation coefficient (r_s). We completed each required computation in Steps 1 and 2. We now substitute these computations into the Spearman correlation coefficient:

$$r_s = 1 - \frac{6(19.50)}{8(8^2 - 1)} = 1 - 0.232 = +0.768.$$

The Spearman correlation coefficient is $r_s = +0.768$. We can test for significance as well. Let's use a two-tailed test at a .05 level of significance. The critical values for a Spearman correlation coefficient are given in Table B.6 in Appendix B. A portion of this table is shown in Table 15.5. Table B6 is similar to that for Pearson except that n (not df) is listed in the rows. Because $n = 8$ in Example 15.2, the critical values at a .05 level of significance are ±0.738. If the value of r_s exceeds ±0.738, then we reject the null hypothesis; otherwise, we retain the null hypothesis.

TABLE 15.5 A portion of the Spearman correlation table in Table B.6 in Appendix B.

	Level of Significance for Two-Tailed Test			
N	.10	.05	.02	.01
4	1.000			
5	0.900	1.000	1.000	
6	0.829	0.886	0.943	1.000
7	0.714	0.786	0.893	0.929
8	0.643	0.738	0.833	0.881
9	0.600	0.700	0.783	0.833
10	0.564	0.648	0.745	0.794

Source: Reprinted with permission from the *Journal of the American Statistical Association.* Copyright 1972 by the American Statistical Association. All rights reserved.

The Spearman correlation coefficient in Example 15.2 was $r_s = 0.768$, which exceeds the critical value, so we reject the null hypothesis. If we were to report this result in a research journal, it would look something like this:

Using the Spearman correlation coefficient, we found evidence of a significant correlation between the order of ranks on each task, $r_s = +0.768$, $p < .05$.

15.8 SPSS IN FOCUS: SPEARMAN CORRELATION COEFFICIENT

In Example 15.2, we concluded that "a significant correlation was evident between the order of ranks on each task, $r_s = +0.768$, $p < .05$," using the Spearman correlation coefficient. Let's confirm this conclusion using SPSS.

1. Click on the **variable view** tab and enter *food* in the **name column;** enter *water* in the name column below it. Reduce the value to 0 in the **decimals column** in both rows.

2. Click on the **data view** tab. Enter the original ranks for the food task and water task in the appropriate columns. You can enter the tied ranks, but entering the original ranks can be easier because SPSS will average the tied ranks by default. Hence, for the food task enter 1, 1, 3, 4, 5, 6, 7, and 8 down the first column. For the water task enter 1, 3, 2, 6, 4, 7, 8, and 5 down the second column.

3. Go to the **menu bar** and click **Analyze,** then **Correlate** and **Bivariate,** to display the dialog box shown in Figure 15.16.

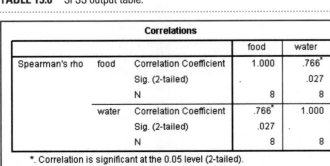

FIGURE 15.16

The dialog box in Steps 3 and 4.

4. Using the arrows, move both variables into the **Variables** box. Uncheck the Pearson box and check the Spearman box in the **Correlation Coefficients** portion of the dialog box.

5. Select **Paste** and click the **Run** command.

The SPSS output table, shown in Table 15.6, shows the value of the correlation coefficient (r_s = .766; this is slightly different than our calculation due to rounding error), the p value (p = .027), and the sample size (N = 8) for this test. If you enter values of each factor that are not ranks, such as the actual times it took subjects to complete the food and water tasks, SPSS will automatically convert the values to ranks and average the tied ranks before computing the Spearman correlation coefficient. To compute the coefficient of determination, square the correlation coefficient.

TABLE 15.6 SPSS output table.

Correlations			food	water
Spearman's rho	food	Correlation Coefficient	1.000	.766*
		Sig. (2-tailed)	.	.027
		N	8	8
	water	Correlation Coefficient	.766*	1.000
		Sig. (2-tailed)	.027	.
		N	8	8
*. Correlation is significant at the 0.05 level (2-tailed).				

LEARNING CHECK 4

1. Name the correlation coefficient used to determine the relationship between two ranked or ordinal factors.

2. Ten employees have their performance ranked by a peer and by management. If we know that $\Sigma D^2 = 21.50$, then what is the value of r_s?

3. Is the Spearman correlation coefficient computed in Question 2 significant using a two-tailed test at a .05 level of significance?

Answers: 1. Spearman correlation coefficient. 2. $r_s = 1 - \dfrac{6(21.50)}{10(10^2 - 1)} = 0.870$; 3. Yes, the correlation coefficient is significant.

15.9 ALTERNATIVE TO PEARSON *R*: POINT-BISERIAL CORRELATION COEFFICIENT

In certain research situations, we measure one factor that is continuous (on an interval or ratio scale of measurement) and a second factor that is dichotomous (on a nominal scale of measurement). A dichotomous factor has only two values or categories, such as gender (male, female) or pet owner (yes, no).

To measure the direction and strength of the linear relationship between one factor that is continuous and one factor that is dichotomous, we use the **point-biserial correlation coefficient.** Again, this formula was derived from the Pearson *r* correlation coefficient, so with some adjustments, the Pearson *r* can also be used. The formula for the point-biserial correlation coefficient is

$$r_{pb} = \left(\frac{M_{Y_1} - M_{Y_2}}{s_Y} \right)\left(\sqrt{pq}\right), \text{ where } s_Y = \sqrt{\frac{SS_Y}{n}}.$$

DEFINITION

The **point-biserial correlation coefficient (r_{pb})** is used to measure the direction and strength of the linear relationship of one factor that is continuous (on an interval or ratio scale of measurement) and a second factor that is dichotomous (on a nominal scale of measurement).

NOTE: The point-biserial correlation coefficient is derived from the Pearson correlation coefficient to determine the correlation between one continuous and one dichotomous factor.

In the point-biserial formula, *p* and *q* are the proportion of scores at each level of the dichotomous factor, s_Y is the standard deviation of *Y* scores (for the continuous factor), and *n* is the number of pairs of scores measured. Using this formula, we will compute the point-biserial correlation coefficient in Example 15.3 using the following three steps:

Step 1: Code the dichotomous factor.

Step 2: Compute preliminary calculations.

Step 3: Compute the point-biserial correlation coefficient (r_{pb}).

In a study investigating how gender is related to perceptions of humor, 12 participants observed a videotape of a female comedian perform a one-minute comedy skit on the topic of being in a college class. The time spent laughing (in seconds) during the videotaped skit was recorded for each participant. The gender of the participant (male, female) is the dichotomous factor, and the time spent laughing during the skit is the continuous factor. Table 15.7 shows the results from this hypothetical study with Step 1 already completed.

EXAMPLE 15.3

TABLE 15.7 The gender and time spent laughing during a one-minute comedy skit for a sample of 12 participants. The dichotomous factor (gender) is coded in the table. Coding the dichotomous factor is Step 1 in Example 15.3.

Gender (1 = male, 2 = female)	Duration of Laughter (in seconds)
X	Y
1	23
1	9
1	12
1	12
1	29
2	32
2	10
2	8
2	20
2	12
2	24
2	34

Step 1: Code the dichotomous factor. In Table 15.7, gender is coded with 1s and 2s, with men coded as *1* and women coded as *2*. The 12 participants consisted of 5 men and 7 women. Hence, the proportion of men is $p = \dfrac{5}{12} = 0.42$, and the proportion of women is $q = \dfrac{7}{12} = 0.58$. The sum of p and q should always be equal to 1.0.

NOTE: To code the dichotomous factor, assign a numeric value to each level of the factor.

Step 2: Compute preliminary calculations. The preliminary calculations are given in Table 15.8. The signs (+ and −) of the values for each factor are essential to making accurate computations. The calculations in Table 15.8, from left to right, are as follows:

TABLE 15.8 Preliminary calculations in Step 2 of Example 15.3. The key values that are substituted into the formula for the point-biserial correlation coefficient are circled.

X	Y	$Y - M_Y$	$(Y - M_Y)^2$	
1	23	4.25	18.06	
1	9	−9.75	95.06	
1	12	−6.75	45.56	
1	12	−6.75	45.56	
1	29	10.25	105.06	
				$M_{Y_1} = 17$ → Mean Y scores for men (coded as "1")
2	32	13.25	175.56	
2	10	−8.75	76.56	
2	8	−10.75	115.56	
2	20	1.25	1.56	
2	12	−6.75	45.56	
2	24	5.25	27.56	
2	34	15.25	232.56	
				$M_{Y_2} = 20$ → Mean Y scores for women (coded as "2")
	$M_Y = 18.75$		$SS_Y = 984.22$	→ The sum of squares for Y

1. Compute the average Y score at each level of the dichotomous variable and overall. In Table 15.8, the mean values for men ($M_{Y_1} = 17$) and women ($M_{Y_2} = 20$) are circled to the right and the overall mean for Y scores (M_Y) is given at the bottom of the column for Y ($M_Y = 18.75$).

2. Subtract each Y score from the overall mean for Y. In the third column, each Y score is subtracted from M_Y. The sum of the differences of scores from the mean should equal 0.

3. Multiply and sum the deviation scores for Y. In this step, multiply the deviation scores for each Y value times itself. The sum of these scores is the sum of squares for Y ($SS_Y = 984.22$).

Step 3: Compute the point-biserial correlation coefficient (r_{pb}). Using the values computed in Steps 1 and 2, first compute s_Y, and then compute the point-biserial correlation coefficient:

$$[1] \quad s_Y = \sqrt{\frac{SS_Y}{n}} = \sqrt{\frac{984.22}{12}} = 9.056.$$

$$[2] \quad r_{pb} = \left(\frac{M_{Y_1} - M_{Y_2}}{s_Y}\right)\left(\sqrt{pq}\right) = \left(\frac{17-20}{9.056}\right)\left(\sqrt{0.42 \times 0.58}\right) = -0.163.$$

The point-biserial correlation coefficient is $r_{pb} = -0.163$. The direction of the correlation is not meaningful because it makes no sense to say that as gender decreases, duration of laughter increases. Gender doesn't increase or decrease, and we must interpret the result differently. If the correlation is significant, then we look back at the data to see which level of the dichotomous variable (gender: male, female) had a larger mean value (mean duration of laughter). If the correlation in Example 15.3 is significant, then we conclude that gender and laughter are related, with women laughing for longer durations than men.

NOTE: The direction (+ or −) of the correlation coefficient is meaningless for a point-biserial correlation because the dichotomous variable can only take on two values.

To test for significance, we compute the two–independent sample *t*-test introduced in Chapter 9 by making each level of the dichotomous factor (men, women) a separate group and duration of laughter the dependent variable in each group. The two–independent sample *t*-test and the point-biserial correlation are related in that the value of the coefficient of determination (r^2) equals the value of eta-squared (η^2) used with the two–independent sample *t*-test. We can convert the value of *r* to a *t*-statistic using the following equation:

NOTE: The t-test and point-biserial test are related in that their measures of effect size (r^2 and η^2) are mathematically the same, which allows the t-test to be used as a test for the significance of a point-biserial correlation.

$$t^2 = \frac{r^2}{(1-r^2)/df}.$$

In Example 15.3, we found that $r_{pb} = -0.163$. In this equation, *df* are the degrees of freedom for the two–independent sample *t*-test, or $n - 2$: $df = 12 - 2 = 10$. We can substitute *r* and *df* into the formula:

$$t^2 = \frac{(-0.163)^2}{(1-(-0.163)^2)/10} = 0.272.$$

The square root of this solution is the *t*-statistic:

$$t = \sqrt{t^2} = \sqrt{0.272} = 0.522.$$

To locate the critical values for this test, we look in Table B.2 in Appendix B for critical values with $df = 10$ for a two-tailed test at a .05 level of significance. The critical values are ±2.228. Because $t = 0.522$ does not exceed the critical values, we retain the null hypothesis. We conclude that the gender of a participant and the duration of laughter are not related. If we were to report this result in a research journal, it would look something like this:

Using the point-biserial correlation coefficient, a correlation between gender and duration of laughter was not significant, $r_{pb} = -0.163$, $p > .05$.

Also, recall that r^2 equals η^2. To demonstrate this equivalence, we can compute eta-squared for the *t*-test introduced in Chapter 9:

$$\text{Eta–squared: } \eta^2 = \frac{t^2}{t^2 + df} = \frac{(0.522)^2}{(0.522)^2 + 10} = 0.027.$$

Coefficient of determination: $r^2 = (0.163)^2 = 0.027.$

Both formulas give the same value of effect size. The proportion of variance for the two–independent sample t-test (η^2) and the coefficient of determination (r^2) for the point-biserial correlation coefficient are equal.

15.10 SPSS IN FOCUS: POINT-BISERIAL CORRELATION COEFFICIENT

There is no command in SPSS to compute a point-biserial correlation coefficient. To compute a point-biserial correlation coefficient using SPSS, we must first code the dichotomous factor and then compute the Pearson correlation coefficient. Because the point-biserial correlation coefficient is derived mathematically from the Pearson correlation coefficient, the value we obtain using SPSS will be identical to that obtained for a point-biserial correlation.

In Example 15.3, we concluded that "a correlation between gender and duration of laughter was not significant, $r_{pb} = -0.163$, $p > .05$," using the point-biserial correlation coefficient. Let's confirm this conclusion using SPSS.

1. Click on the **variable view** tab and enter *gender* in the **name column;** enter *laughter* in the name column below it. Reduce the value to 0 in the **decimals column** in both rows.

2. To code the dichotomous factor, click on the small gray box with three dots in the **Values column** in the row named *gender.* In the **dialog box,** enter *1* in the **Value** cell and *men* in the **Label** cell, then click **Add.** Enter *2* in the **Value** cell and *women* in the **Label** cell, then click **Add.** Click **OK.**

3. Click on the **data view** tab to enter to data. In the first column, enter *1* five times and *2* seven times for gender. In the second column, enter the data for laughter for men and women across from the corresponding code (i.e., enter the data for men next to a code of 1 and the data for women next to a code of 2).

4. Go to the **menu bar** and click **Analyze,** then **Correlate** and **Bivariate,** to display a dialog box.

5. Using the arrows, move both variables into the **Variables** box.

6. Select **Paste** and click the **Run** command.

The SPSS output table, shown in Table 15.9, shows the value of the correlation coefficient ($r = .163$), the p value ($p = .612$), and the sample size ($N = 12$) for this test.

TABLE 15.9   SPSS output table.

Correlations		gender	laughter
gender	Pearson Correlation	1	.163
	Sig. (2-tailed)		.612
	N	12	12
laughter	Pearson Correlation	.163	1
	Sig. (2-tailed)	.612	
	N	12	12

Again, the sign of the correlation is not meaningful for the point-biserial correlation. As long as you code the dichotomous variable, the Pearson and the point-biserial correlation coefficients will be identical. To compute the coefficient of determination, square the correlation coefficient.

LEARNING CHECK 5

1. Name the correlation coefficient used to determine the direction and strength of the linear relationship between one factor that is continuous (on an interval or ratio scale of measurement) and a second factor that is dichotomous (on a nominal scale of measurement).

2. A researcher measures the relationship between political affiliation (Democrat, Republican) and attitudes toward stem cell research (measured on a 7-point rating scale from 1 = *completely against* to 7 = *fully support*).
   a. If the same number of Democrats and Republicans is observed, then what is the value of p and q?
   b. If the same number of Democrats and Republicans is observed, then what is the correlation coefficient when $M_{Y_1} - M_{Y_2} = +3$, and $s_Y = 1.68$?

3. What is the relationship between r^2 and η^2?

Answers: 1. Point-biserial correlation coefficient (r_{pb}); 2. (a) Both p and q equal 0.5; (b) $r_{pb} = \left(\frac{3}{1.68}\right)(\sqrt{0.5 \times 0.5}) =$ 0.893; 3. The formula for each measure is mathematically equivalent.

ALTERNATIVE TO PEARSON *R*: PHI CORRELATION COEFFICIENT 15.11

In certain research situations, we measure two dichotomous factors. Dichotomous factors are typically categorical and are therefore measured on a nominal scale of measurement.

To determine the direction and strength of the linear relationship between two dichotomous factors, we use the **phi correlation coefficient (r_ϕ)**. Again, this formula was derived from the Pearson *r* correlation coefficient, so with some adjustments, the Pearson *r* can also be used. The notation used for the phi correlation coefficient is taken from the outcomes in a 2 × 2 matrix, which is shown in Table 15.10. The formula for the phi correlation coefficient using this notation is

$$r_\phi = \frac{ad - bc}{\sqrt{ABCD}}.$$

TABLE 15.10 A matrix displaying the notation used for the phi correlation coefficient.

		Variable *X*		
		X₁	*X₂*	
Variable *Y*	*Y₁*	a	b	A
	Y₂	c	d	B
		C	D	

DEFINITION

The **phi correlation coefficient (r_ϕ)** is used to measure the direction and strength of the linear relationship of two dichotomous factors on a nominal scale of measurement.

NOTE: The phi correlation coefficient is derived from the Pearson correlation coefficient for measuring the correlation between two dichotomous factors.

A positive correlation occurs when the values in Cells a and d are larger than the values in Cells b and c. A negative correlation occurs when the values in Cells b and c are larger than the values in Cells a and d. The denominator for this test is a mathematical adjustment used to ensure that the phi correlation coefficient always varies between −1.0 and +1.0. We will compute a phi correlation coefficient in Example 15.4.

EXAMPLE 15.4

A researcher wants to determine the relationship between employment (employed, unemployed) and happiness (happy, unhappy) using a sample of 40 participants. The number of participants in each category was recorded. The 2 × 2 matrix in Table 15.11 shows the results of this hypothetical study.

TABLE 15.11   A matrix displaying the results of the hypothetical study in Example 15.4.

		Employment		
		Unemployed 0	Employed 1	Totals
	Unhappy 0	14	6	20
Happiness	Happy 1	6	14	20
	Totals	20	20	$n = 40$

To compute the phi correlation coefficient, we substitute the frequencies (or number of participants) in each cell of the matrix into the formula for the phi correlation coefficient:

$$r_\phi = \frac{(14 \times 14) - (6 \times 6)}{\sqrt{20 \times 20 \times 20 \times 20}} = +0.40.$$

The phi correlation coefficient is $r_\phi = +0.40$. We conclude people who are happy tend to be employed and people who are unhappy tend to be unemployed. Note that the row and the column totals in the 2 × 2 matrix are the same. When this happens, the formula for the phi correlation coefficient can be simplified to

$$r_\phi = \frac{\text{matches} - \text{mismatches}}{\text{sample size}}.$$

To use this simplified formula, we refer to the coding used for each level of the dichotomous factors. The levels of each dichotomous factor are coded (0 or 1) in Table 15.11. Matches occur when the 0s (Cell 0,0) and 1s (Cell 1,1) match. Mismatches occur when they do not match (Cell 0,1 and Cell 1,0). The phi correlation coefficient using this simplified formula is

$$r_\phi = \frac{28 - 12}{40} = +0.40.$$

Both formulas give the same value for the phi correlation coefficient only when row and column totals in the 2 × 2 matrix are the same. When the row and column totals are not the same, use the first formula.

To determine the significance of the phi correlation coefficient, we compute a chi-square (χ^2) test. Although the chi-square test is introduced in detail in Chapter 17, we can use this test here by converting the value of r to a χ^2 statistic using the following equation:

$$\chi^2 = r_\phi^2 n.$$

For this equation, n is the total number of participants in the study ($n = 40$), and r_ϕ^2 is the coefficient of determination. We can substitute these values into the equation:

$$\chi^2 = (0.40)^2 \times 40 = 6.40.$$

To locate the critical value for this test, we look in Table B.7 in Appendix B. A portion of this table is shown in Table 15.12. The levels of significance are listed in each column, and the degrees of freedom are listed in each row in the table. For this test, the degrees of freedom are always equal to 1. If we compute a two-tailed test at a .05 level of significance, then the critical value with one degree of freedom is 3.84. Because the chi-square statistic ($\chi^2 = 6.40$) exceeds the critical value, we reject the null hypothesis. If we were to report this result in a research journal, it would look something like this:

Using the phi correlation coefficient we found a correlation between employment and happiness that was significant, $r_\phi = +0.40$, $p < .05$.

TABLE 15.12 A portion of the chi-square table in Table B.7 in Appendix B.

	Level of Significance	
df	$\alpha = .05$	$\alpha = .01$
1	3.84	6.64
2	5.99	9.21
3	7.81	11.34
4	9.49	13.28
5	11.07	15.09
6	12.59	16.81
7	14.07	18.48
8	15.51	20.09
9	16.92	21.67
10	18.31	23.21

Source: From Table IV of R. A. Fisher and F. Yates, *Statistical Tables for Biological, Agricultural and Medical Research, 6th ed.* London: Longman Group Ltd., 1974 Reprinted with permission of the Addison Wesley Longman Ltd.

TABLE 15.13 The scales of measurement for factors tested using the Pearson, Spearman, point-biserial, and phi correlation coefficients.

Correlation Coefficient	Scale of Measurement for Correlated Variables
Pearson	Both factors are interval or ratio data.
Spearman	Both factors are ranked or ordinal data.
Point-Biserial	One factor is dichotomous (nominal data) and a second factor is continuous (interval or ratio data).
Phi	Both factors are dichotomous (nominal data).

Table 15.13 summarizes when it is appropriate to use each correlation coefficient introduced in this chapter based on the scales of measurement of the data.

15.12 SPSS IN FOCUS: PHI CORRELATION COEFFICIENT

There is no command in SPSS to compute a phi correlation coefficient. To compute a phi correlation coefficient using SPSS, we first code each dichotomous factor, then weight each variable using the **Weight Cases . . .** option in the menu bar, and finally compute a Pearson correlation coefficient. Because the phi correlation coefficient is derived mathematically from the Pearson correlation coefficient, the value we obtain using SPSS will be identical to that obtained for a phi correlation.

In Example 15.4, we concluded that "a correlation between employment and happiness was significant, $r_\phi = +0.40$, $p < .05$," using the phi correlation coefficient. Let's confirm this conclusion using SPSS.

1. Click on the **variable view** tab and enter *employment* in the **name column;** enter *happiness* in the name column below it; enter *count* in the name column below that. Reduce the value in the **decimals column** to 0 in each row.

2. We will code each variable with 0s and 1s to identify each cell in Table 15.11. To code the *employment* variable, click on the small gray box with three dots in the **Values column** in the row named *employment*. In the **dialog box,** enter *0* in the **Value** cell and *unemployed* in the **Label** cell, then click **Add.** Then enter *1* in the **Value** cell and *employed* in the **Label** cell, then click **Add.** Click **OK.**

3. To code the *happiness* variable, click on the small gray box with three dots in the **Values column** in the row named *happiness*. In the **dialog box,** enter *0* in the **Value** cell and *unhappy* in the **Label** cell, then click **Add.** Then enter *1* in the **Value** cell and *happy* in the **Label** cell, then click **Add.** Click **OK.**

4. Click on the **data view** tab to enter the data. For employment, enter 0, 0, 1, and 1. For happiness, enter 0, 1, 0, and 1. For counts, enter 14, 6, 6, and 14 down the column.

5. Go to the menu bar and click **Data,** then **Weight Cases . . .** to display the new dialog box shown in Figure 15.17. Select **Weight cases by** and move *count* into the **Frequency Variable** box, then click **OK.**

6. Go to the **menu bar** and click **Analyze,** then **Correlate** and **Bivariate,** to display a new dialog box. Using the arrows, move *employment* and *happiness* into the **Variables** box.

7. Select **Paste** and click the **Run** command.

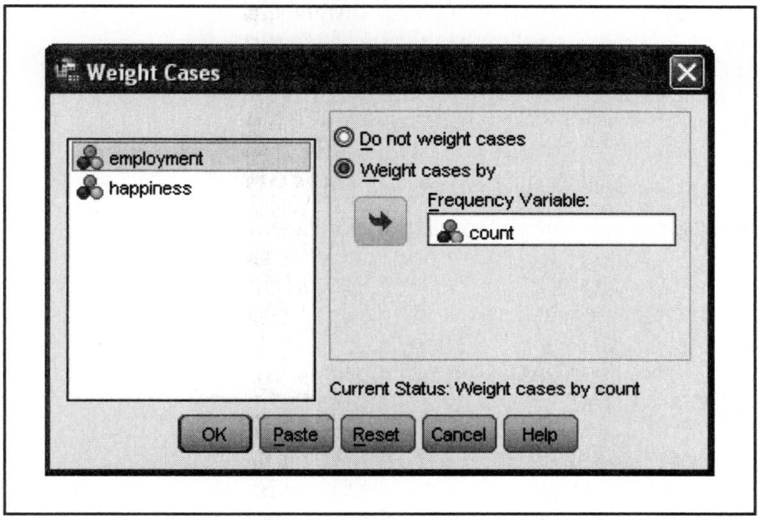

FIGURE 15.17

The dialog box in Steps 3 and 4.

TABLE 15.14 SPSS output table.

Correlations

		employment	happiness
employment	Pearson Correlation	1	.400[*]
	Sig. (2-tailed)		.011
	N	40	40
happiness	Pearson Correlation	.400[*]	1
	Sig. (2-tailed)	.011	
	N	40	40

*. Correlation is significant at the 0.05 level (2-tailed).

The SPSS output table, shown in Table 15.14, shows the value of the correlation coefficient ($r = .400$), the p value ($p = .011$), and the sample size ($N = 40$) for this test. As long as you code and weight the dichotomous factors, the Pearson and phi correlation coefficients will be identical. To compute the coefficient of determination, square the correlation coefficient.

LEARNING CHECK 6

1. The _____ is used to measure the direction and strength of the linear relationship of two dichotomous factors on a nominal scale of measurement.

2. An instructor holds an exam review session and wants to see whether it was effective. He records whether the student attended the review session and whether he or she passed the exam. The following table summarizes the results.

		Review Session		
		Attended	Did Not Attend	Totals
Exam	Passed	12	8	20
	Failed	4	10	14
	Totals	16	18	

   a. How many students were in this study?
   b. What is the value of phi correlation coefficient?

Answers: 1. Phi correlation coefficient (r_ϕ); 2. (a) 34 students, (b) $r_\phi = \dfrac{(12 \times 10) - (8 \times 4)}{\sqrt{20 \times 14 \times 16 \times 18}} = 0.31.$

15.13 APA IN FOCUS: REPORTING CORRELATIONS

To summarize correlations, we report the strength, the direction, and the *p* value for each correlation coefficient. The sample size and effect size should also be reported. The means and standard error or standard deviations measured in a study can be summarized in a figure or table or in the main text. When we compute many correlations in a single study, we often report each correlation coefficient in a table called a *correlation matrix*. For example, Zeidner and Kaluda (2008) measured the relationship between scales for emotional intelligence (EI), verbal ability, and love in a sample of husbands (among many other comparisons not shown here). They reported each correlation in a correlation matrix, as shown in Table 15.15. A correlation matrix provides an informative and concise summary of each correlation measured in a study.

TABLE 15.15 A correlation matrix displaying a portion of the results from a study authored by Zeidner and Kaluda (2008).

Measurement Scales	Husband's Scores		
	1	2	3
1. EI			
2. Verbal ability	0.24*		
3. Love	0.28*	0.10	
* Correlations significant at *p* < .05.			

CHAPTER SUMMARY ORGANIZED BY LEARNING OBJECTIVE

LO 1: Identify the direction and strength of a correlation between two factors.

- A **correlation** is a statistical procedure used to describe the strength and direction of the linear relationship between two factors.
- The value of the **correlation coefficient (r)** is used to measure the strength and direction of the linear relationship between two factors. The value of r ranges from −1.0 to +1.0.
  a. The direction of a correlation is indicated by the sign (+ or −) of r. When a correlation is positive (+), two factors change in the same direction; when a correlation is negative (−), two factors change in opposite directions.
  b. The strength of the correlation is indicated by the value of r, with values closer to ±1.0 indicating stronger correlations and correlations closer to 0 indicating weaker correlations. The closer that data points fall from the regression line, the stronger the correlation.

LO 2–3: Compute and interpret the Pearson correlation coefficient and test for significance; compute and interpret the coefficient of determination.

- The **Pearson correlation coefficient (r)** is used to measure the direction and strength of the linear relationship between two factors in which the data for both factors are measured on an interval or a ratio scale of measurement. The steps to compute the Pearson correlation coefficient are as follows:

  Step 1: Compute preliminary calculations.

  Step 2: Compute the Pearson correlation coefficient: $r = \dfrac{SS_{XY}}{\sqrt{SS_X SS_Y}}$.
- The **coefficient of determination (r^2 or R^2)** measures the extent to which changes in one factor (Y) can be explained by changes in a second factor (X).
- To test for the significance of a Pearson correlation coefficient, follow the four steps to hypothesis testing and use r as the test statistic. The critical values for the test are given in Table B.5 in Appendix B.

LO 4: Define *homoscedasticity*, *linearity*, and *normality* and explain why each assumption is necessary to appropriately interpret a significant correlation coefficient.

- Three assumptions for interpreting a significant correlation coefficient are homoscedasticity, linearity, and normality. **Homoscedasticity** is the assumption that the variance of data points dispersed along the regression line is equal. **Linearity** is the assumption that the best way to describe the pattern of data is using a straight line. Normality is the assumption that data points are normally distributed.

LO 5: Explain how causality, outliers, and restriction of range can limit the interpretation of a significant correlation coefficient.

- Three additional considerations that must be made to accurately interpret a significant correlation coefficient are that (1) correlations do not demonstrate cause, (2) outliers can change the direction and the strength of a correlation, and (3) never generalize the direction and the strength of a correlation beyond the range of data measured (restriction of range).

LO 6: Compute and interpret the Spearman correlation coefficient and test for significance.

- The **Spearman rank-order correlation coefficient (r_s)** is used to measure the direction and strength of the linear relationship between two ranked factors. The formula for the Spearman correlation coefficient is

$$r_s = 1 - \frac{6 \sum D^2}{n(n^2 - 1)}.$$

- The steps to compute a Spearman correlation coefficient are as follows:

  Step 1: Average tied ranks.
  Step 2: Compute preliminary calculations.
  Step 3: Compute the Spearman correlation coefficient (r_s).
- To test for significance, find the critical values for a Spearman correlation coefficient located in Table B.6 in Appendix B.

LO 7: Compute and interpret the point-biserial correlation coefficient and test for significance.

- The **point-biserial correlation coefficient (r_{pb})** is used to measure the direction and strength of the linear relationship of one factor that is continuous (on an interval or ratio scale of measurement) and a second factor that is dichotomous (on a nominal scale of measurement). The formula for the point-biserial correlation coefficient is

$$r_{pb} = \left(\frac{M_{Y_1} - M_{Y_2}}{s_Y} \right)\left(\sqrt{pq}\right), \text{ where } s_Y = \sqrt{\frac{SS_Y}{n}}.$$

- The steps to compute a point-biserial correlation coefficient are as follows:

    Step 1: Code the dichotomous factor.

    Step 2: Compute preliminary calculations.

    Step 3: Compute the point-biserial correlation coefficient (r_{pb}).

- To test for significance, convert a point-biserial correlation coefficient to a *t*-statistic using the first equation given in the LO 9 summary and locate critical values in the *t*-table given in Table B.2 in Appendix B.

LO 8: Compute and interpret the phi correlation coefficient and test for significance.

- The **phi correlation coefficient (r_ϕ)** is used to measure the direction and strength of the linear relationship between two dichotomous factors. The formula for the phi correlation coefficient is

$$r_\phi = \frac{ad - bc}{\sqrt{ABCD}}.$$

- To test for significance, convert a phi correlation coefficient to a chi-square (χ^2) statistic using the second equation given in the LO 9 summary and locate critical values in the chi-square table given in Table B.7 in Appendix B.

LO 9: Convert the value of *r* to a *t* statistic and χ^2 statistic.

- Equation to convert the value of *r* to a *t*-statistic: $t^2 = \dfrac{r^2}{(1 - r^2)/df}.$

- Equation to convert the value of *r* to a χ^2 statistic: $\chi^2 = r_\phi^2 n.$

APA LO 10: Summarize the results of a correlation coefficient in APA format.

- To summarize correlations, report the strength and direction of each correlation coefficient and the *p* value for each correlation. The sample size and the effect size should also be reported. The means and the standard error or standard deviations measured in a study can be summarized in a figure or table or in the main text. To report many correlations in a single study, use a correlation matrix.

SPSS LO 11: Compute the Pearson, Spearman, point-biserial, and phi correlation coefficient using SPSS.

- SPSS can be used to compute the Pearson correlation coefficient using the **Analyze, Correlate,** and **Bivariate** options in the menu bar. These actions will display a dialog box that allows you to identify the variables and to run the correlation (for more details, see Section 15.4).
- SPSS can be used to compute the Spearman correlation coefficient using the **Analyze, Correlate,** and **Bivariate** options in the menu bar. These actions will display a dialog box that allows you to identify the variables, to select the option to compute a Spearman correlation, and to run the correlation (for more details, see Section 15.8).
- There is no command in SPSS to compute a point-biserial correlation coefficient. To compute a point-biserial correlation coefficient using SPSS, first code the dichotomous factor, and then follow the directions for computing a Pearson correlation coefficient (for more details, see Section 15.10).
- There is no command in SPSS to compute a phi correlation coefficient. To compute a phi correlation coefficient using SPSS, first code each dichotomous factor, then weight each variable using the **Weight Cases . . .** option in the menu bar, and finally follow the directions for computing a Pearson correlation coefficient (for more details, see Section 15.12).

KEY TERMS

coefficient of determination
confound variable
correlation
correlation coefficient (r)
covariance
homoscedasticity
linearity

negative correlation
Pearson (product moment)
    correlation coefficient (r)
phi correlation coefficient (r_t)
point-biserial correlation
    coefficient (r_{pb})
positive correlation

regression line
restriction of range
reverse causality
Spearman rank-order correlation
    coefficient (r_s)
Spearman's rho
sum of products (SP)

END-OF-CHAPTER PROBLEMS

Factual Problems

1. What is a correlation?

2. What information does the direction of a correlation coefficient convey?

3. What information does the strength of a correlation coefficient convey?

4. Describe what each of the following statistical terms measure:

   (a) SS_{XY}

   (b) $\sqrt{SS_X SS_Y}$

5. What is the coefficient of determination?

6. State three assumptions for computing linear correlations.

7. True or false: A significant correlation indicates that changes in the values of one factor cause changes in the values of a second factor.

8. When does restriction of range limit the interpretation of a significant correlation?

9. Name four correlation coefficients and describe when it is appropriate to use each.

10. State the formula for the following:

    (a) Converting r to a t-statistic

    (b) Converting r to a χ^2 statistic

Concepts and Application Problems

11. State which correlation coefficient (Pearson, Spearman, point-biserial, or phi) should be used given the following information.

    (a) Both factors are interval or ratio scale.

    (b) Both factors are ranked.

    (c) One factor is dichotomous and a second factor is continuous.

    (d) Both factors are dichotomous.

12. State which correlation coefficient (Pearson, Spearman, point-biserial, or phi) should be used to study each of the following factors:

    (a) Activity (active, inactive) and depression (depressed, not depressed)

    (b) Time spent at school and time spent studying in hours per week

    (c) Veteran (yes, no) and level of patriotism indicated on a rating scale

    (d) The hierarchical ranking of a litter of mice for play and social behavior.

13. State whether each of the following is an example of a positive or negative correlation.

    (a) Higher education level is associated with a larger annual income.

    (b) The smaller the class size, the more students believe they are receiving a quality education.

    (c) Increased testosterone is associated with increased aggression.

    (d) Rising prices of apples are associated with the sale of fewer apples.

14. For each example, state whether one correlation is stronger than the other. If one is stronger, then state which is the stronger correlation.

    (a) $r = +0.04$, $r = -0.40$

    (b) $r = +0.50$, $r = +0.23$

    (c) $r = +0.36$, $r = -0.36$

    (d) $r = -0.67$, $r = -0.76$

15. The graphs display the data points for a linear correlation. Based on the information provided in these graphs, answer the following questions.

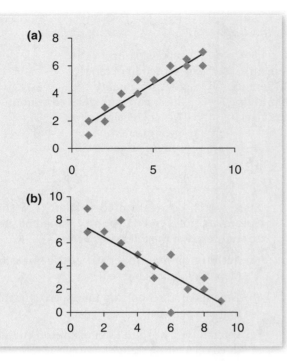

(a) Which graph displays the negative correlation? Explain.

(b) Which graph displays the stronger correlation? Explain.

16. A researcher working with socioeconomic data showed a significant positive correlation between the number of local hospitals and the life expectancy of local residents ($r = 0.19$). Which of the following conclusions is appropriate? Explain why the other is not appropriate.

(a) 3.61% of the variance in life expectancy can be explained by the number of local hospitals.

(b) Increasing the number of local hospitals will cause life expectancy for local residents to increase.

17. A medical study found a negative relationship between exercise (in minutes per week) and stress-related heath problems ($r = -0.26$). Which of the following conclusions is appropriate? Explain why the other is not appropriate.

(a) 6.76% of the variance in stress-related health problems can be explained by the amount of weekly exercise.

(b) Increasing the amount of exercise per week will cause stress-related health problems to decrease.

18. A social scientist measures the relationship between computer use (in hours per day) and daily exercise (in minutes per week). Answer the following questions based on the results provided.

Computer Use	Daily Exercise
3	80
2	60
5	95
4	75

(a) Compute the Pearson correlation coefficient.

(b) Add 2 hours to each measurement of Internet use and recalculate the correlation coefficient.

(c) Subtract 10 minutes from each measurement of daily exercise and recalculate the correlation coefficient.

(d) True or false: Adding and subtracting a constant to one set of scores (X or Y) does not change the correlation coefficient. *Note:* Use your answers in (a) to (c) to answer true or false.

19. A researcher measures the relationship between sleep medication use (times used per week) and time spent working (in hours per week). Answer the following questions based on the results provided.

Sleep Medication Use	Time Spent Working
8	18
3	40
6	20
2	32

(a) Compute the Pearson correlation coefficient.

(b) Multiply each measurement of drug use times 3 and recalculate the correlation coefficient.

(c) Divide each measurement in half for time spent working and recalculate the correlation coefficient.

(d) True or false: Multiplying or dividing a positive constant to one set of scores (X or Y) does not change the correlation coefficient. *Note:* Use your answers in (a) to (c) to answer true or false.

20. A researcher measures the relationship between education (in years) and investment gains (in thousands of dollars). Answer the following questions based on the results provided.

Education	Investment Gains
14	8
12	11
9	10
18	14

(a) Compute the Pearson correlation coefficient.

(b) Multiply each investment gains times −1 (so that it represents investment losses instead of gains). Recalculate the correlation coefficient.

(c) True or false: Multiplying or dividing a negative constant to one set of scores (X or Y) changes the sign of the correlation only, while the strength of the correlation coefficient remains unchanged. *Note:* Use your answers in (a) and (b) to answer true or false.

21. A therapist specializing in family counseling measures the relationship between partners and martial satisfaction. Husbands and wives rated how satisfied they were in their marriage using a 7-point rating scale ranging from 1 (*not satisfied at all*) to 9 (*very satisfied*). Using the hypothetical data given in the following table, compute the Pearson correlation coefficient.

Husband	Wife
X	Y
1	6
2	6
3	6
4	6
5	6
6	6
7	6

22. A community researcher measured the correlation between the average cost of housing and the crime rate in eight local communities. The results of this hypothetical study are listed in the following table.

Average Cost of Housing (in thousands of dollars)	Crime Rates (per 100,000 population)
X	Y
20	96
80	65
220	22
120	31
180	34
90	70
110	30
300	16

(a) Compute the Pearson correlation coefficient.

(b) Compute the coefficient of determination.

(c) Using a two-tailed test at a .05 level of significance, state the decision to retain or reject the null hypothesis.

23. A researcher measures the relationship between Internet use (hours per week) and social interaction (hours per week) in a sample of 10 students. The following table lists the hypothetical results of this study.

Internet Use	Social Interaction
X	Y
6	4
8	6
5	7
7	6
12	5
4	7
3	3
6	5
2	10
11	3

(a) Compute the Pearson correlation coefficient.

(b) Compute the coefficient of determination.

(c) Using a two-tailed test at a .05 level of significance, state the decision to retain or reject the null hypothesis.

24. Using the Pearson correlation coefficient, a study on addiction found a positive correlation between time of cravings and time of relapse ($r = 0.51$) in a sample of 20 addicts. Using a two-tailed test at a .05 level of significance, state the decision to retain or reject the null hypothesis.

25. Using the Pearson correlation coefficient, researchers studying the dangers of cell phone use while driving found a positive correlation between cell phone use while driving and car accidents ($r = 0.24$) in a sample of 52 participants. Using a two-tailed test at a .05 level of significance, state the decision to retain or reject the null hypothesis.

26. A physician measures the relationship between labor pains and infant bonding. The following table lists the ranks for each mother based on the amount of pain she experienced during labor (from lowest to highest) and the amount of time she spent bonding with her infant following birth (from least to most).

Labor Pains	Infant Bonding
X	Y
8	1
7	3
2	7
4	5
3	4
6	2
5	6
1	8

(a) Compute the Spearman correlation coefficient.

(b) Using a two-tailed test at a .05 level of significance, state the decision to retain or reject the null hypothesis.

27. Employers often use standardized measures to gauge how likely it is that a new employee with little to no experience will succeed in their company. One such factor is intelligence, measured using the Intelligence Quotient (IQ). To show that this factor is related to job success, an organizational psychologist measures

the IQ score and job performance (in units sold per day) in a sample of 10 new employees.

IQ	Job Performance
100	16
115	38
108	31
98	15
120	44
147	54
132	40
85	60
105	29
110	35

(a) Convert the following data to ranks and then compute a Spearman correlation coefficient.

(b) Using a two-tailed test at a .05 level of significance, state the decision to retain or reject the null hypothesis.

28. A researcher measures the relationship between political affiliation (Republican, Democrat) and attitudes toward gun control. She had participants state their attitude toward gun control using a 7-point rating scale from 1 (*completely against*) to 7 (*completely support*). The following table lists the results of this hypothetical study.

Political Affiliation 1 = Democrat 2 = Republican	Attitudes Toward Gun Control
X	Y
1	1
1	3
1	1
1	1
1	3
2	7
2	6
2	5
2	6
2	4
2	6
2	5

(a) Compute the point-biserial correlation coefficient.

(b) Using a two-tailed test at a .05 level of significance, state the decision to retain or reject the null hypothesis. *Hint:* You must first convert *r* to a *t*-statistic.

29. To test whether extracurricular activity is a good predictor of college success, a college administrator records whether students participated in extracurricular activities during high school and their subsequent college freshman GPA.

Extracurricular Activity	College Freshman GPA
Yes	3.52
Yes	3.33
Yes	3.91
Yes	3.70
No	2.96
No	3.84
No	3.42
No	2.76
No	3.88
No	2.80

(a) Code the dichotomous variable and then compute a point-biserial correlation coefficient.

(b) Using a two-tailed test at a .05 level of significance, state the decision to retain or reject the null hypothesis. *Hint:* You must first convert *r* to a *t*-statistic.

30. An instructor wants to know the relationship between his review sessions and passing the final exam. He records whether students attended his review session and whether they passed the final exam. The following table lists the results of this hypothetical study using a sample of 64 students.

	Attended Review Session		
Outcome	Yes (0)	No (1)	
	Passed (0)	22	10
	Failed (1)	10	22

(a) Compute the phi correlation coefficient.

(b) Using a two-tailed test at a .05 level of significance, state the decision to retain or reject the null hypothesis. Hint: You must first convert *r* to a χ^2-statistic.

(c) Explain why the simplified formula ((matches – mismatches)/sample size) can be used to compute the phi correlation coefficient using these data.

31. A therapist measures the relationship between a patient's expectations that therapy will be successful and the actual success of the therapy. The following table shows the results of this hypothetical study using a sample of 50 clients.

		Therapy Successful		
		Yes	No	Totals
Client expects success	Yes	22	8	30
	No	5	15	20
	Totals	27	23	

(a) Compute the phi correlation coefficient.

(b) Using a two-tailed test at a .05 level of significance, state the decision to retain or reject the null hypothesis. Hint: You must first convert *r* to χ^2.

Problems in Research

32. **IQ and self-determination.** Nota, Ferrari, Soresi, and Wehmeyer (2007) measured the relationship between IQ and four measures of self-determination in a sample of 141 participants. They reported a negative correlation between IQ and self-determination in daily activities (SDDA), $r = -0.42$, $p < .01$, and a negative correlation between IQ and self-determination in expressing emotions and opinions (SDEO), $r = -0.16$, $p > .05$.

(a) Which correlation is significant?

(b) Which is the stronger correlation?

33. **Emotion and self-body image.** Nobre and Pinto-Gouveia (2008) measured the relationship between emotion and thoughts of low self-body image. The following table shows a portion of their results for the correlations between thoughts of low-self body image and four types of emotions.

Correlations Between Four Emotions and Low Self-Body Image ($n = 163$)	
Emotions	Thoughts of Low Self-Body Image
Sadness	0.24**
Guilt	0.27**
Pleasure	−0.25**
Satisfaction	−0.37**

*$p < .05$. **$p < .01$.

(a) List the emotions that showed a significant positive correlation with thoughts of low self-body image.

(b) List the emotions that showed a significant negative correlation with thoughts of low self-body image.

34. **Masculinity, media, and self-esteem.** Conseur, Hathcote, and Kim (2008) measured the relationship between consumer masculinity and appearance-related self-esteem, consumer masculinity and media influence, and consumer masculinity and overall self-esteem. The researchers reported,

Consumer masculinity was strongly correlated with appearance-related self-esteem ($r = 0.40$, $p < .001$) and media influence ($r = 0.62$, $p < .001$), but not correlated with overall self-esteem ($r = 0.08$, $p > .05$). (p. 553)

(a) State the correlations that were significant.

(b) Which correlation was the strongest?

35. **Vegetable intake among children and parents.** Vejrup, Lien, Klepp, and Bere (2008) measured the relationship between intake and availability of vegetables at dinner in surveys during 2002 and 2005. The correlation matrix summarizes some of the correlations observed in the study. Explain why the last cell in each row is a perfect positive correlation.

Vegetable Intake and Availability at Dinner						
	1	2	3	4	5	6
1. Adolescent intake–02 N	1.00 1,779					
2. Adolescent availability–02 N	0.46 1,766	1.00 1,779				
3. Adolescent intake–05 N	0.52 1,476	0.35 1,476	1.00 1,584			
4. Adolescent availability–05 N	0.33 1,484	0.35 1,483	0.59 1,581	1.00 1,594		
5. Parent intake–02 N	0.25 1,301	0.23 1,298	0.27 1,149	0.22 1,155	1.00 1,320	
6. Parent availability–02 N	0.22 1,299	0.23 1,296	0.21 1,148	0.22 1,154	0.60 1,316	1.00 1,318

All correlations are significant at the 0.01 level (two-tailed).

36. **Factors correlated with job performance.** Ladebo and Awotunde (2007) studied many factors possibly related to job performance, including work overload, emotional exhaustion, and self-efficacy (or the belief in one's own abilities). The researchers reported,

Job performance was unrelated to emotional exhaustion ($r = 0.03$, ns), and [work] overload ($r = −0.04$, ns), but positively related to self-efficacy ($r = 0.22$, $p < .01$). (p. 92)

(a) Which correlation was significant?

(b) Compute the coefficient of determination for the significant correlation.

NOTE: Answers for even numbers are in Appendix C.

Linear Regression

LEARNING OBJECTIVES

After reading this chapter, you should be able to:

1. Define *linear regression* and describe the relationship between a predictor variable and a criterion variable.

2. Compute and interpret the method of least squares.

3. Identify each source of variation in an analysis of regression.

4. Compute an analysis of regression and interpret the results.

5. Compute and interpret the standard error of estimate.

6. Define *multiple regression* and describe when it is used.

7. Summarize the results of an analysis of regression in APA format.

8. Compute an analysis of regression using SPSS.

chapter 16

16.1 FROM RELATIONSHIPS TO PREDICTIONS

In Chapter 15, we described procedures that used the correlation coefficient, r, to measure the extent to which two factors (X and Y) were related. The value of r indicates the direction and strength of a correlation. When r is negative, two factors change in opposite directions; when r is positive, two factors change in the same direction. The closer r is to ±1.0, the stronger the correlation, and the more closely two factors are related.

We can use the information provided by r to predict values of one factor, given known values of a second factor. Recall from Chapter 15 that the strength of a correlation reflects how closely a set of data points fits to a regression line (the straight line that most closely fits a set of data points). In this chapter, we will use the value of r to compute the equation of a regression line and then use this equation to predict values of one factor, given known values of a second factor in a population—this statistical procedure is called **linear regression.** We begin by introducing the fundamentals of linear regression in the next section.

DEFINITION

Linear regression, also called **regression**, is a statistical procedure used to determine the equation of a regression line to a set of data points and to determine the extent to which the regression equation can be used to predict values of one factor, given known values of a second factor in a population.

16.2 FUNDAMENTALS OF LINEAR REGRESSION

Linear regression, like analysis of variance, can be used to analyze any number of factors. In this chapter, however, we will use regression to describe the linear relationship between two factors (X and Y) because many of the behaviors measured by researchers are related in a linear or straight-line pattern.

To use linear regression, we identity two types of variables: the predictor variable and the criterion variable. The **predictor variable** (X) is the variable with values that are known and can be used to predict values of the criterion variable; the predictor variable is plotted on the x-axis of a graph. The **criterion variable** (Y) is the variable with unknown values that we are trying to predict, given known values of the predictor variable; the criterion variable is plotted on the y-axis of a graph.

DEFINITION

The **predictor variable** or **known variable (X)** is the variable with values that are known and can be used to predict values of another variable.

The **criterion variable** or **to-be-predicted variable (Y)** is the variable with unknown values that can be predicted or estimated, given known values of the predictor variable.

NOTE: Linear regression is used to predict values of Y (criterion variable), given values of X (the predictor variable).

We can use linear regression to answer the following questions about the pattern of data points and the significance of a linear equation:

1. Is a pattern evident in a set of data points?

2. Does the equation of a straight line describe this pattern?

3. Are the predictions made from this equation significant?

In Example 16.1, we will ask each question using a hypothetical data set.

A job candidate wants to know how quickly a business tends to promote its employees. He takes a sample of six employees and records the number of years they have been employed and the number of promotions they have received. Figure 16.1 is a scatter plot of the hypothetical data for the six employees.

EXAMPLE 16.1

In this example, the job candidate is interested in predicting the number of promotions, given the number of years an employee has been employed. Thus, years of employment is the predictor variable (X), and the number of promotions is the criterion variable (Y).

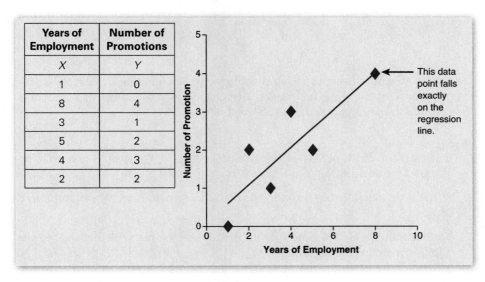

Years of Employment	Number of Promotions
X	Y
1	0
8	4
3	1
5	2
4	3
2	2

This data point falls exactly on the regression line.

FIGURE 16.1

A table and scatter plot showing the number of years six hypothetical workers ($n = 6$) have been employed and the number of promotions each has received in that time. The regression line is given in the scatter plot. Both the table and the scatter plot show the same data.

Is a pattern evident in a set of data points? We want to identify the pattern of the data points to determine whether or not a straight line describes these data. To identify a pattern, we can graph the data. Figure 16.1 shows the data points, which appear to follow a linear pattern. Hence, the equation of a straight line can be fit to these data points.

NOTE: Linear regression is used to describe data points with a pattern that approximates a straight line.

Does the equation of a straight line describe this pattern? Many lines can be fit to the data points in Figure 16.1. We need to find the linear equation that best fits these data points. The equation of the best-fitting straight line, called the *regression line* (defined in Chapter 15), will provide the most accurate predictions of values of the criterion variable, given known values of the predictor variable. To find the equation of the regression line, we use the method of least squares, which was first introduced almost two centuries ago by the French mathematician Adrien Legendre. The method of least squares is described and defined in Section 16.5.

NOTE: The method of least squares is used to find the equation of a best-fitting straight line to a set of data points, called the regression equation.

Are the predictions made from this equation significant? Remember that we use data in a sample to find the regression equation. To determine whether the regression equation we found in the sample can be used to predict values of Y (criterion variable), given values of X (predictor variable) in the population, we use a statistical procedure called analysis of regression. Analysis of regression is described and defined in Section 16.6. Table 16.1 summarizes the questions that organize a study using regression analysis with the methods used to answer each question.

TABLE 16.1   Three questions answered by linear regression and the techniques used to answer each question.

Question	Method for Answering the Question
Is a pattern evident in a set of data points?	Observe a graph of a set of data points to see what pattern emerges
Does the equation of a straight line describe this pattern?	Method of least squares
Are the predictions made from this equation significant?	Analysis of regression

Before we work through an example to answer each question in Table 16.1, let's first explain what the regression line is. Specifically, we will explain what it means to say that a straight line has the best fit for a data set.

 **LEARNING CHECK 1**

1. The equation of the regression line can be used to _____ values of one factor, given known values of a second factor.

2. What is the relationship between the predictor variable and the criterion variable?

3. State whether each description given below best describes the method of least squares or analysis of regression.

   a. The equation of a regression line

   b. The significance of predictions

Answers: 1. Predict; 2. The predictor variable (X) is a known value that is used to predict the value of a criterion variable (Y); 3. (a) The method of least squares, (b) Analysis of regression.

16.3 WHAT MAKES THE REGRESSION LINE THE BEST-FITTING LINE?

Once we have determined that there is a linear pattern in a set of data points, we want to find the regression line, or the straight line that has the best fit. The criterion we use to determine the regression line is the sum of squares (*SS*), or the sum of the squared distances of data points from a straight line. The line, associated with the smallest total value for *SS,* is the best-fitting straight line, called the regression line. Notice that Figure 16.1 shows the regression line for the data in Example 16.1.

In Figure 16.1, data point (8,4) falls on the regression line. The distance between this data point and the regression line, then, is 0. The remaining data points fall a distance from the regression line. The method of least squares is used to square the distance that each data point falls from the regression line and sum the squared distances. The regression line is the line that makes the value of *SS* the smallest. We will use Example 16.2 to explain why each deviation is squared before summing.

NOTE: The regression line is the line that makes the value of SS *the smallest.*

Suppose we measure two factors, one predictor variable plotted on the *x*-axis and one criterion variable plotted on the *y*-axis. Figure 16.2 shows hypothetical data for these two factors.

EXAMPLE 16.2

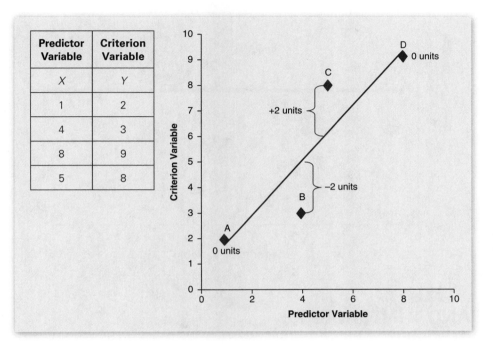

Predictor Variable	Criterion Variable
X	*Y*
1	2
4	3
8	9
5	8

FIGURE 16.2

A table and scatter plot of four hypothetical data points. The regression line and the distances, in units, between the data points and the regression line are shown. Both the table and the scatter plot show the same data.

Figure 16.2 shows the distance of each data point from the regression line. Notice that data points A and D fall on the regression line. The distance of these data points from the regression line is 0. However, data points B and C in the scatter plot fall two units from the regression line. Data point B falls two units below the regression line (–2 units), and data point C falls two units above the regression line (+2 units). The sum of the distances of each data point from the regression line is $0 + 0 + 2 - 2 = 0$.

To avoid a solution of 0, we compute *SS* by squaring the distance of each data point from the regression line, then summing. When we square the distance of each data point in Example 16.2 and then sum, we obtain $SS = 0^2 + 0^2 + 2^2 + (-2)^2 = 8$. This is the smallest possible solution for *SS*. The method of least squares, then, is the method for determining the line associated with the least squares, or the smallest possible value of the sum of squares (*SS*).

Any other line, other than the regression line shown in Figure 16.2, will produce a value of *SS* that is larger than 8 in this example. To illustrate, we fit another straight line to the same data in Figure 16.3. The distance of each data point from this line is +3 units and +4 units above the line and –2 units and —3 units below the line. If we compute the *SS* for these distances, we obtain $SS = 3^2 + (-3)^2 + 2^2 + (-2)^2 = 38$. This result is much larger than $SS = 8$, which is the value we obtained for the least squares regression line. Different lines have different values of *SS*. The regression line, or line of best fit, is the line with the smallest or least value of the *SS*.

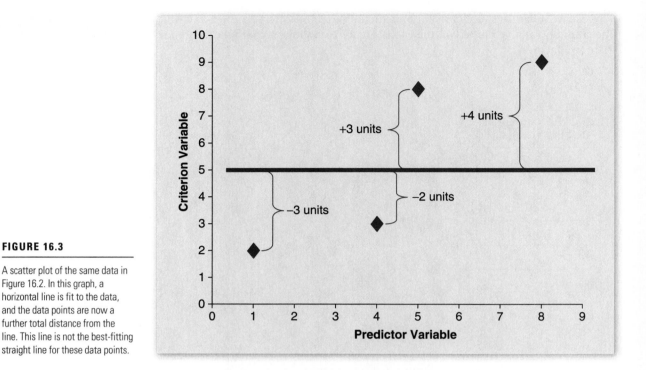

FIGURE 16.3

A scatter plot of the same data in Figure 16.2. In this graph, a horizontal line is fit to the data, and the data points are now a further total distance from the line. This line is not the best-fitting straight line for these data points.

16.4 THE SLOPE AND *Y*-INTERCEPT OF A STRAIGHT LINE

If we know the equation of the regression line, we can predict values of the criterion variable, *Y*, so long as we know values of the predictor variable, *X*. To make use of this equation, we need to know the equation of a straight line. The equation of a straight line is

$$Y = bX + a.$$

In this equation, *Y* is a value we plot for the criterion variable, *X* is a value we plot for the predictor variable, *b* is the slope of a straight line, and *a* is the *y*-intercept (where the line crosses the *y*-axis). To make use of this equation, we need to know the values of *a* and *b* in the equation. In this section, we explain what *a* and *b* measure, and in Section 16.5, we will use the method of least squares to find the values of *a* and *b*.

The **slope,** represented as *b*, is a measure of how much a regression line rises or declines along the *y*-axis as values on the *x*-axis increase. The slope indicates the direction of a relationship between two factors, *X* and *Y*. When the values of two factors change in the same direction, the slope is positive. The regression line will appear as if going uphill, illustrated with a hiker on the regression line in Figure 16.4. When the values of two factors change in opposite directions, the slope is negative. The regression line will appear as if going downhill, illustrated with a skier on the regression line in Figure 16.4.

The slope of a straight line is used to measure the change in *Y* relative to the change in *X:*

$$\text{slope } (b) = \frac{\text{change in } Y}{\text{change in } X}.$$

The **slope (*b*)** of a straight line is used to measure the change in *Y* relative to the change in *X*. When *X* and *Y* change in the same direction, the slope is positive. When *X* and *Y* change in opposite directions, the slope is negative.

DEFINITION

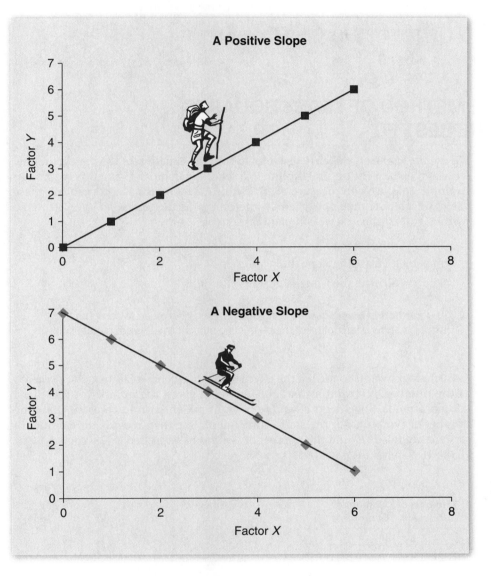

FIGURE 16.4

The slope of a straight line is similar to the slopes of a hill. A positive slope is shown in the top graph; a negative slope is shown in the bottom graph.

The **y-intercept**, represented as *a*, is where a straight line crosses the *y*-axis on a graph. More specifically, the *y*-intercept is the value of *Y*, when *X* = 0. The *y*-intercept is the value of the criterion variable (*Y*), when the predictor variable (*X*) is absent or equal to 0. In Figure 16.4, the *y*-intercept, or value on the *y*-axis where the line crosses, is 0 for the positive slope (top graph) and 7 for the negative slope (bottom graph).

NOTE: The equation of a straight line is Y = bX + a. *In this equation, the slope b measures how* Y *changes as* X *increases, and the y-intercept a is the value of* Y *when* X = 0.

The **y-intercept (*a*)** of a straight line is the value of the criterion variable (*Y*) when the predictor variable (*X*) equals 0.

DEFINITION

LEARNING CHECK 2

1. The regression line, or best-fitting straight line to a set of data points, is the line associated with the smallest possible value of _____.

2. The values of one factor increase as values of a second factor decrease. Does this sentence describe a line with a positive or negative slope?

3. The *y*-intercept is the value of *Y* when *X* equals ____.

Answers: 1. Sum of squares (*SS*); 2. Negative slope; 3. *X* = 0.

16.5 USING THE METHOD OF LEAST SQUARES TO FIND THE BEST FIT

We use the **method of least squares** to find the equation of the regression line, which is the best-fitting straight line to a set of data points. Using this method in Example 16.3, we will measure *SS* for Factor *X* and Factor *Y* and then use these values to compute the slope (*b*) and *y*-intercept (*a*) of the regression line. To use the method of least squares, we complete three steps:

Step 1: Compute preliminary calculations.

Step 2: Calculate the slope (*b*).

Step 3: Calculate the *y*-intercept (*a*).

DEFINITION

The **method of least squares** is a statistical procedure used to compute the slope (*b*) and *y*-intercept (*a*) of the best-fitting straight line to a set of data points.

EXAMPLE 16.3

A psychologist wants to predict the effectiveness of a behavioral therapy (measured as the number of symptoms patients express), given the number of sessions a patient attends. She selects a sample of eight patients who expressed the same number of symptoms at the start of treatment. She then records the number of sessions attended (*X*) and the number of symptoms expressed (*Y*) by each patient. Figure 16.5 shows the data for this study.

FIGURE 16.5

A table and a scatter plot showing the number of sessions eight patients (*n* = 8) have attended and the number of symptoms they express. The regression line for these hypothetical data is shown in the scatter plot. Both the table and the scatter plot show the same data.

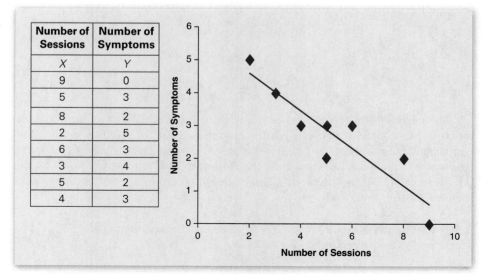

Number of Sessions	Number of Symptoms
X	Y
9	0
5	3
8	2
2	5
6	3
3	4
5	2
4	3

Step 1: Compute preliminary calculations. We begin by making some preliminary calculations shown in Table 16.2. The signs (+ and –) of the values we measure for each factor are essential to making accurate computations. The goal of this step is to compute the sum of squares needed to calculate the slope and y-intercept. We will describe each calculation in Table 16.2 from left to right.

TABLE 16.2 Preliminary calculations in Step 1 for Example 16.3.

X	Y	$X - M_X$	$Y - M_Y$	$(X - M_X)(Y - M_Y)$	$(X - M_X)^2$
9	0	3.75	–2.75	–10.31	14.06
5	3	–0.25	0.25	–0.06	0.06
8	2	2.75	–0.75	–2.06	7.56
2	5	–3.25	2.25	–7.31	10.56
6	3	0.75	0.25	0.19	0.56
3	4	–2.25	1.25	–2.81	5.06
5	2	–0.25	–0.75	0.19	0.06
4	3	–1.25	0.25	–0.31	1.56
$M_X = 5.25$	$M_Y = 2.75$			$SS_{XY} = -22.50$	$SS_X = 39.50$

The deviation of each score (X) from the mean (M_X)

The deviation of each score (Y) from the mean (M_Y)

The product of deviation scores for X and Y

The product of the deviation scores for X

Mean number of sessions (X)

Mean number of symptoms (Y)

The sum of products for X and Y

The sum of squares for X

1. Compute the average X and Y score. In this example, the number of sessions attended is the predictor variable, X, and the number of symptoms expressed is the criterion variable, Y. In Table 16.2, each column of values for X and Y was summed and then averaged:

$$M_X = 5.25.$$
$$M_Y = 2.75.$$

2. Subtract each score from its respective mean. In the third column, each X score is subtracted from M_X; in the fourth column, each Y score is subtracted from M_Y. Remember from Chapter 3 that the sum of each column—the sum of the differences of scores from their mean—is equal to 0.

3. Multiply and sum the deviation scores for X and Y. We computed deviation scores by subtracting each score from its mean. Now multiply across the

rows in the third and fourth columns. The sum of these scores is the sum of squares for XY, also called the sum of products (SP):

$$SP = SS_{XY} = -22.50.$$

4. Multiply and sum the deviation scores for X. Multiply the deviation scores of each X value times itself. The sum of these scores is the sum of squares for X:

$$SS_X = 39.50.$$

MAKING SENSE: SP, *SS*, and the Slope of a Regression Line

Recall from Chapter 4 that the formula for the sum of squares is

$$SS_X = \Sigma (X - M)^2.$$

A mathematically equivalent way to write this formula that gives us the same value of *SS* is

$$SS_X = \Sigma (X - M)(X - M).$$

To compute the sum of products (or the sum of squares for XY), we multiply the deviation of each X value times the deviation of each Y value:

$$SP = SS_{XY} = \Sigma (X - M_X)(Y - M_Y).$$

The structure of the formula for SP, then, is the same as the second formula we stated for SS_X. When we compute SS_X, we multiple each deviation times itself, which makes the solution positive: $SS_X \geq 0$. However, to compute SP, we multiply deviations of X times deviations of Y, so it is possible to obtain negative values of SP. For this reason, the value of SP will determine whether the slope is positive or negative.

NOTE: SS_{XY}, which is the sum of products (SP), determines whether the slope of a straight line is positive or negative.

Step 2: Calculate the slope (b). The slope of a straight line indicates the change in Y relative to the change in X. Because the value of SP can be negative or positive, this value indicates the direction that Y changes as X increases. We will use SP, which is the same as SS_{XY}, to estimate changes in Y and we will use SS_X to estimate changes in X. The formula for computing the slope (b) is

$$b = \frac{\text{change in } Y}{\text{change in } X} = \frac{SS_{XY}}{SS_X} \text{ or } \frac{SP}{SS_X}.$$

We already computed $SS_{XY} = -22.50$ and $SS_X = 39.50$. The slope of the best-fitting straight line is

$$b = \frac{-22.50}{39.50} = -0.57.$$

Step 3: Calculate the y-intercept (a). The y-intercept is the value of Y when $X = 0$. To find this value, we need to know the mean of Y (M_Y), the mean of X (M_X), and the slope we just computed. The formula for determining the y-intercept (a) is

$$a = M_Y - bM_X.$$

We already computed $M_Y = 2.75$, $M_X = 5.25$, and $b = -0.57$. The y-intercept of the regression line is

$$a = 2.75 - [(-0.57)(5.25)] = 5.74.$$

Because we computed the slope, $b = -0.57$, and the y-intercept, $a = 5.74$, we can now state the equation of the least squares regression line as

$$\hat{Y} = -0.57X + 5.74.$$

In this equation, $\hat{Y}$ is the predicted value of Y, given values of X. For example, suppose we want to make a prediction. If one patient has attended four therapy sessions ($X = 4$). We can substitute 4 into the equation to solve for $\hat{Y}$:

$$\hat{Y} = -0.57(4) + 5.74.$$
$$\hat{Y} = 3.46.$$

In this example, we expect or predict that a patient will express 3.46, or between 3 and 4, symptoms following four therapy sessions. In this way, we use the equation to show how many symptoms we expect a patient to exhibit after a particular number of therapy sessions.

NOTE: Once we compute the slope and y-intercept, we can substitute known values of X and solve for $\hat{Y}$, or the predicted value of Y for each known value of X.

LEARNING CHECK 3

1. State the three steps for computing the method of least squares.

2. Assuming these data points have a linear pattern, make the following calculations to find the best-fitting line:

X	Y
1	3
2	2
3	1

   a. Compute the slope.
   b. Compute the y-intercept.
   c. Write the equation of the regression line.

Answers: 1. Step 1: Compute preliminary calculations, Step 2: Calculate the slope, and Step 3: Calculate the y-intercept. 2. (a) $b = -\dfrac{2}{2} = -1.0$, (b) $a = 2.0 - [(-1.0)(-2.0)] = 4.0$, (c) $\hat{Y} = -1X + 4.0$.

16.6 USING ANALYSIS OF REGRESSION TO MEASURE SIGNIFICANCE

In Example 16.3, we used the method of least squares to determine the equation of the regression line for a sample of data. However, we did not determine whether this equation could be used to predict values of Y (criterion variable), given values of X (predictor variable) in the population.

To determine whether the regression equation for a sample of data can be used to make predictions of Y in the population, we use **analysis of regression.** Analysis of regression is similar to an analysis of variance (ANOVA). In an analysis of regression, we measure the variance in Y and split the variance into two sources, similar to how we had two sources of variance using the one-way between-subjects ANOVA in Chapter 12. In this section, we will follow the four steps to hypothesis testing to perform an analysis of regression using the data in Example 16.3.

DEFINITION

Analysis of regression, or **regression analysis**, is a statistical procedure used to test hypotheses for one or more predictor variables to determine whether the regression equation for a sample of data points can be used to predict values of the criterion variable (Y) given values of the predictor variable (X) in the population.

Step 1: State the hypotheses. The null hypothesis is that the variance in Y is not related to changes in X. The alternative hypothesis is that the variance in Y is related to changes in X. The hypotheses in Example 16.3 are as follows:

H_0: The variance in the number of symptoms expressed (Y) is not related to changes in the number of therapy sessions attended (X).

H_1: The variance in the number of symptoms expressed (Y) is related to changes in the number of therapy sessions attended (X).

To evaluate these hypotheses, we measure the variance in Y that is and is not related to changes in X. The variance in Y that is related to changes in X is called **regression variation.** The closer that data points fall to the regression line, the larger the regression variation will be. The variance in Y that is not related to changes in X is called **residual variation.** This is the variance in Y that is residual, left over, or remaining. The farther data points fall from the regression line, the larger the residual variation will be.

DEFINITION

NOTE: Analysis of regression measures two sources of variation in Y: One source of variation is related to changes in X (regression variation), and the other is not (residual variation).

Regression variation is the variance in Y that is related to or associated with changes in X. The closer data points fall to the regression line, the larger the value of regression variation.

Residual variation is the variance in Y that is not related to changes in X. This is the variance in Y that is left over or remaining. The farther data points fall from the regression line, the larger the value of residual variation.

An analysis of regression measures only the variance in Y, the criterion variable, because it is the value we want to predict. The total variance measured, then, equals the variance in Y. As shown in Figure 16.6, we attribute some of the variance in Y

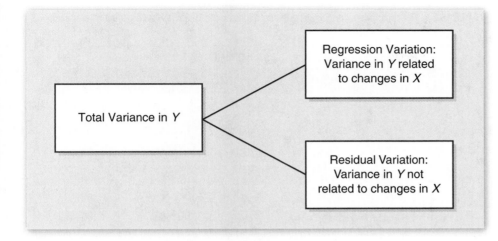

Total Variance in Y

Regression Variation:
Variance in Y related
to changes in X

Residual Variation:
Variance in Y not
related to changes in X

FIGURE 16.6

An analysis of regression measures the variance in Y. Some of the variance is attributed to changes in X; the remaining variance is not attributed to changes in X.

to changes in X (regression variation); the remaining variance in Y is not attributed to changes in X (residual variation). The more variance in Y that we attribute to changes in X (regression variation), the more likely we are to decide to reject the null hypothesis and conclude that values of X significantly predict values of Y.

Step 2: Set the criteria for a decision. We will use a .05 level of significance, as we have for all hypothesis tests. We compute degrees of freedom (*df*) for each source of variation. The degrees of freedom for regression variation, or degrees of freedom numerator, are equal to the number of predictor variables. Because we have one predictor variable (X) in Example 16.3, *df* for regression variation is 1.

The degrees of freedom for residual variation, or degrees of freedom denominator, are equal to the sample size minus 2. We subtract 2 from n because we plot two scores for each data point (one X score and one Y score). In Example 16.3, $n = 8$, so *df* for residual variation is $(8 - 2) = 6$.

The critical value for this test is listed in Table B.3 in Appendix B. The critical value for a test with 1 (*df* numerator) and 6 (*df* denominator) degrees of freedom at a .05 level of significance is 5.99.

Step 3: Compute the test statistic. To compute the test statistic, we measure variance as a mean square, same as we did using the ANOVA tests. We place the variance or mean square (*MS*) attributed to regression variation in the numerator and the variance or mean square attributed to residual variation in the denominator:

$$F = \frac{\text{variance of } Y \text{ related to changes in } X}{\text{variance of } Y \text{ not related to changes in } X} = \frac{MS_{\text{regression}}}{MS_{\text{residual}}}.$$

To compute the test statistic, we first compute the *SS* for each source of variation and then complete the *F*-table.

To compute the sum of squares for the regression variation, we multiply the sum of squares of Y times the *coefficient of determination* or r^2 (this was defined in Chapter 15; it measures the proportion of variance in Y that is related to changes in X):

$$SS_{\text{regression}} = r^2 SS_Y, \text{ where } r = \frac{SS_{XY}}{\sqrt{SS_X SS_Y}}.$$

TABLE 16.3 The calculations for SS_Y using the data in Example 16.3. The first six columns are taken from Table 16.2.

X	Y	$X - M_X$	$Y - M_Y$	$(X - M_X)(Y - M_Y)$	$(X - M_X)^2$	$(X - M_Y)^2$
9	0	3.75	−2.75	−10.31	14.06	7.56
5	3	−0.25	0.25	−0.06	0.06	0.06
8	2	2.75	−0.75	−2.06	7.56	0.56
2	5	−3.25	2.25	−7.31	10.56	5.06
6	3	0.75	0.25	0.19	0.56	0.06
3	4	−2.25	1.25	−2.81	5.06	1.56
5	2	−0.25	−0.75	0.19	0.06	0.56
4	3	−1.25	0.25	−0.31	1.56	0.06
				$SS_{XY} = -22.50$	$SS_X = 39.50$	$SS_Y = 15.50$

The sum of products for X and Y The sum of squares for X The sum of squares for Y

NOTE: $SS_{regression}$ *measures the proportion of variance in* Y *that is related to changes in* X.

Multiplying the coefficient of determination times the variability in Y (SS_Y) will give us the proportion of variance in Y (number of symptoms) that is predicted by or related to changes in X (the number of sessions attended). Using the data given in Table 16.3, we can calculate the value of r:

$$r = \frac{-22.50}{\sqrt{39.50 \times 15.50}} = 0.91.$$

The sum of squares regression is

$$SS_{regression} = r^2 SS_Y = (0.91)^2 \times 15.50 = 12.83.$$

The total variability of Y is 15.50 ($SS_Y = 15.50$), of which we attribute 12.83 units of variability to changes in X. The remaining sum of squares, or sum of squares residual, is computed by multiplying SS_Y times the remaining proportion of variance $(1 - r^2)$:

NOTE: $SS_{residual}$ *measures the proportion of variance in* Y *that is not related to changes in* X.

$$SS_{residual} = (1 - r^2)SS_Y.$$

The residual formula will give us the proportion of variance in Y (number of symptoms) that is not predicted by or related to changes in X (the number of sessions attended). If we substitute the values of r and SS_Y, we obtain the remaining variation in Y measured as the sum of squares residual:

$$SS_{residual} = (1 - 0.91^2) \times 15.50 = 2.67.$$

When we add the sum squares for regression and residual, it will sum to the total variability in Y:

$$SS_Y = SS_{regression} + SS_{residual} = 12.83 + 2.67 = 15.50.$$

To compute the test statistic, we need to complete the F-table, which is set up just as it was for the ANOVA tests. The formulas needed to complete the F-table and the solutions for Example 16.3 are given in Table 16.4. To compute variance or mean square, we divide SS by df for each source of variation, just as we did for the ANOVA tests. The value of the test statistic in Example 16.3 is

$$F_{obt} = \frac{12.83}{0.445} = 28.83.$$

TABLE 16.4 The F-table for an analysis of regression. An asterisk indicates significance at $p < .05$.

Formulas for completing the analysis of regression

Source of Variation	SS	df	MS	F_{obt}
Regression	$r^2 SS_Y$	1	$\dfrac{SS_{regression}}{df_{regression}}$	$\dfrac{MS_{regression}}{MS_{residual}}$
Residual (error)	$(1 - r^2) SS_Y$	$n - 2$	$\dfrac{SS_{residual}}{df_{residual}}$	
Total	$SS_{regression} + SS_{residual}$	$n - 1$		

Solution to Example 16.3

Source of Variation	SS	df	MS	F_{obt}
Regression	12.83	1	12.83	28.83*
Residual (error)	2.67	6	0.445	
Total	15.50	7		

Step 4: Make a decision. To decide whether to retain or reject the null hypothesis, we compare the value of the test statistic to the critical values. Because $F_{obt} = 28.83$ exceeds the critical value (5.99), we reject the null hypothesis. We conclude that the number of symptoms expressed (Y) is related to changes in the number of therapy sessions attended (X). That is, we can predict values of Y, given values of X in the population, using the equation we computed using the method of least squares: $\hat{Y} = -0.57X + 5.74$. If we were to report this result in a research journal, it would look something like this:

An analysis of regression showed a significant negative linear relationship between the number of therapy sessions attended and number of symptoms expressed, $F(1, 6) = 28.83$, $p < .05$.

LEARNING CHECK 4

1. Identify the statistical procedure used to determine whether the equation of a straight line can be used to make predictions in a population.

2. When we sum the value of $SS_{regression}$ and $SS_{residual}$, what value do we obtain?

3. A college administrator measures the SAT scores and high school GPAs of 12 college applicants and computes an analysis of regression. Complete the F-table and state whether the decision is to retain or reject the null hypothesis.

Source of Variation	SS	df	MS	F
Regression	140			
Residual				
Total	600			

Answers: 1. Analysis of regression; 2. The value of SS_y; 3. $SS_{residual} = 460$, $df_{regression} = 1$, $df_{residual} = 10$, $df_{Total} = 11$, $MS_{regression} = 140$, $MS_{residual} = 46$, $F = 3.04$. Decision: Retain the null hypothesis.

16.7 SPSS IN FOCUS: ANALYSIS OF REGRESSION

In Example 16.4, we will use SPSS to compute an analysis of regression using a new set of data adapted from that published in the research journal *Biological Psychology*.

EXAMPLE 16.4

Williams and colleagues (2006) used linear regression to determine the relationship between levels of a brain chemical (5-HT, also known as serotonin) and the positive affect (mood) of participants in their study. The researchers measured 5-HT levels (in micromole/L) in 23 men and their corresponding positive affect on a scale in which higher scores indicated more positive affect. Figure 16.7 displays the approximate data for the 23 participants in their study. Let's use SPSS to compute an analysis of regression for these data.

1. Click on the **variable view** tab and enter X in the **name column;** enter Y in the name column below it. In the **decimals column,** reduce the value to 1 in the first row, X, and 0 in the second row, Y.

2. Click on the **data view** tab. Enter the data for Example 16.4 in the columns for X and Y. Enter the data for 5-HT levels in the column labeled X; enter the data for positive affect in the column labeled Y.

3. Go to the **menu bar** and click **Analyze,** then **Regression** and **Linear,** to display the dialog box shown in Figure 16.8.

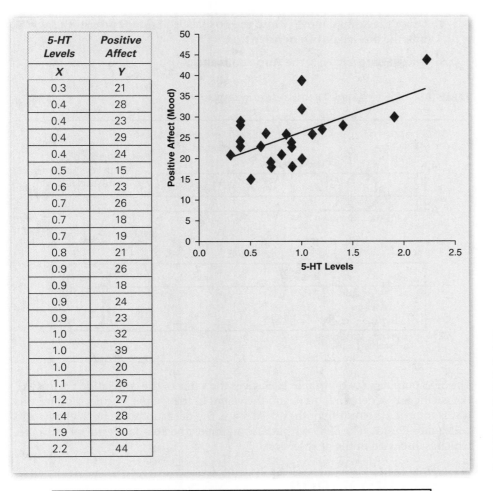

5-HT Levels	Positive Affect
X	Y
0.3	21
0.4	28
0.4	23
0.4	29
0.4	24
0.5	15
0.6	23
0.7	26
0.7	18
0.7	19
0.8	21
0.9	26
0.9	18
0.9	24
0.9	23
1.0	32
1.0	39
1.0	20
1.1	26
1.2	27
1.4	28
1.9	30
2.2	44

FIGURE 16.7

A table and a scatter plot showing the levels of 5-HT in 23 men ($n = 23$) and their corresponding positive affect or mood based on data reported by Williams and colleagues (2006). The regression line is shown in the scatter plot. Both the table and the scatter plot show the same data.

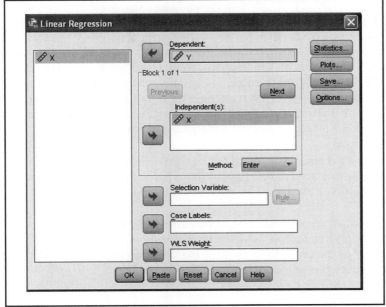

FIGURE 16.8

Dialog box for Steps 3 and 4.

4. Using the arrows, move X into the box labeled **Independent(s);** move Y into the box labeled **Dependent.**

5. Select **Paste** and click the **Run** command.

TABLE 16.5   SPSS output table for an analysis of regression.

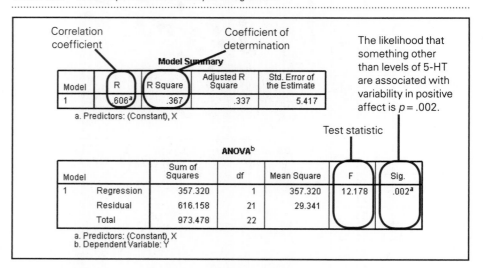

The SPSS output, shown in Table 16.5, gives the value of the correlation coefficient, the coefficient of determination, and the values in the F-table. The decision for this test is to reject the null hypothesis. This was the decision made by Williams and colleagues (2006). The SPSS output also includes the standard error of estimate, which is discussed in the next section.

16.8 USING THE STANDARD ERROR OF ESTIMATE TO MEASURE ACCURACY

In Example 16.3, we concluded that the equation $\hat{Y} = -0.57X + 5.74$ can predict values of Y given values of X in the population. Of course, not all the data points in our sample fell exactly on this line. Many data points fell some distance from the regression line. Whenever even a single data point fails to fall exactly on the regression line, there is error in how accurately the line will predict an outcome. This error can be measured using the **standard error of estimate.**

DEFINITION

The **standard error of estimate (s_e)** is an estimate of the standard deviation or distance that a set of data points falls from the regression line. The standard error of estimate equals the square root of the mean square residual.

The standard error of estimate, s_e, measures the standard deviation or distance that data points in a sample fall from the regression line. The value of s_e estimates the accuracy of the predictions made using the equation of a regression line. It is computed as the square root of the mean square residual:

$$s_e = \sqrt{MS_{\text{residual}}}.$$

In Example 16.3, the mean square residual was 0.445 (given in Table 16.4). Hence, the standard error of estimate is

$$s_e = \sqrt{0.445} = 0.67.$$

The standard error of estimate indicates the accuracy of predictions made using the equation of a regression line, with smaller values of s_e associated with better or more accurate predictions. The standard error of estimate is quite literally a standard deviation (or the square root of the variance) for the residual variation. So it is a measure of the error or deviation of data points from the regression line. To illustrate what the standard error of estimate measures, in this section, we will take a different approach to computing this estimate for Example 16.2.

Because the regression line shows predicted, rather than actual, values of Y, we use a different symbol, $\hat{Y}$, to designate the predicted value. For example, Figure 16.9 shows that when $X = 4$, the actual value, Y, is 3 for the small hypothetical data set first shown in Figure 16.2. The predicted value, however, is $\hat{Y} = 5$. Hence, for each value of Y, the corresponding value of $\hat{Y}$ on the regression line is the value of Y we predict using the equation for the regression line.

NOTE: The standard error of estimate (s_e) is the square root of the mean square residual. This measure gives an estimate for the accuracy in predictions of Y by estimating how far data points fall or deviate from the regression line.

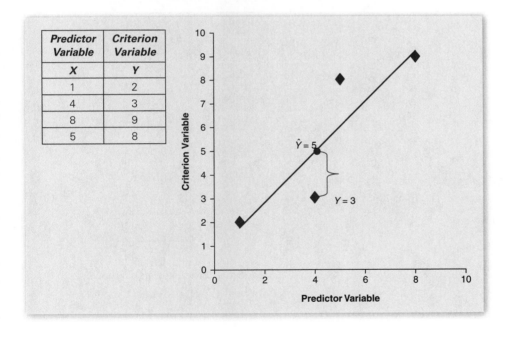

Predictor Variable	Criterion Variable
X	**Y**
1	2
4	3
8	9
5	8

FIGURE 16.9

A table and a scatter plot showing four data points for the small hypothetical data set first shown in Figure 16.2. The scatter plot shows the value of Y when $X = 4$ and the corresponding predicted value of Y (represented by $\hat{Y}$) using the equation of the regression line. Both the table and the scatter plot show the same data.

The standard error of estimate measures the standard deviation of Y scores from the predicted values of Y (or $\hat{Y}$) on the regression line. Hence, we can compute the sum of squares for the difference of $Y - \hat{Y}$ and then divide by the degrees of freedom for the residual variation ($n - 2$). The result is a measure of the variance of data points from the regression line because we divide SS by df. To compute s_e, then, we take the square root of the variance. Therefore, we can state the formula for s_e as

$$s_e = \sqrt{\frac{\sum (Y - \hat{Y})^2}{n - 2}} = \sqrt{\frac{SS_{\text{residual}}}{df}} = \sqrt{MS_{\text{residual}}}.$$

To compute this formula, we (1) compute the *SS* residual, (2) divide by *df* to compute the variance, and (3) take the square root of the variance to obtain the standard error of estimate. Table 16.6 shows these calculations for Example 16.3, which are also summarized here (from left to right in the table).

TABLE 16.6 Preliminary calculations for the standard error of estimate in Step 1 of Example 16.3.

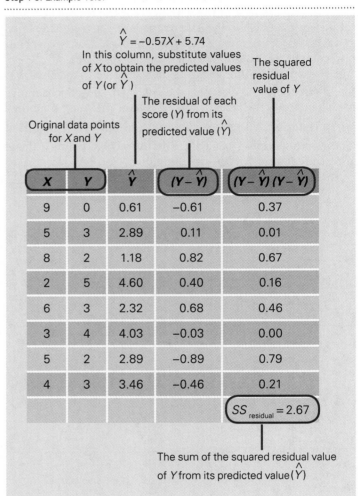

$$\hat{Y} = -0.57X + 5.74$$

In this column, substitute values of *X* to obtain the predicted values of *Y* (or $\hat{Y}$)

The residual of each score (*Y*) from its predicted value ($\hat{Y}$)

The squared residual value of *Y*

Original data points for *X* and *Y*

X	Y	$\hat{Y}$	$(Y - \hat{Y})$	$(Y - \hat{Y})(Y - \hat{Y})$
9	0	0.61	−0.61	0.37
5	3	2.89	0.11	0.01
8	2	1.18	0.82	0.67
2	5	4.60	0.40	0.16
6	3	2.32	0.68	0.46
3	4	4.03	−0.03	0.00
5	2	2.89	−0.89	0.79
4	3	3.46	−0.46	0.21
				$SS_{residual} = 2.67$

The sum of the squared residual value of *Y* from its predicted value ($\hat{Y}$)

1. Substitute each value of *X* into the equation. When we substitute each *X* value into the equation, we obtain the predicted value of *Y*, represented as $\hat{Y}$. For example, in the first row, we substituted *X* = 9 into the equation and obtained

$$\hat{Y} = -0.57(9) + 5.74 = 0.61.$$

The third column of Table 16.6 shows the calculation of $\hat{Y}$ for each *X* value in the data set.

2. Subtract each Y value from its corresponding predicted value, $\hat{Y}$. In each row of Table 16.6, subtract values in the second and third columns: $Y - \hat{Y}$. The result, in the fourth column, is an estimate of the residual or remaining distance between the values of Y and the corresponding predicted values, $\hat{Y}$.

3. Square the residual values of Y, then sum the squares. Square the values in the fourth column: $\left(Y - \hat{Y}\right)^2$. The sum in the fifth column of Table 16.6 is an estimate of the sum of squares residual:

$$SS_{\text{residual}} = \sum \left(Y - \hat{Y}\right)^2 = 2.67.$$

To compute variance, we divide SS_{residual} by the degrees of freedom for error $(df = 6)$ to obtain MS_{residual}. The square root of MS_{residual} is the standard error of estimate:

$$s_e = \sqrt{\frac{SS_{\text{residual}}}{df}} = \sqrt{\frac{2.67}{6}} = 0.67.$$

NOTE: *The standard error of estimate is an estimate of the error in predictions made by a regression line.*

These calculations match those given in Table 16.4 for Example 16.3 and illustrate that the standard error of estimate is a measure of the standard deviation of data points from the regression line. In a practical sense, the standard error of estimate uses the standard deviation of data points as an estimate of the error in predictions made by a regression line. The smaller the standard error of estimate, the closer values of Y will be to their predicted values, $\hat{Y}$, on the regression line and the more accurate the predictions of Y will be using known values of X.

 **LEARNING CHECK 5**

1. What measure is used to describe the accuracy of predictions made by the equation of a regression line?

2. Compute the standard error of estimate for each of the following values of MS_{residual}.

   a. 16   b. 36   c. 64   d. 81

3. Will smaller or larger values of the standard error of estimate result in more accurate predictions of Y using known values of X?

Answers: 1. Standard error of estimate; 2. (a) $\sqrt{16} = 4$, (b) $\sqrt{36} = 6$, (c) $\sqrt{64} = 8$, (d) $\sqrt{81} = 9$; 3. Smaller.

MULTIPLE REGRESSION   16.9

In this chapter, we have described research situations where we use one variable (the predictor variable) to predict another variable (the criterion variable). While a single variable can be used to make accurate predictions, many behaviors are often too complex to be represented by a simple linear equation. That is, often, the changes in a single predictor variable do not allow us to accurately predict changes in a criterion variable.

We find that our predictions of many behaviors improve when we consider more information—specifically, when we consider more predictor variables. When we use multiple predictor variables to predict changes in a criterion variable, we use an analysis called **multiple regression.** In Example 16.3, for example, we could include other factors besides the number of sessions attended to better predict the effectiveness of a therapy. Examples of possible added predictor variables include how often the patient arrives on time for a therapy session, the level of support the patient receives from others, and the age of the patient. Including any of these additional factors would undoubtedly improve our predictions regarding the effectiveness of a therapy.

DEFINITION

Multiple regression is a statistical method that includes two or more predictor variables in the equation of a regression line to predict changes in a criterion variable.

To accommodate more predictor variables in the equation of a regression line, we add the slope, *b,* and the predictor variable, *X,* for each additional variable. To illustrate, the linear equations for one, two, and three variables are as follows:

[1] $\hat{Y} = bX + a$ (one predictor variable)

[2] $\hat{Y} = b_1X_1 + b_2X_2 + a$ (two predictor variables)

[3] $\hat{Y} = b_1X_1 + b_2X_2 + b_3X_3 + a$ (three predictor variables)

NOTE: Multiple regression is used to predict changes in a criterion variable with two or more predictor variables.

Notice that we add another *bX* to the regression equation for each predictor variable we add. One advantage of including multiple predictors in the regression equation is that we can detect the extent to which two or more predictor variables interact. Example 16.5 illustrates what this means using a research example involving the extent to which two factors predict symptoms of depression.

EXAMPLE 16.5

Harrell and Jackson (2008) conducted a study in which they measured the extent to which restrained eating and ruminative coping could predict changes in mood—specifically, depression—using a sample of female college students.

When people are depressed, they can change their mood in several ways. Harrell and Jackson (2008) focused on two possible predictor variables related to changes in mood: restrained eating and ruminative coping. A *restrained eater* is someone who spends an inordinate amount of time thinking, planning, and obsessing over food choices and the consequences of those choices. *Ruminative coping* occurs when a person focuses repetitively on the meaning, causes, and consequences of his or her mood. In a depressed state, this focus tends to be negative, thereby making mood or depression worse.

The researchers first tested restrained eating as the only predictor variable of changes in depression using equation [1] from that listed above. The results showed that restrained eating was a significant predictor of changes in depression. They then added ruminative coping into the linear equation. Because they were now testing two predictor variables (restrained eating and ruminative coping), they used equation [2] from that listed above. With two predictor variables, they concluded that ruminative coping, and not restrained eating, significantly predicted changes in depression. While restrained eating did predict changes in depression using equation [1], this factor no longer predicted changes in depression when ruminative coping was added as a factor using regression equation [2]. How can these two equations lead to such different conclusions?

To answer these questions, think of stealing cookies from a cookie jar. If cookies are stolen 10 times and your brother was near the cookie jar 8 of the 10 times, then there is a predictive relationship between your brother and the stolen cookies. However, if you add your friend who was near the cookie jar 10 out of 10 times the cookies were stolen, then now you can fully predict the stolen cookies based on this new factor (your friend). In the observation using two factors, the significance of your brother being near the cookie jar is smaller. Similarly, restrained eating predicted symptoms of depression when considered alone but was no longer a significant predictor when ruminative coping was added as a factor. Using multiple regression in this study allowed the researchers to detect the extent to which these two predictor variables interacted, in a way that would not be possible unless they were both included in the same regression equation.

LEARNING CHECK 6

1. What statistical method includes two or more predictor variables in the equation of a regression line to predict changes in a criterion variable?

2. What two values are added to the regression equation when a new predictor variable is added to the regression equation?

3. What is a key advantage of using multiple regression?

Answers: 1. Multiple regression; 2. *b* and *X* are added to the regression equation for each additional predictor variable; 3. Multiple regression makes it possible to detect the extent to which two or more predictor variables interact.

APA IN FOCUS: REPORTING
REGRESSION ANALYSIS 16.10

To summarize an analysis of regression involving a single predictor variable, we report the test statistic, degrees of freedom, and *p* value for the regression analysis. The data points for each pair of scores are often summarized in a scatter plot or a figure displaying the regression line. The regression equation can be stated in the scatter plot. For example, here is an appropriate summary for the results we obtained in Example 16.4:

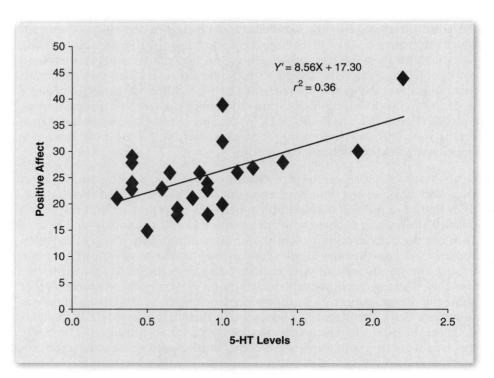

FIGURE 16.10

The linear association between 5-HT levels and positive affect. The data are adapted from that reported by Williams et al. (2006).

An analysis of regression showed a significant positive linear relationship between levels of 5-HT and positive affect, $F(1, 21) = 12.18$, $p < .05$. Figure 16.10 displays the data points, the coefficient of determination, and the regression equation of these data.

CHAPTER SUMMARY ORGANIZED BY LEARNING OBJECTIVE

LO 1: Define *linear regression* and describe the relationship between a predictor variable and a criterion variable.

- **Linear regression** is a statistical procedure used to determine the equation of a regression line to a set of data points and the extent to which the regression equation can be used to predict values of one factor, given known values of a second factor in a population.
- We can use regression to answer these questions:

  1. Is a pattern evident for a set of data points?

  2. Does the equation of a straight line describe this pattern?

  3. Are the predictions made from this equation significant?

LO 2: Compute and interpret the method of least squares.

- The **method of least squares** is a statistical procedure used to compute the slope (*b*) and *y*-intercept (*a*) of the best-fitting straight line to a set of data points, called the regression line. The three steps needed to find the equation of the regression line are as follows:
  Step 1: Compute preliminary calculations.
  Step 2: Calculate the slope (*b*).
  Step 3: Calculate the *y*-intercept (*a*).
- The equation of a straight line is $Y = bX + a$.
  - The **slope (b)** of a straight line is a measure of the change in *Y* relative to the change in *X*. When *X* and *Y* change in the same direction, the slope is positive. When *X* and *Y* change in opposite directions, the slope is negative. The formula for the slope is

  $$b = \frac{\text{change in } Y}{\text{change in } X} = \frac{SS_{XY}}{SS_X}.$$

  - The ***y*-intercept (a)** of a straight line indicates the value of *Y* when *X* equals 0. The formula for the *y*-intercept is

  $$a = M_Y - bM_X.$$

LO 3–4: Identify each source of variation in an analysis of regression; compute an analysis of regression and interpret the results.

- **Analysis of regression** is a statistical procedure used to test hypotheses for one or more predictor variables to determine whether the regression equation for a sample of data points can be used to predict values of the criterion variable (*Y*) given values of the predictor variable (*X*) in the population.
- An analysis of regression for one predictor variable includes two sources of variation:

  1. Regression variation is a measure of the variance in *Y* that is related to changes in *X*. The closer that data points fall to the regression line, the larger the value of regression variation. The formula for regression variation is

  $$SS_{\text{regression}} = r^2 SS_Y.$$

  2. Residual variation is a measure of the variance in *Y* that is not related to changes in *X*. This is the variance in *Y* that is residual, left over, or remaining. The farther that data points fall from the regression line, the larger the value of residual variation. The formula for regression variation is

  $$SS_{\text{residual}} = (1 - r^2)SS_Y.$$

- The proportion of variance (r^2) is a measure of the proportion of variance in *Y* that can be explained or predicted by known values of *X*.

LO 5: Compute and interpret the standard error of estimate.

- The **standard error of estimate** (s_e) is an estimate of the standard deviation or distance that a set of data points falls from the regression line. The standard error of estimate equals the square root of the mean square residual:

  $$s_e = \sqrt{MS_{\text{residual}}}.$$

- The standard error of estimate uses the standard deviation of data points as an estimate of the error in predictions made by a regression line. The smaller the standard error of estimate, the closer values of Y will be to their predicted values, $\hat{Y}$, on the regression line and the more accurate the predictions of Y will be using known values of X.

LO 6: Define *multiple regression* and describe when it is used.

- **Multiple regression** is a statistical method that includes two or more predictor variables in the equation of a regression line to predict changes in a criterion variable.
- One advantage of including multiple predictors in the regression equation is that we can detect the extent to which two or more predictor variables interact.

APA LO 7: Summarize the results of an analysis of regression in APA format.

- To summarize an analysis of regression involving a single predictor variable, we report the test statistic, the degrees of freedom, and the p value for the regression analysis. The data points for each pair of scores are often summarized in a scatter plot or figure displaying the regression line. The regression equation can be stated in the scatter plot.

SPSS LO 8: Compute an analysis of regression using SPSS.

- SPSS can be used to compute an analysis of regression. An analysis of regression is computed using the **Analyze, Regression,** and **Linear** options in the menu bar. These actions will display a dialog box that allows you to identify the variables and run the analysis (for more details, see Section 16.7).

KEY TERMS

analysis of regression	multiple regression	residual variation
criterion variable (Y)	predictor variable (X)	slope (b)
known variable (X)	regression	standard error of estimate
linear regression	regression analysis	to-be-predicted variable (Y)
method of least squares	regression variation	y-intercept (a)

END-OF-CHAPTER PROBLEMS

Factual Problems

1. State the equation of the regression line used to predict values of the criterion variable.

2. Distinguish between the predictor variable and the criterion variable.

3. What method is used to determine the equation of the regression line for a set of data points?

4. Explain why it is necessary to square the deviation of each data point from the regression line to compute the method of least squares.

5. Define the following terms.
   (a) Slope
   (b) y-intercept

6. State three steps used to compute the method of least squares.

7. An analysis of regression measures the variability of which variable (X or Y)?

8. Describe regression variation in terms of variation in Y.

9. Describe residual variation in terms of variation in Y.

10. State the formula for the standard error of estimate. What does this error value measure?

11. What is multiple regression?

12. State a key advantage for using multiple regression.

Concepts and Application Problems

13. Which is the predictor variable (X) and which is the criterion variable (Y) for each of the following examples?

    (a) A researcher tests whether the size of an audience can predict the number of mistakes a student makes during a classroom presentation.

    (b) A social psychologist tests whether the size of a toy in cereal boxes can predict preferences for that cereal.

    (c) A military officer tests whether the duration of an overseas tour can predict the morale among troops overseas.

14. Which scatter plot displays a regression line with a positive slope? Which displays a regression line with a negative slope?

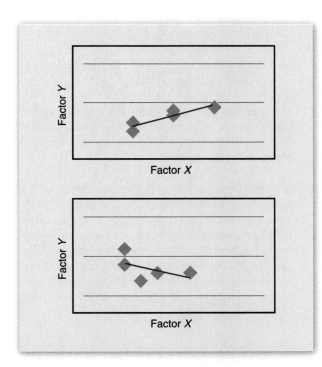

15. For each of the following regression equations, explain how the criterion variable (Y) changes as the predictor variable (X) increases.

Hint: You can find the answer by looking at the equation.

(a) $\hat{Y} = 0.75X - 2.40$

(b) $\hat{Y} = -3.02X - 0.90$

(c) $\hat{Y} = 2.10X + 10$

(d) $\hat{Y} = -3.14X + 12$

16. A researcher reports the following equation for the relationship between income and height among men.

    The method of least squares showed a positive linear relationship, $\hat{Y} = 2.1X + 0.80$, indicating that the height of men predicts income.

    (a) Based on this description, what was the predictor variable (X)?

    (b) Describe the direction of this relationship in words.

17. An animal trainer tests whether the number of hours of obedience training can predict where a dog places in a dog show. The hypothetical data are given below.

Hours of Training	Place in Breed Show
X	**Y**
18	1
4	6
10	2
7	4

In terms of the method of least squares, which of the following regression lines is the best fit for these data?

(a) $\hat{Y} = -0.338X + 6.545$ (b) $\hat{Y} = 0.338X - 6.545$

(c) $\hat{Y} = -1.3X + 5.25$ (d) $\hat{Y} = 1.3X - 5.25$

18. A researcher reports the following regression equation for the relationship between two variables: $\hat{Y} = 1.3X + 2$. Find the predicted value of Y, given that X = 0, 2, 4, and 8.

19. A forensic psychologist tests the extent to which the age of a criminal (X) predicts the age of the victim (Y) for nonviolent crimes. The psychologist uses the case files to record the age of five criminals and the age of the victim in those cases. The hypothetical data are listed in the following table.

Age of Criminal	Age of Victim
X	Y
32	24
24	20
28	25
17	22
12	16

(a) Compute the method of least squares to find the equation of the regression line.

(b) Use the regression equation to determine the predicted age of a victim of a nonviolent crime when the criminal is 20 years old.

20. A developmental psychologist tests the extent to which birth order predicts the amount of attention a child receives from his or her parents. The psychologist records the time (in minutes) that parents spend with their children during a 20-minute session. All children were the same age at the time of this test. The hypothetical data are listed in the following table.

Birth Order	Time Attending to the Child
X	Y
1	12
1	14
5	9
2	10
3	15
2	16
4	8
5	7

(a) Compute the method of least squares to find the equation of the regression line.

(b) Use this regression equation to determine the predicted amount of time a parent spends with his or her second-born child.

21. An instructor measured quiz scores and the number of hours studying among a sample of 20 college students. If $SS_{XY} = 43$, $SS_X = 99$, $M_Y = 6$, and $M_X = 5$, then what is the regression equation for this sample?

22. A team of clinical psychologists tested the extent to which levels of cognitive functioning were related to the number of symptoms for some disorder expressed in 15 patients. The researchers recorded the following values: $SS_{XY} = 48.60$, $SS_X = 355.73$, and $SS_Y = 96.40$.

(a) What is the proportion of variance, r^2, in symptoms (Y) that can be explained by levels of cognitive functioning (X)?

(b) If the total variation in Y is 96.40 ($SS_Y = 96.40$), then what is the $SS_{regression}$, or the amount of variation that is predicted by X?

(c) What is the $SS_{residual}$, or the amount of variation in Y that is remaining?

23. A researcher tested whether time of day could predict mood in a sample of 14 college students. If $SS_{residual} = 108$, then what is the standard error of estimate in this sample?

24. A health psychologist hypothesizes that students who study more also exercise less because they spend so much time studying. She measures whether the number of hours studying (per week) could predict the number of hours exercising in a sample of 62 students. Complete the following regression table for this hypothetical study and make a decision to retain or reject the null hypothesis.

Source of Variation	SS	df	MS	F_{obt}
Regression			80	
Residual (error)				
Total	1440			

25. A psychologist noted that people have more difficulty sleeping in a bright room than in a dark room. She measured whether the intensity of the light could predict the time it took a sample of 4 participants to fall asleep. The data for this hypothetical study are listed in the following table. Compute an analysis of regression for this hypothetical study and make a decision to retain or reject the null hypothesis.

Intensity of Light (in watts)	Time It Took to Sleep (in minutes)
X	Y
5	10
10	18
20	30
40	35

26. A psychologist believed that as children get older, they engage in more "inactive activities" such as playing computer games, watching TV, and surfing online. She tested whether there was a relationship between age (X) and amount of activity per week (Y) in a sample of 10 participants. Compute an analysis of regression for this hypothetical study and make a decision to retain or reject the null hypothesis.

Age (years)	Amount of Activity (hours)
X	Y
7	4.3
9	3.2
10	1.0
13	1.5
12	1.2
15	0.8
9	3.0
12	4.0
15	1.5
14	1.9

27. A sports psychologist tested whether the number of team wins in the previous season can predict the number of wins in the following season in a sample of 32 teams. Complete the regression table for this hypothetical study and make a decision to retain or reject the null hypothesis.

Source of Variation	SS	df	MS	F_{obt}
Regression				
Residual (error)			8	
Total	44			

Problems in Research

28. **Serotonin (5-HT) and positive affect.** Williams and colleagues (2006) used linear regression to determine the relationship between levels of a brain chemical (5-HT, also known as serotonin) and the positive affect (or mood) of participants in their study. Identify the predictor variable and the criterion variable in their study based on this description of their study:

> A positive relationship was observed between 5-HT and positive affect, $F(1,21) = 12.045$, $p = 0.002$. 5-HT may reflect the subjective experience of . . . mood states. (p. 173)

29. **Brain volume and neurocognitive deficits.** Bonilha and colleagues (2008) measured brain volume reduction in a region of the prefrontal cortex called Brodmann Area 9 (BA9) in a sample of 14 adult patients with schizophrenia. Participants completed a cognitive performance test called the Wisconsin Card Sorting Test (WCST). The relationship between brain volume reduction and the number of errors on the WCST was measured. The following scatter plot shows the approximate standardized values they measured.

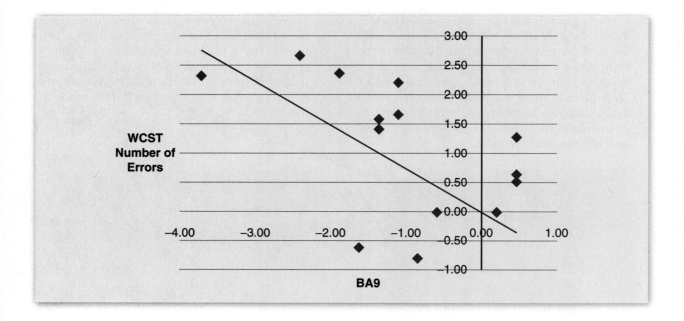

(a) Is the slope positive or negative?

(b) Describe the relationship between prefrontal brain volume in BA9 and cognitive performance on the WCST test.

30. **Sleep length and life satisfaction.** Kelly (2004) studied the relationship between sleep length and global (i.e., overall) life satisfaction in a large sample of college students. The Satisfaction With Life Scale (SWLS) was used to measure global life satisfaction, where higher scores indicated greater satisfaction. She reported the following results:

> A simple regression was calculated using sleep length as the criterion and SWLS scores as the predictor. The result was significant, $F(1,210) = 12.30$, $p < .001$, [indicating] a positive relationship. (p. 429)

(a) How many college students were tested in this study?

(b) Describe the relationship between length of sleep and global life satisfaction.

31. **Depression associated with treatment of disease.** Raison and colleagues (2005) measured the relationship between baseline (pretreatment) depression and depression during treatment with a drug used to treat a type of disease unrelated to depression. They found that levels of depression during treatment (Y) could be predicted by baseline levels of depression (X) using the following regression equation: $\hat{Y} = 0.55X + 32.7$. Estimate the levels of depression during treatment when:

(a) $X = 40$

(b) $X = 60$

(c) $X = 80$

(d) $X = 100$

32. **Measuring procrastination.** Chen, Dai, and Dong (2008) measured the relationship between scores on a revised version of the Aitken Procrastination Inventory (API) and actual procrastination among college students. Higher scores on the API indicate greater procrastination. They found that procrastination (Y) among college students could be predicted by API scores (X) using the following regression equation: $\hat{Y} = 0.146X - 2.922$. Estimate procrastination when:

(a) $X = 30$

(b) $X = 40$

(c) $X = 50$

NOTE: Answers for even numbers are in Appendix C.

Nonparametric Tests
Chi-Square Tests

LEARNING OBJECTIVES

After reading this chapter, you should be able to:

1. Distinguish between nonparametric and parametric tests.

2. Explain how the test statistic is computed for a chi-square test.

3. Calculate the degrees of freedom for the chi-square goodness-of-fit test and locate critical values in the chi-square table.

4. Compute the chi-square goodness-of-fit test and interpret the results.

5. Identify the assumption and the restriction of expected frequency size for the chi-square test.

6. Calculate the degrees of freedom for the chi-square test for independence and locate critical values in the chi-square table.

7. Compute the chi-square test for independence and interpret the results.

8. Compute effect size for the chi-square test for independence.

9. Summarize the results of a chi-square test in APA format.

10. Compute the chi-square goodness-of-fit test and the chi-square test for independence using SPSS.

17.1   TESTS FOR NOMINAL DATA

In Chapters 8 to 16, we computed a variety of hypothesis tests using data on an interval or ratio scale of measurement. These hypothesis tests include the z-test, t-test, analysis of variance (ANOVA), correlation, and analysis of regression. Each of these hypothesis tests are types of **parametric tests** because they are used to test hypotheses about parameters in a population in which the data in the population are normally distributed and measured on an interval or ratio scale of measurement.

DEFINITION

Parametric tests are hypothesis tests that are used to test hypotheses about parameters in a population in which the data in the population are normally distributed and are measured on an interval or a ratio scale of measurement.

When data are measured on an interval or ratio scale of measurement, the test statistic used for each hypothesis test can measure variance in the formula. In the z-test and t-test, standard error was used in the denominator of the test statistic. In the other hypothesis tests, the variance was placed in both the numerator and denominator of the test statistic. However, the variance can only meaningful convey differences when data are measured on a scale in which the distance that scores deviate from their mean is meaningful. While data on an interval and a ratio scale do meaningfully convey distance, data on a nominal and ordinal scale do not. Hence, when we measure data on a nominal or an ordinal scale, we require hypothesis tests that use test statistics that do not analyze the variance of the data. In this chapter, we introduce such a hypothesis test used to analyze nominal data.

Let's use an example to illustrate why the variance of nominal data is not meaningful. Suppose a marketing team asks a group of children which of two products they prefer (one with or one without a picture of a cartoon character). Table 17.1 shows that 20 children chose the product with the cartoon character and 10 children chose the other product. Measuring the variance in this example is meaningless because we only recorded counts or frequencies—specifically, the number of children choosing one of two products. We do not record a dependent variable for each participant; instead, we record a single count in each category, and it is meaningless to measure the variance of a single measure or count in each group or category.

TABLE 17.1   The count or frequency of 30 children choosing one of two products. A single count or frequency is recorded in each category.

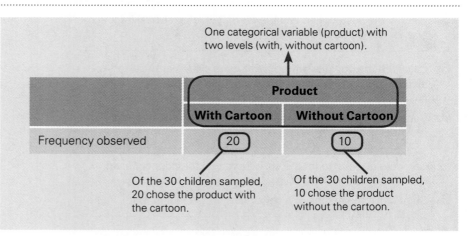

A research situation in which we count the number of participants or items in two or more categories is an example of a **nonparametric test.** A nonparametric test has the following three characteristics that distinguish it from parametric tests:

1. Nonparametric tests can be used even when we do not make inferences about parameters in a population, although they can be used to test hypothesized relationships in a population.

2. Nonparametric tests do not require that the data in the population are normally distributed. Because the data can have any type of distribution, nonparametric tests are often called distribution-free tests.

3. Nonparametric tests can be used to analyze data on a nominal or ordinal scale of measurement.

Nonparametric tests are hypothesis tests that are used (1) to test hypotheses that do not make inferences about parameters in a population, (2) to test hypotheses about data that can have any type of distribution, and (3) to analyze data on a nominal or ordinal scale of measurement.

DEFINITION

In this chapter, we introduce the **chi-square (χ^2) test** (pronounced "kie-square"), which is used to test hypotheses about the discrepancy between the observed and the expected frequencies in different nominal categories. Table 17.1 shows the basic setup of such a test, with a single count or frequency being recorded in each group or category. This test can be used to test hypotheses about a single categorical variable or about two categorical variables observed together. Each type of chi-square test is introduced in this chapter.

NOTE: The chi-square test is a nonparametric test that measures counts or frequencies in different categories.

The **chi-square (χ^2) test** is a statistical procedure used to test hypotheses about the discrepancy between the observed and expected frequencies in two or more nominal categories.

DEFINITION

THE CHI-SQUARE GOODNESS-OF-FIT TEST   17.2

When we record a single count for the levels of a single categorical variable, we use the **chi-square goodness-of-fit test.** This type of test was illustrated in Table 17.1. In Table 17.1, the categorical variable was the product, and the levels were 2 (cartoon, no cartoon). If children didn't prefer one product to the other, then we would expect half to choose each product, meaning that out of 30 children, we would expect 15 children to choose each product. We conduct the chi-square goodness-of-fit test to determine whether the frequencies we observed (20 and 10) fit well with what we expected (15 and 15). We will compute this test using new data in Example 17.1.

NOTE: A goodness-of-fit chi-square indicates how well a set of observed frequencies fits with what was expected.

The **chi-square (χ^2) goodness-of-fit test** is a statistical procedure used to determine whether observed frequencies at each level of one categorical variable are similar to or different from the frequencies we expected at each level of the categorical variable.

DEFINITION

EXAMPLE 17.1

A team of researchers conducted a study about dreaming by observing 80 participants as they slept overnight in a laboratory. As part of the study, the researchers woke each participant during rapid eye movement (REM) sleep, the stage of sleep in which people dream, and they asked participants whether or not they were dreaming. Table 17.2 is a frequency table showing the number of participants who did recall a dream, did not recall a dream, or were unsure if they were dreaming. On the basis of previous studies, the researchers expected 80% of participants to recall their dream, 10% to not recall, and 10% to be unsure. Compute a chi-square goodness-of-fit test at a .05 level of significance.

TABLE 17.2 The observed frequency of dreams recalled and the expected frequency based on proportions in each category that were reported in previous studies.

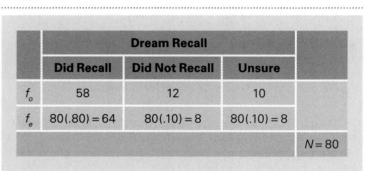

	Dream Recall			
	Did Recall	**Did Not Recall**	**Unsure**	
f_o	58	12	10	
f_e	80(.80) = 64	80(.10) = 8	80(.10) = 8	
				$N = 80$

Table 17.2 displays two rows of frequencies. The top row lists the **frequency observed (f_o)** in each category. This is the number of participants we observed in the study who said that they did recall a dream, did not recall a dream, or were unsure if they dreamed. In this study, 80 participants ($N = 80$) were observed, of whom 58 did recall a dream, 12 did not, and 10 were unsure.

The bottom row in Table 17.2 lists the **frequency expected (f_e)** in each category. This value is computed based on the proportions expected in each category. In this example, 80 participants were observed, of whom we expected 80% of them to recall their dream, 10% to not recall, and 10% to be unsure. We can multiply the total sample size (N) times the proportion expected in each category (p) to find the frequency expected in each category:

$$f_e = Np.$$

DEFINITION

The **frequency observed (f_o)** is the count or frequency of participants recorded in each category or at each level of the categorical variable.

The **frequency expected (f_e)** is the count or frequency of participants in each category, or at each level of the categorical variable, as determined by the proportion expected in each category.

Table 17.2 shows the calculation of the frequency expected in each category. In a sample of 80 participants, we expect 64 to recall their dream, 8 to not recall, and 8 to be unsure. The chi-square goodness-of-fit test statistic will determine how well the observed frequencies fit with the expected frequencies.

THE TEST STATISTIC

The null hypothesis for the chi-square goodness-of-fit test is that the expected frequencies are correct. The alternative hypothesis is that the expected frequencies are not correct. The test statistic for the chi-square goodness-of-fit test is 0 when the observed and expected frequencies are equal and gets larger (more positive) as the discrepancies (or differences) get larger. The larger the discrepancies, the more likely we are to reject the null hypothesis. The test statistic for the chi-square goodness-of-fit test is

$$\chi^2_{obt} = \sum \frac{(f_o - f_e)^2}{f_e}.$$

NOTE: The chi-square test statistic measures the size of the discrepancy between observed and expected frequencies.

The difference between the observed and expected frequency at each level of the categorical variable is squared in the numerator of the test statistic to eliminate negative values. The value in the numerator is divided by the expected frequency to determine the relative size of the discrepancy. To illustrate, suppose we observe a discrepancy of 10 in two studies. In Study 1, the expected frequency was 100 and we observed 110, and in Study 2, the expected frequency was 10 and we observed 20. The discrepancy in the second study is much larger in this example because 20 is twice as large as 10, whereas 110 is not nearly that different from 100.

MAKING SENSE: The Relative Size of a Discrepancy

The test statistic measures the relative size of the discrepancy in each category or at each level of the categorical variable. To further illustrate what a relative discrepancy is, suppose we observe 10 people ($f_o = 10$) in a category that we expected to observe 5 people ($f_e = 5$). The discrepancy between the observed and the expected frequency is 5 ($10 - 5 = 5$). If we substitute these values into the formula, we find

$$\chi^2_{obt} = \frac{(10 - 5)^2}{5} = 5.00.$$

Now suppose we observe 30 people ($f_o = 30$) in a category that we expected to observe 25 people ($f_e = 25$). In this category, the discrepancy between the observed and the expected frequency is again 5 ($30 - 25 = 5$). However, if we substitute these values into the formula, we find

$$\chi^2_{obt} = \frac{(30 - 25)^2}{25} = 1.00.$$

Notice that the value of χ^2_{obt} is smaller in the second example, even though the discrepancy was 5 in both. The reason is that, relatively speaking, 10 is twice as large as 5, whereas 30 is not nearly that different from 25. The difference may be more easily appreciated using an analogy to weight lifting. Lift 5 pounds, then 10 pounds, and you will likely notice the difference. Lift 45 pounds, then 50 pounds, and you will likely not notice the difference as much. As you lift heavier weights, a 5-pound difference becomes less and less noticeable. In a similar way, the denominator of the chi-square test statistic accounts for the relative size of a discrepancy.

THE DEGREES OF FREEDOM

To make a decision, we compare the test statistic we obtain to the distribution of chi-square test statistic values in the positively skewed **chi-square distribution.** The chi-square distribution is a set of chi-square test statistic values for all possible samples when the null hypothesis is true. Figure 17.1 shows the general shape of a chi-square distribution. There is an entire family of chi-square distributions, with each distribution having specified degrees of freedom. The degrees of freedom for each chi-square distribution are equal to the number of levels of the categorical variable (k) minus 1:

$$df = k - 1.$$

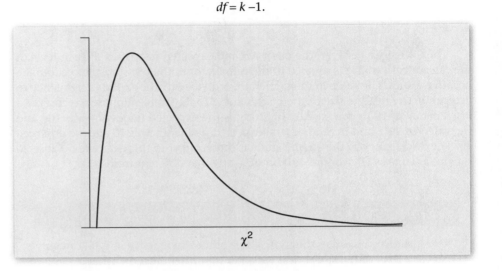

FIGURE 17.1

The general shape of the chi-square distribution.

DEFINITION

The **chi-square distribution** is a positively skewed distribution of chi-square test statistic values for all possible samples when the null hypothesis is true.

To compute the test statistic, we sum the discrepancy between observed and expected frequencies at each level of the categorical variable. The more categories we observe, the more discrepancies we sum, and the larger we can expect the test statistic to be. For this reason, the critical value of a chi-square test increases as the number of levels of the categorical variable, k, increases. Hence, as the degrees of freedom for a goodness-of-fit test ($k - 1$) increase, the critical value also increases.

> ### MAKING SENSE: Degrees of Freedom
>
> The degrees of freedom reflect the number of levels of the categorical variable, k, that are free to vary. When we compute expected frequencies, the last expected frequency is not free to vary because it must make the total expected frequency equal to N (or the total sample size). Suppose, for example, that three studies each had a sample size of 400 participants. The categorical variable had $k = 2$ levels in one study, $k = 4$ levels in a second study, and $k = 8$ levels in a third study. The levels of each categorical variable are shown in Table 17.3. For each categorical variable, the expected frequency is free to vary except in one level—the last level must make the total expected frequency equal 400 (the total sample size). Hence, each level of the categorical variable is free to vary except one, or $k - 1$.

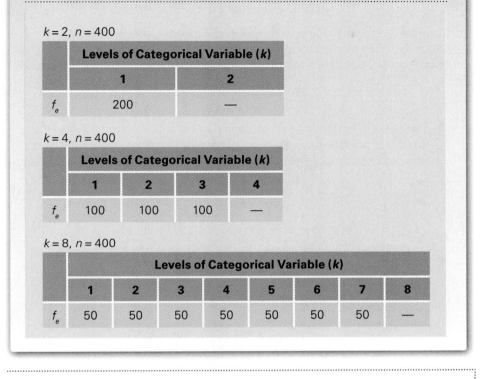

TABLE 17.3 Expected frequencies when $k = 2$, $k = 4$, and $k = 8$ in a sample of 400 participants ($n = 400$). The expected frequency at each level of the categorical variable is free to vary except one because the last level must make the total expected frequency equal 400 (the total sample size).

$k = 2$, $n = 400$

	Levels of Categorical Variable (k)	
	1	**2**
f_e	200	—

$k = 4$, $n = 400$

	Levels of Categorical Variable (k)			
	1	**2**	**3**	**4**
f_e	100	100	100	—

$k = 8$, $n = 400$

	Levels of Categorical Variable (k)							
	1	**2**	**3**	**4**	**5**	**6**	**7**	**8**
f_e	50	50	50	50	50	50	50	—

LEARNING CHECK 1

1. Why is the variance inappropriate for studies in which we count the number of participants who fall into each category?

2. Why is the chi-square called a goodness-of-fit test?

3. The following table summarizes the results of a study concerning the frequency of student participation in classes taught by three different instructors.

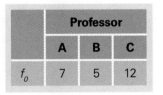

	Professor		
	A	**B**	**C**
f_0	7	5	12

   a. How many participants were observed in this study (N)?
   b. What are the degrees of freedom for this test?
   c. Compute the expected frequencies assuming equal proportions.

4. Two studies find a 6-point discrepancy between the observed and expected frequency. If the discrepancy in Study A is 17 (observed) compared to 11 (expected), and the discrepancy in Study B is 82 (observed) compared to 76 (expected), which study will produce a larger chi-square test statistic value?

HYPOTHESIS TESTING FOR GOODNESS OF FIT

We now have the components we need to use the chi-square goodness-of-fit test to evaluate a hypothesis. We will continue with Example 17.1 and follow the four steps to hypothesis testing.

EXAMPLE 17.1 CONTINUED

In Example 17.1, participants recalled their dreams, did not recall them, or were unsure if they recalled them. There were 58, 12, and 10 individuals in each of those categories. These observations were recorded in Table 17.2 and reproduced in Table 17.4.

TABLE 17.4 The observed frequency of dreams recalled and the expected frequency based on proportions in each category as stated by the null hypothesis. This table reproduces the same data given in Table 17.2.

	Dream Recall			
	Did Recall	**Did Not Recall**	**Unsure**	
f_o	58	12	10	
f_e	80(.80) = 64	80(.10) = 8	80(.10) = 8	
				$N = 80$

Step 1: State the hypotheses. The null hypothesis states the proportions (p) expected in each category. We used these proportions to determine the expected frequencies. The alternative hypothesis states that the proportions stated by the null hypothesis are not correct:

H_0: The distribution of proportions (8:1:1) is the same as expected.

$p_{did\ recall} = 0.80$.

$p_{did\ not\ recall} = 0.10$.

$p_{unsure} = 0.10$.

H_1: Not H_0. The distribution of proportions differs from that stated by the null hypothesis.

Step 2: Set the criteria for a decision. The level of significance for this test is .05. The degrees of freedom are $k - 1$. With $k = 3$ levels of dream recall, $df = 3 - 1 = 2$. To locate the critical value for this test, find the intersection of the row for

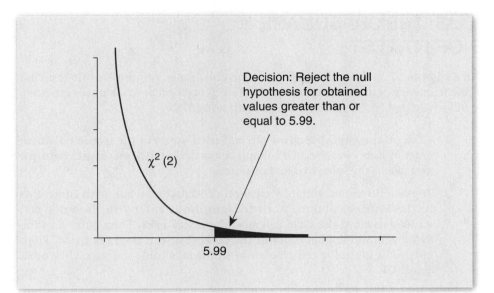

Decision: Reject the null hypothesis for obtained values greater than or equal to 5.99.

χ^2 (2)

5.99

FIGURE 17.2

The rejection region for a chi-square with 2 degrees of freedom. The critical value is 5.99.

2 degrees of freedom and the column for a .05 level of significance in Table B.7 in Appendix B. The critical value is 5.99. Figure 17.2 shows the chi-square distribution, with the rejection region beyond the critical value given. Because the chi-square distribution is positively skewed, the rejection region is always placed in the upper tail.

NOTE: The rejection region is always placed in the upper tail of the positively skewed chi-square distribution.

Step 3: Compute the test statistic. To compute the test statistic, we substitute the frequencies recorded in Table 17.4 into the test statistic formula and sum the discrepancy between the observed and expected frequency one column at a time:

$$\chi^2_{obt} = \frac{(58-64)^2}{64} + \frac{(12-8)^2}{8} + \frac{(10-8)^2}{8}$$
$$= 0.56 + 2.00 + .50$$
$$= 3.06.$$

Step 4: Make a decision. We compare the value of the test statistic with the critical value. If the test statistic falls beyond the critical value, which is 5.99, then we reject the null hypothesis. In this example, $\chi^2_{obt} = 3.06$, and it fails to exceed the critical value of 5.99. We therefore retain the null hypothesis. If we were to report this result in a research journal, it would look something like this:

A chi-square goodness-of-fit test showed that the frequency of dream recall during REM sleep was similar to what was expected, $\chi^2(2) = 3.06$, $p > .05$.

17.3 SPSS IN FOCUS: THE CHI-SQUARE GOODNESS-OF-FIT TEST

In Example 17.1, we concluded from the chi-square goodness-of-fit test that "the frequency of dream recall during REM sleep was similar to what was expected, $\chi^2(2) = 3.06$, $p > .05$." Let's confirm this result using SPSS.

1. Click on the **variable view** tab and enter *dream* in the **name column;** enter *frequency* in the name column below it. Go to the **decimals column** and reduce the value to 0 for both rows.

2. To code the *dream* variable: click on the small gray box with three dots in the **Values** column. In the **dialog box,** enter *1* in the value cell and *did recall* in the label cell, and then click **add.** Then enter *2* in the value cell and *did not recall* in the label cell, and then click *add.* Then enter *3* in the value cell and *unsure* in the label cell, and then click **add.** Select **OK.**

3. Click on the **data view** tab. In the *dream* column, enter a 1 in the first cell, 2 in the next cell, and 3 in the next cell. In the frequency column, enter the corresponding observed frequencies: 58, 12, and 10, respectively.

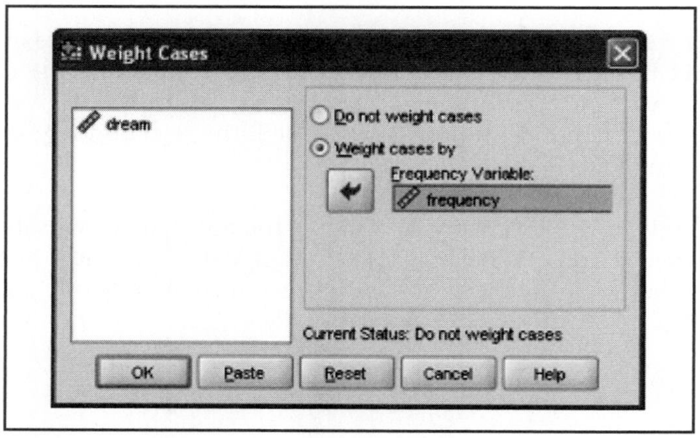

FIGURE 17.3

SPSS dialog box for Step 4.

4. Go to the menu bar and click **Data,** then **Weight cases** to display the dialog box shown in Figure 17.3. Select **Weight cases by** and move *frequency* into the **Frequency Variable** cell, and then click **OK.**

5. Go to the **menu bar** and click **Analyze,** then **Nonparametric tests** and **Chi-square,** to display the dialog box shown in Figure 17.4.

6. Using the arrows, move *dream* into the **Test Variables List** box. In the **Expected Values** box, notice that we have two options: assume all categories (or expected frequencies) are equal or enter the expected frequencies in the cell provided. Because the expected frequencies were not equal, we enter the expected frequencies one at a time and click **Add** to move them into the cell, same as shown in Figure 17.4.

7. Select **Paste** and click the **Run** command.

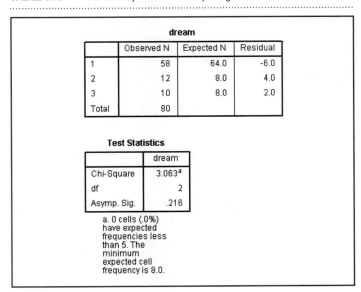

FIGURE 17.4

SPSS dialog box for Steps 5 and 6.

TABLE 17.5 The SPSS output for the chi-square goodness-of-fit test.

dream

	Observed N	Expected N	Residual
1	58	64.0	-6.0
2	12	8.0	4.0
3	10	8.0	2.0
Total	80		

Test Statistics

	dream
Chi-Square	3.063[a]
df	2
Asymp. Sig.	.216

a. 0 cells (.0%) have expected frequencies less than 5. The minimum expected cell frequency is 8.0.

The SPSS output displays two tables, which are both shown in Table 17.5. The top table displays the observed and expected frequencies. The bottom table lists the value of the test statistic, the degrees of freedom (*df*), and the *p* value (Asymp. Sig.) for the test. These data match the values we computed for Example 17.1.

1. The following table summarizes the results of a study of preferences for one of four types of milk.

	Milk Products			
	1%	**2%**	**Whole**	**Skim**
f_o	35	40	10	15
f_e	30	30	20	20

   a. How many participants were observed in this study (N)?
   b. What are the degrees of freedom for this test?
   c. Based on the given expected frequencies, what is the null hypothesis?
   d. What is the critical value for this test at a .05 level of significance?
   e. Compute the test statistic and decide whether to retain or reject the null hypothesis.

2. When observed frequencies are a "good fit" with expected frequencies, do we reject or retain the null hypothesis?

Answers: 1. (a) $N = 100$, (b) $df = 4 - 1 = 3$, (c) The null hypothesis is that the proportion of each product is 3:3:2:2, respectively, (d) Critical value is 7.81, (e) $\chi^2_{obt} = \frac{(35-30)^2}{30} + \frac{(40-30)^2}{30} + \frac{(10-20)^2}{20} + \frac{(15-20)^2}{20} = 10.42$. Decision: Reject the null hypothesis. 2. Retain the null hypothesis.

17.4 INTERPRETING THE CHI-SQUARE GOODNESS-OF-FIT TEST

Interpreting the chi-square goodness-of-fit test is different than any other test taught in this book in two ways: The chi-square test (1) is not interpreted in terms of differences between categories and (2) can be used to confirm that a null hypothesis is correct. Each way of interpreting the chi-square goodness-of-fit test is described in this section.

INTERPRETING A SIGNIFICANT CHI-SQUARE GOODNESS-OF-FIT TEST

It is not appropriate to make comparisons *across the levels* of the categorical variable using a chi-square goodness-of-fit test, meaning that this test can't be interpreted in terms of differences between categories. In Example 17.1, we do not compare whether 58 (did recall), 12 (did not recall), and 10 (unsure) are significantly different from each other. Instead, we compare the discrepancy between observed and expected frequencies *at each level* of the categorical variable, thereby making a total of k comparisons.

To show how we interpret the results for Example 17.1, Table 17.6 shows each comparison in the table we used to summarize the data. Because the null hypothesis was retained, we conclude that there were no discrepancies for each comparison; hence, each comparison was as expected.

TABLE 17.6 The three comparisons for the categorical variable in Example 17.1. Because we retained the null hypothesis, no comparisons are significant.

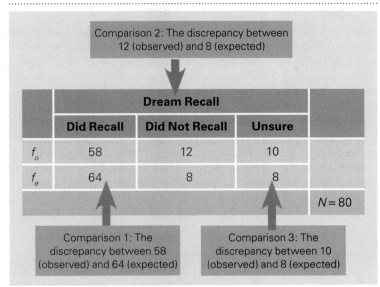

Comparison 2: The discrepancy between 12 (observed) and 8 (expected)

	Dream Recall			
	Did Recall	**Did Not Recall**	**Unsure**	
f_o	58	12	10	
f_e	64	8	8	$N = 80$

Comparison 1: The discrepancy between 58 (observed) and 64 (expected)

Comparison 3: The discrepancy between 10 (observed) and 8 (expected)

NOTE: To interpret a significant chi-square goodness-of-fit test, we compare observed and expected frequencies at each level of the categorical variable.

Comparisons are made at each level of the categorical variable because this is how the test statistic measures the discrepancies. The test statistic adds the discrepancy at each level of the categorical variable. Because the test statistic does not compare differences between the discrepancies, there is no statistical basis for identifying which discrepancies are actually significant. When a chi-square goodness-of-fit test is significant, we mostly speculate as to which observed frequencies were significantly different from the expected frequencies (i.e., which observed frequencies were unexpected). The more discrepancies we add (the larger k is), the more difficult it becomes to identify which observed frequencies were significantly different from the expected frequencies. One strategy is to identify the most obvious or largest discrepancies. Using this strategy, the largest discrepancies tend to be the focus of a significant result, with smaller discrepancies tending to be ignored.

USING THE CHI-SQUARE GOODNESS-OF-FIT TEST TO SUPPORT THE NULL HYPOTHESIS

Unlike parametric tests, the chi-square goodness-of-fit test is one of the few hypothesis tests used to confirm that a null hypothesis is correct. In Example 17.1, we found that the proportion of participants recalling dreams was consistent with what we would expect. This was the result we were looking for—we had no reason to think this wouldn't be the case, based on previous research studies.

Other examples of studies trying to show support for a null hypothesis are not hard to find. A researcher may want to show that a local community has traffic accident rates that are similar to the general population or that a marketing company may want to show that sales for a certain product are still expectedly higher than other competing brands. In each situation, the researcher or company tests a hypothesis to show that the observed frequencies are similar to the expected frequencies. So a decision to retain the null hypothesis is actually the goal of the hypothesis test. The chi-square goodness-of-fit test is a rare example of a test used for this purpose.

NOTE: The chi-square goodness-of-fit test is a rare example of a test used to show that a null hypothesis is correct.

17.5 INDEPENDENT OBSERVATIONS AND EXPECTED FREQUENCY SIZE

A key assumption for the chi-square test is that the observed frequencies are recorded independently, meaning that each observed frequency must come from different and unrelated participants. You can't count the same person twice. In addition, we would violate this assumption if we compared preferences for a certain product among identical twins because these participants are related. Likewise, this assumption would be violated if we compared preferences over a series of trials because the same participants would be counted more than once.

One restriction on using a chi-square test is that the size of an expected frequency should never be smaller than 5 in a given category. In Example 17.1, this means that the expected frequency should be at least 5 for each category of dream recall, and this was the case. To illustrate further, suppose we have two situations:

Situation A: $f_0 = 2, f_e = 1$ ⟶ $\chi^2_{obs} = \dfrac{(2-1)^2}{1} = 1.00$

Situation B: $f_0 = 21, f_e = 20$ ⟶ $\chi^2_{obs} = \dfrac{(21-20)^2}{20} = 0.05$

In both situations, the difference between observed and expected frequencies is 1. Yet, if you compute χ^2 for each situation, you obtain very different values. In Situation A, you divided by an expected frequency of 1, whereas you divided by 20 in Situation B. The result is that smaller expected frequencies, those less than 5, tend to overstate the size of a discrepancy. There are two ways to overcome this limitation:

1. Increase the sample size so that it is five times larger than the number of levels of the categorical variable. With three levels, we would need at least 15 participants ($3 \times 5 = 15$); with five levels, we would need at least 25 participants ($5 \times 5 = 25$), and so on.

2. Increase the number of levels of the categorical variable. The more levels, or the larger k is, the larger the critical value for the hypothesis test. As a general rule, when k is greater than 4, then having one expected frequency less than 5 is not as problematic.

✔ **LEARNING CHECK 3**

1. State whether each of the following examples violates an assumption or is a restriction for the chi-square test.
   a. A large sample size
   b. An expected frequency less than 5
   c. Observed frequencies are independently recorded
   d. There are at least three levels of a categorical variable

2. How is a chi-square goodness-of-fit test interpreted?

3. What is the key assumption for the chi-square test?

Answers: 1. (a) No, (b) Yes, this is a restriction for the test, (c) Yes, this is an assumption for the test, (d) No; 2. We compare discrepancies between observed and expected frequencies at each level of one categorical variable; 3. Observed frequencies are independently recorded in each category.

THE CHI-SQUARE TEST FOR INDEPENDENCE   17.6

The chi-square test can also be used to test for independence. Specifically, when we record frequencies for two categorical variables, we can determine the extent to which the two variables are related, using an analysis similar to a correlation. This hypothesis test is called the **chi-square test for independence.**

The chi-square test for independence has two categorical variables with any number of levels. Table 17.7 shows three examples of a chi-square test for independence. It helps to organize the data for such studies into tables, as shown. We describe these tables just as we did for the two-way ANOVA tests. That is, we refer to this test by referencing the levels of each categorical variable, as shown in Table 17.7. Each cell in the table represents a group or category where we record frequencies. We can determine the number of cells in a table by multiplying the levels of each variable. That is, the first table has a gender variable with two levels (male, female) and an exam variable with two levels (pass, fail), and so this study has four groups ($2 \times 2 = 4$) or four cells in the table representing the study.

TABLE 17.7   Three examples of two-way chi-square tests for independence, as organized in a table. The cells in each table represent a group or category where we record frequencies. To find the number of cells, multiply the levels of each categorical variable. A 2×2 chi-square has $2 \times 2 = 4$ cells. A 2×3 chi-square has $2 \times 3 = 6$ cells. A 3×4 chi-square has $3 \times 4 = 12$ cells. The cells are numbered in each example.

2×2 Chi-square:

		Gender	
		Male	**Female**
Physical Exam	Pass	1	2
	Fail	3	4

2×3 Chi-square:

		Trimester		
		First	**Second**	**Third**
Stress Levels	Low	1	2	3
	High	4	5	6

3×4 Chi-square:

		Season of Birth			
		Spring	**Summer**	**Fall**	**Winter**
Time of Day	Morning	1	2	3	4
	Noon	5	6	7	8
	Night	9	10	11	12

DEFINITION

The **chi-square test for independence** is a statistical procedure used to determine whether frequencies observed at the combination of levels of two categorical variables are similar to frequencies expected.

NOTE: A chi-square test for independence can be used for two categorical variables with any number of levels.

The chi-square test for independence is interpreted similar to a correlation. If two categorical variables are independent, they are not related or correlated. And conversely, if two categorical variables are dependent, they are related or correlated. To illustrate how to identify independent and dependent relationships in a frequency table, refer to Table 17.8. Table 17.8a shows that depression and serotonin (a brain chemical) have a dependent relationship. Table 17.8b shows that depression and preferences for Coke or Pepsi have an independent relationship. The table shows that the more frequencies vary across the table, the less independent, and therefore the more related, the two variables are.

TABLE 17.8   A dependent (a) and an independent (b) relationship between two categorical variables. A dependent relationship is evident when frequencies vary across the table.

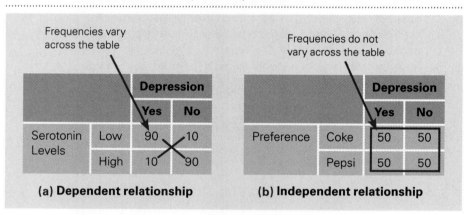

(a) Dependent relationship   (b) Independent relationship

In Example 17.2, we will demonstrate how to compute a chi-square test for independence.

EXAMPLE 17.2

Previous studies show that patients often discontinue scheduled counseling prematurely. Suppose that we hypothesize that more patients will complete counseling when the family is involved with the counseling. To test this hypothesis, we measure the relationship between the type of counseling (family vs. individual) and the counseling outcome (completion vs. premature termination). Table 17.9 shows the results of this study. Compute a chi-square test for independence using a .05 level of significance.

The categorical variables in Example 17.2 are the type of counseling (2 levels) and the outcome (2 levels). Each cell in the table represents a group where we can record frequencies. In Table 17.9, we find there are $2 \times 2 = 4$ cells, and a frequency observed is listed in each cell. The row totals show that 34 patients participated in family counseling and 76 in individual counseling. The column totals show that

TABLE 17.9 Observed frequency. The observed frequency at each combination of levels of two categorical variables using a sample of 110 patients. Row and column totals are given.

Frequency Expected (f_e)		Outcome		
		Completion	Premature Termination	
Type of Counseling	Family	22	12	34
	Individual	31	45	76
		53	57	$N = 110$

53 patients completed counseling, and 57 ended counseling prematurely. The total sample size is 110 patients.

DETERMINING EXPECTED FREQUENCIES

Table 17.9 lists only the observed frequencies. To determine the expected frequencies, we need to know the sample size for each level of the categorical variables. To do this, we refer to the row and column totals in the table. When the row and column totals are equal, the expected frequencies in each cell will also be equal. In this case, we would divide the total sample size by the number of cells to find the expected frequency for each cell.

However, in Table 17.9, the row and the column totals are not equal. The number of patients in family and individual counseling is different; the number of patients completing and prematurely terminating counseling is different. To find the expected frequencies in this case, we must ask how many patients we expect to observe in each cell, given the number of patients who were observed. The size of the expected frequency in a given cell, then, is directly related to the number of patients observed. To determine expected frequencies:

NOTE: The size of the expected frequency in a given cell is directly related to the number of participants observed.

1. Identify the row and column totals for each cell. These totals represent the sample size for each cell.

2. Compute the following formula for each cell:

$$f_e = \frac{\text{row total} \times \text{column total}}{N}.$$

Each calculation is shown in Table 17.10. The sum of the expected frequencies will equal the total sample size. The expected frequencies in each cell are the frequencies we expect to observe when the categorical variables are independent. Table 17.10 shows the frequencies we expect to observe when the outcome for counseling is independent of the type of counseling.

TABLE 17.10 Expected frequency. The expected frequencies of for type of counseling and counseling outcome. Calculations are given in each cell.

Frequency Expected (f_e)		Outcome		
		Completion	Premature Termination	
Type of Counseling	Family	$(34 \times 53)/110 = 16.38$	$(34 \times 57)/100 = 17.62$	34
	Individual	$(76 \times 53)/110 = 36.62$	$(76 \times 57)/100 = 39.38$	76
		53	57	$N = 110$

THE TEST STATISTIC

The test statistic for the chi-square test for independence determines how similar the expected frequencies are to the observed frequencies. The computation of the test statistic does not change from that used with a chi-square goodness-of-fit test. For the chi-square test for independence, the formula will measure the discrepancy between the observed and expected frequency in each cell. Larger discrepancies make the value of the test statistic larger and increase the likelihood that we will reject the null hypothesis. A decision to reject the null hypothesis indicates that the levels of two categorical variables are dependent or related. The formula for the test statistic is

NOTE: The test statistic for a chi-square goodness-of-fit and a chi-square test for independence is the same.

$$\chi^2_{obt} = \sum \frac{(f_o - f_e)^2}{f_e}.$$

THE DEGREES OF FREEDOM

To compute the degrees of freedom for a chi-square test for independence, we multiply the degrees of freedom for each categorical variable. Each categorical variable is associated with $k - 1$ degrees of freedom. The chi-square test for independence, then, is found by multiplying the degrees of freedom for each factor:

$$df = (k_1 - 1)(k_2 - 1).$$

Solving for the degrees of freedom in Example 17.2, we get

$$df = (2 - 1)(2 - 1) = 1.$$

As with the chi-square goodness-of-fit test, the degrees of freedom reflect the number of cells or categories that are free to vary in a frequency table. To illustrate, Table 17.11 shows the expected frequency for one cell in Example 17.2. Because we know the row and column totals, we only need to compute the expected frequency for one cell; the remaining cells are not free to vary—the values in the remaining cells must make the cells sum to the row and column totals. Hence, $df = 1$ in Example 17.2.

TABLE 17.11   The degrees of freedom. The degrees of freedom are the number of cells that are free to vary. In a 2×2 chi-square, once we compute the expected frequency of one cell, the remaining cells are not free to vary—they must sum to the row and column totals. Hence, $df = 1$ for a 2×2 chi-square.

Frequency Expected (f_e)		Outcome		
		Completion	Premature Termination	
Type of Counseling	Family	16.38	—	34
	Individual	—	—	76
		53	57	$N = 110$

HYPOTHESIS TESTING FOR INDEPENDENCE

We now have the components we need to use the chi-square test for independence to evaluate a hypothesis. We will continue with Example 17.2 and follow the four steps to hypothesis testing.

In Example 17.2, we are testing the relationship between type of counseling (family, individual) and counseling outcome (completion, premature termination). Table 17.12 lists the observed and expected frequencies (given in parentheses) for Example 17.2. We will compute a chi-square test for independence at a .05 level of significance to determine whether the categorical variables in this example are independent or related.

EXAMPLE 17.2 CONTINUED

TABLE 17.12   The observed and expected frequencies for Example 17.2. Expected frequencies are given in parentheses.

		Outcome		
		Completion	Premature Termination	
Type of Counseling	Family	22 (16.38)	12 (17.62)	34
	Individual	31 (36.62)	45 (39.38)	76
		53	57	$N = 110$

Step 1: State the hypotheses. The null hypothesis states that the two categorical variables are independent or not related. The alternative hypothesis states that the two variables are dependent or related.

H_0: The type of counseling and outcome of counseling are independent or not related. The observed frequencies will be equal to the expected frequencies in each cell.

H_1: The type of counseling and outcome of counseling are dependent or related. The observed frequencies will not be equal to the expected frequencies in each cell.

Step 2: Set the criteria for a decision. The level of significance for this test is .05, and the degrees of freedom are $df = 1$. To locate the critical value for this test, find the intersection of the row at one degree of freedom and the column at a .05 level of significance in Table B.7 in Appendix B. The critical value is 3.84. Figure 17.5 shows the chi-square distribution and the rejection region beyond the critical value.

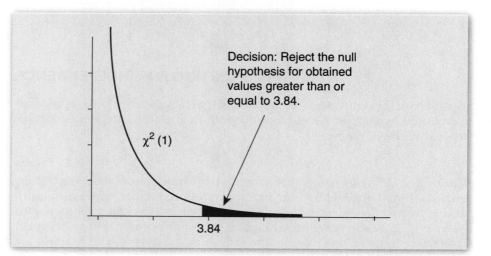

FIGURE 17.5

The rejection region for a chi-square with 1 degree of freedom. The critical value is 3.84.

NOTE: Always place the rejection region in the upper tail of the positively skewed chi-square distribution.

Step 3: Compute the test statistic. To compute the test statistic, we substitute the observed frequencies and expected frequencies, given in Table 17.12, into the formula for the test statistic. Using the values in the table, sum the discrepancy between observed and expected frequencies one cell at a time:

$$\chi^2_{obt} = \frac{(22-16.38)^2}{16.38} + \frac{(12-17.62)^2}{17.62} + \frac{(31-36.62)^2}{36.62} + \frac{(45-39.38)^2}{39.38}$$

$$= 1.928 + 1.793 + 0.863 + 0.802$$

$$= 5.386.$$

Step 4: Make a decision. To make a decision, we compare the value of the test statistic to the critical value. If the test statistic falls beyond the critical value of 3.84, then we reject the null hypothesis; otherwise, we retain the null hypothesis. Because $\chi^2_{obt} = 5.386$ exceeds the critical value of 3.84, we reject the null hypothesis. If we were to report this result in a research journal, it would look something like this:

A chi-square test for independence showed a significant relationship between the type of counseling and outcome, $\chi^2(1) = 5.386$, $p < .05$. The data indicate that family involvement in counseling is associated with a greater number of patients completing counseling.

1. A researcher conducts a 2×3 chi-square test for independence.

   a. How many cells are in this study?

   b. What are the degrees of freedom for this hypothesis test?

2. What is the null hypothesis for a chi-square test for independence?

3. The following table summarizes the results of a study concerning the relationship between use of tanning beds and gender.

		Use Tanning Beds		
		Yes	No	Totals
Gender	Men	10	12	22
	Women	14	8	22
	Totals	24	20	

   a. How many total participants were in this study?

   b. What is the critical value for this test at a .05 level of significance?

   c. Compute the test statistic and decide whether to retain or reject the null hypothesis.

Answers: 1. (a) 6 cells, (b) $df = (2-1)(3-1) = 2$; 2. The null hypothesis states that two categorical variables are independent or unrelated, or that each observed frequency will be equal to each expected frequency; 3. (a) $N = 44$, (b) 3.84, (c) $\chi^2_{obt} = \frac{(10-12)^2}{12} + \frac{(12-10)^2}{10} + \frac{(14-12)^2}{12} + \frac{(8-10)^2}{10} = 1.47$. Decision: Retain the null hypothesis.

THE RELATIONSHIP BETWEEN CHI-SQUARE AND THE PHI COEFFICIENT   17.7

The phi correlation coefficient that we computed in Chapter 15 indicated the direction and strength of the linear relationship between two dichotomous variables. This coefficient also can be used for the same types of data as those in the chi-square test for independence. Specifically, the phi correlation coefficient can be used in place of a 2×2 chi-square test for independence. Example 17.3 restates the data for this type of research situation first given in Chapter 15.

A researcher wants to determine the relationship between employment (employed, unemployed) and happiness (happy, unhappy) using a sample of 40 participants. The number of participants in each category was recorded. Table 17.13 shows the results of this hypothetical study.

EXAMPLE 17.3

When the row and column totals are the same value in a table representing a chi-square test for independence, the expected frequencies in each cell are also equal. Using a phi correlation coefficient for this test in Chapter 15, we concluded the following:

Using the phi correlation coefficient, a significant relationship between employment and happiness was evident, $r_\phi = +0.40$, $p < .05$.

TABLE 17.13 The observed and expected frequencies for the relationship between employment status and happiness. This table was originally given without expected frequencies for an example using the phi correlation coefficient in Table 15.11 in Chapter 15.

		Employment		
		Unemployed	Employed	Totals
Happiness	Unhappy	14 (10)	6 (10)	20
	Happy	6 (10)	14 (10)	20
	Total	20	20	

To determine the significance of the phi correlation coefficient, we converted the phi coefficient to a chi-square test statistic using the following equation:

$$\chi^2 = r_\phi^2 n.$$

NOTE: The phi correlation coefficient (r_ϕ) and chi-square test for independence can be used to analyze the relationship between two categorical variables, each with two levels.

In this equation, r_ϕ is the correlation coefficient and n is the total sample size. In Example 17.3, this conversion is

$$\chi^2 = (0.40)^2 \times 40 = 6.40.$$

In Example 17.3, a phi coefficient of .40 is equivalent to a chi-square test statistic of 6.40. We can confirm that the chi-square test statistic is indeed 6.40 by summing the discrepancies between observed and expected frequencies in each cell in Table 17.13. The value of the test statistic is

$$\chi^2_{obt} = \frac{(14-10)^2}{10} + \frac{(6-10)^2}{10} + \frac{(6-10)^2}{10} + \frac{(14-10)^2}{10}$$
$$= 1.60 + 1.60 + 1.60 + 1.60$$
$$= 6.40.$$

The conversion equation and the computation of the chi-square test statistic produce the same value of χ^2_{obt}. Consequently, the phi correlation coefficient and the chi-square test statistic are related in that we can use the value of one to compute the other. The relationship between these statistics also allows us to use the phi coefficient to estimate effect size with the chi-square test for independence.

17.8 MEASURES OF EFFECT SIZE

There are three common measures of effect size for the chi-square test for independence: the proportion of variance, the phi coefficient, and Cramer's *V.* Any of these measures can be used to estimate effect size for this test. Each measure of effect size is described in this section.

EFFECT SIZE USING PROPORTION OF VARIANCE: $\phi^2 = \dfrac{\chi^2}{n}$

The coefficient of determination or proportion of variance (ϕ^2) is one measure of effect size. When stated as an effect size measure with a chi-square test for independence, the r term for the correlation coefficient is replaced with ϕ. In Example 17.2, we selected a sample of 110 participants and computed $\chi^2(1) = 5.386$. The proportion of variance using the formula given in the heading is

$$\phi^2 = \frac{5.386}{110} = 0.05.$$

We conclude that the type of counseling attended (family vs. individual) accounts for 5% of the total variance for completing counseling.

EFFECT SIZE USING THE PHI COEFFICIENT: $\phi = \sqrt{\dfrac{\chi^2}{n}}$

The square root of the proportion of variance can also be reported as an estimate of effect size. The square root of the proportion of variance is the phi coefficient. Using the phi coefficient to estimate effect size in Example 17.2, we take the square root of the proportion of variance (the formula is given in the heading):

$$\phi = \sqrt{0.05} = 0.224.$$

This value, $\phi = 0.224$, is the value of the phi coefficient, when the chi-square test statistic is 5.386, using a sample of 110 participants.

EFFECT SIZE USING CRAMER'S V: $\sqrt{\dfrac{\chi^2}{n \times df_{smaller}}}$

The proportion of variance and phi coefficient can only be used for a 2×2 chi-square test for independence. When the levels of one or more categorical variables are greater than two, we use **Cramer's V** or **Cramer's phi** to estimate effect size.

> **Cramer's V**, also called **Cramer's phi (ϕ)**, is an estimate of effect size for the chi-square test for independence for two categorical variables with any number of levels.

DEFINITION

In the formula, the term $df_{smaller}$ is the smaller of the two set of degrees of freedom. For a 2×2 chi-square, both degrees of freedom equal 1, so the smaller degree of freedom is 1. If we compute this formula, we will reproduce the effect size that we already obtained using the phi coefficient:

$$V = \sqrt{\frac{5.386}{110 \times 1}} = \sqrt{0.05} = 0.224.$$

Table 17.14 shows the effect size conventions for interpreting Cramer's V, as proposed by Cohen (1988). These conventions are guidelines, not cutoffs for effect size. They are meant to help identify the importance of a result. Referring to Table 17.14, the discrepancy we observed in Example 17.2 was a medium effect size.

TABLE 17.14 Effect size conventions for Cramer's V as proposed by Cohen (1988).

$df_{smaller}$	Effect Size		
	Small	**Medium**	**Large**
1	0.10	0.30	0.50
2	0.07	0.21	0.35
3	0.06	0.17	0.29

17.9 SPSS IN FOCUS: THE CHI-SQUARE TEST FOR INDEPENDENCE

In Example 17.2, a 2 × 2 chi-square test for independence showed "a significant relationship between the type of counseling and outcome of counseling, $\chi^2(1) = 5.386$, $p < .05$." Let's confirm this conclusion using SPSS.

1. Click on the **variable view** tab and enter *row* in the **name column;** enter *column* in the name column below it; enter *frequency* in the name column below that. Go to the **decimals column** and reduce the value to 0 for all rows.

2. To code the *row* variable, click on the small gray box with three dots in the **Values** column for *row*. In the **dialog box,** enter *1* in the value cell and *family* in the label cell, and then click **add.** Then enter *2* in the value cell and *individual* in the label cell, and then click **add.** To code the *column* variable, click on the small gray box with three dots in the **Values** column for *column*. In the **dialog box,** enter *1* in the value cell and *completion* in the label cell, and then click **add.** Then enter *2* in the value cell and *premature termination* in the label cell, and then click **add.** Select **OK.**

3. Click on the **data view** tab. In the *row* column enter 1, 1, 2, and 2 in the first four cells. For the column labeled *column*, enter 1, 2, 1, and 2 in each cell respectively. Enter the corresponding observed frequencies in the *frequency* column: 22, 12, 31, and 45 respectively.

4. Go to the menu bar and click **Data,** then **Weight cases** to display a dialog box. In the dialog box, click **Weight cases by,** move *frequency* into the **Frequency Variable** cell, and then click **OK.**

5. Go to the **menu bar** and click **Analyze,** then **Descriptive statistics** and **Crosstabs,** to display a new dialog box.

6. Using the arrows, move *row* into the **Row(s)** box and *column* into the **Column(s)** box. Click **Statistics . . .** to display another dialog box.

7. Select **Chi-square.** To compute effect size, select **Phi and Cramer's V** in the box labeled **Nominal,** and then click **Continue.**

8. Select **Paste** and click the **Run** command.

Table 17.15 shows the SPSS output for the chi-square test for independence. The frequency table (top table) shows the observed and expected frequencies. The first row of the bottom table lists the value of the chi-square test statistic, the degrees of freedom (*df*), and the *p* value (Asymp. Sig.) for the test. Read only the top row in the bottom table. Table 17.16 displays the results of the effect size estimate. The values in the SPSS output tables are similar to those we compute by hand for Example 17.2.

TABLE 17.15 SPSS output for the chi-square frequency table (top) and for the chi-square test for independence (bottom).

row * column Crosstabulation

Count

		column		Total
		1	2	
row	1	22	12	34
	2	31	45	76
Total		53	57	110

Chi-Square Tests

	Value	df	Asymp. Sig. (2-sided)	Exact Sig. (2-sided)	Exact Sig. (1-sided)
Pearson Chi-Square	5.382[a]	1	.020		
Continuity Correction[b]	4.466	1	.035		
Likelihood Ratio	5.433	1	.020		
Fisher's Exact Test				.024	.017
Linear-by-Linear Association	5.333	1	.021		
N of Valid Cases	110				

a. 0 cells (.0%) have expected count less than 5. The minimum expected count is 16.38.
b. Computed only for a 2x2 table

TABLE 17.16 SPSS output for effect size using phi and Cramer's *V*.

Symmetric Measures

		Value	Approx. Sig.
Nominal by Nominal	Phi	.221	.020
	Cramer's V	.221	.020
N of Valid Cases		110	

LEARNING CHECK 5

1. True or false: The phi coefficient can be converted to a chi-square and vice versa.

2. Which effect size measure or measures can be used with a 3 × 3 chi-square test for independence?

3. State the effect size using Cramer's *V* for each of the following tests:

   a. 2 × 3 chi-square, $N = 60$, $\chi^2 = 8.12$

   b. 4 × 3 chi-square, $N = 80$, $\chi^2 = 9.76$

   c. 2 × 2 chi-square, $N = 100$, $\chi^2 = 3.88$

Answers: 1. True. 2. Cramer's V; 3. (a) $\sqrt{\dfrac{8.12}{60 \times 1}} = 0.368$, (b) $\sqrt{\dfrac{9.76}{80 \times 2}} = 0.247$, (c) $\sqrt{\dfrac{3.88}{100 \times 1}} = 0.197$.

17.10 APA IN FOCUS: REPORTING THE CHI-SQUARE TEST

To summarize the chi-square goodness-of-fit test, we report the test statistic, the degrees of freedom, and the p value. The observed frequencies can be summarized in a figure or a table or in the main text. To summarize the chi-square test for independence, we also report the effect size. For example, here is a summary of the results for Example 17.2 using Cramer's V as the measure of effect size:

A chi-square test for independence showed a significant relationship between the type of counseling and outcome, $\chi^2(1) = 5.386$, $p < .05$ ($V = 0.224$). The data indicate that family involvement in counseling is associated with a greater number of patients completing counseling.

CHAPTER SUMMARY ORGANIZED BY LEARNING OBJECTIVE

LO 1: Distinguish between nonparametric and parametric tests.

- **Parametric tests** are hypothesis tests that are used to test hypotheses about parameters in a population in which the data in the population are normally distributed and measured on an interval or a ratio scale of measurement.
- **Nonparametric tests** are hypothesis tests that are used (1) to test hypotheses that do not make inferences about parameters in a population, (2) to test hypotheses about data that can have any type of distribution, and (3) to analyze data on a nominal or ordinal scale of measurement.

LO 2: Describe how the test statistic is computed for a chi-square test.

- The test statistic for a chi-square test is

$$\chi^2_{obt} = \sum \frac{(f_o - f_e)^2}{f_e}.$$

- The test statistic compares the discrepancy between observed frequencies and the expected frequencies stated in a null hypothesis. The larger the discrepancy between observed and expected frequencies, the larger the value of the test statistic.

LO 3–4: Calculate the degrees of freedom for the chi-square goodness-of-fit test and locate critical values in the chi-square table; compute the chi-square goodness-of-fit test and interpret the results.

- The **chi-square goodness-of-fit test** is a statistical procedure used to determine whether observed frequencies at each level of one categorical variable are similar to or different from the frequencies we expected at each level of the categorical variable. The degrees of freedom for this test are $k - 1$.
- There is no statistical basis for interpreting which discrepancies are significant. The more discrepancies we add, or the larger k is, the more difficult it is to interpret a significant

test. One strategy is to identify the largest discrepancies, which tend to be the focus of a significant result, with smaller discrepancies tending to be ignored.

LO 5: Identify the assumption and the restriction of expected frequency size for the chi-square test.

- An assumption for the chi-square test is that observed frequencies are independently recorded in each category. A restriction of this test is that expected frequencies should be greater than 5 in each category. This restriction can be overcome when we increase the sample size such that it is five times larger than the number of levels of the categorical variable or increase the number of levels of the categorical variable.

LO 6–7: Calculate the degrees of freedom for the chi-square test for independence and locate critical values in the chi-square table; compute the chi-square test for independence and interpret the results.

- The **chi-square test for independence** is a statistical procedure used to determine whether frequencies observed at the combination of levels of two categorical variables are similar to expected frequencies.
- To find the expected frequency in each cell of a frequency table for a chi-square test for independence, first find the row and the column totals for each cell, then calculate the following formula for each cell:

$$f_e = \frac{\text{row total} \times \text{column total}}{N}.$$

- The test statistic is the same as that for the chi-square goodness-of-fit test. The degrees of freedom are $(k_1 - 1)(k_2 - 1)$. A significant outcome indicates that two categorical variables are related or not independent.

LO 8: Compute effect size for the chi-square test for independence.

- Effect size for a chi-square test for independence measures the size of an observed effect. Three measures of effect size are as follows:

Effect size using proportion of variance: $\phi^2 = \dfrac{\chi^2}{n}$.

Effect size using the phi coefficient: $\phi = \sqrt{\dfrac{\chi^2}{n}}$.

Effect size using **Cramer's V**: $V = \sqrt{\dfrac{\chi^2}{n \times df_{smaller}}}$.

APA LO 9: Summarize the results of a chi-square test in APA format.

- To summarize the chi-square goodness-of-fit test, report the test statistic, the degrees of freedom, and the p value. The observed frequencies can be summarized in a figure or table or in the main text. For the chi-square test for independence, an estimate for effect size should also be reported.

SPSS LO 10: Compute the chi-square goodness-of-fit test and the chi-square test for independence using SPSS.

- The chi-square goodness-of-fit test is computed using the **Analyze, Nonparametric tests,** and **Chi-square** options in the menu bar. These actions will display a dialog box that allows you to identify the groups and run the test. A **weight cases** option must also be selected from the menu bar (for more details, see Section 17.3).
- The chi-square goodness-of-fit test is computed using the **Analyze, Descriptive statistics,** and **Crosstabs** options in the menu bar. These actions will display a dialog box that allows you to identify the groups and run the test. A **weight cases** option must also be selected from the menu bar (for more details, see Section 17.9).

KEY TERMS

chi-square distribution
chi-square goodness-of-fit test
chi-square (χ^2) test
chi-square test for independence

Cramer's phi (ϕ)
Cramer's V
frequency expected (f_e)
frequency observed (f_o)

nonparametric tests
parametric tests

END-OF-CHAPTER PROBLEMS

Factual Problems

1. State three ways that nonparametric tests differ from parametric tests.

2. A chi-square test is used when we measure data on what scale of measurement?

3. Why is a chi-square called a goodness-of-fit test?

4. Define the following terms:
   (a) Frequency observed (f_o)
   (b) Frequency expected (f_e)

5. Write the formula for finding the expected frequency for a chi-square goodness-of-fit test.

6. What is the decision likely to be for values of χ^2_{obt} close to 0?

7. How are the degrees of freedom computed for each test listed below?
   (a) A chi-square goodness-of-fit test
   (b) A chi-square test for independence

8. What is the shape of the chi-square distribution?

9. Name one assumption and one restriction for the chi-square test.

10. Write the formula for the frequency expected for a chi-square test for independence.

11. Write the formula for each of the following effect size measures for the chi-square test for independence:
    (a) Proportion of variance
    (b) Phi coefficient
    (c) Cramer's V

12. When is Cramer's *V* the only measure of effect size that can be used with the chi-square test for independence?

Concepts and Application Problems

13. Based on the scale of measurement for the data, which of the following tests is parametric? Which is nonparametric?

    (a) A researcher measures the average age that schizophrenia is diagnosed in a sample of male and female patients.

    (b) A researcher measures the proportion of schizophrenic patients born in each season.

    (c) A researcher tests whether frequency of Internet use and social interaction are independent.

    (d) A researcher measures the amount of time (in seconds) that a group of teenagers uses the Internet for school-related and non-school-related purposes.

14. For each of the following examples, state whether the chi-square goodness-of-fit test or the chi-square test for independence is appropriate.

    (a) A study concerning the number of individuals who prefer one of four career options

    (b) A study concerning the frequency of aberrant behavior among high school freshmen, sophomores, juniors, and seniors

    (c) A study testing the relationship between the frequency of intimacy (low, high) and personality type (extravert, introvert)

15. For each of the following examples, state whether the chi-square goodness-of-fit test or the chi-square test for independence is appropriate, and state the degrees of freedom (*df*) for the test.

    (a) An instructor tests whether class attendance (low, high) and grade point average (low, average, high) are independent.

    (b) A student tests whether the professor's speaking style (monotone, dynamic) and student interest (low, high) are independent.

    (c) A health psychologist records the number of below average, average, overweight, and obese individuals in a sample of college students.

    (d) A personality psychologist compares the number of single mothers with Type A or Type B personality traits.

16. A chi-square goodness-of-fit test has the following expected frequencies: 12, 4, and 8. Should a chi-square goodness-of-fit test be used to analyze these data? Explain.

17. Students are asked to rate their preference for one of four video games. The following table lists the observed preferences in a sample of 120 students. State whether to reject or retain the null hypothesis for a chi-square goodness-of-fit test given the following expected frequencies.

	Video Games			
	McStats	**Tic-Tac-Stats**	**Silly Stats**	**Super Stats**
Frequency observed	30	30	30	30

    (a) Expected frequencies: 25%, 25%, 25%, 25%, respectively

    (b) Expected frequencies: 70%, 10%, 10%, 10%, respectively

18. The Better Business Bureau (BBB) wants to determine whether a certain business is engaging in fair hiring practices. The BBB finds that a local business employs 66 men and 34 women. The general population of workers in this industry is 60% men and 40% women. Using a chi-square goodness-of-fit test, decide to retain or reject the null hypothesis that the distribution of men and women in the local business is consistent with, or proportional to, that in the general population of workers. Use a .05 level of significance.

19. A local brewery produces three premium lagers named Half Pint, XXX, and Dark Night. Of its premium lagers, they bottle 40% Half Pint, 40% XXX, and 20% Dark Night lagers. In a marketing test of a sample of consumers, 26 preferred the Half Pint lager, 42 preferred the XXX lager, and 12 preferred the Dark Night

lager. Using a chi-square goodness-of-fit test, decide to retain or reject the null hypothesis that production of the premium lagers matches these consumer preferences using a .05 level of significance.

20. A behavioral therapist records the number of children who are spanked and not spanked by their parents as a form of punishment in a sample of parents who were spanked by their parents as children. The following table shows the results of a chi-square goodness-of-fit test. If we expect to observe equal frequencies, then compute a chi-square goodness-of-fit test using a .05 level of significance and decide to retain or reject the null hypothesis.

Child Is Not Spanked	Child Is Spanked
28	46

21. A psychologist studying addiction tests whether cravings for cocaine and relapse are independent.

The following table lists the observed frequencies in the small sample of people who use drugs.

Obs. Freq.		Relapse Yes	No	
Cravings	Yes	20	10	30
	No	8	17	25
		28	27	$N = 55$

(a) Conduct a chi-square test for independence at a .05 level of significance. Decide whether to retain or reject the null hypothesis.

(b) Compute effect size using ϕ and Cramer's V. *Hint:* Both should give the same estimate of effect size.

22. A developmental psychologist tests whether a family's religious affiliation is independent of their child's religious affiliation. The psychologist records the religious affiliation of 136 children and their parents' religious affiliation. The following table lists the observed frequencies for this test.

		Religious Affiliation of Parent				
		Protestant	Catholic	Jewish	Muslim	
Religious Affiliation of Child	Protestant	20	2	4	7	33
	Catholic	5	19	2	4	30
	Jewish	2	4	22	8	36
	Muslim	8	6	7	16	37
		35	31	35	35	$N = 136$

(a) Conduct a chi-square test for independence at a .05 level of significance. Decide whether to retain or reject the null hypothesis.

(b) Compute effect size using Cramer's V.

23. A professor tests whether the loudness of noise during an exam (low, medium, and high) is independent of exam grades (pass, fail). The following table shows the observed frequencies for this test.

		Noise Level Low	Medium	High	
Exam	Pass	20	18	8	46
	Fail	8	6	10	24
		28	24	18	$N = 70$

(a) Conduct a chi-square test for independence at a .05 level of significance. Decide whether to retain or reject the null hypothesis.

(b) Compute effect size using Cramer's V.

24. What is the proportion of variance (ϕ^2) for each of the following values in a 2 × 2 chi-square test for independence?

(a) $\chi^2 = 3.96$, $n = 50$

(b) $\chi^2 = 5.23$, $n = 75$

(c) $\chi^2 = 12.00$, $n = 100$

25. What is Cramer's V for each of the following values for the chi-square test for independence?

(a) $\chi^2 = 4.36$, $n = 80$, $df_{smaller} = 1$

(b) $\chi^2 = 8.12$, $n = 120$, $df_{smaller} = 2$

(c) $\chi^2 = 11.54$, $n = 150$, $df_{smaller} = 3$

26. Based on Cohen's effect size conventions, what is the size of the effect for each of the following values of Cramer's V?

(a) $V = 0.08$, $df_{smaller} = 1$

(b) $V = 0.24$, $df_{smaller} = 2$

(c) $V = 0.30$, $df_{smaller} = 3$

Problems in Research

27. **Choosing effect size.** Volker (2006) analyzed methods and approaches for reporting effect size in psychological research. In his assessment of estimates for effect size using the chi-square test, he wrote,

Given that Cramer 's V is an extension of the coefficient, the values of effect size ϕ and Cramer 's V will be identical when a 2 × 2 [chi-square] is analyzed. (p. 666)

(a) Which coefficient is Volker (2006) referring to?

(b) Why are the two values of effect size identical when analyzing a 2 × 2 chi-square?

28. **Undercover officers and marital stress.** Love, Vinson, Tolsma, and Kaufmann (2008) studied the psychological effects of being an undercover officer, including the stress it places on a marriage. In a sample of 239 former undercover officers, the researchers recorded the following number of officers reporting symptoms of marital stress, as listed in the following table. If

we expect to observe equal frequencies, then compute a chi-square goodness-of-fit test at a .05 level of significance. Decide whether to retain or reject the null hypothesis.

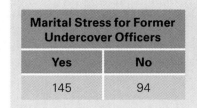

Marital Stress for Former Undercover Officers	
Yes	**No**
145	94

29. **Attitudes toward race among Americans.** In June 2008, a Princeton Survey Research group asked a sample of 1,984 Americans this question:

In your view, is the growing variety of ethnic and racial groups in the U.S. very good, good, bad or very bad for the country?

The following table lists the survey results listed at pollingreport.com. If we expect to observe equal frequencies, then compute a chi-square goodness-of-fit test at a .05 level of significance. Decide whether to retain or reject the null hypothesis.

Very Good	Good	Bad	Very Bad	Unsure
381	1,022	301	140	160

30. **Issues, priorities, and politics.** In July 2008, an NBC News/Wall Street Journal poll asked a sample of Americans to state which issue (taken from a list) should be the top priority for the U.S. federal government. The following table lists the top three priorities cited most frequently according to those listed at pollingreport.com. If we expect to observe equal frequencies, then compute a chi-square goodness-of-fit test at a .05 level of significance. Decide whether to retain or reject the null hypothesis.

Job Creation/ Economic Growth	Energy and the Cost of Gas	The War in Iraq
231	201	161

31. **Gender and depression.** Altamura, Dell'Osso, Vismara, and Mundo (2008) measured the relationship between gender and duration of untreated illness (DUI) among a sample of those suffering from major depressive disorder (MDD). The following table lists the observed frequencies from this study. Compute a chi-square test for independence at a .05 level of significance. Decide whether to retain or reject the null hypothesis.

		Duration of Untreated Illness		
		DUI ≤ 12 Months	DUI > 12 Months	
Gender	Men	20	5	25
	Women	55	33	88
		75	38	$N = 113$

32. **Gender discrimination among the elderly.** Keskinoglu and colleagues (2007) studied gender discrimination among the elderly. As part of their study, they recorded whether participants were involved in or made decisions concerning personal income and earnings (personal income) and whether they were exposed to negative gender discrimination. The following table lists the observed frequencies from this study. Compute a chi-square test for independence at a .05 level of significance. Decide whether to retain or reject the null hypothesis.

		Negative Gender Discrimination		
		Yes	No	
Personal Income	Yes	32	71	103
	No	26	19	45
		58	90	$N = 148$

NOTE: Answers for even numbers are in Appendix C.

Nonparametric Tests

Tests for Ordinal Data

LEARNING OBJECTIVES

After reading this chapter, you should be able to:

1. Explain why ordinal data are computed using nonparametric tests.

2. Compute the one-sample and related samples sign test and interpret the results.

3. Compute the normal approximation for the sign test.

4. Compute the Wilcoxon signed-ranks *T* test and interpret the results.

5. Compute the normal approximation for the Wilcoxon signed-ranks *T* test.

6. Compute the Mann-Whitney *U* test and interpret the results.

7. Compute the normal approximation for the Mann-Whitney *U* test.

8. Compute the Kruskal-Wallis *H* test and interpret the results.

9. Compute the Friedman test and interpret the results.

10. Summarize the results of nonparametric tests for ordinal data in APA format.

11. Compute the related samples sign test, the Wilcoxon signed-ranks *T* test, the Mann-Whitney *U* test, the Kruskal-Wallis *H* test, and the Friedman test using SPSS.

18.1 TESTS FOR ORDINAL DATA

In Chapter 17, we described the use of nonparametric tests for nominal data. Nonparametric tests are also used for ordinal data, and in this chapter, we introduce several hypothesis tests adapted for analyzing the significance of ordinal data.

SCALES OF MEASUREMENT AND VARIANCE

When we computed a *t*-test and an analysis of variance (ANOVA), we found that each test used variance to measure the error or deviation of scores in a sample. However, as described in Chapter 17, variance can only meaningful convey differences when data are measured on a scale in which the distance that scores deviate from their mean is meaningful, and ordinal data do not meaningfully convey distance.

To show that ordinal data do not convey distance, suppose we measure four scores: 6, 8, 9, and 98. The variance of these scores measures the distance that the scores deviate from their mean. However, if we covert the scores to ranks, by ranking them from smallest to largest, the ranks would be 1, 2, 3, and 4. The ranks do not indicate the actual distance between the scores because the scores are now all one rank apart. Hence, ranked data, which is an ordinal scale measurement, do not covey the distance between scores; the data only indicate that one score is larger or smaller than another. The variance, then, can't be used to analyze data on an ordinal scale. In this chapter, we introduce five nonparametric hypothesis tests for ordinal data. These tests are used as alternatives to the parametric tests taught in Chapters 9, 10, 12, and 13. Each test taught in this chapter and the parametric test it replaces is listed in Table 18.1.

NOTE: The variance can't be used to analyze ranked data because ordinal data do not meaningfully convey distance.

TABLE 18.1 A list of each nonparametric test and its alternative parametric test to be described in this chapter.

Parametric Test	Nonparametric Test
One–independent sample *t*-test	Sign test
Two–independent sample *t*-test	Mann-Whitney *U* Test
Related samples *t*-test	The sign test and Wilcoxon signed-ranks T test
One-way between-subjects ANOVA	Kruskal-Wallis *H* test
One-way within-subjects ANOVA	Friedman test

MAKING SENSE: Reducing Variability

For the *t*-tests and ANOVA tests, we used the variance as a measure of error. Error was measured by the estimated standard error with the *t*-tests and by the mean square error with the ANOVA tests. For each test, the larger the variability in a study, the larger the error and the smaller the power to detect an effect (i.e., to decide to reject the null hypothesis). To illustrate, suppose we measure four scores: 2, 4, 6, and 40. One score, 40, is an outlier in this data set, which increases variability and reduces power. Now, suppose we convert these scores to ranks by ranking the lowest score as *1*, the next lowest as *2*, and so on. The original four scores and the ranks of those scores are as follows:

Original scores (outlier skews data and increases variability):

Sample ($n = 4$): 2, 4, 6, 40

Ranks (eliminates variability due to outliers):

Sample ($n = 4$): 1, 2, 3, 4

Notice that the outlier, 40, is gone. The data were reduced to ranks beginning at 1 and increasing incrementally one rank at a time. The key advantage of measuring ranked data is that it minimizes variability caused by outliers. This variability would be attributed to error if we computed a parametric test, thereby reducing the power to detect an effect. Because measuring ranked data minimizes variability, a test for ordinal data can actually increase the power to detect an effect when data are skewed with outliers.

MINIMIZING BIAS: TIED RANKS

There is one additional concern when measuring ordinal data: tied ranks. When tied ranks are present, this can bias the decision to reject or to retain the null hypothesis. To avoid bias, we average the tied ranks. The steps for averaging tied ranks are the same as those described for the Spearman rank-order correlation coefficient (see Chapter 15). To review the steps, suppose we record four ranks, where two ranks are tied: 1, 2, 2, and 3. To average the tied ranks, follow three steps:

NOTE: Tied ranks should be averaged before computing a nonparametric test.

1. Assume the ranks are in order. We treat the tied ranks as if they are not tied. That is, we treat ranks 2 and 2 as if they were ranked in numerical order: 2, then 3.

2. Compute the mean of the tied ranks. We average the tied ranks as if they are not tied. We add the ordered tied ranks and divide by the number of tied ranks we added:

$$\text{Mean rank} = \frac{\text{sum of tied ranks}}{\text{number of tied ranks added}} = \frac{2+3}{2} = 2.5.$$

We will replace the tied ranks with this average rank, 2.5.

3. Shift the remaining ranks accordingly. We averaged ranks 2 and 3, so the next rank is 4. Hence, the final list of ranks is 1, 2.5, 2.5, and 4.

We will avoid working with tied ranks in this chapter, although note that when the data include tied ranks, these three steps must be completed for all tied ranks before performing the hypothesis test.

LEARNING CHECK 1

1. Is the variance of ordinal scale data meaningful? Explain.

2. Nonparametric tests have greater power than parametric tests for what types of data?

3. Rewrite each of the following rankings after averaging the tied ranks.
   a. 1, 2, 3, 4, 4, 5, 6
   b. 1, 2, 3, 3, 3, 4, 5
   c. 1, 1, 2, 2, 3, 3, 4

Answers: 1. No, because ordinal data do not meaningfully convey distance; 2. Data with outliers or skewed data sets; 3. (a) 1, 2, 3, 4.5, 4.5, 6, 7; (b) 1, 2, 4, 4, 4, 6, 7; (c) 1.5, 1.5, 3.5, 3.5, 5.5, 5.5, 7.

18.2 THE SIGN TEST

A nonparametric alternative to the one–independent sample *t*-test and the related samples *t*-test is the **sign test.** In this section, we describe how to use the sign test as an alternative to these parametric tests. The sign test is used to find the binomial probability that an observed number of scores fall above or below the median.

DEFINITION

The **sign test** is a statistical procedure used to determine the binomial probability that an observed number of scores fall above and below the median (one sample) or are positive and negative (related samples). The sign test is used as a nonparametric alternative to the one–independent sample *t*-test and the related samples *t*-test.

ONE-SAMPLE SIGN TEST

NOTE: To compute a one-sample sign test, count the number of scores above and below the median. The larger number is the test statistic.

We begin the sign test by reducing all measures to pluses and minuses. We assign a plus sign (+) to any score above the median; we assign a negative sign (–) to any score below the median using the one-sample sign test. In doing so, we are converting measured values to ordinal data, with a plus indicating a value greater than a minus. The test statistic (x) is the number of pluses or the number of minuses, whichever occurs more often. For a one-sample sign test, the null hypothesis is that there are an equal number of scores above and below the median (so, an equal number of pluses and minuses), as illustrated in Figure 18.1. In this section, we compute the one-sample sign test in Example 18.1, and we compute the related samples sign test in Example 18.2.

EXAMPLE 18.1

A researcher finds that the median body mass index (BMI) score in the general U.S. population is 28.3. The BMI is used as a measure of health, where higher scores indicate greater health risks. The researcher hypothesizes that professional athletes will have lower BMI scores than the general U.S. population, and records the BMI scores for six professional athletes, listed in Table 18.2. Conduct a one-sample sign test using a .05 level of significance.

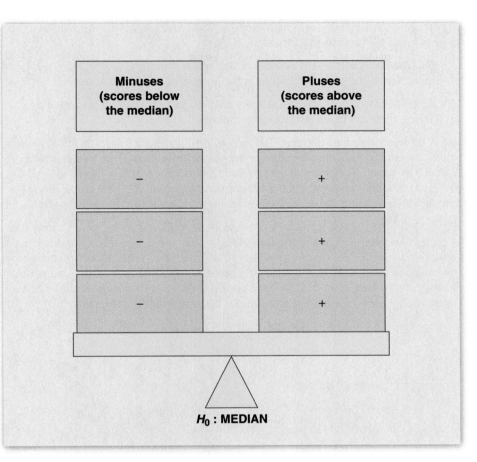

FIGURE 18.1

The null hypothesis for the one-sample sign test is that an equal number of scores will fall above and below the median, which occurs when an equal number of scores are positive and negative. The fulcrum represents the null hypothesis in this illustration.

TABLE 18.2 The difference between the BMI scores in the sample and the median BMI score in the general population (as stated by the null hypothesis). Only the sign of the difference is needed to make this test.

Sport Athlete	BMI Score in Sample	BMI Score in General Population	Difference
Golfer	29.8	28.3	+
Basketball player	24.5	28.3	−
Baseball player	28.3	28.3	0 (discard)
Swimmer	23.2	28.3	−
Hockey player	27.6	28.3	−
UFC fighter	28.0	28.3	−

Step 1: State the hypotheses. The median is 28.3, and we are testing whether this value is lower for professional athletes:

H_0: Median = 28.3   The number of BMI scores above and below 28.3 is the same. Hence, there is no difference in the number of pluses and minuses.

H_1: Median < 28.3   There are more BMI scores below 28.3 than above it. Hence, there are more minuses than pluses.

Step 2: Set the criteria for a decision. The level of significance for this test is .05. To set the criteria, we refer to a distribution of binomial probabilities when $n = 6$, which is given in Table B.8 in Appendix B. We will refer to Table B.8 in Appendix B in Step 4 to see if the binomial probability of obtaining the test statistic is less than .05. If the probability is less than .05, then we reject the null hypothesis; otherwise, we retain the null hypothesis.

Step 3: Compute the test statistic. To compute the test statistic, we assign a plus sign to each value above 28.3 (the median), assign a negative sign to each value below 28.3, and discard or get rid of any values that equal 28.3. Table 18.2 lists the pluses and minuses. If the null hypothesis is true, then we should find the same number of pluses and minuses. Most BMI scores were assigned a negative sign, as illustrated in Figure 18.2. For this reason, the test statistic is the number of minuses:

Test statistic: $x = 4$ minuses.

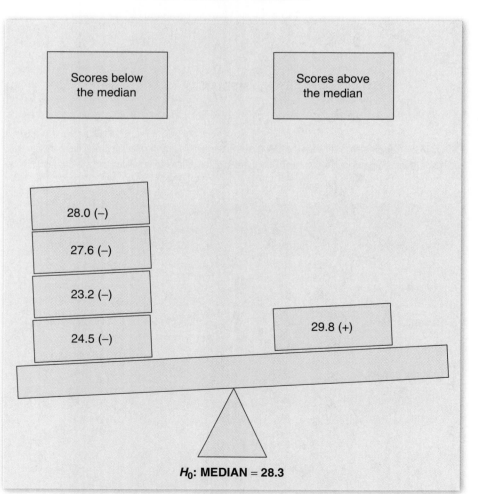

FIGURE 18.2

The number of pluses and minuses in Example 18.1. In this example, the scale is obviously tipped to the negative end of the scale.

Step 4: Make a decision. To make a decision we find the probability of obtaining at least $x = 4$ when $n = 6$. Because there are only two outcomes of interest (pluses and minuses), we use the list of binomial probabilities given in Table B.8 in Appendix B to make a decision. The table shows the binomial probability distribution of x, for samples ranging in size from 2 to 20. For $n = 6$ in this example, search down the column at $n = 6$ and across the row at $x = 4$. The probability of obtaining at least four scores below the median is the sum of the probabilities at $x = 4$, $x = 5$, and $x = 6$:

$$p = 0.234 + .094 + .016 = 0.344.$$

In Example 18.1, $p = .344$ is larger than the level of significance, $\alpha = .05$. The decision is to retain the null hypothesis. We conclude that the median BMI score of professional athletes is the same as the general American population. If we were to report this result in a research journal, it would look something like this:

> In a sample of six athletes, the one-sample sign test showed no evidence that the median BMI score of professional athletes differs from that in the general U.S. population, $x = 4$, $p > .05$.

NOTE: There are two possible outcomes for a one-sample sign test: pluses (scores above the median) and minuses (scores below the median). For this reason, we use a binomial distribution to determine the probability of outcomes for this test.

RELATED SAMPLES SIGN TEST

When the sign test is used to compare differences between two related samples, we call it the related samples sign test. The related samples sign test can be used as a nonparametric alternative to the related samples *t*-test. We will compute the related samples sign test in Example 18.2.

An instructor notices an increase in student outbursts during class. To test this observation, she compares the difference in the number of student outbursts in a class of 11 students taught by a substitute teacher one day and by a full-time teacher the next day. Table 18.3 shows the number of outbursts in each class. She hypothesizes that there will be more outbursts in the class taught by the substitute teacher. Conduct the related samples sign test using a .05 level of significance.

EXAMPLE 18.2

Step 1: State the hypotheses. The null hypothesis and alternative hypothesis are as follows:

H_0: Pluses = Minuses   Half the students will show more outbursts in the class taught by the substitute teacher, and half will show more outbursts in the class taught by the full-time teacher. Hence, the number of pluses and minuses will be the same.

H_1: Pluses > Minuses   More students will show more outbursts in the class taught by the substitute teacher than in the class taught by the full-time teacher. Hence, there will be more pluses than minuses.

Step 2: Set the criteria for a decision. The level of significance for this test is .05. The test statistic is again the number of pluses or minuses, whichever occurs more often. We will refer to Table B.8 in Appendix B in Step 4 to see if the binomial probability of obtaining the test statistic is less than .05. If the probability is less than .05, then we reject the null hypothesis; otherwise, we retain the null hypothesis.

TABLE 18.3 The difference between the number of outbursts in a classroom with a substitute teacher and a full-time teacher. Only the sign of the difference is needed to make this test.

Student	Substitute Teacher	Full-Time Teacher	Difference
1	3	2	+
2	2	0	+
3	5	4	+
4	3	3	0 (discard)
5	4	2	+
6	2	0	+
7	0	2	–
8	3	1	+
9	1	0	+
10	6	4	+
11	4	3	+

Step 3: Compute the test statistic. To compute the test statistic, we subtract across the rows in Table 18.3, which lists the pluses and minuses. Assign a plus sign (+) for positive differences and a negative sign (–) for negative differences. If the difference is 0, then discard the value. If the null hypothesis is true, then we should find the same number of pluses and minuses. Because most differences in this study were positive, as illustrated in Figure 18.3, the test statistic is the number of pluses:

$$\text{Test statistic: } x = 9 \text{ pluses.}$$

Step 4: Make a decision. To make a decision, we find the probability of obtaining at least $x = 9$ when $n = 11$ pairs of scores. To find the binomial probability, we search down the column at $n = 11$ and across the row at $x = 9$ in Table B.8 in Appendix B. The probability of obtaining at least nine positive scores is the sum of the probabilities at $x = 9$, $x = 10$, and $x = 11$:

$$p = 0.027 + .005 + \text{---} = 0.032.$$

The missing value for $n = 11$ is negligible, meaning that the probability is less than or equal to .0005. Probabilities less than or equal to .0005 are omitted from the table. In Example 18.2, $p = .032$ is smaller than the level of significance, $p = .05$. The decision is to reject the null hypothesis. If we were to report this result in a research journal, it would look something like this:

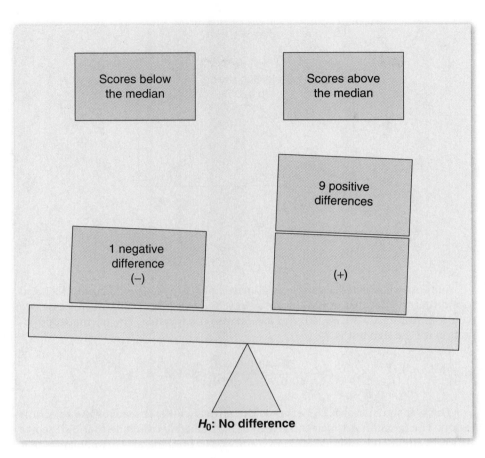

FIGURE 18.3

The number of pluses and minuses in Example 18.2. In this example, the scale is obviously tipped to the positive end of the scale.

In a sample of 11 students, the related samples sign test showed that outbursts were more common in a class taught by a substitute teacher compared to a class taught by a full-time teacher, $x = 9$, $p < .05$.

THE NORMAL APPROXIMATION FOR THE SIGN TEST

With larger samples, the binomial distribution approximates a normal distribution (see Chapter 6). Therefore, when we have a large sample size, we can approximate the binominal probabilities of the sign test using the following formula:

$$z = \frac{x - np}{\sqrt{np(1-p)}}.$$

NOTE: With larger samples, a binominal distribution approximates a normal distribution. For this reason, the normal approximation can be used to compute the sign test.

In the formula, x is the value of the test statistic, n is the sample size, and p is the probability that we obtain scores above or below the median when the null hypothesis is true. The null hypothesis is that the number of pluses and minuses will be equal, so $p = .50$ for this test. We will use the normal approximation formula for Example 18.1. We compute a two-tailed test at a .05 level of significance, so the critical values for this test are $z = \pm 1.96$. Figure 18.4 shows the z-distribution, with rejection regions beyond the critical values.

FIGURE 18.4

The critical values and rejection region for a two-tailed test at a .05 level of significance. If the test statistic exceeds the critical values, then we choose to reject the null hypothesis; otherwise, we retain the null hypothesis.

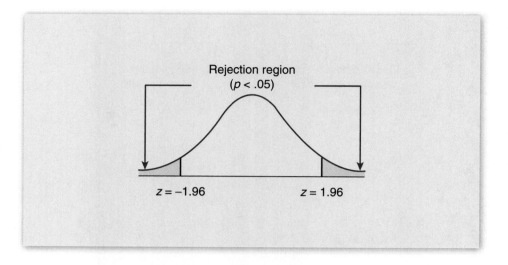

Suppose we selected a sample of 40 participants ($n = 40$) in Example 18.1 and found that the number of BMI scores below 28.3 was 30 ($x = 30$). In this case, we would substitute $x = 30$, $n = 40$, and $p = .50$ into the formula. The normal approximation for the sign test is

$$z = \frac{30 - 40(0.50)}{\sqrt{40(0.50)(1 - 0.50)}} = 3.162.$$

The test statistic of 3.162 exceeds the critical value; it reaches the rejection region. The decision is to reject the null hypothesis. We conclude that BMI scores are lower among professional athletes compared to the general U.S. population. For a related samples sign test, the normal approximation can be used as well, where n is the number of pairs of scores measured.

18.3 SPSS IN FOCUS: THE RELATED SAMPLES SIGN TEST

There is no command in SPSS to compute a one-sample sign test, but there is a command to compute a related samples sign test. In Example 18.2, we concluded that "outbursts were more common in a class taught by a substitute teacher compared to a class taught by a full-time teacher, $x = 9$, $p < .05$." Let's confirm this conclusion using SPSS.

1. Click on the **variable view** tab and enter *substitute* in the **name column;** enter *fulltime* in the name column below it. In the **decimals column**, reduce the value to 0 for both rows.

2. Click on the **data view** tab. Enter the number of outbursts for each variable that is listed in the middle two columns of Table 18.3.

3. Go to the **menu bar** and click **Analyze,** then **Nonparametric tests** and **2 Related Samples . . .** to display the dialog box shown in Figure 18.5.

4. Using the arrows, move *fulltime* into the **Test Pairs** box, and move *substitute* into the same box, as shown in Figure 18.5. In the **Test Type** box, make sure **Sign** is checked and **Wilcoxon** is unchecked.

5. Select **Paste** and click the **Run** command.

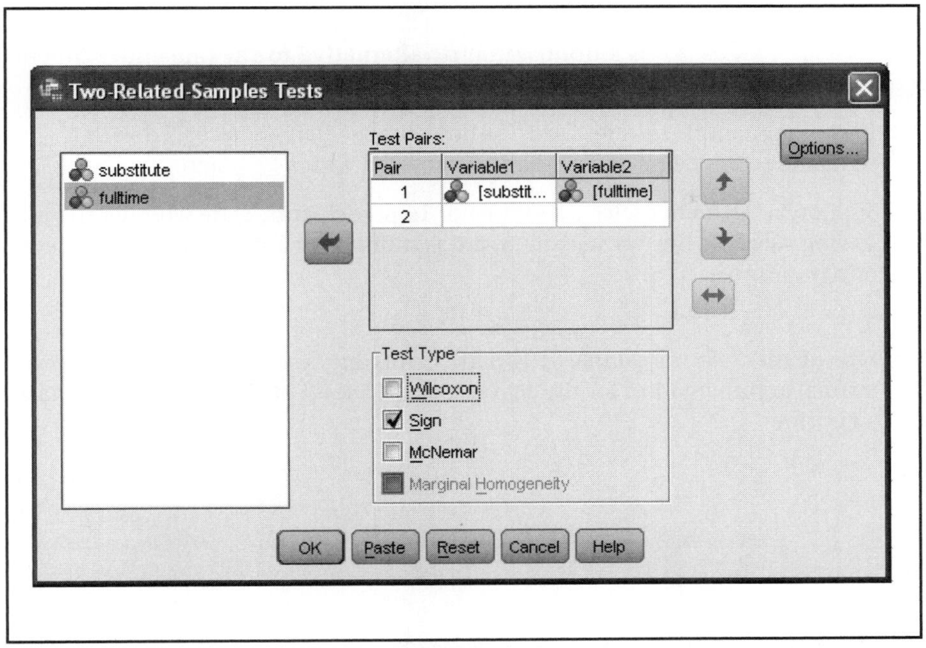

FIGURE 18.5

SPSS dialog box in Steps 3 and 4.

TABLE 18.4 SPSS output table for the related samples sign test.

Frequencies

		N
fulltime - substitute	Negative Differences[a]	1
	Positive Differences[b]	9
	Ties[c]	1
	Total	11

a. fulltime < substitute
b. fulltime > substitute
c. fulltime = substitute

Test Statistics[b]

	fulltime - substitute
Exact Sig. (2-tailed)	.021[a]

a. Binomial distribution used.
b. Sign Test

The SPSS output table, shown in Table 18.4, shows the number of positive differences, negative differences, and ties in the **Frequencies** box. The p value, but not the test statistic, is given in the **Test Statistics** box. In this example, the sample size was $n = 11$, and SPSS will only give the value of the test statistic for the sign test when $n > 25$.

LEARNING CHECK 2

1. _____ is a nonparametric alternative to the one–independent sample *t*-test and the related samples *t*-test.

2. In the one-sample sign test, scores above the median are recorded with a ____ sign, and scores below the median are recorded with a ____ sign.

3. Suppose a researcher selects a sample of 16 participants. State whether the following values of the test statistic, *x*, are significant for a sign test. Use a .05 level of significance.

   a. *x* = 8   b. *x* = 12   c. *x* = 15

4. A researcher selects a sample of 30 participants and records *x* = 24. Compute the normal approximation for the sign test at a .05 level of significance, and make a decision.

Answers: 1. The sign test; 2. Plus, Minus; 3. (a) Not significant, (b) Significant, (c) Significant;

$$4.\ z = \frac{24 - 30(0.5)}{\sqrt{30(0.5)(1 - 0.5)}} = 3.286.\ \text{Decision: Reject the null hypothesis.}$$

18.4 THE WILCOXON SIGNED-RANKS T TEST

NOTE: The Wilcoxon signed-ranks T test compares differences in the total ranks in two related groups.

A more popular nonparametric alternative to the related samples *t*-test is the **Wilcoxon signed-ranks T test.** This test is used to determine whether the total ranks in two related groups are significantly different. To compute the Wilcoxon signed-ranks T test, we follow three steps:

Step 1: Rank each difference score regardless of the sign.

Step 2: Separate the ranks into two groups: those associated with positive differences (+) and those associated with negative differences (–).

Step 3: Sum the ranks in each group. The smaller total is the test statistic (T).

The null hypothesis for the Wilcoxon signed-ranks T test is that there is no difference in ranks between groups. The alternative hypothesis is that there is a difference in ranks between groups. In Example 18.3, we will compute the Wilcoxon signed-ranks T test.

DEFINITION

The **Wilcoxon signed-ranks T test** is a statistical procedure used to determine whether the total ranks in two related groups are significantly different. The Wilcoxon signed-ranks T test is used as a nonparametric alternative to the related samples *t*-test.

EXAMPLE 18.3

A researcher measures the number of cigarettes patients smoked (per day) in a sample of 12 patients before and 6 months following diagnosis of heart disease. Table 18.5 shows the pre- and postdiagnosis results. Test whether patients significantly reduced smoking 6 months following diagnosis using the Wilcoxon signed-ranks T test at a .05 level of significance.

TABLE 18.5 The number of cigarettes smoked per day before (column a) and six months following (column b) diagnosis of heart disease. The difference in cigarette use before and following diagnosis (column c) and the ranking of the differences (column d) are also shown.

Cigarettes Smoked Per Day			
Before Diagnosis (a)	Following Diagnosis (b)	Difference (c)	Rank (d)
23	20	3	3
12	16	−4	4
11	10	1	1
15	0	15	9
25	5	20	11
20	8	12	8
11	0	11	7
9	15	−6	6
13	8	5	5
15	13	2	2
30	12	18	10
21	0	21	12

Step 1: Rank each difference score regardless of the sign. The difference between columns (a) and (b) in Table 18.5 is given in column (c) of the table. In column (d), all numbers are treated as positive numbers, and the difference scores are ranked in numerical order. Rankings begin with the lowest nonnegative difference score (1) and continue incrementally until all difference scores have been ranked.

Step 2: Separate the ranks into two groups. In this step, use the sign of the difference scores in column (c) to sort the ranks into positive and negative groups. If a difference score is negative in column (c), then assign the corresponding rank in column (d) to the Negatives group. If a difference score is positive in column (c), then assign the corresponding rank in column (d) to the Positives group. Table 18.6 shows the result of this procedure. Notice that the ranks from column (d) in Table 18.5 are assigned to each group and not the original difference scores.

Step 3: Sum the ranks in each group. Table 18.6 shows the sum of ranks for each group. The smaller total is the test statistic, which in this example is T = 10. To determine whether this result is significant, we compare the value of T to the critical

TABLE 18.6 Assigning ranks to groups. The ranks associated with positive differences are in the Positives group; ranks associated with negative differences are in the Negatives group. The smaller group total is the test statistic (T = 10).

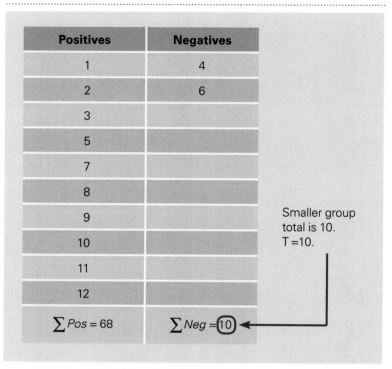

Positives	Negatives
1	4
2	6
3	
5	
7	
8	
9	
10	
11	
12	
$\sum Pos = 68$	$\sum Neg = 10$

Smaller group total is 10. T = 10.

value that is listed in Table B.9 in Appendix B. The table is organized with the level of significance for one- and two-tailed tests placed across the columns and sample size listed down the rows. The critical value for a two-tailed test with $n = 12$ at a .05 level of significance is 13.

To decide whether to retain or reject the null hypothesis, we compare the value of the test statistic T to the critical value of 13. When the test statistic T is smaller than the critical value, we reject the null hypothesis; otherwise, we retain the null hypothesis. Because the test statistic (T = 10) is smaller than the critical value, we reject the null hypothesis. If we were to report this result in research journal, it would look something like this:

> In a sample of 12 patients, the Wilcoxon signed-ranks T test showed that patients significantly reduced their cigarette use 6 months following diagnosis of heart disease, T = 10, $p < .05$.

INTERPRETATION OF THE TEST STATISTIC T

In the Wilcoxon signed-ranks T test, the smaller the test statistic, the more likely we are to reject the null hypothesis. Notice that this is the first hypothesis test with this decision rule. The reason is that when most of the ranks are given to one group, the sum of the leftover ranks is small. This was the case in Example 18.3, where most ranks were assigned to the Positives group, so the sum of ranks left over in the Negatives group was small (T = 10). A smaller value of T reflects larger differences between groups, meaning that smaller values of T are less likely to occur if the null hypothesis is true.

NOTE: Using a Wilcoxon signed-ranks T test, the smaller the value of the test statistic, T, the more likely we are to reject the null hypothesis.

THE NORMAL APPROXIMATION FOR THE WILCOXON T

With large samples, we can use the normal approximation of the Wilcoxon signed-ranks T test to find the probability of obtaining the test statistic T. The null hypothesis for the normal approximation test is that positive and negative difference scores are associated with equal ranks. When the null hypothesis is true, the test statistic for the Wilcoxon signed-ranks T test has a mean and standard deviation equal to

$$\text{Mean: } \mu_T = \frac{n(n+1)}{4}.$$

$$\text{Standard deviation: } \sigma_T = \sqrt{\frac{n(n+1)(2n+1)}{24}}.$$

The test statistic for the Wilcoxon signed-ranks T test corresponds to a z-distribution and takes the basic form of a z-transformation:

$$z = \frac{T - \mu_T}{\sigma_T}.$$

In Example 18.3, we will compute the normal approximation formula for a two-tailed test at a .05 level of significance. The critical values for this test are $z = \pm1.96$. In this example, T = 10 and n = 12. Once we know T and n, we can substitute values for the mean and the standard deviation into the test statistic. The mean and the standard deviation for the normal approximation test are

$$\mu_T = \frac{12(12+1)}{4} = 39.$$

$$\sigma_T = \sqrt{\frac{12(12+1)(2(12)+1)}{24}} = 12.75.$$

We substitute T = 10, μ_T = 39, and σ_T = 12.75 into the z-statistic formula:

$$z = \frac{10-39}{12.75} = -2.28.$$

The obtained value of –2.28 exceeds the critical value of –1.96; it reaches the rejection region. The decision is to reject the null hypothesis. This analysis showed that patients significantly reduced their cigarette use following diagnosis.

18.5 SPSS IN FOCUS: THE WILCOXON SIGNED-RANKS T TEST

In Example 18.3, we concluded that "patients significantly reduced their cigarette use 6 months following diagnosis of heart disease, $z = -2.28$, $p < .05$." Let's confirm this conclusion using SPSS.

1. Click on the **variable view** tab and enter *before* in the **name column;** enter *after* in the name column below it. In the **decimals column**, reduce the value to 0 for both rows.

2. Click on the **data view** tab. Enter the number of cigarettes for each variable that is listed in the first two columns in Table 18.5. SPSS will automatically convert these to ranks and organize them into groups.

3. Go to the **menu bar** and click **Analyze,** then **Nonparametric tests** and **2 Related Samples . . .** to display a dialog box.

4. Using the arrows in the dialog box, move *before* into the **Test Pairs** box and move *after* into the same box. In the **Test Type** box, make sure **Wilcoxon** is checked (this option should be checked by default).

5. Select **Paste** and click the **Run** command.

The SPSS output table, shown in Table 18.7, displays the number of positive and negative ranks, the mean ranks, and the sum of ranks in the **Ranks** box. The

TABLE 18.7   SPSS output table for the Wilcoxon signed-ranks T test.

Ranks

		N	Mean Rank	Sum of Ranks
after - before	Negative Ranks	10[a]	6.80	68.00
	Positive Ranks	2[b]	5.00	10.00
	Ties	0[c]		
	Total	12		

a. after < before
b. after > before
c. after = before

Test Statistics[b]

	after - before
Z	-2.275[a]
Asymp. Sig. (2-tailed)	.023

a. Based on positive ranks.
b. Wilcoxon Signed Ranks Test

test statistic for the normal approximation of this test and the *p* value are given in the **Test Statistics** box. SPSS will compute the normal approximation for the Wilcoxon signed-ranks T test, regardless of the sample size.

LEARNING CHECK 3

1. _____ is a nonparametric alternative to the related samples *t*-test.

2. True or false: In the Wilcoxon signed-rank T test, the larger the value of the test statistic T, the more likely we are to reject the null hypothesis.

3. In a sample of 11 participants, state whether each of the following values of T is significant using a .05 level of significance.

   a. T = 8   b. T = 10   c. T = 15

4. A researcher computes the Wilcoxon signed-ranks T test using a sample of 15 participants and records T = 25. Compute the normal approximation for the Wilcoxon signed-ranks T test at a .05 level of significance and decide whether to retain or reject the null hypothesis.

THE MANN-WHITNEY *U* TEST   13.2

A nonparametric alternative to the two–independent sample *t*-test is the Mann-Whitney *U* test. This test is used to determine whether the total ranks in two independent groups are significantly different. The steps for computing the Mann-Whitney *U* test are similar to those for the Wilcoxon signed-ranks T test. To compute the Mann-Whitney *U* test, we follow three steps:

> Step 1: Combine scores from both samples and rank them in numerical order. (Keep track of the group that scores came from.)
>
> Step 2: Assign points when a score in one group outranks scores in another group.
>
> Step 3: Sum the points in each group to find the test statistic (*U*). The smaller total is the test statistic.

The **Mann-Whitney *U* test** is a statistical procedure used to determine whether the dispersion of ranks in two independent groups is equal. The Mann-Whitney *U* test is used as a nonparametric alternative to the two–independent sample *t*-test.

DEFINITION

The null hypothesis for the Mann-Whitney *U* test is that the ranks in two groups are equally dispersed. The alternative hypothesis is that the ranks in two groups are not equally dispersed. Think of dispersion in terms of a deck of playing cards. There are 26 black cards and 26 red cards in a deck of 52 playing cards. If we

NOTE: The Mann-Whitney U test compares the dispersion of ranks in two independent groups.

shuffle the deck and spread out the cards, the black and red cards should be evenly dispersed; that is, the same number of black and red cards should be in the front, middle, and end of the deck. This outcome of even dispersion would be the null hypothesis for this test. The more lopsided the dispersion, the more likely we are to reject the null hypothesis. In Example 18.4, we will compute the Mann-Whitney U test.

EXAMPLE 18.4

A business owner measured the job satisfaction of his day-shift and night-shift employees. Employees rated their job satisfaction on a rating scale from 1 (*not satisfied at all*) to 100 (*completely satisfied*). Table 18.8 lists each worker's rating. Test whether ratings of job satisfaction differed between these two groups using the Mann-Whitney U test at a .05 level of significance.

TABLE 18.8 Job satisfaction scores among day-shift (D) and night-shift (N) employees.

Day Shift (D)	Night Shift (N)
88	24
72	55
93	70
67	60
62	50

Step 1: Combine scores from both samples. Treat all scores as if they came from a single group and list them in numerical order, as shown in Table 18.9, column (a). Keep track of the original group that scores came from—this information is needed in Step 2. The groups are shown in column (b) of Table 18.9, with the letter D listed next to each score in the day-shift group and the letter N listed next to each score in the night-shift group.

Step 2: Award points when a score in one group outranks scores in another group. We assign each score points based on how many scores in the other group that the score outranks. The number of points assigned is equal to the number of scores that it outranks in the other group. For example, 5 points were assigned to each of the top three scores because each of the top three scores from the day-shift group (D) outranked all five scores from the night-shift group (N). The largest score from the night shift outranked only two scores from the day shift, so it was assigned 2 points. The next two scores from the day shift outranked four scores from the night shift, so each was assigned 4 points. The last four night-shift scores failed to outrank any scores from the day shift, so those scores were not assigned points.

TABLE 18.9 Group satisfaction scores are combined in numerical order. Column (b) lists the group that the scores came from. Points are assigned whenever a score from one group is ranked higher than the other.

(a) Score	(b) Group	(c) Points
93	D	5
88	D	5
72	D	5
70	**N**	**2**
67	D	4
62	D	4
60	**N**	—
55	**N**	—
50	**N**	—
24	**N**	—

TABLE 18.10 Assigning points to groups. The points assigned to each group are summed. The smaller group total is the test statistic ($U = 2$).

Day Shift (D)	Night Shift (N)
5	2
5	—
5	—
4	—
4	—
$\sum$ points = 23	$\sum$ points = 2

Smaller group total is 2: $U = 2$

Step 3: Sum the points in each group to find the test statistic (U). Table 18.10 reorganizes the data into groups. Group D was assigned a total of 23 points, and Group N was assigned 2 points. The smaller total is the test statistic:

$$\text{Test statistic: } U = 2.$$

To decide whether to retain or reject the null hypothesis, we compare the value of the test statistic to the critical value found in Table B.10 in Appendix B. The critical value is located at the interaction of the sample size for each group: The critical value for U is 2. When the test statistic is equal to or smaller than the critical value, we reject the null hypothesis; otherwise, we retain the null hypothesis. Because the test statistic ($U = 2$) is equal to the critical value, we reject the null hypothesis. If we were to report this result in a research journal, it would look something like this:

The Mann-Whitney U test showed that job satisfaction was significantly higher among day shift compared to night shift employees, $U = 2$, $p < .05$.

INTERPRETATION OF THE TEST STATISTIC U

For the Mann-Whitney U test, smaller values of U are associated with a greater likelihood of rejecting the null hypothesis. The null hypothesis for this test is that the ranks in two groups are equally dispersed. In terms of the groups in Example 18.4, the null hypothesis is that we should observe the following dispersion:

Expected distribution: D, N, D, N, D, N, D, N, D, N

The expected dispersion is an even dispersion of scores between Groups D (day shift) and N (night shift). When groups are dispersed in this way, the scores are similarly dispersed between groups. The more lopsided or uneven the dispersion, the larger the difference is between two groups. In terms of the groups in Example 18.4, the observed dispersion was as follows:

Observed distribution: D, D, D, N, D, D, N, N, N, N

NOTE: For a Mann-Whitney U test, the more uneven the dispersion of ranks between two independent groups, the more likely we are to reject the null hypothesis.

We observed that most scores, or job satisfaction ratings in Example 18.4, were larger in Group D than in Group N. This uneven dispersion resulted in a small value of U and a decision to reject the null hypothesis. This was the decision because smaller values of U reflect larger differences between groups, meaning that smaller values of U are less likely to occur if the null hypothesis is true.

COMPUTING THE TEST STATISTIC U

With large sample sizes, the steps to compute U can be tedious. When the sample size is large, the test statistic for two independent groups (A and B) can be computed using the following formulas for each group:

$$\text{Group A}: U_A = n_A n_B + \frac{n_A(n_A + 1)}{2} - \sum R_A.$$

$$\text{Group B}: U_B = n_A n_B + \frac{n_B(n_B + 1)}{2} - \sum R_B.$$

In the formulas, n_A and n_B are the sample size for each group, and R is the rank for each group. For Example 18.4, we will represent the day-shift group as Group A and the night-shift group as Group B. For Group A, the sum of the ranks is

$$\sum R_A = 1+2+3+5+6 = 17.$$

And the value of U is

$$U_A = 5(5) + \frac{5(5+1)}{2} - 17 = 23.$$

This is the same value of U given in Table 18.10 for the day-shift group. For Group B, the sum of the ranks is

$$\sum R_B = 4+7+8+9+10 = 38.$$

And the value of U is

$$U_B = 5(5) + \frac{5(5+1)}{2} - 38 = 2.$$

This is the same value of U given in Table 18.10 for the night shift group. The value of U_B is the test statistic because it is the smaller value. To make a decision, we compare the test statistic to the same critical value given in Table B.10 in Appendix B. The decision for this test is to reject the null hypothesis.

THE NORMAL APPROXIMATION FOR U

With large samples, we can use the normal approximation for the Mann-Whitney U test to find the probability of obtaining the test statistic. The null hypothesis for the normal approximation test is that scores are evenly dispersed between groups. When the null hypothesis is true, the test statistic for the Mann-Whitney U test has a mean and a standard deviation equal to

$$\text{Mean}: \mu_U = \frac{n_A n_B}{2}.$$

$$\text{Standard deviation}: \sigma_U = \sqrt{\frac{n_A n_B (n_A + n_B + 1)}{12}}.$$

The test statistic for the Mann-Whitney U test corresponds to a z-distribution and takes the basic form of a z-transformation:

$$z = \frac{U - \mu_U}{\sigma_U}.$$

In Example 18.4, we will compute the normal approximation formula for a two-tailed test at a .05 level of significance. The critical values for this test are

$z = \pm 1.96$. In this example, $U = 2$, $n_A = 5$, and $n_B = 5$. Once we know U, n_A, and n_B, we can substitute values of the mean and standard deviation into the test statistic. The mean and standard deviation for the normal approximation test are

$$\mu_U = \frac{5 \times 5}{2} = 12.50.$$

$$\sigma_U = \sqrt{\frac{5(5)(5+5+1)}{12}} = 4.79.$$

We substitute $U = 2$, $\mu_U = 12.50$, and $\sigma_U = 4.79$ into the z-statistic formula:

$$z = \frac{2 - 12.50}{4.79} = -2.19.$$

The obtained value of -2.19 exceeds the critical value of -1.96; it reaches the rejection region. The decision is to reject the null hypothesis. This analysis showed that job satisfaction was higher among day-shift compared to night-shift employees.

18.7 SPSS IN FOCUS: THE MANN-WHITNEY U TEST

In Example 18.4, we concluded that "job satisfaction was significantly higher among day-shift compared to night-shift employees, $U = 2$, $p < .05$." Let's confirm this conclusion using SPSS.

1. Click on the **variable view** tab and enter *groups* in the **name column;** enter *scores* in the name column below it. In the **decimals column,** reduce the value to 0 for all rows.

2. To label the *groups* variable, click on the small gray box with three dots in the **Values** column to display a **dialog box.** Enter *1* in the **value** cell and *day shift* in the **label** cell, and then click **add.** Then enter *2* in the **value** cell and *night shift* in the **label** cell, and then click **add.** Select **OK.**

3. Click on the **data view** tab to enter the data. In the *groups* column, enter *1* five times and *2* five times below that. In the *scores* column, list the scores that correspond to each group code. Hence, the scores 88, 72, 93, 67, and 62 should be listed next to a code of 1; the scores 24, 55, 70, 60, and 50 should be listed next to a code of 2 in the second column.

4. Go to the **menu bar** and click **Analyze,** then **Nonparametric Tests** and **2 Independent Samples,** to display a dialog box.

5. The **Mann-Whitney U** is selected by default in the dialog box. Using the arrows, move *scores* into the **Test Variable List** box and *groups* into the **Grouping Variable** box. Click **Define Groups . . .** to open a new dialog box.

6. In the new dialog box, enter *1* in the top cell and *2* in the bottom cell. Select **Continue.**

7. Select **Paste** and click the **Run** command.

The SPSS output table, shown in Table 18.11, shows the sample size, mean rank, and sum of ranks for each group in the **Ranks** box. The **Test Statistics** box lists the test statistic U (first row), the z-score for the normal approximation (third row), and the p value for a two-tailed test (fourth row).

TABLE 18.11   SPSS output table for the Mann-Whitney U test.

Ranks

	groups	N	Mean Rank	Sum of Ranks
scores	day shift	5	7.60	38.00
	night shift	5	3.40	17.00
	Total	10		

Test Statistics[b]

	scores
Mann-Whitney U	2.000
Wilcoxon W	17.000
Z	-2.193
Asymp. Sig. (2-tailed)	.028
Exact Sig. [2*(1-tailed Sig.)]	.032[a]

a. Not corrected for ties.
b. Grouping Variable: groups

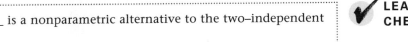

LEARNING CHECK 4

1. _____ is a nonparametric alternative to the two–independent sample t-test.

2. State the null hypothesis for the Mann-Whitney U test.

3. For a sample of 14 participants ($n = 7$ per group), state whether each of the following values of U is significant using a .05 level of significance.

   a. $U = 8$ b. $U = 12$ c. $U = 15$

4. A researcher computes the Mann-Whitney U test with $n = 25$ in each group and $U = 100$. Compute the normal approximation for the Mann-Whitney U test at a .05 level of significance and decide whether to retain or reject the null hypothesis.

Answers: 1. Mann-Whitney U test; 2. The ranks in two groups are equally dispersed; 3. (a) Significant, (b) Not significant, (c) Not significant; 4. Mean: $\mu_U = \dfrac{25(25)}{2} = 312.5$; Standard deviation: $\sigma_U = \sqrt{\dfrac{25(25)(25+25+1)}{12}} = 51.54$; Test statistic: $z = \dfrac{100 - 312.5}{51.54} = -4.12$. Decision: Reject the null hypothesis.

18.8 THE KRUSKAL-WALLIS *H* TEST

A nonparametric alternative to the one-way between-subjects ANOVA is the Kruskal-Wallis *H* test. This test is used to determine whether the total ranks in two or more independent groups are significantly different. To compute the Kruskal-Wallis *H* test, we follow three steps:

Step 1: Combine scores from each group and rank them in numerical order. (Keep track of the group that scores came from.)

Step 2: Sum the ranks for each group.

Step 3: Compute the test statistic (*H*).

DEFINITION

The **Kruskal-Wallis *H* test** is a statistical procedure used to determine whether the total ranks in two or more independent groups are significantly different. The Kruskal-Wallis *H* test is used as a nonparametric alternative to the one-way between-subjects ANOVA.

NOTE: The Kruskal-Wallis H test compares differences in the sum of ranks for two or more independent groups.

The null hypothesis for this test is that the sum of ranks in each group does not differ. The alternative hypothesis is that the sum of ranks in each group differs. When the null hypothesis is true and *n* is greater than or equal to 5 per group, the test statistic *H* is approximately distributed as a chi-square distribution with $k - 1$ degrees of freedom, where *k* is the number of groups. For this reason, we will use the chi-square distribution to make a decision for this test. In Example 18.5, we will compute the Kruskal-Wallis *H* test.

EXAMPLE 18.5

A researcher asks a sample of 15 students ($n = 5$ per group) to view and rate how effectively they think one of three short video clips promoted safe driving. The participants rated these clips from 1 (*not effective at all*) to 100 (*very effective*). Table 18.12 lists the ratings by participants in each group. Test whether ratings differ between groups using the Kruskal-Wallis *H* test at a .05 level of significance.

Step 1: Combine scores from each group and rank them in numerical order. Table 18.13a lists the ratings in numerical order (far-left column) and the

TABLE 18.12 Ratings of effectiveness for three different short safe driving video clips in a sample of 15 students.

Clip A	Clip B	Clip C
88	92	50
67	76	55
22	80	43
14	77	65
42	90	39

TABLE 18.13 The ranking of all scores irrespective of group assignment in Step 1 (a), and the sum of ranks for each group in Step 2 (b).

Rating	Group	Rank
92	Clip B	1
90	Clip B	2
88	Clip A	3
80	Clip B	4
77	Clip B	5
76	Clip B	6
67	Clip A	7
65	Clip C	8
55	Clip C	9
50	Clip C	10
44	Clip A	11
43	Clip C	12
39	Clip C	13
22	Clip A	14
14	Clip A	15

(a)

Clip A	Clip B	Clip C
3	1	81
7	2	92
11	4	104
14	5	125
15	6	136
$\sum R_1 = 50$	$\sum R_2 = 18$	$\sum R_3 = 52$

(b)

corresponding group that each rating came from (middle column). The ratings are ranked in order from most to least in the last column of the table. Keep track of the original group that scores came from—this information is needed in Step 2.

Step 2: Sum the ranks for each group. We reorganize the ranks listed in Table 18.13a by listing the ranks for each group in separate columns, as shown in the Table 18.13b. Sum the ranks in each group. The sum of ranks will be used to find the test statistic.

Step 3: Compute the test statistic (H). The formula for the test statistic of the Kruskal-Wallis H test is

$$H = \frac{12}{N(N+1)}\left(\sum \frac{R^2}{n}\right) - 3(N+1).$$

In the formula, N is the total sample size, n is the sample size per group, and R is the total rank in each group. In Example 18.5, $N = 15$, $n = 5$, and the total ranks are listed in Table 18.13b. When we substitute these values into the formula, the test statistic for the Kruskal-Wallis H is

$$H = \frac{12}{15(15+1)}\left(\frac{(50)^2}{5} + \frac{(18)^2}{5} + \frac{(52)^2}{5}\right) - 3(15+1)$$
$$= (.05)(500 + 64.80 + 540.80) - 48$$
$$= 55.28 - 48$$
$$= 7.28.$$

To find the critical values, we look in the chi-square table (Table B.7 in Appendix B) for a test with $k - 1$ degrees of freedom. Because there are three groups in Example 18.5, the degrees of freedom are $3 - 1 = 2$, and the critical value is 5.99, as shown in Figure 18.6. If the test statistic exceeds the critical value, then we reject the null hypothesis; otherwise, we retain the null hypothesis. The test statistic of 7.28 exceeds the critical value of 5.99; it reaches the rejection region. The decision is to reject the null hypothesis. If we were to report this result in a research journal, it would look something like this:

> The Kruskal-Wallis H test showed that rankings of three safe driving video clips were significantly different, $H = 7.28$, $p < .05$.

INTERPRETATION OF THE TEST STATISTIC H

To compute the test statistic for the Kruskal-Wallis H test, we rank scores listed in numerical order, then place the ranks back into groups. The null hypothesis for this

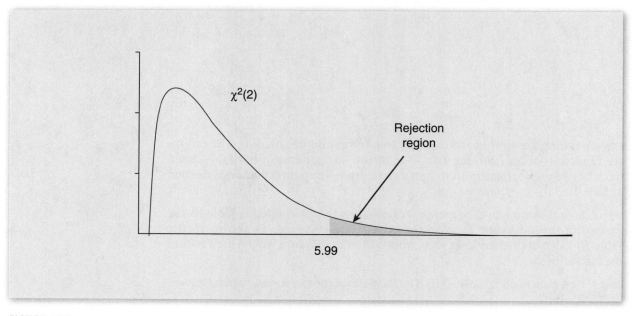

FIGURE 18.6

The critical value for the Kruskal-Wallis H test. In Example 18.5, the obtained value exceeds the critical value, so we reject the null hypothesis.

test is that the sum of ranks in each group does not differ. When the null hypothesis is true, the ranks will be evenly dispersed between groups. In Example 18.5, we had three groups (Clips A, B, and C). The null hypothesis, then, is that we should expect the following dispersion:

Expected distribution: A, B, C, A, B, C, A, B, C, A, B, C, A, B, C

The expected dispersion is an even dispersion of ranks between groups. When groups are dispersed in this way, the scores are similarly dispersed between groups. The more lopsided or uneven the dispersion, the larger the difference is between groups. In terms of the groups in Example 18.5, the observed dispersion was as follows:

Observed distribution: B, B, A, B, B, B, A, C, C, C, A, C, C, A, A

We observed that all five ratings for Clip B were in the top six ranks, which made this is a very lopsided distribution. When ranks are dispersed unevenly, the total ranks, R, will be very different between groups and result in a larger value of the test statistic H. Hence, larger values of H reflect larger differences between groups, meaning that larger values of H are less likely to occur if the null hypothesis is true.

NOTE: For a Kruskal-Wallis H test, the more uneven the dispersion of ranks between two or more independent groups, the more likely we are to reject the null hypothesis.

SPSS IN FOCUS: THE KRUSKAL-WALLIS *H* TEST   18.9

In Example 18.5, we concluded that "rankings of three safe driving video clips were significantly different, $H = 7.28$, $p < .05$." Let's confirm this conclusion using SPSS.

1. Click on the **variable view** tab and enter *groups* in the **name column;** enter *ratings* in the name column below it. In the **decimals column**, reduce the value to 0 for all rows.

2. To label the *groups* variable, click on the small gray box with three dots in the **Values** column to display a dialog box. In the **dialog box,** enter *1* in the value cell and *Clip A* in the label cell, and then click **add.** Then enter *2* in the value cell and *Clip B* in the label cell, and then click **add.** Then enter *3* in the value cell and *Clip C* in the label cell, and then click **add.** Select **OK.**

3. Click on the **data view** tab to enter the data. In the *groups* column, enter *1* five times, *2* five times below that, and *3* five times below that. In the *ratings* column, list the scores that correspond to each group code.

4. Go to the **menu bar** and click **Analyze,** then **Nonparametric Tests** and **k Independent Samples,** to display a dialog box.

5. The **Kruskal-Wallis H** option is selected by default. Using the arrows, move *ratings* into the **Test Variable List** box and *groups* into the **Grouping Variable** box. Click **Define Groups . . .** to open a new dialog box.

6. In the dialog box, enter *1* in the top cell and enter *3* in the bottom cell to identify the range of codes for the groups. Select **Continue.**

7. Select **Paste** and click the **Run** command.

TABLE 18.14 SPSS output table for the Kruskal-Wallis *H* test.

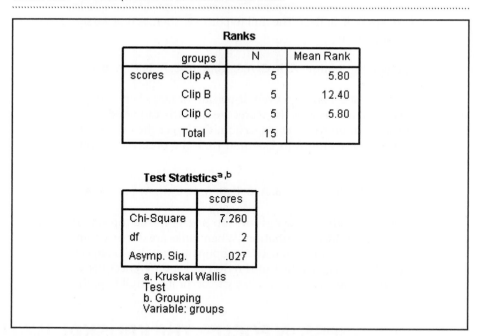

Ranks

	groups	N	Mean Rank
scores	Clip A	5	5.80
	Clip B	5	12.40
	Clip C	5	5.80
	Total	15	

Test Statistics[a,b]

	scores
Chi-Square	7.260
df	2
Asymp. Sig.	.027

a. Kruskal Wallis Test
b. Grouping Variable: groups

The SPSS output table, shown in Table 18.14, shows the sample size and mean rank per group in the **Ranks** box. The chi-square test statistic, the degrees of freedom, and the *p* value (Asymp. Sig.) are given in the **Test Statistics** box.

LEARNING CHECK 5

1. _____ is a nonparametric alternative to the one-way between-subjects ANOVA.

2. When the null hypothesis is true and the sample size per group is at least $n = 5$, the test statistic H approximates what kind of distribution?

3. For a study concerning the differences in five groups ($k = 5$), state whether each of the following values of H are significant at a .05 level of significance.
    a. $H = 8.00$ b. $H = 12.00$ c. $H = 15.00$

Answers: 1. Kruskal-Wallis H test; 2. Chi-square distribution; 3. (a) Not significant, (b) Significant, (c) Significant.

18.10 THE FRIEDMAN TEST

A nonparametric alternative to the one-way within-subjects ANOVA is the Friedman test. This test is used to determine whether the total ranks in two or more groups are significantly different when the same participants are observed in each group. To compute the Friedman test, we follow three steps:

Step 1: Rank scores across each row for each individual participant.

Step 2: Sum the ranks for each group.

Step 3: Compute the test statistic $\left(\chi_R^2\right)$.

The **Friedman test** is a statistical procedure used to determine whether the total ranks in two or more groups are significantly different when the same participants are observed in each group. The Friedman test is used as a nonparametric alternative to the one-way within-subjects ANOVA.

DEFINITION

The null hypothesis for the Friedman test is that the sum of ranks in each group does not differ. The alternative hypothesis is that the sum of ranks in each group differs. When the null hypothesis is true and n is greater than or equal to 5 per group, the test statistic for the Friedman test is approximately distributed as a chi-square distribution with $k - 1$ degrees of freedom, where k is the number of groups. For this reason, we will use the chi-square distribution to make a decision for this test. In Example 18.6, we will compute the Friedman test.

NOTE: The Friedman test compares differences in the sum of ranks in two or more related groups.

An obstetrician is concerned that women without health insurance will fail to make regular office visits during the course of their pregnancy. To test this concern, she selects a sample of seven expecting women who do not have health insurance and records the number of hospital visits made during each trimester of their pregnancy. The data are shown in Table 18.15a. Test whether the number of office visits during each trimester of pregnancy is different using the Friedman test at a .05 level of significance.

EXAMPLE 18.6

TABLE 18.15   The number of hospital visits expecting mothers made during each trimester of their pregnancy (a), and the rankings across the rows for each woman in Step 1 (b). In Step 2, the ranks in each group are summed.

Participant	Trimester				First	Second	Third
	First	Second	Third				
A	3	5	8	Scores converted to ranks for each participant	1	2	3
B	6	4	7		2	1	3
C	2	0	5		2	1	3
D	4	3	2		3	2	1
E	4	6	9		1	2	3
F	4	3	7		2	1	3
G	8	6	5		3	2	1
					$\sum R_1 = 14$	$\sum R_2 = 11$	$\sum R_3 = 17$

(a)   (b)

Step 1: Rank scores across each row for each individual participant. We rank the number of visits for each woman from least to most. For example, Participant A had 3, 5, and 8 visits. We rank these 1, 2, and 3, respectively. Participant B had 6, 4, and 7 visits. We rank these 2, 1, and 3, respectively. Table 18.15b shows the ranks for the number of visits for each woman. In the table, we rank across the rows for each individual woman.

Step 2: Sum the ranks for each group. Once all scores are ranked, we sum the ranks in each group or trimester for this study. In Table 18.15b, this means that we sum down the columns. The sum of the ranks will be used to compute the test statistic.

Step 3: Compute the test statistic $\left(\chi_R^2\right)$. The formula for the test statistic, χ_R^2, for the Friedman test is

$$\chi_R^2 = \frac{12}{nk(k+1)}\sum R^2 - 3n(k+1).$$

In the formula, R is the total ranks in each group, n is the sample size in each group, and k is the number of groups. In Example 18.6, $n = 7$, $k = 3$, and the total ranks are listed in Table 18.15b. When we substitute these values into the formula, the test statistic for the Freidman test is

$$\chi_R^2 = \frac{12}{7(3)(3+1)}\left((14)^2 + (11)^2 + (17)^2\right) - 3(7)(3+1)$$

$$= \frac{12}{84}(196 + 121 + 289) - 84$$

$$= (0.143)(606) - 84$$

$$= 2.658.$$

To find the critical values, we look in the chi-square table (Table B.7 in Appendix B) for a test with $k - 1$ degrees of freedom. Because there are three groups in Example 18.5, the degrees of freedom are $3 - 1 = 2$, and the critical value is 5.99. When the test statistic exceeds the critical value, we reject the null hypothesis; otherwise, we retain the null hypothesis. The test statistic of 2.658 does not exceed the critical value of 5.99; it fails to reach the rejection region. The decision is to retain the null hypothesis. If we were to report this result in a research journal, it would look something like this:

> The Friedman test showed no significant differences in the number of office visits made by women in each trimester of their pregnancy, $\chi_R^2(2) = 2.658$, $p > .05$.

INTERPRETATION OF THE TEST STATISTIC χ_R^2

NOTE: For a Friedman test, the more consistent the order of ranks across participants, the larger the group differences will be, and the more likely we are to reject the null hypothesis.

The Freidman test statistic reflects the consistency of ranks across groups. The more consistent the ranks, the larger the differences will be in the total ranks for each group, and the more likely we are to reject the null hypothesis. In Example 18.6, the most consistent situation would be when all women had the same order of ranks. For example, suppose the ranks for all women were 1, 2, 3 in consecutive semesters. In this situation, all ranks would be 1 in the first trimester, 2 in the second trimester, and 3 in the third trimester. The sum of the ranks for each trimester would be 7, 14, and 21, respectively, producing the largest group differences in total ranks and the largest value of the test statistic. Hence, larger values of χ_R^2 reflect larger differences between groups, meaning that larger values of χ_R^2 are less likely to occur if the null hypothesis is true.

SPSS IN FOCUS: THE FRIEDMAN TEST 18.11

In Example 18.6, we concluded that there are "no significant differences in the number of office visits made by women in each trimester of their pregnancy, $\chi_R^2(2) = 2.658, p > .05$." Let's confirm this conclusion using SPSS.

1. Click on the **variable view** tab and enter *first* in the **name column;** enter *second* in the name column below it; enter *third* in the name column below that. In the **decimals column**, reduce the value to 0 for all rows.

2. Click on the **data view** tab to enter the data. Enter the number of visits for the first, second, and third trimester in the appropriately labeled columns.

3. Go to the **menu bar** and click **Analyze,** then **Nonparametric Tests** and **k Related Samples,** to display a dialog box.

4. The **Friedman** option is selected by default. Use the arrows to move each variable into the **Test Variables** box.

5. Select **Paste** and click the **Run** command.

TABLE 18.16 SPSS output table for the Freidman test.

Ranks

	Mean Rank
first	2.00
second	1.57
third	2.43

Test Statistics[a]

N	7
Chi-Square	2.571
df	2
Asymp. Sig.	.276

a. Friedman Test

The SPSS output table, shown in Table 18.16, shows the mean ranks for each group in the **Ranks** box. The sample size per group (n), the chi-square test statistic, the degrees of freedom, and the p value (Asymp. Sig.) are given in the **Test Statistics** box. The chi-square statistic is a bit different in the SPSS output compared to our calculation because SPSS did not round and we did round to compute the test statistic.

LEARNING CHECK 6

1. _____ is a nonparametric alternative to the one-way within-subjects ANOVA.

2. When the null hypothesis is true and the sample size per group is at least $n = 5$, the test statistic χ_R^2 approximates what kind of distribution?

3. Suppose we test three groups (A, B, and C). All scores are ranked 1 in Group A, 2 in Group B, and 3 in Group C. In this study, what is the likely decision for a Freidman test? Explain.

3. For a study concerning the differences in ranks for four groups ($k = 4$), state whether each of the following values of χ_R^2 is significant at a .05 level of significance.

   a. $\chi_R^2 = 6.00$ b. $\chi_R^2 = 8.00$ c. $\chi_R^2 = 10.00$

Answers: 1. The Friedman test; 2. Chi-square distribution; 3. Reject the null hypothesis because this situation would produce the largest value of χ_R^2; 4. (a) Not significant, (b) Significant, (c) Significant.

18.12 APA IN FOCUS: REPORTING NONPARAMETRIC TESTS

To summarize any nonparametric test, you must report the test statistic, the degrees of freedom (if applicable), and the p value for the test. The degrees of freedom would be applicable for the Friedman test and the Kruskal-Wallis H test because both tests use the chi-square distribution to set the criteria for a decision. The sign test, the Wilcoxon signed-ranks T test, and the Mann-Whitney U test can be computed two ways because each test has a normal approximation alternative with large samples. For each test, you can report the original test statistic value (X for the sign test, T for the Wilcoxon signed-ranks T test, or U for the Mann-Whitney U test) or the z-score for the normal approximation of these tests.

CHAPTER SUMMARY ORGANIZED BY LEARNING OBJECTIVE

LO 1: Explain why ordinal data are computed using nonparametric tests.

- Variance can only meaningfully convey the distance that scores deviate from the mean when data are measured on an interval or ratio scale. Ordinal data do not meaningfully convey the distance that scores deviate from their mean. For this reason, nonparametric tests are most appropriate for analyzing ordinal data.

LO 2–3: Compute the one-sample and related samples sign test and interpret the results; compute the normal approximation for the sign test.

- The **sign test** is a statistical procedure used to determine the binomial probability that an observed number of scores fall above and below the median (one sample) or are positive and negative (related samples). This test is used as a nonparametric alternative to the one–independent sample *t*-test and the related samples *t*-test.
- For the one-sample sign test, count the number of scores above or below the median. Assign a plus sign to each value above the median, assign a negative sign to each value below the median, and discard values that equal the median. When the null hypothesis is true, the number of pluses and minuses will be the same; the larger the discrepancy between pluses and minuses, the more likely we are to reject the null hypothesis.
- For the related samples sign test, subtract pairs of scores for each participant. Count the number of difference scores that are positive and negative, and discard values that equal 0. When the null hypothesis is true, the number of positive and negative difference scores will be the same; the larger the discrepancy between positive and negative difference scores, the more likely we are to reject the null hypothesis.
- The formula for the normal approximation of the sign test is

$$z = \frac{x - np}{\sqrt{np(1-p)}}, \text{ where } p = .50.$$

LO 4–5: Compute the Wilcoxon signed-ranks T test and interpret the results; compute the normal approximation for the Wilcoxon signed-ranks T test.

- The **Wilcoxon signed-ranks T test** is a statistical procedure used to determine whether the total ranks in two related groups are significantly different. This test is used as a nonparametric alternative to the related samples *t*-test.
- The steps for completing the Wilcoxon signed-ranks T test are as follows:
  Step 1: Rank each difference score regardless of the sign.
  Step 2: Separate the ranks into two groups: those associated with positive differences (+) and those associated with negative differences (–).
  Step 3: Sum the ranks in each group. The smaller total is the test statistic.
- The null hypothesis for this test is that there is no difference in ranks between groups. The alternative hypothesis is that there is a difference in ranks between groups. The smaller the value of the test statistic, the more likely we are to reject the null hypothesis.
- The formula for the normal approximation of the Wilcoxon signed-rank T test is

$$z = \frac{T - \mu_T}{\sigma_T}, \text{ where } \mu_T = \frac{n(n+1)}{4},$$

$$\text{and } \sigma_T = \sqrt{\frac{n(n+1)(2n+1)}{24}}.$$

LO 6–7: Compute the Mann-Whitney *U* test and interpret the results; compute the normal approximation for the Mann-Whitney *U* test.

- The **Mann-Whitney *U* test** is a statistical procedure used to determine whether the dispersion of ranks in two independent groups is equal. This test is used as a nonparametric alternative to the two–independent sample *t*-test.
- The steps for completing this test are as follows:
  Step 1: Combine scores from both samples and rank them in numerical order. (Keep track of the group that scores came from.)

Step 2: Assign points when a score in one group outranks scores in another group.
Step 3: Sum the points in each group to find the test statistic (U). The smaller total is the test statistic.

- The null hypothesis for this test is that the ranks in two groups are equally dispersed. The alternative hypothesis is that the ranks in two groups are not equally dispersed. The smaller the value for the test statistic, the more likely we are to reject the null hypothesis.

- The formula for the normal approximation of the Mann-Whitney U test is

$$z = \frac{U - \mu_U}{\sigma_U}, \text{ where } \mu_U = \frac{n_A n_B}{2};$$

$$\sigma_U = \sqrt{\frac{n_A n_B (n_A + n_B + 1)}{12}}.$$

LO 8: Compute the Kruskal-Wallis H test and interpret the results.

- The **Kruskal-Wallis H test** is a statistical procedure used to determine whether the total ranks in two or more independent groups are significantly different. This test is used as a nonparametric alternative to the one-way between-subjects ANOVA.

- The steps for completing this test are as follows:
Step 1: Combine scores from each group and rank them in numerical order. (Keep track of the group that scores came from.)
Step 2: Sum the ranks for each group.
Step 3: Compute the test statistic (H):

$$H = \frac{12}{N(N+1)} \left(\sum \frac{R^2}{n} \right) - 3(N+1).$$

- The null hypothesis for this test is that the sum of ranks in each group does not differ. The alternative hypothesis is that the sum of ranks in each group differs. When the null hypothesis is true and n is greater than or equal to 5 per group, the test statistic H is approximately distributed as a chi-square distribution. For this reason, we use the chi-square distribution to make a decision for this test.

LO 9: Compute the Friedman test and interpret the results.

- The **Friedman test** is a statistical procedure used to determine whether the total ranks in two or more groups are significantly different when the same participants are observed in each group. This test is used as a nonparametric alternative to the one-way within-subjects ANOVA.

- The steps for completing this test are as follows:
Step 1: Rank scores across each row for each individual participant.
Step 2: Sum the ranks for each group.
Step 3: Compute the test statistic (χ_R^2):

$$\chi_R^2 = \frac{12}{nk(k+1)} \sum R^2 - 3n(k+1).$$

- The null hypothesis for this test is that the sum of ranks in each group does not differ. The alternative hypothesis is that the sum of ranks in each group differs. When the null hypothesis is true and n is greater than or equal to 5 per group, the test statistic χ_R^2 is approximately distributed as a chi-square distribution. For this reason, we use the chi-square distribution to make a decision for this test.

APA LO 10: Summarize the results of nonparametric tests for ordinal data in APA format.

- To summarize any nonparametric test, report the test statistic and the p value for the test. The degrees of freedom for the chi-square distribution are also reported for the Friedman and the Kruskal-Wallis H tests.

SPSS LO 11: Compute the related samples sign test, the Wilcoxon signed-ranks T test, the Mann-Whitney U test, the Kruskal-Wallis H test, and the Friedman test using SPSS.

- SPSS can be used to compute the related samples sign test by selecting the **Analyze,** then **Nonparametric tests** and **2 Related Samples . . .** options in the menu bar. These actions will display a dialog box that allows you to choose the sign test, identify the groups, and run the test (for more details, see Section 18.3).

- SPSS can be used to compute the Wilcoxon signed-ranks T test by selecting the **Analyze,** then **Nonparametric tests** and **2 Related Samples . . .** options in the menu bar. These actions will display a dialog box that allows you to identify the groups and run the test (for more details, see Section 18.5).
- SPSS can be used to compute the Mann-Whitney U test by selecting the **Analyze,** then **Nonparametric Tests** and **2 Independent Samples** options in the menu bar. These actions will display a dialog box that allows you to identify the groups and run the test (for more details, see Section 18.7).

- SPSS can be used to compute the Kruskal-Wallis H test by selecting the **Analyze,** then **Nonparametric Tests** and **k Independent Samples** options in the menu bar. These actions will display a dialog box that allows you to identify the groups and run the test (for more details, see Section 18.9).
- SPSS can be used to compute the Friedman test by selecting the **Analyze,** then **Nonparametric Tests** and **k Related Samples** options in the menu bar. These actions will display a dialog box that allows you to identify the groups and run the test (for more details, see Section 18.11).

KEY TERMS

Friedman test	Mann-Whitney U test	Wilcoxon signed-ranks
Kruskal-Wallis H test	sign test	T test

END-OF-CHAPTER PROBLEMS

Factual Problems

1. What tests are appropriate for analyzing ordinal scale data?

2. Why is the variance not meaningful to analyze ordinal scale data?

3. Can nonparametric tests have greater power to detect an effect compared to parametric tests? Explain.

4. Which nonparametric test can be used as an alternative to both the one–independent sample t-test and the related samples t-test?

5. Which parametric tests do the following tests replace?
   (a) Sign test
   (b) Wilcoxon signed-ranks T test
   (c) Mann-Whitney U test
   (d) Kruskal-Wallis H test
   (e) Friedman test

6. What are the dichotomous outcomes for the related samples sign test?

7. Explain how to interpret the test statistic T.

8. Explain how to interpret the test statistic U.

9. Which nonparametric tests can be computed using a normal approximation formula to compute the test statistic?

10. What are the degrees of freedom for the Kruskal-Wallis H test and the Friedman test?

11 Explain how to interpret the test statistic H.

12. When the null hypothesis is true and n is greater than or equal to 5 per group, the test statistic for the Friedman test is approximately distributed as what type of distribution?

Concepts and Application Problems

13. State the appropriate nonparametric alternative test for each of the following parametric tests.
   (a) One–independent sample t-test
   (b) Two–independent sample t-test
   (c) Related samples t-test
   (d) One-way between-subjects ANOVA
   (e) One-way within-subjects ANOVA

14. State the appropriate nonparametric test for each of the following examples.

    (a) A physiological psychologist compares differences in the amount of chemical activity in a certain brain region between a group of cocaine-dependent rats and a group of nicotine-dependent rats.

    (b) A social psychologist surveys a sample of women to test the claim that the average person drinks 32 ounces of soda per week.

    (c) A clinician measures the difference in metabolic rates between pairs of identical twins.

    (d) Each day for one week, a consultant records the amount of physical activity in a sample of patients suffering from depression.

    (e) A personality psychologist measures neuroticism in a sample of teenage university students, community college students, and high school dropouts.

15. State the appropriate nonparametric test for each of the following examples.

    (a) A researcher measures the time it takes to complete a surgical procedure in a sample of surgeons with low, medium, or high skill level.

    (b) A clinical researcher records the number of calories a group of obese patients consumes each day for 5 days.

    (c) A social psychologist measures the time it takes children to complete a creativity task first in the presence and then in the absence of a parent.

    (d) A cognitive psychologist measures the time it takes a sample of students to complete a memory task. The students were divided into one of three groups: A no distraction group, a moderate level of distraction group, and a high level of distraction group.

16. Transform the following 12 scores ($n = 12$) into ranked data. Convert tied scores into tied ranks.
    - 12, 14, 15, 15, 21, 24,
    - 25, 29, 31, 31, 31, 40

17. Transform the following scores ($n = 6$ for each sample) into ranked data for each sample. In which sample will a nonparametric test likely increase power the most? Explain.
    - Sample A: 1, 4, 5, 6, 9, 75
    - Sample B: 2, 3, 4, 7, 8, 10

18. The null hypothesis for the normal approximation for the sign test is that the probability of scores falling above and below the median equals

what value? What type of probability distribution is used to make the sign test?

19. A community psychologist selects a sample of 16 local police officers to test whether their physical endurance is better than the median score of 72. She measures their physical endurance on a 100-point physical endurance rating scale. Based on the data given below, compute the one-sample sign test at a .05 level of significance and state whether to retain or reject the null hypothesis.

Performance Scores			
76	90	75	95
65	92	82	73
77	70	86	50
85	68	80	81

20. A local school introduces a new academic program designed to improve students' grade point average (GPA) scores. To test the program, they select a sample of 10 students and measure the difference in their GPA scores before and after this program. Test whether or not scores improved following this program using the related samples sign test at a .05 level of significance and state whether to retain or reject the null hypothesis.

Change in GPA Following the Program	
+0.20	+0.05
−1.99	+0.55
+0.25	+0.63
+0.23	+0.10
+0.54	+1.09

21. Compute the Wilcoxon signed-ranks T test on the data in Question 20. Is your conclusion the same? Explain why or why not.

22. Practitioners measured spiritual well-being (SWB) in a sample of 16 adults who were alcoholic before and following treatment for alcoholism. Test whether or not SWB changed following treatment using the Wilcoxon signed-ranks T test at a .05 level of significance and state whether to retain or reject the null hypothesis.

Change in SWB Following Treatment	
−6	−1
+12	+20
+10	−3
−2	+7
−5	+11
+13	+15
+8	+14
−4	+9

23. Use the normal approximation for the Wilcoxon signed-ranks T test to analyze the data in Question 22 and state whether to retain or reject the null hypothesis.

24. A professor has a teaching assistant record the amount of time (in minutes) that a sample of 16 students engaged in an active discussion. The assistant observed 8 students in a class who used a slide show presentation and 8 students in a class who did not used a slide show presentation. Based on the results shown in the table, test whether active discussion times differed using the Mann-Whitney U test at a .05 level of significance. State whether to retain or reject the null hypothesis.

With Microsoft PowerPoint	Without Microsoft PowerPoint
7	23
14	11
12	15
8	18
10	21
13	5
6	4
9	19

25. Use the normal approximation for the Mann-Whitney U test to analyze the data in Question 24 and state whether to retain or reject the null hypothesis.

26. A psychologist hypothesizes that playing music or news radio during work may increase worker productivity. To test this hypothesis, she measured worker productivity (in units per hour) at three locations in a small business. Employees listened to music in one location, listened to news radio in a second location, or did not listen to radio during work in a third location. Based on the results shown in the table, test whether or not productivity levels differed using the Kruskal-Wallis H test at a .05 level of significance. State whether to retain or reject the null hypothesis.

Music	News Radio	No Radio
32	29	26
34	30	38
36	31	20
40	25	18
28	23	27

27. A statistics instructor measured student attitudes toward a statistics course prior to lectures, at the midterm, and after the final exam. Attitudes were measured on a 16-point scale, with higher scores indicating more positive attitudes toward the statistics course. Based on the results shown in the table, test whether or not attitudes differed using the Friedman test at a .05 level of significance. State whether to retain or reject the null hypothesis.

Student	Prior to Lectures	At the Midterm	After the Final
A	6	8	12
B	4	9	16
C	8	12	14
D	12	11	16
E	5	6	11

Problems in Research

28. **Power and variability.** Serlin and Harwell (2004) analyzed the power of statistical designs when distributions are not normally distributed. In their article, they reported, "It is well-known that for normally distributed errors parametric tests are optimal statistically, but perhaps less

well-known is that when normality does not hold, nonparametric tests frequently possess greater statistical power than parametric tests" (p. 492). Explain why power can be greater using a nonparametric test when data are not normally distributed.

29. **Preferences for a mirror among mice.** Sherwin (2004) tested whether or not mice prefer having a mirror in their cage. He set up 16 pairs of connected cages, one with a mirror and one without, and put a solitary mouse in each pair of cages. He then measured the amount of time each mouse spent in the two cages. He found that 13 mice spent more time in the cage without a mirror; 3 spent more time in the cage with a mirror.

    (a) If you must choose between the one-sample or related samples sign test, which would be most appropriate for these data?

    (b) Compute the sign test at a .05 level of significance and state whether to retain or reject the null hypothesis.

30. **Breast cancer and stress.** Palesh and colleagues (2007) tested the relationship between stress and the progression of breast cancer in women. They measured the progression of breast cancer among 94 women who experienced serious traumatic life events, standard stressful life events, or no stressful life events. They reported the following result: "A Kruskal-Wallis test found . . . differences among the three groups $[\chi^2 (2) = 6.09, p = .047]$" (p. 237).

    (a) How many groups were in this study, and what are the degrees of freedom for this test?

    (b) Was this nonparametric test significant at a .05 level of significance?

31. **Screening for substance abuse among adolescents.** Rojas, Sherrit, Harris, and Knight (2008) conducted a study using the Car, Relax, Alone, Forget, Friends, Trouble (CRAFFT) substance abuse screening test in 14- to 18-year-old patients. This screening test is a 16-item test for substance-related problems and disorders among adolescents. They screened patients and compared the

scores in their study (Study 2) to those from a previous study (Study 1). They reported,

Because the CRAFFT score distributions were highly skewed, we used the nonparametric Mann-Whitney U test for differences in mean rank. The mean rank in Study 1 was significantly higher than in Study 2 (mean rank 362 vs. 325, $p = .02$). (p. 195).

(a) Why was the Mann-Whitney U used in this study?

(b) Based on the description of the results, did Study 1 or Study 2 generate the test statistic? Explain.

32. **Teacher stress and coping.** Austin, Shah, and Muncer (2005) measured different coping strategies that teachers use for different types of stress. They had teachers complete the Total Teacher Concern Inventory (TTCI) to determine how stressful five stress-related areas were among teachers and reported the results shown in the following table. Assuming that higher scores indicate greater stress, which stress-related area was considered the most stressful among teachers? Which was considered the least stressful?

Stress Areas	Mean	*SD*
Work-related stress	3.632	0.858
Time management	3.194	0.844
Discipline and motivation	3.140	1.038
Professional distress	2.516	0.901
Professional investment	2.276	0.786

Mean ($\pm$ *SD*) scores for the five stress-related areas of the TTCI ($n = 38$).

As can be seen in the table above, there are significant differences between the five stress-related areas on a Friedman test ($\chi^2 = 61.95, df = 4, p = .0005$). (p. 69).

NOTE: Answers for even numbers are in Appendix C.

AFTERWORD

A Final Thought on the Role of Statistics in Research Methods

One of the goals for this book has been to introduce statistics in the context of the types of research problems that behavioral scientists study. This goal is important because many of you will take a research methods course at some point at the college level. To understand research methods, you will need to bring knowledge of statistics with you to your research methods course. To give you a sense of how statistics fits in research, Figure 19.1 provides a general overview of the process researchers engage in to study behavior.

I. The research process begins with exploration. In this phase, researchers, among other things, review published literature and the statistical conclusions reported in them, conduct pilot studies (small, inexpensive studies) to determine the power or likelihood of showing an effect, and collaborate or work together with other researchers to share ideas.

II. This initial phase is used to generate hypotheses. In this book, hypotheses have been primarily given to you. But hypotheses just don't appear. Instead, they are explored and extensively developed before ever being tested. Researchers use statistics to gauge the significance of a result and the power of detecting an effect. These types of analyses play a central role in determining which hypotheses are eventually tested and which are not.

III. Once hypotheses are generated, they are tested using hypothesis testing. Choosing an appropriate hypothesis test is determined by a variety factors, including, but not limited to, the number of participants and groups being tested, how often participants are observed, the design of the study (can the study show cause?), the types of hypotheses being tested (parametric or nonparametric), and the scales of measurement of the data being measured (nominal, ordinal, interval, or ratio). Many of these factors have been reviewed in this book.

IV. These tests then require interpretation. You are already aware of the fact that interpretation can be tricky. For example, conclusions concerning different scales of measurement require different interpretations. Conclusions for tests that show cause (experimental design) are different from those that show relationships (quasi-experimental and correlational designs). It follows that once an effect is shown or not shown, researchers must go back and reconsider whether changes should be made to existing hypotheses or whether they should begin testing new hypotheses. Correctly interpreting an effect and making the appropriate changes requires statistical know-how, much of which you have already attained by reading this book.

The general phases of the research process are cyclic—researchers continue to work through each phase to explore and test new ideas and stronger hypotheses. Statistics plays a large role in each phase of the research process from the development of hypotheses to the testing of hypotheses. It is an important tool in the process of conducting research in the behavioral sciences. So rest assured that the knowledge you have gained by studying statistics in this book will prove invaluable as you continue to develop as a critical consumer of knowledge and to explore methods of discovery in your own pursuits.

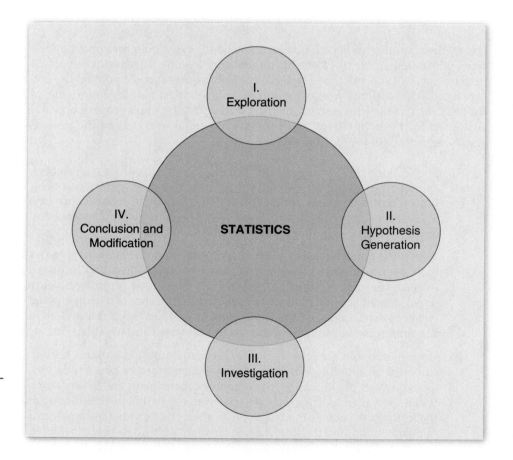

FIGURE 19.1

A general overview of conducting research. Statistics plays a role in each phase of the research process.

APPENDIX A

Mathematics in Statistics

A.1 POSITIVE AND NEGATIVE NUMBERS

While an understanding of mathematics becomes more important as you advance in your use of statistics, you need only a basic level of mathematics to do well in an introductory statistics course. The fundamentals of statistics are based largely on basic addition, subtraction, multiplication, division, and problem solving. That being said, we begin this appendix with an introduction to positive and negative numbers.

Theoretically, numbers can range from $-\infty$ to $+\infty$ (negative infinity to positive infinity), with the average value of all numbers that could possibly exist being equal to 0. Anything less than 0 is negative, and anything greater than 0 is positive. For every positive value, there is a negative counterpart. If we think of numbers as units away from 0, then +5 and –5 would each be 5 units away from 0: One is 5 units above 0 (+5), and one is 5 units below 0 (–5). As shown in Figure A.1, each number is the same distance from 0 but in the opposite direction.

A positive number isn't necessarily one with a positive outlook on life—a "glass half full" kind of number—although you may have seen smiling numbers like that on *Sesame Street* or *Blue's Clues* as a kid. It means, of course, that the value of the number is greater than 0. Zero (0) is not positive, and it is not negative; it is considered a neutral number. We can define positive and negative numbers using the following rules.

[1] A constant written without a sign is positive (+).

$$+2 = 2 \quad +x = x, \text{ where } x \neq 0$$

[2] A constant preceded by a negative sign (–) is negative.

$$-2 \neq 2 \quad -x \neq x, \text{ where } x \neq 0$$

These rules apply mostly to constants (as opposed to variables). A **variable** is a characteristic or property that can take on different values at different times. In contrast, a **constant** is a characteristic or a property that can take on only a single value. Variables are typically expressed alphabetically.

> **DEFINITION**
>
> A **variable** is a characteristic or a property that can take on different values at different times.
>
> A **constant** is a characteristic or property that can take on only a single value.

For example, x and y are variables that are commonly used to represent numbers. The value of one of these variables can be anything you define it to be. You could even assign a negative number for x, making $+x$ a negative number and thus violating Rule [1]. You could similarly violate Rule [2], which is why these rules apply mostly to constants. Constants are represented as numbers. You will be introduced to many constants and variables in statistics.

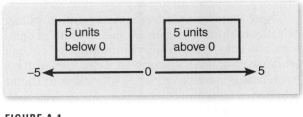

FIGURE A.1

Positive and negative signs indicate units above and below 0, respectively.

A.2 ADDITION

Addition is arguably the most basic mathematical function. Both positive and negative numbers can be added. The following rules apply to adding positive and negative numbers.

[3] **When adding numbers with the same sign, add them and keep the sign of the individual numbers the same.**

$$+2 + (+4) = +6 \qquad 2 + 4 = 6 \qquad -2 + (-4) = -6$$

Notice that Rule [3] applies to both positive and negative numbers. So long as the individual numbers have the same sign, all you do is add them and not change the sign. Adding positive numbers yields a solution of greater magnitude or value; adding negative numbers yields a solution of lesser magnitude or value.

[4] **When adding numbers with different signs, either add the numbers in the order they are listed or reorganize them so that all positive numbers precede all negative numbers.**

$$(+8) + (-3) + (+2) + (-4) = +3$$

Consider the problem given above. One way to approach it, particularly for students who are good at these kinds of problems, is to just do the math in order. The thought process would be something like this: $8 + (-3) = 5$, $5 + 2$ equals 7, and $7 + (-4)$ equals 3. Thus, the answer is +3. A second approach for those not as comfortable with math would be to reorganize the problem by the sign of the numbers as follows:

$$(+8) + (+2) + (-3) + (-4) = +3$$

Notice that all the positive values precede the negative values. This makes it easier to do the problem because you separated the positive and negative values. The thought process for this approach would be something like this: $8 + 2 = 10$, $10 + (-3) = 7$, and $7 + (-4) = 3$. Thus, the answer is +3. This becomes particularly useful when the string of numbers in the problem is longer, as in the one below. In this case, reorganizing the problem may be very helpful. Try it yourself and see whether you find it easier to do the problem this way.

$$(+9) + (-3) + (-7) + (+2) + (-4)$$
$$+ (+5) + (+6) + (-1) + (+8) = +15$$

Also, note that whenever there are two ways to approach a problem, you can check your work by doing it both ways, particularly on an exam. You can lose a lot of points because of simple math errors that can be avoided by checking your work. On multiple-choice exams, simple math errors can cost you the entire value of the problem because partial credit isn't an option in most cases. If you have time to go through a problem two ways, then why not check your work? It can only help you redeem points that you otherwise would have lost.

A.3 SUBTRACTION

Subtraction and addition are opposites: Addition increases the value of the number, and subtraction decreases the value. Two rules can be stated for positive and negative numbers.

[5] **A positive sign preceding a negative sign makes a negative, and vice versa.**

$$5 + (-3) = 5 - 3 = 2$$
$$12 - (+7) = 12 - 7 = 5$$
$$-6 + (-6) = -6 - 6 = -12$$

Whether we add a negative number or subtract a positive number, the sign between the two numbers will be negative. In a sense, adding a negative number and subtracting a positive number are two ways of describing the same thing.

[6] **A negative sign preceding a negative sign makes a positive.**

$$5 - (-5) = 5 + 5 = 10$$
$$(-4) - (-4) = -4 + 4 = 0$$
$$0 - (-5) = 0 + 5 = 5$$

Note that two negatives make a positive. It may be easier to think of negative values in terms of debt, which is something often too familiar to college students. Suppose you are in debt four dollars (represented numerically as −$4.00). If your friend subtracts or takes away four dollars of your debt, then he or takes away the amount of your debt: −$4.00 − (−$4.00) = $0; he erased your debt. Hence, when you subtract a negative number, you are actually adding.

1. A _____ is defined as a characteristic or property that can take on different values at different times.

2. True or false: Zero (0) is neither a positive nor a negative number.

3. Compute the following problems: a. $7 + (-3) + 6 = ?$ b. $7 - 3 + 6 = ?$

4. Compute the following problems: a. $7 - (-3) - 6 = ?$ b. $-7 - 3 - 6 = ?$

Answers: 1. Variable; 2. True; 3. (a) 10, (b) 10; 4. (a) +4, (b) −16.

A.4 MULTIPLICATION

Multiplication is really a simplified way to add a lot of numbers together. For example, suppose you have six 5-dollar bills. You could add them all up to get the total amount of money: $5.00 + $5.00 + $5.00 + $5.00 + $5.00 + $5.00 = $30.00. However, an easier calculation is to multiply the $5.00 times the number of bills you have (6). Thus, $5.00 × 6 bills = $30.00.

There are four ways to indicate or symbolize multiplication: a × sign, a center dot (·), parentheses with no operational sign between the numbers, and an asterisk (*). Each symbol means the same thing: Multiply the numbers between them. Below is an example of each:

$$6 \times 4 = 24 \quad 6 \cdot 4 = 24 \quad 6\,(4) = 24 \quad 6 * 4 = 24$$

As for addition and subtraction, you can multiply negative and positive numbers. There are a few rules to follow when multiplying numbers.

[7] When multiplying two numbers with the same sign, the answer is always *positive*.

Whether we multiply two positive numbers or two negative numbers, the result is the same: It produces a positive solution. To illustrate, the following is an example in which the solution to each example is the same (+63).

$$9 \times 7 = +63$$
$$-9 \times -7 = +63$$

[8] When multiplying two numbers with different signs, the answer is always *negative*.

When multiplying one positive and one negative number, the solution will always be negative. To illustrate, the following is an example in which the solution to each example is the same (−63).

$$-9 \times 7 = -63$$
$$9 \times -7 = -63$$

Whether the 9 or the 7 is the negative number, the result is the same—the solution is always negative (−63). In this way, multiplication can be used as a shortcut for adding because it does not violate the general rules of addition.

A.5 DIVISION

There are three ways to indicate division: a ÷ sign, a fraction, and a $\overline{)}$ sign. Each of these signs means the same thing: Divide the numbers among them. The following is an example of each:

$$6 \div 2 = 3$$
$$\frac{6}{2} = 3$$
$$2\overline{)6} = 3$$

You can think of division as the opposite of multiplication. If we multiply 7×3, then we obtain 21. But we can do the opposite: We can divide $21 \div 7$ to obtain 3, or we can divide $21 \div 3$ to obtain 7. Hence, we can multiply two numbers to obtain 21, or we can divide those numbers to get 3 and 7. Because these two operations are similar in this way, so also are the rules.

[9] When dividing two numbers with the same sign, the answer is always *positive*.

$$-9 \div -3 = 3$$
$$9 \div 3 = 3$$

It is sometimes easier to make sense of this by looking at the process in a different way. The first problem is actually asking how many –3s we must add to get –9. The answer is 3 (–3 + –3 + –3 = –9). Hence, we must add (–3) three times to get 9. The answer is positive. The second problem would be calculated likewise (3 + 3 + 3 = 9). In this case, +3 would be added three times to get 9.

[10] When dividing two numbers with different signs, the answer is always *negative*.

$$-9 \div 3 = -3$$
$$9 \div -3 = -3$$

For this rule, same signs mean positive values; different signs mean negative values. However, this rule is true only when two numbers are calculated. For instances in which more than two numbers are multiplied or divided, the following rule applies:

[11] When more than two numbers are multiplied or divided: If there are an even number of negative values, the answer will be positive; if there are an odd number of negative numbers, the answer will be negative.

$$2 \times -4 \times 2 \times -4 = +64$$
$$2 \times -4 \times 2 \times 4 = -64$$

Let's work through each of these problems, two numbers at a time. For the first example, $2 \times -4 = -8$, because numbers with different signs yield a negative result. Next, $-8 \times 2 = -16$, because the signs again are different for each number. Finally, $-16 \times -4 = +64$. The sign changed because now both numbers have the same sign—both numbers are negative (–16 and –4).

The second problem starts out the same way: $2 \times -4 = -8$, because numbers with different signs yield a negative result. For the same reason, the next solution is again negative: $-8 \times 2 = -16$. The last calculation is where the solution changes, $-16 \times 4 = -64$. Because the signs for this last calculation are different, the answer becomes negative. Hence, an even number of negative values will produce a positive solution (such as two negative values in the first problem), and an odd number of negative values will produce a negative solution (such as one negative value in the second problem).

✔ LEARNING CHECK 2

1. True or false: When multiplying two numbers with the same sign, the answer is always *negative*.

2. Compute: a. $6 \times 8 = ?$ b. 9×-5

3. True or false: When dividing two numbers with different signs, the answer is always *negative*.

4. Compute: a. $20 \div 4 = ?$ b. $\dfrac{16}{4} = ?$ c. $2\overline{)6} = ?$

Answers: 1. False. The answer is always positive; 2. (a) 48, (b) –45; 3. True; 4. (a) 5, (b) 4, (c) 3.

A.6 FRACTIONS

Fractions represent a division operation. A fraction is the division of the numerator (the top expression) by the denominator (the bottom expression). Fractions are used more often to represent values to the right of the decimal point than values to the left. For example, because $\dfrac{6}{2}$ is 3, it makes more sense to represent that value as the whole number 3. Yet if the expression reads $\dfrac{2}{6}$, then the division would produce a value less than 1. In this case, leaving the expression as a fraction might be easier to read.

Fractions are important in statistics because many statistical formulas include them. In many cases, you will probably find it easier to leave a solution as a fraction. The following rules are used for fractions.

[12] Dividing 0 into any number is undefined.

$$\frac{0}{100} = 0$$

$$\frac{100}{0} = \text{undefined}$$

The term *undefined* is used because it doesn't make sense to say that 0 goes into anything except itself. Statistical theorists recognize this rule and take care not to allow undefined problems. Therefore, if your answer to a problem in statistics is "undefined," it is likely an arithmetic mistake, and you should probably do the problem again.

[13] Whole numbers are also fractions, with the whole number in the numerator and a 1 in the denominator.

$$5 = \frac{5}{1}$$

$$10 = \frac{10}{1}$$

$$1,000 = \frac{1,000}{1}$$

Making any whole number a fraction is as simple as placing the whole number over 1. This rule will be especially useful when you need to add, subtract, multiply, or divide fractions using whole numbers.

[14] To add or subtract fractions, you must find the *least common denominator* and then add the numerators together.

$$\frac{2}{5} + \frac{3}{10} = \frac{(2 \times 2)}{(5 \times 2)} + \frac{(3 \times 1)}{(10 \times 1)} = \frac{4}{10} + \frac{3}{10} = \frac{7}{10}$$

$$\frac{2}{5} - \frac{3}{10} = \frac{(2 \times 2)}{(5 \times 2)} - \frac{(3 \times 1)}{(10 \times 1)} = \frac{4}{10} - \frac{3}{10} = \frac{1}{10}$$

The *least common denominator* is a fancy way of saying that only fractions with the same denominator can be added and subtracted. Each example above shows how this works. Note that multiplying the numerator and denominator times the same number does not change the value of a fraction. For example, $\frac{2}{4}$ is the same as $\frac{4}{8}$. If we multiply both the numerator and denominator times 2, it would be $\frac{4}{8}$. Both values are equal. Therefore, in the above example, we determine that 10 is the least common denominator—it is the lowest multiple that makes the denominators equal. This is because $5 \times 2 = 10$, and $10 \times 1 = 10$. This will make both denominators 10, but whatever we do to the denominator, we must also do to the numerator. This gives us a new, but equal, problem: $\frac{4}{10} + \frac{3}{10}$. Now that the denominators are the same, we add the numerators together and leave the denominator alone. We do the same for subtraction, except that we subtract the numerators.

[15] To multiply fractions, multiply the numerators together and multiply the denominators together.

$$\frac{2}{3} \times \frac{4}{5} = \frac{8}{15}$$

$$\frac{1}{5} \times 3 = \frac{1}{5} \times \frac{3}{1} = \frac{3}{5}$$

$$\frac{3}{4} \times \frac{2}{3} = \frac{6}{12} = \frac{1}{2}$$

When multiplying fractions, multiply across the numerator and denominator. It is also worth remembering that fractions are a way of representing a division operation. Therefore, you are allowed to simplify or reduce values before multiplying across. You can reduce any value in the numerator with any value in the denominator. Consider the following example:

$$\frac{4}{12} \times \frac{6}{8} = \frac{1}{4}$$

Here we could reduce $\frac{4}{12}$ to $\frac{1}{3}$ by dividing the numerator and denominator by 4, and we could reduce $\frac{6}{8}$ to $\frac{3}{4}$ by dividing each by 2. It follows that $\frac{1}{3} \times \frac{3}{4} = \frac{3}{12}$, which could be further reduced to $\frac{1}{4}$ by dividing each by 3. We could also reduce across the multiplication sign. For example, the 4 and 8 are divisible by 2 (i.e., 4 reduces to 1 and 8 to 2), and the 6 and 12 are divisible by 2 as well (i.e., 6 reduces to 1 and 12 to 2). It follows that $\frac{1}{2} \times \frac{1}{2} = \frac{1}{4}$. Both methods result in the same answer, and many times it is easier to reduce the fractions before you multiply.

[16] To divide fractions, invert the second fraction and multiply.

$$\frac{3}{5} \div \frac{2}{3} = \frac{3}{5} \times \frac{3}{2} = \frac{9}{10}$$

When dividing fractions, invert the fraction that is doing the dividing (the divisor) and multiply it into the fraction you were going to divide (the dividend). You never actually perform the division operation.

In statistics, it is also common to see this problem written as

$$\frac{\frac{3}{5}}{\frac{2}{3}}$$

To solve this problem, move the bottom fraction to the right, and follow Rule [16]:

$$\frac{3}{5} \div \frac{2}{3} = \frac{3}{5} \times \frac{3}{2} = \frac{9}{10}$$

LEARNING CHECK 3

1. The _____ is the lowest multiple that makes the denominators of more than one fraction equal.

2. Compute: a. $\frac{15}{21} + \frac{2}{7} = ?$ b. $\frac{3}{4} - \frac{3}{12} = ?$

3. Compute: a. $\frac{5}{9} \div \frac{2}{3} = ?$ b. $\frac{\frac{4}{5}}{\frac{4}{3}} = ?$

Answers: 1. Least common denominator. 2. (a) $\frac{15}{21} + \frac{6}{21} = \frac{21}{21} = 1.0$, (b) $\frac{9}{12} - \frac{3}{12} = \frac{6}{12} = \frac{1}{2}$; 3 (a) $\frac{5}{9} \times \frac{3}{2} = \frac{5}{6}$, (b) $\frac{4}{5} \div \frac{4}{3} = \frac{4}{5} \times \frac{3}{4} = \frac{3}{5}$.

A.7 DECIMALS AND PERCENTS

Because decimals are another way to express fractions, you can write decimals as fractions and fractions as decimals.

[17] The decimal is a fraction with 10, 100, 1,000, and so on as the denominator.

$$2.6 = 2\frac{6}{10}$$

$$4.35 = 4\frac{35}{100}$$

$$5.004 = 5\frac{4}{1,000}$$

If the decimal is to the tenths place, then put the decimal over 10 when making it a fraction; if to the hundredths place, then place it over 100; if to the thousandths place, then place it over 1,000; and so on. When converting decimals to fractions, remember that you can leave any whole numbers alone; simply change the decimal to a fraction.

[18] To combine whole numbers with fractions, multiply the denominator times the whole number; then add that result to the numerator.

$$2\frac{6}{10} = \frac{26}{10}$$

$$3\frac{2}{3} = \frac{11}{3}$$

In the first problem, you first multiply the denominator times the whole number: $10 \times 2 = 20$, then add the result to the numerator: $20 + 6 = 26$. This makes the new numerator 26; the denominator does not change. Similarly, in the second problem, $3 \times 3 = 9$, and $9 + 2 = 11$. This makes the new numerator 11; the denominator does not change.

[19] Percentages are fractions to the hundredths place.

$$25\% = \frac{25}{100} = 0.25$$

A.8 EXPONENTS AND ROOTS

[20] An exponent tells how many times a number or expression is multiplied times itself.

$$2^4 = 2 \times 2 \times 2 \times 2 = 16$$
$$4^2 = 4 \times 4 = 16$$
$$3^3 = 3 \times 3 \times 3 = 27$$

The exponent is placed to the upper right of a number. In the three examples above, the exponents are (from left) 4, 2, and 3. It is common to see numbers squared (x^2) in statistics because this gets rid of negative values; remember, *any negative number multiplied times itself will be positive.*

[21] Roots are the reverse of exponents: A root represents a value that, when multiplied times itself, equals that number.

$$\sqrt[4]{16} = 2$$
$$\sqrt{16} = 4$$
$$\sqrt[3]{27} = 3$$

$$3\% = \frac{3}{100} = .03$$

$$4.7\% = \frac{4.7}{100} = .047$$

Decimal places go from tenths (one place), to hundredths (two places), to thousandths (three places), and so on. A percentage is two places to the right of the decimal and ranges between 0% and 100%.

Roots are expressed using radical signs: $\sqrt{\ }$. You take the root of everything under the radical. Consider the examples given above. The fourth root of 16 is 2, the square root of 16 is 4, and the third root (cube root) of 27 is 3. This means 2 must be multiplied four times to equal 16 (i.e., $2 \times 2 \times 2 \times 2 = 16$), 4 must be multiplied twice to equal 16 (i.e., $4 \times 4 = 16$), and 3 must be multiplied three times to equal 27 (i.e., $3 \times 3 \times 3 = 27$). The number on the "tail" of the radical represents the root.

$$\sqrt[2]{4} = \sqrt{4} = 2$$

No number needs to "sit on the radical" for square roots—it is assumed that you are taking the square root of the number under the radical unless otherwise indicated. This is important because we will rarely deal with anything beyond square roots in statistics.

 **LEARNING CHECK 4**

1. True or false: A fraction can be stated as a decimal.

2. State each of the following as a fraction.
   a. 0.08   b. 2.45   c. –0.952   d. 13%

3. True or false: Roots are the reverse of exponents.

4. Perform the following computations:
   a. $\sqrt{25} = ?$ b. $\sqrt{81} = ?$ c. $7^2 = ?$ d. $15^2 = ?$

Answers: 1. True; 2. (a) $\frac{8}{100}$, (b) $2\frac{45}{100}$ or $\frac{245}{100}$, (c) $-\frac{952}{1000}$, (d) $\frac{13}{100}$; 3. True; 4. (a) 5, (b) 9, (c) 49, (d) 225.

A.9 ORDER OF COMPUTATION

Statistics include calculations of addition, subtraction, division, multiplication, parentheses, exponents, and roots, and sometimes all in the same problem. "Doing the math" often becomes confusing, even with a calculator. It truly is "math errors" that needlessly cost many students points on exams. The following rules will make it easier to work your way through many problems in this book.

[22] Always perform mathematical operations in the parentheses first.

To begin, you should treat whatever is inside parentheses as a single number. For example, $5(4 + 6) = 5(10) = 50$. In this example, first added 4 and 6, then multiply that result times 5. It is a good idea to start with the parentheses before you perform any other calculations. The following are additional examples with parentheses.

$$7 + (4 - 2) = 7 + 2 = 9$$

$$4(\sqrt{4}) = 4(2) = 8$$

$$32 - (4^2) = 32 - 16 = 16$$

$$\frac{(3+2)}{\sqrt{25}} = \frac{5}{\sqrt{25}} = 1$$

[23] When parentheses are nested, start working from the inside out.

Nested parentheses are those located inside other parentheses. In this case, you should begin doing mathematical operations for all parentheses inside other ones. Keep working your way out until you have calculated operations in every parenthesis. Below are a few examples of how this works.

$$2\left(\left(\sqrt{9} - \sqrt{4}\right) - (3+4)\right) = 2((3-2) - 7)$$
$$= 2(1 - 7) = 2 \times (-6) = -12$$

$$4 + \left(\left(5 - 4\right) + \left(3 \times \frac{1}{3}\right)\right) = 4 + (1+1) = 4 + 2 = 6$$

$$\frac{8}{((3+3) - (\sqrt{4} - 0))} = \frac{8}{(6-2)} = \frac{8}{4} = 2$$

$$\frac{((5+2) \times (7-4))}{((5+2) - (7-7))} = \frac{(7 \times 3)}{(7-0)} = \frac{21}{7} = 3$$

[24] In problems without parentheses, calculate square roots and exponents first (they are treated as a single numbers). Then do all multiplication and division before any addition and subtraction.

This rule can be memorized by using the acronym: Please Roughly Excuse My Dear Aunt Sally, which stands for Parentheses, Roots, Exponents, Multiplication, Division, Addition, and Subtraction. Make sure to follow all the previous rules when performing the order of computation. Below is an example to help guide you through each of the steps.

$$= 4 - 20 + (16 - 8)\ 2^2 \div \sqrt{64} \quad (parentheses)$$
$$= 4 - 20 + 8 \times 2^2 \div \sqrt{64} \quad (roots)$$
$$= 4 - 20 + 8 \times 2^2 \div 8 \quad (exponents)$$
$$= 4 - 20 + 8 \times 4 \div 8 \quad (multiplication)$$
$$= 4 - 20 + 32 \div 8 \quad (division)$$
$$= 4 - 20 + 4 \quad (addition)$$
$$= 4 - 16 \quad (subtraction)$$
$$= -12$$

✔ **LEARNING CHECK 5**

1. True or false: The correct order of computation is parentheses, roots, exponents, multiplication, division, addition, and subtraction.

2. True or false: When parentheses are nested, start working from the inside out.

3. Perform the following computations:
   a. $8^2 - \sqrt{9}$ b. $8^2 - \sqrt{9} + (4 \times 2^2)^2$
   c. $\dfrac{8^2 - \sqrt{9} + (4 \times 2^2)^2}{\sqrt{144} - \sqrt{4}}$

Answers: 1. True. 2. True. 3. (a) 61, (b) 317, (c) 31.7.

A.10   EQUATIONS: SOLVING FOR x

An equation is two expressions joined by an equal sign. The values on each side of the equal sign must be equal—otherwise they would be unequal. Because both sides are equal, anything you do to one side of the equation, you must also do to the other. You can perform almost any mathematical operation on an equation, so long as both sides of the equation remain equal. This is why you must treat both sides the same—so that they remain equal.

[25] Adding and subtracting from both sides of the equation is allowed.

$$6 + 2 = 8 \qquad 5 + 7 + 3 = 20 - 5 \qquad 30 - 4 + 14 = 50 - 10$$
$$8 = 8 \qquad\qquad 15 = 15 \qquad\qquad 40 = 40$$

$$55 + 2 = 33 + 24 \qquad 2 - 1 + 3 = 8 - 4 \qquad 7 + 21 - 3 = 25$$
$$57 = 57 \qquad\qquad 4 = 4 \qquad\qquad 25 = 25$$

[26] Multiplying and dividing from both sides of the equation is allowed.

$$6 + 4 = 100 \div 10 \quad 10 + 11 = 7 \times 3 \quad 5 + 3 \times 2 = 7 \times 5 - 5$$
$$10 = 10 \qquad\qquad 21 = 21 \qquad\qquad 30 = 30$$

$$21 \div \sqrt{49} = 3 \qquad 6 \times 4 \div 2 = 12^2 \div 12 \qquad 4^2 = 8 \times 2$$
$$3 = 3 \qquad\qquad 12 = 12 \qquad\qquad 16 = 16$$

[27] When solving for x, you must follow Rules [25] and [26] until x is alone on one side of the equation.

When given an equation with undefined variables (such as x), we can often solve for x. In other words, we can apply Rules [25] and [26] to find the value for x. Also, it is worth noting that an x alone is assumed to have a 1 in front of it (i.e., $x = 1x$). Consider the following example:

$$x - 3 + 9 = 2x$$

$-3 + 9 = x$ (subtract $1x$ from each side of the equation)

$6 = x$ (add $-3 + 9$ to solve for x)

In this example, the first step we made was to subtract $1x$ from each side of the equation. Ultimately, we want to get x alone on one side of the equation. By subtracting $1x$ from each side, we got rid of x on the left side ($1x - 1x = 0x$). Because zero times anything is zero, then $0x$ must equal 0 ($0x = 0$). Subtracting $1x$ on the right side resulted in x being alone on that side ($2x - 1x = 1x$ or x). Here is another example with x in the numerator of a fraction:

$$\frac{x - 5}{5} = 4$$

$5(4) = 1(x - 5)$ (cross multiply)

$20 = x - 5$ (do the multiplication on each side of the equation)

$25 = x$ (add 5 to each side of the equation to solve for x)

You will need to solve for x in certain cases, such as for problems in Chapter 6. In that chapter, we will work with problems where we need to find scores and percentages. To illustrate, suppose your professor says he or she will give the top 15% of students an A in the class. For this problem, we will solve for x to find the cutoff score (x) for an A grade. In this way, being familiar with solving equations is going to help you with some of the topics covered in this book.

LEARNING CHECK 6

1.   True or false: Adding, subtracting, multiplying, and dividing from both sides of an equation is allowed.

2.   Solve for x:

   a. $x + 4 = 9$ b. $2x - 6 = 8$ c. $-x + 6 = -12$

   d. $8 = \dfrac{x}{2}$ e. $\dfrac{2}{3} = \dfrac{x}{6}$ f. $5 = \dfrac{x - 2}{6}$

Answers: 1. True. 2. (a) $x = 5$, (b) $x = -1$, (c) $x = 18$, (d) $x = 16$, (e) $x = 4$, (f) $x = 32$.

A.11 SUMMATION NOTATION

A summation sign looks like an *M* on its side: Σ. This symbol is referred to as *sigma,* and it is used throughout statistics. A summation sign that precedes some value is telling you to sum everything that comes next. For example, suppose you are asked to sum three values: $x_1 = 2$, $x_2 = 3$, $x_3 = 4$. To make this calculation, sum the values.

$$\sum x = x_1 + x_2 + x_3$$
$$= 2 + 3 + 4$$
$$= 9$$

The sigma notation can be a bit more complicated than this. For example, suppose you are given the three values above but asked instead to add only x_2 and x_3. To use summation notation, we have to identify where to begin and where to stop adding. To do this, we use the following notation: $\sum_{i=2}^{i=3} x_i$. The *i* represents different values of *x*, such that each *x* (i.e., x_1, x_2, and x_3) is represented as x_i. This notation reads "sum of *x* from x_2 to x_3." The notation underneath sigma tells you where to start adding; the notation above sigma tells you where to stop adding. This notation system works only when *adding in order.* The solution to this problem is given below.

$$\sum_{i=2}^{i=3} x = x_2 + x_3$$
$$= 3 + 4$$
$$= 7$$

For the formulas used in statistics, you will rarely be asked to sum a limited number of scores or values. Instead, when you see a sigma sign in a statistical formula, you will be asked to sum all scores. In situations where you are asked to add all numbers in a data set, the *i* notation is not necessary. If nothing is above or below the sigma, then add all values.

[28] $\sum x = \sum_{i=1}^{i=n} x$, **where *n* represents the subscript of *x* where we stop adding.**

Certain types of summation will appear often in statistics. Using the formulas in this book, summation requires summing all the given scores. In this section, we will focus on the types of summation commonly used in statistics.

In some cases, a summation sign is located inside parentheses, and it is squared: $\left(\sum x\right)^2$. Using the acronym Please Roughly Excuse My Dear Aunt Sally, we compute the summation in the parentheses first. Then we square the total; this notation reads "sum of *x*, quantity squared." Using the same *x* values given previously ($x_1 = 2$, $x_2 = 3$, $x_3 = 4$), we will solve the following problem.

$$\left(\sum x\right)^2 = \left(x_1 + x_2 + x_3\right)^2$$
$$= (2 + 3 + 4)^2$$
$$= 9^2$$
$$= 81$$

In another case, we use a similar notation, except without the parentheses: $\sum x^2$. In this case, you must square each individual score, and then add. Using the acronym Please Roughly Excuse My Dear Aunt Sally, we know that exponents are calculated first (there are no parentheses or roots here, so we skip the "P" [Please] and the "R" [Roughly] in the acronym and start with the "E" [Excuse]), then add. Using the same *x* values given previously ($x_1 = 2$, $x_2 = 3$, $x_3 = 4$), let's solve this problem.

$$\sum x^2 = x_1^2 + x_2^2 + x_3^2$$
$$= 2^2 + 3^2 + 4^2$$
$$= 4 + 9 + 16$$
$$= 29$$

A few problems using summation also involve two or more variables. In this section, we limit the discussion to the summation of two variables. Suppose we have three rectangles with the following lengths and widths:

Length	Width
8	3
10	12
20	2

To find the area of a rectangle, we use the following formula: Area = Length × Width ($A = l \times w$). Therefore, if we were asked to sum the areas of these rectangles, we could represent that as $\sum (l \times w)$, where $l_1 = 8$, $l_2 = 10$, $l_3 = 20$, $w_1 = 3$, $w_2 = 12$, and $w_3 = 2$. The following is the solution for summing the areas of these rectangles:

$$\sum (l \times w) = (l_1 \times w_1) + (l_2 \times w_2) + (l_3 \times w_3)$$
$$= (8 \times 3) + (10 \times 12) + (20 \times 2)$$
$$= 24 + 120 + 40 = 184$$

Now suppose we are interested in knowing the squared sum of the areas. To do this, we represent the summation notation as $\sum (l \times w)^2$.

$$\sum (l \times w)^2 = (l_1 \times w_1)^2 + (l_2 \times w_2)^2 + (l_3 \times w_3)^2$$
$$= (8 \times 3)^2 + (10 \times 12)^2 + (20 \times 2)^2$$
$$= 576 + 14{,}400 + 1{,}600$$
$$= 16{,}576$$

Finally, suppose we are interested in knowing the sum of the areas, quantity squared. To do this, we represent the summation notation as $\left(\sum l \times w\right)^2$.

$$\left(\sum l \times w\right)^2 = ((l_1 \times w_1) + (l_2 \times w_2) + (l_3 \times w_3))^2$$
$$= ((8 \times 3) + (10 \times 12) + (20 \times 2))^2$$
$$= (24 + 120 + 40)^2$$
$$= (184)^2$$
$$= 33{,}856$$

In all, the math covered in this appendix is as much math as you need to do well in this course topic. Sure, there is a lot of math in statistics, but this is as hard as the math will get. You can calculate any statistic by applying the basic principles discussed in this appendix.

....

✔ **LEARNING CHECK 7**

1. True or false: The summation problem $\left(\sum x\right)^2$ reads "sum of x, quantity squared."

2. Perform the following computations for two scores, where $x_1 = 5$, $x_2 = 4$:
   a. $\sum x$ b. $\sum x^2$ c. $\left(\sum x\right)^2$

3. Perform the following computations with the same values of x given in Question 2:
   a. $\sqrt{\sum x}$ b. $\sqrt{\sum x^2}$ c. $\left(\sqrt{\sum x}\right)^2$

Answers: 1. True; 2. (a) $5 + 4 = 9$, (b) $5^2 + 4^2 = 41$, (c) $(5 + 4)^2 = 9^2 = 81$; 3. (a) $\sqrt{(5+4)} = \left(\sqrt{9}\right) = 3$, (b) $\sqrt{5^2 + 4^2} = \sqrt{41} = 6.4$, (c) $\left(\sqrt{(5+4)}\right) = \left(\sqrt{9}\right) = 3 = 3^2 = 9$.

....

KEY TERMS

constant   variable

REVIEW PROBLEMS

SECTION A1—Positive and Negative Numbers

Identify whether the following are negative, positive, or neither.

1. 2.8   2. −36

3. 10   4. −5.99

5. +20   6. 700

7. 0   8. x

9. $-y$ 10. y

Identify whether the following are constants or variables.

11. 8   12. −5

13. $-x$ 14. y

15. 0   16. xy

SECTIONS A2–A3—Addition and Subtraction

1. $1 + 5 = ?$
2. $(+2) + (+8) = ?$
3. $(-3) + 3 = ?$
4. $3 + (-8) = ?$
5. $(-3) + (-6) = ?$
6. $3 + 10 + 6 = ?$
7. $(-7) + 3 + (-4) = ?$
8. $9 - (-9) = ?$
9. $10 - 4 + 6 = ?$
10. $(-3) - (-3) = ?$

SECTIONS A4–A5—Multiplication and Division

Compute the following:

1. $6 \times 5 = ?$
2. $8(4) = ?$
3. $-7 \times -3 = ?$
4. $12 \times 5 = ?$
5. $8 \times 4 \times -1 = ?$
6. $7(2)(-3)(-2) = ?$
7. $-4 \times 4 = ?$
8. $-8 \div 8 = ?$
9. $12 \div 12 = ?$
10. $5\overline{)15} = ?$
11. $\dfrac{18}{2} = ?$
12. $-\dfrac{3}{6} = ? = ?$
13. $-18 \div -9 = ?$
14. $10 \div (-2) = ?$
15. $-20\overline{)5} = ?$
16. $9(2)(-3) = ?$

State whether the following statements are true or false:

17. $\dfrac{1}{2} = 0.50$
18. $\dfrac{9}{2} = 2 \div 9$
19. $6 \times 5 = 5 \times 6$
20. $2\overline{)3} = \dfrac{3}{2}$

SECTIONS A6–A7—Fractions, Decimals, and Percents

Identify whether the following are equal to 0 or undefined.

1. $\dfrac{2}{0}$
2. $\dfrac{0}{10}$
3. $\dfrac{0}{81}$
4. $\dfrac{16}{0}$

Convert the following mixed fractions into a single fraction:

5. $2\dfrac{5}{8}$
6. $1\dfrac{1}{2}$
7. $-5\dfrac{2}{7}$
8. $-12\dfrac{2}{3}$

Convert the following decimals into fractions:

9. 0.20
10. -0.35
11. 0.002
12. 0.0052
13. -0.8
14. 1.25

Convert the following decimals into percents:

15. $.1000$
16. $.0250$
17. $.0500$
18. $.5000$

Compute the following:

19. $\dfrac{2}{3} \times \dfrac{4}{5} = ?$
20. $\dfrac{5}{8} + \dfrac{3}{2} = ?$
21. $\dfrac{1}{3} + \dfrac{1}{5} + \dfrac{2}{3} = ?$
22. $-\dfrac{2}{7} \times \dfrac{1}{2} \times \dfrac{4}{5} = ?$
23. $\dfrac{2}{3} \div \dfrac{4}{5} = ?$
24. $\dfrac{2}{3} - \dfrac{3}{7} = ?$
25. $\dfrac{5}{6} - \dfrac{11}{12} = ?$
26. $-\dfrac{5}{3} \div \dfrac{10}{6} = ?$

SECTIONS A8–A9—Exponents, Roots, and Order of Computation

1. $4^1 = ?$
2. $\sqrt{81} = ?$
3. $\sqrt[3]{8} = ?$
4. $12^2 = ?$
5. $5^3 = ?$
6. $\sqrt{2+7} = ?$
7. $\sqrt{16^2} = ?$
8. $(\sqrt{16})^2 = ?$
9. $8 \cdot 4 + 3 = ?$
10. $3 + 8 \div 4 = ?$
11. $1 + 2 \times 3 \div 5 = ?$
12. $(3 + 2 \times 4) \div 5 = ?$
13. $(6 \div 11) \times 1 \div 12 = ?$
14. $\dfrac{\frac{1}{2} + \frac{2}{4}}{\frac{1}{2}} = ?$

SECTIONS A10–A11—Equations and Summation Notation

Solve for x.

1. $x + 3 = 12$
2. $\dfrac{x}{2} = 4$
3. $6x = 18$
4. $5x + 10 = 20$
5. $\dfrac{x+3}{2} = 1.96$
6. $\dfrac{x-15}{7} = -1.96$
7. $\dfrac{x+9}{3} = 1.645$
8. $\dfrac{x+4}{8} = -1.645$

Using the following values of x and y to compute the following problems:

$$x_1 = 2, \ x_2 = 4, \ x_3 = 6$$
$$y_1 = 3, \ y_2 = 5, \ y_3 = 7$$

9. $\left(\sum x\right)^2 = ?$
10. $\sum y^2 = ?$
11. $\sum x + \sum y = ?$
12. $\sum xy = ?$
13. $\sqrt{\sum x^2} = ?$
14. $\sqrt{\sum xy} = ?$
15. $\sum (x+y)^2 = ?$
16. $\sum (x^2 + y^2) = ?$

APPENDIX B

TABLE B.1 Proportions of Area under the Standard Normal Curve: The Unit Normal Table

Column (A) lists z-score values. Column (B) lists proportion of the area between the mean and the z-score value. Column (C) lists the proportion of the area beyond the z-score in the tail of the distribution. (Note: Because the normal distribution is symmetrical, areas for negative z-scores are the same as those for positive z-scores.)

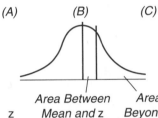
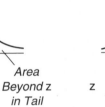
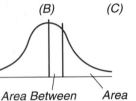
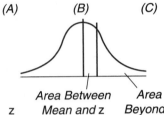

(A) z	(B) Area Between Mean and z	(C) Area Beyond z in Tail	(A) z	(B) Area Between Mean and z	(C) Area Beyond z in Tail	(A) z	(B) Area Between Mean and z	(C) Area Beyond z in Tail
0.00	.0000	.5000	0.15	.0596	.4404	0.30	.1179	.3821
0.01	.0040	.4960	0.16	.0636	.4364	0.31	.1217	.3783
0.02	.0080	.4920	0.17	.0675	.4325	0.32	.1255	.3745
0.03	.0120	.4880	0.18	.0714	.4286	0.33	.1293	.3707
0.04	.0160	.4840	0.19	.0753	.4247	0.34	.1331	.3669
0.05	.0199	.4801	0.20	.0793	.4207	0.35	.1368	.3632
0.06	.0239	.4761	0.21	.0832	.4168	0.36	.1406	.3594
0.07	.0279	.4721	0.22	.0871	.4129	0.37	.1443	.3557
0.08	.0319	.4681	0.23	.0910	.4090	0.38	.1480	.3520
0.09	.0359	.4641	0.24	.0948	.4052	0.39	.1517	.3483
0.10	.0398	.4602	0.25	.0987	.4013	0.40	.1554	.3446
0.11	.0438	.4562	0.26	.1026	.3974	0.41	.1591	.3409
0.12	.0478	.4522	0.27	.1064	.3936	0.42	.1628	.3372
0.13	.0517	.4483	0.28	.1103	.3897	0.43	.1664	.3336
0.14	.0557	.4443	0.29	.1141	.3859	0.44	.1700	.3300

(A) z	(B) Area Between Mean and z	(C) Area Beyond z in Tail	(A) z	(B) Area Between Mean and z	(C) Area Beyond z in Tail	(A) z	(B) Area Between Mean and z	(C) Area Beyond z in Tail
0.45	.1736	.3264	0.78	.2823	.2177	1.11	.3665	.1335
0.46	.1772	.3228	0.79	.2852	.2148	1.12	.3686	.1314
0.47	.1808	.3192	0.80	.2881	.2119	1.13	.3708	.1292
0.48	.1844	.3156	0.81	.2910	.2090	1.14	.3729	.1271
0.49	.1879	.3121	0.82	.2939	.2061	1.15	.3749	.1251
0.50	.1915	.3085	0.83	.2967	.2033	1.16	.3770	.1230
0.51	.1950	.3050	0.84	.2995	.2005	1.17	.3790	.1210
0.52	.1985	.3015	0.85	.3023	.1977	1.18	.3810	.1190
0.53	.2019	.2981	0.86	.3051	.1949	1.19	.3830	.1170
0.54	.2054	.2946	0.87	.3078	.1922	1.20	.3849	.1151
0.55	.2088	.2912	0.88	.3106	.1894	1.21	.3869	.1131
0.56	.2123	.2877	0.89	.3133	.1867	1.22	.3888	.1112
0.57	.2157	.2843	0.90	.3159	.1841	1.23	.3907	.1093
0.58	.2190	.2810	0.91	.3186	.1814	1.24	.3925	.1075
0.59	.2224	.2776	0.92	.3212	.1788	1.25	.3944	.1056
0.60	.2257	.2743	0.93	.3238	.1762	1.26	.3962	.1038
0.61	.2391	.2709	0.94	.3264	.1736	1.27	.3980	1020
0.62	.2324	.2676	0.95	.3289	.1711	1.28	.3997	.1003
0.63	.2357	.2643	0.96	.3315	.1685	1.29	.4015	.0985
0.64	.2389	.2611	0.97	.3340	.1660	1.30	.4032	.0968
0.65	.2422	.2578	0.98	.3365	.1635	1.31	.4049	.0951
0.66	.2454	.2546	0.99	.3389	.1611	1.32	.4066	.0934
0.67	.2486	.2514	1.00	.3413	.1587	1.33	.4082	.0918
0.68	.2517	.2483	1.01	.3438	.1562	1.34	.4099	.0901
0.69	.2549	.2451	1.02	.3461	.1539	1.35	.4115	.0885
0.70	.2580	.2420	1.03	.3485	.1515	1.36	.4131	.0869
0.71	.2611	.2389	1.04	.3508	.1492	1.37	.4147	.0853
0.72	.2642	.2358	1.05	.3531	.1469	1.38	.4162	.0838
0.73	.2673	.2327	1.06	.3554	.1446	1.39	.4177	.0823
0.74	.2704	.2296	1.07	.3577	.1423	1.40	.4192	.0808
0.75	.2734	.2266	1.08	.3599	.1401	1.41	.4207	.0793
0.76	.2764	.2236	1.09	.3621	.1379	1.42	.4222	.0778
0.77	.2794	.2206	1.10	.3643	.1357	1.43	.4236	.0764

(A) z	(B) Area Between Mean and z	(C) Area Beyond z in Tail	(A) z	(B) Area Between Mean and z	(C) Area Beyond z in Tail	(A) z	(B) Area Between Mean and z	(C) Area Beyond z in Tail
1.44	.4251	.0749	1.77	.4616	.0384	2.10	.4821	.0179
1.45	.4265	.0735	1.78	.4625	.0375	2.11	.4826	.0174
1.46	.4279	.0721	1.79	.4633	.0367	2.12	.4830	.0170
1.47	.4292	.0708	1.80	.4641	.0359	2.13	.4834	.0166
1.48	.4306	.0694	1.81	.4649	.0351	2.14	.4838	.0162
1.49	.4319	.0681	1.82	.4656	.0344	2.15	.4842	.0158
1.50	.4332	.0668	1.83	.4664	.0336	2.16	.4846	.0154
1.51	.4345	.0655	1.84	.4671	.0329	2.17	.4850	.0150
1.52	.4357	.0643	1.85	.4678	.0322	2.18	.4854	.0146
1.53	.4370	.0630	1.86	.4686	.0314	2.19	.4857	.0143
1.54	.4382	.0618	1.87	.4693	.0307	2.20	.4861	.0139
1.55	.4394	.0606	1.88	.4699	.0301	2.21	.4864	.0136
1.56	.4406	.0594	1.89	.4706	.0294	2.22	.4868	.0132
1.57	.4418	.0582	1.90	.4713	.0287	2.23	.4871	.0129
1.58	.4429	.0571	1.91	.4719	.0281	2.24	.4875	.0125
1.59	.4441	.0559	1.92	.4726	.0274	2.25	.4878	.0122
1.60	.4452	.0548	1.93	.4732	.0268	2.26	.4881	.0119
1.61	.4463	.0537	1.94	.4738	.0262	2.27	.4884	.0116
1.62	.4474	.0526	1.95	.4744	.0256	2.28	.4887	.0113
1.63	.4484	.0516	1.96	.4750	.0250	2.29	.4890	.0110
1.64	.4495	.0505	1.97	.4756	.0244	2.30	.4893	.0107
1.65	.4505	.0495	1.98	.4761	.0239	2.31	.4896	.0104
1.66	.4515	.0485	1.99	.4767	.0233	2.32	.4898	.0102
1.67	.4525	.0475	2.00	.4772	.0228	2.33	.4901	.0099
1.68	.4535	.0465	2.01	.4778	.0222	2.34	.4904	.0096
1.69	.4545	.0455	2.02	.4783	.0217	2.35	.4906	.0094
1.70	.4554	.0446	2.03	.4788	.0212	2.36	.4909	.0091
1.71	.4564	.0436	2.04	.4793	.0207	2.37	.4911	.0089
1.72	.4573	.0427	2.05	.4798	.0202	2.38	.4913	.0087
1.73	.4582	.0418	2.06	.4803	.0197	2.39	.4916	.0084
1.74	.4591	.0409	2.07	.4808	.0192	2.40	.4918	.0082
1.75	.4599	.0401	2.08	.4812	.0188	2.41	.4920	.0080
1.76	.4608	.0392	2.09	.4817	.0183	2.42	.4922	.0078

(A) z	(B) Area Between Mean and z	(C) Area Beyond z in Tail	(A) z	(B) Area Between Mean and z	(C) Area Beyond z in Tail	(A) z	(B) Area Between Mean and z	(C) Area Beyond z in Tail
2.43	.4925	.0075	2.74	.4969	.0031	3.05	.4989	.0011
2.44	.4927	.0073	2.75	.4970	.0030	3.06	.4989	.0011
2.45	.4929	.0071	2.76	.4971	.0029	3.07	.4989	.0011
2.46	.4931	.0069	2.77	.4972	.0028	3.08	.4990	.0010
2.47	.4932	.0068	2.78	.4973	.0027	3.09	.4990	.0010
2.48	.4934	.0066	2.79	.4974	.0026	3.10	.4990	.0010
2.49	.4936	.0064	2.80	.4974	.0026	3.11	.4991	.0009
2.50	.4938	.0062	2.81	.4975	.0025	3.12	.4991	.0009
2.51	.4940	.0060	2.82	.4976	.0024	3.13	.4991	.0009
2.52	.4941	.0059	2.83	.4977	.0023	3.14	.4992	.0008
2.53	.4943	.0057	2.84	.4977	.0023	3.15	.4992	.0008
2.54	.4945	.0055	2.85	.4978	.0022	3.16	.4992	.0008
2.55	.4946	.0054	2.86	.4979	.0021	3.17	.4992	.0008
2.56	.4948	.0052	2.87	.4979	.0021	3.18	.4993	.0007
2.57	.4949	.0051	2.88	.4980	.0020	3.19	.4993	.0007
2.58	.4951	.0049	2.89	.4981	.0019	3.20	.4993	.0007
2.59	.4952	.0048	2.90	.4981	.0019	3.21	.4993	.0007
2.60	.4953	.0047	2.91	.4982	.0018	3.22	.4994	.0006
2.61	.4955	.0045	2.92	.4982	.0018	3.23	.4994	.0006
2.62	.4956	.0044	2.93	.4983	.0017	3.24	.4994	.0006
2.63	.4957	.0043	2.94	.4984	.0016	3.25	.4994	.0006
2.64	.4959	.0041	2.95	.4984	.0016	3.30	.4995	.0005
2.65	.4960	.0040	2.96	.4985	.0015	3.35	.4996	.0004
2.66	.4961	.0039	2.97	.4985	.0015	3.40	.4997	.0003
2.67	.4962	.0038	2.98	.4986	.0014	3.45	.4997	.0003
2.68	.4963	.0037	2.99	.4986	.0014	3.50	.4998	.0002
2.69	.4964	.0036	3.00	.4987	.0013	3.60	.4998	.0002
2.70	.4965	.0035	3.01	.4987	.0013	3.70	.4999	.0001
2.71	.4966	.0034	3.02	.4987	.0013	3.80	.4999	.0001
2.72	.4967	.0033	3.03	.4988	.0012	3.90	.49995	.00005
2.73	.4968	.0032	3.04	.4988	.0012	4.00	.49997	.00003

Source: Based on J. E. Freund, *Modern Elementary Statistics* (11th edition). Pearson Prentice Hall, 2004.

TABLE B.2 THE *t*-DISTRIBUTION

Table entries are values of *t*-corresponding to proportions in one tail or in two tails combined.

One tail
(either right or left)

Two tails
combined

	Proportion in One Tail					
	0.25	0.10	0.05	0.25	0.01	0.005
	Proportion in Two Tails Combined					
df	0.50	0.20	0.10	0.05	0.02	0.01
1	1.000	3.078	6.314	12.706	31.821	63.657
2	0.816	1.886	2.920	4.303	6.965	9.925
3	0.765	1.638	2.353	3.182	4.541	5.841
4	0.741	1.533	2.132	2.776	3.747	4.604
5	0.727	1.476	2.015	2.571	3.365	4.032
6	0.718	1.440	1.943	2.447	3.143	3.707
7	0.711	1.415	1.895	2.365	2.998	3.499
8	0.706	1.397	1.860	2.306	2.896	3.355
9	0.703	1.383	1.833	2.282	2.821	3.250
10	0.700	1.372	1.812	2.228	2.764	3.169
11	0.697	1.363	1.796	2.201	2.718	3.106
12	0.695	1.356	1.782	2.179	2.681	3.055
13	0.694	1.350	1.771	2.160	2.650	3.012
14	0.692	1.345	1.761	2.145	2.624	2.977
15	0.691	1.341	1.753	2.131	2.602	2.947
16	0.690	1.337	1.746	2.120	2.583	2.921
17	0.689	1.333	1.740	2.110	2.567	2.898
18	0.688	1.330	1.734	2.101	2.552	2.878
19	0.688	1.328	1.729	2.093	2.539	2.861
20	0.687	1.325	1.725	2.086	2.528	2.845
21	0.686	1.323	1.721	2.080	2.518	2.831
22	0.686	1.321	1.717	2.074	2.508	2.819
23	0.685	1.319	1.714	2.069	2.500	2.807
24	0.685	1.318	1.711	2.064	2.492	2.797
25	0.684	1.316	1.708	2.060	2.485	2.787
26	0.684	1.315	1.706	2.056	2.479	2.779
27	0.684	1.314	1.703	2.052	2.473	2.771
28	0.683	1.313	1.701	2.048	2.467	2.763
29	0.683	1.311	1.699	2.045	2.462	2.756
30	0.683	1.310	1.697	2.042	2.457	2.750
40	0.681	1.303	1.684	2.021	2.423	2.704
60	0.679	1.296	1.671	2.000	2.390	2.660
120	0.677	1.289	1.658	1.980	2.358	2.617
∞	0.674	1.282	1.645	1.960	2.326	2.576

Source: Table III of R.A. Fisher and F. Yates, *Statistical Tables for Biological, Agricultural and Medical Research, 6th ed.* London: Longman Group Ltd., 1974 (previously published by Oliver and Boyd Ltd., Edinburgh). Adapted and reprinted with permission of the Addison Wesley Longman.

TABLE B.3 Table entries indicate critical values for the *F*-distribution.

Critcial values at a .05 level of significance are given in lightface type.

Critcial values at a .01 level of significance are given in boldface type.

df_{BG}

		Degrees of Freedom Numerator											
		1	**2**	**3**	**4**	**5**	**6**	**7**	**8**	**9**	**10**	**20**	**∞**
Degrees of Freedom Denominator	1	161 **4052**	200 **5000**	216 **5403**	225 **5625**	230 **5764**	234 **5859**	237 **5928**	239 **5928**	241 **6023**	242 **6056**	248 **6209**	254 **6366**
	2	18.51 **98.49**	19.00 **99.00**	19.16 **99.17**	19.25 **99.25**	19.30 **99.30**	19.33 **99.33**	19.36 **99.34**	19.37 **99.36**	19.38 **99.38**	19.39 **99.40**	19.44 **99.45**	19.5 **99.5**
	3	10.13 **34.12**	9.55 **30.92**	9.28 **29.46**	9.12 **28.71**	9.01 **28.24**	8.94 **27.91**	8.88 **27.67**	8.84 **27.49**	8.81 **27.34**	8.78 **27.23**	8.66 **26.69**	8.5 **26.1**
	4	7.71 **21.20**	6.94 **18.00**	6.59 **16.69**	6.39 **15.98**	6.26 **15.52**	6.16 **15.21**	6.09 **14.98**	6.04 **14.80**	6.00 **14.66**	5.96 **14.54**	5.80 **14.02**	5.6 **13.5**
	5	6.61 **16.26**	5.79 **13.27**	5.41 **12.06**	5.19 **11.39**	5.05 **10.97**	4.95 **10.67**	4.88 **10.45**	4.82 **10.27**	4.78 **10.15**	4.74 **10.05**	4.56 **9.55**	4.37 **9.02**
	6	5.99 **13.74**	5.14 **10.92**	4.76 **9.78**	4.53 **9.15**	4.39 **8.75**	4.28 **8.47**	4.21 **8.26**	4.15 **8.10**	4.10 **7.98**	4.06 **7.87**	3.87 **7.39**	3.67 **6.88**
	7	5.59 **13.74**	4.74 **9.55**	4.35 **8.45**	4.12 **7.85**	3.97 **7.46**	3.87 **7.19**	3.79 **7.00**	3.73 **6.84**	3.68 **6.71**	3.63 **6.62**	3.44 **6.15**	3.23 **5.65**
	8	5.32 **11.26**	4.46 **8.65**	4.07 **7.59**	3.84 **7.01**	3.69 **6.63**	3.58 **6.37**	3.50 **6.19**	3.44 **6.03**	3.39 **5.91**	3.34 **5.82**	3.15 **5.36**	2.93 **4.86**
	9	5.12 **10.56**	4.26 **8.02**	3.86 **6.99**	3.63 **6.42**	3.48 **6.06**	3.37 **5.80**	3.29 **5.62**	3.23 **5.47**	3.18 **5.35**	3.13 **5.26**	2.93 **4.80**	2.71 **4.31**
	10	4.96 **10.04**	4.10 **7.56**	3.71 **6.55**	3.48 **5.99**	3.33 **5.64**	3.22 **5.39**	3.14 **5.21**	3.07 **5.06**	3.02 **4.95**	2.97 **4.85**	2.77 **4.41**	2.54 **3.91**
	11	4.84 **9.65**	3.98 **7.20**	3.59 **6.22**	3.36 **5.67**	3.20 **5.32**	3.09 **5.07**	3.01 **4.88**	2.95 **4.74**	2.90 **4.63**	2.86 **4.54**	2.65 **4.10**	2.40 **3.60**
	12	4.75 **9.33**	3.89 **6.93**	3.49 **5.95**	3.26 **5.41**	3.11 **5.06**	3.00 **4.82**	2.92 **4.65**	2.85 **4.50**	2.80 **4.39**	2.76 **4.30**	2.54 **3.86**	2.30 **3.36**
	13	4.67 **9.07**	3.80 **6.70**	3.41 **5.74**	3.18 **5.20**	3.02 **4.86**	2.92 **4.62**	2.84 **4.44**	2.77 **4.30**	2.72 **4.19**	2.67 **4.10**	2.46 **3.67**	2.21 **3.17**
	14	4.60 **8.86**	3.74 **6.51**	3.34 **5.56**	3.11 **5.03**	2.96 **4.69**	2.85 **4.46**	2.77 **4.28**	2.70 **4.14**	2.65 **4.03**	2.60 **3.94**	2.39 **3.51**	2.13 **3.00**
	15	4.54 **8.68**	3.68 **6.36**	3.29 **5.42**	3.06 **4.89**	2.90 **4.56**	2.79 **4.32**	2.70 **4.14**	2.64 **4.00**	2.59 **3.89**	2.55 **3.80**	2.33 **3.36**	2.07 **2.87**

df_{E}

Degrees of Freedom Denominator	Degrees of Freedom Numerator: 1	2	3	4	5	6	7	8	9	10	20	∞
16	4.49 **8.53**	3.63 **6.23**	3.24 **5.29**	3.01 **4.77**	2.85 **4.44**	2.74 **4.20**	2.66 **4.03**	2.59 **3.89**	2.54 **3.78**	2.49 **3.69**	2.28 **3.25**	2.01 **2.75**
17	4.45 **8.40**	3.59 **6.11**	3.20 **5.18**	2.96 **4.67**	2.81 **4.34**	2.70 **4.10**	2.62 **3.93**	2.55 **3.79**	2.50 **3.68**	2.45 **3.59**	2.23 **3.16**	1.96 **2.65**
18	4.41 **8.28**	3.55 **6.01**	3.16 **5.09**	2.93 **4.58**	2.77 **4.25**	2.66 **4.01**	2.58 **3.85**	2.51 **3.71**	2.46 **3.60**	2.41 **3.51**	2.19 **3.07**	1.92 **2.57**
19	4.38 **8.18**	3.52 **5.93**	3.13 **5.01**	2.90 **4.50**	2.74 **4.17**	2.63 **3.94**	2.55 **3.77**	2.48 **3.63**	2.43 **3.52**	2.38 **3.43**	2.15 **3.00**	1.88 **2.49**
20	4.35 **8.10**	3.49 **5.85**	3.10 **4.94**	2.87 **4.43**	2.71 **4.10**	2.60 **3.87**	2.52 **3.71**	2.45 **3.56**	2.40 **3.45**	2.35 **3.37**	2.12 **2.94**	1.84 **2.42**
21	4.32 **8.02**	3.47 **5.78**	3.07 **4.87**	2.84 **4.37**	2.68 **4.04**	2.57 **3.81**	2.49 **3.65**	2.42 **3.51**	2.37 **3.40**	2.32 **3.31**	2.09 **2.88**	1.81 **2.36**
22	4.30 **7.94**	3.44 **5.72**	3.05 **4.82**	2.82 **4.31**	2.66 **3.99**	2.55 **3.76**	2.47 **3.59**	2.40 **3.45**	2.35 **3.35**	2.30 **3.26**	2.07 **2.83**	1.78 **2.31**
23	4.28 **7.88**	3.42 **5.66**	3.03 **4.76**	2.80 **4.26**	2.64 **3.94**	2.53 **3.71**	2.45 **3.54**	2.38 **3.41**	2.32 **3.30**	2.28 **3.21**	2.04 **2.78**	1.76 **2.26**
24	4.26 **7.82**	3.40 **5.61**	3.01 **4.72**	2.78 **4.22**	2.62 **3.90**	2.51 **3.67**	2.43 **3.50**	2.36 **3.36**	2.30 **3.25**	2.26 **3.17**	2.02 **2.74**	1.73 **2.21**
25	4.24 **7.77**	3.38 **5.57**	2.99 **4.68**	2.76 **4.18**	2.60 **3.86**	2.49 **3.63**	2.41 **3.46**	2.34 **3.32**	2.28 **3.21**	2.24 **3.13**	2.00 **2.70**	1.71 **2.17**
26	4.22 **7.72**	3.37 **5.53**	2.98 **4.64**	2.74 **4.14**	2.59 **3.82**	2.47 **3.59**	2.39 **3.42**	2.32 **3.29**	2.27 **3.17**	2.22 **3.09**	1.99 **2.66**	1.69 **2.13**
27	4.21 **7.68**	3.35 **5.49**	2.96 **4.60**	2.73 **4.11**	2.57 **3.79**	2.46 **3.56**	2.37 **3.39**	2.30 **3.26**	2.25 **3.14**	2.20 **3.06**	1.97 **2.63**	1.67 **2.10**
28	4.20 **7.64**	3.34 **5.45**	2.95 **4.57**	2.71 **4.07**	2.56 **3.76**	2.44 **3.53**	2.36 **3.36**	2.29 **3.23**	2.24 **3.11**	2.19 **3.03**	1.96 **2.60**	1.65 **2.07**
29	4.18 **7.60**	3.33 **5.42**	2.93 **4.54**	2.70 **4.04**	2.54 **3.73**	2.43 **3.50**	2.35 **3.33**	2.28 **3.20**	2.22 **3.08**	2.18 **3.00**	1.94 **2.57**	1.63 **2.04**
30	4.17 **7.56**	3.32 **5.39**	2.92 **4.51**	2.69 **4.02**	2.53 **3.70**	2.42 **3.47**	2.34 **3.30**	2.27 **3.17**	2.21 **3.06**	2.16 **2.98**	1.93 **2.55**	1.61 **2.01**
31	4.16 **7.53**	3.30 **5.36**	2.91 **4.48**	2.68 **3.99**	2.52 **3.67**	2.41 **3.45**	2.32 **3.28**	2.25 **3.15**	2.20 **3.04**	2.15 **2.96**	1.92 **2.53**	1.60 **1.89**
32	4.15 **7.50**	3.29 **5.34**	2.90 **4.46**	2.67 **3.97**	2.51 **3.65**	2.40 **3.43**	2.31 **3.26**	2.24 **3.13**	2.19 **3.02**	2.14 **2.93**	1.91 **2.51**	1.59 **1.88**

		Degrees of Freedom Numerator											
		1	**2**	**3**	**4**	**5**	**6**	**7**	**8**	**9**	**10**	**20**	**∞**
33		4.14	3.28	2.89	2.66	2.50	2.39	2.30	2.23	2.18	2.13	1.90	1.58
		7.47	**5.31**	**4.44**	**3.95**	**3.63**	**3.41**	**3.24**	**3.11**	**3.00**	**2.91**	**2.49**	**1.87**
34		4.13	3.28	2.88	2.65	2.49	2.38	2.29	2.23	2.17	2.12	1.89	1.57
		7.44	**5.29**	**4.42**	**3.93**	**3.61**	**3.39**	**3.22**	**3.09**	**2.98**	**2.89**	**2.47**	**1.86**
35		4.12	3.27	2.87	2.64	2.49	2.37	2.29	2.22	2.16	2.11	1.88	1.56
		7.42	**5.27**	**4.40**	**3.91**	**3.59**	**3.37**	**3.20**	**3.07**	**2.96**	**2.88**	**2.45**	**1.85**
36		4.11	3.26	2.87	2.63	2.48	2.36	2.28	2.21	2.15	2.11	1.87	1.55
		7.40	**5.25**	**4.38**	**3.89**	**3.57**	**3.35**	**3.18**	**3.05**	**2.95**	**2.86**	**2.43**	**1.84**
37		4.11	3.25	2.86	2.63	2.47	2.36	2.27	2.20	2.14	2.10	1.86	1.54
		7.37	**5.23**	**4.36**	**3.87**	**3.56**	**3.33**	**3.17**	**3.04**	**2.93**	**2.84**	**2.42**	**1.83**
38		4.10	3.24	2.85	2.62	2.46	2.35	2.26	2.19	2.14	2.09	1.85	1.53
		7.35	**5.21**	**4.34**	**3.86**	**3.54**	**3.32**	**3.15**	**3.02**	**2.92**	**2.83**	**2.40**	**1.82**
39		4.09	3.24	2.85	2.61	2.46	2.34	2.26	2.19	2.13	2.08	1.84	1.52
		7.33	**5.19**	**4.33**	**3.84**	**3.53**	**3.30**	**3.14**	**3.01**	**2.90**	**2.81**	**2.39**	**1.81**
40		4.08	3.23	2.84	2.61	2.45	2.34	2.25	2.18	2.12	2.07	1.84	1.51
		7.31	**5.18**	**4.31**	**3.83**	**3.51**	**3.29**	**3.12**	**2.99**	**2.88**	**2.80**	**2.37**	**1.80**
42		4.07	3.22	2.83	2.59	2.44	2.32	2.24	2.17	2.11	2.06	1.82	1.50
		7.27	**5.15**	**4.29**	**3.80**	**3.49**	**3.26**	**3.10**	**2.96**	**2.86**	**2.77**	**2.35**	**1.78**
44		4.06	3.21	2.82	2.58	2.43	2.31	2.23	2.16	2.10	2.05	1.81	1.49
		7.24	**5.12**	**4.26**	**3.78**	**3.46**	**3.24**	**3.07**	**2.94**	**2.84**	**2.75**	**2.32**	**1.76**
60		4.00	3.15	2.76	2.53	2.37	2.25	2.17	2.10	2.04	1.99	1.75	1.39
		7.08	**4.98**	**4.13**	**3.65**	**3.34**	**3.12**	**2.95**	**2.82**	**2.72**	**2.63**	**2.20**	**1.60**
120		3.92	3.07	2.68	2.45	2.29	2.18	2.09	2.02	1.96	1.91	1.66	1.25
		6.85	**4.79**	**3.95**	**3.48**	**3.17**	**2.96**	**2.79**	**2.66**	**2.56**	**2.47**	**2.03**	**1.38**
∞		3.84	3.00	2.60	2.37	2.21	2.10	2.01	1.94	1.88	1.83	1.57	1.00
		6.63	**4.61**	**3.78**	**3.32**	**3.02**	**2.80**	**2.64**	**2.51**	**2.41**	**2.32**	**1.88**	**1.00**

Degrees of Freedom Denominator

Source: The entries in this table were computed by the author.

TABLE B.4 The Studentized Range Statistic (q)

The critical values for q correspond to alpha = .05 (lightface type) and alpha = .01 (boldface type)

df_E	Range								
	2	**3**	**4**	**5**	**6**	**7**	**8**	**9**	**10**
6	3.46 **5.24**	4.34 **6.32**	4.90 **7.02**	5.30 **7.55**	5.63 **7.98**	5.91 **8.33**	6.13 **8.62**	6.32 **8.87**	6.50 **9.10**
7	3.34 **4.95**	4.17 **5.91**	4.68 **6.54**	5.06 **7.00**	5.36 **7.38**	5.60 **7.69**	5.82 **7.94**	5.99 **8.17**	6.15 **8.38**
8	3.26 **4.75**	4.05 **5.64**	4.53 **6.21**	4.89 **6.63**	5.17 **6.97**	5.41 **7.26**	5.60 **7.47**	5.78 **7.70**	5.93 **7.89**
9	3.20 **4.60**	3.95 **5.43**	4.42 **5.95**	4.76 **6.34**	5.03 **6.67**	5.24 **6.91**	5.43 **7.13**	5.60 **7.33**	5.74 **7.50**
10	3.15 **4.48**	3.88 **5.27**	4.33 **5.77**	4.66 **6.14**	4.92 **6.43**	5.12 **6.67**	5.30 **6.89**	5.46 **7.06**	5.60 **7.22**
11	3.11 **4.38**	3.82 **5.16**	4.27 **5.63**	4.59 **5.98**	4.83 **6.25**	5.03 **6.48**	5.21 **6.69**	5.36 **6.85**	5.49 **7.01**
12	3.08 **4.32**	3.78 **5.05**	4.20 **5.50**	4.51 **5.84**	4.75 **6.10**	4.96 **6.32**	5.12 **6.52**	5.26 **6.67**	5.39 **6.82**
13	3.05 **4.26**	3.73 **4.97**	4.15 **5.41**	4.47 **5.74**	4.69 **5.98**	4.88 **6.19**	5.06 **6.39**	5.21 **6.53**	5.33 **6.68**
14	3.03 **4.21**	3.70 **4.90**	4.11 **5.33**	4.41 **5.64**	4.64 **5.88**	4.83 **6.10**	4.99 **6.28**	5.13 **6.41**	5.25 **6.56**
15	3.01 **4.17**	3.68 **4.84**	4.09 **5.26**	4.38 **5.56**	4.59 **5.80**	4.79 **6.01**	4.95 **6.18**	5.09 **6.31**	5.21 **6.46**
16	2.99 **4.13**	3.65 **4.79**	4.05 **5.19**	4.33 **5.50**	4.56 **5.72**	4.74 **5.94**	4.89 **6.10**	5.03 **6.23**	5.15 **6.37**
17	2.98 **4.10**	3.63 **4.75**	4.02 **5.15**	4.30 **5.44**	4.52 **5.66**	4.70 **5.86**	4.85 **6.02**	4.99 **6.14**	5.11 **6.28**
18	2.97 **4.07**	3.62 **4.71**	4.01 **5.10**	4.29 **5.39**	4.49 **5.60**	4.68 **5.80**	4.84 **5.95**	4.97 **6.08**	5.08 **6.21**
19	2.96 **4.05**	3.59 **4.68**	3.98 **5.05**	4.26 **5.35**	4.47 **5.56**	4.65 **5.75**	4.80 **5.91**	4.93 **6.03**	5.04 **6.15**

df_E	Range								
	2	3	4	5	6	7	8	9	10
20	2.95 **4.02**	3.58 **4.64**	3.96 **5.02**	4.24 **5.31**	4.45 **5.51**	4.63 **5.71**	4.78 **5.86**	4.91 **5.98**	5.01 **6.09**
22	2.94 **3.99**	3.55 **4.59**	3.93 **4.96**	4.20 **5.27**	4.41 **5.44**	4.58 **5.62**	4.72 **5.76**	4.85 **5.87**	4.96 **6.00**
24	2.92 **3.96**	3.53 **4.55**	3.91 **4.92**	4.17 **5.17**	4.37 **5.37**	4.54 **5.55**	4.69 **5.70**	4.81 **5.81**	4.92 **5.93**
26	2.91 **3.94**	3.52 **4.51**	3.89 **4.87**	4.15 **5.13**	4.36 **5.33**	4.53 **5.49**	4.67 **5.63**	4.79 **5.74**	4.90 **5.86**
28	2.90 **3.91**	3.50 **4.48**	3.87 **4.83**	4.12 **5.09**	4.33 **5.28**	4.49 **5.45**	4.63 **5.58**	4.75 **5.69**	4.86 **5.81**
30	2.89 **3.89**	3.49 **4.45**	3.85 **4.80**	4.10 **5.05**	4.30 **5.24**	4.47 **5.40**	0.60 **5.54**	4.73 **5.64**	4.84 **5.76**
40	2.86 **3.82**	3.45 **4.37**	3.79 **4.70**	4.05 **4.93**	4.23 **5.11**	4.39 **5.26**	4.52 **5.39**	4.65 **5.49**	4.73 **5.60**
60	2.83 **3.76**	3.41 **4.28**	3.75 **4.60**	3.98 **4.82**	4.16 **4.99**	4.31 **5.13**	4.44 **5.25**	4.56 **5.36**	4.65 **5.45**
100	2.81 **3.72**	3.36 **4.22**	3.70 **4.52**	3.93 **4.74**	4.11 **4.90**	4.26 **5.04**	4.39 **5.15**	4.50 **5.23**	4.59 **5.34**
∞	2.77 **3.64**	3.31 **4.12**	3.63 **4.40**	3.86 **4.60**	4.03 **4.76**	4.17 **4.88**	4.28 **4.99**	4.39 **5.08**	4.47 **5.16**

Source: The entries in this table were computed by the author.

TABLE B.5 Critical Values for the Pearson Correlation*

*To be significant, the sample correlation, r, must be greater than or equal to the critical value in the table.

	Level of Significance for One-Tailed Test			
	.05	.025	.01	.005
	Level of Significance for Two-Tailed Test			
$df = n - 2$	.10	.05	.02	.01
1	.988	.997	.9995	.99999
2	.900	.950	.980	.990
3	.805	.878	.934	.959
4	.729	.811	.882	.917
5	.669	.754	.833	.874
6	.622	.707	.789	.834
7	.582	.666	.750	.798
8	.549	.632	.716	.765
9	.521	.602	.685	.735
10	.497	.576	.658	.708
11	.476	.553	.634	.684
12	.458	.532	.612	.661
13	.441	.514	.592	.641
14	.426	.497	.574	.623
15	.412	.482	.558	.606
16	.400	.468	.542	.590
17	.389	.456	.528	.575
18	.378	.444	.516	.561
19	.369	.433	.503	.549

df = n − 2	Level of Significance for One-Tailed Test			
	.05	.025	.01	.005
	Level of Significance for Two-Tailed Test			
	.10	.05	.02	.01
20	.360	.423	.492	.537
21	.352	.413	.482	.526
22	.344	.404	.472	.515
23	.337	.396	.462	.505
24	.330	.388	.453	.496
25	.323	.381	.445	.487
26	.317	.374	.437	.479
27	.311	.367	.430	.471
28	.306	.361	.423	.463
29	.301	.355	.416	.456
30	.296	.349	.409	.449
35	.275	.325	.381	.418
40	.257	.304	.358	.393
45	.243	.288	.338	.372
50	.231	.273	.322	.354
60	.211	.250	.295	.325
70	.195	.232	.274	.302
80	.183	.217	.256	.283
90	.173	.205	.242	.267
100	.164	.195	.230	.254

Source: Table VI of R. A. Fisher and F. Yates, *Statistical Tables for Biological, Agricultural and Medical Research, 6th ed.* London: Longman Group Ltd., 1974 (previously published by Oliver and Boyd Ltd., Edinburgh). Adapted and reprinted with permission of the Addison Wesley Longman.

TABLE B.6   Critical Values for the Spearman Correlation*

*To be significant, the sample correlation, r, must be greater than or equal to the critical value in the table.

	Level of Significance for One-Tailed Test			
	.05	**.025**	**.01**	**.005**
	Level of Significance for Two-Tailed Test			
n	**.10**	**.05**	**.02**	**.01**
4	1.000			
5	0.900	1.000	1.000	
6	0.829	0.886	0.943	1.000
7	0.714	0.786	0.893	0.929
8	0.643	0.738	0.833	0.881
9	0.600	0.700	0.783	0.833
10	0.564	0.648	0.745	0.794
11	0.536	0.618	0.709	0.755
12	0.503	0.587	0.671	0.727
13	0.484	0.560	0.648	0.703
14	0.464	0.538	0.622	0.675
15	0.443	0.521	0.604	0.654
16	0.429	0.503	0.582	0.635
17	0.414	0.485	0.566	0.615
18	0.401	0.472	0.550	0.600
19	0.391	0.460	0.535	0.584
20	0.380	0.447	0.520	0.570
21	0.370	0.435	0.508	0.556
22	0.361	0.425	0.496	0.544
23	0.353	0.415	0.486	0.532
24	0.344	0.406	0.476	0.521
25	0.337	0.398	0.466	0.511
26	0.331	0.390	0.457	0.501
27	0.324	0.382	0.448	0.491
28	0.317	0.375	0.440	0.483
29	0.312	0.368	0.433	0.475
30	0.306	0.362	0.425	0.467
35	0.283	0.335	0.394	0.433
40	0.264	0.313	0.368	0.405
45	0.248	0.294	0.347	0.382
50	0.235	0.279	0.329	0.363
60	0.214	0.255	0.300	0.331
70	0.190	0.235	0.278	0.307
80	0.185	0.220	0.260	0.287
90	0.174	0.207	0.245	0.271
100	0.165	0.197	0.233	0.257

Source: Reprinted with permission from the *Journal of the American Statistical Association.* Copyright 1972 by the American Statistical Association. All rights reserved.

TABLE B.7 Critical Values of Chi-Square (χ^2)

	Level of Significance	
df	$\alpha = .05$	$\alpha = .01$
1	3.84	6.64
2	5.99	9.21
3	7.81	11.34
4	9.49	13.28
5	11.07	15.09
6	12.59	16.81
7	14.07	18.48
8	15.51	20.09
9	16.92	21.67
10	18.31	23.21
11	19.68	24.72
12	21.03	26.22
13	22.36	27.69
14	23.68	29.14
15	25.00	30.58
16	26.30	32.00
17	27.59	33.41
18	28.87	34.80
19	30.14	36.19
20	31.41	37.47
21	32.67	38.93
22	33.92	40.29
23	35.17	41.64
24	36.42	42.98
25	37.65	44.31
26	38.88	45.64
27	40.11	46.96
28	41.34	48.28
29	42.56	49.59
30	43.77	50.89
40	55.76	63.69
50	67.50	76.15
60	79.08	88.38
70	90.53	100.42

Source: From Table IV of R. A. Fisher and F. Yates, *Statistical Tables for Biological, Agricultural and Medical Research, 6th ed.* London: Longman Group Ltd., 1974 Reprinted with permission of the Addison Wesley Longman Ltd.

TABLE B.8 Distribution of Binomial Probabilities When $p = 0.50$

	Sample Size (n)																		
x	2	3	4	5	6	7	8	9	10	11	12	13	14	15	16	17	18	19	20
0	0.250	0.125	0.062	0.032	0.016	0.008	0.004	0.002	0.001	...	...	...	...	...	...	...	...	...	...
1	0.500	0.375	0.250	0.156	0.094	0.055	0.031	0.018	0.010	0.005	0.003	0.002	0.001	...	...	...	...	...	...
2	0.250	0.375	0.376	0.312	0.234	0.164	0.109	0.070	0.044	0.027	0.016	0.010	0.006	0.003	0.002	0.001	0.001	...	...
3		0.125	0.250	0.312	0.234	0.273	0.219	0.164	0.117	0.081	0.054	0.035	0.022	0.014	0.008	0.006	0.003	0.002	0.001
4			0.062	0.156	0.234	0.273	0.274	0.246	0.205	0.161	0.121	0.087	0.061	0.042	0.028	0.019	0.012	0.007	0.005
5				0.032	0.094	0.164	0.219	0.246	0.246	0.226	0.193	0.157	0.122	0.092	0.067	0.047	0.033	0.022	0.015
6					0.016	0.055	0.109	0.164	0.205	0.226	0.226	0.209	0.183	0.153	0.122	0.094	0.071	0.053	0.037
7						0.008	0.031	0.070	0.117	0.161	0.193	0.209	0.210	0.196	0.175	0.148	0.121	0.096	0.074
8							0.004	0.018	0.044	0.081	0.121	0.157	0.183	0.196	0.196	0.185	0.167	0.144	0.120
9								0.002	0.010	0.027	0.054	0.087	0.122	0.152	0.175	0.185	0.184	0.176	0.160
10									0.001	0.005	0.016	0.035	0.061	0.092	0.122	0.148	0.167	0.176	0.176
11										...	0.003	0.010	0.022	0.042	0.067	0.094	0.121	0.144	0.160
12											...	0.002	0.006	0.014	0.028	0.047	0.071	0.096	0.120
13												...	0.001	0.003	0.008	0.019	0.033	0.053	0.074
14													...	...	0.002	0.006	0.012	0.022	0.037
15														...	...	0.001	0.003	0.007	0.015
16															...	...	0.001	0.002	0.005
17																...	...	...	0.001
18																	...	...	...
19																		...	...
20																			...

" ... " relfects omited values for probabilities of 0.0005 or less.

Source: The entries in this table were computed by the author.

TABLE B.9   Wilcoxon Signed-Ranks T Criticial Values

*For values of T to be significant, T must be equal to or less than the critical value listed in the table for a given level of significance and sample size *n*. Dashes (--) indicate that a decision is not possible.

n	Level of Significance (Two-Tailed test)		Level of Significance (One-Tailed test)	
	0.05	0.01	0.05	0.01
5	--	--	0	--
6	0	--	2	--
7	2	--	3	0
8	3	0	5	1
9	5	1	8	3
10	8	3	10	5
11	10	5	13	7
12	13	7	17	9
13	17	9	21	12
14	21	12	25	15
15	25	15	30	19
16	29	19	35	23
17	34	23	41	27
18	40	27	47	32
19	46	32	53	37
20	52	37	60	43
21	58	42	67	49
22	65	48	75	55
23	73	54	83	62
24	81	61	91	69
25	89	68	100	76
26	98	75	110	84
27	107	83	119	92
28	116	91	130	101
29	126	100	140	110
30	137	109	151	120

Source: The entries in this table were computed by the author.

TABLE B.10A Critical Values of the Mann-Whitney U for $\alpha = .05$*

*Critical values are provided for a one-tailed test at $\alpha = .05$ (lightface type) and for a two-tailed test at $\alpha = .05$ (bold-face type). To be significant for any given n_A and n_B, the obtained U must be equal to or less than the critical value in the table. Dashes (-) in the body of the table indicate that no decision is possible at the stated level of significance and values off n_A and n_B.

$n_B\backslash n_A$	1	2	3	4	5	6	7	8	9	10	11	12	13	14	15	16	17	18	19	20
1	–	–	–	–	–	–	–	–	–	–	–	–	–	–	–	–	–	–	0	0
	–	–	–	–	–	–	–	–	–	–	–	–	–	–	–	–	–	–	–	–
2	–	–	–	–	0	0	0	1	1	1	1	2	2	2	3	3	3	4	4	4
	–	–	–	–	–	–	–	**0**	**0**	**0**	**0**	**1**	**1**	**1**	**1**	**1**	**2**	**2**	**2**	**2**
3	–	–	0	0	1	2	2	3	3	4	5	5	6	7	7	8	9	9	10	11
	–	–	–	–	**0**	**1**	**1**	**2**	**2**	**3**	**3**	**4**	**4**	**5**	**5**	**6**	**6**	**7**	**7**	**8**
4	–	–	0	1	2	3	4	5	6	7	8	9	10	11	12	14	15	16	17	18
	–	–	–	**0**	**1**	**2**	**3**	**4**	**4**	**5**	**6**	**7**	**8**	**9**	**10**	**11**	**11**	**12**	**13**	**13**
5	–	0	1	2	4	5	6	8	9	11	12	13	15	16	18	19	20	22	23	25
	–	–	**0**	**1**	**2**	**3**	**5**	**6**	**7**	**8**	**9**	**11**	**12**	**13**	**14**	**15**	**17**	**18**	**19**	**20**
6	–	0	2	3	5	7	8	10	12	14	16	17	19	21	23	25	26	28	30	32
	–	–	**1**	**2**	**3**	**5**	**6**	**8**	**10**	**11**	**13**	**14**	**16**	**17**	**19**	**21**	**22**	**24**	**25**	**27**
7	–	0	2	4	6	8	11	13	15	17	19	21	24	26	28	30	33	35	37	39
	–	–	**1**	**3**	**5**	**6**	**8**	**10**	**12**	**14**	**16**	**18**	**20**	**22**	**24**	**26**	**28**	**30**	**32**	**34**
8	–	1	3	5	8	10	13	15	18	20	23	26	28	31	33	36	39	41	44	47
	–	**0**	**2**	**4**	**6**	**8**	**10**	**13**	**15**	**17**	**19**	**22**	**24**	**26**	**29**	**31**	**34**	**36**	**38**	**41**
9	–	1	3	6	9	12	15	18	21	24	27	30	33	36	39	42	45	48	51	54
	–	**0**	**2**	**4**	**7**	**10**	**12**	**15**	**17**	**20**	**23**	**26**	**28**	**31**	**34**	**37**	**39**	**42**	**45**	**48**
10	–	1	4	7	11	14	17	20	24	27	31	34	37	41	44	48	51	55	58	62
	–	**0**	**3**	**5**	**8**	**11**	**14**	**17**	**20**	**23**	**26**	**29**	**33**	**36**	**39**	**42**	**45**	**48**	**52**	**55**
11	–	1	5	8	12	16	19	23	27	31	34	38	42	46	50	54	57	61	65	69
	–	**0**	**3**	**6**	**9**	**13**	**16**	**19**	**23**	**26**	**30**	**33**	**37**	**40**	**44**	**47**	**51**	**55**	**58**	**62**
12	–	2	5	9	13	17	21	26	30	34	38	42	47	51	55	60	64	68	72	77
	–	**1**	**4**	**7**	**11**	**14**	**18**	**22**	**26**	**29**	**33**	**37**	**41**	**45**	**49**	**53**	**57**	**61**	**65**	**69**
13	–	2	6	10	15	19	24	28	33	37	42	47	51	56	61	65	79	75	80	84
	–	**1**	**4**	**8**	**12**	**16**	**20**	**24**	**28**	**33**	**37**	**41**	**45**	**50**	**54**	**59**	**63**	**67**	**72**	**76**
14	–	2	7	11	16	21	26	31	36	41	46	51	56	61	66	71	77	82	87	92
	–	**1**	**5**	**9**	**13**	**17**	**22**	**26**	**31**	**36**	**40**	**45**	**50**	**55**	**59**	**64**	**67**	**74**	**78**	**83**
15	–	3	7	12	18	23	28	33	39	44	50	55	61	66	72	77	83	88	94	100
	–	**1**	**5**	**10**	**14**	**19**	**24**	**29**	**34**	**39**	**44**	**49**	**54**	**59**	**64**	**70**	**75**	**80**	**85**	**90**
16	–	3	8	14	19	25	30	36	42	48	54	60	65	71	77	83	89	95	101	107
	–	**1**	**6**	**11**	**15**	**21**	**26**	**31**	**37**	**42**	**47**	**53**	**59**	**64**	**70**	**75**	**81**	**86**	**92**	**98**
17	–	3	9	15	20	26	33	39	45	51	57	64	70	77	83	89	96	102	109	115
	–	**2**	**6**	**11**	**17**	**22**	**28**	**34**	**39**	**45**	**51**	**57**	**63**	**67**	**75**	**81**	**87**	**93**	**99**	**105**
18	–	4	9	16	22	28	35	41	48	55	61	68	75	82	88	95	102	109	116	123
	–	**2**	**7**	**12**	**18**	**24**	**30**	**36**	**42**	**48**	**55**	**61**	**67**	**74**	**80**	**86**	**93**	**99**	**106**	**112**
19	0	4	11	18	25	32	39	47	54	62	69	77	84	92	100	107	115	123	130	138
	–	**2**	**8**	**13**	**20**	**27**	**34**	**41**	**48**	**55**	**62**	**69**	**76**	**83**	**90**	**98**	**105**	**112**	**119**	**1**
20	0	4	11	18	25	32	39	47	54	62	69	77	84	92	100	107	115	123	130	138
	–	**2**	**8**	**13**	**20**	**27**	**34**	**41**	**48**	**55**	**62**	**69**	**76**	**83**	**90**	**98**	**105**	**112**	**119**	**127**

Source: From KIRK. Statistics, 5E. © 2008 Wadsworth, a part of Cengage Learning, Inc. Reproduced by permission. www.cengage.com/permissions.

TABLE B.10B   Critical Values of the Mann-Whitney U For $\alpha = .01$*

*Critical values are provided for a one-tailed test at $\alpha = .01$ (lightface type) and for a two-tailed test at $\alpha = .01$ (bold-face type). To be significant for any given n_A and n_B, the obtained U must be equal to or less than the critical value in the table. Dashes (-) in the body of the table indicate that no decision is possible at the stated level of significance and values off n_A and n_B.

n_B\n_A	1	2	3	4	5	6	7	8	9	10	11	12	13	14	15	16	17	18	19	20
1	—	—	—	—	—	—	—	—	—	—	—	—	—	—	—	—	—	—	—	—
	—	—	—	—	—	—	—	—	—	—	—	—	—	—	—	—	—	—	—	—
2	—	—	—	—	—	—	—	—	—	—	—	—	0	0	0	0	0	0	1	1
	—	—	—	—	—	—	—	—	—	—	—	—	—	—	—	—	—	—	**0**	**0**
3	—	—	—	—	—	—	0	0	1	1	1	2	2	2	3	3	4	4	4	5
	—	—	—	—	—	—	—	—	**0**	**0**	**0**	**1**	**1**	**1**	**2**	**2**	**2**	**2**	**3**	**3**
4	—	—	—	—	0	1	1	2	3	3	4	5	5	6	7	7	8	9	9	10
	—	—	—	—	—	**0**	**0**	**1**	**1**	**2**	**2**	**3**	**3**	**4**	**5**	**5**	**6**	**6**	**7**	**8**
5	—	—	—	0	1	2	3	4	5	6	7	8	9	10	11	12	13	14	15	16
	—	—	—	—	**0**	**1**	**1**	**2**	**3**	**4**	**5**	**6**	**7**	**7**	**8**	**9**	**10**	**11**	**12**	**13**
6	—	—	—	1	2	3	4	6	7	8	9	11	12	13	15	16	18	19	20	22
	—	—	—	**0**	**1**	**2**	**3**	**4**	**5**	**6**	**7**	**9**	**10**	**11**	**12**	**13**	**15**	**16**	**17**	**18**
7	—	—	0	1	3	4	6	7	9	11	12	14	16	17	19	21	23	24	26	28
	—	—	—	**0**	**1**	**3**	**4**	**6**	**7**	**9**	**10**	**12**	**13**	**15**	**16**	**18**	**19**	**21**	**22**	**24**
8	—	—	0	2	4	6	7	9	11	13	15	17	20	22	24	26	28	30	32	34
	—	—	—	**1**	**2**	**4**	**6**	**7**	**9**	**11**	**13**	**15**	**17**	**18**	**20**	**22**	**24**	**26**	**28**	**30**
9	—	—	1	3	5	7	9	11	14	16	18	21	23	26	28	31	33	36	38	40
	—	—	**0**	**1**	**3**	**5**	**7**	**9**	**11**	**13**	**16**	**18**	**20**	**22**	**24**	**27**	**29**	**31**	**33**	**36**
10	—	—	1	3	6	8	11	13	16	19	22	24	27	30	33	36	38	41	44	47
	—	—	**0**	**2**	**4**	**6**	**9**	**11**	**13**	**16**	**18**	**21**	**24**	**26**	**29**	**31**	**34**	**37**	**39**	**42**
11	—	—	1	4	7	9	12	15	18	22	25	28	31	34	37	41	44	47	50	53
	—	—	**0**	**2**	**5**	**7**	**10**	**13**	**16**	**18**	**21**	**24**	**27**	**30**	**33**	**36**	**39**	**42**	**45**	**48**
12	—	—	2	5	8	11	14	17	21	24	28	31	35	38	42	46	49	53	56	60
	—	—	**1**	**3**	**6**	**9**	**12**	**15**	**18**	**21**	**24**	**27**	**31**	**34**	**37**	**41**	**44**	**47**	**51**	**54**
13	—	0	2	5	9	12	16	20	23	27	31	35	39	43	47	51	55	59	63	67
	—	—	**1**	**3**	**7**	**10**	**13**	**17**	**20**	**24**	**27**	**31**	**34**	**38**	**42**	**45**	**49**	**53**	**56**	**60**
14	—	0	2	6	10	13	17	21	24	28	31	35	38	43	47	51	55	59	63	67
	—	—	**1**	**4**	**7**	**11**	**15**	**18**	**21**	**24**	**27**	**31**	**34**	**38**	**42**	**45**	**49**	**53**	**56**	**60**
15	—	0	3	7	11	15	19	24	28	33	37	42	47	51	56	61	66	70	75	80
	—	—	**2**	**5**	**8**	**12**	**16**	**20**	**24**	**29**	**33**	**37**	**42**	**46**	**51**	**55**	**60**	**64**	**69**	**73**
16	—	0	3	7	12	16	21	26	31	36	41	46	51	56	61	66	71	76	82	87
	—	—	**2**	**5**	**9**	**13**	**18**	**22**	**27**	**31**	**36**	**41**	**45**	**50**	**55**	**60**	**65**	**70**	**74**	**79**
17	—	0	4	8	13	18	23	28	33	38	44	49	55	60	66	71	77	82	88	93
	—	—	**2**	**6**	**10**	**15**	**19**	**24**	**29**	**34**	**39**	**44**	**49**	**54**	**60**	**65**	**70**	**75**	**81**	**86**
18	—	0	4	9	14	19	24	30	36	41	47	53	59	65	70	76	82	88	94	100
	—	—	**2**	**6**	**11**	**16**	**21**	**26**	**31**	**37**	**42**	**47**	**53**	**58**	**64**	**70**	**75**	**81**	**87**	**92**
19	—	1	4	9	15	20	26	32	38	44	50	56	63	69	75	82	88	94	101	107
	—	**0**	**3**	**7**	**12**	**17**	**22**	**28**	**33**	**39**	**45**	**51**	**56**	**63**	**69**	**74**	**81**	**87**	**93**	**99**
20	—	1	5	10	16	22	28	34	40	47	53	60	67	73	80	87	93	100	107	114
	—	**0**	**3**	**8**	**13**	**18**	**24**	**30**	**36**	**42**	**48**	**54**	**60**	**67**	**73**	**79**	**86**	**92**	**99**	**105**

Source: From KIRK. Statistics, 5E. © 2008 Wadsworth, a part of Cengage Learning, Inc. Reproduced by permission. www.cengage.com/permissions.

APPENDIX C

Chapter Solutions for Even-Numbered Problems

SECTION A1

2. Negative
4. Negative
6. Positive
8. Positive
10. Positive
12. Constant
14. Variable
16. Variable

SECTIONS A2–A3

2. 10
4. –5
6. 19
8. 18
10. 0

SECTIONS A4–A5

2. 32
4. 60
6. 84
8. –1
10. 3
12. $-\dfrac{1}{2} = 0.50$

14. –5
16. –54
18. False
20. False

SECTIONS A6–A7

2. 0
4. Undefined
6. $\dfrac{3}{2}$
8. $-\dfrac{38}{3}$
10. $-\dfrac{35}{100}$
12. $\dfrac{52}{10,000}$

14. $\dfrac{125}{100}$
16. 2.5%
18. 50%
20. $\dfrac{17}{8}$
22. $-\dfrac{8}{70}$
24. $\dfrac{5}{21}$
26. $-\dfrac{2}{2} = -1.00$

SECTIONS A8–A9

2. 9
4. 144
6. $\sqrt{9} = 3$
8. 16
10. 5
12. 2.2
14. 2

SECTIONS A10–A11

2. $x = 8$
4. $x = 2$
6. $x = 1.28$
8. $x = -17.16$
10. 83
12. 68
14. $\sqrt{68} = 8.25$
16. 139

CHAPTER 1

2. Data describe a set of measurements (made up of raw scores); a raw score describes individual measurements.

4. Experimental, quasi-experimental, and correlational research methods.

6. The four scales of measurement are nominal, ordinal, interval, and ratio. Ratio scale measurements are the most informative.

8. Interval variables DO NOT have a true zero, and ratio variables DO have a true zero.

10. Continuous and discrete numbers.

12. (a) False. (b) True. (c) True.

14. The statistics class has a *population* of 25 students enrolled, but a *sample* of only 23 students attended.

16. An experimental research method because the researcher claims to have demonstrated *cause*.

18. (a) Quasi-independent variable. (b) Quasi-independent variable. (c) Independent variable. (d) Independent variable. (e) Quasi-independent variable. (f) Independent variable.

20. (a) Cocaine use (dependent vs. inexperienced). (b) Impulsive behavior.

22. Nominal, ordinal, interval, and ratio.

24. (a) Qualitative. (b) Quantitative. (c) Quantitative. (d) Qualitative.

26.

Variable	Type of Data (qualitative vs. quantitative)	Type of Number (continuous vs. discrete)	Type of Measurement
Gender	Qualitative	Discrete	Nominal
Seasons	Qualitative	Discrete	Nominal
Time of day	Quantitative	Continuous	Ratio
Rating scale score	Quantitative	Discrete	Interval
Movie ratings (one to four stars)	Quantitative	Discrete	Ordinal
Number of students in your class	Quantitative	Discrete	Ratio
Temperature (degrees Fahrenheit)	Quantitative	Continuous	Interval
Time (in minutes) to prepare dinner	Quantitative	Continuous	Ratio
Position standing in line	Quantitative	Discrete	Ordinal

28. Yes, this is an experiment. The race conditions were created by the researchers (manipulation), students were randomly assigned to each condition (randomization), and racial attitudes in two groups were compared (comparison).

30. An operational definition.

32. Equidistant scales. Variables on an interval scale have equidistant scales, meaning that differences on this scale are informative.

CHAPTER 2

2. Grouped data are distributed in intervals; ungrouped data are not.

4. To ensure that a single score can't be counted in more than one interval.

6. Ungrouped data sets with only a few different scores, and qualitative or categorical variables.

8. Midpoint; Upper boundary.

10. The *x*-axis.

12. (a)

Classes	f(x)
L	9
C	16
R	5

(b) Yes, the rat did press the center lever the most.

14. Three errors are (1) the intervals overlap, (2) the class width for each interval is not equal, and (3) the distribution includes an open interval.

16. The upper class boundaries are 3, 6, 9, 12, 15, and 18.

18. The interval width for each interval is 3.

20. Sixty children qualify for the new cognitive-behavioral therapy.

22. (a) 13, 17, 32, 32, 32, 40, 41, 49, 66, and 68. (b) Ten scores.

24. (a) Histogram. (b) Bar chart. (c) Histogram. (d) Bar chart.

26. (a) A = 78, B = 86, C = 68, D = 13. (b) Yes, this was a difficult test because half the class would fail.

28.

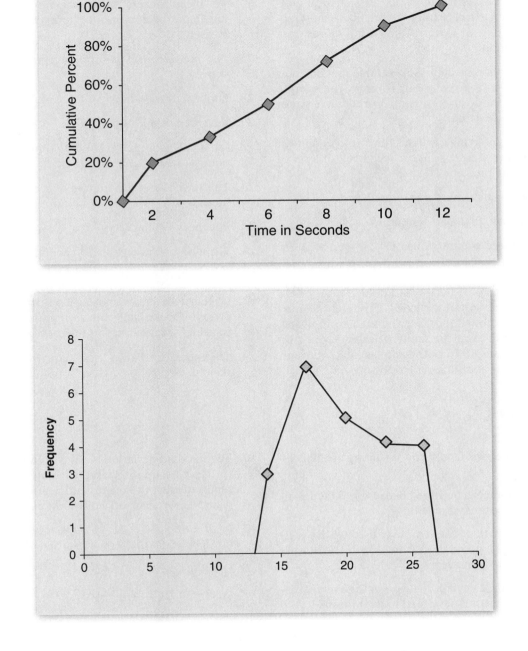

30.

32. Yes, as values on the x-axis increase (partying), values on the y-axis decrease (GPA).

34. (a) While more men earned a bachelor's degree in psychology in 1970–1971, women earn more than three times the number of bachelor's degrees in psychology as of 2005–2006. (b) Ungrouped data, because years are not distributed consecutively.

36. (a) 31–50 age group. (b) Two problems with this table are that the interval width is not equal, and the table includes an open class (51+).

38. (a) A pictorial frequency distribution. (b) Yes, these data reflect the distribution of wealth by country, so it is meaningful to "map" the distribution of these data because the data are distributed by country.

CHAPTER 3

2. Measures of central tendency are statistical measures used to locate a single score that is most representative or descriptive of all scores in a distribution.

4. A population mean is the mean for a set of scores in an entire population, whereas the sample mean is the mean for a sample, or subset of scores from a population.

6. The weighted mean equals the arithmetic mean when the sample sizes or "weights" for a set of scores are the same or equal.

8. Data that are skewed and ordinal data.

10. (a) Median. (b) Mean. (c) Mean.

12. (a) College students: mean = 25, median = 18, mode = 21. Parents: mean = 14, median = 18, mode = 21. (b) Because both distributions are skewed, the median would be the appropriate measure of central tendency. This might be misleading, though, because the median indicates that texting was the same between groups (the median was 18 in both samples), even though differences exist in regard to the mean.

14. The mean because the data are normally distributed, and the duration (in hours) is a ratio scale measure.

16. The median because the data are negatively skewed.

18. Bimodal distribution.

20. Weighted mean = 3.65.

22. (a) $M = 22$ points. (b) $M = 10$ points. (c) $M = 24$ points. (d) $M = 6$ points.

24. The sum of the differences of scores from the mean is 0.

26. The mean will increase.

28. The new mean weight is 190 pounds.

30. The data are skewed.

32. (a) The mode for nonsmoking Black participants was concern about a family member; the mode for nonsmoking White participants was concern for a friend.

34. The median because these data are negatively skewed.

CHAPTER 4

2. Two scores; the largest and smallest score in a distribution.

4. The variance is preferred because it includes all scores to estimate variability.

6. The variance of the sample will equal the variance of the population from which the sample was selected, on average.

8. The standard deviation measures the average distance that scores deviate from their mean.

10. The standard deviation is always positive, is used to describe quantitative variables, typically reported with the mean, and is affected by the value of every score in a distribution.

12. (a) $R = 98 - 77 = 21$. (b) $IQR = 96 - 85 = 11$. (c) $SIQR = 5.5$. (d) $s^2 = 55.41$. (e) $SD = 7.44$.

14. $Q_1 = 4.0$, $Q_2 = 5.5$, $Q_3 = 8.0$.

16. (a) $df = 30$. (b) $s^2 = \dfrac{120}{30} = 4.0$, $SD = \sqrt{4} = 2$.

18. No, in both cases, the standard deviation is the square root the variance. Hence, the population and the sample standard deviation will be $\sqrt{9} = 3.0$.

20. (a) Decrease. (b) Increase. (c) No effect.

22. The population variance.

24. $s^2 = \dfrac{240}{60-1} = 4.07; SD = \sqrt{4.07} = 2.02.$

26. (a) $SD = 4$. (b) $SD = 8$.

28. $SS = 37.50, s^2 = 5.36, SD = 2.31.$

30. $SD = 0.5.$

32. (a) $df = 60$ for men; $df = 92$ for women.

(b) Men are more likely to smoke at least half a pack per day because 10 cigarettes is within 1 SD of the mean for men but greater than 1 SD from the mean for women.

34. No, the data are likely skewed because the mean is pulled toward the larger scores in the distribution.

36. Men, because they reported an ideal height that was less than 4 inches shorter than the mean height of female participants. Women reported ideal heights that were over 6 inches taller than the mean height of male participants.

CHAPTER 5

2. A random event is any event where the outcomes for that event can vary. Outcomes do not vary in a fixed event.

4. Probability and relative frequency vary between 0 and 1 and can never be negative. The relative frequency of an outcome is the probability of its occurrence.

6. Two outcomes (A and B) are complementary when the sum of their probabilities is equal to 1.

8. A probability distribution is the distribution of probabilities for each outcome of a random variable. A binomial probability distribution is unique in that it distributes the probabilities for a random variable with only two possible outcomes.

10. (a) $\mu = np$. (b) $\sigma^2 = np(1-p)$ or $\sigma^2 = npq$. (c) $\sigma = \sqrt{\sigma^2}$.

12. 3,000 mothers were not satisfied.

14. (a) $p = .22$. (b) $p = .19$. (c) $p = .69$. (d) $p = .53$.

16. (a) The probability that an executive's rank holds great influence. (b) The probability that employees are directly influenced by an executive's decision. (c) The probability that an executive's rank holds great influence and that his or her decisions

directly influence employees. (d) The probability that an executive's rank holds great influence or that his or her decision directly influences employees.

18. $p = .12 \times .12 = .014.$

20. $p = .95.$

22. Using Bayes' theorem: $p(S \mathbin{/} P) = \dfrac{.50 \times .25}{.63} = .20.$

24. The probability falling in love and playing a sport is $p = .72 \times .55 = .396$. This does not match the last probability given.

26. $p = .19.$

28. We expect students to have an average of two dreams per night.

30. (a) 184 employees. (b) 168 employees.

32. (a) $p = .17 \times .17 \times .17 = .004913.$

34. (a) $p(\text{kicked right}) = \dfrac{112}{286} = .39$. (b) p(kicked right $\cap$ jumped right) $= \dfrac{59}{286} = .21$. (c) From the table: $p(\text{jumped right} \mathbin{/} \text{kicked right}) = \dfrac{59}{112} = .53$, and using the conditional probability formula: $p(\text{jumped right} \mathbin{/} \text{kicked right}) = \dfrac{.21}{.39} = .53.$

CHAPTER 6

2. Normality arises naturally in many physical, behavioral, and social measurement studies.

4. The mean equals 0 and the standard deviation equals 1.

6. The standard normal transformation is the difference between a score and the mean, divided by the standard deviation.

8. Step 1: Locate the z-score associated with a given proportion in the unit normal table. Step 2: Transform the z-score into a raw score (x).

10. Both np and nq must be greater than 10.

12. (a) .6915. (b) .0934. (c) .5000. (d) .0250. (e) .4602.

14. (a) The areas are equal. (b) The first area is bigger. (c) The first area is bigger. (d) The second area is bigger. (e) The second area is bigger.

16. (a) $z = 1.645$. (b) $z = -1.96$. (c) $z = -0.51$. (d) $z = 0$ (e) $z = 0$.

18. Students with a 3.56 GPA or better will be offered a scholarship.

20. (a) .0548. (b) .1587. (c) .4452. (d) .8413. (e) .9452.

22. $SD = 1.50$.

24. $M = 10$.

26. She knows that very few people will be highly accurate at lie detection because the data are normally distributed—the probability of behaviors far from the mean (e.g., highly accurate lie detection) will be associated with a low probability of occurrence.

28. (a) $p = .9049$. (b) $p = .0418$.

30. (a) $p = .0110$. (b) $p = .3790$.

32. (a) A rating of 22.16 marks the top 10% of ratings for this joke. (b) $np = 86(.8078) = 69.5$ undergraduates.

CHAPTER 7

2. Sampling without replacement and conditional probabilities are related in that when we sample without replacement, the probability of each selection is conditional or dependent on the person or item that was selected in the previous selection.

4. Sampling with replacement is a method of sampling in which each participant or item selected is replaced before the next selection. Sampling without replacement is a method of sampling in which each participant or item selected is not replaced before the next selection.

6. The central limit theorem is a theorem that states that regardless of the distribution of scores in a population, the sampling distribution of sample means selected from that population will be approximately normally distributed.

8. It means that we must divide SS by df to ensure that when we select a random sample of a given size, the sample variance will be equal to the value of the population variance on average.

10. It is more important that the sample variance be unbiased.

12. (a) The standard error would increase. (b) The standard error would decrease.

14. No, because each student is not selected at random, and each student's name is not replaced before selecting another student.

16. (a) 625 samples. (b) 4,096 samples. (c) 65,536 samples. (d) 6,250,000 samples.

18. (a) $\mu_M = 8$. (b) $\mu_M = 0$. (c) $\mu_M = -20$. (d) $\mu_M = \infty$. (e) $\mu_M = -\infty$. (f) $\mu_M = .03$.

20. (a) True. (b) True. (c) False. (d) True.

22. (a) True. (b) False. (c) True. (d) False.

24. (a) $\mu_M = -30$. (b) $\sigma_M = \dfrac{4}{\sqrt{16}} = 1.00$. (c) Sketch of sampling distribution with $M \pm 3\ SD$:

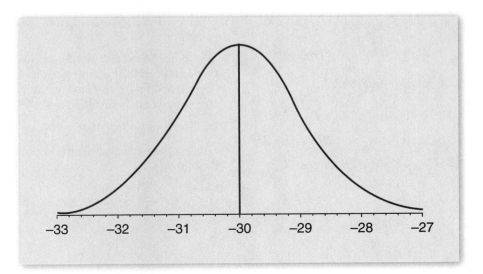

26. (a) Decreases. (b) Increases. (c) Decreases. (d) Increases.

28. (a) $5^3 = 125$ possible samples. (b) $\mu = \dfrac{9}{5} = 1.80$. The population mean is 1.80. (c) $\sigma = \sqrt{\dfrac{28.80}{5}} = \sqrt{5.76} = 2.40$. The population standard deviation is 2.40.

30. $\sigma_M = \dfrac{2.40}{\sqrt{3}} = 1.39$.

32. The sample statistics we measure do not always equal the population parameters they are meant to estimate.

CHAPTER 8

2. Reject the null hypothesis and retain the null hypothesis.

4. A Type II error is the probability of retaining a null hypothesis that is actually false. Researchers do not directly control for this type of error.

6. Critical values = ±1.96.

8. All four terms describe the same thing. The level of significance is represented by alpha, which defines the rejection region or the region associated with the probability of committing a Type I error.

10. Alpha level, sample size, and effect size.

12. In hypothesis testing, the significance of an effect determines whether an effect exists in some population. Effect size is used as a measure of how big the effect is in the population.

14. All decisions are made about the null hypothesis and not the alternative hypothesis. The only appropriate decisions are to retain or reject the null hypothesis.

16. The sample size in the second sample was larger. Therefore, the second sample had more power to detect the effect, which is likely why the decisions were different.

18. (a) $\alpha = .05$. (b) $\alpha = .01$. (c) $\alpha = .001$.

20. (1a) Reject the null hypothesis. (1b) Reject the null hypothesis. (1c) Reject the null hypothesis. (1d) Retain the null hypothesis. (2a) Retain the null hypothesis. (2b) Retain the null hypothesis. (2c) Reject the null hypothesis. (2d) Reject the null hypothesis.

22. (a) $\sigma_M = \dfrac{7}{\sqrt{49}} = 1.0$; hence, $z_{obt} = \dfrac{74-72}{1} = 2.00$. The decision is to reject the null hypothesis.

(b) $d = \dfrac{74-72}{7} = .29$. A medium effect size.

24. (a) $d = \dfrac{0.05}{0.4} = 0.125$. A small effect size.

(b) $d = \dfrac{0.1}{0.4} = 0.25$. A medium effect size.

(c) $d = \dfrac{0.4}{0.4} = 1.00$. A large effect size.

26. (a) $d = \dfrac{1}{1} = 1.00$. Large effect size. (b) $d = \dfrac{1}{2} = 0.50$. Medium effect size. (c) $d = \dfrac{1}{4} = 0.25$. Medium effect size. (d) $d = \dfrac{1}{6} = .17$. Small effect size.

28. This will decrease standard error, thereby increasing power.

30. The point Good and Hardin are making is that it is possible with the same data to retain the null hypothesis for a two-tailed test and reject the null hypothesis for a one-tailed test.

32. (a) Two-tailed z-test. (b) $\alpha = .05$.

34. We use the z-test because the population variance is known.

CHAPTER 9

2. Because the sample variance is an unbiased estimator of the population variance—the sample variance will equal the value of the population variance on average.

4. The t-distribution is a sampling distribution with a standard error that is computed using the sample variance to estimate the population variance. Hence, the degrees of freedom for sample variance $(n-1)$ are also associated with each t-distribution.

6. Estimated Cohen's d, eta-squared, and omega-squared.

8. The pooled sample standard deviation, which is the square root of the pooled sample variance.

10. The value for the test statistic, the degrees of freedom, and the p value for the test.

12. (1a) Reject the null hypothesis. (1b) Retain the null hypothesis. (1c) Reject the null hypothesis. (1d) Reject the null hypothesis. (2a) Retain the null hypothesis. (2b) Retain the null hypothesis. (2c) Reject the null hypothesis. (2d) Retain the null hypothesis.

14. (a) ±2.201. (b) −2.602. (c) ±2.779. (d) +1.699.

16. (a) Increase. (b) No effect. (c) Decrease.

18. (a) $t_{obt} = \dfrac{3.0 - 1.4}{0.535} = 2.991 = 2.991$. The decision is to reject the null hypothesis. (b) Estimated Cohen's d: $\dfrac{3.0 - 1.4}{1.512} = 1.06$ (large effect size).

20. (a) $t_{obt} = \dfrac{(6-3)-0}{1.00} = 3.00$. The decision is to reject the null hypothesis. (b) Estimated Cohen's d: $\dfrac{6-3}{1.581} = 1.90$ (large effect size).

22. The sample size is 40 classrooms. The decision was to reject the null hypothesis ($p < .05$). The study showed a medium effect size.

24. (a) Large. (b) Medium. (c) Medium. (d) Small.

26. The tails of the t-distribution will approach the x-axis faster, and the t-distribution will more closely approximate the z-distribution.

28. $t_{obt} = \dfrac{30.4 - 50}{3.614} = -5.424$. The decision is to reject the null hypothesis.

30. (a) $\omega^2 = \dfrac{(-2.47)^2 - 1}{(-2.47)^2 + 136} = 0.04$ (small proportion of variance). (b) Estimated Cohen's d: $\dfrac{2.79 - 2.47}{0.74} = 0.43$ (medium effect size).

32. (a) $t_{obt} = \dfrac{(86.36 - 104.09) - 0}{\sqrt{\dfrac{188.12}{11} + \dfrac{188.12}{11}}} = -3.035$. The decision is to reject the null hypothesis. (b) Estimated Cohen's d: $\dfrac{86.36 - 104.09}{\sqrt{188.12}} = -1.29$ (large effect size). (c) $\eta^2 = \dfrac{(-3.035)^2}{(-3.035)^2 + 20} = 0.32$ (large effect size).

CHAPTER 10

2. The repeated measures design and the matched-pairs design.

4. Participants can be matched through experimental manipulation and natural occurrence.

6. The degrees of freedom for the related samples *t*-test are the number of difference scores minus 1.

8. Computing difference scores eliminates between-persons error.

10. No, both research designs are associated with selecting related samples. The way that participants are selected is different, but not the computation of the test statistic for a related samples *t*-test.

12. To report the results of a related samples *t*-test, state the test statistic, the degrees of freedom, the *p* value, and the effect size. Also, summarize the means and the standard error or standard deviations measured in the study in a figure, a table, or in the text.

14. (a) Matched-pairs design, $df = 19$. (b) Repeated measures design, $df = 29$. (c) Matched-pairs design, $df = 24$. (d) Repeated measures design, $df = 11$.

16. (a) $M_D = \dfrac{-4}{5} = -0.8$; $s_D = \sqrt{\dfrac{30.8}{5-1}} = 2.8 = 2.8$; $s_{MD} = \dfrac{2.8}{\sqrt{5}} = 1.3$.

(b)

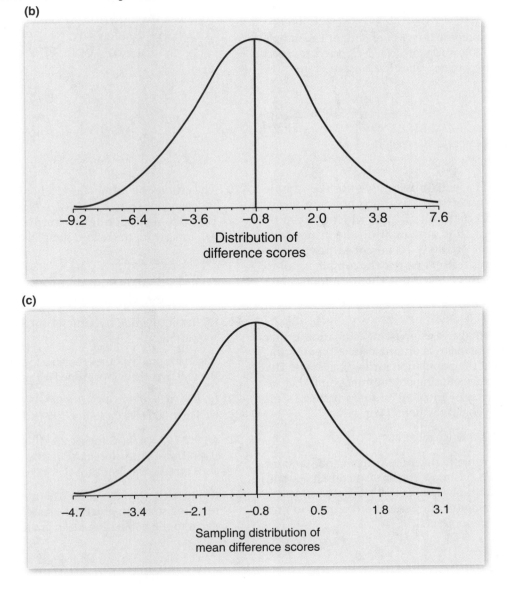

Distribution of difference scores

(c)

Sampling distribution of mean difference scores

18. (a) $t_{obt} = \frac{4}{2} = 2.0$. (b) $t_{obt} = \frac{4}{8} = 0.5$. (c) $t_{obt} = \frac{8}{2} = 4.0$. (d) $t_{obt} = \frac{8}{16} = 0.5$.

20. (a) $t_{obt} = \frac{-5.5 - 0}{1.18} = -4.660$. The decision is to reject the null hypothesis. (b) Estimated Cohen's $d = \frac{-5.5}{3.338} = 1.65$ (large effect size).

22. (a) $t_{obt} = \frac{-195}{180.19} = -1.082$. The decision is to retain the null hypothesis. (b) Omega-squared: $\omega^2 = \frac{(-1.082)^2 - 1}{(-1.082)^2 + 9} = 0.02$ (small effect size). (c) The researcher did not find support for her hypothesis; the decision is that there is no mean difference in number of calories consumed between normal-weight and overweight siblings.

24. This was a repeated measures design. The sample size was 120 participants. The decision was to reject the null hypothesis. This was a large effect size.

26. (a) Decrease. (b) No effect. (c) Increase.

28. (a) Repeated measures design. (b) Yes, rats increased responding on the lever for the sucrose–corn oil mixture compared to sucrose alone.

30. (a) Matched-pairs design. (b) The results show that teachers perceive children with cancer as having greater social problems compared to their peers in terms of showing greater social withdrawal, somatic complaints, and social problems.

32. (a) Reject the null hypothesis for each measure. (b) Opportunity to promote: $\omega^2 = \frac{(3.65)^2 - 1}{(3.65)^2 + 254} = .05$ (small effect size). High pay: $\omega^2 = \frac{(5.50)^2 - 1}{(5.50)^2 + 254} = .10$ (medium effect size). Pay according to performance: $\omega^2 = \frac{(5.61)^2 - 1}{(5.61)^2 + 254} = .11$ (medium effect size).

CHAPTER 11

2. When we use estimation, we use the sample mean as an estimate of the population mean, then find the limits within which we can be confident that a population mean or mean difference is likely to be contained. Using hypothesis testing, we use the sample mean to make decisions regarding the likelihood that a population mean stated by a null hypothesis is correct.

4. The advantage of using point estimation is that the sample mean is an unbiased estimator and will equal the population mean on average. The disadvantage of using point estimation is that we have no way of knowing for sure whether a sample mean equals the population mean.

6. A 95% confidence interval.

8. Step 1: Compute the sample mean and standard error. Step 2: Choose the level of confidence and find the critical values at that level of confidence. Step 3: Compute the estimation formula to find the confidence limits.

10. The estimation formula is $M \pm t(s_M)$ for the one–independent sample t-test, $M_1 - M_2 \pm t(s_{M_1 - M_2})$ for the two–independent sample t-test, and $M_D \pm t(s_{MD})$ for the related samples t-test.

12. The point estimate.

14. (a) Related samples t-test. (b) Two–independent sample t-test. (c) One–independent sample t-test.

16. (a) Retain the null hypothesis. (b) Reject the null hypothesis.

18. Retain the null hypothesis because the value stated in the null hypothesis is contained within the 95% CI.

20. (a) 95% CI = 9.7 to 14.3. (b) 94 ± 6.684; 95% CI = 87.316 to 100.684. (c) 4 ± 1.47; 95% CI = 2.53 to 5.47.

22. (a) 90% CI = 478.78 to 541.23. (b) Reject the null hypothesis. The value stated in the null hypothesis is outside the limits for the 90% CI.

24. (a) 90% CI = 66.39 to 73.61. (b) No, the new teaching strategy actually decreased grades compared to the population mean grade of 75 points.

26. (a) 99% CI = –16.85 to –3.15. (b) Yes, using hand gestures to count increased the speed of counting between 3.15 seconds and 16.85 seconds in the population.

28. (a) 95% CI = 7.03 to 16.97. (b) Yes, children took between 7.03 and 16.97 more bites of food

wrapped in familiar packaging compared to plain packaging.

30. Effect size.

32. (a) Alcohol abuse. (b) Drug abuse.

CHAPTER 12

2. Yes, in situations when we select a sample from a single population and randomly assign participants to two or more groups.

4. Between-groups variation and within-groups variation.

6. A sample variance, or SS divided by df.

8. Compute post hoc tests.

10. Fisher's LSD.

12. Two measures are eta-squared $\left(\eta^2\right)$ and omega-squared $\left(\omega^2\right)$. Omega-squared is the more conservative estimate.

14. (a) Environmental conditions (levels = 6). (b) Brain regions (levels = 5). (c) Seasons of birth (levels = 4). (d) Leadership styles (levels = 3).

16. (a) No, because $k = 2$. (b) Yes, because $k > 2$ and the result is significant. (c) No, because the result is not significant.

18. $F = 0$. Because all group means are the same ($M = 6$), there is no variability between groups. The mean square between groups in the numerator is equal to 0, making the value of the test statistic equal to 0.

20. $k = 3$, $N = 60$, $n = 20$, and it was a medium effect size.

22. (a)

Source of Variation	SS	df	MS	F
Between groups	30	2	15	11.72*
Within groups (error)	50	39	1.28	
Total	80	41		

(b) $\eta^2 = \dfrac{30}{80} = 0.38$. Large effect size. (c) Reject the null hypothesis.

24. (a)

Source of Variation	SS	df	MS	F
Between groups	27.27	2	13.64	3.47*
Within groups (error)	106.20	27	3.93	
Total	133.47	29		

(b) A one-way ANOVA was significant, $F(2, 27) = 3.47$, $p < .05$, with polycose consumption being significantly greater than saccharin consumption (Tukey HSD, $p < .05$). Otherwise, no significant differences were evident.

26. (a)

Source of Variation	SS	df	MS	F
Between groups	56.37	2	28.19	12.78*
Within groups (error)	46.32	21	2.21	
Total	102.69	23		

(b) A one-way ANOVA was significant, $F(2, 21) = 12.78$, $p < .05$, with the difficult task arousing greater stress compared to the easy and typical tasks (Fisher LSD, $p < .05$). Otherwise, no significant differences were evident.

28. (a) Increase. (b) Increase. (c) Decrease. (d) Decrease.

30. If the decision is to retain the null hypothesis, then we conclude that the group means in the population do not vary. Computing effect size is not meaningful because we just concluded that there is no effect.

CHAPTER 13

2. Three source of variation: between groups, between persons, and within groups. The between-groups source of variation is associated with variance between group means.

4. Twelve participants are observed 4 times.

6. When the within-groups variation is 0, this makes the denominator of the test statistic equal to 0. Hence, the test statistic is undefined. There is no solution.

8. Testwise alpha is the alpha level, or probability of committing a Type I error, per test or pairwise comparison made on the same data. The Bonferroni procedure can be used to determine the testwise for multiple pairwise comparisons.

10. Sum of squares between persons.

12. The power increases.

14. (a) $df_{BG} = 5$, $df_E = 100$. (b) $df_{BG} = 2$, $df_E = 18$. (c) $df_{BG} = 3$, $df_E = 24$. (d) $df_{BG} = 3$, $df_E = 60$.

16. $n = 20$ participants.

18. The test statistic will be undefined in both data sets because participant scores do not vary between groups.

20. (a)

Source of Variation	SS	df	MS	F_{obt}
Between groups	**396**	**2**	198	**5.50**
Between persons	234	**9**	**26**	
Within groups (error)	**648**	**18**	**36**	
Total	1,278	29		

The decision is to reject the null hypothesis.

(b) $\eta_P^2 = \dfrac{396}{1,278 - 234} = 0.38$ or 38%.

32. $SS_E = 3,511.51$, $df_{BG} = 1$, $MS_{BG} = 1,134.91$. The decision is to reject the null hypothesis.

34. $SS_E = 2,635.84$, $MS_{BG} = 1,236.29$, $MS_E = 25.59$, $F_{obt} = 48.31$. The decision is to reject the null hypothesis.

22. (a)

Source of Variation	SS	df	MS	F_{obt}
Between groups	77.46	3	25.82	17.77
Between persons	33.50	5	6.70	
Within groups (error)	21.79	15	1.45	
Total	132.75	23		

(b) A one-way ANOVA was significant, $F(3, 15) = 17.81$, $p < .05$. Using the Bonferroni procedure, related samples t-tests showed that participants committed significantly fewer errors in the first and last 15-minute intervals compared with intervals two and three ($p < .05$). There were four significant related samples t-tests:

First > Second, $t(5) = -4.66$, $p < .05$.

First > Third, $t(5) = -7.42$, $p < .05$.

Last > Second, $t(5) = 5.22$, $p < .05$.

Third > Fourth, $t(5) = 4.60$, $p < .05$.

24. (a)

Source of Variation	SS	df	MS	F_{obt}
Between groups	0.58	2	0.29	0.277
Between persons	15.63	7	2.23	
Within groups (error)	14.75	14	1.05	
Total	30.96	23		

The decision is to retain the null hypothesis, $F(2, 14) = 0.277$, $p > .05$. The number of tours a soldier has served does not significantly affect morale.

26. (a)

Source of Variation	SS	df	MS	F_{obt}
Between groups	30	1	30	2.00
Between persons	27	9	3	
Within groups (error)	135	9	15	
Total	192	19		

The decision is to retain the null hypothesis. The number of outbursts during class did not significantly vary by the type of teacher, $F(1, 9) = 2.00$, $p > .05$.

28. Housing rat pups together could influence how they respond during a study. Any differences between groups in a given group could be related to their housing situation. This would violate the assumption of independence within groups.

30. (a) 11 types of power. (b) A partial eta-squared would have been more appropriate for a within-subjects test. But the partial estimate would have been larger than the eta-squared estimate they reported. So reporting eta-squared is acceptable because it is a more conservative estimate.

32. (a)

Source of Variation	SS	df	MS	F_{obt}
Between groups	23.53	4	5.88	10.44
Between persons	29.90	5	5.98	
Within groups (error)	11.27	20	0.56	
Total	64.70	29		

Decision: Reject the null hypothesis. A placebo significantly decreased the frequency of binge eating over an 8-week period, $F(4, 20) = 10.44$, $p < .05$.

(b) The results indicate that a placebo (fake drug) significantly decreases binging. This might cast doubt on studies that show that a real drug for treating binge eating disorder also reduces binging.

CHAPTER 14

2. The 2-between or between-subjects design, the 1-between 1-within or mixed design, and the 2-within or within-subjects design.

4. (a) Main effects are located in the row and column totals outside the table. (b) An interaction is located in the cells inside the table.

6. (a) $N = 135$ total subjects. (b) 9 cells of groups.

8. The within-groups or error source of variation.

10. The interaction because it is potentially more informative.

12. Omega-squared.

14. Factor A: Gender (two levels: men, women). Factor B: Reason for immoral act in the vignette (three levels: preservation, protection, self-gain).

16. (a) $M = 3$, $M = 7$ for the column totals. (b) $M = 4$, $M = 6$ for the row totals. (c) $M = 2$, $M = 6$, $M = 4$, $M = 8$ for each cell.

18. Reject the null hypothesis.

20. The value of the test statistic will decrease.

22. (a)

Source of Variation	SS	df	MS	F
Season	44,204.17	1	44,204.17	5.139*
Shift	1,900.00	2	950.00	0.110
Season × Shift	233.34	2	116.67	0.014
Error	154,825.00	18	8,601.39	
Total	201,162.51	23		

Decision: Reject the null hypothesis for the main effect of season. Retain the null hypothesis for the other main effect and the interaction.

(b) The main effect of season has only two levels. Multiple comparisons are not needed. Participants consumed more calories in winter compared to summer.

24. (a)

Source of Variation	SS	df	MS	F
Exam	190	2	95	6.33*
Student class	60	3	20	1.33
Exam × Student Class	540	6	90	6.00*
Error	1,620	108	15	
Total	2,410	119		

26. (a)

Source of Variation	SS	df	MS	F
Adult	226.08	2	113.04	5.79*
Consequence	3,504.17	1	3504.17	179.45*
Adult × Consequence	343.58	2	171.79	8.80*
Error	351.50	18	19.53	
Total	4,425.33	23		

Decision: Reject the null hypothesis for both main effects and the interaction.

(b) Simple effect test for type of adult with rewarding consequence:

Source of Variation	SS	df	MS	F
Adult	26.17	2	13.08	1.30
Within groups (error)	90.75	9	10.08	
Total	116.92	11		

Decision: Retain the null hypothesis—times did not vary by type of adult for a rewarding consequence.

Simple main effect test for type of adult with punishing consequence:

Source of Variation	SS	df	MS	F
Adult	543.50	2	271.75	9.38*
Within groups (error)	260.75	9	28.97	
Total	804.25	11		

Decision: Reject the null hypothesis—times did vary by type of adult for a punishing consequence.

Conclusion: A two-way ANOVA showed a significant Adult × Consequence interaction, $F(4, 27) = 4.45$, $p < .05$. Simple effect tests indicated that the three types of adults had similar influence in the reward condition ($p > .05$) but not in the punishment condition, $F(2, 9) = 9.38$, $p < .05$. Post hoc tests showed that parents and siblings had more influence in the punishment condition compared to strangers (Tukey's HSD, $p < .05$).

28. (a)

Source of Variation	SS	df	MS	F
Living status	0.06	1	0.06	0.04
Pet owner status	14.06	1	14.06	9.00*
Living × Owner	0.56	1	0.56	0.36
Error	18.75	12	1.56	
Total	33.43	15		

Decision: Reject the null hypothesis for the main effect of pet owner status. Retain the null hypothesis for the other main effect and the interaction.

(b) There is only a significant main effect of pet owner status. Because there are only two levels of this factor, post hoc tests are not necessary.

30. (a)

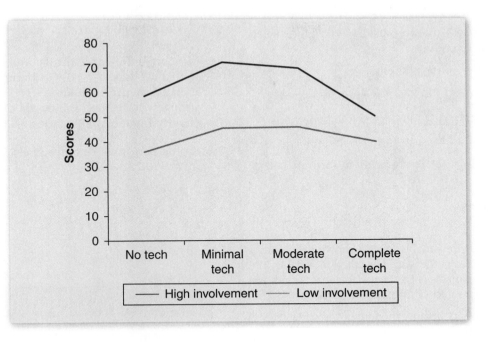

(b) Yes, an interaction is possible because the lines are not parallel.

32. (a) Yes, this study found a significant main effect of species. (b) Conduct pairwise comparisons for the species factor.

34. (a) Yes, this study found a significant main effect of emoticon style. (b) Post hoc tests are not required because there are only two levels of emoticon style; the two levels of this factor must significantly differ.

CHAPTER 15

2. The sign of the correlation coefficient (– or +) indicates the direction or slope of a correlation. A positive correlation indicates that the values of both factors change in the same direction. A negative correlation indicates that the values of two factors changes in opposite directions.

4. (a) SS_{XY} is used to measure the covariance in X and Y or the extent to which X and Y vary together. (b) $\sqrt{SS_X SS_Y}$ is used to measure the independent variance of X and Y.

6. Homoscedasticity, linearity, and normality.

8. Restriction of range limits the interpretation of a significant correlation when the range of data

measured in a sample is smaller than the range of data in the population from which the sample was selected.

10. (a) $t^2 = \dfrac{r^2}{(1-r^2)/df}$. (b) $\chi^2 = r_\phi^2 n$.

12. (a) Phi. (b) Pearson. (c) Point-biserial. (d) Spearman.

14. (a) $r = -0.40$ is the stronger correlation. (b) $r = +0.50$ is the stronger correlation. (c) These correlations are equal strength. (d) $r = -0.76$ is the stronger correlation.

16. (a) Is the appropriate conclusion. (b) Is not appropriate because correlations do not demonstrate cause.

18. (a) $r = 0.894$. (b) $r = 0.894$. (c) $r = 0.894$. (d) True.

20. (a) $r = 0.574$. (b) $r = -0.574$. (c) True.

22. (a) $r = -0.843$. (b) $r^2 = (-0.843)^2 = 0.711$. (c) Reject the null hypothesis.

24. Reject the null hypothesis.

26. (a) $r_s = -0.881$. (b) Reject the null hypothesis.

28. (a) $r_{pb} = -0.893$. (b) Reject the null hypothesis.

30. (a) $r_\phi = \dfrac{44 - 20}{64} = 0.375$. (b) Reject the null hypothesis. (c) The simplified formula can be used because the row and column totals are equal.

32. (a) $r = -0.42$. (b) $r = -0.42$.

34. (a) Consumer masculinity and appearance-related self-esteem, $r = 0.40$. Consumer masculinity and media influence, $r = 0.62$. (b) The strongest correlation is between consumer masculinity and media influence, $r = 0.62$.

36. (a) Job performance and self-efficacy, $r = 0.22$. (b) $r^2 = (0.22)^2 = .048$.

CHAPTER 16

2. The predictor variable (X) is a known value that is used to predict the value of a criterion variable. The criterion variable (Y) is the variable that is predicted by known values of the predictor variable.

4. It is necessary because the sum of the differences of data points from the regression line equals zero. To avoid this problem, each deviation score is squared.

6. The steps for the method of least squares are as follows: Step 1: Compute preliminary calculations. Step 2: Calculate the slope (b). Step 3: Calculate the y-intercept (a).

8. Regression variation is a measure of the variance in Y that is related to or associated with changes in X. The closer that data points fall to the regression line, the larger the value of regression variation.

10. $s_e = \sqrt{MS_{\text{residual}}}$. The standard error of estimate measures the standard deviation or distance that a set of data points falls from the regression line.

12. Multiple regression can detect the extent to which two predictor variables interact because two or more predictor variables are included in the same regression equation.

14. Regression Line A is a positive slope. Regression Line B is a negative slope.

16. (a) Height of men. (b) As height increases, income increases.

18. $\hat{Y} = 2.0, 4.6, 7.2,$ and 12.4, respectively.

20. (a) The regression equation is $\hat{Y} = -1.41X + 15.43$. (b) $\hat{Y} = -1.41(2) + 15.43 = 12.61$ minutes.

22. (a) $r^2 = (0.26)^2 = 0.07$. (b) $SS_{\text{regression}} = 0.07(96.40) = 6.75$. (c) $SS_{\text{residual}} = (1 - 0.07)96.40 = 89.65$.

24. (a)

Source of Variation	SS	df	MS	F_{obt}
Regression	80	1	80	3.53
Residual (error)	1,360	60	22.67	
Total	1,440	61		

The decision is to retain the null hypothesis.

26. (a)

Source of Variation	SS	df	MS	F_{obt}
Regression	6.41	1	6.41	6.15*
Residual (error)	8.33	8	1.04	
Total	14.74	9		

The decision is to reject the null hypothesis.

28. The predictor variable is levels of 5-HT. The criterion variable is mood.

30. (a) $n = 212$ students. (b) Students who sleep more have higher SWLS scores, or higher global life satisfaction.

32. (a) $\hat{Y} = 0.146(30) - 2.922 = 1.458$. (b) $\hat{Y} = 0.146(40) - 2.922 = 2.918$. (c) $\hat{Y} = 0.146(50) - 2.922 = 4.378$.

CHAPTER 17

2. Nominal scale of measurement.

4. (a) The frequency observed (f_o) is the count or frequency of participants recorded in each cell or category. (b) The frequency expected (f_e) is the count or frequency of participants in each cell or category, as determined by the proportion in each group or category stated by the null hypothesis.

6. Retain the null hypothesis.

8. Positively skewed.

10. The frequency expected in each cell is:
$$f_e = \frac{\text{row total} \times \text{column total}}{N}.$$

12. When the levels of one or more categorical variables are greater than two.

14. (a) Chi-square goodness-of-fit test. (b) Chi-square goodness-of-fit test. (c) Chi-square test for independence.

16. No, because at least one expected frequency is less than 5.

18. $\chi^2_{obt} = \frac{(66-60)^2}{60} + \frac{(34-40)^2}{40} = 1.50$. Decision:
Retain the null hypothesis. The distribution of men and women employed is "fair" or consistent with that in the general population for this industry.

20. $\chi^2_{obt} = \frac{(28-37)^2}{37} + \frac{(46-37)^2}{37} = 4.378$. Decision:
Reject the null hypothesis. Parents who were spanked by their parents as children more frequently spank their own children.

22. (a)
$$\chi^2_{obt} = \frac{(20-8.5)^2}{8.5} + \frac{(10-7.5)^2}{7.5} + \frac{(8-8.5)^2}{8.5} + \frac{(7-8.5)^2}{8.5}$$
$$+ \frac{(5-7.7)^2}{7.7} + \frac{(19-6.8)^2}{6.8} + \frac{(2-7.7)^2}{7.7} + \frac{(4-7.7)^2}{7.7}$$
$$+ \frac{(2-9.3)^2}{9.3} + \frac{(4-8.2)^2}{8.2} + \frac{(22-9.3)^2}{9.3} + \frac{(8-9.3)^2}{9.3}$$
$$+ \frac{(8-9.5)^2}{9.5} + \frac{(6-8.5)^2}{8.5} + \frac{(7-9.5)^2}{9.5} + \frac{(16-9.5)^2}{9.5}$$
$$= 82.46.$$

The decision is to reject the null hypothesis. The religious affiliation of parents and children is related.

(b) Cramer's $V = \sqrt{\frac{82.46}{136 \times 3}} = 0.45$.

24. (a) $\phi^2 = \frac{3.96}{50} = .079$. (b) $\phi^2 = \frac{5.23}{75} = .070$.

(c) $\phi^2 = \frac{12.00}{100} = .120$.

26. (a) Small effect size. (b) Medium effect size. (c) Large effect size.

28. $\chi^2_{obt} = \frac{(145-119.5)^2}{119.5} + \frac{(94-119.5)^2}{119.5} = 10.884$. The decision is to reject the null hypothesis.

30. $\chi^2_{obt} = \frac{(231-197.7)^2}{197.7} + \frac{(201-197.7)^2}{197.7} + \frac{(161-197.7)^2}{197.7} =$

12.477. The decision is to reject the null hypothesis.

32. $\chi^2_{obt} = \frac{(32-40.4)^2}{40.4} + \frac{(71-62.6)^2}{62.6} + \frac{(26-17.6)^2}{17.6} +$

$\frac{(19-27.4)^2}{27.4} = 9.375$. The decision is to reject the null hypothesis.

CHAPTER 18

2. Variance can only meaningful convey differences when data are measured on a scale in which the distance that scores deviate from their mean is meaningful, and ordinal data do not convey distance.

4. The sign test.

6. The number of positive or negative difference scores.

8. The smaller the value of U, the more uneven the dispersion of ranks between two groups. Hence, smaller values of U are less likely to occur if the null hypothesis is true.

10. The degrees of freedom for both tests are $k - 1$.

12. A chi-square distribution.

14. (a) Mann-Whitney U test. (b) One-sample sign test. (c) Related samples sign test or Wilcoxon signed-ranks T test. (d) Friedman test. (e) Kruskal-Wallis H test.

16. The ranks for these data are as follows: 1, 2, 3.5, 3.5, 5, 6, 7, 8, 10, 10, 10, 12.

18. The null hypothesis states that $p = .50$ for scores falling above and below the median. The binomial probability distribution is used to make this test.

20. The test statistic is $x = 9$. The p value is $p = .010 + .001 = .011$. The decision is to reject the null hypothesis.

22. The test statistic is $T = 21$. The decision is to reject the null hypothesis.

24. The test statistic is $U = 19$. The decision is to retain the null hypothesis.

26. $H = \dfrac{12}{15(16)} \left(\dfrac{58^2}{5} + \dfrac{34^2}{5} + \dfrac{28^2}{5} \right) - 3(16)$

$\quad = (0.05)(1060.80) - 48$

$\quad = 5.040$

The decision is to retain the null hypothesis.

28. Nonparametric tests reduce variability to ranks, thereby reducing variability that would have otherwise been attributed to error using a parametric test. Reducing nonnormal data to ranks can therefore increase the power to detect an effect.

30. (a) There were 3 groups and 2 degrees of freedom. (b) Yes, this test was significant because $p = .047$.

32. Work-related stress was rated the most stressful; professional investment was rated the least stressful.

Glossary

This glossary includes all terms and symbols that were boxed and defined in each chapter. The number in parentheses following each definition states the chapter(s) where the term was boxed and defined.

1-between 1-within or mixed design a research design for a two-way analysis of variance (ANOVA) in which different participants are observed at each level of the between-subjects factor and are repeatedly observed across the levels of the within-subjects factor; also called a *mixed design* (14).

2-between or between-subjects design a research design for a two-way ANOVA in which different participants are observed in each cell or group (14).

2-within or within-subjects design a research design for the two-way ANOVA in which the same participants are observed in each cell or group (14).

Additive law see *additive rule* (5).

Additive rule states that when two outcomes for a given event are mutually exclusive, the probability that any one of these outcomes occurs is equal to the sum of their individual probabilities; also referred to as the *additive law* (5).

Alpha level (α) is the level of significance or criterion for a hypothesis test. It is the largest probability of committing a Type I error that researchers will allow and still decide to reject the null hypothesis (8).

Alternative hypothesis (H_1) a statement that directly contradicts a null hypothesis by stating that the actual value of a population parameter, such as the mean, is less than, greater than, or not equal to the value stated in the null hypothesis (8).

Analysis of regression a statistical procedure used to test hypotheses for one or more predictor variables to determine whether the regression equation for a sample of data points can be used to predict values of the criterion variable (Y) given values of the predictor variable (X) in the population; also called *regression analysis* (16).

Analysis of variance (ANOVA) a statistical procedure used to test hypotheses for one or more factors concerning the variance among two or more group means ($k \geq 2$), where the variance in one or more populations is unknown; also called an *F-test* (12).

Arithmetic mean see *mean* (3).

Average see *mean* (3).

Bar chart a graphical display used to summarize the frequency of discrete and categorical data that are distributed in whole units or classes; also called a *bar graph* (2).

Bar graph see *bar chart* (2).

Bayes' law see *Bayes' theorem* (5).

Bayes' theorem a mathematical formula that relates the conditional and the marginal (unconditional) probabilities of two conditional outcomes that occur at random (5).

Bell-shaped distribution see *normal distribution* (3, 6).

Beta (β) error see *Type II error* (8).

Between-groups variation the variation attributed to mean differences between groups (12).

Between-persons variation the variation attributed to differences between person means averaged across groups. Because the same participants are observed across groups, this source of variation is removed from the error term in the denominator of the test statistic for the one-way within-subjects ANOVA (13).

Between-subjects design a research design in which we select independent samples, meaning that different participants are observed at each level of a factor (12, 14).

Between-subjects factor a type of factor where different participants are observed at each level of the factor (14).

Biased estimator any sample statistic, such as a sample mean, obtained from a randomly selected sample that does not equal the value of its respective population parameter, such as a population mean, on average (4).

Bimodal distribution a distribution of scores, where two scores occur most often or most frequently. A bimodal distribution has two modes (3).

Binomial distribution see *binomial probability distribution* (5).

Binomial probability distribution the distribution of probabilities for each outcome of a bivariate random variable (5).

Bivariate plots see *data points* (2).

Bivariate random variable any random variable with only two possible outcomes; also called a *dichotomous variable* (5).

Cell the combination of one level from each factor. Each cell is a group in a research study (14).

Central limit theorem a theorem that states that regardless of the distribution of scores in a population, the sampling distribution of sample means selected from that population will be approximately normally distributed (7).

Central tendency statistical measures for locating a single score that is most representative or descriptive of all scores in a distribution. Examples include the mean, the median, and the mode (3).

Chebyshev's theorem defines the percent of data from *any* distribution that will be contained within any number of standard deviations from the mean, where $SD > 1$ (4).

Chi-square distribution a positively skewed distribution of chi-square test statistic values for all possible samples when the null hypothesis is true (17).

Chi-square goodness-of-fit test a statistical procedure used to determine whether observed frequencies at each level of one categorical variable are similar to or different from the frequencies we expected at each level of the categorical variable (17).

Chi-square (χ^2) test a statistical procedure used to test hypotheses about the discrepancy between the observed and expected frequencies in two or more nominal categories (17).

Chi-square test for independence a statistical procedure used to determine whether frequencies observed at the combination of levels of two categorical variables are similar to frequencies expected (17).

Class width see *interval width* (2).

Coding the procedure of converting a nominal value to a numeric value (1).

Coefficient of determination (r^2 or R^2) is used to measure the proportion of variance in one factor (Y) that can be explained by known values of a second factor (X) (15).

Cohen's effect size conventions standard rules for identifying small, medium, and large effects based on typical findings in behavioral research (8).

Cohen's *d* a measure for effect size in terms of the number of standard deviations that mean scores have shifted above or below the population mean stated by the null hypothesis. The larger the value for *d*, the larger the effect in the population (8).

Complementary outcomes a probability relationship where the sum of the probabilities for two outcomes is equal to 1. When two outcomes are complementary, they are exhaustive of all possible outcomes—so the two outcomes constitute 100% of the sample space (5).

Complete factorial design a research design where each level of one factor is combined or crossed with each level of the other factor, with participants observed in each cell or combination or levels (14).

Computational formula for variance a way to calculate the population variance and the sample variance without needing to sum the squared differences of scores from their mean to compute the *SS* in the numerator; also called the *raw scores method* (4).

Conditional outcomes a probability relationship where the probability of one outcome is dependent on the occurrence of the other outcomes. An outcome is dependent when the probability of its occurrence is changed by the occurrence of the other outcome; also referred to as *dependent outcomes* (5).

Confidence boundaries see *confidence limits* (11).

Confidence interval (CI) the interval or range of possible values within which an unknown population parameter is likely to be contained (11).

Confidence limits the upper and lower boundaries of a confidence interval given within a specified level of confidence; also called *confidence boundaries* (11).

Confound variable an unanticipated variable not accounted for in a research study that could be causing or associated with observed changes in one or more measured variables; also called a *third variable* (15).

Constant a characteristic or property that can take on only a single value (A).

Continuous variable measured along a continuum at any place beyond the decimal point. These data can be measured in whole units or fractional units (1).

Correlation a statistical procedure used to describe the strength and direction of the linear relationship between two factors (15).

Correlation coefficient (*r*) is used to measure the strength and direction of the linear relationship, or correlation, between two factors. The value of *r* ranges from –1.0 to +1.0 (15).

Covariance a measure for the extent to which the values of two factors (*X* and *Y*) vary together. The closer data points fall to the regression line, the more that the values of two factors vary together (15).

Cramer's phi (φ) see *Cramer's V* (17).

Cramer's V the standard effect size estimate for the chi-square test for independence; also called *Cramer's* phi (17).

Criterion variable (*Y*) the variable with unknown values that can be predicted or estimated, given known values of the predictor variable; also called the *to-be-predicted variable* (16).

Critical value a cutoff value that defines the boundaries beyond which 5% or less of sample means can be obtained if the null hypothesis is true. Sample means obtained beyond a critical value result in a decision to reject the null hypothesis (8).

Cumulative frequency a summary display that distributes the sum of frequencies across a series of intervals. The frequencies can be added or cumulated from the bottom up or the top down in a frequency distribution (2).

Cumulative percents a summary display that distributes the sum of relative percents across a series of intervals. This summary is presented from the bottom up and is referred to as a *percentile rank* (2).

Cumulative relative frequency a summary display that distributes the sum of relative frequencies across a series of intervals. Relative frequencies can be added or cumulated from the bottom up or the top down in a frequency distribution (2).

Data (plural) measurements or observations that are typically numeric (1).

Data points the *x*- and *y*-coordinates for each plot in a scatter gram (2).

Datum (singular) a single measurement or observation, usually referred to as a *score* or *raw score* (1).

Deciles measures that divide a set of data into 10 equal parts (4).

Definitional formula for variance a way to calculate the population variance and sample variance that requires summing the squared differences of scores from their mean to compute the *SS* in the numerator (4).

Degrees of freedom (*df*) for the *t*-test, the sample size minus 1 ($n - 1$) for each sample of scores or each sample of difference scores. For two independent samples, the degrees of freedom are equal to the sum of the degrees of freedom for each sample (9).

Degrees of freedom between groups (*df*$_{BG}$) the degrees of freedom associated with the variance for the group means in the numerator of the test statistic. It is equal to the number of groups (*k*) minus 1; also called *degrees of freedom numerator* (12).

Degrees of freedom between persons (*df*$_{BP}$) the degrees of freedom associated with the variance of person means averaged across groups. It is equal to the number of participants (*n*) minus 1 (13).

Degrees of freedom denominator (*df*$_{den}$) see *degrees of freedom error* (12).

Degrees of freedom error (df_E) the degrees of freedom associated with the error variance in the denominator. It is equal to the total sample size (N) minus the number of groups (k); also called *degrees of freedom denominator* or *degrees of freedom within groups* (12).

Degrees of freedom for sample variance the number of scores in a sample that are free to vary. All scores except one are free to vary in a sample: $n-1$ (4).

Degrees of freedom numerator (df_{num}) see *degrees of freedom between groups* (12).

Degrees of freedom within groups see *degrees of freedom error* (12).

Dependent outcomes see *conditional outcomes* (5).

Dependent sample see *related sample* (10).

Dependent variable (DV) the variable that is believed to change in the presence of the independent variable. It is the "presumed effect," so to speak (1).

Descriptive statistics procedures used to summarize, organize, and make sense of a set of scores or observations. These are typically presented graphically, in tabular form, or as summary statistics (1).

Deviation the difference of each score from its mean. Denoted $(x-\mu)$ for a population and denoted $(x-M)$ for a sample (4).

Dichotomous variable any random variable with only two possible outcomes; also called a *bivariate variable* (5).

Difference scores a score or value obtained by subtracting two scores (10).

Directional (one-tailed) tests hypothesis tests where the alternative hypothesis is stated as "greater than" (>) or "less than" (<) a value stated in the null hypothesis. Hence, the researcher is interested in a specific alternative from the null hypothesis (8).

Discrete variable measured in whole units or categories that are not distributed along a continuum (1).

Effect the difference between a sample mean and the population mean stated in the null hypothesis. In hypothesis testing, an effect is not significant when we retain the null hypothesis; an effect is significant when we reject the null hypothesis (8).

Effect size a statistical measure of the size of an observed effect in a population, which allows researchers to describe how far scores shifted in the population, or the percentage of variance that can be explained by a given variable. (8).

Empirical rule a rule that states that for any normally distributed set of data, at least 99.7% of data lie within 3 SD of the mean, at least 95% of data lie within 2 SD of the mean, and at least 68% of data lie within 1 SD of the mean (4).

Equidistant scales a set of numbers distributed in equal units (1).

Error refers to any unexplained difference that cannot be attributed to, or caused by, having different groups or treatments. The standard error of the mean is used to estimate the error or unexplained differences in a statistical design. For the ANOVA, the term *error* refers to the within-groups source of variation, even though other sources of error exist in the within-subjects ANOVA designs (10).

Estimated Cohen's d a measure of effect size in terms of the number of standard deviations that mean scores shift above or below the population mean stated by the null hypothesis. The larger the value of estimated Cohen's d, the larger the effect is in the population (9).

Estimated standard error (s_M) an estimate of the standard deviation of a sampling distribution of sample means selected from a population with an unknown variance. It is an estimate of the standard error or the standard distance that sample means can be expected to deviate from the value of the population mean stated in the null hypothesis (9).

Estimated standard error for difference scores (s_{MD}) an estimate of the standard deviation of a sampling distribution of mean difference scores. It is an estimate of the standard error or standard distance that mean difference scores can be expected to deviate from the mean difference score stated in the null hypothesis (10).

Estimated standard error for the difference ($s_{M_1-M_2}$) an estimate of the standard deviation of a sampling distribution of mean differences between two sample means. It is an estimate of the standard error or the standard distance that mean differences can be expected to deviate from the mean difference stated in the null hypothesis (9).

Estimation a statistical procedure in which a sample statistic is used to estimate the value of an unknown population parameter. Two types of estimation are point estimation and interval estimation (11).

Expected value see *mathematical expectation* (5).

Experiment a research study that specifically controls the conditions under which observations are made to isolate cause-and-effect relationships between variables (1).

Experimentwise alpha the alpha level, or probability of committing a Type I error for all tests, when a multiple tests are conducted on the same data (12).

F-distribution a positively skewed distribution derived from a sampling distribution of *F*-ratios (12).

Fixed event any event where the outcome observed in that event is always the same (5).

F-obtained see *F-statistic* (12).

Fractiles measures that divide a set of data into two or more equal parts; examples include the median, deciles, quartiles, and percentiles (4).

Frequency the number of times or how often a category, a score, or a range of scores occurs (2).

Frequency distribution a summary display for a distribution of data organized or summarized in terms of how often a category, a score, or a range of scores occurs (2).

Frequency expected (f_e) the count or frequency of participants in each category, or at each level of the categorical variable, as determined by the proportion expected in each category (17).

Frequency observed (f_0) the count or frequency of participants recorded in each category or at each level of the categorical variable (17).

Frequency polygon a dot-and-line graph used to summarize the frequency of continuous data at the midpoint of each interval (2).

Friedman test a statistical procedure used to determine whether the total ranks in two or more groups are significantly different when the same participants are observed in each group. This test is used as a nonparametric alternative to the one-way within-subjects ANOVA (18).

F-statistic (F_{obt}) the test statistic for an ANOVA. It is computed as the mean square (or variance) between groups divided by the mean square (or variance) within groups; also called *F-obtained* (12).

F-test see *analysis of variance* (12).

Gaussian distribution see *normal distribution* (3, 6).

Grouped data a set of scores distributed into intervals, where the frequency of each score can fall into any given interval (2).

Histogram a graphical display used to summarize the frequency of continuous data that are distributed in numeric intervals (2).

Homoscedasticity the assumption that there is an equal ("homo") variance or scatter ("scedasticity") of data points dispersed along the regression line (15).

Hypothesis a statement or proposed explanation for an observation, a phenomenon, or a scientific problem that can be tested or observed. A hypothesis is often a statement about the value for a parameter in a population (8).

Hypothesis testing a method for testing a claim or hypothesis about a parameter in a population, using data measured in a sample. In this method, we test some hypothesis by determining the likelihood that a sample statistic could have been selected, if the hypothesis regarding the population parameter were true. Also called *significance testing* (8).

Independent outcomes a probability relationship where the probability of one outcome does not affect the probability of the second outcome (5).

Independent sample the selection of participants to each group or sample, where the participants are unrelated in that they are observed once in only one sample. To collect independent samples, participants are selected from two or more populations or selected from a single population and randomly assigned to different groups (10).

Independent variable (IV) the variable that is manipulated in an experiment. This variable remains unchanged (or "independent") between conditions being observed in an experiment. It is the "presumed cause," so to speak (1).

Inferential statistics procedures used that allow researchers to *infer* or generalize observations made with samples to the larger population from which they were selected. Examples include *z*-tests, *t*-tests, and *F*-tests (1).

Interaction a source of variation associated with the variance of group means across the combination of levels of two factors. It is a measure of how cell means at each level of one factor change across the levels of a second factor (14).

Interquartile range (IQR) range of a distribution of scores falling within the upper and lower quartiles of a distribution (4).

Interval a discrete range of values within which the frequency of a subset of scores is contained (2).

Interval boundaries the upper and lower limits for each interval in a grouped frequency distribution (2).

Interval estimation a statistical procedure in which a sample of data is used to find the interval or range of possible values within which a population parameter is likely to be contained (11).

Interval scales measurements where the values have no true zero and the distance between each value is equidistant. Examples include Likert scores, temperature, latitude, and longitude (1).

Interval width the range for each interval of a grouped frequency distribution; also called the *class width* (2).

Known variable (X) see *predictor variable* (16).

Kruskal-Wallis *H* test a statistical procedure used to determine whether the total ranks in two or more independent groups are significantly different. This test is used as a nonparametric alternative to the one-way between-subjects ANOVA (18).

Law of large numbers a theorem or a rule that increasing the number of observations or sample size in a study will decrease the standard error. The smaller the standard error, the closer a distribution of the sample means will be from the population mean (7).

Leaf the number(s) located to the right of the vertical line in a stem-and-leaf display. A leaf lists the last digit or digits for each number in each row (2).

Level of confidence the probability or likelihood that an interval estimate will contain an unknown population parameter (11).

Level of significance refers to criterion of judgment upon which a decision is made regarding the value stated in a null hypothesis. The criterion is based on the probability of obtaining a statistic measured in a sample if the value stated in the null hypothesis were true. Also called *significance level* (8).

Levels of the factor (*k*) the number of groups or different ways that an independent or quasi-independent variable is observed; also called the *levels of the independent variable* for groups in experimental research designs (12).

Levels of the independent variable specific conditions of the independent variable; also called the *levels of the factor* for groups in quasi-experiments and correlational research designs (1).

Likert scales numeric response scales used to indicate a participant's level of agreement or opinion with some statement (1).

Linear regression a statistical procedure used to determine the equation of a regression line to a set of data points and the extent to which the regression equation can be used to predict values of one factor, given known values of a second factor in a population; also called *regression* (16).

Linearity the assumption that the best way to describe a pattern of data is using a straight line (15).

Lower boundary the smallest value in each interval of a grouped frequency distribution (2).

Lower confidence limit the smallest possible value of a population parameter in a confidence interval with a specified level of confidence (11).

Lower quartile (*Q*₁) data that fall in the bottom 25% of a distribution of scores (4).

Main effect a source of variation associated with mean differences across the levels of a single factor (14).

Mann-Whitney *U* test a statistical procedure used to determine whether the dispersion of ranks in two independent groups is equal. This test is used as a nonparametric alternative to the two-independent sample *t*-test (18).

Matched-pairs design an experimental method in which pairs of participants are matched (either experimentally or naturally) based on common characteristics or traits that they share; also called a *matched-samples design* and a *matched-subjects design* (10).

Matched-samples design see *matched-pairs design* (10).

Matched-subjects design see *matched-pairs design* (10).

Mathematical expectation the mean, or average expected outcome, for a given random variable. The expected outcome for a random variable is the sum of the products for each random outcome times the probability of its occurrence; also called an *expected value* (5).

Mean the sum of a set of scores in a distribution, divided by the total number of scores summed; also called an *arithmetic mean* or *average* (3).

Mean square between groups (MS_{BG}) the variance attributed to differences between group means. It is the numerator for the test statistic of an ANOVA (12).

Mean square between persons (MS_{BP}) the variance attributed to mean differences in scores between persons (13).

Mean square error (MS_E) the variance attributed to differences within each group. It is the denominator for the test statistic for an ANOVA; also called *mean square within groups* (12).

Mean square within groups see *mean square error* (12).

Median the middle value in a distribution of data listed in numeric order (3, 4).

Median quartile (Q_2) data that fall between the 25th and 50th percentiles of a distribution of scores (4).

Method of least squares a statistical procedure used to compute the slope (*b*) and *y*-intercept (*a*) of the best-fitting straight line to a set of data points (16).

Mixed design see *1-between, 1-within or mixed design* (14).

Modal distribution a distribution of scores, where one or more scores occur most often or most frequently (3).

Mode the value in a data set that occurs most often or most frequently (3).

Multimodal distribution a distribution of scores, where more than two scores occur most often or most frequently. A multimodal distribution has more than two modes (3).

Multiple regression a statistical method that includes two or more predictor variables in the equation of a regression line to predict changes in a criterion variable (16).

Multiplicative law see *multiplicative rule* (5).

Multiplicative rule states that when two outcomes for a given event are independent, the probability that both outcomes occur is equal to the product of their individual probabilities; also called the *multiplicative law* (5).

Mutually exclusive outcomes a probability relationship where two outcomes can't occur together. The probability of two mutually exclusive outcomes occurring together is 0 (5).

Negative correlation ($-1.0 \leq r < 0$) a negative value for *r*, which indicates that the values of two factors change in different directions, meaning that as the values of one factor increase, the values of the second factor decrease (15).

Negatively skewed a distribution of scores where a few outliers are substantially smaller (toward the left tail in a graph) than most other scores (3).

Nominal scales measurements where a number is assigned to represent something or someone. Nominal variables are typically categorical variables that have been coded (1).

Nondirectional (two-tailed) tests hypothesis tests where the alternative hypothesis is stated as *not equal to* ($\neq$). The researcher is interested in any alternative from the null hypothesis (8).

Nonmodal (rectangular) distribution a distribution of scores with no mode; hence, all scores occur at the same frequency; also called a *rectangular distribution* (3).

Nonparametric tests hypothesis tests that are used (1) to test hypotheses that do not make inferences about parameters in a population, (2) to test hypotheses about data that can have any type of distribution, and (3) to analyze data on a nominal or ordinal scale of measurement (17).

Normal distribution a theoretical distribution with data that are symmetrically distributed around the mean, median, and mode; also called a *symmetrical, Gaussian,* or *bell-shaped distribution* (3, 6).

Null hypothesis (H_0) a statement about a population parameter, such as the population mean, that is assumed to be true (8).

Observed power a type of post hoc or retrospective power analysis. The observed power is used to estimate the likelihood of detecting a population effect, assuming that the observed results in a study reflect a true effect in the population (12).

Obtained value the value of a test statistic that is compared to the critical value(s) for a hypothesis test to make a decision. When the obtained value exceeds a critical value, we decide to reject the null hypothesis; otherwise, we retain the null hypothesis (8).

Ogive a dot-and-line graph used to summarize the cumulative percent of continuous data at the upper boundary of each interval (2).

One–independent sample *t*-test a statistical procedure used to test hypotheses concerning the mean in a single population with an unknown variance (9).

One–independent sample *z*-test a statistical procedure used to test hypotheses concerning the mean in a single population with a known variance (8).

One-way between-subjects ANOVA a statistical procedure used to test hypotheses for one factor with two or more levels concerning the variance among the group means. This test is used when different participants are observed at each level of a factor and the variance in any one population is unknown (12).

One-way within-subjects ANOVA a statistical procedure used to test hypotheses for one factor with two or more levels concerning the variance among the group means. This test is used when the same participants are observed at each level of a factor and the variance in any one population is unknown (13).

Open class see *open interval* (2).

Open interval an interval with no defined upper or lower boundary; also called an *open class* (2).

Operational definition a description of some observable event in terms of the specific process or manner by which it was observed or measured (1).

Ordinal scales measurements where values convey order or "rank" alone (1).

Outcome space see *sample space* (5).

Outliers extreme scores that fall substantially above or below most of the scores in a particular data set (2).

p value the probability of a obtaining a sample outcome, given that the value stated in the null hypothesis is true. The p value for obtaining a sample outcome is compared to the level of significance or criterion for making a decision (8).

Pairwise comparison a statistical comparison for the difference between two group means. A post hoc test evaluates all possible pairwise comparisons for an ANOVA with any number of groups (12).

Parametric tests hypothesis tests that are used to test hypotheses about parameters in a population in which the data in the population are normally distributed and measured on an interval or ratio scale of measurement (17).

Pearson (product moment) correlation coefficient (r) a measure used to determine the direction and strength of the linear relationship of two factors in which the data for both factors are measured on an interval or ratio scale of measurement (15).

Percentile rank a cumulative percent summary. The ranks indicate the percent of scores at or below a given value and must be added from the lowest value (2).

Percentiles measures that divide a set of data into 100 equal parts (4).

Phi correlation coefficient (r_ϕ) a measure used to determine the direction and strength of the linear relationship of two dichotomous factors on a nominal scale of measurement (15).

Pictogram a summary display that uses symbols or illustrations to represent a concept, an object, a place, or an event (2).

Pie chart a graphical display in the shape of a circle that is used to summarize the relative percent of discrete and categorical data into sectors (2).

Point-biserial correlation coefficient (r_{pb}) a measure used to determine the direction and strength of the linear relationship of one factor that is continuous (on an interval or ratio scale of measurement) and a second factor that is dichotomous (on a nominal scale of measurement) (15).

Point estimation a statistical procedure that involves the use of a sample statistic to estimate a population parameter (11).

Pooled sample standard deviation $\left(\sqrt{s_p^2}\right)$ the combined sample standard deviation of two samples. It is computed by taking the square root of the pooled sample variance. This measure estimates the standard deviation for the difference between two population means (9).

Pooled sample variance (s_p^2) the combined sample variance of two samples. When the sample size is unequal, the variance in each sample is weighted by its respective degrees of freedom (9).

Population a set of *all* individuals, items, or data of interest. This is the group about which scientists will generalize (1).

Population mean (μ) the sum of a set of scores in a population, divided by the total number of scores summed (3).

Population parameter a characteristic (usually numeric, such as the mean or variance) that describes a population. The population characteristic typically of greatest interest to a researcher is the mean score in a population (1).

Population size (N) the number of individuals that constitute an entire group or population (3).

Population standard deviation (σ) a measure of variability for the average distance that scores in a population deviate from their mean. It is calculated by taking the square root of the population variance (4).

Population variance (σ^2) a measure of variability for the average squared distance that scores in a population deviate from the mean. It is computed only when all scores in a given population are known (4).

Positive correlation ($0 < r \leq +1.0$) a positive value of r that indicates that the values of two factors change in the same direction: As the values of one factor increase, values of the second factor also increase; as the values of one factor decrease, values of the second factor also decrease (15).

Positively skewed a distribution of scores where a few outliers are substantially larger (toward the right tail in a graph) than most other scores (3).

Post hoc test a statistical procedure computed following a significant ANOVA to determine which pair or pairs of group means significantly differ. These tests are necessary when $k > 2$ because multiple comparisons are needed. When $k = 2$, the two means must significantly differ; this is the only comparison (12).

Power the probability of rejecting a false null hypothesis. Specifically, it is the probability that a randomly selected sample will show that the null hypothesis is false when the null hypothesis is in fact false (8).

Predictor variable (X) the variable with values that are known and can be used to predict values of another variable; also called the *known variable* (16).

Pre-post design a type of repeated measures design in which researchers measure a dependent variable for participants before (pre) and following (post) some treatment (10).

Probability (p) the frequency of times an outcome occurs divided by the total number of possible outcomes (5).

Probability distribution the distribution of probabilities for each outcome of a random variable. The sum of probabilities in a probability distribution is equal to 1.0 (5).

Proportion a part or portion of all measured data. The sum of all proportions for a distribution of data is 1.0 (2).

Proportion of variance (η^2, ω^2) is a measure of effect size in terms of the proportion or percentage of variability in a dependent variable that can be explained or accounted for by a treatment (9).

Qualitative variable varies by class. This is often represented as a label and describes nonnumeric aspects of phenomena (1).

Quantitative variable varies by amount. This is measured numerically and is often collected by measuring or counting (1).

Quartile deviation see *semi-interquartile range* (4).

Quartiles dividing data evenly into four parts or quartiles (4).

Quasi-independent variable a variable whose levels are not randomly assigned to participants (nonrandom). This variable differentiates the groups or conditions being compared in a quasi-experimental research design (1).

Random assignment a random procedure used to ensure that participants in a study have an equal chance of being assigned to a particular group or condition (1).

Random event any event where the outcomes observed in that event can vary (5).

Random variable a variable obtained or measured in a random experiment. Unlike other mathematical variables, a random variable is not the actual outcome of a random experiment but rather describes the possible, as-yet-undetermined outcomes in a random experiment (5).

Range the difference between the largest (L) and the smallest value (S) in a data set (4).

Ratio scales measurements where a set of values has a true zero and are equidistant. Examples include counts and measures of weight, height, time, and calories (1).

Raw score a single measurement or observation; see *datum* (1).

Raw scores method for variance see *computational formula for variance* (4).

Real limits the upper and lower values within which the probability for obtaining a binomial outcome is contained (6).

Real range one more than the difference between the largest value and the smallest value in a data set (2).

Rectangular distribution see *nonmodal distribution* (3).

Regression see *linear regression* (16).

Regression analysis see *analysis of regression* (16).

Regression line the best-fitting straight line to a set of data points. A best-fitting line is the line that minimizes the distance of all data points that fall from it (15).

Regression variation the variance in *Y* that is related to or associated with changes in *X*. The closer that data points fall to the regression line, the larger the value of regression variation (16).

Rejection region the region beyond a critical value in a hypothesis test. When the value of a test statistic is in the rejection region, the decision is to reject the null hypothesis; otherwise, the decision is to retain the null hypothesis (8).

Related sample the selection of participants to each group or sample where the participants are related. Participants can be related in two ways: They are observed in more than one group (repeated measures design), or they are matched, experimentally or naturally, based on the common characteristics or traits that they share (matched pairs design); also called a *dependent sample* (10).

Related samples *t*-test an inferential statistic used to test hypotheses concerning two related samples selected from populations in which the variance in one or both populations is unknown (10).

Relative frequency a summary display that distributes the proportion of scores occurring in each interval of a frequency distribution. It is computed as the frequency in each interval divided by the total number of frequencies recorded (2).

Relative percent a summary display that distributes the percentage of scores occurring in each class interval relative to all scores distributed (2).

Repeated measures design a research design in which the same participants are observed in each group or treatment. Two types of repeated measures designs are called the pre-post design and the within-subjects design (10).

Residual variation the variance in *Y* that is not related to changes in *X*. This is the variance in *Y* that is left over or remaining. The farther that data points fall from the regression line, the larger the value of residual variation (16).

Restriction of range a problem that arises when the range of data for one or both correlated factors in a sample is limited or restricted, compared to the range of data in the population from which the sample was selected (15).

Reverse causality a problem that arises when the direction of causality between two factors can be in either direction (15).

Root mean square deviation see *standard deviation* (4).

Sample a set of *selected* individuals, items, or data taken from a population of interest (1).

Sample design a specific plan or protocol for how individuals will be selected or sampled from a population of interest (7).

Sample mean (M or $\bar{X}$) the sum of a set of scores in a sample, divided by the total number of scores summed (3).

Sample size (n) the number of individuals that constitute a subset of those selected from a larger population (3).

Sample space the total number of possible outcomes that can occur in a given random event; also called *outcome space* (5).

Sample standard deviation (s or SD) a measure of variability for the average distance that scores in a sample deviate from their mean. It is calculated by taking the square root of the sample variance (4).

Sample statistic a characteristic (usually numeric, such as the mean or variance) that describes a sample (1).

Sample variance (s^2 or SD^2) a measure of variability for the average squared distance that scores in a sample deviate from the mean. It is computed when only a portion or sample of data is measured in a population (4).

Sampling distribution a distribution of all sample means or sample variances that could be obtained in samples of a given size from the same population (7).

Sampling error the extent to which sample means selected from the same population differ from one another. This difference, which occurs by chance, is measured by the standard error of the mean (7).

Sampling with replacement a method of sampling, where each participant or item selected is replaced before the next selection. This method of sampling is used in the development of statistical theory (7).

Sampling without replacement a method of sampling, where each participant or item selected

is not replaced before the next selection. This method of sampling is the most common method used in behavioral research (7).

Scales of measurement identifies how the properties of numbers can change with different uses. Four scales of measurement are nominal, ordinal, interval, and ratio (1).

Scatter diagram see *scatter gram* (2).

Scatter gram a graphical display of discrete data points (x, y) used to summarize the relationship between two variables; also called a *scatter diagram* or *scatter plot* (2).

Scatter plot see *scatter gram* (2).

Science the study of phenomena, such as behavior, through strict observation, evaluation, interpretation, and theoretical explanation (1).

Score a single measurement or observation; see *datum* (1).

Sector the particular portion of a pie chart that represents the relative percentage of a particular class or category. To find the central angle for each sector, multiply each relative percent times 3.6 (2).

Semi-interquartile range (SIQR) a measure of half the distance between the cutoffs for the upper and lower quartiles of a distribution. The SIQR is computed by dividing the IQR in half; also called a *quartile deviation* (4).

Sign test a statistical procedure used to determine the binomial probability that an observed number of scores fall above and below the median (one sample) or are positive and negative (related samples). This test is used as a nonparametric alternative to the one–independent sample t-test and the related samples t-test (18).

Significance a decision made concerning a value stated in the null hypothesis. When the null hypothesis is rejected, we reach significance. When the null hypothesis is retained, we fail to reach significance. Also called *statistical significance* (8).

Significance level see *level of significance* (8).

Significance testing see *hypothesis testing* (8).

Simple frequency distribution a summary display for the frequency of each individual score (ungrouped data) in a distribution, or the frequency of scores falling within defined groups or intervals (grouped data) in a distribution (2).

Simple main effect tests hypothesis tests used to analyze a significant interaction by comparing the mean differences or simple main effects of one factor at each level of a second factor (14).

Skewed distribution a distribution of scores that includes outliers or scores that fall substantially above or below most other scores in a data set (3).

Slope (b) a measure of the change in Y relative to the change in X. When X and Y change in the same direction, the slope is positive. When X and Y change in opposite directions, the slope is negative (16).

Source of variation any variation that can be measured in a study (12).

Spearman rank-order correlation coefficient (r_s) a measure used to determine the direction and strength of the linear relationship of two ranked factors on an ordinal scale of measurement; also called *Spearman's rho* (15).

Spearman's rho see *Spearman rank-order correlation coefficient* (15).

Standard deviation a measure of variability for the average distance that scores deviate from their mean. It is calculated by taking the square root of the variance; also called the *root mean square deviation* (4).

Standard deviation of a probability distribution a measure of variability for the average distance that outcomes for a given random variable deviate from the expected value or mean of a probability distribution. It is calculated by taking the square root of the variance of a probability distribution (5).

Standard error see *standard error of the mean* (7).

Standard error of estimate (s_e) an estimate of the standard deviation or distance that a set of data points falls from the regression line. The standard error of estimate equals the square root of the mean square residual (16).

Standard error of the mean (σ_M) the standard deviation of a sampling distribution of sample means. It is the standard error or distance that sample mean values deviate from the value of the population mean; also stated as *standard error* (7).

Standard normal distribution a normal distribution with a mean equal to 0 and a standard deviation equal to 1. It is distributed in z-score units along the x-axis; also called a *z-distribution* (6).

Standard normal transformation an equation that converts any normal distribution with any mean and any variance to a standard normal distribution with a mean equal to 0 and a standard deviation equal to 1; also called a *z-transformation* (6).

Statistical significance see *significance* (8).

Statistics a branch of mathematics used to summarize, analyze, and interpret a group of numbers or observations (1).

Stem the number(s) located to the left of the vertical line in a stem-and-leaf display. A stem lists the first digit or digits for each number in each row (2).

Stem-and-leaf display a graphical display where each individual score from an original set of data is listed. The data are organized such that the common digits shared by all scores are listed to the left (in the stem), with the remaining digits for each score listed to the right (in the leaf); also called a *stem-and-leaf plot* (2).

Stem-and-leaf plot see *stem-and-leaf display* (2).

Student's t see *t-distribution* (9).

Studentized range statistic (q) a statistic used to determine critical values for comparing pairs of means at a given range. This statistic is used in the formula to find the critical value for the Tukey's honestly significant difference (HSD) post hoc test (12).

Sum of products (SP) the sum of squares for two factors, X and Y; also represented as SS_{XY}. SP is the numerator for the Pearson correlation formula. To compute SP, multiply the deviation of each X value times the deviation of each Y value (15).

Sum of squares (SS) the sum of the squared deviations of scores from their mean. SS is the numerator in the variance formula (4).

Sum of squares between groups (SS_{BG}) the sum of squares attributed to variability between groups (12).

Sum of squares between persons (SS_{BP}) the sum of squares attributed to variability in participant scores across groups (13).

Sum of squares error (SS_E) the sum of squares attributed to variability within each group; also called *sum of squares within groups* (12).

Sum of squares total (SS_T) the overall sum of squares across all groups (12).

Sum of squares within groups (SS_{WG}) see *sum of squares error* (12).

Symmetrical distribution see *normal distribution* (3, 6).

t-distribution a normal-like distribution with greater variability in the tails because the sample variance is substituted for the population variance to estimate the standard error in this distribution (9).

Test statistic a mathematical formula that allows researchers to determine the likelihood or probability of obtaining sample outcomes if the null hypothesis were true. The value of the test statistic can be used to make a decision regarding the null hypothesis (8).

Testwise alpha the alpha level, or probability of committing a Type I error, for each test or pairwise comparison made on the same data (13).

Third variable see *confound variable* (15).

To-be-predicted variable (Y) see *criterion variable* (16).

t-observed see *t-statistic* (9).

t-obtained see *t-statistic* (9).

Treatment any unique characteristic of a sample or any unique way that a researcher treats a sample in hypothesis testing (9).

True zero describes values where the value 0 truly indicates nothing. Examples of variables with no true zero are Likert scores, temperature, latitude, and longitude; examples of variables with a true zero are weight, height, time, and calories (1).

t-statistic an inferential statistic used to determine the number of standard deviations in a *t*-distribution that a sample mean deviates from the mean value or mean difference stated in the null hypothesis. Also referred to as *t-observed* or *t-obtained* (9).

Two–independent sample t-test a statistical procedure used to test hypotheses concerning the difference between two population means, where the variance in one or both populations is unknown (9).

Two-way ANOVA a statistical procedure used to test hypotheses concerning the variance of groups created by combining the levels of two factors. This test is used when the variance in any one population is unknown (14).

Two-way between-subjects ANOVA a statistical procedure used to test hypotheses concerning the combination of levels of two factors using the 2-between or between-subjects design (14).

Type I error the probability of rejecting a null hypothesis that is actually true. Researchers directly control for the probability of committing this type of error by stating an alpha level (8).

Type II error the probability of retaining a null hypothesis that is actually false. Also called *beta (β) error* (8).

Type III error a source of error that occurs for one-tailed tests where the researcher decides to retain the null hypothesis because the rejection region was located in the wrong tail (8).

Unbiased estimator any sample statistic, such as a sample mean, obtained from a randomly selected sample that equals the value of its respective population parameter, such as a population mean, on average (4, 7).

Ungrouped data a set of scores or categories distributed individually, where the frequency for each individual score or category is counted (2).

Unimodal distribution a distribution of scores, where one score occurs most often or most frequently. A unimodal distribution has one mode (3).

Unit normal table a type of probability distribution table displaying a list of *z*-scores and the corresponding proportions of area or probabilities associated with each *z*-score listed (6).

Upper boundary the largest value in each interval of a grouped frequency distribution (2).

Upper confidence limit the largest possible value of a population parameter in a confidence interval with a specified level of confidence (11).

Upper quartile the portion of data that fall between the 50th and 75th percentiles of a distribution of scores (4).

Variability a measure of the dispersion or spread of scores in a distribution that ranges from 0 and $+\infty$. Examples include the range, the variance, and the standard deviation (4).

Variable a characteristic or property that can take on different values at different times (A).

Variance a measure of variability for the average squared distance that scores deviate from their mean (4).

Variance of a probability distribution a measure of variability for the average squared distance that outcomes for a given random variable deviate from the expected value or mean of a probability distribution (5).

Weighted mean (M_w) the combined mean of two or more groups of scores, where the number of scores in each group is disproportionate or unequal (3).

Wilcoxon signed-ranks T test a statistical procedure used to determine whether the total ranks in two related groups are significantly different. This test is used as a nonparametric alternative to the related samples t-test (18).

Within-group variation the variation attributed to mean differences within each group. This source of variation cannot be attributed to or caused by having different groups and is therefore called error variation (12).

Within-subjects design a research design in which the same participants are observed across many groups but not necessarily before and after a treatment (10, 14).

Within-subjects factor a type of factor where the same participants are observed across the levels of the factor (14).

y-intercept (a) the value of the criterion variable (Y) when the predictor variable (X) equals 0 (16).

z-distribution see *standard normal distribution* (6).

z-score a unit of measurement distributed along the x-axis of a standard normal distribution (6).

z-statistic an inferential statistic used to determine the number of standard deviations in a standard normal distribution that a sample mean deviates from the population mean stated in the null hypothesis (8).

z-table see *unit normal table* (6).

z-transformation see *standard normal transformation* (6).

References

Agrawal, A., Madden, P. A. F., Buchholz, K. K., Heath, A. C., & Lynskey, M. T. (2008). Transitions to regular smoking and to nicotine dependence in women using cannabis. *Drug and Alcohol Dependence, 95,* 107–114.

Albert, U., Salvi, V., Saracco, P., Bogetto, P., & Maina, G. (2007). Health-related quality of life among first-degree relatives of patients with obsessive-compulsive disorder in Italy. *Psychiatric Services, 58*(7), 970–976.

Altamura, A. C., Dell'Osso, B., Vismara, S., & Mundo, E. (2008). May duration of untreated illness influence the long-term course of major depressive disorder? *European Psychiatry, 23,* 92–96.

American Psychological Association. (2009). *Publication manual of the American Psychological Association* (6th ed.). Washington, DC: Author.

Austin, V., Shah, S., & Muncer, S. (2005). Teacher stress and coping strategies used to reduce stress. *Occupational Therapy International, 12*(2), 63–80.

Bar-eli, M., Azar, O. H., Ritov, I., Keidar-Levin, Y., & Schein, G. (2007). Action bias among elite soccer goalkeepers: The case of penalty kicks. *Journal of Economic Psychology, 28,* 606–621.

Bellou, V. (2007). Psychological contract assessment after a major organizational change: The case of mergers and acquisitions. *Employee Relations, 29*(1), 68–88.

Bernstein, I. L. (1978). Learned taste aversions in children receiving chemotherapy. *Science, 200,* 1302–1303.

Bernstein, P. L. (1998). *Against the Gods: The remarkable story of risk.* New York: John Wiley.

Blouin, D. C., & Riopelle, A. J. (2004). The difference between *t* and *z* and the difference it makes. *Journal of General Psychology, 131*(1), 77–84.

Bonache, J. (2005). Job satisfaction among expatriates, repatriates and domestic employees: The perceived impact of international assignments on work-related variables. *Personnel Review, 34*(1), 110–124.

Bonilha, L., Molnar, C., Horner, M. D., Anderson, B., Forster, L., George, M. S., et al. (2008). Neurocognitive deficits and prefrontal cortical atrophy in patients with schizophrenia. *Schizophrenia Research, 101,* 142–151.

Capaldi, E. D., & Privitera, G. J. (2008). Decreasing dislike for sour and bitter in children and adults. *Appetite, 50*(1), 139–145.

Centers for Disease Control and Prevention. (2002). Cohabitation, marriage, divorce, and remarriage in the United States. *Vital and Health Statistics, 23*(22), 1–94.

Chen, X.-L., Dai, X.-Y., & Dong, Q. (2008). A research of Aitken Procrastination Inventory applied to Chinese college students. *Chinese Journal of Clinical Psychology, 16*(1), 22–23.

Cheng, R. W., & Lam, S. (2007). Self-construal and social comparison effects. *British Journal of Educational Psychology, 77,* 197–211.

Cohen, B. H. (2002). Calculating a factorial ANOVA from means and standard deviations. *Understanding Statistics, 1*(3), 191–203.

Cohen, J. (1988). *Statistical power analysis for the behavioral sciences.* Hillsdale, NJ: Lawrence Erlbaum.

Collins, M. W., & Morris, S. B. (2008). Testing for adverse impact when sample size is small. *Journal of Applied Psychology, 93*(2), 463–471.

Conners, C. K., Epstein, J. N., Angold, A., & Klaric, J. (2003). Continuous performance test performance in a normative epidemiological sample. *Journal of Abnormal Child Psychology, 31*(5), 555–562.

Conseur, A., Hathcote, J. M., & Kim, S. (2008). Consumer masculinity behavior among college students and its relationship to self-esteem and media influence. *Sex Roles, 58,* 549–555.

Dai, X., Wertenbroch, K., & Brendl, C. M. (2008). The value heuristic in judgments of relative frequency. *Psychological Science, 19,* 18–19.

DellaValle, D. M., Roe, L. S., & Rolls, B. J. (2005). Does the consumption of caloric and non-caloric beverages with a meal affect energy intake? *Appetite, 44,* 187–193.

Drakou, A., Kambitsis, C., Charachousou, Y., & Tzetzis, G. (2006). Exploring life satisfaction of sport coaches in Greece. *European Sport Management Quarterly, 6*(3), 239–252.

Edenborough, M., Jackson, D., Mannix, J., & Wilkes, L. M. (2008). Living in the red zone: The experience of child-to-mother violence. *Child and Family Social Work, 13,* 464–473.

Elias, S. M. (2007). Influence in the ivory tower: Examining the appropriate use of social power in the university classroom. *Journal of Applied Social Psychology, 37*(11), 2532–2548.

Erkal, S., Copur, Z., Dogan, N., & Safak, S. (2007). Examining the relationship between parents' gender roles and responsibilities towards their children (a Turkish example). *Social Behavior and Personality, 35*(9), 1221–1234.

Eskesen, S. T., Eskesen, F. N., & Ruvinsky, A. (2004). Natural selection affects frequencies of AG and GT dinucleotides at the 5' and 3' ends of exons. *Genetics, 167,* 543–550.

Evans, S. W., Langberg, J., Raggi, V., Allen, J., & Buvinger, E. C. (2005). Development of a school-based treatment program for middle school youth with ADHD. *Journal of Attention Disorders, 9,* 343–353.

Freitas, J. N. S., El-Hani, C. N., & da Rocha, P. L. B. (2008). Affiliation in four echimyid rodent species based on intrasexual dyadic encounters: Evolutionary implications. *Ethology, 114,* 389–397.

Gibson, D. M., & Myers, J. E. (2006). Perceived stress, wellness, and mattering: A profile of first-year Citadel cadets. *Journal of College Student Development, 47*(6), 647–660.

Gilman, R., Huebner, E. S., Tian, L., Park, N., O'Byrne, J., Schiff, M., et al. (2008). Cross-national adolescent multidimensional life satisfaction reports: Analyses of mean scores and response style differences. *Journal of Youth Adolescents, 37,* 142–154.

Gmitrova, V. & Gmitrov, J. (2004). The primacy of child-directed pretend play on cognitive competence in a mixed-age environment: Possible interpretations. *Early Child Development and Care, 174*(3), 267–279.

Good, P. I., & Hardin, J. W. (2003). *Common errors in statistics (and how to avoid them).* New York: John Wiley.

Gottesman, I. I., & Bertelsen, A. (1989). Confirming unexpressed genotypes for schizophrenia: Risks in the offspring of Fischer's Danish identical and fraternal discordant twins. *Archives of General Psychiatry, 46*(10), 867–872.

Guan, J., McBride, R., & Xiang, P. (2005). Chinese teachers' attitudes toward teaching physical activity and fitness. *Asia-Pacific Journal of Teacher Education, 33*(2), 147–157.

Gulledge, A. K., Stahmann, R. F., & Wilson, C. M. (2004). Seven types of nonsexual romantic physical affection among Brigham Young University students. *Psychological Reports, 95,* 609–614.

Harrell, Z. A., & Jackson, B. (2008). Thinking fat and feeling blue: Eating behaviors, ruminative coping, and depressive symptoms in college women. *Sex Roles, 58,* 658–665.

Harrell, Z. A., & Karim, N. M. (2008). Is gender relevant only for problem alcohol behaviors? An examination of correlates of alcohol use among college students. *Addictive Behaviors, 33,* 359–365.

Harwell, M. R., & Gatti, G. G. (2001). Rescaling ordinal data to interval data in educational research. *Review of Educational Research, 71,* 105–131.

Hentges, B. A., Meier, J. A., & Bartsch, R. A. (2007). The effect of race, gender, and bias on liking of commercials with perceived stereotypes. *Current Research in Social Psychology, 13*(6), 65–78.

Hilari, K., & Northcott, S. (2006). Social support in people with chronic aphasia. *Aphasiology, 20*(1), 17–36.

Hoenig, J. M., & Heisey, D. M. (2001). The abuse of power: The pervasive fallacy of power calculations in data analysis. *The American Statistician, 55,* 19–24.

Hollands, J. G., & Spence, I. (1992). Judgments of change and proportion in graphical perception. *Human Factors, 34,* 313–334.

Hollands, J. G., & Spence, I. (1998). Judging proportions with graphs: The summation model. *Applied Cognitive Psychology, 12,* 173–190.

Holmes, V. M., Malone, A. M., & Redenbach, H. (2008). Orthographic processing and visual sequential memory in unexpectedly poor spellers. *Journal of Research in Reading, 31*(1), 136–156.

Horne, J. J. (2008). Short sleep is a questionable risk factor for obesity and related disorders: Statistical versus clinical significance. *Biological Psychology, 77,* 266–276.

Jamieson, P. E., & Romer, D. (2008). Unrealistic fatalism in U.S. youth ages 14 to 22: Prevalence and characteristics. *Journal of Adolescent Health, 42,* 154–160.

Jones, N., Blackey, H., Fitzgibbon, K., & Chew, E. (2010). Get out of MySpace! *Computers & Education, 54,* 776–782.

Kaiser, H. F. (1960). Directional statistical decisions. *Psychological Review, 67,* 160–167.

Kausch, O., Loreen, R., & Douglas, R. (2006). Lifetime histories of trauma among pathological gamblers. *American Journal on Addictions, 15*(1), 35–43.

Kelly, W. E. (2004). Sleep-length and life satisfaction in a college student sample. *College Student Journal, 38*(3), 428–430.

Keskinoglu, P., Ucuncu, T., Yildirim, I., Gurbuz, T., Ur, I., & Ergor, G. (2007). Gender discrimination in the elderly and its impact on the elderly health. *Archives of Gerontology and Geriatrics, 45,* 295–306.

Kruger, J., & Savitsky, K. (2006). *The persuasiveness of one- vs. two-tailed tests of significance: When weak results are preferred over strong* [Abstract]. Retrieved from http://ssrn.com/abstract=946199

Ladebo, J., & Awotunde, J. M. (2007). Emotional and behavioral reactions to work overload: Self-efficacy as a moderator. *Current Research in Social Psychology, 13*(8), 86–100.

Laming, D. (2006). Predicting free recalls. *Journal of Experimental Psychology: Learning, Memory, and Cognition, 32*(5), 1146–1163.

Leventhal, L. (1999). Answering two criticisms of hypothesis testing. *Psychological Reports, 85,* 3–18.

Levitt, J. T., Malta, L. S., Martin, A., Davis, L., & Cloitre, M. (2007). The flexible applications of a manualized treatment for PTSD symptoms and functional impairment related to the 9/11 World Trade Center attack. *Behaviour Research and Therapy, 45,* 1419–1433.

Liang, H.-F., Chiang, Y.-C., Chien, L.-Y., & Yeh, C.-H. (2007). A comparison of emotional/behavioural problems between Taiwanese children with cancer and healthy controls. *Journal of Clinical Nursing, 16*(2), 304–311.

Lopata, C., Hamm, E., Volker, M. A., & Sowinski, J. E. (2007). Motor and visuomotor skills of children with Asperger's disorder: Preliminary findings. *Perceptual and Motor Skills, 104,* 1183–1192.

Love, K. G., Vinson, J., Tolsma, J., & Kaufmann, G. (2008). Symptoms of undercover police officers: A comparison of officers currently, formerly, and without undercover experience. *International Journal of Stress Management, 15*(2), 136–152.

Lumeng, J., Somashekar, D., Appugliese, D., Kaciroti, N., Corwyn, R. F., & Bradley, R. H. (2007). Shorter sleep duration is associated with increased risk of being overweight at ages 9 to 12 years. *Pediatrics, 120,* 1020–1029.

Malcolm, B. P. (2004). Evaluating the effects of self-esteem on substance abuse among homeless men. *Journal of Alcohol & Drug Education, 48*(3), 39–61.

McCabe, M. P., Ricciardelli, L. A., & James, T. (2007). A longitudinal study of body change strategies of fitness center attendees. *Eating Behaviors, 8,* 492–496.

McDonald, B. (2002). Self-assessment skills used by high school students without formal training. *School Psychology International, 23*(4), 416–424.

Mennella, J. A., Kennedy, J. M., & Beauchamp, G. K. (2006). Vegetable acceptance by infants: Effects of formula flavors. *Early Human Development, 82,* 463–468.

Miltenberger, R. G., Redlin, J., Crosby, R., Stickney, M., Mitchell, J., Wonderlich, S., et al. (2003). Direct and retrospective assessment of factors contributing to compulsive buying. *Journal of Behavior Therapy and Experimental Psychiatry, 34,* 1–9.

Miyoshi, R., Yamakawa, M., Shigenobu, K., Makimoto, K., Zhu, C., Segawa, N., et al. (2008). Association between activity level and changes in bodyweight in dementia patients. *Psychogeriatrics, 8,* 170–174.

Montoya, R. M. (2007). Gender similarities and differences in preferences for specific body parts. *Current Research in Social Psychology, 13*(11), 133–144.

Naleid, A. M., Grimm, J. W., Kessler, D. A., Sipols, A. J., Aliakban, S., Bennett, J. L., et al. (2008). Deconstructing the vanilla milkshake: The dominant effects of sucrose on self-administration of nutrient-flavor mixtures. *Appetite, 50,* 128–138.

Nicholls, A. R., Polman, R. C. J., Levy, A. R., & Backhouse, S. H. (2009). Mental toughness in sport: Achievement level, gender, age, experience, and sport type differences. *Personality and Individual Differences, 47,* 73–75.

Nobre, P. J., & Pinto-Gouveia, J. (2008). Cognitions, emotions, and sexual response: Analysis of the relationship among automatic thoughts, emotional responses, and sexual arousal. *Archives of Sexual Behavior, 37,* 652–661.

Nota, L., Ferrari, L., Soresi, S., & Wehmeyer, M. (2007). Self-determination, social abilities, and the quality of life of people with intellectual disability. *Journal of Intellectual Disability Research, 51,* 850–865.

Okpala, C. O., Bell, G. C., & Tuprah, K. (2007). A comparative study of student achievement in traditional schools and schools of choice in North Carolina. *Urban Education, 42*(4), 313–325.

Orathinkal, J., Vansteenwegen, A., & Burggraeve, R. (2008). Forgiveness: A perception and motivation study among married adults. *Scandinavian Journal of Psychology, 49,* 155–160.

O'Sullivan, M. (2007). Unicorns or Tiger Woods: Are lie detection experts myths or rarities? A response to *On Lie Detection "Wizards"* by Bond and Uysal. *Law and Human Behavior, 31,* 117–123.

Ottenbacher, K. J. (1993). The interpretation of averages in health professions research. *Evaluation & The Health Professions, 16*(3), 333–341.

Painter, J. E., Wansink, B., & Hieggelke, J. B. (2002). How visibility and convenience influence candy consumption. *Appetite, 38,* 237–238.

Palesh, O., Butler, L. D., Koopman, C., Giese-Davis, J., Carlson, R., & Spiegel, D. (2007). Stress history and breast cancer recurrence. *Journal of Psychosomatic Research, 63,* 233–239.

Pastizzo, M. J., & Carbone, R. F., Jr. (2007). Spoken word frequency counts based on 1.6 million words in American English. *Behavior Research Methods, 39*(4), 1025–1028.

Patten, C. A., Brockman, T. A., Ames, S. C., Ebbert, J. O., Stevens, S. R., Thomas, J. L., et al. (2008). Differences among Black and White young adults on prior attempts and motivation to help a smoker quit. *Addictive Behaviors, 33,* 496–502.

Powers, J. R., & Young, A. F. (2008). Longitudinal analysis of alcohol consumption and health of middle-aged women in Australia. *Addiction, 103,* 424–432.

Raison, C. L., Borisov, A. S., Broadwell, S. D., Capuron, L., Woolwine, B. J., Jacobson, I. M., et al. (2005). Depression during pegylated interferon-alpha plus ribavirin therapy: Prevalence and prediction. *Journal of Clinical Psychiatry, 66*(1), 41–48.

Reese, H. W. (1999). Problems of statistical inference. *Revista Mexicana de Análisis de la Conducta, 25*(1), 39–68.

Riopelle, A. J. (2003). Functional anatomy of the null hypothesis and of tests of it. *Journal of General Psychology, 130*(1), 47–57.

Rojas, N. L., Sherrit, L., Harris, S., & Knight, J. R. (2008). The role of parental consent in adolescent substance use research. *Journal of Adolescent Health, 42,* 192–197.

Rollag, K. (2007). Defining the term 'new' in new employee research. *Journal of Occupational and Organizational Psychology, 80,* 63–75.

Rolls, B. J., & Roe, L. S. (2002). Effect of the volume of liquid food infused intragastrically on satiety in women. *Physiology & Behavior, 76,* 623–631.

Ryan, R. S. (2006). Hands-on exercise improves understanding of the standard error of the mean. *Teaching of Psychology, 33*(3), 180–183.

Salska, I., Frederick, D. A., Pawlowski, B., Reilly, A. H., Laird, K. T., & Rudd, N. A. (2008). Conditional mate preferences: Factors influencing preferences for height. *Personality and Individual Differences, 44,* 203–215.

Sanchez, D. T., Kiefer, A. K., & Ybarra, O. (2006). Sexual submissiveness in women: Costs for sexual autonomy and arousal. *Personality and Social Psychology Bulletin, 32*(4), 512–524.

Sanchez-Meca, J., & Marin-Martinez, F. (2008). Confidence intervals for the overall effect size in random-effects meta-analysis. *Psychological Methods, 13*(1), 31–48.

Serlin, R. C., & Harwell, M. R. (2004). More powerful tests of predictor subsets in regression analysis under nonnormality. *Psychological Methods, 9*(4), 492–509.

Sherwin, C. M. (2004). Mirrors as potential environmental enrichment for individually housed laboratory mice. *Applied Animal Behaviour Science, 87,* 95–103.

Shook, N. J., & Fazio, R. H. (2008). Roommate relationships: A comparison of interracial and same-race living situations. Group Processes and Intergroup *Relations, 11,* 425–437.

Sinacore, J. M., Chang, R. W., & Falconer, J. (1992). Seeing the forest despite the trees: The benefit of exploratory data analysis to program evaluation research. *Evaluation & The Health Professions, 15,* 131–146.

Spinks, R., Arndt, S., Caspers, K., Yucuis, R., McKirgan, L. W., Pfalzgraf, C., et al. (2007). School achievement strongly predicts midlife IQ. *Intelligence, 35,* 563–567.

Stevens, S. S. (1946). On the theory of scales of measurement. *Science, 103,* 677–680.

Stillman, T. F., Baumeister, R. F., & DeWall, C. N. (2007). What's so funny about not having money? The effects of power on laughter. *Personality and Social Psychology Bulletin, 33*(11), 1547–1558.

Stipanicic, A., Nolin, P., Fortin, G., & Gobeil, M.-F. (2008). Comparative study of the cognitive sequelae of school-aged victims of shaken baby syndrome. *Child Abuse & Neglect, 32,* 415–428.

Szklarska, A., Koziel, S., Bielicki, T., & Malina, R. (2007). Influence of height on attained level of education in males at 19 years of age. *Journal of Biosocial Science, 39,* 575–582.

Tekinarslan, E. (2008). Computer anxiety: A cross-cultural comparative study of Dutch and Turkish university students. *Computers in Human Behavior, 24,* 1572–1584.

Templer, D. I., & Tomeo, M. E. (2002). Mean graduate record examination (GRE) score and gender distribution as function of academic discipline. *Personality and Individual Differences, 32,* 175–179.

Thompson, B. (2007). Effect sizes, confidence intervals, and confidence intervals for effect sizes. *Psychology in the Schools, 44*(5), 423–432.

Thorndike, E. L. (1898). Animal intelligence: An experimental study of the associate processes in animals. *Psychological Review Monograph Supplement, 2*(4), 1–8.

Tung, F.-W., & Deng, Y.-S. (2007). Increasing social presence of social actors in e-learning environments: Effects of dynamic and static emoticons on children. *Displays, 28,* 174–180.

Tunney, R. J. (2006). Preference reversals are diminished when gambles are presented as relative frequencies. *Quarterly Journal of Experimental Psychology, 59*(9), 1516–1523.

Vejrup, K., Lien, N., Klepp, K.-I., & Bere, E. (2008). Consumption of vegetables at dinner in a cohort of Norwegian adolescents. *Appetite, 51,* 90–96.

Volker, M. A. (2006). Reporting effect size estimates in school psychology research. *Psychology in the Schools, 43*(6), 653–672.

Wainwright, P. E., Leatherdale, S. T., & Dublin, J. A. (2007). Advantages of mixed models over traditional ANOVA models in developmental studies: A worked example in a mouse model of fetal alcohol syndrome. *Developmental Psychobiology, 49,* 664–674.

Wan, L., Friedman, B. H., Boutros, N. N., & Crawford, H. J. (2008). Smoking status affects men and women differently on schizotypal traits and cognitive failures. *Personality and Individual Differences, 44,* 425–435.

Wickham, L. H. V., Morris, P. E., & Fritz, C. O. (2000). Facial distinctiveness: Its measurement, distribution and influence on immediate and delayed recognition. *British Journal of Psychology, 91,* 99–123.

Wild, C. (2006). The concept of distribution. *Statistics Education Research Journal, 5*(2), 10–25.

Wilens, T. E., Biederman, J., Adamson, J. J., Henin, A., Sgambati, S., Gignac, M., et al. (2008). Further evidence of an association between adolescent bipolar disorder with smoking and substance abuse disorders: A controlled study. *Drug and Alcohol Dependence, 95,* 188–198.

Wilfley, D. E., Crow, S. J., Hudson, J. I., Mitchell, J. E., Berkowitz, R. I., Blakesley, V., et al. (2008). Efficacy of sibutramine for the treatment of binge-eating disorder: A randomized multicenter placebo-controlled double-blind study. *American Journal of Psychiatry, 165,* 51–58.

Williams, E., Stewart-Knox, B., Helander, A., McConville, C., Bradbury, I., & Rowland, I. (2006). Associations between whole-blood serotonin and subjective mood in healthy male volunteers. *Biological Psychology, 71,* 171–174.

Witt, P. L., & Schrodt, P. (2006). The influence of instructional technology use and teacher immediacy on student affect for teacher and course. *Communication Reports, 19*(1), 1–15.

Yuan, K., & Maxwell, S. (2005). On the post hoc power in testing mean differences. *Journal of Educational and Behavioral Statistics, 30,* 141–167.

Zeidner, M., & Kaluda, I. (2008). Romantic love: What's emotional intelligence (EI) got to do with it? *Personality and Individual Differences, 44,* 1684–1695.

Zou, G. Y. (2007). Toward using confidence intervals to compare correlations. *Psychological Methods, 12*(4), 399–413.

Zwick, R., & Sklar, J. C. (2005). Predicting college grades and degree completion using high school grades and SAT scores: The role of student ethnicity and first language. *American Educational Research Journal, 42,* 439–464.

Index

SAGE Research Methods Online

The essential tool for researchers

Sign up now at www.sagepub.com/srmo for more information.

An expert research tool

- An **expertly designed taxonomy** with more than 1,400 unique terms for social and behavioral science research methods

- **Visual and hierarchical search tools** to help you discover material and link to related methods

- Easy-to-use navigation tools
- Content organized by complexity
- Tools for citing, printing, and downloading content with ease
- Regularly updated content and features

A wealth of essential content

- The most comprehensive picture of quantitative, qualitative, and mixed methods available today

- More than **100,000 pages of SAGE book and reference material** on research methods as well as editorially selected material from SAGE journals

- More than **600 books** available in their entirety online

Launching 2011!

⑤SAGE research methods online

DECISION TREES

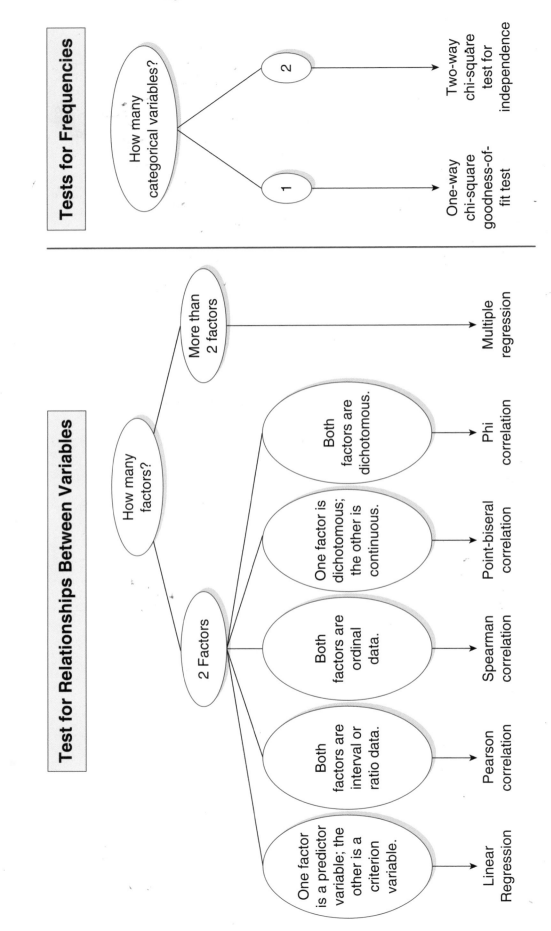

Tests for Frequencies

How many categorical variables?

1 → One-way chi-square goodness-of-fit test

2 → Two-way chi-square test for independence

Test for Relationships Between Variables

How many factors?

More than 2 factors → Multiple regression

2 Factors:

One factor is a predictor variable; the other is a criterion variable. → Linear Regression

Both factors are interval or ratio data. → Pearson correlation

Both factors are ordinal data. → Spearman correlation

One factor is dichotomous; the other is continuous. → Point-biseral correlation

Both factors are dichotomous. → Phi correlation